AF707314

OPTIMISING PUBLIC INTERESTS THROUGH COMPETITIVE TENDERING

Governments are increasingly trying to achieve a variety of public interests through competitive tendering of public contracts, authorisations, subsidies as well as public assets. Over the past decades, domestic and EU law has developed for these 'limited rights' at different speeds and is extremely fragmented: there is no coherent legal framework. This book provides information on the legal aspects of competitive allocation of all types of limited rights on the basis of an overarching perspective. It explains the impact of the legal framework on the ability of governments to achieve the public interests they pursue through competitive tendering. The book is relevant for domestic and EU public authorities, legislators, courts of law as well as academics. It discusses and connects in a consistent manner legal questions arising in the framework of competitive allocation of public contracts, authorisations, subsidies and public assets.

CHRIS JANSEN is Professor of Private Law at the Faculty of Law, Vrije Universiteit Amsterdam and Deputy Justice at the Courts of Appeal in The Hague and 's-Hertogenbosch. He is a leading authority on European public procurement law and its relevance for the allocation by governments of scarce rights outside the domain of public contracts. He is advisor of the Dutch government on the Dutch Public Procurement Act and was formerly chairman of the Dutch Public Procurement Ombudsman.

FRANK VAN OMMEREN is Professor of Constitutional and Administrative Law and Dean at the Faculty of Law, Vrije Universiteit Amsterdam. He is a member of the Dutch Council for Public Administration and a member of the Dutch 'Trade and Industry Appeals Tribunal'. He delivered his inaugural lecture on 'Limited Licenses; The Allocation of Limited Licenses as Part of General Administrative Law' (2004). His research was awarded by the Royal Holland Society of Sciences and Humanities. Together with Chris Jansen, he received a grant from the Dutch Research Council to further research and develop a coherent legal framework for the competitive allocation of limited rights by the government.

JOHAN WOLSWINKEL is Professor of Administrative Law at Tilburg Law School, Tilburg University. He has developed an impressive track record with various thought-provoking publications on issues of competitive decision-making, including the co-edited volume *Scarcity and the State* (2016). He was awarded a prestigious Vidi grant from the Dutch Research Council to further research on open government, transparency and administrative decision-making.

SUE ARROWSMITH is Professor Emerita at the School of Law, University of Nottingham. She is the author of the *Law of Public and Utilities Procurement* (3rd edn, 2018) which is recognised by the English courts as the 'leading academic authority' and has been cited in the courts of numerous European countries as well as in the jurisprudence of the ECJ. In addition, she is founding editor of the *International Public Procurement Law Review*; is a former member of the advisory committees on procurement and reform of the EU, World Bank, UNCITRAL and UK government; and has been awarded the Swinbank Medal of the Chartered Institute of Procurement and Supply for contribution to thought innovation in procurement and supply. In 2019 she was created Kings Counsel honoris causa in recognition of her contribution to legal development.

OPTIMISING PUBLIC INTERESTS THROUGH COMPETITIVE TENDERING

Concept, Context and Challenges

Edited by

CHRIS JANSEN

Vrije Universiteit Amsterdam

FRANK VAN OMMEREN

Vrije Universiteit Amsterdam

JOHAN WOLSWINKEL

Tilburg University

SUE ARROWSMITH

University of Nottingham

CAMBRIDGE
UNIVERSITY PRESS

CAMBRIDGE
UNIVERSITY PRESS

Shaftesbury Road, Cambridge CB2 8EA, United Kingdom

One Liberty Plaza, 20th Floor, New York, NY 10006, USA

477 Williamstown Road, Port Melbourne, VIC 3207, Australia

314–321, 3rd Floor, Plot 3, Splendor Forum, Jasola District Centre, New Delhi – 110025, India

103 Penang Road, #05-06/07, Visioncrest Commercial, Singapore 238467

Cambridge University Press is part of Cambridge University Press & Assessment, a department of the University of Cambridge.

We share the University's mission to contribute to society through the pursuit of education, learning and research at the highest international levels of excellence.

www.cambridge.org
Information on this title: www.cambridge.org/9781009443777

DOI: 10.1017/9781009443739

© Cambridge University Press & Assessment 2025

This publication is in copyright. Subject to statutory exception and to the provisions of relevant collective licensing agreements, no reproduction of any part may take place without the written permission of Cambridge University Press & Assessment.

First published 2025

A catalogue record for this publication is available from the British Library

A Cataloging-in-Publication data record for this book is available from the Library of Congress

ISBN 978-1-009-44377-7 Hardback

Cambridge University Press & Assessment has no responsibility for the persistence or accuracy of URLs for external or third-party internet websites referred to in this publication and does not guarantee that any content on such websites is, or will remain, accurate or appropriate.

CONTENTS

CONTRIBUTORS

SUE ARROWSMITH, Professor Emerita of Public Procurement Law and Policy at University of Nottingham, School of Law

BENEDETTA BIANCARDI, Legal expert at Italian National Anticorruption Authority

JACOBINE VAN DEN BRINK, Professor of Administrative Law at University of Amsterdam (UvA), Faculty of Law

ANOESKA BUIJZE, Professor of National and European Administrative Law at Utrecht University, Faculty of Law, Economics and Governance

ROBERTO CARANTA, Professor of Administrative Law at University of Turin, Department of Law

STEVEN VAN GARSSE, Professor of Administrative Law at University of Hasselt, Faculty of Law; Associate Professor at University of Antwerp, Faculty of Law; and Professor at Antwerp Management School

JOHAN VAN DE GRONDEN, Professor of European Law, Centre for State and Law, Radboud University Nijmegen; and State Counsellor in extraordinary service at the Dutch Council of State

RIANNE JACOBS, Judge at the Dutch Trade and Industry Appeals Tribunal and Endowed Professor of Legal and Regulatory Issues at Vrije Universiteit Amsterdam, Faculty of Law

CHRIS JANSEN, Professor of Private Law at Vrije Universiteit Amsterdam, Faculty of Law

FRANK VAN OMMEREN, Professor of Constitutional and Administrative Law at Vrije Universiteit Amsterdam, Faculty of Law

ILENIA VANDORPE, Associate at Equator Attorneys Antwerp

FERDINAND WOLLENSCHLÄGER, Professor of Public Law and European Law at Augsburg University, Faculty of Law

JOHAN WOLSWINKEL, Professor of Administrative Law at Tilburg University, Tilburg Law School

PREFACE

Whenever the number of applicants exceeds the number of government rights – licenses, subsidies, contracts, and so on – available for grant, these rights are limited. A fundamental and returning issue here is to what extent governments are required to apply some form of competitive tendering to allocate these limited rights. In addressing this issue, it is key to acknowledge that governments are expected to act in the public interest. The public interest, however, is not a monolith, but covers many, sometimes conflicting public interests. Therefore, this edited volume puts central the question of how governments can pursue these different public interests when resorting to competitive tendering, or refraining therefrom.

To answer this central question, this edited volume aims at bringing together four different types of limited rights: public (procurement) contracts, licenses, subsidies and government sales. The fundamental and innovative challenge is to investigate whether and to what extent these different types of limited rights are subject to similar 'allocation rules'.

It is striking that each of these rights has been subject to detailed analysis within its own subdiscipline, both in legal scholarship and in legal practice. However, the indispensable exercise of cross-fertilisation between these different types of limited rights is lacking. This edited volume overcomes this compartmentalisation of limited rights by adopting a unique approach of bringing together experts from these different subfields and starting a conversation between them.

This edited volume is the final result of two international expert meetings organised in 2018 and 2019 to foster the exchange of ideas and insights between experts from different subfields and jurisdictions. Both expert meetings were hosted by the Centre for Public Contract Law and Governance at the Faculty of Law of Vrije Universiteit Amsterdam. While the first expert meeting welcomed a wide range of participants from different (European) jurisdictions, the second expert meeting had a more focused approach in which only the authors of this edited volume participated. We are very grateful to the participants of both expert meetings for sharing their inspiring thoughts with others. Without any doubt, this very diverse and thought-provoking input has been vital in realising this edited volume.

It should come as no surprise that the initiative for this edited volume can be traced to the Netherlands. The Dutch legal system has turned out to be very adaptive and flexible in moving between domestic and EU law and between public law and private law when settling legal issues on the allocation of limited rights by governments. Moreover, the Centre for Public Contract Law and Governance has established a strong track record in conducting 'bridging' research on the allocation of different limited rights for almost two decades.

In particular, this edited volume builds on the book project *Scarcity and the State: The Allocation of Limited Rights by the Administration* (2016), which gave the first impetus to a Europe-wide exploration of building blocks for a consistent and general legal theory on the allocation of limited rights by governments.[1]

The edited volume that we present here has been realised in different stages. Based on the input that we received during both expert meetings, we have drafted a questionnaire for the authors who have contributed to Part I of this volume, which aims at characterising four different types of limited rights in a similar and therefore comparable way. Thanks to their willingness to follow this uniform format, the chapters in Part I have a similar structure. Next, we have asked the authors of Part II of this volume to connect these different limited rights on a various number of topics, after having considered the draft chapters of Part I. Following an iterative process, the authors of both parts have been enabled to clarify and elaborate upon remaining issues that were deemed crucial for the comparison between different kinds of limited rights. The chapters were finalised in spring 2023.

It goes without saying that we are indebted to the different authors for their willingness to participate in this phased and therefore lengthy process. We are indebted to them even more because of their excellent and highly valuable contributions. This holds in particular for Sue Arrowsmith. The larger size of her contribution to this volume and her

[1] Paul Adriaanse, Frank van Ommeren, Willemien den Ouden and Johan Wolswinkel (eds.), *Scarcity and the State I: The Allocation of Limited Rights by the Administration* (Cambridge: Intersentia, 2016); Paul Adriaanse, Frank van Ommeren, Willemien den Ouden and Johan Wolswinkel (eds.), *Scarcity and the State II: Member State Reports on Gambling Licences, Radio Frequencies and CO2 Emission Permits* (Cambridge: Intersentia, 2016).

being mentioned as co-editor on the cover is justified thanks to her great efforts during the expert meetings in paving the way and providing the structure for the comparison of different limited rights.

Finally, we would like to thank our student assistants Anne van Leeuwen, Michelle Rijnen and Terēze Tiesniece for their indispensable support in realising and finalising this edited volume.

Chris Jansen
Frank van Ommeren
Johan Wolswinkel

TABLE OF CASES

European Court of Justice

Case 7/61 *Commission of the European Economic Community* v. *Government of the Italian Republic* [1961] ECR 00635, ECLI:EU:C:1961:31 | 2.4.2

Case 5/77 *Tedeschi* [1977] ECR 01555, ECLI:EU:C:1977:144 | 8.3

Case 149/79 *Commission* v. *Belgium I* [1980] ECR 3881, ECLI:EU:C:1980:297 | 3.4.1

Case 149/79 *Commission* v. *Belgium II* [1982] ECR 1845, ECLI:EU:C:1982:195 | 3.4.1

Case C-40/85 *Belgium* v. *Commission* [1986] ECLI:EU:C:1986:305 | 5.4.1

Case C-234/84 *Belgium* v. *Commission* [1986] ECLI:EU:C:1986:302 | 5.4.2

Case 205/84 *Commission* v. *Germany* [1986] ECR 03755, ECLI:EU:C:1986:463 | 8.3.1

Case 199/85 *Commission of the European Communities* v. *Italian Republic* [1987] ECR 1039, ECLI:EU:C:1987:115 | 2.4.1, 2.4.2

Case 118/85 *Commission* v. *Italy* [1987] ECR 02599, ECLI:EU:C:1987:283 | 8.2

Case 222/86 *Heylens* [1987] ECR 4097 | 3.4.3

Case 263/86 *Belgian State* v. *Humbel* [1988] ECR 05365, ECLI:EU:C:1988:451 | 8.2

Case 31/87 *Gebroeders Beentjes BV* v. *State of the Netherlands* [1988] ECR 4635, ECLI:EU:C:1988:422 | 2.3, 2.4.2, 7.3.2

Case C-21/88 *Du Pont de Nemours Italiana SpA* v. *Unità sanitaria locale No.2 di Carrara* [1990] ECR I-889, EU:C:1990:121 | 2.4.2

Case C-113/89 *Rush Portuguesa Lda* v. *Office national d'immigration (National Immigration Office)* [1990] ECR I-1417, EU:C:1990:142 | 2.4.2

Case C-41/90 *Höfner* [1991] ECR I-01979, ECLI:EU:C:1991:161 | 8.2

Case C-76/90 *Säger* [1991] ECR I-04221, ECLI:EU:C:1991:331 | 8.3.1

Case C-340/89 *Vlassopoulou* [1991] ECR I-2357, ECLI:EU:C:1991:193 | 3.4.3

Joined Cases C-159/91 and C-160/91 *Poucet and Pistre* [1993] ECR I-00637, ECLI:EU:C:1993:63 | 8.2

Case C-109/92 *Wirth* v. *Landeshauptstadt Hannover* [1993] ECR I-06447, ECLI:EU:C:1993:916 | 8.2

Case C-328/92 *Commission of the European Communities* v. *Kingdom of Spain* [1994] ECR I-1569, ECLI:EU:C:1994:178 | 2.4.1, 2.4.2

Case C-91/92 *Faccini Dori* [1994] ECR I-03325, ECLI:EU:C:1994:292 | 8.2

Joined Cases C-278/92, C-279/92 and C-280/92 *Kingdom of Spain* v. *Commission* [1994] ECR 1994 I-04103, ECLI:EU:C:1994:325 | 5.4.2

Case C-153/02 *Neri* v. *European School of Economics (ESE Insight World Education System Ltd)* [2003] ECR I-13555, ECLI:EU:C:2003:614 | 8.2
Case C-495/99 *Commission* v. *CAS Succhi di Frutta SpA* [2004] ECLI:EU:C:2004:236 | 9.3
Case C-496/99 P *Commission of the European Communities* v. *CAS Succhi di Frutta* [2004] ECLI:EU:C:2004:236 | 1.4.2, 3.4.3, 7.4.2, 10.3.4
Case C-277/00 *Germany* v. *Commission* [2004] EU:C:2004:238 | 5.4.1, 5.4.2
Case C-247/02 *Sintesi SpA* v. *Autorità per la Vigilanza sui Lavori Pubblici* [2004] ECLI:EU:C:2004:593 | 1.4.2
Case C-201/02 *Wells* [2004] ECR I-00723, ECLI:EU:C:2004:12 | 8.3.2
Case C-331/04 *ATI EAC Srl e Viaggi di Maio Snc, EAC Srl and Viaggi di Maio Snc* v. *ACTV Venezia SpA, Provincia di Venezia and Comune di Venezia* [2005] ECR I-10109, ECLI:EU:C:2005:718 | 2.3
Case C-525/03 *Commission of the European Communities* v. *Italian Republic* [2005] ECR I-9405, ECLI:EU:C:2005:343 | 2.4.1
Case C-29/04 *Commission of the European Communities* v. *Republic of Austria* [2005] ECLI:EU:C:2005:670 | 6.2.2
Case C-231/03 *Consorzio Aziende Metano (Coname)* v. *Comune di Cingia de' Botti* [2005] ECR I-7287, ECLI:EU:C:2005:487 | 2.4.1
Case C-458/03 *Parking Brixen* [2005] ECR I-8612 | 3.4.2, 6.2.3
Case C-390/98 *Banks* [2006] ECR I-6117, ECLI:EU:C:2006:528 | 5.4.2.
Case C-323/03 *Commission* v. *Spain* [2006] ECLI:EU:C:2006:159 | 3.4.2, 3.4.3, 7.4.1
Case C-372/04 *Watts* v. *Bedford Primary Care Trust and Secretary of State for Health* [2006] ECR I-04325, ECLI:EU:C:2006:325 | 8.2
Case C-260/04 *Commission of the European Communities* v. *Italian Republic* [2007] ECLI:EU:C:2007:508 | 1.1.2, 3.4.2, 3.4.4
Case C-220/05 *Jean Auroux and Others* v. *Commune de Roanne* [2007] ECLI:EU:C:2007:31 | 6.2.2
Case C-6/05 *Medipac-Kazantzidis* [2007] ECR I-4557, ECLI:EU:C:2007:337 | 3.4.3
Joined Cases C-338/04, C-359/04 and C-360/04 *Placanica* [2007] ECR I-1891 | 3.4.2
Case C-250/06 *United Pan-Europe Communications* [2007] ECR I-11135, ECLI:EU:C:2007:783 | 8.3.2
Case C-347/06 ASM *Brescia* [2008] ECR I-05641, ECLI:EU:C:2008:416 | 8.3.2
Case C-380/05 *Centro Europa 7 Srl* [2008] ECR I-349 | 3.4.2, 3.4.3
Joined Cases C-147/06 and C-148/06 *SECAP et al.* [2008] ECR I-3565 | 3.4.3
Case C-214/07 *Commission* v. *France* [2008] ECR I-8357, ECLI:EU:C:2008:619 | 5.4.2
Case C-152/05 *Commission of the European Communities* v. *Federal Republic of Germany* [2008] ECLI:EU:C:2008:17 | 7.2.4
Case C-346/06 *Dirk Ruffert* v. *Land Niedersachsen* [2008] ECR I-01989, ECLI:EU:C:2008:189 | 2.4.2
Case C-532/06 *Emm. G. Lianakis AE, Sima Anonymi Techniki Etairia Meleton kai Epivlepseon and Nikolaos Vlachopoulos* v. *Dimos Alexandroupolis and Others* [2008] ECR I-00251, ECLI:EU:C:2008:40 | 2.3

General Court of the European Union

Case T-242/12 *SNCF Mobilités* v. *Commission* [2018] ECLI:EU:T:2015:1003 | 5.4.1, 5.4.2, 9.4.3

Case T-223/19 *Casa Regina Apostolorum* [2021] ECLI:EU:T:2021:315 | 8.2

EFTA Court

Case E-16/16 *Fosen-Linjen AS* v. *AtB AS* [2017] EFTA Court judgment of 31 October 2017 | 2.4.2

Case E-7/18 *Fosen-Linjen AS, supported by the Confederation of Norwegian Enterprise (Næringslivets Hovedorganisasjon)* v. *AtB AS (Fosen-Linjen 2)* [2019] EFTA Court judgment of 1 August 2019 | 2.4.2

ABBREVIATIONS

AB	Administratiefrechtelijke Beslissingen Rechtspraak Bestuursrecht
AG	attorney general
AHURI	Australian Housing and Urban Research Institute
All ER	All England Law Reports
BayVGH	Bayerischer Verwaltungsgerichtshof (Higher Administrative Court of Bavaria)
BVerfGE	Bundesverfassungsgericht (German Federal Constitutional Court)
BVerwGE	Bundesverwaltungsgericht (German Federal Administrative Court)
BVVG	Bodenverwertungs- und -verwaltungs GmbH
CAN. Buss. L.J.	Canadian Business Law Journal
CASE	Centre for Social and Economic Research
cf.	*confer* (compare)
CFI	court of first instance
CFR	Charter of Fundamental Rights of the European Union
CIPS	Chartered Institute of Procurement and Supply
Cm	Command Papers
COM	Documents of the European Commission
COMESA	Common Market for Eastern and Southern Africa
Cornell Int'l L.J.	Cornell International Law Journal
COVID-19	coronavirus disease 2019
DCRF	Draft Common Frame of Reference
DDR	Deutsche Demokratische Republik
DG	directorate general
DG GROW	Directorate General for Internal Market, Industry, Entrepreneurship and SMEs
DVBl	Deutsches Verwaltungsblatt
EAFRD	European Agricultural Fund for Rural Development
EC	European Commission
ECJ	European Court of Justice
ECLI	European Case Law Identifier

ECR	European Court Reports
EEA	European Economic Area
EEC	European Economic Community
EFTA	European Free Trade Association
EGC	European General Court
EMFF	European Maritime and Fisheries Fund
EPL	European Public Law
ERC	European Research Council
ERDF	European Regional Development Fund
ESF	European Social Fund
ESI Funds	European Structural and Investment Funds
EU	European Union
EuR	Europarecht
Euratom	European Atomic Energy Community
FRF	French Franc
GALA	General Administrative Law Act (Netherlands)
GBER	General Block Exemption Regulation
GDP	gross domestic product
GewArch	Gewerbearchiv
GG	Grundgesetz (German Constitution)
GPA	Agreement on Government Procurement
GRAWE	Grazer Wechselseitige Versicherung
GSA	General Services Administration
GWB	Gesetz gegen Wettbewerbsbeschränkungen (German Competition Act)
HR	Hoge Raad der Nederlanden (Dutch Supreme Court)
IAMO	Institute of Agricultural Development in Transition Economies
IBM	International Business Machines Corporation
IMF	International Monetary Fund
IPPP	institutional public–private partnership
MEAT	most economically advantageous tender
MEIP	market economy investor principle
MEO	market economy operator
MEVP	market economy vendor principle
MiFID	Markets in Financial Instruments Directive
MoU	memorandum of understanding
NBER	National Bureau of Economic Research
NHS	National Health Service
NJW	Neue Juristische Wochenschrift
NL	Netherlands
NVwZ	Neue Zeitschrift für Verwaltungsrecht
NVwZ-RR	Neue Zeitschrift für Verwaltungsrecht Rechtsprechungs-Report

OECD	Organisation for Economic Co-operation and Development
OJ	Official Journal
PPLR	Public Procurement Law Review
PPP	public–private partnerships
PIN	prior information notice
PSO	public service obligations
R&R	rescue and restructuring
REALaw	Review of European Administrative Law
ReM	Recht en Methode in onderzoek en onderwijs
ReNEUAL	Research Network on EU Administrative Law
RIS	Raadsinformatiesysteem
SA	state aid
SCR	Supreme Court Reports (Canada)
SGEI	service of general economic interest
SGI	service of general interest
SI	statutory instrument
SIP	share issue privatisation
SMEs	small and medium-sized enterprises
SNCF	Société Nationale des Chemins de fer Français
SNCM	Société Nationale Maritime Corse-Méditerranée
SOE	state-owned enterprise
SSGI	social services of general interest
SWD	staff working document
TAP	Transportes Aéreos Portugueses
TEU	Treaty on European Union
TFEU	Treaty on the Functioning of the European Union
UN	United Nations
UNCAC	United Nations Convention Against Corruption
UNCITRAL	United Nations Commission on International Trade Law
VAT	value-added tax
VGH	Verwaltungsgerichtshof (German Higher Administrative Court)
VPS	visual protection surface
VVDStRL	Vereinigung der Deutschen Staatsrechtslehrer
WTO	World Trade Organization

1

Optimising Public Interests through Competitive Tendering

Connecting Limited Rights

JOHAN WOLSWINKEL, CHRIS JANSEN AND FRANK VAN OMMEREN

1.1 Connectivity in a Fragmented Landscape

1.1.1 A Fragmented Landscape

Making choices is inherent to administrative action. Take the example of governments involved in the procurement of works or services. Every time again, they have to decide which party will get the desired contract and which parties will not.[1] However, making choices is not unique for public contracts.[2] In fact, it is essential to government as such. Which behaviour shall be forbidden and which behaviour shall not? Which infrastructures shall be restored first? Which people or businesses should pay more taxes? Which activities should receive financial support?

Not only do governments have to make choices over and over again, they also have to do so 'in the public interest'. However, getting a grasp of *the* public interest is a difficult exercise. Instead, we can observe a rich variety of public interests, ranging from general concerns such as consumer protection, public safety or compliance with fundamental legal values, to more concrete policy objectives, such as the delivery of vaccines

[1] See Case C-410/14, *Dr. Falk Pharma GmbH* v. *DAK-Gesundheit* ECLI:EU:C:2016:399, paras. 37–38 and 40; and Case C-9/17, *Maria Tirkkonen* ECLI:EU:C:2018:142, paras. 29–31.

[2] Public contracts are understood here in a narrow sense as contracts where public authorities *acquire* certain goods or services. See for this understanding of 'public contracts' in procurement law: Article 1(2) and Article 2(1)(5) of Directive 2014/24/EU of the European Parliament and of the Council of 26 February 2014 on public procurement and repealing Directive 2004/18/EC, OJ 2014, No. L94/65.

within the shortest time frame possible. When observing this variety of public interests, governments are faced with an optimisation problem: since it is impossible to realise all public interests involved to the full extent, they need to find the right balance between these interests.

Although making choices is at the very heart of every administrative action, the immediate consequences thereof are nowhere as clear as in those situations where governments[3] award only a limited number of rights to a selected number of private parties. In such circumstances where governments 'allocate limited rights',[4] the decision to award such a limited right to one party implies the exclusion of other parties from obtaining that right. For example, where the government aims at authorising one gambling casino only, it has to make a choice between several applicants if more than one is interested in obtaining that authorisation. Equally, when the government aims at encouraging scientific research in combatting the COVID-19 pandemic, the limited availability of the financial budget will lead to disappointed scholars, even though their ideas might be brilliant. Similarly, where a government aims to commission the restoration of bridges or to sell some real estate, the resulting contract will usually be awarded to one party only.

From a legal perspective, it is striking that this context of scarcity, allocation and choice has been regulated in such a fragmented manner in the European Union so far. Instead of providing for common, overarching rules on making selective choices, EU regulation is characterised by 'right-dependent' frameworks: the set of applicable rules is determined largely by the concrete *type* of limited rights (e.g. public contracts, authorisations, etc.). Thus, the award of public contracts is governed by a rather detailed regime consisting of the public procurement directives,[5] whereas limited authorisations are governed by a distinct legal regime, found either in

[3] We use the terms 'governments' and 'public authorities' interchangeably in this chapter.

[4] Although the use of the term 'limited-issued rights' or – shortly – 'limited rights' is not very widespread, reference is made to this term occasionally in official legal documents. See, for example, the amendments 2 and 11 in the Opinion of the Committee of the Regions on the award of concessions contracts, OJ 2012, No. C391/49.

[5] Directive 2014/23/EU of the European Parliament and of the Council of 26 February 2014 on the award of concession contracts, OJ 2014, No. L94/1 (hereinafter: Concessions Directive), Directive 2014/24/EU of the European Parliament and of the Council of 26 February 2014 on public procurement and repealing Directive 2004/18/EC, OJ 2014, No. L94/65 (hereinafter: Public Procurement Directive), and Directive 2014/25/EU of the European Parliament and of the Council of 26 February 2014 on procurement by entities operating in the water, energy, transport and postal services sectors and repealing Directive 2004/17/EC, OJ 2014, No. L94/243 (hereinafter: Utilities Directive).

sectoral EU legislation[6] or in transversal legislation such as the Services Directive.[7] For subsidies, the regulatory landscape is even more diffuse with a great variety of subsidy schemes and cooperation mechanisms between EU and national institutions,[8] while sales of public assets by governments have hardly received attention in secondary EU legislation so far.[9]

1.1.2 The Need for Connection

As long as legal scholars and practitioners are only concerned with a certain domain of limited rights (e.g. public contracts, authorisations, etc.), this lack of connection with other, adjacent areas of limited rights is not problematic. However, for several reasons, there is a strong need for a connecting approach that transcends existing legal demarcations between limited rights.

First and foremost, there is the need for coherence in the allocation of limited rights. Admittedly, each type of limited rights has its own characteristics which may justify the application of different rules. At the same time, however, the allocation of limited rights is not only governed by sector-specific or 'right-specific' rules but also by general legal principles, such as the principles of equal treatment and legal certainty and the market freedoms of the Treaty on the Functioning of the European Union (TFEU). These general principles force us to examine which meaning is given thereto in the context of scarcity, allocation and choice, irrespective of the type of limited rights at issue. A well-known example thereof is the development regarding the obligation of transparency in the case-law of the Court of Justice of the European Union (hereinafter:

[6] See, for example, Directive 94/22/EC of the European Parliament and of the Council of 30 May 1994 on the conditions for granting and using authorisations for the prospection, exploration and production of hydrocarbons, OJ 1994, No. L164/3 (hereinafter: Hydrocarbons Directive).

[7] Directive 2006/123/EC of the European Parliament and of the Council of 12 December 2006 on services in the internal market, OJ 2006, No. L376/36 (hereinafter: Services Directive).

[8] Regulation (EU, Euratom) 2018/1046 of the European Parliament and of the Council of 18 July 2018 on the financial rules applicable to the general budget of the Union, amending Regulations (EU) No. 1296/2013, (EU) No. 1301/2013, (EU) No. 1303/2013, (EU) No. 1304/2013, (EU) No. 1309/2013, (EU) No. 1316/2013, (EU) No. 223/2014, (EU) No. 283/2014, and Decision No. 541/2014/EU and repealing Regulation (EU, Euratom) No. 966/2012, OJ 2018, No. L193/1 (hereinafter: Financial Regulation).

[9] See most explicitly the Commission Communication on State aid elements in sales of land and buildings by public authorities, OJ 1997, No. C209/3, which has been replaced by the Commission Notice on the notion of State aid as referred to in Article 107(1) of the Treaty on the Functioning of the European Union, OJ 2016, No. C262/1.

ECJ). Where this obligation has mainly evolved under Article 49 and 56 TFEU with respect to concession contracts (and prior under the procurement directives with respect to public contracts),[10] this obligation also applies to (exclusive) authorisations. The reason therefore is that the effects of such an exclusive authorisation on undertakings established in other Member States and potentially interested in that activity are the same as those of a service concession contract.[11]

Following this first point, looking beyond the domain of a certain type of limited rights can be fruitful in order to identify and solve existing gaps with regard to the award of that type of limited rights. In cases where the applicable 'right-dependent' regulation does not provide for an answer on certain allocation issues, solutions may be available in other domains of limited rights. For example, the provision in the Concessions Directive on the duration of concessions[12] has not been the result of simply copy-pasting a similar provision in the Public Procurement Directive, but has been inspired by the ECJ's case-law on authorisations and the provisions on duration in the Services Directive.[13]

Finally, the legal arrangements that we encounter in practice cannot always be reduced to a single type of limited rights, but have a hybrid nature. An example of this hybridity can be found in the context of subsidies, where a (unilateral) grant award decision is complemented by a written grant agreement.[14] Likewise, the Public Procurement Directive has conflict rules for so-called mixed contracts that fall within different legal regimes.[15] The ECJ's case-law also gives examples where some parts of a legal arrangement are subject to a specific legal regime, whereas other parts are not. In those circumstances, case-law has to develop its own conflict rules.[16] This

[10] Case C-87/94, *Commission of the European Communities* v. *Kingdom of Belgium* ECLI:EU:C:1996:161, para. 54.

[11] Case C-203/08, *Sporting Exchange Ltd* v. *Minister van Justitie* ECLI:EU:C:2010:307, paras. 46–47.

[12] See Article 18 Concessions Directive.

[13] See for a detailed analysis: C. J. Wolswinkel, 'The Magic of Five in the Duration of Concessions: Refining Corollaries in the Concessions Directive', in Grith Skovgaard Olykke and Albert Sanchez-Graells (eds.), *Reformation or Deformation of the EU Public Procurement Rules* (Cheltenham: Edward Elgar Publishing, 2016), pp. 318–342.

[14] See, e.g., Article 201 Financial Regulation.

[15] See Article 3 Public Procurement Directive.

[16] See, for example, Joined Cases C-145/08 and C-149/08, *Club Hotel Loutraki AE and Others* v. *Ethnico Symvoulio Radiotileorasis* and *Ypourgos Epikrateias and Aktor Anonymi Techniki Etaireia (Aktor ATE)* v. *Ethnico Symvoulio Radiotileorasis* ECLI:EU:C:2010:247, paras. 59 and 63, combining the privatisation of a public undertaking with the procurement of services and works.

hybridity is also visible with regard to services of general economic interest: where Member States are free to adopt a system of exclusive rights, financial compensation or a combination thereof, the different types of limited rights (exclusive rights or financial compensation) turn out not to be separated worlds, but heavily connected.[17]

This hybridity also comes to the fore when we compare classifications under domestic law with classifications under EU law. The ECJ's case-law shows multiple examples where domestic categorisations do not coincide with categorisations used in EU law. For example, in *Promoimpresa*, the ECJ held that Italian 'concessioni' for tourist beach activities did not classify as concession contracts under the Concessions Directive, but as authorisations under the Services Directive.[18] Reversely, Italian 'concessioni' for organising games of chance were not considered as licences, but as service concession contracts.[19] In other words, legal arrangements that are classified as an authorisation or a concession in some legal regime could classify as another type of limited rights (or a mixed type) in another legal regime.

1.1.3 The Bridging Function of Competitive Tendering

Despite all the differences between public contracts, authorisations, subsidies and (government) sales,[20] the need for *choice* is the common denominator once these rights are limited in number. Such limitation implies the need for allocation, but not necessarily for competition. However, recent developments in both legislation and case-law show

[17] See, for example, Article 3(1) of Regulation (EC) No. 1370/2007 of the European Parliament and of the Council of 23 October 2007 on public passenger transport services by rail and by road and repealing Council Regulations (EEC) Nos. 1191/69 and 1107/70, OJ 2007, No. L315/1, as amended afterwards (hereinafter: PSO Regulation): 'Where a competent authority decides to grant the operator of its choice an exclusive right and/or compensation, of whatever nature, in return for the discharge of public service obligations, it shall do so within the framework of a public service contract.'

[18] Joined Cases C-458/14 and C-67/15, *Promoimpresa srl and Others v. Consorzio dei comuni della Sponda Bresciana del Lago di Garda e del Lago di Idro and Others*, ECLI: EU:C:2016:558, para. 47. For more detail, refer to C. J. Wolswinkel, 'Concession Meets Authorisation: New Demarcations Lines under the Concessions Directive?' (2017) 12 *European Procurement & Private Partnership Law Review* 396–407.

[19] Case C-260/04, *Commission of the European Communities* v. *Italian Republic* ECLI:EU: C:2007:508, para. 20.

[20] We refer to '(government) sales' to indicate that the government is selling certain public assets to private parties. In case of public contracts, by contrast, the government is acquiring certain goods or services from private parties (see footnote 2).

an increased preference for 'allocation through competition'. Admittedly, the developments on this issue are not entirely in sync across the different limited rights we envisage: where the obligation to call for competition has been familiar to public contracts for decades already,[21] this obligation is relatively new to authorisations.[22] Nonetheless, it goes without saying that allocation through competition has evolved into the default option in the allocation of limited rights. In short, the dominating idea is that a competitive procedure between interested parties will enable governments to put 'their' rights in the hands of those who value them most while at the same time enabling them to realise other public interests than value for money.

This book aims to provide an integrative approach to limited rights by putting central the issue of 'competitive allocation' or 'competitive tendering'[23] as the connecting topic between limited rights. By doing so, competitive tendering can also function as a starting point for the analysis of other rules on the allocation of limited rights, for example, on the duration of these rights or on the contents of the award criteria. Competitive tendering is understood here broadly as an (administrative) decision-making process where potential candidates are invited to express their interest in obtaining a limited right. Resorting to competitive tendering may offer possibilities to (better) achieve certain public interests, but it may also be detrimental to achieving other public interests. Since the legal choices made to realise competition differ across limited rights, it is essential to map these differences in order to understand the different trade-offs in the balancing of public interests involved.

The central question we aim to answer in this book is how the applicable legal framework impacts the realisation of different public interests through competitive tendering. The perspective we have in mind is that of a public authority faced with a limited number of rights available for grant. This 'allocating authority' has a certain level of administrative discretion, dependent on the choices that have been made by the competent legislatures. These choices, together referred to as the legal framework, cover primary EU law (Treaty on European Union (TEU) and TFEU), secondary EU legislation, domestic legislation and

[21] See already Article 12 of Council Directive 71/305/EEC of 26 July 1971 concerning the co-ordination of procedures for the award of public works contracts, OJ 1971, No. L185/5.

[22] See in this direction Article 12 of the Services Directive as well as Case C-203/08, *Sporting Exchange Ltd* v. *Minister van Justitie* ECLI:EU:C:2010:307.

[23] The terms 'competitive allocation', 'competitive tendering' and 'competitive procedure' will be used interchangeably throughout this chapter. For more detail on this terminology, see Section 1.2.3.

delegated rule-making. At each of these rule-making levels, choices are made on how to award limited rights in a competitive way and therefore on how to pursue or reconcile different public interests. These choices can be very general, merely prescribing the principles the allocating authority should take into account, but can also be quite specific, thereby further limiting the authority's discretion in selecting an allocation procedure or in determining the steps to be taken in an allocation procedure. But irrespective of their rule- or principle-based character, such legal constraints usually address only one or a few public interests, thereby leaving the other interests unaffected. Thus, the allocative choices made at these rule-making levels determine the discretion left to the allocating authorities in pursuing different public interests. In other words, the allocative choices made at the different rule-making levels and the discretion left to the allocating authority are two sides of the same coin.

The underlying aim of this book project is to identify general legal patterns (or the lack thereof) in the regulation of the allocation of limited rights. First of all, this exercise is indispensable for legal scholars in deepening their theoretical understanding of the allocation of limited rights as a distinct field in (EU) administrative law. Besides, this analysis also helps legal practitioners to look beyond their distinct fields of law (procurement law, subsidy law, etc.) by offering them concrete examples and instruments from adjacent types of limited rights.

In order to structure the current landscape of limited rights and to facilitate further (legal) comparison, we use this introductory contribution to present an overarching analytical framework. This framework consists of three elements. First, we introduce terminology and categorisations that are capable of transcending existing (legal) demarcations in the allocation of limited rights (Section 1.2). Next, we argue that the issue of which public interests are pursued in the allocation of limited rights, is a fruitful lens to unite and compare insights from different subfields of limited rights (Section 1.3). Finally, while reflecting upon the role of the legal framework in optimising public interests through competitive tendering, we propose three dimensions of legal comparison that enable the differences across the limited rights to be highlighted and explained (Section 1.4). The resulting framework is the point of departure for this book, the set-up of which will be further sketched in Section 1.5. In this section, we will also discuss the main overarching results that follow from the interplay between the different parts and chapters of this book. We conclude by pointing out some research directions that should further close the gap between different types of limited rights (Section 1.6).

1.2 Building Blocks for a Connecting Approach towards Limited Rights

1.2.1 Different Avenues for Categorising Limited Rights

Limited-issued rights – or shortly, limited rights – have in common that the number (or amount) of rights available for grant is limited to a maximum.[24] If the number of applicants or interested parties exceeds this number of available rights, public authorities face a *choice* between these applicants. This element of choice (selection) is distinctive for limited rights in comparison with other, non-limited rights.[25]

The notion of 'limited rights' is absent in EU legislation. However, the notion of 'exclusive and special rights' in Article 106(1) TFEU comes close to this notion. In *Pawlak*, the ECJ reiterated that a State measure may be regarded as granting a special or exclusive right within the meaning of Article 106(1) TFEU 'where it confers protection on a limited number of undertakings and which may substantially affect the ability of other undertakings to exercise the economic activity in question in the same geographical area under substantially equivalent conditions'.[26] The element in the ECJ's reasoning on the *limited* number of protected undertakings is essential to our understanding of limited rights. In fact, the concept of 'exclusive and special rights' in Article 106 TFEU introduces a subcategorisation of limited rights based on the *size* of the restriction by distinguishing between one (exclusive) right on the one hand and two or more (special) rights on the other hand.

Limited rights can also be categorised in other ways. The best way to get a better idea of the characteristics of limited rights and the regulation

[24] See already on this definition of 'limited rights': P. C. Adriaanse, F. J. van Ommeren, W. den Ouden and C. J. Wolswinkel, 'The Allocation of Limited Rights by the Administration: A Quest for a General Legal Theory', in P. C. Adriaanse, F. J. van Ommeren, W. den Ouden and C. J. Wolswinkel (eds.), *Scarcity and the State I: The Allocation of Limited Rights by the Administration* (Cambridge: Intersentia, 2016), pp. 9–10.

[25] Case C-410/14, *Dr. Falk Pharma GmbH* v. *DAK-Gesundheit* ECLI:EU:C:2016:399, para. 38: 'It is therefore apparent that the choice of a tender and, thus, of a successful tenderer, is intrinsically linked to the regulation of public contracts by that directive and, consequently, to the concept of "public contract" within the meaning of Article 1(2) of that directive.' See also on this characteristic of selectivity: R. Caranta, 'The Changes to the Public Contract Directives and the Story They Tell about How EU Law Works' (2015) 52 *Common Market Law Review* 391–460, at 447–448.

[26] Case C-545/17, *Mariusz Pawlak* v. *Prezes Kasy Rolniczego Ubezpieczenia Społecznego* ECLI:EU:C:2019:260, para. 43.

thereof is to consider specific examples of limited rights in specific sectors. This 'sector-based' approach is also followed in several pieces of EU legislation. A good example thereof is the public service obligation (PSO) Regulation on public passenger transport services by rail and by road.[27] Other well-known examples include the Hydrocarbons Directive,[28] the Postal Services Directive[29] and the EU Electronic Communications Code.[30] Although applicable to a specific sector only, it is interesting to note that such sectoral regulation more than once acknowledges the existence of different types of limited rights that might sometimes overlap. For example, the PSO Regulation states explicitly that where a competent authority decides to grant the operator of its choice an exclusive right *and/or* compensation, of whatever nature, in return for the discharge of PSO, it shall do so within the framework of a 'public service contract'.[31] Furthermore, this regulation states explicitly that a 'public service contract' may also consist of a decision adopted by the competent authority taking the form of an individual legislative or regulatory act.[32] Thus, a limited right in the context of the PSO Regulation clearly has different appearances. The Hydrocarbons Directive, adopted already in 1994, defines an 'authorization' broadly as any law, regulation, administrative or *contractual* provision or instrument issued thereunder by which the competent authorities of a Member State entitle an entity to exercise, on its own behalf and at its own risk, the exclusive right to prospect or explore for or produce hydrocarbons in

[27] Regulation (EC) No. 1370/2007 of the European Parliament and of the Council of 23 October 2007 on public passenger transport services by rail and by road and repealing Council Regulations (EEC) Nos. 1191/69 and 1107/70, OJ 2007, L315/1.

[28] Directive 94/22/EC of the European Parliament and of the Council of 30 May 1994 on the conditions for granting and using authorisations for the prospection, exploration and production of hydrocarbons, OJ 1994, No. L164/3.

[29] Directive 97/67/EC of the European Parliament and of the Council of 15 December 1997 on common rules for the development of the internal market of community postal services and the improvement of quality of service, OJ 1998, No. L15/14.

[30] Directive (EU) 2018/1972 of the European Parliament and of the Council of 11 December 2018 establishing the European Electronic Communications Code (Recast), OJ 2018, No. L321/36.

[31] Article 3(1) PSO Regulation.

[32] Article 2(i) PSO Regulation. In the context of transfers of undertaking, even (governmental) asset sales can be involved in the award of contracts for public passenger transport services. See Case C-172/99, *Oy Liikenne Ab* v. *Pekka Liskojärvi and Pentti Juntunen* ECLI:EU:C:2001:59 and more recently Case C-298/18, *Reiner Grafe and Jürgen Pohle* v. *Südbrandenburger Nahverkehrs GmbH and OSL Bus GmbH* ECLI:EU:C:2020:121.

a geographical area.[33] Again, the limited right at issue can have different appearances. Finally, where public contracts are at the very heart of public procurement law, the Public Procurement Directive (as well as its predecessors) is aware of the possible entanglement of public contracts with unilateral instruments, as it excludes public service contracts from its scope whenever these contracts are awarded by a contracting authority to another contracting authority on the basis of an 'exclusive right' which they enjoy pursuant to *a law, regulation or published administrative provision* which is compatible with the TFEU.[34]

This sector-based approach shows us that we should not restrict our attention to either unilateral instruments (e.g. licenses) or bilateral (contractual) instruments of public authorities when analysing limited rights. At the same time, the restricted scope of this sectoral legislation can act as a barrier to adopting a broader, cross-sectoral perspective on the issue of competitive tendering. In that sense, the development towards adopting more horizontal EU legislation, such as the public procurement directives and the Services Directive, which apply beyond the scope of a specific sector, can function as a catalyst for adopting a broader view on the allocation of limited rights. But even this transversal legislation is still usually restricted to specific *types* of limited rights.

1.2.2 A Right-Oriented Approach: Types of Limited Rights

Our challenge here is to develop a common understanding that allows us to connect different types of limited rights. Since we aim to adopt a legal perspective on the issue of competitive tendering of limited rights, we cannot ignore existing demarcations in EU law. Let us start with the Concessions Directive (2014/23/EU) to identify several types of limited rights. This relatively new legal instrument is a very useful starting point, as this directive pays ample attention to the relationship between concessions and adjacent legal arrangements, which we will discuss here (Figure 1.1).

First of all, concessions can be contrasted with *public contracts* (as defined in public procurement law). These public contracts, which are

[33] Article 1(3) Hydrocarbons Directive.

[34] Article 11 Public Procurement Directive. For more details on the origins of this provision, refer to C. J. Wolswinkel, 'Article 11: Service Contracts Awarded on the Basis of an Exclusive Right', in Roberto Caranta and Albert Sanchez-Graells (eds.), *Commentary on the Public Procurement Directive (2014/24/EU)* (Cheltenham: Edward Elgar Publishing 2021), pp. 112–125.

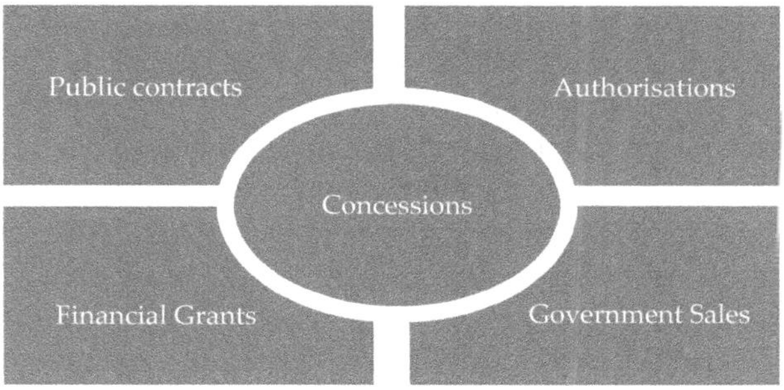

Figure 1.1 Limited rights.

characterised by the *acquisition* of certain goods or services by public authorities,[35] have always dominated the regulatory landscape of limited rights within EU law. Starting with separate directives for works, supplies and services in the 1970s and 1990s, the Public Procurement Directive (2014/24/EU) currently contains a general legal framework for the procurement of works, supplies and services. Both public contracts and concessions are contracts for pecuniary interest concluded in writing by means of which one or more contracting authorities or contracting entities entrust the provision and the management of services[36] to one or more economic operators. The relevant difference is that the consideration of a concession consists either solely in the right to exploit the services that are the subject of the contract or in that right together with payment, whereas the consideration of a public contract is payment only.[37]

Secondly, concessions can be contrasted with *authorisations*. The Services Directive (2006/123/EC) defines an authorisation as any (formal or implied) decision from a competent authority, concerning access to a service activity or the exercise thereof.[38] Both the Concessions Directive and the ECJ's case-law make clear that these authorisations have to be

[35] See Article 1(2) Public Procurement Directive: 'Procurement within the meaning of this Directive is the acquisition by means of a public contract of works, supplies or services by one or more contracting authorities from economic operators chosen by those contracting authorities [. . .].'

[36] For convenience, this provision of services includes the execution of works and the supply of products here.

[37] Article 5(1) Concessions Directive and Article 2(6) Public Procurement Directive.

[38] Article 4(6) Services Directive.

distinguished from concessions,[39] although the dividing line is not always clear and unambiguous.[40] While selectivity or choice is certainly not characteristic of each authorisation scheme,[41] the Services Directive introduces some specific provisions on limited-issued authorisations.[42]

The third type of rights that can be contrasted with concessions is that of *public facilities*. The most prominent example of this category is financial grants (subsidies), but also other forms of access to public facilities *in natura* (e.g. access to high school or university)[43] are part of this type. Again, the recitals of the Concessions Directive make clear that these grants should not be considered as concessions.[44] Unlike public contracts and authorisations, general EU legislation on the distribution of public facilities in general and subsidies in particular is lacking. To some extent, the EU Financial Regulation provides guidance for a generalised approach as it contains a separate title on the award of grants (next to public contracts).[45]

Finally, concessions are contrasted with the *disposal of public assets* by sale, lease or otherwise. The Concessions Directive states that those

[39] Recital 14 Concessions Directive. See also recital 57 of the Services Directive:

> The provisions of this Directive relating to authorisation schemes should concern cases where the access to or exercise of a service activity by operators requires a decision by a competent authority. This concerns neither decisions by competent authorities to set up a public or private entity for the provision of a particular service nor the conclusion of contracts by competent authorities for the provision of a particular service which is governed by rules on public procurement, since this Directive does not deal with rules on public procurement.

[40] For more detail, refer to Wolswinkel, 'Concession Meets Authorisation', 403–405.

[41] See also recital 13 Concessions Directive.

[42] In particular, the Services Directive distinguishes between the situation where the number of available authorisations is limited by overriding reasons related to the public interests ('artificially limited authorisations'; Article 11) and the situation where the number of available authorisations is limited because of the scarcity of available natural resources or technical capacity ('naturally limited authorisations'; Article 12). For more details, see C. J. Wolswinkel, 'The Allocation of a Limited Number of Authorisations: Some General Requirements from European Law' (2009) 2 *Review of European Administrative Law*, 2, 61–104.

[43] Case C-73/08, *Nicolas Bressol and Others* and *Céline Chaverot and Others* v. *Gouvernement de la Communauté française* ECLI:EU:C:2010:181.

[44] Recital 12 Concessions Directive: '[. . .] the mere financing, in particular through grants, of an activity, which is frequently linked to the obligation to reimburse the amounts received where they are not used for the purposes intended, does not fall under the scope of this Directive.'

[45] See in particular Title VIII of the Financial Regulation.

arrangements do not classify as concessions if the State or contracting authority establishes only general conditions for the use of these resources 'without procuring specific works or services'. Although choice or selectivity is also present in situations where the public authority decides with whom it concludes a contract for lease or sale (and with whom not accordingly),[46] the distinct feature between these sale or lease arrangements and concessions (or public contracts) is that the public authority acts as a seller, not as a buyer.[47]

Given the similarities between these different legal arrangements, especially when the available number is limited to a maximum, it is tempting to unite them under the umbrella of 'limited rights'. However, we should not neglect the inherent differences between these types of limited rights. In this sense, the more general legal debate on the multi-faced meaning of 'rights' has direct implications for our approach to 'limited rights' as a subset thereof. It is especially the American legal scholar Wesley Newcomb Hohfeld who can be credited for the criticism that the notion of 'rights' is sometimes used too easily, thereby providing for incorrect instances of analogous or deductive reasoning.[48] While the aim of this book is not to give a full characterisation of limited rights following Hohfeld's conceptualisation of rights (in privileges (permissions), claims, powers and immunities), his criticism forces us to apply analogous reasoning with regard to limited rights carefully. What is more, his disentanglement of the notion of 'rights' makes us aware that the limited rights we observe in practice do not always fit one to one in our theoretical legal concepts. Instead, the limited rights that we observe in (legal) practice do usually combine elements of different concepts. Well-known legal figures such as 'authorisations', 'grants' and 'public contracts' are often compounds of the theoretical legal concepts of 'permissions' and 'claims' as defined by Hohfeld.[49] In other words, limited rights are hybrid concepts in themselves more than once. For example, public contracts combine a (monetary) *claim* against the State

[46] Recital 15 Concessions Directive.

[47] See explicitly C-451/08, *Helmut Müller GmbH* v. *Bundesanstalt für Immobilienaufgaben* ECLI:EU:C:2010:168, para. 41: '[. . .] such a [public works] contract requires that the public authority assume the position of purchaser and not seller.'

[48] W. N. Hohfeld, 'Some Fundamental Legal Conceptions as Applied in Judicial Reasoning' (1913) 23 *Yale Law Journal* 16–59.

[49] See also Adriaanse et al., 'The Allocation of Limited Rights by the Administration', p. 29: 'Allocation of complex legal positions that comprise both rights and duties, obligations or charges'.

Table 1.1 *Limited rights*

	'Buying State'	*'Selling State'*
Bilateral	Public contracts	Government sales
Unilateral	Subsidies	Authorisations

with an *obligation* for the economic operator to provide a service to the State.[50] The grant of an authorisation, which could be considered a *permission* in itself, can go hand in hand with a monetary claim of the State, in particular if the number of authorisations is limited and these limited authorisations are granted by means of an auction. Thus, how we categorise limited rights depends on the perspective that we adopt. For example, privatisation could be equated with authorisation in the sense that the State acts in its selling capacity, disposing of something, while both public procurement and subsidisation assume that the State spends money to private parties in order to acquire something for the public interest. At the same time, authorisation and subsidisation could be grouped together as unilateral decisions, vested in public law, whereas public procurement and privatisation assume a bilateral process where public authorities act in their contracting capacity (see Table 1.1). Thus, the relevant dividing lines between limited rights are constantly moving.

1.2.3 Allocation and Competition

Whenever the number of applicants exceeds this limited number of rights available for grant, public authorities have to choose who gets what. In other words, limited rights cannot be granted easily to everyone, but have to be *allocated*, which assumes a choice to be made between applicants. Competition, however, is not a necessary consequence of limitation and allocation. However, once rights are limited, public authorities can use competition to allocate these rights. They can transform the administrative decision-making procedure into a contest with winning and losing candidates who compete with each other.

In this project, we understand 'competitive tendering' in a very broad sense as any decision-making process in which candidates can compete

[50] See C. E. C. Jansen, 'Allocation of Limited Rights from a European Public Procurement Law Perspective', in Adriaanse, Van Ommeren, Den Ouden and Wolswinkel, *Scarcity and the State*, pp. 252–253.

with one another in order to obtain the limited rights available for grant. The element of competition presupposes that these candidates are aware that they are competing with one another. Thus, competitive tendering always starts with an invitation for competition to potential candidates for the limited rights at stake. Although as a default option this invitation will be made public and generally accessible, the invitation could also be sent to a limited group of potential candidates. If only one potential candidate is addressed, there is no situation of competitive tendering. Admittedly, one could argue that there is indirect competition in the sense that if the candidate does not meet the authority's needs, the authority can address other candidates. However, direct competition where candidates are aware that they are competing with one another is lacking here.[51]

The term 'tendering' is less familiar outside the domain of public procurement law. Within the context of public procurement, 'tendering' has a specific meaning.[52] When the term 'tendering' is used outside this context, it is usually an equivalent to a 'beauty contest' as opposed to other allocation procedures, such as the auction. In as far as this notion of 'tendering' may cause some misunderstanding, it is also appropriate to refer to a 'competitive procedure' or 'competitive allocation' here.

In our broad definition of 'competitive tendering' or 'competitive procedure', the distinct element with other (non-competitive) decision-making procedures is the call for competition, which makes potential candidates aware that they are competing with one another for limited rights. To put it somewhat differently, it does not matter on the basis of what criterion the public authority makes its choice, as long as this choice has been preceded by some call for competition. Thus, allocation procedures such as a lottery or a 'first come, first served' allocation can also be included in this notion of competitive procedure, provided a call for competition has preceded this allocation procedure. This broad definition does not aim to exclude a more narrow understanding of competitive tendering in certain domains of limited rights. Instead, it is highly useful to make explicit several understandings of competitive tendering across limited rights by starting with the most general understanding thereof. Thus, what may count as non-competitive tendering in

[51] Jansen, 'Allocation of Limited Rights from a European Public Procurement Law Perspective', p. 241.

[52] Article 2(11) Public Procurement Directive defines a tenderer as an economic operator that has submitted a tender.

one domain of limited rights (e.g. authorisations) may count as competitive tendering in another domain (e.g. public contracts). For example, in some domains, allocation on a 'first come, first served' basis or allocation after a lottery are not included as competitive procedures, whereas such allocation procedures are included as being competitive in other domains. As a consequence, it is necessary to take into account non-competitive tendering as the logical counterpart of competitive tendering: whether or not competitive tendering is able to *optimise* the public interests involved also depends on the issue of how competitive tendering performs in comparison with the alternative of non-competitive tendering.

The broad definition of 'competitive procedure' adopted in this project fits with the approach taken in EU legislation. The PSO Regulation on public passenger transport services, for example, defines 'direct award' as the award of a public service contract to a given public service operator 'without any prior competitive tendering procedure'.[53] However, this regulation remains silent on the question of what competitive tendering entails. In the Public Procurement Directive, the publication of a call for competition is the constituent element to guarantee competitive tendering in the award of public contracts.[54] When it comes to adequate publicity with respect to limited authorisations, the requirement of transparency is also imposed to facilitate competition.[55] Thus, a broad definition of competitive tendering focussing on transparency prior to the allocation of limited rights seems useful for analysing the balancing of public interests across different types of limited rights.

1.3 Optimising Public Interests: A Legal Perspective

1.3.1 A Wide Range of Public Interests

To answer the central question of how the applicable legal framework impacts the realisation of different public interests through competitive tendering, it is also necessary to have a more or less shared understanding of 'public interests'. In general, public interests can be understood as a subset of social interests. Where interests are social whenever their promotion is desired by society as a whole, a public interest only arises

[53] Article 2(h) PSO Regulation.
[54] Article 26(1) Public Procurement Directive.
[55] Case C-203/08, *Sporting Exchange Ltd* v. *Minister van Justitie* ECLI:EU:C:2010:307, para. 41.

if the government takes up the promotion of a social interest in the belief that this interest will otherwise not be realised properly. Adopting social interests as public interests therefore means that the government makes it an *aim* of its policy to promote that interest.[56] Since we focus on governments allocating limited rights, we restrict our attention to 'allocation-oriented' public interests. Therefore, we understand a public interest specifically as any interest that a government aims to promote when *allocating* limited rights.[57]

Which public interests do we have in mind when focussing on the allocation of limited rights? The field of public procurement is a very useful starting point for identifying 'allocation-oriented' public interests. Sue Arrowsmith identifies eight different public interests involved in public procurement: (1) value for money, (2) achieving additional policies, (3) opening of markets, (4) equal treatment, (5) fair treatment, (6) integrity, (7) accountability and (8) efficiency of the process.[58] In this introductory chapter – and in the book as such – we take this approach in public procurement as the starting point for our analysis, but add three other public interests that seem to play a more distinct role in the allocation of other types of limited rights: (9) satisfying 'inherent needs', (10) safeguarding fundamental rights and (11) transparency.

While the resulting set of eleven allocation-oriented objectives seems rather heterogeneous, it is possible to cluster them. First of all, we have the public interest of satisfying the needs inherent to a certain type of limited rights. This public interest of 'inherent needs' adheres to the inherent characteristics of types of limited rights, for example acquiring something in the case of public contracts or permitting an activity in the case of authorisations. Next, we can cluster five 'output-related' interests, all relating to the outcome of the allocation procedure: value for money,

56 Netherlands Scientific Council for Government Policy, *Safeguarding the Public Interest: Summary of the 56th Report* (The Hague: Scientific Council for Government Policy, 2001), pp. 12–13.

57 Having in mind the perspective of an allocating authority acting within the boundaries set by the applicable legal framework, some public interests will be considered a constraint rather than an aim when awarding limited rights.

58 For a more detailed discussion of these public interests involved in the allocation of limited rights by public procurement, we refer to Chapter 2, Section 2.3, and to S. Arrowsmith, 'Public Procurement: Basic Concepts and the Coverage of Public Procurement Rules', in S. Arrowsmith (ed.), *Public Procurement Regulation: An Introduction* (Nottingham: EU Asia Inter University Network for Teaching and Research in Public Procurement Regulation, University of Nottingham, 2011), pp. 1–32 at pp. 4–19.

achieving additional policies, opening of markets, safeguarding fundamental rights and integrity. As opposed to this set of output-related objectives, we identify a set of five 'process-related' interests: equal treatment, fair treatment, transparency, accountability and efficiency of the process.[59]

While neither this inventory of public interests nor its categorisation is set in stone, we use this introductory chapter to reflect upon the specific role that the legal framework fulfils in the pursuit of these public interests when public authorities allocate limited rights. To that end, we make use of the public management theory of Mark Moore on creating and recognising public value.[60]

1.3.2 Towards a Strategic Triangle for Allocating Limited Rights

According to Moore, governments (and in particular public managers within those governments) should focus on creating *public value*. The core idea is that public authorities are responsible for using the powers entrusted to them to achieve the maximum public value possible in the particular context in which they find themselves. At first sight, *public value* could be considered as the achievement of collectively valued or desired social outcomes. This conception of 'public value', however, does not only focus on achieving 'social justice' for the society as a whole, but also on the idea of 'client satisfaction', with clients being understood here as the *direct* beneficiaries of government services.[61]

The resulting framework takes both the complex and the dynamic conditions into account that public authorities are confronted with. These conditions are complex in the sense that public authorities are held responsible for producing and protecting many different kinds of value, while they are also dynamic in the sense that public interests change over time. For those reasons, it is insufficient for governments to focus on the creation of public value only. Instead, there are three dimensions which have to be balanced to align them successfully:[62]

[59] This inventory of eleven allocation-oriented public interests has also been communicated to the authors of the chapters of this edited volume in the author guidelines.

[60] M. H. Moore, *Creating Public Value* (Cambridge, MA: Harvard University Press, 1995) and M. H. Moore, *Recognizing Public Value* (Cambridge, MA: Harvard University Press, 2013), p. 101 ff.

[61] Moore, *Recognizing Public Value*, pp. 59–60.

[62] Ibid., p. 102.

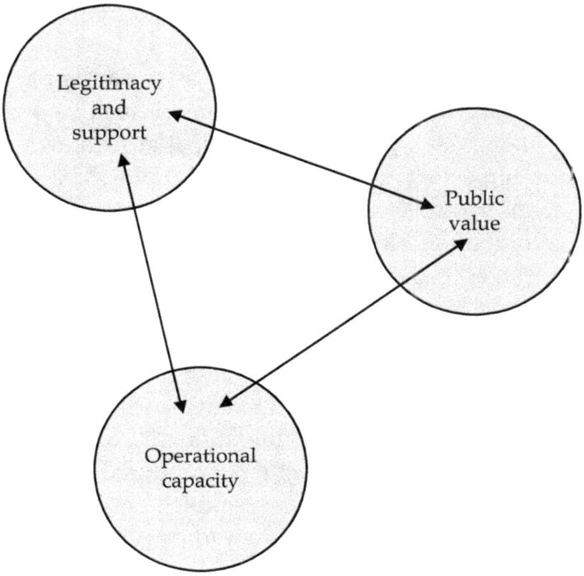

Figure 1.2 Strategic triangle.

1. a conception of public value that public authorities could produce using the assets entrusted to them;
2. sources of legitimacy and support for that vision of public value; and
3. operational capacity they would need to materially produce the envisioned public value.

The analytic framework developed to guide that effort is known as the strategic triangle (Figure 1.2).[63]

1.3.2.1 Public Value

The first part of this strategic triangle is the creation of public value in the aforesaid sense of combining socially desired outcomes with client satisfaction. Public authorities[64] should be explicit about the dimensions of public value they intend to produce. These dimensions of public value can be derived primarily from the authority's mission. The mission of a public authority, whether established by tradition, statute, professional

[63] Figure derived from ibid., p. 103.

[64] While Moore refers to public agencies (ibid., p. 53), we apply this strategic triangle to any public authority faced with the allocation of limited rights.

aspiration or informal agreement, embodies a collective conception of the purposes for which the authority exists and how it ought to behave in trying to achieve those purposes. Dependent on the authority at issue, we can think of a wide range of public purposes, such as public health, climate and sustainability, public housing, spatial planning, public education, telecommunication, public transport, employment opportunities, culture, and so on. However, in addition to this idea of mission achievement, three other dimensions of public value can be distinguished: unintended positive consequences, client satisfaction and justice and fairness. Side effects of an authority's behaviour that are not part of its existing mission can still contribute to the creation of public value. Client satisfaction embraces the idea that public authorities sometimes contract individually with certain individuals ('clients'), whereas the social outcomes (whether intentional or unintentional, positive or negative) defined above are ultimately enjoyed or endured by the collective public.[65] Justice and fairness, finally, complement the perspective of effectiveness and efficiency that is inherent to private organisations: once a public authority engages state authority, justice and fairness in both operations and outcomes become just as important as efficiency and effectiveness in achieving outcomes and satisfying clients.[66]

Once we apply this broad understanding of public value to the specific context of a public authority allocating limited rights, it is obvious that this understanding covers a wide variety of allocation-oriented public interests defined. First of all, the so-called satisfaction of inherent needs fits with the authority's mission. This interest combines the characteristics of the limited right at stake with the underlying public purpose. For example, the need inherent to public procurement is to acquire something in order to promote some public interest; the 'inherent' objective of sale is to dispose of something, again in the interest of some public purpose. The 'inherent' objective of licensing as such is to permit some activity under certain conditions. From a more general perspective, the licensing scheme as a whole has a different aim, like limiting how often or where a harmful activity is performed, or making the performance of such activities subject to control, for example in the interest of consumer protection or public safety. In other words, the aim of authorisation is to restrict *and* permit in the interest of some public purpose. Finally, the

[65] Ibid., p. 36.

[66] Ibid., p. 42 and pp. 55–56.

'inherent' objective of subsidising is to stimulate some desirable activity by a financial incentive.

Given that public authorities acquire or dispose of something or that they regulate an activity by licensing or subsidising, they can impose additional conditions on the allocation of the limited right at stake, for example by imposing requirements on employment, sustainability, and so on. These public interests are called 'additional' or 'subsequent' as they can only be taken into account *after* the initial choice has been made to award a specific type of limited rights. The use of the word 'additional' does therefore not express any form of hierarchy, but merely indicates some form of sequencing. Unlike the satisfaction of inherent needs, pursuing these additional policies – also called 'horizontal policy objectives'[67] – is less clearly linked to the authority's mission. It seems more appropriate to consider the achievement of additional policies as a socially desired outcome situated somewhere between the authority's mission and unintended positive consequences, whereas so-called necessary side effects, which have also been recognised in the ECJ's case-law,[68] clearly link to this latter category of unintended positive consequences of administrative action.

Allocation-oriented public interests such as safeguarding fundamental rights, integrity, equal treatment and fair treatment could also be considered as contributing to public value from the dimension of fairness and justness. This is perhaps less evident for the public interest of transparency, which is often conceived of as instrumental – as a means to an end, for example to ensure equal treatment or to increase economic performance and market efficiency[69] – but can also be considered as an intrinsic value of its own. In particular, transparency could be understood as a public interest relating to 'client satisfaction': the competing economic operators who are directly involved in the allocation process should have access to all relevant information, both *ex ante* and *ex post*. Accountability, finally, has a more ambiguous character in the strategic triangle since it combines the three dimensions of this triangle: the necessity of accountability for the allocation of limited rights forces

[67] See Chapter 2, Section 2.3.

[68] See, e.g., Case C-258/08, *Ladbrokes Betting & Gaming Ltd* and *Ladbrokes International Ltd* v. *Stichting de Nationale Sporttotalisator* ECLI:EU:C:2010:308, para. 28, referring to revenues as 'an incidental beneficial consequence'.

[69] A. Buijze, *The Principle of Transparency in EU Law* (Utrecht: Utrecht University, 2013), p. 35 ff.

public authorities to define concretely the dimensions of public value they create, helps them to mobilise support and legitimacy and guides them in using operational capacity to produce the desired effects.

1.3.2.2 Legitimacy: A Legal Framework

The second part of the strategic triangle is that of legitimacy and support. It is here that our legal perspective on the allocation of limited rights enters the scene. Although Moore distinguishes several sources of legitimacy, we focus on one of them: the law, as produced by the legislature (legislation) and courts (case-law).[70] These institutions (as well as other institutions, such as the media or interest groups) make external demands for accountability of public authorities. Since the external actors demanding accountability are the same as those who can authorise public action, authorisation and accountability are two sides of the same coin. In fact, authorisation is what gives legitimacy and support to a new public value proposition.

Thus, new legislation or a development in case-law authorises and guides allocating authorities in the choices they make in the design of their allocation procedure. In other words, since the legislature and courts act as the authorising environment for allocating authorities, the legal framework these external actors produce for allocating authorities functions as authorisation for their behaviour. From a legal perspective, this authorisation can take different forms. An important distinction is that between rule-based and principle-based regulation. Rule-based regulation lays down concrete rules public authorities should comply with when allocating limited rights. Principle-based regulation, either in legislation or in case-law, requires public authorities to act in accordance with some general legal principles without stipulating the exact meaning of those principles in a particular allocation context.

1.3.2.3 Operational Capacity: Efficiency and Effectiveness

The third and final part of the strategic triangle is about operational capacity, which is needed to materially produce the envisioned public value. Since public value cannot be realised without sufficient operational capacity, public authorities should constantly have attention for developing and directing operational capacity to achieve desired social outcomes.[71] This operational capacity not only should be conceived as the

[70] Moore, *Recognizing Public Value*, p. 115, refers to these institutions as 'formal overseers'.
[71] Ibid., p. 120.

use of public authorities' own assets but also includes the operational capacity this authority is able to purchase or to receive from society otherwise.

Whereas the relationship between operational capacity and public value is clear, it is equally important to highlight the dynamics between, on the one hand, legitimacy and support and, on the other hand, operational capacity. The legal framework, acting as an authorising environment, provides for assets to produce public value. These assets are not restricted to financial assets (money), but do also cover 'State authority'. More than considering operational capacity in itself, operational capacity should be considered in terms of a 'value chain' that links inputs of public resources (money and authority) into a production system consisting of public policies, programes, procedures and activities that produce transactions with clients and, ultimately, create some socially desired outcome. In the context of the allocation of limited rights, this means that allocation-oriented public interests such as value for money, opening of markets and efficiency of the process should not be seen as exclusively associated with this dimension of operational capacity, but should be taken into account when creating public value and assessing the costs thereof.[72]

The law also has a role to play when including 'operational' public interests such as effectiveness and efficiency in an authority's mission. By incorporating these interests into the applicable legal framework, legislators and courts highlight the importance of taking these interests into account. Thus, even though it can be highly debated whether efficiency and effectiveness are economic values that belong to the operational part only,[73] the law can act as an authorising environment to take these interests into account. Considering the authorising role of the law in more detail, rule-based action has arguably an efficiency element of its own, since it decreases the chance for arbitrariness when public authorities use their authority to create public value. However, the drawback of this approach is that allocating authorities lose sight of the underlying public interests, while totally neglecting other public interests that have not been touched upon in the legal framework.

[72] Ibid., p. 42.

[73] See two different approaches: T. Bingham, *The Rule of Law* (London: Allen Lane, 2010), not considering efficiency as an essential characteristic of the 'rule of law' versus J. Jowell, 'The Rule of Law and Its Underlying Values', in Jeffrey Jowell and Dawn Oliver (eds.), *The Changing Constitution*, 6th ed. (Oxford: Oxford University Press, 2007), p. 5 ff., considering efficiency as part of the 'rule of law'.

1.3.3 Towards a Public Value Account in the Allocation of Limited Rights?

As mentioned before, the starting point of our analysis is that of a public authority allocating limited rights within the boundaries of the applicable legal framework. For several reasons, the public management theory of creating public value is a helpful tool to reflect upon the role of this legal framework as an authorising environment for the allocating behaviour of public authorities.

First, from the perspective of the allocating authority, this legal framework should be seen as an element of legitimacy for its allocating behaviour. Thus, where the legal framework stipulates the mission of an authority and confers well-defined powers for predetermined purposes to pursue that mission, the authority can adapt its behaviour to this framework. By contrast, where the legal framework remains silent about the dimensions of public values that allocating authorities should produce or where it does not provide for the legal instruments to act accordingly, these authorities either stick to 'outdated' interests they were always assumed to pursue or take into account new, 'foreign' interests, for which they will be held accountable. For example, as long as EU procurement legislation had not addressed the question of whether contracting authorities could include additional policies in their procurement procedures (e.g. on 'green procurement'), they were often reluctant to do so. Similarly, where the legislature or case-law is explicitly prescribing some form of competitive tendering, it is clear for allocating authorities (at least to some extent) how they should act. By contrast, in the absence of such a clear-cut obligation, allocating authorities will continue to struggle with the question of whether they are obliged to organise some form of competitive tendering.

Secondly, the strategic triangle and the corresponding need to account for the creation of public value show that allocating authorities should strive for compliance with the law as such.[74] While both the legal framework and the available operational capacity have to be taken into account by allocating authorities, these dimensions are not the public values being produced. Instead, the concept of the strategic triangle is an invitation or even an incentive to make explicit the various public

[74] See Moore, *Recognizing Public Value*, p. 179, referring to the example of the Minnesota Department of Revenue, which stated 'compliance with tax law' as its envisioned public value.

interests involved in the allocation of limited rights. These different dimensions of public value, ranging from pursuing its mission or additional interests to respecting fundamental rights and equal treatment, can all be included in a so-called public value account, which can unveil the ongoing balancing of public interests.

Thirdly, it is important to stress that such a public value account does not assume any hierarchy between the various public interests involved. Thus, where in so-called green public procurement protection of the environment or climate is considered to be a secondary goal (with value for money being the primary one), this goal is primary in the allocation of emission permits (with value for money being a secondary one). The framework on the creation of public value, however, has a more neutral character: labels such as 'primary' and 'secondary' are considered to be irrelevant since they depend on the chosen perspective. Instead, the public value account offers a tool for allocating authorities to focus on various public interests, distinguish between them and report on them in order to create public value. It does, however, not prescribe *how* these public interests should be balanced against each other, but is a *condition sine qua non* to reflect upon this trade-off. In the absence of such a public value account, it is hard to unveil the balancing of public interests taking place.

Focussing in particular on competitive tendering, the underlying idea behind the choice for a competitive tendering procedure is its presumed capacity to achieve certain public interests. To an increasing extent, both legislatures and courts require public authorities to use some form of competitive tendering. From the perspective of the different public interests involved, there is no guarantee in advance that competitive tendering is the most ideal procedure to realise public interests; perhaps these public interests could be better served by a non-competitive procedure. Therefore, when assessing the merits of competitive tendering on the basis of a public value account, we should not lose sight of the ability of non-competitive procedures to create public value in a particular context.

1.4 Regulating Competitive Tendering: Dimensions of Comparison

1.4.1 The Unique Stages of Competitive Tendering

Following Moore's theory on strategic public management, we should consider the legal framework as an instrument used by external institutional actors (legislature, courts) to steer public authorities' behaviour in creating public value. With our focus on the allocation of limited rights, we should reflect in more detail upon the specific 'points of support' that the legal framework – as an authorising environment – offers to allocating authorities. In order to unveil whether and, if so, how the legal framework supports public authorities in dealing with the different public interests involved, it is necessary to distinguish between the different stages involved in the allocation of limited rights.

First, there is the *limitation* of the number of rights available for grant. In some cases, limitation and creation of government rights will almost go hand in hand. If the government has something (for sale) or needs something (to buy), the size of this demand or supply will be inherently limited. For example, if the government needs a certain amount of materials (computers, etc.) to fulfil its public tasks, it will conclude a public contract with a market party delivering this amount of materials (assuming it will not produce these materials itself). In other cases, however, there is no limitation *in advance* to the number of rights available for grant. In those cases, the creation of the right, for example by introducing a licensing or a subsidy scheme, should be distinguished from the limitation of that right: while the mere creation of some right does not need to imply a quantitative restriction, a limitation to the number of available rights allows for capacity restrictions.

Only once some government right has been (created and) limited does the stage of *allocation* come into play: an allocation procedure needs to be designed and applied resulting in a selection of winning applicants. Governments can choose among different allocation procedures with their own characteristics, such as an auction, a beauty contest, a lottery and a first come, first served mechanism. As said before, it is at this stage of allocation where competition enters the scene. However, it occurs more than often that legislative attention is restricted to the stages of creation and limitation only, thereby offering public authorities administrative discretion (or lack of guidance) when designing and applying the allocation procedure.

Even in cases where the legal framework has addressed the allocation stage in more detail, it should be noted that the allocation of limited rights is only a prelude to the stage where these rights can be enjoyed by the receiving party: once a limited right has been granted, the legal relationship between the public authority and the holder of that right is only to start (perhaps with the exception of sales). This *execution* stage, however, cannot be seen in isolation from its prior stages. Even where the legal framework is silent about this relationship, it is necessary to underline that the choice for competitive tendering can, for example, affect the duration of the right and the possibility of making amendments to the initial agreements during the execution stage. Thus, regulating competitive tendering is not only about regulating the allocation stage *stricto sensu*, but extends to prior and subsequent stages that are affected by the choice for competitive tendering and the way public interests are pursued.

1.4.2 *The Interplay between EU Law and Domestic Law*

As soon as public authorities allocate limited rights, the applicable rules of the 'allocation game' should be clear, both for the allocating authority and for the competing applicants.[75] What is less clear, though, is who should set these allocation rules. Is it a matter of discretion for the allocating authority or should the legislator provide legal guidance for the allocating authority? And even if the amount of discretion left to the allocating authority should be reduced by the legislator, is this up to the EU legislator or to the domestic legislator? This relationship between competent legislators is complex. For example, the ECJ ruled in *Sintesi* that the abstract and general fixing by the national legislature of a single criterion for the award of public works contracts deprives the contracting authorities of the possibility of taking into consideration the nature and specific characteristics of such contracts, taken in isolation, by choosing for each of them the criterion most likely to ensure free competition and thus to ensure that the best tender will be accepted.[76] In other words, the European legislator prohibited the national legislator from providing more support (or constraints) in the choice of the allocation procedure. In other cases, however, the EU legislator leaves it deliberately to the

[75] Case C-496/99 P, *Commission of the European Communities* v. *CAS Succhi di Frutta* ECLI:EU:C:2004:236, para. 111:

> [. . .] all the conditions and detailed rules of the award procedure must be drawn up in a clear, precise and unequivocal manner, to make it possible for all reasonably informed tenderers exercising ordinary care to understand their exact significance and interpret them in the same way, and to circumscribe the contracting authority's discretion and enable it to ascertain effectively whether the tenders submitted satisfy the criteria applying to the relevant procedure.

[76] Case C-247/02, *Sintesi SpA* v. *Autorità per la Vigilanza sui Lavori Pubblici* ECLI:EU:C:2004:593, para. 40.

domestic legislator to determine which allocation procedures public authorities are allowed to use.

Undoubtedly, European Union law plays an important role in regulating the allocation of limited rights.[77] This holds in particular for internal market law and to a lesser extent for competition law. Thus, the domestic legislator is bound by the legal constraints defined by EU law. The intensity of constraints provided for by EU legislation differs across limited rights. For example, with regard to the award of public contracts and concession contracts, the EU legislator has adopted monetary thresholds below which the EU public procurement directives do not apply.[78] By contrast, when regulating service authorisations under the Services Directive, the EU legislator has removed any requirement of cross-border interest. As a consequence, the allocation regime of the Services Directive does also apply to limited authorisations in purely internal situations.[79] These dynamics between EU and domestic law have immediate consequences for the institutional actors that allocating authorities should focus on when exercising their discretion in awarding limited rights.

1.4.3 Rule-Based and Principle-Based Regulation

Finally, irrespective of the different stages involved in the allocation of limited rights and irrespective of the competent legislator, there is the issue of *how* this legislator should authorise and steer public authorities' allocating behaviour. When we take EU law as the starting point of this legislative process and the allocation rules to be applied as the end point, there needs to be a transformation of 'principles' enshrined in (primary) EU law into concrete allocation rules in a regulatory process starting at EU level and ending at some domestic level. While not referring to allocation issues in particular, the market freedoms (principles) of the TFEU imply some general 'allocation principles', such as equal treatment of tenderers and transparency, as the ECJ's case-law shows. These principles can be further concretised, with more specific allocation rules being derived from these principles (e.g. on the duration of limited rights). However, there is

[77] See Chapter 8 of Van de Gronden.

[78] Article 4 of the Public Procurement Directive and Article 4 of the Concessions Directive.

[79] Joined Cases C-360/15 and C-31/16, *College van Burgemeester en Wethouders van de gemeente Amersfoort* v. *X BV* and *Visser Vastgoed Beleggingen BV* v. *Raad van de gemeente Appingedam* ECLI:EU:C:2018:44.

an inherent limit to this process of transforming general legal principles into concrete allocation rules: not every concrete rule on the allocation procedure can be considered a direct consequence of some general legal principle.[80] Thus, such a concrete rule should be codified separately to be applicable. In particular, if the EU legislator limits itself by referring to general principles only, then the domestic legislator could define more concrete rules under the umbrella of these general principles. But even at the level of EU legislation itself, the different types of limited rights show different legislative choices. For example, whereas the Public Procurement Directive describes five kinds of procedures in more detail, the Services Directive merely requires an impartial and transparent selection procedure.[81] Ultimately, the resulting degree of discretion for the allocating authority in choosing the applicable allocation rules and therefore in pursuing public interests will be the result of all these legislative choices, made by the EU and the domestic legislator.

1.5 Introducing the Book

1.5.1 A Transversal Research Project

The analytical framework that we have outlined above in Sections 1.2, 1.3 and 1.4 to study the allocation of limited rights as a *general* phenomenon in public law has been the point of departure for the research project ending up in this edited volume. Based on two expert meetings hosted by the Centre for Public Contract Law & Governance of the Vrije Universiteit Amsterdam, we have decided to adopt a two-stage approach to studying the allocation of limited rights in a transversal way. First, we have asked experts in different subfields of administrative law to characterise 'their' limited right and to give an 'account' of the way public interests are pursued and balanced against each other, either by competitive tendering or not. To that end, we have selected four types of limited rights: public contracts (*Sue Arrowsmith*), licences (*Ferdinand Wollenschläger*), subsidies (*Jacobine van den Brink*) and government sales (*Roberto Caranta* and *Benedetta Biancardi*). Without being the only limited rights that can be envisaged, these four rights can be considered

[80] See Case C-95/10, *Strong Segurança SA* v. *Município de Sintra and Securitas-Serviços e Tecnologia de Segurança*, ECLI:EU:C:2011:161, para. 42, where the ECJ held that a broad approach to the applicability of the principle of equal treatment could lead to the application of essential provisions of a directive to contracts not covered by that directive.

[81] See Article 12 Services Directive.

the most important ones, especially from a regulatory perspective, also because legislation on the allocation of limited rights is currently compartmentalised along these four types. What is more, all these limited rights have different intensities of legal frameworks in EU and/or domestic law, which also sheds light on the question of how the applicable legal framework impacts the pursuit of public interests by means of a competitive allocation of limited rights. In characterising 'their' limited rights, the experts have followed a uniform questionnaire, which we have drafted such as to facilitate comparison between limited rights.[82] The chapters in Part I of this book provide for these characterisations of different types of limited rights, starting with public contracts given its impact on other legal subdomains.

Next, we have asked other legal scholars to use these contributions as building blocks for transversal contributions in which they compare the different limited rights on a particular dimension described in the previous sections. *Steven Van Garsse* and *Ilenia Vandorpe* compare the different contributions by focussing on the differences between the limited rights involved to provide some insights into the possibilities and impossibilities of the idea of a common allocation mechanism (cf. Section 1.2.2). *Johan Wolswinkel* takes another point of departure, by comparing the different contributions as to the public interests involved (cf. Sections 1.3 and 1.4.1). *Johan van de Gronden* discusses the impact of EU law in regulating limited rights, with a particular interest in services of general economic interest (cf. Section 1.4.2). *Anoeska Buijze* analyses how one particular public interest, the multifaced concept of transparency, relates to other public interests in the context of competitive allocation and takes shape across the different limited rights (cf. Sections 1.2.3 and 1.3.1). Finally, *Chris Jansen*, *Rianne Jacobs* and *Frank van Ommeren* reflect upon the dynamics between rule-based and principle-based regulation across limited rights (cf. Section 1.4.3). Together, these transversal contributions form Part II of this book.

1.5.2 Overarching Observations: Concept, Context and Challenges

Where the aim of this edited volume is to overcome the legal fragmentation characterising the allocation of limited rights by public authorities,

[82] For this reason, the chapters in Part I of this book have a similar structure.

the different contributions to this volume show that this comparative view has added value to the legal analysis of the allocation of limited rights. We present our overarching observations in three steps here.

First, the book enriches our understanding of the *concept* of 'competitive allocation of limited rights'. Where limited rights can be defined quite straightforwardly as government rights that are available in limited amounts only, the characteristics of different types of limited rights vary greatly. For example, the decision to limit the number of rights attracts a lot of separate attention in the case of licensing, but is considered a given when public contracts or sales are concerned.

In addition, the book also makes clear that the concept of 'competitive tendering' or 'competitive allocation' is perceived differently across different types of limited rights. Although for every limited right discussed in the book there is a tendency to consider allocation by competition as the default rule, this notion of competition is operationalised differently. In the context of public contracts, competition has been operationalised in different procedures, which all aim to establish some form of competition. With regard to sales, State aid law seems to consider an unconditional bidding procedure as the only viable way to sell State assets in accordance with State aid law. As far as subsidising is concerned, there is also a tendency, especially at the EU level, to restrict competitive tendering to beauty contests, thereby ruling out the application of a lottery or a first come, first served mechanism. In case of limited licensing, competitive allocation does not seem to be restricted to a particular allocation procedure in advance. Thus, even the allocation of a licence on a first come, first served basis is not excluded in advance to be of a competitive nature, thereby allowing for a rather broad understanding of competition, which is almost equivalent to the transparency requirement.

Our second set of general observations relates to the *context* of the allocation of limited rights. In this regard, it should be stressed first that legal scholars should not be obsessed solely with the legal rules applicable to the allocation of a certain type of limited rights, but also with the objectives or public interests underlying these legal rules. In this regard, it is striking that Arrowsmith shows how the (detailed) rules on the procurement of public contracts reflect the continuous struggle to reconcile different public interests involved in the allocation of limited rights. As far as licensing or subsidising is concerned, this contextual approach, taking into account the underlying public interests involved, seems less developed, whereas State aid law seems very hesitant about incorporating (other) public interests in the process of selling public assets. At this point, those other subfields could learn from public procurement law how to make the balancing of public interests explicit.

Once we take into account this broader context of the allocation of limited rights, our attention shifts from the issue of whether certain legal rules have been complied with, to the issue of how the allocation of limited rights contributes to the realisation of public value. This focus on what Mark Moore would call the 'public value account' of limited rights does not nullify the legal perspective in the allocation of limited rights. On the contrary, a 'public value account' recognises explicitly the legal framework as an authorising environment to pursue public interests involved in the allocation of limited rights.

This context of realising public interests introduces new *challenges* for a legal approach to the allocation of limited rights. First, legal scholars and practitioners should pay attention to the public interests underlying the applicable rules. In particular, they should be aware of the trade-off between public interests that takes place when setting allocation rules, but also when interpreting general principles. Only by incorporating these public interests, can they establish to what extent the applicable legal framework functions as an authorising environment to create public value. Second, legal scholars and practitioners should be willing to consider other limited rights than the limited rights they are acquainted with. Even though the ultimate goal of the comparative approach in this book is not to harmonise the applicable allocation regime across all limited rights, taking notice of the (competitive) allocation of other limited rights can serve as an important source of inspiration. In some cases, there may be good reason to apply a legal rule that has been developed for another limited right. In other cases, however, the characteristics of the limited right at stake might oppose an analogous application of an 'allocation rule'. In those cases, legal scholars should try to justify that divergent application by the characteristics of the different limited rights. Third, legal practitioners should not only pursue process-related interests, such as equal treatment or transparency, but also be explicit about the output-related interests involved in the allocation of limited rights. In fact, the default rule to allocate limited rights through competitive and transparent tendering urges public authorities to make explicit in advance which output-related interests they pursue. At the same time, it is clear from several contributions in this book that the currently applicable legal framework, in particular the EU State aid regime, does not allow for sufficient flexibility in pursuing different output-related interests, such as additional policies. Thus, a final challenge this book entails is to reflect upon the applicable legal frameworks and their relationship to different public interests. One example thereof is the need to modernise State aid law in order to incorporate other public interests than value for money in the process of selling public assets. Another example is the returning question of whether the public interest of the opening of markets, which underlies the market freedoms of EU internal market law, has a similar impact as far as the interpretation of equality principles in domestic law is concerned. The answer to this question will determine whether similar requirements flow from domestic law as compared with EU law as far as the allocation of limited rights is concerned.[83]

1.6 Concluding Remarks: Towards a *ius distributiva commune*?

Limited rights occur in different areas of government intervention in different appearances. These differences between limited rights, further strengthened by the applicability of different legal regimes, may obscure the commonalities and similarities that public contracts, limited licences, financial grants and government sales have. What is necessary, therefore, is a common language that allows for a comparative examination of the allocation of different types of limited rights.

This book contributes to the development of that common language and shows that the legal frameworks for different limited rights are slowly but surely converging. This does not mean, however, that the allocation of each limited right should take place in the same way. On the contrary, the similarities between the different rights in being available in limited quantity only and being subject to general legal principles should be weighed against the differences between the different types of limited rights and their respective legal frameworks. Thus, this book calls for a continuous effort to analyse to what extent a certain limited right is similar to another limited right when addressing the question of whether some legal rule reflecting the balancing of public interests for a certain type of limited rights could also apply to other types of limited rights.

Inspired by the extensive set of rules developed in the context of public procurement law, at least some common core of 'allocation law' has

[83] See C. J. Wolswinkel, F. J. van Ommeren and W. den Ouden, 'Limited Authorisations between EU and Domestic Law: Comparative Remarks from Dutch Law' (2019) 25 *European Public Law* 559–586.

emerged, clearly indicating that the allocation of other limited rights is no longer a matter of administrative discretion from the side of public authorities. Instead, these allocating authorities should be aware that the allocation of limited rights is subject to general legal principles that need to be contextualised when being applied to allocation issues, requiring a level playing field with equal opportunities. In particular, the obligation to organise competition has evolved into the default rule for allocation for (almost) every limited right, even though public authorities enjoy a lot of discretion in organising that competition. That being said, the trade-off between the different public interests involved turns out to be a dynamic one, not only between but also within limited rights. This volume aims at contributing to a better understanding of those dynamics.

PART I

Characterising Limited Rights

2

Public Procurement

SUE ARROWSMITH

2.1 Introduction

Public procurement refers to a public authority's activity of purchasing goods or services (including construction services) from an external source,[1] from pens to satellites, and from street cleaning to long-term facilities management. It is an activity of great economic importance, accounting for a significant proportion of gross domestic product (GDP) in most countries – around 13.4 per cent of the European Union (EU) GDP in 2016.[2] Obviously, it is therefore of much interest from a public expenditure perspective. However, it is also important for many other reasons, including its role in ensuring quality public services, its significance in the fight against corruption and the role it can play in tackling other societal problems, ranging from climate change to modern slavery.

From the perspective of this book, public procurement is relevant because it involves the allocation of rights in the form of economically valuable contracts. These are limited rights in that the potential right to payment under a contract will generally attract the interest of more than one economic operator but can only be awarded to one.[3]

[1] This is the definition used by Jansen in the book to which this present book is a follow-up, except that here the word procurement is replaced by buying to provide a synonym for the 'procurement' element of the definition, for reasons explained below: see C. Jansen, 'Allocation of Limited Rights from a European Public Procurement Law Perspective', in P. Adriaanse, F. van Ommeren, W. den Ouden and J. Wolswinkel (eds.), *Scarcity and the State I: The Allocation of Limited Rights by the Administration* (Cambridge: Intersentia, 2016), pp. 239–276, at p. 240.

[2] For a summary of more recent data from the EU and elsewhere, see Z. Kutlina-Dimitrova, 'Government Procurement: Data, Trends and Protectionist Tendencies', European Commission Chief Economist Note – Trade (Issue 3, September 2018), in particular section 3.1, pp. 7–8, available at https://trade.ec.europa.eu/doclib/docs/2018/september/tradoc_157319.pdf.

[3] Jansen, 'Allocation of Limited Rights', pp. 253–254.

Further, it is of particular interest from the perspective of balancing interests through competitive tendering in allocating limited rights – the theme of this book – for a number of (often related) reasons.

First, as elaborated later, referring to the distinction employed in *Scarcity and the State I*,[4] on which this present book builds, public procurement usually entails allocation of limited rights based on substantive (material) criteria rather than some other approach (order of receipt, drawing of lots or proportional or *pro rata* division). This underlies competitive tendering processes in all fields, making procurement a useful analogy.

Secondly, such allocation has in fact generally been made in practice in public procurement through competitive tendering rather than some alternative, such as partnership sourcing (as elaborated below),[5] making the experience of public procurement very relevant for a general study of competitive tendering.

Thirdly – a point that does not necessarily follow from the second – there is a long and detailed history of *regulating* competitive tendering in procurement and regulating it in detail.[6] (As Jansen points out, at the EU level, the allocation of public contracts is regulated in more detail than the allocation of any other scarce right.[7]) This results in a wealth of both legal material *and* related commentary that can inform debate.

[4] P. Adriaanse, F. van Ommeren, W. den Ouden and J. Wolswinkel, 'The Allocation of Limited Rights by the Administration: A Quest for a General Legal Theory', in P. Adriaanse, F. van Ommeren, W. den Ouden and J. Wolswinkel (eds.), *Scarcity and the State I: The Allocation of Limited Rights by the Administration* (Cambridge: Intersentia, 2016), pp. 3–26, at p. 11; and in the same volume, L. Arroyo Jiménez and D. U. Fernández-Bermejo, 'The Allocation of Limited Public Rights: An Analytical and Constitutional Approach', pp. 27–53, at p. 34, dividing the criteria into substantive/material and other criteria.

[5] D. Parker and K. Hartley, 'The Economics of Partnership Sourcing versus Adversarial Competition: A Critique' (1997) 3 *European Journal of Purchasing and Supply Management* 115–125.

[6] For a general perspective on regulating this activity, see S. L. Arrowsmith, J. Linarelli and D. Wallace Jr, *Regulating Public Procurement: National and International Perspectives* (London: Kluwer Law International, 2000); P. Trepte, *Regulating Procurement: Understanding the Ends and Means of Public Procurement Regulation* (Oxford: Oxford University Press, 2004). On regulation at the EU level, see S. Arrowsmith, *The Law of Public and Utilities Procurement: Regulation in the EU and UK*, 3rd ed. (London: Sweet & Maxwell, vol. 1, 2014, and vol. 2, 2018) and the many works cited there; and on national approaches in the EU, see S. Treumer and M. Comba (eds.), *Modernising Public Procurement: The Approach of EU Member States*, European Procurement Law Series (Cheltenham: Edward Elgar Publishing, 2018).

[7] Jansen, 'Allocation of Limited Rights', p. 249.

Fourthly, this regulation has occurred at both the national level (including in EU Member States) and at the EU level, and there has been significant interaction between these different levels. Thus, the significant material that exists on the topic covers both the dimensions relevant to this book and also the relationship between them.

Fifthly, this is a type of limited right that has been studied from an international and comparative perspective,[8] creating useful input into the debate from a range of sources beyond the EU. These include, in particular, the United Nations Commission on International Trade Law (UNCITRAL) Model Law on Public Procurement 2011,[9] which is based on, and serves as a model for, national procurement systems on a global basis and to which this chapter will refer to illustrate certain points about national regulation; and the World Trade Organization's (WTO) Agreement on Government Procurement (GPA),[10] which provides open market and governance rules on a global level and also serves as a model for many regional and bilateral trade agreements in procurement.[11] A study of these instruments can help in assessing the EU position in procurement as a suitable model for regulation.

Sixthly, at the EU level it is in the context of public procurement that the European Court of Justice (ECJ) has in fact mainly developed and applied a more general principle of transparency – which will often be implemented through competitive tendering – to govern allocation of

[8] On this, see Arrowsmith et al., *Regulating Public Procurement*; Trepte, *Regulating Procurement: Understanding the Ends and Means*. Since these works, the literature has expanded significantly: recent brief summaries of various systems and developments are found in, for example, M. Audit and S. W. Schill (eds.), *Transnational Law of Public Contracts* (Bruxelles: Bruylant, 2016).

[9] See, in particular, S. Arrowsmith, 'Public Procurement: An Appraisal of the UNCITRAL Model Law as a Global Standard' (2004) 53 *International and Comparative Law Quarterly* 17–46; C. Nicholas, 'The 2011 UNCITRAL Model Law on Public Procurement' (2012) 21 *Public Procurement Law Review* NA 111–123; C. Nicholas, 'UNCITRAL and the Internationalization of Government Procurement Regulation', in A. Georgopoulos, B. Hoekman and P. C. Mavroidis (eds.), *The Internationalization of Government Procurement Regulation* (Oxford: Oxford University Press, 2017), pp. 86–110.

[10] See generally S. Arrowsmith and R. D. Anderson (eds.), *The WTO Regime on Government Procurement: Challenge and Reform* (Cambridge: Cambridge University Press, 2011) and the works cited there.

[11] R. D. Anderson, A. C. Müller, K. Osei-Lah, J. Pardo De Leon and P. Pelletier, 'Government Procurement Provisions in Regional Trade Agreements: A Stepping Stone to GPA Accession?', in S. Arrowsmith and R. D. Anderson (eds.), *The WTO Regime on Government Procurement: Challenge and Reform* (Cambridge: Cambridge University Press, 2011), pp. 561–656.

certain types of limited rights covered by the Treaty on the Functioning of the European Union (TFEU), leveraging the approach developed in the secondary legislation on public procurement (an interpretative device termed by Werlauff and Treumer as 'the leverage principle').[12] This makes an examination of the approach in that secondary legislation particularly important for our broader topic in an EU context.

In addition, as is evident from what was said above (and as we will elaborate below), public procurement activities typically involve a wide range of interests that need to be balanced, some or all of which are also relevant for allocating other types of limited rights; and public procurement has significant elements in common with certain other transactions involving allocation of limited rights, such as the indivisible nature of allocations (common to certain authorisations (monopoly or other limited licences) and certain other types of claims (sales, competitively awarded grants or entry into joint venture commercial partnerships)) and the fact that awards are sometimes time-critical for the potential awardees. These points mean that the public procurement experience provides insights for a range of relevant problems in allocating limited rights through competitive tendering.

Of course, as Jansen emphasises in *Scarcity and the State I*,[13] public procurement is one specific area with its own characteristics that must be kept in mind in developing a general theory of regulation. It is also essential to examine the solutions of both the court and the legislature with a critical eye, making use of the abundant literature, and not to assume that because a particular solution is firmly embedded in EU procurement law it is an appropriate solution that can be transferred to other contexts, even when the issues that arise are directly equivalent. However, subject to these caveats, a study of procurement can make a particularly valuable contribution, both in identifying the problems to be solved – the myriad different interests to consider and the often complex relationships between these interests and the mechanisms to implement them – and in providing examples of solutions.

Against this background, this chapter explains how the different interests involved in public procurement are balanced in the procedures for awarding public procurement contracts in the EU, both at the EU level and by the Member States, in the context of competitive tendering.

[12] S. Treumer and E. Werlauff, 'The Leverage Principle: Secondary Law as a Lever for the Development of Primary Community Law' (2003) 28 *European Law Review* 124–133.

[13] Jansen, 'Allocation of Limited Rights', p. 250.

After some preliminary observations on the concept of public procurement (Section 2.2), our question will be pursued by, first, identifying the various interests involved and explaining how these interests are relevant in principle to the regulatory systems of the EU and its Member States in public procurement in Section 2.3.[14] In Section 2.3 we also provide a brief analysis of the general concept of competitive tendering in the procurement context by way of essential background to the legal discussion. Here we will refer back to the theoretical analysis of these concepts in the book *Scarcity and the State I* that laid the foundation for the current work and further nuance and develop that analysis in the context of public procurement, where relevant for this chapter.

We then turn to the central question of how the issue of competitive tendering is addressed in the legal frameworks of the EU, as the regulator of the Member States, and of Member States within that EU framework (Section 2.4).

As there is such a significant volume of material on public procurement, we will look at this issue primarily from the perspective of three key interests, namely value for money in relation to commercial aspects of the procurement, effective implementation of industrial, social and environmental policies ('additional' or 'horizontal' policies) and efficiency of the procurement procedure, considering each of these three interests in turn. However, during the analysis of these three interests we will also touch on many of the other interests involved, by examining the way in which they are balanced against these three key interests. We will also look separately at the balancing of interests in the specific context of remedies, although again focusing mainly on these three interests.

2.2 The Concept of Public Procurement

The concept of public procurement, like any in legal discourse, can have different meanings in different systems and contexts, as well as fuzzy boundaries. The definition of public procurement at the start of this chapter, as the activity of a public authority in purchasing goods or services from an external source, serves to highlight the general scope of the chapter. However, it is appropriate at the outset to make some further preliminary points regarding this definition and, consequently, the scope of this chapter.

14 The EU itself also acts as a purchaser as well as a regulator of the Member States, but this dimension is outside the scope of this book.

The first is that the concept of public procurement is used here (as reflected in the definition) to include acquisitions through concession arrangements, namely arrangements under which a contracting partner is remunerated by exploiting the goods, works or services provided: for example, a toll road where the contractor is remunerated for building and maintaining the road. These are treated as distinct from public procurement in some regulatory systems, especially those of the Civil Law. However, they are included here since they involve the same essential features as other acquisitions and involve exactly the same interests and same considerations in balancing those interests. This is reflected in the fact that they are now regulated by the EU in an almost identical manner to other public procurement, albeit in a discrete legal instrument.[15] (In the author's view, they do not in fact warrant a different classification or instrument, nor is their actual treatment much different from other types of public procurement, despite the decision to regulate them separately and certain superficial differences.[16] They are also considered to fall within the descriptive notion of public procurement – not a technical term in English law – as used by English lawyers.) Such concessions are, on the other hand, to be distinguished as a practical phenomenon from simple authorisations that confer a right of exploitation without any *obligation* to provide goods, works or services, and thus without any element of acquisition that is central to the procurement concept, even though these are sometimes referred to as concessions.[17]

The second preliminary point is that the term 'public procurement' is sometimes used to refer not to the acquisition *process* but only to activity governed by a formal process and/or system of rules. For example, Jansen

[15] Directive 2014/23/EU of the European Parliament and of the Council of 26 February 2014 on the award of concession contracts, OJ 2014, No. L94/1 ('the Concessions Directive').

[16] S. Arrowsmith, 'Revisiting the Case against a Separate Concessions Regime in the Light of the Concessions Directive: A Specific Directive without Specificities?', in F. Amtenbrink, G. Davies, D. Kochenov and J. Lindeboom (eds.), *The Internal Market and the Future of European Integration – Essays in Honour of Laurence W. Gormley* (Cambridge: Cambridge University Press, 2019), pp. 370–395.

[17] Nor governed by the EU's procurement Directives: see Arrowsmith, *The Law of Public and Utilities Procurement*, vol. 2 (2018), at para. 14–24; J. Wolswinkel, 'From Public Contracts to Limited Authorisations and Vice Versa: Exploring General Award Requirements from the ECJ's Corollary Approach' (2015) 24 *Public Procurement Law Review* 137–163; G. S. Ølykke, 'Is the Granting of Special and Exclusive Rights Subject to the Principles Applicable to the Award of Concessions? Recent Development in Case Law and Their Implications for One of the Last Sanctuaries for Protectionism' (2014) 23 *Public Procurement Law Review* 1–20. On authorisations, see Chapter 3 of Wollenschläger.

in *Scarcity and the State I* states: 'Although the notion of "procurement" has much in common with "purchasing" or simply "buying", procurement is considered to relate to a more or less elaborate and staged process of decisions, eventually resulting in works, goods or services to be supplied in accordance with the public authority's expectation as to quality, delivery time and budget.'[18] This perhaps results from translating concepts that have this meaning in other legal systems and languages into the English term 'public procurement'. However, the concept does not generally convey that narrower meaning to English lawyers, and there is no direct equivalent of such a concept, perhaps as a result of the absence of a significant tradition of legal regulation of procurement in the English legal system prior to the advent of the EU regime.[19] In fact, the word procurement came into common use in English more to distinguish a type of acquisition in an organisational setting that is proactive and strategic, rather than – as implied by 'buying' or 'purchasing' – purely reactive, but is also commonly used as synonymous with buying in an organisational (as opposed to personal) context.[20] Thus 'public procurement' refers merely to the practical phenomenon of purchasing activity in the public sector rather than conveying any information about the approach to the function or to control. It is this use of the concept to refer merely to that practical phenomenon which is adopted here.

The third preliminary point is that there are some transactions sharing certain features with the 'central' case of procurement, or which involve both these features plus additional elements that are not of themselves in the nature of procurement, on which there has been legal debate over classification for the purpose of the EU's procurement Directives. These include sponsorship arrangements that involve providing some goods, works or services without direct financial payment; various forms of agreement for developing land; institutional public–private partnerships (IPPPs);[21] and arrangements under which procuring entities set up a list

18 Jansen, 'Allocation of Limited Rights', p. 240.

19 C. Turpin, *Government Procurement and Contracts* (London: Longman, 1989); J. M. Fernández Martín, *The EC Public Procurement Rules: A Critical Analysis* (Oxford: Clarendon Press, 1996).

20 Reflected in the fact that the UK-based global body for professionals, the Chartered Institute of Procurement and Supply (CIPS), adopted that name in 2014 to replace the Chartered Institute of Purchasing and Supply.

21 See Arrowsmith, *The Law of Public and Utilities Procurement*, vol. 1 (2014), at, respectively, paras. 6-12–6-13 (sponsorship and payment in kind), paras. 6-261–6-264 (development agreements), and paras. 6-238–6-241 (IPPPs).

of suppliers as the basis for selection by private parties using public funds.[22] Very often, these involve allocating limited rights, and competitive tendering or a procedure involving some similar elements is suitable to realise and balance the interests involved. In the absence of explicit secondary legislation on allocation, there is potentially a temptation to classify these as procurement in order to apply a detailed and certain system to the allocation, even when the full detailed rules of the procurement Directives are not necessarily appropriate. In general, however, it is submitted that other than for a false start in the area of development agreements,[23] the ECJ has generally classified these transactions appropriately. These situations, of course, provide an excellent illustration of the value of developing and applying a more general theory on the allocation of limited rights outside secondary legislation that can import elements of the public procurement rules that are suitable for these situations while rejecting or modifying those that are not.

Finally, this chapter only considers the situation in which a public authority has already both identified its need for particular goods, works or services and decided to satisfy these needs through undertaking a procurement – that is a purchase from an external source – rather than by some other method, such as providing services with its own employees (in-house provision). These earlier decisions of identifying needs and determining the method of provision fall broadly within the area studied as public procurement.[24] They involve a certain balancing of interests, such as balancing Member States' interests in freedom to organise their administration against EU interests in promoting a competitive market and, further, this could involve competitive tendering (which can potentially be used to decide whether operations should be carried on in-house or through procurement in the first place, as under the United Kingdom's (UK) regime of Compulsory Competitive Tendering in the

[22] Case C-410/14, *Dr. Falk Pharma GmbH* v. *DAK-Gesundheit* ECLI:EU:C:2016:399, and Case C-9/17, *Maria Tirkonnen* ECLI:EU:C:2018:142.

[23] See Arrowsmith, *The Law of Public and Utilities Procurement*, vol. 1 (2014), paras. 6-261–6-264.

[24] E.g. the Organisation for Economic Co-operation and Development (OECD) Recommendation of the Council on Public Procurement includes within the definition of public procurement 'the process of identifying what is needed; determining who the best person or organisation is to supply this need . . .' – OECD Directorate for Public Governance and Territorial Development, OECD Recommendation of the Council on Public Procurement (2015), p. 6, at www.oecd.org/gov/public-procurement/OECD-Recommendation-on-Public-Procurement.pdf.

1980s and 1990s).[25] However, following the approach adopted in considering public procurement law in the book *Scarcity and the State I*,[26] these decisions are outside the scope of this chapter, which will consider the manner of allocation of rights once these have come into existence and are to be the subject of some kind of competitive allocation procedure.

2.3 An Overview of Public Interests in Public Procurement

In general, the inherent objective or interest of public procurement, in the sense that the term is used in this chapter, is for a public body to acquire something that it needs. This is not invariably the sole or even main reason for undertaking a procurement: for example, public works programmes are commonly undertaken to boost employment, as well as for the benefit of the resulting works. However, even in those exceptional cases when acquiring something is not the sole or main reason for the procurement, acquiring something is still the inherent objective that explains the award of the limited right.

Once a public authority has made the initial decision to undertake a procurement, there are many interests to balance during the subsequent allocation procedure and thus to take into account in regulatory rules. As we will see, these interests differ between systems. As we will elaborate, their operation is also complicated by the multi-layered nature of procurement regulation in which different actors, such as the EU, national regulators, local regulators and individual contracting authorities, might want to pursue different, and possibly conflicting, interests. In general, however, as is elaborated below, competitive tendering is the key tool used to promote procurement objectives and to balance the interests involved, regardless of the goals and interests of the particular system.

Legal academics have offered various classifications of the various interests in the public procurement context. For example, Trepte has based his analysis of regulation on what he considers the three 'most readily identifiable' objectives of public procurement, namely economic efficiency, promotion of social and political objectives, and trade

[25] For an overview and further literature, see Arrowsmith, *The Law of Public and Utilities Procurement*, vol. 1, paras. 2-27–2-30.

[26] Jansen, 'Allocation of Limited Rights', p. 245 and also p. 259.

objectives;[27] Dekel analyses public tenders in terms of the interests of integrity, economic efficiency and equal opportunities;[28] while Schooner refers to nine (non-exhaustive) 'desiderata' of regulation: competition, integrity, transparency, efficiency, customer satisfaction, best value, wealth distribution, risk avoidance and uniformity.[29] The present author has previously adopted an eight-fold classification that provides a more comprehensive and nuanced approach and also serves to distinguish between, on the one hand, interests that can be considered as objectives in the sense of outcomes and, on the other hand, the means to achieve those outcomes.[30] (Some of Schooner's desiderata, for example, such as uniformity, and also competition in the sense used by Schooner, refer to means.) This eight-fold classification refers to value for money in relation to commercial aspects of acquiring the goods or services (commercial objectives); integrity; effective and efficient implementation of industrial, social and environmental policy (horizontal objectives); opening of markets to trade; equal opportunities and equal treatment for suppliers; fair treatment; accountability; and efficiency in the procurement procedure. All these interests, it is submitted, can be considered 'objectives' of the procurement process in the sense of desired outcomes and are certainly 'interests' that may need to be taken into account in conducting or regulating procurement. Kelman prefers an approach that, from the perspective of public procurement as an activity, sees as the only goal (or objective) for the public authority as obtaining best-value products and services; he contends that other interests often referred to as goals or objectives, such as integrity, are better characterised as 'constraints' that must be observed in achieving that goal.[31]

As Chapter 1 has explained, the present book builds on this eight-fold analysis of interests in public procurement to provide a framework for analysing the interests involved in the allocation of limited rights more

[27] Trepte, *Regulating Procurement: Understanding the Ends and Means*, p. 59.

[28] O. Dekel, 'The Legal Theory of Competitive Bidding for Government Contracts' (2008) 37 *Public Contract Law Journal* 237–268.

[29] S. Schooner, 'Desiderata: Objectives for a System of Government Contract Law' (2002) 11 *Public Procurement Law Review* 103–110.

[30] S. Arrowsmith, 'Public Procurement: Basic Concepts and the Coverage of Public Procurement Rules', in S. Arrowsmith (ed.), *Public Procurement Regulation: An Introduction* (EU Asia Inter University Network for Teaching and Research in Public Procurement Regulation, 2011), pp. 1–32 at pp. 4–19, at www.nottingham.ac.uk/pprg/documentsarchive/asialinkmaterials/publicprocurementregulationintroduction.pdf.

[31] S. Kelman, 'Reinventing Government, 25 Years On: Has the Procurement System Improved?' (2018) 27 *Public Procurement Law Review* 101–108.

broadly. Thus, the book takes as the basis for analysis these eight interests along with the 'inherent' interest involved in each type of right (as already referred to above) and two further 'interests'. One is transparency, which the present author has previously classified not as an objective or interest of the procurement process, since (as distinct from the interest of accountability, as elaborated below) in the way the terms are used in EU procurement law as well as in some national systems it has a different quality from the 'interests' above, being one of the means – or tools – to achieving desired objectives or interests,[32] rather than an objective or interest per se. This is elaborated further in the discussion of transparency below. The second further interest that this book refers to is safeguarding fundamental rights.

Before turning to the specific interests, we should finally mention that an important issue in examining the interests involved in public procurement has been that of a hierarchy of interests and the use of language that might imply such a hierarchy, whether in a particular procurement, in a particular system (including in its regulatory rules) or at an abstract level. In this respect, we sometimes find that even when various other interests are characterised as objectives, or goals, in the context of public procurement, commercial interests are sometimes characterised as 'primary'. This is seen at an abstract level, for example, in the OECD Recommendation on Public Procurement, 2015, which states in its definitions section: 'Primary procurement objective refers to delivering goods and services necessary to accomplish government mission in a timely, economical and efficient manner.'[33] This labels the interests referred to above as commercial objectives and efficiency of the process (an aspect of efficiency in a more general sense)[34] as 'primary'. These objectives are then contrasted with the objectives referred to above as horizontal objectives, which the Recommendation characterises as 'secondary': 'Secondary policy objectives refers to any of a variety of objectives such as sustainable green growth, the development of small and medium-sized enterprises, innovation, standards for responsible business conduct or broader industrial policy objectives, which governments increasingly pursue through use of procurement as a policy lever, in

[32] E.g. Arrowsmith, 'Public Procurement: Basic Concepts', pp. 21–23.

[33] OECD Recommendation of the Council on Public Procurement, p. 6.

[34] The term 'efficiency' generally refers to undertaking the task at hand in a manner that uses the minimum resources, including resources on processes.

addition to the primary procurement objective.'[35] A similar approach has also been seen at the EU level and in discussing national systems, including (in earlier days) by the present author;[36] in literature, the terminology of 'secondary' policies is often employed[37] (including by Jansen in *Scarcity and the State I*),[38] while those discussing the United States (US) federal system, for example, refer to 'collateral' policies,[39] with a similar connotation. A quite different view of procurement objectives at an abstract level, on the other hand, is espoused by Dekel, who asserts (with little argumentation) that from a normative perspective integrity is the most critical and 'primary' goal and that efficiency and equal opportunities are 'equally important' as each other but far less so than integrity[40] (and criticises the US federal system for failing to implement this hierarchy clearly).

A close study of public procurement at a system level reveals that, to the extent that the interests involved *are* articulated clearly, the relevant objectives and the hierarchy between them in fact vary significantly, as Trepte emphasises[41] and as is illustrated below; and there is also wide variation between individual procurements in particular systems. There is thus a danger in using hierarchical terminology: it may provide a misleading description, as it does not capture the phenomenon described accurately or completely, or may carry normative connotations detrimental to developing an appropriate balance between interests. Such language therefore needs to be avoided unless used with the specific and careful intention of describing such a hierarchy or promoting a

[35] OECD Recommendation of the Council on Public Procurement, p. 6.

[36] S. Arrowsmith, *Government Procurement and Judicial Review* (Toronto: Carswell, 1988), p. 81 (in relation to Canada) and (in relation to EU law and certain Member States), S. Arrowsmith, 'Public Procurement as a Tool of Policy and the Impact of Market Liberalisation' (1995) 111 *Law Quarterly Review* 235–284, note 1.

[37] E.g. H.-J. Priess and C. Pitschas, 'Secondary Criteria and Their Compatibility with EC and WTO Procurement – The Case of the German Scientology Declaration' (2000) 9 *Public Procurement Law Review* 171–195; R. H. Weber, 'Development Promotion as a Secondary Policy in Public Procurement? An Answer in the Light of Digital Solidarity Clause' (2009) 18 *Public Procurement Law Review* 184–200; D. C. Dragoş, B. Neamţu and R. Velişcu, 'Secondary Considerations in Public Procurement in Romania', in R. Caranta and M. Trybus (eds.), *The Law of Green and Social Procurement in Europe* (Copenhagen: DJØF Publishing, 2010), pp. 189–233.

[38] Jansen, 'Allocation of Limited Rights', p. 241.

[39] J. Cibinic Jr, R. C. Nash Jr and C. R. Yukins, *Formation of Government Contracts*, 4th ed. (Wolters Kluwer Law & Business, 2011), chapter 11 'Collateral Policies'.

[40] Dekel, 'The Legal Theory of Competitive Bidding', 267.

[41] Trepte, *Regulating Procurement: Understanding the Ends and Means*, *passim*.

particular normative approach. In the context of EU procurement law, for example, Arrowsmith and Kunzlik argue that using the label 'secondary' to describe industrial, social and environmental policies tends to suggest that these are of lesser importance than commercial policies, even when promoting important interests such as health and human rights, and even to de-normalise such policies by implying that they are not rational, normal or legitimate; thus, they prefer the value-neutral term 'horizontal policies' to ensure that regulators treat these policies on their merits (including in accordance with what they argue is a principle in EU law of the equal status of these policies with other procurement policies, as discussed below).[42] Taking account of this experience and literature in public procurement, the present book recognises the need to avoid assuming any hierarchy of objectives at an abstract level and therefore uses value-neutral terminology. As has been explained, the book uses the neutral terminology of 'additional' interests to describe some of these types of policies.

We can now outline briefly the various interests involved in allocating limited rights with reference to the public procurement setting.

2.3.1 Value for Money in Relation to the Commercial Aspects of Acquiring the Goods, Works or Services (Commercial Objectives)

The basic concept of value for money in procurement is used in various senses including – in a very broad sense – to refer to the notion of obtaining the overall best value in a procurement, taking account of, and balancing, *all* the interests that the procurement system seeks to achieve, and not merely the commercial aspects. In this chapter, we characterise the second interest in the list of interests in Chapter 1 for allocating limited rights,[43] which refers simply to 'value for money', as 'value for *money in relation to the commercial aspects* of acquiring the goods or services'. This definition refers explicitly to the commercial aspects in recognition that the notion of value for money is also often used in the much broader sense mentioned above.

[42] See further S. Arrowsmith and P. Kunzlik, 'Public Procurement and Horizontal Policies in EC Law: General Principles', in S. Arrowsmith and P. Kunzlik (eds.), *Social and Environmental Policies in EC Procurement Law: New Directives and New Directions* (Cambridge: Cambridge University Press, 2009), pp. 9–54.

[43] See Chapter 1, Section 1.4.2.

As highlighted by Arrowsmith, Linarelli and Wallace,[44] this can be seen to cover three matters: ensuring that goods or services procured are both suitable for purpose and not over-specified ('gold-plated'); ensuring that they are acquired on the best possible terms, which may involve considering not just price but also other commercial elements such as quality and delivery time; and ensuring that the supplier(s) actually provide the goods or services on the agreed terms. In *Scarcity and the State I*, Jansen separates the successful acquisition of the goods or services themselves, which he refers to as the 'primary' goal, from the interest in achieving value for the taxpayer's money in doing so,[45] and this is reflected in the identification in Chapter 1 of the present book of the separate 'inherent' interest in a limited right, which in procurement is the acquisition of the goods, works or services. Even if we separate the inherent interest in actually making the acquisition from implementation of value for money in relation to commercial aspects in general, however, the definition of value for money in the commercial aspects of the acquisition still embraces all three elements of the definition in Arrowsmith, Linarelli and Wallace since the interest is not just in securing delivery but doing so on the terms that were agreed.

As Jansen explains, we should also note that this broad objective of value for money (in relation to the commercial aspects of the procurement) itself entails a need to decide and implement a balance between different interests;[46] these include (among many others) security in delivery, price, different quality elements, aesthetics of products or services and timing of delivery (which may need to be balanced against both security of delivery and each other).

Value for money in relation to the procurement's commercial aspects is an ostensible goal of all procurement allocation procedures, and its attainment is also a goal of most – probably the overwhelming majority – regulatory systems at the national or sub-national level,[47] or at the level of individual procuring entities (which often adopt regulatory rules for their own procurements, as with standing orders of English local authorities). The balance of the different interests potentially involved

[44] Arrowsmith et al., *Regulating Public Procurement*, pp. 28–31.

[45] Jansen, 'Allocation of Limited Rights', p. 240.

[46] Ibid.

[47] As reflected in the UNCITRAL Model Law on Public Procurement 2011, available at https://uncitral.un.org/en/texts/procurement/modellaw/public_procurement (which is discussed further below).

(such as the relative importance of price and quality) may, of course, vary greatly, but criteria relating in some way to these commercial elements will generally provide important substantive (material) criteria for allocating the 'limited right' of a procurement contract. This is an interest that is reflected in the output of the process, as manifested in the undertaking to supply the subject matter, its features, the price paid and so forth.

However, while it is an objective of all processes and of the regulatory rules of most systems, it is not the case that *all* procurement *systems* have value for money in relation to commercial aspects as an objective in the sense of an outcome that the system aims to achieve. In particular, as the present author has argued elsewhere,[48] this is not in fact an objective of the EU procurement regime, since that is based on the internal market competences of the EU and as such the EU procurement Directives are – and, indeed, can be – largely concerned only with achieving free movement and opening markets to undistorted competition (as acknowledged also by Adriaanse et al. in *Scarcity and the State I*).[49]

Thus, for example, the Directives do not, and cannot, determine how different commercial elements should be traded off with each other, such as the extent to which public authorities should pay more for an aesthetically pleasing building or less delivery risk.[50] Nor do, or can, the Directives determine all the details of the procurement procedure directed at *efficient realisation* of the chosen interests – for example, by *requiring* use of negotiations where this could secure better products and prices. Under the Directives and the TFEU free movement rules, the

48 See, in particular, S. Arrowsmith, 'The Purpose of the EU Public Procurement Directives: Ends, Means, and the Implications for National Regulatory Space for Commercial and Horizontal Procurement Policies' (2011–2012) 14 *Cambridge Yearbook of European Legal Studies* 1–47.

49 Adriaanse et al., 'The Allocation of Limited Rights by the Administration', p. 18.

50 It is submitted that such decisions are also excluded from judicial scrutiny under a doctrine of 'excluded buying decisions', unless they result in indistinctly applicable measures or are made in bad faith, since they never create obstacles to participation in the market but simply define that market (i.e. what the public authority wants to buy) – a doctrine supported by policy considerations such as the limited potential for discrimination and limited impact on trade, avoidance of the costs of scrutiny of such commercial decisions and the lack of suitability of the judiciary for such an exercise: see S. Arrowsmith and P. Kunzlik, 'EC Regulation of Public Procurement', in Arrowsmith and Kunzlik, *Social and Environmental Policies in EC Procurement Law*. Case C-413/17, *'Roche Lietuva' UAB* ECLI:EU:C:2018:865 recently suggests that such decisions are reviewable under a proportionality test, but the judgment was given without an Opinion of the Advocate General.

relevance of value for money in relation to commercial elements is that it is an *interest of Member States that must be taken into account by the EU* in adopting and interpreting EU procurement rules. It is also the case that achieving EU objectives can enhance value for money of Member States by, for example, lowering prices, and that since – as we will see – the same tools of transparency and competitive tendering are the primary means to ensure both EU objectives and national value for money objectives, the EU regulatory framework tends to support, rather than conflict with, national value for money goals. However, it is important to bear in mind that value for money in relation to commercial elements of a procurement is not an objective of the Directives per se, remaining a matter of Member State policy within the framework set by the EU and that, as we discuss below, there may in some cases be a trade-off between this and EU objectives. The EU state aid rules also do not have value for money in relation to commercial elements as an objective as such although, as we will see, procurement that does not result in value for money may involve unlawful state aid.

2.3.2 Effective and Efficient Implementation of Industrial, Social and Environmental Policy (Horizontal Policies or 'Additional' Policies)

As alluded to above, public procurement is used as a tool to support or promote a variety of industrial, social or environmental objectives that are not *necessarily* connected with the objective for which the goods or services themselves are required. For example, a public authority procuring building works might create jobs working on the contracts for the unemployed or for disadvantaged minorities. Policy areas explicitly promoted or supported in the EU's procurement legislation or policy include promoting innovation, small and medium-sized enterprise (SME) development, provision of employment opportunities for disadvantaged persons, safeguarding labour standards and protection of the environment.[51] The safeguarding of national security – for example, through maintenance of domestic capability or security of supply – is also important in defence procurement.[52] The effective and efficient implementation of

[51] See further Arrowsmith, *The Law of Public and Utilities Procurement*, vol. 2 (2018), paras. 20-33–20-38 and the literature cited there.

[52] On the EU position, see Arrowsmith, *The Law of Public and Utilities Procurement*, vol. 2 (2010), chapter 15, and the literature cited there.

these kinds of policies is a further interest in public procurement that is reflected in the output of the allocation process.

We define this interest not just as an interest in achieving these 'additional' policies but in implementing them in an effective and efficient way. This is the equivalent of the 'value for money' element in relation to the commercial aspects of the acquisition of the goods, works or services themselves: public authorities aim not just to ensure the policy in question is put in place but that it is a policy that achieves its end and does so on the best possible terms – for example, that any premium paid for including a condition requiring long-term unemployed persons to be engaged on the contract is as small as possible – as well as a possible need to balance different horizontal policy concerns against each other. Chapter 1 seems to include the fact that 'conditions' are imposed as an element of the concept of additional policies but the concept of horizontal policies in public procurement (albeit equated with the concept of additional policies in Chapter 1)[53] is broader.[54] Chapter 1 also suggests that such policies are 'less clearly linked to the authority's mission' than satisfaction of inherent needs and their achievement more 'a socially desired outcome situated somewhere between the authority's mission and unintended positive consequences'.[55] However, often (except for policies concerned solely with legal compliance) this is emphatically not the case, with legal powers to pursue such additional policies limiting entities to policies that pursue their legally authorised mission, with efforts to pursue policies outside that mission giving rise to legal controversies.[56]

As mentioned, this dimension of procurement has sometimes been characterised as a 'secondary' one. However, it was suggested above that neutral terminology is preferable in examining this topic to ensure a balanced approach, bearing in mind that the treatment of this dimension may vary between different systems, entities and procurements. As already noted, Arrowsmith and Kunzlik use the term horizontal policies, since such policies are spread across procurements of goods, works and services used for many different objectives (the 'vertical'

[53] See Chapter 1, Section 1.3.2.

[54] See the taxonomy in S. Arrowsmith, 'Horizontal Policies in Public Procurement: A Taxonomy' (2010) 10 *Journal of Public Procurement* 149–186.

[55] See Chapter 1, Section 1.3.2.

[56] See, for example, in England and Wales, *R* v. *Lewisham LBC ex parte Shell UK* [1988] 1 All ER 938 and, in Canada, *Shell Canada Products* v. *City of Vancouver* [1994] 1 SCR 231.

objectives of the procurement). The concept of horizontal policies is not precise or intended to have any legal significance with reference to the EU or any other system, but merely to describe a general phenomenon with fuzzy boundaries: for example, contract terms limiting the adverse impact of a product's production or use on the environment (e.g. requirements for use of recycled materials or low-energy lightbulbs) could be seen as commercial policy (relating to the value of what is procured) or horizontal (relating to a cross-cutting environmental policy). Legislators and policymakers have sometimes drawn a distinction that relates broadly to the horizontal and vertical aspects, however – as in the case of rules in the EU Directives and UNCITRAL Model Law on Public Procurement 2011 that refer to the 'subject matter' of the contract, as discussed below – and then need to consider carefully how the distinction is to be made, depending on the specific objective of the rule in question. Other, helpfully neutral, terminology now in common use in the procurement field is that of 'sustainable procurement', defined by the United Nations Environment Programme as procurement that seeks to 'achieve the appropriate balance between the three pillars of sustainable development, i.e. economic, social and environmental'.[57] This latter term refers to all dimensions of the procurement on an equal level, the reference to sustainability highlighting the activity envisaged by the term horizontal policies.

Effective and efficient implementation of horizontal policies is an objective of many national procurement systems. Although this use of procurement is sometimes referred to in the EU context as if it were a novel phenomenon, in fact it has a long history, certainly in Anglo-Saxon countries;[58] and there is an extensive literature, including from an EU legal perspective.[59] What is recent, however, is greater recognition of this

[57] Quoted by B. Sjåfjell and A. Wiesbrock, 'Why Should Public Procurement Be about Sustainability?', in B. Sjåfjell and A. Wiesbrock (eds.), *Sustainable Public Procurement under EU Law: New Perspectives on the State as Stakeholder* (Cambridge: Cambridge University Press, 2015), pp. 1–22 at p. 2.

[58] See, e.g., J. E. Nagle, *The History of Government Contracting*, 2nd ed. (Washington, DC: George Washington University Press, 1999), pp. 361–378 (on the US); B. Bercusson, *The Fair Wages Resolutions* (London: Mansell Information Publishing, 1978) (on labour law issues); Arrowsmith, *Government Procurement and Judicial Review* (Canada); Turpin, *Government Procurement and Contracts* (UK).

[59] For a sense of the evolution of this topic, see, in particular, Arrowsmith, 'Public Procurement as a Tool of Policy'; Fernández Martín, *The EC Public Procurement Rules: A Critical Analysis*, chapters 2 and 3; C. McCrudden, *Buying Social Justice: Equality, Government Procurement, & Legal Change* (Oxford: Oxford University Press, 2007);

dimension of procurement in the EU's own legislation and policy,[60] especially in the 2014 procurement Directives, leading to this being given greater attention in some Member States.[61]

With respect to the EU itself, we should first emphasise that the EU-level open markets policy in procurement is in fact an industrial horizontal policy that must be implemented by national regulators and their public authorities. This policy needs to be balanced not only against Member State interests in commercial value for money and integrity, but also to an extent against Member States' interests in pursuing their own horizontal policies (including by supporting their national industry), and it is the constraint that the EU places on these national interests that has been most prominent in considering horizontal policies from an EU law perspective. In addition, however, the EU increasingly requires Member States positively to promote some other horizontal policies of EU interest, such as preventing climate change,[62] supporting SMEs[63] and

Arrowsmith and Kunzlik, *Social and Environmental Policies in EC Procurement Law*; B. Sjåfjell and A. Wiesbrock, *Sustainable Public Procurement under EU Law: New Perspectives on the State as Stakeholder* (Cambridge: Cambridge University Press, 2015). See further Arrowsmith, *The Law of Public and Utilities Procurement*, vol. 2 (2018), chapter 20 and the further current and historical literature cited there on different topics.

60 See Arrowsmith, *The Law of Public and Utilities Procurement*, vol. 2 (2018), paras. 20-33–20-38 and the legal provisions and literature cited there. Ensuring greater uptake of green and social procurement is one of the EU's six strategic priorities in its 2017 Communication from the Commission to the European Parliament, the Council, the European Economic and Social Committee and the Committee of the Regions: 'Making Public Procurement work in and for Europe' (Strasbourg, 3 October 2017, COM(2017) 572 final).

61 See, for example, PwC, Study on 'Strategic use of public procurement in promoting green, social and innovation policies' – Final Report (European Commission, DG GROW, Framework Contract No. MARKT/2011/023/B2/ST/FC for Evaluation, Monitoring and Impact Assessment of Internal Market DG Activities, 2015), available at https://ec.europa.eu/docsroom/documents/17261 (along with related individual country studies).

62 E.g. Directive 2009/33/EC of the European Parliament and of the Council of 23 April 2009 on the promotion of clean and energy-efficient road transport vehicles CJ 2009, No. L120/5, Art. 5; Directive 2012/27/EU of the European Parliament and of the Council of 25 October 2012 on energy efficiency, amending Directives 2009/125/EC and 2010/30/EU and repealing Directives 2004/8/EC and 2006/32/EC, OJ 2012, No. L315/1.

63 In particular, by requiring Member States to justify any decision not to divide contracts into lots: e.g. Directive 2014/24/EU of the European Parliament and of the Council of 26 February 2014 on public procurement and repealing Directive 2004/18/EC, OJ 2014, No. L94/65 ('Public Procurement Directive'), Art. 46(1).

promoting accessibility,[64] or encourages them to do so. The EU's recent activity on horizontal policies has two main dimensions. The first is that, following decades of debate in which there was a certain hostility towards horizontal policies within the Commission, the EU legislator has proactively relaxed and clarified the area of discretion for Member States in a way that tilts the balance of interests away from open markets and more towards other horizontal policies, both to recognise Member States' own policy interests and to allow Member States to use procurement to promote EU policies.[65] The second is that, as referred to above, the EU has increasingly sought to extend the *obligations* on Member States to use their procurement to support EU policies.

As with value for money in relation to commercial aspects, integrity and (as discussed below) open market goals, transparency and competitive tendering are key tools for realising horizontal policies; in the same way that tendering is the tool for seeking the best suppliers and inducing them to make the best offers from a commercial perspective, so also this tool enables the procuring entity to discover and incentivise those suppliers who can offer the best terms for the combined commercial and horizontal aspects of a procurement in those cases in which horizontal aspects are included.

2.3.3 Opening of Markets to Trade

As Arrowsmith, Linarelli and Wallace have highlighted,[66] one of the key reasons for the 'global reformation' in procurement regulation in the last few decades has been the development growth of international agreements aimed at opening public procurement to trade. As mentioned, this is the objective of the EU regime, with the procurement Directives (outlined below) seeking to ensure free movement and to open markets to undistorted competition. While this is, as mentioned, in fact one type

[64] E.g. Public Procurement Directive, Art. 42(2) requires that except in justified cases specifications must take into account accessibility criteria for persons with disabilities or design for all users and also must be established by reference to any EU mandatory accessibility requirements (as to which see now Directive (EU) 2019/882 of the European Parliament and of the Council of 17 April 2019 on the accessibility requirements for products and services, OJ 2019, No. L151/70, setting out such requirements, and also encouraging their use in public procurement where not mandatory under Directive 2019/882: see recital 90).

[65] On this point, see Arrowsmith, *The Law of Public and Utilities Procurement*, vol. 2 (2018), paras. 20-33–20-37.

[66] Arrowsmith et al., *Regulating Public Procurement*, chapter 1.

of horizontal (additional) policy, it is considered a distinct objective here in the light of its central role in the EU and, as a consequence, in shaping both the approach and detail of Member States' procurement regimes.

There are various different means by which states may seek to open markets to trade. One approach, for example, is greater standardisation of procedures to make it easier for foreign suppliers to operate (the focus of, for example, the Common Market for Eastern and Southern Africa (COMESA),[67] and the UNCITRAL Model Law on Public Procurement 2011).[68] However, while this is one *effect* of the EU procurement directives, it is not ostensibly – or even permissibly – the means adopted by the EU regime to this end. Rather, the EU regime seeks to open markets primarily through the approach employed by most trade regimes – including the WTO's GPA that forms a model for many other agreements – of prohibiting discrimination on grounds of nationality; requiring transparent procedures and a competitive tendering process based on verifiable non-discriminatory criteria, to prevent discrimination from being hidden; and requiring proactive removal of certain barriers to access, such as short time limits for responding to opportunities.[69] As mentioned, the use of transparency and competitive tendering to achieve open market goals means that the tools used to achieve these goals dovetail to a large extent with those used to give effect to national interests, including commercial value for money, integrity and national horizontal policies, as well as with the objective of equal treatment (see below). However, again a balancing exercise is sometimes required which, as we explain below, is sometimes seen, for example, in the clash between the EU policy of limiting discretion to prevent hidden discrimination and Member States' interests in allowing discretion for commercial reasons.

2.3.4 *Integrity*

'Integrity' refers to the need to avoid corruption ('abuse of entrusted power for private gain',[70] such as bribery or award of contracts based on

[67] See E. Nwogwugwu, 'Towards the Harmonisation of International Procurement Policies and Practices' (2005) 14 *Public Procurement Law Review* 131–152.

[68] Arrowsmith, 'Public Procurement: An Appraisal of the UNCITRAL Model Law'.

[69] Arrowsmith, 'The Purpose of the EU Public Procurement Directives'.

[70] Transparency International – the global coalition against corruption, 'The Anti-corruption Plain Language Guide' (Berlin: Transparency International, July 2009), p. 14, available at www.transparency.org/whatwedo/publication/the_anti_corruption_plain_language_guide.

personal interest) or collusion (bid-rigging), and also might be considered to embrace the need to avoid the perception of such behaviour,[71] such as in terms of the existence of conflicts of interest.

There is a close relationship between integrity and other objectives since integrity problems often have an adverse impact on those other objectives, including value for money in implementing commercial or horizontal objectives – that is, the absence of integrity can affect the outcomes of the allocation process.[72] (Trepte in fact examines anti-corruption strategy mainly under the efficiency objective.[73]) For example, awarding a contract on the basis of a bribe can mean that it is not awarded to the supplier offering the best terms.

As with commercial value for money and open market objectives, competitive tendering and transparency are key tools for delivering this objective. Both these points mean that the implementation of these two objectives in procurement is largely complementary rather than entailing a balancing exercise between commercial value and integrity.

However, it is appropriate to categorise integrity as a separate objective because the reasons for seeking integrity sometimes transcend its role in securing commercial value.[74] Thus, for example, this may be important for tackling organised crime funded through corruptly awarded contracts[75] or because of corruption's wider detrimental effect on economic development. Public authorities may also be particularly concerned with corruption because of its particularly serious effect on reputation. This can lead to integrity being given significant weight – some would argue too much weight.[76] While, as noted, there is significant complementarity between integrity and commercial value, there is also, however, a potential need for a balance here: for example, as we will discuss below, limits

[71] In this respect, the preamble to the UNCITRAL Model Law on Public Procurement 2011 refers in recital (e) to the objective of 'Promoting the integrity of, *and* fairness and public confidence in, the procurement process' [emphasis added].

[72] Although the relationship is complex and multifaceted; see, e.g., S. Rose-Ackerman, *Corruption and Government: Causes, Consequences and Reform*, 2nd ed. (Cambridge: Cambridge University Press, 2016), pp. 27–38.

[73] Trepte, *Regulating Procurement: Understanding the Ends and Means.*

[74] Arrowsmith et al., *Regulating Public Procurement*, pp. 37–38.

[75] See, for example, F. Anechiarico and J. B. Jacobs, 'Purging Corruption from Public Contracting: The "Solutions" Are Now Part of the Problem' (1995) 40 *New York Law School Law Review* 143–176.

[76] See, e.g., J. Branstetter, 'Darleen Druyun: An Evolving Case Study in Corruption, Power, and Procurement' (2005) 34 *Public Contract Law Journal* 443–468.

on discretion that can help prevent corruption can also hinder the ability of procuring entities to take optimal commercial decisions.

2.3.5 *Equal Opportunities and Equal Treatment for Suppliers*

Many national public procurement systems refer to a principle of equal treatment of participants.[77] Equal treatment has also been recognised by the ECJ as a 'fundamental' principle of EU procurement law, going beyond merely precluding discrimination on grounds of nationality, and defined by reference to the more general EU law principle of equality as requiring that comparable situations must not be treated differently and different situations must not be treated in the same way, unless objectively justified.[78] The principle has now been written into the Directives[79] and is used extensively not merely to interpret ambiguous provisions but also effectively to add obligations to the Directives' explicit rules.[80]

It is important to realise, however, that in general a concept of equal treatment may play one of two essentially different roles in public procurement.

First, it may serve simply as a means to implement other interests, including commercial value for money, integrity, effective implementation of horizontal policies and opening up markets. Providing all interested suppliers with an equal opportunity to compete, for example, seeks to ensure both that the best suppliers participate and that those suppliers are motivated by competition to put forward their best possible offers.

In addition, however, equal treatment may be an objective of the procurement process in its own right – what Dekel refers to as an 'intrinsic objective' of the process:

[77] See Dekel, 'The Legal Theory of Competitive Bidding', pp. 248–249 and note 37, regarding the concept of equal treatment as a 'fundamental' principle of the US procurement system. In the UK, the government stated in the 1995 White Paper, Setting New Standards: A Strategy for Government Procurement, Cm 1-2840 (1995) that competition is important not only as an aid to value for money 'but because it provides fair access to work paid for by the taxpayer'. The UNCITRAL Model Law lists equal treatment as an objective in the preamble to the Model Law (recital (d)).

[78] Joined Cases C-21/03 and C-34/03, *Fabricom SA* v. *État Belge* [2005] ECR I-1559, ECLI: EU:C:2005:127 at para. 27.

[79] E.g. Public Procurement Directive, Art. 18(1).

[80] See Arrowsmith, *The Law of Public and Utilities Procurement*, vol. 1 (2014), para. 7–15.

> In selecting its business partners, a procuring entity determines who will benefit from the economic advantage inherent in a contractual relationship with it. . . . The fact that the transaction involves public funds or assets, coupled with the fact that Government owes a fiduciary duty to the public at large, obliges the contracting authority to accord all members of the public an equal opportunity to enjoy this public benefit that the government has decided to allocate.[81]

Equal treatment as an intrinsic objective of procurement policy can potentially be derived from a more general constitutional principle of equal treatment, as found in some Member States or, in the EU context, from its role as a constitutional principle of EU law itself. It is often not entirely clear what status equal treatment holds in this respect in a given system. From the perspective of the procurement law of individual Member States, equal treatment may potentially be an intrinsic objective, although its actual status in this respect also may not actually be clear in individual systems. From the perspective of EU procurement law, equal treatment is arguably simply a means to the economic ends that flow from open markets, however, although again this is not wholly clear.

As Arroyo Jiménez and Fernández-Bermejo explain in *Scarcity and the State I*, the concept of equality of opportunity in the allocation of limited rights does not necessarily imply either transparency or competition.[82] However, in public procurement equal treatment as an intrinsic objective is generally given effect through a system involving competitive tendering and transparency since those are features of public procurement systems for other reasons, as is elaborated below. To the extent that equal treatment is merely a means to an end, it influences the way in which the competitive tendering system operates, with the aim of ensuring that the competition is fair. It may, for example, lead to accepting procedural costs in inviting and assessing large numbers of applications or tenders that cannot be justified by reference simply to the likely benefits of greater participation in terms of better tenders, which might be the sole concern in a system in which equal treatment is seen simply as a means for obtaining the best contract. The value placed on equal treatment from either perspective – as intrinsic objective or means to an end – may vary and affect the balance between this and other interests of the system.

[81] Dekel, 'The Legal Theory of Competitive Bidding', 246. It can be noted that Dekel considers that this duty is owed to the country's own citizens, but not to others (note 25).

[82] Arroyo Jiménez and Fernández-Bermejo, 'The Allocation of Limited Public Rights: An Analytical and Constitutional Approach', pp. 38–39.

Recognition of equal treatment as an intrinsic objective could lead to the principle being given more weight in the balancing exercise than it might be afforded if seen merely as a means to other ends.

2.3.6 *Fair Treatment*

Like equal treatment, fair treatment of suppliers is also sometimes regarded as a separate value in procurement. This can involve, for example, concepts of procedural fairness (or 'due process'), such as the right to input prior to an adverse decision. There is a debate in some legal systems, such as in the UK, over whether certain general administrative law standards, including due process, should extend to public procurement and other functions that are commercial and/or common to private parties.[83] In fact, many rules associated with fair treatment again support other objectives; for example, allowing representations prior to debarment can improve the quality of debarment decisions that can enhance commercial value. However, as with equal treatment, recognition of fair treatment as an independent value can have implications for the balance of interests in the process, in particular influencing the extent of procedural costs (financial costs or delay to the process) that are considered acceptable.

2.3.7 *Accountability*

Accountability, in the sense of enabling citizens and other interested parties to establish whether procurement objectives are being met, can also be seen as a goal of procurement systems or processes. Ensuring that applicable objectives and rules can be monitored and enforced is one dimension of what we discuss below as the concept of transparency, and, as explained there, transparency in general, including this accountability aspect, is important as a *means* to achieve many procurement objectives, including commercial value for money. In addition, however, accountability is a value in its own right, in particular in a democratic society, as expressed by Branstetter: 'Whilst [transparency] may play some role in

[83] For example, in the UK see S. Arrowsmith, 'Judicial Review and the Contractual Powers of Public Authorities' (1990) 106 *Law Quarterly Review* 277–292; S. H. Bailey, 'Judicial Review of Contracting Decisions' [2007] *Public Law* 444–463; E. Aspey, 'The Search for the True Public Law Element: Judicial Review of Procurement Decisions' [2016] *Public Law* 35–53.

prevention [of corruption] by making it more difficult for the culprit to get away with it, transparency is of more importance to restore faith in the system for contractors and the taxpayers by allowing them to see exactly what transpires in the government contracting arena.'[84] As a *separate* objective, it may justify costs – for example, financial costs of publishing information – that go beyond what is warranted by their contribution to other specific objectives such as financial savings or an actual reduction in corruption.

2.3.8 *Efficiency of the Process*

There is a further interest in any procurement in ensuring that the process is carried out efficiently – that is, without unnecessary or disproportionate delay or waste of resources for public authorities or unreasonable costs for suppliers. This is different from *effectiveness*, in the sense that the process is well designed to achieve its objectives (e.g. that the type of tendering procedure chosen is suitable for identifying the best offers), which can be considered as an element of the objectives already discussed above.

Efficiency in the process is obviously an important concern at the domestic level, including among EU Member States. There are some ways in which this interest complements other goals, in that lowering supplier costs attracts more participants. However, this interest also involves balancing time and resource costs against other objectives – for example, the costs of evaluating more tenders against the likelihood of more tenders producing better offers, as is elaborated later. From an EU perspective, delay and resource costs of the process are relevant from two perspectives in that, first, they are important concerns of Member States that the EU must consider when designing the procedures that Member States must apply, thus requiring a balance between open market objectives and this interest of Member States. Second, limiting costs of supplier participation is relevant to the EU's own objectives as these costs create obstacles to competition, and this has influenced the 2014 procurement Directives, as discussed later below.

2.3.9 *Safeguarding Fundamental Rights*

As mentioned, Chapter 1 treats safeguarding fundamental rights as a separate interest pursued in allocation procedures. Like other elements of

[84] Branstetter, 'Darleen Druyun'.

legal compliance set at a level beyond the regulating entity, this is not an interest that can be balanced against other considerations in regulating public procurement but one that must be fully respected in all cases. Thus, for example, to the extent that equal treatment is a constitutional principle that governs public procurement activity, as mentioned above, the need to respect this principle may limit the regulatory options.

2.3.10 *Transparency*

Finally, as mentioned above, transparency plays a key role in most public procurement systems as reflected in references to this in, for example, the Preamble to the UNCITRAL Model Law on Public Procurement 2011[85] and in other key models.[86] As noted by Arroyo Jiménez and Fernández-Bermejo in *Scarcity and the State I*, in general transparency is an open and ambiguous concept, or 'umbrella' notion.[87] In broad terms, it refers to openness and publicity, but is used with various more precise meanings and functions in different contexts,[88] and by different authors. As noted above, in procurement law[89] and literature, including by the current author,[90] it has been used to refer to open procurement processes as a *tool* for promoting many of the interests outlined above, rather than as an end in itself and in this respect is distinguished from what we call 'accountability', as just discussed. For this reason also, it is included in this chapter on public procurement at the end of the list of 'interests' identified in this book, since it has a subsidiary character to those interests, and is in fact better labelled as a tool than an interest as such.

In this context, the concept of transparency has four dimensions, as identified by Arrowsmith, Linarelli and Wallace:[91]

85 UNCITRAL Model Law on Public Procurement 2011, recital (f).

86 World Trade Organization, The Revised Agreement on Government Procurement (2012) (Annex to the Protocol Amending the Agreement on Government Procurement, adopted on 30 March 2012 (GPA/113)), sixth recital, available at www.wto.org/english/docs_e/legal_e/rev-gpr-94_01_e.htm.

87 Arroyo Jiménez and Fernández-Bermejo, 'The Allocation of Limited Public Rights: An Analytical and Constitutional Approach', p. 37.

88 See, e.g., A. W. G. J. Buijze, 'Transparency: The Swiss Knife of EU Law' (2015) 26 *European Review of Public Law* 1123–1161.

89 E.g. Case C-324/98, *Telaustria Verlags GmbH and Telefonadress GmbH* v. *Telekom Austria AG* [2000] ECR I-10745, ECLI:EU:C:2000:669.

90 E.g. Arrowsmith et al., *Regulating Public Procurement*, p. 73; Arrowsmith, *The Law of Public and Utilities Procurement*, vol. 1 (2014), paras. 3-13–3-15.

91 Arrowsmith et al., *Regulating Public Procurement*, pp. 74–75. These are reflected in the requirements of the United Nations Convention Against Corruption (UNCAC) in its

(i) *Publicity for contract opportunities.* This is regarded as a cornerstone of good national procurement systems that supports various interests, as reflected in the UNCITRAL Model Law requirement for a public advertisement under many procurement methods, including the 'default' method of open tendering.[92] From the domestic perspective, this allows the best suppliers to identify the opportunity, facilitating access by the procuring entity to the offers that best promote value for money in its commercial and horizontal policy goals; allows for monitoring to determine whether goals are achieved; and ensures equal treatment of interested suppliers and accountability. Publicity is also required by the EU procurement Directives for major contracts of EU Member States in the Official Journal of the European Union,[93] with only limited exceptions, to open markets by ensuring availability of opportunities across the EU and monitoring of the obligation not to discriminate; and the ECJ famously ruled in *Telaustria* that a similar publicity requirement derives from the TFEU free movement rules for contracts outside the Directives that are of cross-border interest[94] – a ruling that has formed the basis of parallel obligations relating to the allocation of other limited rights, as discussed in some of the other chapters of this book.

(ii) *Publicity for the rules governing each procedure.* Transparency in public procurement also entails publicity for both the general rules of the system – for example, on what type of procurement methods can be used and in what circumstances – and (for participants) the rules for specific procurements, such as the evaluation criteria and rules for their application. Again, these features are seen in national

requirements for dealing with corruption in Arts. 9(1)(a)-(d). The United Nations Convention Against Corruption was adopted by the UN General Assembly in New York on 31 October 2003 by Resolution 58/4 and entered into force on 14 December 2005; further details and the text available at www.unodc.org/unodc/en/corruption/uncac.html.

92 UNCITRAL Model Law on Public Procurement 2011, Art. 33(1) (open tendering) and see, e.g., Art. 35(1).

93 E.g. Public Procurement Directive, Art. 49 and Art. 26(5), with the exceptions (discussed later below) in Art. 32.

94 E.g. Case C-324/98, *Telaustria Verlags GmbH and Telefonadress GmbH* v. *Telekom Austria AG* [2000] ECR I-10745, ECLI:EU:C:2000:669.

systems, as reflected in the UNCITRAL Model Law,[95] and in trade instruments, including the EU Directives.[96]

This element of transparency again serves various functions in different systems and procedures. Thus, as stated by Arroyo Jiménez and Fernández-Bermejo in *Scarcity and the State I*,[97] such obligations are designed to limit and control the margin of discretion in allocating contracts and other limited rights to ensure that improper factors are not considered and that all interests are properly weighed;[98] in the procurement context this can clearly contribute both to commercial and horizontal interests; to integrity and to opening markets – like publicity for the opportunity, allowing for monitoring for the presence of corrupt motives or unlawful discrimination); to equal treatment – again through monitoring of treatment; and to accountability. Publicity for the rules of the procedure also has benefits for these interests that are separate from the role of transparency in controlling discretion, in particular giving bidders information to formulate submissions that best respond to the purchaser's needs and priorities – for example, on the balance between cost and quality – and so enhancing the value for of commercial or horizontal interests in this way, also.

(iii) *Rule-based decision-making that limits discretion.* Also important are substantive limits on discretion, which provide a degree of precision in decision-making. This dimension is often neglected and is apparently not per se regarded by Arroyo Jiménez and Fernández-Bermejo as an element of transparency in allocation procedures. However, it is submitted that this is fundamental to transparency, as well as having other benefits (such as enhancing the quality of decisions by sharing experience and inputs with

[95] UNCITRAL Model Law on Public Procurement 2011, Art. 5 (publication of legislation, administrative measures, case law etc. of general application) and Art. 11(5) (evaluation material).

[96] E.g. Public Procurement Directive, Art. 67(5) and as developed in the case law, in particular Case C-532/06, *Emm. G. Lianakis AE, Sima Anonymi Techniki Etairia Meleton kai Epivlepseon and Nikolaos Vlachopoulos* v. *Dimos Alexandroupolis and Others* [2008] ECR I-00251, ECLI:EU:C:2008:40; Case C-331/04, *ATI EAC Srl e Viaggi di Maio Snc, EAC Srl and Viaggi di Maio Snc* v. *ACTV Venezia SpA, Provincia di Venezia and Comune di Venezia* [2005] ECR I-10109, ECLI:EU:C:2005:718.

[97] Arroyo Jiménez and Fernández-Bermejo, 'The Allocation of Limited Public Rights: An Analytical and Constitutional Approach'.

[98] Ibid., p. 37.

individual decision-makers through rules).[99] From a transparency perspective, substantive limits on discretion are a condition for the visibility of the decision-making process that allows monitoring for corrupt and discriminatory motives and to ensure equality of treatment, and also for other benefits of transparency referred to in terms of allowing suppliers to understand how best to formulate submission. For example, a process that uses a sole award criterion of 'best value for money' does not secure the visibility needed for monitoring or other purposes,[100] even if it is publicised (in accordance with elements (i) and (ii) above) and there are mechanisms for monitoring and redress in accordance with element (iv) below.

This is again generally a prominent element in national procurement systems, as reflected in the UNCITRAL Model Law and – as is clear from the Directives' history – in the EU Directives.[101] For example, these rules limit award criteria to those relating to the subject matter of the contract[102] (which in the EU is a rule originally aimed at limiting discretion[103] and also has this as one of its functions in the Model Law);[104] require the formulation of criteria and rules on their application (weightings or at least order of importance of the criteria) in advance of tenders;[105] and include various limits that aim to reduce subjective discretion in applying the criteria.[106] Similarly, detailed rules in both the Model Law and

[99] See generally K. C. Davis, *Discretionary Justice: A Preliminary Inquiry* (Baton Rouge: Louisiana State University Press, 1969).

[100] Thus, for example, Case 31/87, *Gebroeders Beentjes BV* v. *State of the Netherlands* [1988] ECR 4635, ECLI:EU:C:1988:422, the ECJ indicated that simply awarding the contract based on a criterion of 'most acceptable tender' without further elaboration would give an unrestricted freedom of choice that would not be compliant with the directives.

[101] See, in particular, Arrowsmith, 'The Purpose of the EU Public Procurement Directives'.

[102] UNCITRAL Model Law on Public Procurement 2011, Art. 11(1); Public Procurement Directive, Art. 67(2).

[103] See the discussion in Arrowsmith, *The Law of Public and Utilities Procurement*, vol. 1 (2014), para. 7-170.

[104] See Guide to Enactment of the UNCITRAL Model Law on Public Procurement (adopted 2012), p. 85, available at https://uncitral.un.org/en/texts/procurement/modellaw/public_procurement/guide. See also the discussion later below.

[105] UNCITRAL Model Law on Public Procurement 2011, Art. 11(5); Public Procurement Directive, Art. 67(5).

[106] E.g. UNCITRAL Model Law on Public Procurement 2011, Art. 11(4), requiring that 'To the extent practicable, all non-price evaluation criteria shall be objective, quantifiable and expressed in monetary terms.' On the EU rule, developed in detail in the case law, see Arrowsmith, *The Law of Public and Utilities Procurement*, vol. 1 (2014), paras. 7-203–7-209.

EU Directives on the scope of exceptions to obligations to use competitive award procedures[107] can be seen as concerned with curtailing discretion to facilitate monitoring.

While limits on discretion play an important positive role, they can also, however, potentially be detrimental to procurement goals, as analysed notably by Kelman: 'As a strategy of organizational design, rules have a cautious character. When we design organizations based on rules, we guard against disaster, but at the cost of stifling excellence.'[108] For example, rules forbidding or limiting discussions with suppliers may be imposed to safeguard against abuse of discretion in negotiations for corrupt or discriminatory motives.[109] However, such discussions can be useful to ensure a specification is workable, enable products or services offered to be best adapted to the public authority's needs or prevent bid-rigging, leading to better value.[110] The appropriate balance between rules and discretion is a major issue for public procurement regulation.[111] This debate is relevant in determining the best *means* to promote particular interests – for example, whether and in what circumstances value for money can be obtained by limiting negotiation rather than allowing it, balancing the benefits of negotiation against the potential for abuse of discretion (and against other possible disadvantages of negotiations). It is also relevant, however, to balancing different interests against each other, and thus to the theme

[107] UNCITRAL Model Law on Public Procurement 2011, Art. 35; Public Procurement Directive, Art. 32.

[108] S. Kelman, *Procurement and Public Management: The Fear of Discretion and the Quality of Government Performance* (Washington, DC: The AEI Press, 1999), p. 28 S. Kelman, 'Remaking the Federal Procurement System' (2002) 31 *Public Contract Law Journal* 581–622.

[109] K. Krueger, 'The Scope for Post-Tender Negotiations in International Tendering Procedures', in S. Arrowsmith and A. Davies (eds.), *Public Procurement: Global Revolution* (London: Kluwer Law International, 1999); P. Bajari and S. Tadelis, 'Incentives and Award Procedures: Competitive Tendering vs. Negotiations in Procurement', in N. Dimitri, G. Piga and G. Spagnolo (eds.), *Handbook of Procurement* (Cambridge: Cambridge University Press, 2006), pp. 121–142.

[110] Ibid.

[111] See Kelman, *Procurement and Public Management*, p. 28; Kelman, 'Remaking the Federal Procurement System'; S. L. Schooner, 'Fear of Oversight: The Fundamental Failure of Businesslike Government' (2001) 50 *American University Law Review* 627–723; S. Arrowsmith, 'The EC Procurement Directives, National Procurement Policies and Better Governance: The Case for a New Approach' (2002) 27 *European Law Review* 3–24.

of the current chapter. For example, the EU Directives have limited use of flexible award procedures in order to prevent abuse to favour national suppliers, but have widened the grounds for their use successively in the 2004 and 2014 reforms to give greater freedom to Member States to use such procedures to obtain value for money where considered appropriate by the contracting authority.[112] The tension between different interests that results from this dimension of transparency is discussed further below in examining the specific interests of commercial value and horizontal policies.

(iv) *The possibility for verification and enforcement.* This fourth element of transparency includes information obligations, such as requirements to give reasons for decisions, requirements to record and/or publicise decisions and the reasons for them, and – less common – requirements to retain and/or give access to contractual documents, including concluded contracts. Many such obligations are found in both the UNCITRAL Model Law and EU Directives, with some EU Member States going further than required (e.g. in publication of or access to contractual documents, as in the UK).[113] This fourth

[112] In 2004, use was widened by introducing the competitive dialogue procedure for particularly complex contracts (see Directive 2004/18/EC of the European Parliament and of the Council of 31 March 2004 on the coordination of procedures for the award of public works contracts, public supply contracts and public service contracts, OJ 2004, No. L134/114, Arts. 28 and 29). In 2014, the possibility for using procedures involving some dialogue was extended even further; this was done by widening the grounds for competitive dialogue and also for the other flexible procedure in the Directive, a version of the negotiated procedure but with a call for competition (although the discretion available under the latter procedure – which was also renamed competitive procedure with negotiation – was tightened). See Public Procurement Directive Art. 26(4) and Arts. 29–30. For analysis, see S. Arrowsmith and S. Treumer, 'Competitive Dialogue in EU Law: A Critical Review', in S. Arrowsmith and S. Treumer (eds.), *Competitive Dialogue in EU Procurement* (Cambridge: Cambridge University Press, 2012), pp. 3–143, and M. Burnett and M. Oder, *Competitive Dialogue and Negotiated Procedures – A Practical Guide*, 2nd ed. (Maastricht: European Institute of Public Administration, 2015).

[113] See currently Crown Commercial Service, Procurement Policy Note – Promoting Greater Transparency (Information Note PPN 02/17, December 2017), available at https://assets.publishing.service.gov.uk/government/uploads/system/uploads/attachment_data/file/667054/17_v1.0.docx__1___1_.pdf; Crown Commercial Service, Procurement Policy Note 01/17 – Update to Transparency Principles (Action Note PPN 01/17, February 2017), available at www.gov.uk/government/publications/procurement-policy-note-0117-update-to-transparency-principles; Crown Commercial Service, The Transparency of Suppliers and Government to the Public (Crown Commercial Service, 2017), available at https://assets.publishing.service.gov.uk/government/uploads/system/uploads/attachment_data/file/592358/TransparencyPrinciplesFebruary2017.pdf. For a recent review of several Member States, see K. M. Halonen, R. Caranta and A. Sanchez Graells (eds.), *Transparency in EU*

element also demands mechanisms for enforcement, the most prominent in international models being supplier review. This is required by the UNCAC as an anti-corruption measure[114] and is included in the UNCITRAL Model Law since its revision in 2011.[115] This fourth element of transparency, by ensuring application of the regulatory rules, generally supports all interests that are pursued by those rules, although as we noted in the case of UNCAC they may be motivated by a focus on particular concerns (in that case, integrity) and, as we discuss below, different interests in the procurement process need to be balanced in devising and applying the rules on enforcement themselves.

In *Scarcity and the State I*, Arroyo Jiménez and Fernández-Bermejo suggested that at least *ex ante* transparency 'should always be obligatory' in procedures allocating limited rights that are seeking to achieve public interest goals (as do public procurement procedures in seeking a supplier to deliver what is needed for the public interest and on the best terms); they consider this necessary in accordance with principles of impartiality and objectivity, because of transparency's role in ensuring selection only of those who can fulfil the relevant interest and, of those, of the party who can do that in the best way.[116]

However, the need to ensure goods or services are actually acquired in the best way cannot alone explain the role of transparency in these procedures, given that private commercial procurement often does not involve *ex ante* transparency, despite the same imperative to acquire needed goods or services on the best terms. The private sector, instead, often employs 'relational' approaches, focusing on building long-term relationships with certain suppliers, rather than using 'transactional' approaches that entail a transparent award procedure (usually involving competitive tendering, as explained later below), which is focused on identifying the best supplier for each contract in isolation.[117] Such relational approaches (or 'partnership sourcing') can, for example, allow the

Procurements: Disclosure within Public Procurement and During Contract Execution, European Procurement Law Series (Cheltenham: Edward Elgar, 2019).

114 UNCAC, Art. 9(1)(d).

115 UNCITRAL Model Law on Public Procurement 2011, Ch. VIII (Arts. 64–69).

116 Arroyo Jiménez and Fernández-Bermejo, 'The Allocation of Limited Public Rights: An Analytical and Constitutional Approach', p. 48.

117 Parker and Hartley, 'The Economics of Partnership Sourcing'.

parties to work together investing resources in product development.[118] The reason for the dominance of a very different model in public procurement arguably lies in a combination of the different interests and/or the weight given to them in the public sector, and the institutional differences between the public and private sectors. Relevant from the former perspective can be the greater weight placed on integrity as a separate goal and the open market objectives of public procurement, for both of which transparency is a particularly relevant tool, and the existence of the separate equal treatment and accountability objectives. From the institutional perspective, factors such as low pay and lack of performance-related pay, absence of a profit motive, bureaucratic rules and budgets unrelated to particular goals, and political involvement, as well as lower commercial procurement skills and training, may mean that efficiency incentives are lower in the public sector and that therefore different strategies, including transparency are needed.[119] Higher levels of corruption, as well as greater importance attached to integrity, may also drive the use of transparency.[120]

Since the public sector environment and the existence and importance of different national goals differ between states, different levels of transparency may be appropriate for each. While, as noted, transparency is employed by most national systems to a degree, a central problem of any international or supranational system is the trade-off between the international/supranational interests and national interests, where the degree of transparency that is ideal for supporting the former interests in the variety of states that are subject to regulation goes beyond that considered optimum from the perspective of national interests in some of those states.[121] This has been an issue for the EU: as noted above, it has, for example, arisen in relation to the availability of flexible award

[118] See, e.g., M. Bensaou, 'Portfolios of Buyer–Supplier Relationships' (1999) 40:4 *Sloan Management Review* 35–44 and A. Lindgreen, J. Vanhamme, E. M. van Raaij and W. J. Johnston, 'Go Configure: The Mix of Purchasing Practices to Choose for Your Supply Base' (2013) 55 *California Management Review* 72–96. Parker and Hartley present such relationships as points on a continuum, the optimum approach depending on the circumstances: Parker and Hartley, 'The Economics of Partnership Sourcing'.

[119] See generally Trepte, *Regulating Procurement: Understanding the Ends and Means*; Rose-Ackerman, *Corruption and Government*, chapter 3.

[120] See OECD, Survey on Managing Conflict of Interest in the Executive Branch and Whistleblower Protection (2014), available at www.oecd.org/gov/ethics/2014-survey-managing-conflict-of-interest.pdf.

[121] In the EU context see Arrowsmith, 'The EC Procurement Directives, National Procurement Policies and Better Governance'.

procedures allowing discussion with suppliers. It has also been manifested, inter alia, in efforts to balance the open market interest with the interests of Member States in discretion to choose and implement horizontal policies in procurement, as discussed below.

2.4 Optimising Public Interests: Legal Choices and Assumptions

2.4.1 Competitive Tendering or Not?

2.4.1.1 The Rationale for Competitive Tendering as a General Principle for Allocating Public Procurement Contracts

We have discussed above the importance of four elements of transparency in procurement some, or possibly all, of which are also features of the transparency concept in the state's allocation of other limited rights. As we have already noted, however, Arroyo Jiménez and Fernández-Bermejo have rightly suggested that such transparency in the allocation of limited rights does not, on the one hand, always entail a competitive process; impartiality in allocation can also be achieved by other transparent methods, such as random selection or 'first come, first served'.[122]

They do suggest, on the other hand, that in those cases – including public procurement – where the selection of rights holders aims at realising a public interest, the principle of objectivity that requires a weighing of relevant interests entails, prima facie, 'genuine comparative or competitive procedures',[123] to ensure the best realisation of the objective. All processes of this kind can be considered as 'competitive tendering' in a broad sense, in accordance with the use of that term as defined in Chapter 1 of this book.[124] In public procurement, the relevant comparison is generally achieved for all but small procurements[125]

[122] Arroyo Jiménez and Fernández-Bermejo, 'The Allocation of Limited Public Rights: An Analytical and Constitutional Approach', p. 48.

[123] Ibid., and see also p. 45.

[124] See Chapter 1, Section 1.1.3.

[125] And for small procurement that involves a repeat element, both the EU procurement Directives and UNCITRAL Model Law provide for procuring entities to use broader ongoing arrangements. These involve competitive tendering either for access to be a supplier for the smaller orders (as with what the EU calls framework agreements) or systems that provide an efficient process for tendering the repeat orders (as with the EU's concepts of a dynamic purchasing system and a qualification system or what the UNCITRAL Model Law calls an 'open' framework agreement). Entities are pushed or required to use these processes through guidance or the impact of aggregation rules. See

through very structured tendering processes, usually ending with bids submitted to a common deadline, and it is for these kinds of formal processes that the label of competitive tendering is often reserved in the public procurement context.[126] As reflected in the UNCITRAL Model Law, tendering processes are publicly advertised and open to all qualified suppliers as the default approach,[127] although the label competitive tendering is also used for structured procedures involving invited suppliers only, such as the Model Law's restricted tendering procedure. Such competitive tendering, whether in the broad or narrow sense, serves to identify the supplier offering the best value in terms of relevant commercial and horizontal considerations for the specific contract. From a national perspective, competitive tendering is also a good means to ensure transparency within a context that requires a comparison based on substantive criteria, and hence to secure the benefits that transparency has for many of the interests in the process separately from the benefits provided by competition (monitoring of decision-making, etc., as just outlined above).

Since, however, much private procurement is undertaken without competitive tendering even in a broad sense but on a relational basis, as already explained above, as with transparency the choice of the 'default' public sector position of competitive tendering cannot, it is submitted, be explained *solely* by the need to select the best supplier for the public interest. Rather, it reflects the fact that tendering is the *preferred approach* to making such a selection *in the light of the additional factors mentioned earlier of different procurement objectives and weightings and a different institutional environment between the public sector and private sectors.* This is a point that is often missed when presenting the benefits of competitive tendering in a public law context.[128]

passim G. L. Albano and C. Nicholas, *The Law and Economics of Framework Agreements: Designing Flexible Solutions for Public Procurement* (Cambridge: Cambridge University Press, 2016).

126 Usage differs on attaching this label to less structured processes, such as the Model Law's competitive negotiations procedure or informal parallel negotiations with more than one supplier.

127 UNCITRAL Model Law on Public Procurement 2011, Art. 28(1).

128 There has long been debate over the related questions of whether public procurement would benefit from less reliance than at present on hard law to regulate public procurement and/or from formal competitive tendering as a tool, including in the UK where – in contrast with many civil law countries – there was in fact no general legal duty to undertake competitive tendering prior to the entry into force of legal obligations under EU law (as noted in Section 2.4.1.2). (This is related to the more general debate over the merits of rules versus discretion.) See Arrowsmith, 'The EC Procurement Directives,

In the author's view, the requirement of the EU procurement Directives for competitive tendering for major contracts (outlined below) is explained by the fact that tendering is both the most suitable method to secure the transparency that is necessary to open markets and at the same time consistent both with the need to ensure competition in EU markets and with the approach used by Member States to secure their national procurement interests. However, as mentioned, and as elaborated below, these national interests are not exactly the same as EU interests.[129] Further, differences between Member States in the existence and weighting of national objectives and their institutional environments – including levels of corruption and commercial skills – means that the most appropriate form of tendering from a national perspective may differ, making more difficult the task of balancing EU and national interests when designing the EU process. Country differences in this respect are clearly acknowledged in the UNCITRAL Model Law, which provides a toolbox of competitive procurement methods for different circumstances, rather than a 'one size fits all' solution.[130]

Competitive tendering also plays a role in EU state aid law. Preventing distortion of markets through aid to national industry is one EU policy that can be considered a horizontal policy relevant to public procurement, since public procurement awards can involve unlawful state aid, as discussed below. As we will see, competitive tendering has not been *required* as a tool to prevent unlawful state aid but is recognised in EU law as having a role in helping Member States to avoid unlawful aid by ensuring that contracts are awarded on market terms.

2.4.1.2 The Legal Framework for Competitive Tendering in the EU and Its Member States

As already explained, the EU's procurement Directives aim at achieving free movement and opening EU public markets to undistorted competition.

National Procurement Policies and Better Governance', pp. 21–23; Fernández Martín, *The EC Public Procurement Rules: A Critical Analysis*; Kelman, *Procurement and Public Management*, p. 28.

[129] S. Arrowsmith, 'The National and International Perspectives on the Regulation of Public Procurement: Harmony or Conflict?', in H. Olszewskiego and B. Popowskiej (eds.), *Gospodarka Administracja Samorzad* (Poznań: Wyd. Printer, 1997), pp. 9–36; also published in S. Arrowsmith and A. Davies (eds.), *Public Procurement Global Revolution* (The Hague: Kluwer Law International, 1998), pp. 1–26.

[130] See Guide to Enactment of the UNCITRAL Model Law on Public Procurement (2012), e.g. pp. 128–130 (in the commentary on methods of tendering).

These Directives date back to the 1970s and have gradually expanded in scope and rigour.[131] The current instruments are Directive 2014/24/EU ('Public Procurement Directive'), governing most major public contracts, which will be the focus of our discussion; Directive 2014/25/EU ('Utilities Directive') on procurement by entities operating in the utility sectors of water, transport, energy and postal services; Directive 2014/23/EU ('Concessions Directive') regulating concessions; and Directive 2009/81/EC ('Defence and Security Directive') on defence and security procurement.[132]

As we have already alluded to above, these Directives seek to achieve their objectives by requiring a transparent approach to procurement. This transparency is implemented by requiring the use of competitive tendering as the starting point, in line with the theories just discussed above of competitive tendering as the appropriate instrument to realise procurement goals in the public sector context.

The rules on competitive tendering in the Directives implement a 'strong' version of transparency across all four dimensions, as we have already illustrated by some of the examples given in the earlier discussion of the transparency concept. They contain a huge amount of detail implementing the four dimensions across all stages of the allocation process covering, in particular, publication of the notice, the procedures and criteria (and evidence thereof) for determining eligibility, criteria and procedures for reducing numbers of participants where the procuring entity has reasons to do this (such as excessive procedural costs of allowing tenders by any interested party), criteria and procedures comparing tenders and otherwise dealing with tenders and the scope for discussions with tenderers at various stages of the procedure.[133] The

[131] For a history, see Arrowsmith, *The Law of Public and Utilities Procurement*, vol. 1 (2014), paras. 3-27–3-54.

[132] Respectively Directive 2014/24/EU of the European Parliament and of the Council of 26 February 2014 on public procurement and repealing Directive 2004/18/EC, OJ 2014, No. L94/65; Directive 2014/25/EU of the European Parliament and of the Council of 26 February 2014 on procurement by entities operating in the water, energy, transport and postal services sectors and repealing Directive 2004/17/EC, OJ 2014, No. L94/243; Directive 2014/23/EU of the European Parliament and of the Council of 26 February 2014 on the award of concession contracts, OJ 2014, No. L94/1; and Directive 2009/81/EC of the European Parliament and of the Council of 13 July 2009 on the coordination of procedures for the award of certain works contracts, supply contracts and service contracts by contracting authorities or entities in the fields of defence and security, and amending Directives 2004/17/EC and 2004/18/EC, OJ 2009, No. L216/76.

[133] For a detailed analysis, see Arrowsmith, *The Law of Public and Utilities Procurement*, vol. 1 (2014) and vol. 2 (2018), and for an overview A. Semple, *A Practical Guide to Public Procurement* (Oxford: Oxford University Press, 2015).

competitive tendering procedures prescribed in the different Directives are in practice very similar; such differences as existed at one time between the predecessors to the Public Procurement Directive and Utilities Directive have been gradually eroded – for example, as regards the availability of flexible procedures involving discussions with suppliers.[134] The new Concessions Directive is also little different in practical terms.[135] A stringent supplier enforcement system (enhanced in 2007) is also provided for in secondary legislation.[136] Both the high level of detail in the procurement rules and the 'hard law' approach were already found in many Member State systems, being a characteristic of Civil Law systems on which the Directives were largely based, but involved a significant change of approach to procurement in both respects in some countries, including the UK,[137] which had previously operated a system that was both more principle-based and regulated the procurement of individual entities more through soft law than binding and enforceable legal rules.[138] In many Member States, the Directives' rules on tendering are supplemented with even more detailed national legal rules, the extent to which this is the case often (although not always)[139] reflecting the national traditions just referred to.

Procurement outside the Directives but still of cross-border interest is subject to the *Telaustria* transparency jurisprudence. This jurisprudence originated in a concern over the Directives' limited application in relation

[134] Such procedures are available for any contract covered by the Utilities Directive and under the Defence and Security Directive in the form of the negotiated procedure with a call for competition and are now also very widely available under the Public Procurement Directive following the reforms of 2004 and 2014 as discussed above, even if not universally available. Open procedures are not available under the Defence and Security Contracts Directive, which is an anomaly.

[135] Arrowsmith, 'Revisiting the Case against a Separate Concessions Regime'.

[136] For contracts governed by the Public Procurement Directive, the rules are found in Council Directive 89/665/EEC of 21 December 1989 on the coordination of the laws, regulations and administrative provisions relating to the application of review procedures to the award of public supply and public works contracts, OJ 1989, No. L395/33 ('Remedies Directive'). Substantial amendments were made by Directive 2007/66/EC of the European Parliament and the Council of 11 December 2007 amending Council Directives 89/665/EEC and 92/13/EEC with regard to improving the effectiveness of review procedures concerning the award of public contracts, OJ 2007, No. L335/31. For analysis, see Arrowsmith, *The Law of Public and Utilities Procurement*, vol. 2 (2018), chapter 22.

[137] See Fernández Martín, *The EC Public Procurement Rules: A Critical Analysis.*

[138] See Turpin, *Government Procurement and Contracts.*

[139] See, e.g., S. Treumer, 'Denmark as a Daredevil in EU Public Procurement Law: Implementation of Directive 2014/24 EU' (2019) 28 *Public Procurement Law Review* 173–185.

to concessions and leveraged the Directives to develop the Treaty rules both for these contracts and, later (as mentioned in this chapter's introduction), for allocation of other limited rights. This jurisprudence has been less relevant to procurement itself since 2014 when the Directives were extended to concessions and also applied more stringently to services contracts but is still relevant, in particular, to below-threshold contracts of cross-border interest.

The ECJ has never squarely stated whether the TFEU's transparency concept requires some kind of competitive tendering for procurement or instead permits other approaches that can secure impartiality (such as random or first-come-first-served approaches), since the jurisprudence has concerned either what obligations are implied when competitive tendering has already been chosen or what circumstances justify dispensing with transparency altogether.[140] However, given that competitive tendering is the general starting point in national procurement systems, it seems likely that the ECJ will follow the logic of Arroyo Jiménez and Fernández-Bermejo by requiring a comparative or competitive approach as the starting point. This seems to be also the view of the European Commission, which envisages at least a flexible competitive process with scope for discussions.[141] Non-transparent approaches akin to those used by the private sector that can achieve public interest goals but without securing impartiality can be ruled out as inconsistent with the very requirement of the *Telaustria* transparency principle.

As regards other aspects of transparency, there is much uncertainty over how far and in what respect obligations reflect those of the Directives themselves, although it is clear they do not do so in full,[142]

[140] For details, see Arrowsmith, *The Law of Public and Utilities Procurement*, vol. 1 (2014), paras. 4-43–4-46; C. Risvig Hansen, *Contracts Not Covered, or Not Fully Covered, by the Public Sector Directive* (Copenhagen: DJØF Publishing, 2012).

[141] European Commission, Commission Interpretative Communication on the Community law applicable to contract awards not or not fully subject to the provisions of the Public Procurement Directives, OJ 2006, No. C179/2 (hereafter 'Communication on non-covered contracts').

[142] Advocate General Fennelly stated in *Telaustria* that transparency is concerned with ensuring the 'fundamental fairness and openness of the award procedures' and that awards are not 'shrouded in secrecy or opacity', and do not require entities 'to apply by analogy the provisions of the most relevant of the EU directives' (para. 43 of the Opinion in Case C-324/98, *Telaustria Verlags GmbH and Telefonadress GmbH* v. *Telekom Austria AG* [2000] ECR I-10745 at I-10766, ECLI:EU:C:2000:270; and see Case C-231/03, *Consorzio Aziende Metano (Coname)* v. *Comune di Cingia de' Botti* [2005] ECR I-7287, ECLI:EU:C:2005:487).

and there is some EU-level case law indicating that certain obligations either do or do not apply.[143] For example, the ECJ has clarified that obligations to limit discretion by formulating the rules for the award in advance (an aspect of the third element of transparency referred to above) are less stringent than under the Directives, as the Directives generally require weightings in advance for award criteria, whereas the TFEU's transparency obligation does not (although, as under the Directives, if weightings *are* given, they cannot be changed after submission of tenders).[144] However, much more case law will be needed before it is known fully which of the Directives' many detailed rules on the four dimensions of transparency are applicable also under the TFEU. This case law is, of course, helpful in establishing the common element of obligations relating to allocation of limited rights and hence the balance of interests in relation to allocation of those other rights, where the allocation procedures used have a close analogy to those of public procurement; for example, the rule that evaluation criteria cannot be changed is likely to be equally relevant for competitive procedures for allocating government assets or grants. Supplier review of these obligations is required in accordance with general TFEU rules on remedies for enforcing individual rights[145] (again a less stringent standard than under secondary legislation on procurement);[146] and this also forms a common element of the general transparency obligation for allocation of limited rights.

As regards the discretion remaining to Member States to implement national interests, given the Directives' wide coverage and detailed obligations, this is now quite limited for major contracts and has gradually

[143] Again, for further detail see Arrowsmith, *The Law of Public and Utilities Procurement*, vol. 1 (2014), paras. 4-43–4-46.

[144] Case C-226/09, *European Commission* v. *Ireland* [2010] ECR I-11807, ECLI:EU:C:2010:697.

[145] See, e.g., Joined cases C-145/08 and C-149/08, *Club Hotel Loutraki AE, Athinaïki Techniki AE and Evangelos Marinakis* v. *Ethniko Simvoulio Radiotileorasis and Ipourgos Epikratias* (C-145/08) and *Aktor Anonimi Tekhniki Etairia (Aktor ATE)* v. *Ethniko Simvoulio Radiotileorasis* (C-149/08), [2010] ECR I-04165, ECLI:EU:C:2010:247; and for analysis Arrowsmith, *The Law of Public and Utilities Procurement*, vol. 2 (2018), paras. 22-43–22-47.

[146] Case C-91/08, *Wall AG* v. *Stadt Frankfurt am Main and Frankfurter Entsorgungs- und Service (FES) GmbH* [2010] ECR I-02815, ECLI:EU:C:2009:659, para. 141 of the Opinion of Advocate General Bot (a position also supported in the ruling in that case); Case C-203/14, *Consorci Sanitari del Maresme* v. *Corporació de Salut del Maresme i la Selva* ECLI:EU:C:2015:445, para. 16 of the Opinion of Advocate General Jääskinen.

diminished since the 1970s. While national governments have traditionally relied on competitive tendering to promote national interests and the EU's use of tendering to open markets dovetails with this, as we have seen national and EU interests are not identical: measures that promote open markets may be detrimental to national goals and, moreover, there may be differences between the EU regulator and national authorities on what measures *best* promote national goals, creating a need for a balance between EU and national interests, in designing EU procedures.

There is in theory more national flexibility in the award of below-threshold contracts. For those of cross-border interest, only the limited and uncertain principle-based obligations of the TFEU apply. However, the flexibility provided by principle-based obligations that are of a hard law nature and uncertain in content can be illusory, since this situation can impel Member States (or their entities) to fall back on the safety of detailed 'Directive-type' procedures; this is quite different from a scenario (such as applied in the UK prior to EU membership) in which the regulated party enjoys discretion to set its own procedures in the light of principles without legal interference. For contracts not of cross-border interest, Member States have complete discretion.[147] In practice, many below-threshold contracts are subject to competitive tendering for reasons of national interest (or still would be even if the EU did not require tendering). The fact that there are no EU Directives requiring tendering says nothing about whether or not competitive tendering is appropriate from a national perspective, since the Directives' thresholds are not aimed at identifying which contracts are suitable for competitive tendering for reasons of value for money, integrity and so on, but only at identifying contracts likely to be of interest to cross-border trade, requiring tendering to open markets.

It is also relevant to mention that public procurement activity may constitute unlawful state aid under Art. 107 TFEU, as receipt of a public contract may amount to an economic advantage that an undertaking would not have received under normal market conditions when the procurement is not in the nature of a 'normal commercial transaction'. This may apply when the contract is awarded on particularly favourable terms – for example, with an excessive price; when a contract amendment benefits the contracting partner without corresponding consideration;

[147] On Member State approaches, see, for example, D. Dragos and R. Caranta (eds.), *Outside the EU Procurement Directives – Inside the Treaty?* (Copenhagen: DJØF Publishing, 2012).

when the state purchases something for which it has no genuine need; and in certain cases in which the purchaser takes into account considerations not related to the contract's subject matter.[148] The fact that a contract is awarded under the EU's procurement rules is a significant consideration in helping to determine if the award involves state aid, following the EU procurement rules being considered as a mechanism to ensure that the transaction is a normal commercial transaction.[149]

2.4.1.3 Exceptions to Competitive Tendering

While an obligation to use competitive tendering is the starting point when allocating public procurement contracts in both EU and national systems, there are, however, exceptions. Under EU law these apply in cases in which there are countervailing interests that are considered to prevail over the public interests promoted by competitive tendering. As we will illustrate below in considering the balance between some key interests, often these countervailing interests are those in an efficient procurement process, as competitive tendering uses significant resources, but other interests are also relevant – for example, urgency in delivery. The derogations from tendering under the Directives are stated expressly,[150] and it appears that these derogations,[151] and possibly others,[152] also apply under the TFEU. As a general matter, since com-

[148] Case T-14/96, *Bretagne Angleterre Irlande (BAI)* v. *Commission of the European Communities* [1999] ECR II-139, ECLI:EU:T:1999:12.

[149] E.g. on the precise relevance of the Directives' award procedures, see Arrowsmith, *The Law of Public and Utilities Procurement*, vol. 1 (2014), paras. 4-82–4-86 and the literature cited there, and also European Commission, Commission Notice on the notion of State aid as referred to in Art. 107(1) of the Treaty on the Functioning of the European Union, OJ 2016, No. C262/1, available at https://ec.europa.eu/competition/state_aid/modernisation/notice_aid_en.html, confirming the view that following any of the competitive award procedures in the Directive is generally sufficient to preclude state aid, although not conclusive; and G. S. Ølykke, 'Commission Notice on the Notion of State Aid as Referred to in Article 107(1) TFEU – Is the Conduct of a Public Procurement Procedure Sufficient to Eliminate the Risk of Granting State Aid?' (2016) 25 *Public Procurement Law Review* 197–212.

[150] E.g. Public Procurement Directive, Art. 32.

[151] For example, Case T-258/06, *Federal Republic of Germany* v. *European Commission* [2010] ECR II-02027, ECLI:EU:T:2010:214, paras. 140–141; Case C-525/03, *Commission of the European Communities* v. *Italian Republic* [2005] ECR I-9405, ECLI:EU:C:2005:343, para. 47 of the Opinion of Advocate General Jacobs.

[152] This was accepted by the Commission in argument in Case T-258/06, *Federal Republic of Germany* v. *European Commission* [2010] ECR II-02027, ECLI:EU:T:2010:214.

petitive tendering is a starting point that is considered the best means to promote the relevant public interests, any exceptions are treated strictly. Thus, under EU law the exceptions are to be interpreted narrowly and the burden of proof that grounds for an exception exist is on the party invoking the exception, the reason given being that they are derogations from rules designed to ensure the effectiveness of the free movement rules.[153]

2.4.2 *Balancing Interests through Competitive Tendering*

2.4.2.1 Introduction

In the light of the many relevant interests and different levels of regulation, Section 2.4.2 takes the following approach, in order to focus on the most important and interesting issues.[154]

First, given that Member States must pursue national interests within a common framework that aims at opening markets, we will consider the relationship between, on the one hand, the EU's interest in open markets that provides the foundation for that framework and, on the other hand, national commercial interests, and the way in which these interests are balanced in the current competitive tendering rules of the common framework (Section 2.4.2.2).

We then focus on horizontal ('additional') policies. Here we consider, first, briefly, the issue of balancing horizontal and commercial interests at the national level and, secondly, how the EU's competitive tendering framework balances the EU's open market objectives with the horizontal policy interests of Member States (Section 2.4.2.3).

Third, we will look at the way in which the interest in an efficient procurement process is balanced against other interests in designing competitive tendering procedures (Section 2.4.2.4).

Finally, we will consider how all the main interests involved in public procurement – including the interest in an efficient procurement process, which is critical in this context – are balanced in the context of a supplier

[153] Case 199/85, *Commission of the European Communities* v. *Italian Republic* [1987] ECR 1039, ECLI:EU:C:1987:115, para. 14; Case C-328/92, *Commission of the European Communities* v. *Kingdom of Spain* [1994] ECR I-1569, ECLI:EU:C:1994:178, para. 16.

[154] The focus at the EU level will be on the rules in the EU Directives, rather than the much more skeletal rules stemming from the TFEU under the *Telaustria* principle, where the balance of interests is yet to emerge clearly and which are much less important in practice.

remedies system (Section 2.4.2.5). This is worthy of special attention since the issue of remedies in public procurement is of particular interest as a model for other areas.

2.4.2.2 National Commercial Objectives and the EU's Objective of Opening Markets

Competitive Tendering as a Tool for Achieving National Commercial Objectives in the Context of the EU Directives Competitive tendering is a mechanism designed to achieve commercial value for money, namely ensuring that goods, works or services are suitable, are obtained on the best possible commercial terms and are actually delivered and on the terms promised. It does so by making the contract opportunity widely known and accessible, and then using competition for that specific contract to induce suppliers to put forward their best possible offers.[155]

The common framework for opening markets in the Public Procurement Directive, within which Member States must fit their competitive tendering processes, uses as the default model (like the UNCITRAL Model Law) a procedure that is open in the sense that any interested supplier, first, is able to find the opportunity and, second, has a right to be considered based on objective criteria. The default model is also one that can be described as formal, or inflexible, tendering, involving a single tendering phase to a specified deadline, without opportunity to discuss, supplement or amend tenders after submission.

This default position takes the form of two separate methods, both freely available for all procurements.

One is the 'open procedure', which requires any interested supplier to be allowed to tender; a supplier cannot be prevented from tendering because it does not meet qualification conditions, although its tender can be rejected for this reason after submission.[156]

The second is called the 'restricted procedure' but is in fact an open method in the above sense of being openly accessible and giving all interested persons a right to be considered.[157] It is different from the Directive's open procedure, however, in two ways. First, there is a pretendering phase in which the contracting authority may reject suppliers

[155] See, e.g., Bajari and Tadelis, 'Incentives and Award Procedures'.

[156] For full details of the open procedure, see Arrowsmith, *The Law of Public and Utilities Procurement*, vol. 1 (2014), chapter 7.

[157] For full details of the restricted procedure, see Arrowsmith, *The Law of Public and Utilities Procurement*, vol. 1 (2014), chapter 8.

that do not meet eligibility conditions – a process that in many systems (unlike in the EU) forms part of procedures that are called 'open' and is referred to as 'pre-qualification' (as in the UNCITRAL Model Law, which allows prequalification as a phase in its open tendering method).[158] The second way in which the EU's restricted procedure differs from its 'open procedure' is that it also allows the contracting authority to invite to tender only a limited number of those meeting the eligibility conditions,[159] provided they are chosen on the basis of objective conditions (the 'reduction of numbers' process) in order to balance the cost of the procedure against other considerations. This is often allowed also in procurements systems outside the EU, but often only in limited circumstances, such as for complex procurement, and often in procedures where there is no open solicitation and no general right to be considered, and which are not classified as 'open' procedures.[160] However, it seems most useful to classify as 'open' all those procedures to which there is an open right of access based on merit-based criteria, as this right of access for all is the most important feature. It is important to emphasise here that the EU's 'restricted procedure' is very different from 'restricted tendering' in the UNCITRAL Model Law, which involves neither an open solicitation nor a right of anyone to be considered.[161]

This default form of competitive tendering under the EU's common framework involves the main phases below,[162] as well as detailed rules about both procedures in general (such as in the form of communications and record keeping) and the specific phases.[163]

(i) *Establishing the main specification and terms.* The open and restricted procedures envisage a fairly complete specification and set of contract terms prior to formally commencing the procedure (usually when the publicity for the contract occurs), as these must

158 See UNCITRAL Model Law on Public Procurement 2011, Art. 18.

159 This is provided for in Art. 65 of the Public Procurement Directive.

160 This is the case under the UNCITRAL Model Law on Public Procurement 2011, where no reduction in numbers process (but only pre-qualification possibility) is provided for in the default open tendering method.

161 See UNCITRAL Model Law on Public Procurement 2011, Art. 45 and see also Arts. 34 (1) and (5).

162 Referring to phases in the sense of processes that are envisaged by the Directive rather than phases of the procedure in a temporal sense, although it largely follows the order set out below, with some variation for different award procedures and national choices.

163 See again Arrowsmith, *The Law of Public and Utilities Procurement*, vol. 1 (2014), chapters 7 and 8.

be available electronically and free of charge at the start.[164] From a value for money perspective, it is in this phase that the authority ensures that what it is buying is appropriate (a process that may have involved research and consultation before launching the procedure) and also that it is defined so that everyone meeting the need can participate. The Directives and TFEU contain rules to ensure that suitable products, works and services are not arbitrarily excluded[165] (e.g. by requiring the use of a particular material when other materials are just as effective)[166] – important if the benefits of competition for commercial aspects of the procurement are to be realised, as well as for opening markets.

(ii) *Public solicitation*. There must be a public call for tenders in the EU's Official Journal, in a specific form that includes certain listed information and also must meet general requirements of transparency in its presentation.[167] Under the Public Procurement Directive, this notice can be either for a single procurement or (for some entities and procedures only) through a 'prior information notice' (PIN) covering a series of procurements. From an EU perspective, this serves the purpose of opening markets, but in practice also supports national objectives through wide competition, including commercial value.

(iii) *Qualification and/or reduction of numbers*. The qualification phase involves assessing whether suppliers meet eligibility conditions, generally including conditions on technical and financial competence to deliver, important from the perspective of national commercial objectives (as well as horizontal policy objectives).[168] From a national perspective, the extent and nature of the conditions set

[164] Public Procurement Directive, Art. 53(1).

[165] In the Public Procurement Directive, these rules are mainly in Art. 42. For details, see Arrowsmith, *The Law of Public and Utilities Procurement*, vol. 2 (2019), chapter 18.

[166] The ECJ has ruled that procuring entities must always be willing to accept equivalent products or services to those in detailed specifications: Case C-359/93, *Commission of the European Communities* v. *Kingdom of the Netherlands* (UNIX) [1995] ECR I-157, ECLI: EU:C:1995:14; and this is inherent also in the rule in Art. 42(3) of the Public Contacts Directive, requiring acceptance of equivalents where detailed specifications are used rather than performance or functional specifications, while Art. 42(4) also expressly requires reference to equivalents in the exceptional cases in which the procuring entity can refer to a specific make or source.

[167] See Public Procurement Directive, Art. 48(2), Art. 49 and Art. 51.

[168] See ibid., Arts. 56–64; and for details and analysis Arrowsmith, *The Law of Public and Utilities Procurement*, vol. 1 (2014), chapter 12.

and the assessment procedure will involve balancing the need to ensure delivery (taking account of such factors as the consequences of non-delivery, the difficulty of replacing a supplier and the risk in the sector concerned) against other interests, in particular procedural costs.

Under the Directive's restricted procedure, the qualification assessment takes place when firms are selected to tender, while under an open procedure, it takes place only at the tendering phase. The Directives limit the criteria and evidence that can be used, to prevent unreasonable barriers to market access in terms of procedural costs to suppliers, as discussed later below, and ensure transparency of the process from the perspective of the second and third dimensions of transparency[169] – publicity for applicable rules and limits on discretion.[170] The effect of these rules is to restrict Member States' discretion in taking assessment decisions in pursuit of national commercial objectives, for example by limiting Member States to considering only performance for the past three years for supply and services contracts or five years for works contracts.[171]

The reduction in numbers phase (in the restricted procedure) is again optional for Member States/contracting authorities so far as the Directive is concerned – that is, they may choose to invite all qualified suppliers or reduce numbers, which for the most part involves balancing the benefits for commercial value for money of wider competition against procedural costs (including the impact that high participation costs might have on the commercial terms achieved). Often such a process is suitable where the costs of preparing and evaluating tenders are high, as with complex service contracts.

(iv) *Award phase*. In the award phase, qualified suppliers submit tenders for comparison. The comparison induces suppliers to put forward the most competitive offers that respond to the authority's needs. The comparison may be made on the basis solely of the lowest price but also (as reflected in the UNCITRAL Model Law)[172] taking into account other interests, such as aesthetics or other quality features.

169 See, in particular, Public Procurement Directive, Art. 58(5).

170 On the purpose of these provisions, see Arrowsmith, 'The Purpose of the EU Public Procurement Directives', in particular pp. 18–20.

171 Public Procurement Directive, Art. 60(4) and Annex XII Part II, a) ii).

172 UNCITRAL Model Law on Public Procurement 2011, Art. 11.

Such other criteria are relevant where the products or services of suppliers may differ, and allow the authority to learn of, and take account of, these differences. Such a process is envisaged in the Directive, which requires the award to the 'most economically advantageous tender' (MEAT) that is compliant,[173] and allows MEAT to be assessed on the basis of price or cost *or* 'the best price–quality ratio', that is, including consideration of non-price factors.[174] The Directives' history indicates that the MEAT obligations, including an obligation to disclose the MEAT criteria, were originally introduced to secure the second and third dimensions of transparency – publicity for applicable rules and limits on discretion – and to facilitate the fourth dimension – verification and enforcement – to prevent national discrimination, in accordance with rules that were *consistent with* national interests in securing the award to the 'best' tender for commercial value for money purposes.[175] However, arguably these rules have since been 'reinterpreted' by judicial decisions and the later Directive as concerned additionally with ensuring the award to the best tenderer in the interests of ensuring a competitive market.[176]

(v) *Contract execution*. Finally, ensuring commercial value also involves some control over contract execution since a failure at the execution stage – whether because of non-delivery or change of terms (e.g. to increase the price) – can undermine the value achieved through the initial allocation of the right. Traditionally, control over this phase has relied less on transparency and legally enforceable general rules than has the allocation phase, reflected in the fact that the UNCITRAL Model Law on Public Procurement 2011 does not deal with this phase.

Actions in this phase likewise have potential implications for EU objectives – for example, by allowing a price rise to national suppliers – and the 2014 Directives thus introduced detailed rules[177] which codify and elaborate rules developed by the ECJ[178] based on

173 Public Procurement Directive, Art. 67(1).
174 Ibid., Art. 67(2).
175 Arrowsmith, 'The Purpose of the EU Public Procurement Directives', pp. 18–20.
176 Public Procurement Directive, recital 90; see Arrowsmith, *The Law of Public and Utilities Procurement*, vol. 1 (2014), at para. 7-169.
177 Public Procurement Directive, Art. 72.
178 Case C-454/06, *pressetext Nachrichtenagentur GmbH* v. *Republik Österreich (Bund), APA-OTS Originaltext – Service GmbH, APA Austria Presse Agentur registrierte Genossenschaft mit beschränkter Haftung* [2008] ECR I-04401, ECLI:EU:C:2008:351.

the Directives' general principles. These prohibit contract amendments except in specified cases in which there is either considered no risk to the open market objectives[179] (e.g. with change provided for in advance in transparent review clauses)[180] or in which this interest is considered to be outweighed by national interests, including in value for money, such as in continuity of supply and avoiding procedural costs (e.g. allowing contract amendments to deal with unforeseeable circumstances).[181]

As with many other rules, the Directives' minimum transparency requirements here often dovetail with national commercial interests by preventing the allocation process from being undermined from this perspective, as well as from an open market perspective. However, there is again a potential clash as national regulators could prefer to make wider exceptions to the general rules than judged appropriate by the EU, when they balance this national interest against the disruption and procedural costs of holding a new award procedure instead of extending an existing contract or against other benefits of modification. The circumstances of the *Finn Frogne* case,[182] in which a modification was made to settle a commercial dispute but the ECJ considered that this did not provide grounds for modification under EU law, are perhaps an example of how such a clash could occur.

As Jansen notes in *Scarcity and the State I*[183] the concept of value for money (in relation to commercial elements) itself involves deciding on a balance between different interests, which is implemented through the various phases above. This includes balancing security of delivery – the 'inherent' interest in public procurement – against, for example, elements of price and other costs, different quality elements, aesthetics and timing of delivery, and then balancing these elements against each other. For example, a specific element – availability of a telephone helpline for tenants in a housing services contract, for example – could be omitted

179 For details, see Arrowsmith, *The Law of Public and Utilities Procurement*, vol. 1 (2014), paras. 6-267–6-305 and the works cited there.
180 Public Procurement Directive, Art. 72(1)(a).
181 Ibid., Art. 72(1)(c)(i).
182 Case C-549/14, *Finn Frogne A/S* v. *Rigspolitiet ved Center for Beredskabskommunikation* (Centre for Emergency Communication of the National Police, Denmark) ECLI:EU:C:2016:634.
183 Jansen, 'Allocation of Limited Rights'.

altogether because the contracting authority is not willing to pay anything for it; could be specified as a minimum requirement (e.g. availability of the helpline for a certain number of hours a day), effectively meaning that quality element is indispensable regardless of tendered cost (although perhaps subject to a budgetary limit); and/or could be included in the award criteria along with price, in which case the contracting authority must decide how to balance the price/cost and other element (how much more it is willing to pay for that element), with the result that the exact extent of its inclusion in the contract will be determined by the tenders submitted.

Formal, single-stage tendering is not always, however, the most suitable form of competitive tendering for obtaining value for money; as mentioned earlier, more flexible forms – which may include multiple tendering stages and/or discussions with suppliers, including the chance to amend or improve initial offers – may sometimes be preferable, despite the reduced transparency. Reasons for this[184] include the value of discussions in formulating workable specifications and contract terms or in developing offers that meet the authority's needs, the potential of discussions for improving offers and risks of collusion from formal tendering in some markets. As reflected in the UNCITRAL Model Law,[185] procurement systems thus tend to provide for more flexible competitive procedures for certain contracts, but with the conditions for their use closely defined[186] and subject to controls, such as higher approvals.[187] The need for such procedures for commercial reasons in EU Member States is recognised in the Public Procurement Directive, in particular[188] in the competitive dialogue procedure[189] and competitive procedure with negotiation[190] (procedures that, for historical reasons, largely duplicate each other), available on the (overlapping) grounds of where the authority's needs require adapting readily available solutions;

184 Krueger, 'The Scope for Post-Tender Negotiations'; Bajari and Tadelis, 'Incentives and Award Procedures'.

185 See UNCITRAL Model Law on Public Procurement 2011, chapter II on the different flexible procurement methods.

186 For the conditions applicable to flexible methods under the UNCITRAL Model Law on Public Procurement 2011, see Art. 30(1)-(4).

187 Although such a requirement is now provided for under the UNCITRAL Model Law on Public Procurement 2011 only for the request for proposals with dialogue procedure (Art. 30(2)).

188 See also the innovation partnership procedure in Art. 31.

189 Public Procurement Directive, Art. 30.

190 Ibid., Art. 29.

those needs include design or innovative solutions; negotiations are required because of the nature, the complexity or the legal and financial make-up of the contract or risks attached; or technical specifications cannot be established with sufficient precision using established standards.[191] The experiences – both positive and negative – of the Directives in designing such procedures for complex procurement, and national experiences with implementation, are potentially valuable for the allocation of other limited rights of a complex nature, such as authorisations for complex activities.[192]

Further, total exemptions are sometimes appropriate from competitive tendering, even in its very broad sense and even for major contracts; this is sometimes because of the need to balance value for money with other interests, often the resource costs of the award procedure, but sometimes for reasons of value for money itself.

Thus, for example, procurement systems often allow a single-source process that dispenses with any form of comparison of offers for at least some cases of urgency. This prioritises the need to acquire goods and services when needed above other value for money elements, including price and cost, as well as above other interests protected by competitive tendering. However, balancing these different interests is tricky, and for this reason and as well as because of different national conditions and values (as noted later below), systems differ on the scope of this kind of exemption. Thus, some allow a single-source approach for extreme urgency in general albeit subject often to conditions, as reflected in the UNCITRAL Model Law of 1994,[193] while others restrict the single-source approach to the most exceptional cases, such as catastrophic events, a position reflected in the 2011 version of the Model Law, which now requires a quick and informal competitive process for other cases of urgency.[194] The many different approaches to balancing different interests in this context are illustrated in the varying national responses to the COVID-19 pandemic, which led some states to amend their laws and

[191] Ibid., Art. 26(4).

[192] For analysis, see Arrowsmith, *The Law of Public and Utilities Procurement*, vol. 1 (2014), chapters 8 and 9; S. Arrowsmith and S. Treumer (eds.), *Competitive Dialogue in EU Procurement* (Cambridge: Cambridge University Press, 2012); and Burnett and Oder, *Competitive Dialogue and Negotiated Procedures.*

[193] UNCITRAL Model Law on Procurement of Goods, Services and Construction 1994, Art. 22(1)(b).

[194] The competitive negotiations procedure, as provided for in cases of urgency in Art. 30 (4).

some to dispense with regular procurement rules altogether and has provided an opportunity to reflect on and revisit the complexities of balancing different interests in emergency scenarios.[195]

Such single sourcing is often subject to other controls to protect commercial and other interests, such as higher approvals or (as under UNCITRAL) a public notice of use[196] or a requirement to conduct negotiations,[197] including to collect market data or cost information in appropriate cases to avoid unreasonable prices.[198] Publication of a broad range of documentation and data on public procurement, promoted by the open contracting movement, is also becoming increasingly important to allow all stakeholders to monitor both legal compliance and procurement outcomes, and has been boosted in some countries as a result of the significant use of single-source procurement (and less formal comparison processes) in the pandemic.[199]

In the EU, the Public Procurement Directive includes several exemptions from competitive tendering[200] that can be attributed to Member States' commercial interests, namely for: 'extreme urgency' under certain conditions (see later below); research and development contracts for supplies; purchases from a commodity market or on particularly advantageous terms because of winding up or similar; purchases needed to avoid incompatibility or technical difficulties; and procurement from a winner of a design contest. Some of the rules allowing modification to concluded contracts are also justified by Member States' commercial interests, such as a rule allowing further works, supplies or services to be added to an existing contract where a change of supplier would cause 'significant inconvenience'.[201]

[195] See S. Arrowsmith and L. Butler, 'The Experiences and Lessons of the Covid-19 Pandemic: Public Procurement Regulation in (a) Crisis?', in S. Arrowsmith, L Butler, A. La Chimia and C. Yukins (eds.), *Public Procurement Regulation in (a) Crisis? Global Lessons from the COVID-19 Pandemic* (Oxford: Hart, 2021), pp. 559–615.

[196] UNCITRAL Model Law on Public Procurement 2011, Art. 34(5), although this is not required in the case of a catastrophic event (Art. 34(6)).

[197] UNCITRAL Model Law on Public Procurement 2011, Art. 52.

[198] Guide to Enactment of the UNCITRAL Model Law on Public Procurement (2012), p. 225.

[199] Arrowsmith and Butler, 'The Experiences and Lessons of the Covid-19 Pandemic', pp. 587–588.

[200] See Public Procurement Directive, Art. 30(2); for analysis see Arrowsmith, *The Law of Public and Utilities Procurement*, vol. 1 (2014), chapter 10.

[201] Public Procurement Directive, Art. 72(1)(b).

As mentioned, different systems and entities may differ in their approach to implementing value for money, both in designing the detail of tendering procedures and in defining the scope of exceptions to tendering. This includes determining the balance between transparency and discretion; this is a different matter from the balance between different elements of commercial value (security of delivery, price, etc.) but relates to the *technique* for implementing the chosen balance. Thus, as noted, limited commercial skills or a high level of corruption might require a high level of transparency for value for money reasons including, for example, very limited use of flexible procedures and single-source procurement, or limited discretion in conducting tendering, such as allowing only award criteria that do not involve discretion (such as price only).

One aspect of tendering in which this balance between transparency and discretion plays out that is particularly interesting for the broader subject of allocating other limited rights is the area of non-compliant applications or tenders. Maximum transparency, eliminating discretion, leaves extremely limited room for a procuring entity to allow corrections, allowing these at most only when the correct content is evident on the face of the application or tender document itself and perhaps requiring correction in such cases so that no discretion comes into play at all. However, eliminating all discretion can prejudice value for money as it may mean that good suppliers or offers are excluded simply because of a mistake (e.g. failing to attach a required document giving evidence of qualifications). The need for a trade-off between the benefits of reduced discretion and the potential costs can lead to a variety of different rules, which are often also very complex because of the variety and complexity of different fact situations and the policy considerations involved.

Also in terms of the technique for implementing commercial value for money (as opposed to the trade-off between different commercial elements), competitive tendering can involve trade-offs between short-term considerations – obtaining value for money in the context of the specific transaction – and longer-term considerations relating to operation of the system. The problem of non-compliant applications and tenders is again a useful illustration: while permitting a correction can allow acceptance of better offers in the immediate procurement, the costs can include damaging the confidence of suppliers and thus deterring participation and discouraging careful preparation.

All the above issues and others need to be considered carefully in deciding how to achieve value in relation to a complex area such as non-compliant submissions, and the exercise is further complicated by the need also to consider other interests, including the value of transparency from an integrity and open market perspective and procedural costs. It is outside the scope of this piece to provide a full analysis of this one area, which is examined from both a national and EU perspective in the author's other work.[202] What is important here is simply to highlight that a study of public procurement is invaluable when addressing parallel issues in the context of other limited rights – for example, where applicants for grants or bidders seeking to purchase public property make mistakes in their submissions – since the case law and literature provide a starting point for identifying the many interests and issues, a framework for analysing them and a guide to possible solutions.

Balancing National Interests in Commercial Value with the EU's Interest in Open Markets We have already referred to the general need for a balance between Member State interests in value for money and the EU's open market interests, which has been discussed by the author elsewhere.[203] In this section, we will further elaborate on this and consider some key points relating to the way that the Directives approach that balance.

First, as mentioned, to a large extent the rules for opening markets are consistent with and supportive of national commercial objectives, since both rely on competitive tendering. (From a substantive point of view, open market policy can also enhance value for money as a result of both greater competition in specific transactions and the beneficial effect of market competition in general in terms of restructuring effects.)[204]

However, as we have also seen, this is not always so. In particular, as we explained in examining rule-based decision-making as the third element of transparency, there may be some tension between EU and

[202] For a full analysis of the policy considerations and case law under EU and UK law, for example, see Arrowsmith, *The Law of Public and Utilities Procurement*, vol. 1 (2014), paras. 7-271–7-293.

[203] See, in particular, Arrowsmith, 'The EC Procurement Directives, National Procurement Policies and Better Governance'; Arrowsmith, *The Law of Public and Utilities Procurement*, vol. 1 (2014) and vol. 2 (2018), *passim*. And see also the important early work on this subject in Fernández Martín, *The EC Public Procurement Rules: A Critical Analysis*.

[204] See generally W. S. Atkins Management Consultants, *The Cost of Non-Europe in Public Sector Procurement* (Luxembourg: Office for Official Publications of the European Communities, 1988), vol. 5A of W. S. Atkins Management Consultants, *The Cost of Non-Europe, Basic Findings*.

national interests when the Directives choose a higher level of constraint on discretion than is deemed optimum for value for money by the national decision-maker (regulator, contracting authority, etc.).

This can occur at many points in competitive tendering. Thus in the case of correction of non-compliant submissions that we looked at earlier, the main concerns of the rules in the Public Procurement Directive (quite skeletal rules that have been elaborated in the case law) seem to be that allowing suppliers discretion to correct submissions may give an opportunity to favour national suppliers and undermine equal treatment; but, as we saw, limiting discretion may require a trade-off with national commercial interests if the national regulator considers that the commercial benefits of allowing correction to gain access to better offers outweigh any short- and long-term costs. A significant example of this tension over transparency versus discretion is also seen in the evolution of provision in the public sector Directives to allow discussions with suppliers during tendering procedures, which we alluded to earlier. This became a controversial subject in the 1980s and 1990s with the development of more complex procurement, including privately financed infrastructure and major information technology projects, that some Member States, including France and the UK, found difficult to implement from a value for money perspective using open and restricted procedures, but which the Commission claimed did not generally fall within the one flexible competitive procedure that existed, the negotiated procedure in its competitive form (although the UK courts took a different view).[205] This problem was finally addressed in 2004 by introducing competitive dialogue for complex projects.[206] Some of the provisions exempting procurement from competitive tendering altogether that we mentioned above also involve a trade-off between the EU's open market objectives and commercial value – for example, allowing the use of single sourcing for reasons of urgency increases the risk of national favouritism.

More generally, in the most recent – 2014 – Directives, the initial impetus for reform seemed to come from a general desire to adjust the Directives' balance more generally towards greater flexibility for Member States in the area of commercial value,[207] and this was reflected in some

[205] On this history, see Arrowsmith and Treumer, 'Competitive Dialogue in EU Law: A Critical Review', pp. 16–29.

[206] Now found, as mentioned above, mainly in Public Procurement Directive, Art. 30.

[207] This impetus came from a Report from Mario Monti to the President of the European Commission, of 9 May 2010, 'A new strategy for the Single Market: at the service of

innovations in the Public Procurement Directive, such as wider grounds for using the flexible procedures,[208] shorter time limits for certain procedural phases, less strict requirements for the operation of dynamic purchasing systems, and a possibility for advertising contracts through a PIN for sub-central entities.[209] However, there were also changes in the opposite direction, such as stricter conditions for the automatic exclusion of suppliers for poor past performance.[210]

Given the complexity of public procurement and the skeletal nature of the original Directives, much of the detail of the rules – for example, on correction of non-compliant submissions – and hence the balance between national interests and the single market are determined by case law, often based on general principles. In this respect, the ECJ's approach to interpretation is important. In the past, the ECJ has tended to adopt principles of interpretation that favour the single market in this balance. For example, as mentioned, the ECJ has adopted a principle of narrow interpretation of exceptions to tendering,[211] and it has also applied a principle of proportionality that limits Member States' discretion in seeking commercial value or reduced procedural costs (e.g. requiring a case-by-case approach to exclusions)[212] but has not been applied in reverse to protect Member States' own interests in the commercial elements of the acquisition (or, as discussed later below, efficient

Europe's economy and society', available at www.irpa.eu/en/a-new-strategy-for-the-single-market/, which gave significant attention to this issue although key specific reforms that were proposed were not all adopted. On the background to the 2014 Directives see Arrowsmith, *The Law of Public and Utilities Procurement*, vol. 1 (2014), paras. 3-46–3-48.

208 Stated in Public Procurement Directive, Art. 26(4).

209 On these new flexibilities see J. Davey, 'Procedures Involving Negotiation in the New Public Procurement Directive: Key Reforms to the Grounds for Use and the Procedural Rules' (2014) 23 *Public Procurement Law Review* 103; G. Fletcher, 'Minimum Time Limits under the New Public Procurement Directive' (2014) 23 *Public Procurement Law Review* 94; C. Risvig Hamer, 'Regular Purchases and Aggregated Procurement: The Changes in the New Public Procurement Directive regarding Framework Agreements, Dynamic Purchasing Systems and Central Purchasing Bodies' (2014) 23 *Public Procurement Law Review* 201–210.

210 Arrowsmith, *The Law of Public and Utilities Procurement*, vol. 1 (2014), paras. 12-104–12-106.

211 Case 199/85, *Commission of the European Communities* v. *Italian Republic* [1987] ECR 1039, ECLI:EU:C:1987:115, para. 14; Case C-328/92, *Commission of the European Communities* v. *Kingdom of Spain* [1994] ECR I-1569, ECLI:EU:C:1994:178, para. 16.

212 Joined Cases C-21/03 and C-34/03, *Fabricom SA* v. *État Belge* [2005] ECR I-1559, ECLI: EU:C:2005:127. See Arrowsmith, *The Law of Public and Utilities Procurement*, vol. 1 (2014), para. 7-24.

process).[213] It is questionable whether EU interests should be given priority over Member State interests in this way either in public procurement or in other areas involving the allocation of limited rights, and the present author has argued elsewhere for a more neutral approach including by applying the proportionality principle in both directions.[214] This issue of the principles of interpretation to be used in balancing different interests is equally relevant in allocating other limited rights.

2.4.2.3 Horizontal (Additional) Policy Objectives and the Balance with Other Objectives

Competitive Tendering and National Horizontal Policies In recent years, the ebb and flow of horizontal policies in EU Member States has been closely linked with EU measures, as discussed below. The nature of horizontal policies has also changed, in particular with the curtailment of Member States' power to use procurement as a tool to protect national industry, and an increasing emphasis on environmental issues but – as we mentioned earlier – current policies still cover many areas of more long-standing interest, such as safeguarding labour standards and providing employment opportunities for disadvantaged persons. This subject raises interesting questions of constitutionality and policy effectiveness that themselves involve balancing different interests. For example, there are questions over whether using procurement as a policy tool compared with more direct methods, such as subsidies, provides for an efficient balance of interests, given that procurement may be a more costly tool but more politically attractive because of limited visibility of the costs or because of political convenience.[215] However, here we are concerned solely with balancing horizontal policy interests against other interests from the perspective of competitive tendering, assuming an appropriate decision to choose procurement as a policy tool.

[213] Although it was referred to in the context of procedural burdens by Advocate General Kokott in Case C-368/10, *European Commission* v. *Kingdom of the Netherlands* ECLI: EU:C:2011:840 who stated, in para. 57 of the Opinion: '... the administrative burden involved in laying down the requirements on contracting authorities cannot be overlooked. That burden should always be proportionate to the objectives pursued in public procurement law' and on this basis concluded that cross-reference to the provisions of a private eco-label was sufficient to comply with transparency requirements for contract requirements, although the ECJ did not agree with that conclusion.

[214] Arrowsmith, *The Law of Public and Utilities Procurement*, vol. 1 (2014), para. 7-25.

[215] See, e.g., Arrowsmith, 'Horizontal Policies in Public Procurement'.

The approach towards implementing horizontal policies in competitive tendering, and the advantages of using competitive tendering, are the same as those outlined above in relation to commercial value. Effectively, a horizontal policy element is an additional non-price element that can be implemented in the same way as commercial non-price elements, such as quality or aesthetics. Some horizontal policies lend themselves more naturally to implementation through contract conditions than to award criteria. For example, concern with child labour overseas, even if legal in the country concerned, is likely to be manifested through terms prohibiting this or exclusion of suppliers, rather than award criteria that allow contractors to 'bargain' to use child labour with the inducement of lower prices. However, with other policies various mechanisms may be used. For example, employment opportunities for disadvantaged persons can be implemented through mandatory contract terms (e.g. specifying a certain number of unemployed persons to be engaged for the contract); through award criteria, that is, one element to be balanced against price and other elements (with the supplier's offer then incorporated as a contract term to ensure that the chosen balance of interests is delivered); or both in the same procurement. The points made earlier about balancing different commercial elements in tendering are equally relevant in principle to horizontal policies, as the present author has examined elsewhere,[216] and competition and transparency play the same role: thus competition aims to ensure that the suppliers offering the best balance of all elements, including horizontal elements, are able to participate and that those suppliers are induced to make their best offers; while transparency ensures that the chosen balance is implemented – for example, that the chosen criteria, both commercial and horizontal, are actually used to award the contract.

A particular concern in the balancing exercise in this context is the use of award criteria that do not focus simply on the supplier's ability to deliver the contract's subject matter, but go beyond that – for example, focusing on the nature of the supplier (as with price preferences for small suppliers or suppliers owned by disadvantaged ethnic groups) or on the supplier's actions outside the contract (such as whether it invests in the tobacco industry). As acknowledged in UNCITRAL's Guide to Enactment for its Model Law, concerns over such policies from a national perspective are

[216] On the different implementation mechanisms, see Arrowsmith, 'Horizontal Policies in Public Procurement'.

twofold.[217] The first concern relates to what the Guide calls 'best value for money', referring to the overall balance between commercial and other elements of the procurement, and the fear that going beyond the subject matter can involve high costs for the horizontal element. The second is fear of abuse, in that a carte blanche to pursue such policies can give contracting authorities wide discretion in both choosing[218] and applying policies, which authorities could use to favour particular suppliers. For these reasons, the Model Law provides as a starting point that award criteria must 'relate to the subject matter of the procurement'[219] and contemplates the use of criteria that do not relate to the subject matter only when explicitly provided for by the procurement regulations or other legal provisions.[220] This requirement for legislation encourages states to set horizontal policies at the central level as a safeguard against the potential problems, so ensuring that the balance of commercial and horizontal elements is carefully considered.

It is also not uncommon to implement horizontal policies by restricting contracts to limited, and quite narrow, groups, such as to suppliers devoted to providing work opportunities for disadvantaged groups or to small businesses.[221] Clearly, this potentially has a significant adverse impact on both commercial aspects and (other) horizontal aspects, both because of the reduced competitive pressure from the limited pool and because the 'preferred' suppliers may not be as competitive as other types of suppliers. In comparison with award criteria relating to the supplier, which reveal the 'price' of the horizontal policy in terms of higher prices, reduced quality and so on (and also control this through *ex ante* limits on these costs via the weighting of criteria), the costs also are not potentially visible through the results of the tendering procedure. Clearly, both the appropriate balance and the difficulty of achieving it in practice need careful consideration before this approach is used (consideration which may be sacrificed, however, to political expediency given that such approaches can produce quick and visible results without visibility of costs).

One way to reduce the trade-offs and so obtain a better overall balance of interests is through a variation of the set-aside approach, sometimes

[217] Guide to Enactment of the UNCITRAL Model Law on Public Procurement (2012), p. 85.

[218] The Guide to Enactment mentions choosing policies but concern over abuse of discretion is also relevant to their application.

[219] UNCITRAL Model Law on Public Procurement 2011, Art. 11(1).

[220] UNCITRAL Model Law on Public Procurement 2011, Art. 11(3).

[221] Arrowsmith, 'Horizontal Policies in Public Procurement', pp. 175–176.

called 'offer back'. This involves holding a tendering procedure in accordance with the usual rules on tendering and then setting aside ('offering back') part of the tendered requirement to the best bidder from the preferred group only if that bidder will match the best terms tendered in the competitive procedure. This approach was once used by the UK government to award contracts for workshops for persons with disabilities (the 'Priority Suppliers' scheme)[222] before being abandoned as being contrary to EU law (see below).

Finally, in the same way that exemptions from competitive tendering may be applied for commercial reasons, they may also be made for reasons of horizontal policy. Examples include developing 'national champions' for either commercial reasons (again now precluded by EU law)[223] or security reasons (common in the defence field), or maintaining industrial capacity or a particular type of capacity (e.g. of non-profit entities).[224] The difficulty of ensuring that commercial objectives are met in the absence of competition and transparency is particularly acute when there is dependence on a single firm and may require specific and detailed mechanisms, such as detailed pricing formulae based on contractor costs, market rates and/or general industry profit.[225]

Balancing Effective and Efficient Implementation of Horizontal (Additional) Policy Objectives with the EU's Policy on Open Markets The balance drawn by the EU competitive tendering regime between, on the one hand, the EU' s open market and policy and, on the other hand, the national horizontal policy interests of Member States has been extensively analysed, including by the present author.[226] To see how these interests are balanced, it is important to understand that there are

[222] See Arrowsmith, 'Public Procurement as a Tool of Policy', pp. 243–244.

[223] On such historical policies in the UK and the impact of EU law, see again Arrowsmith, 'Public Procurement as a Tool of Policy', pp. 243–244.

[224] On these policies in the defence field, see Arrowsmith, *The Law of Public and Utilities Procurement*, vol. 2 (2018), chapter 15.

[225] See, for example, in the UK regime under Part 2 of the Defence Reform Act 2014 and Single Source Contracts Regulation (SI 2014, No. 3337), as amended. See Arrowsmith, *The Law of Public and Utilities Procurement*, vol. 2 (2018), paras. 15-164–15-167; L. Butler, 'Single Source Wars, The Saga Continues' (2019) 28 *Public Procurement Law Review* NA 28–38; L. Butler, 'Single Source Wars, The Saga Continues 2: The Single Source Contract (Amendment) (No. 2) Regulations 2018' (2019) 28 *Public Procurement Law Review* 92–107.

[226] See further Arrowsmith, *The Law of Public and Utilities Procurement*, vol. 2 (2018), chapter 20, and the extensive literature on the topic that is cited there.

three main ways in which the TFEU and directives curtail the substance of national policies for reasons of market-opening.[227]

One is by prohibiting discrimination.[228] Most obviously, this diminishes the scope for Member States to use procurement to support national industry that does not enjoy a comparative advantage, since this is the basic purpose of the open market rules.[229] We can also note that possible justifications for discrimination have been very narrowly drawn in the sphere of economic policy so that, for example, regional policy cannot be pursued at all through procurement.[230] Outside the economic sphere, however, the fact that a policy is directly or indirectly discriminatory does not necessarily rule it out.[231]

Second, the policy of limiting discretion to prevent abuse is also important. We have just seen that this is a concern from a national perspective itself in balancing national horizontal and commercial interests (the main concern here being the risk of corruption), and it is also a major issue at the EU level, where the concern is with the risk of national favouritism. The concern with discretion is, as we have seen, a major factor in the EU controlling the manner in which Member States seek to implement their *commercial* objectives, resulting in rules that both limit discretion extensively and require disclosure of rules and criteria to suppliers. All these EU rules are also relevant for controlling national discretion over horizontal policies. However, in the case of horizontal policies certain further constraints are also applied. These might be explained by the additional concerns that horizontal policies generate in this regard and/or by the fact that Member State horizontal policies have been afforded a lower status in the hierarchy of interests set by EU law, as explained below.

The risk of discrimination can arise here, first, from abuse of the discretion in creating and defining horizontal policies, which may be

[227] Arrowsmith, 'The Purpose of the EU Public Procurement Directives'.

[228] Under the free movement rules of the TFEU and the more general equal treatment principle in the directives, e.g. Public Procurement Directive, Art. 18(1).

[229] Case 7/61, *Commission of the European Economic Community* v. *Government of the Italian Republic* [1961] ECR 00635 (English special edition 00317), ECLI:EU:C:1961:31.

[230] Case C-21/88, *Du Pont de Nemours Italiana SpA* v. *Unità sanitaria locale No.2 di Carrara* [1990] ECR I-889, EU:C:1990:121.

[231] E.g. Case C-513/99, *Concordia Bus Finland Oy Ab, formerly Stagecoach Finland Oy Ab* v. *Helsingin kaupunki and HKL-Bussiliikenne* [2002] ECR I-7213, EU:C:2002:495; Case C-113/89, *Rush Portuguesa Lda* v. *Office national d'immigration (National Immigration Office)* [1990] ECR I-1417, EU:C:1990:142, para. 18.

done to favour national industry rather than out of genuine support for the policy (reflecting a more general problem in international trade law of balancing national social and environment regulations with the interest in preventing abuse for protectionist reasons). For example, a specification requiring a level of environmental performance that tends to be met by national producers but not those from most other Member States could be adopted in order to favour national industry. This concern is arguably behind rules in the Directives that (subject to exceptions) limit contract conditions and award criteria to those linked to the subject matter of the contract. This rule means, for example, that horizontal policies concerned with the supplier (price preferences for small suppliers, etc.) or its actions outside the contract cannot generally be taken into account. These limits were originally introduced through the case law and are now stated in the Directives and the reason for them has never been clearly articulated in either source; but the risk of abuse is one plausible reason for them, and – as already explained above – the historical material shows that curtailing abuse of discretion was in fact the reason for the directives' original restrictions on award criteria.

Alongside a risk of discrimination in creating and defining horizontal policies, a risk of discrimination also arises from the possibility of implementing such policies in specific tendering procedures. Again, this can explain the requirement for conditions and award criteria to be linked to the subject matter of the contract, since the introduction of broad horizontal considerations potentially enhances the scope of discretionary decision-making about specific suppliers. This is arguably manifested in the rule resulting from the *Beentjes* case,[232] interpreting the concept of 'technical capacity' under the directives. Contracting authorities may refuse contracts to suppliers who do not have the technical capacity to perform, allowing them to exclude suppliers who cannot, for example, provide products of the specified quality. However, *Beentjes* is generally interpreted to mean that technical capacity does not cover the ability to perform certain types of social or environmental conditions, which the ECJ called 'special conditions', to distinguish them from the commercial conditions – a distinction now carried explicitly into the Directives.[233] The consequence is that a supplier cannot be rejected even

[232] Case 31/87, *Gebroeders Beentjes BV* v. *State of the Netherlands* [1988] ECR 4635, ECLI: EU:C:1988:422.

[233] Public Procurement Directive, Art. 70. For analysis see Arrowsmith, *The Law of Public and Utilities Procurement*, vol. 2 (2018), paras. 20-79–20-89.

if the contracting authority believes that the supplier cannot fulfil a special condition; provided that the supplier accepts the conditions, they must be considered, and adherence to the condition can only be enforced by the threat of sanctions for non-compliance. This approach can be criticised for creating an unjustified hierarchy in which social and environmental conditions set by Member States are unjustifiably given a lower value in EU law than commercial conditions – a point to which we will return below – as well as because it creates significant uncertainty given the unclear and arbitrary nature of the dividing line between special conditions and others.[234]

Third, the free movement rules and the Directives are concerned not merely with removing discrimination based on nationality but also with removing non-discriminatory obstacles. This consideration, also, could justify constraints on horizontal policies, including limiting policies to the subject matter of the contract. This may have influenced arguments made by the European Commission in the 1990s for a narrow interpretation of the concept of the subject matter of the contract, to preclude policies relating to the production of products supplied under the contract:[235] such policies can have significant restrictive effects as they may de facto entail changes to production across a whole factory or business.

Conversely, it is important to reiterate in this context that it is not an objective of EU policy to realise commercial value, which is for Member States, and the EU has no role, actual or potential, in setting the balance between national horizontal and commercial interests, as opposed to balancing those national interests with its own open market objectives.[236] This is not always understood. Thus, in its Green Paper on Modernisation of EU Public Procurement Policy, the Commission states, after discussing

[234] Arrowsmith, *The Law of Public and Utilities Procurement*, vol. 2 (2018), paras. 20-79–20-89.

[235] See European Commission, Interpretative Communication on the Community law applicable to public procurement and the possibilities for integrating environmental considerations into public procurement (COM(2001) 274 final), OJ 2001, No. C333/12, p. 20; and for discussion S. Arrowsmith, 'Application of the EC Treaty and Directives to Horizontal Policies: A Critical Review', in Arrowsmith and Kunzlik, *Social and Environmental Policies in EC Procurement Law*, pp. 147–248 at pp. 219–220; P. Kunzlik, 'The Procurement of "Green" Energy', in Arrowsmith and Kunzlik, *Social and Environmental Policies in EC Procurement Law*, pp. 369–407.

[236] See, again, Arrowsmith, 'The Purpose of the EU Public Procurement Directives'; P. Kunzlik, 'Neoliberalism and the European Public Procurement Regime' (2012–2013) 15 *Cambridge Yearbook of European Legal Studies* 283–356; Arrowsmith, *The Law of Public and Utilities Procurement*, vol. 1 (2014), paras. 3-18–3-20.

the possibility of using horizontal considerations in procurement: 'when considering such a possibility, the trade-offs with other policy considerations must be carefully assessed. The link with the subject-matter of the contract ensures that the purchase itself remains central to the process in which taxpayers' money is used. This is an important guarantee to ensure that contracting authorities obtain the best possible offer with efficient use of public monies'.[237] This suggests that EU law seeks to curtail horizontal policies going beyond the contract in order to ensure that Member States do not incur high costs on such policies. However, this cannot provide an explanation for the rule limiting policies to the subject matter of contracts given the objectives of the Directives and limits on EU competence, and we suggested above that the rule is in fact concerned with curtailing discretion to prevent protectionism and with removing obstacles to market participation.

One consequence of this is that EU law cannot generally decide the weight that Member States may give to social and environmental criteria as compared with commercial criteria. This issue was raised in *EVN/Wienstrom*,[238] where the ECJ indicated that Member States may adopt a weighting of 45 per cent for environmental criteria and stated a general principle that the authority is free to choose both the award criteria and their weighting.[239] However, further statements in this case could be read as placing limits on that principle. In this respect, the Court first stated that the weighting must enable an overall evaluation to be made to identify the MEAT;[240] then highlighted the value of renewable energy sources for reducing emissions of greenhouse gas and the existence of EU legislation promoting renewable energy;[241] and finally concluded that *in the light of the importance of encouraging renewable energy* the 45 per cent weighting was acceptable.[242] This reasoning, especially the reference to the Court's own view of the importance of environmental matters and the existence of an EU policy, could indicate that weightings that

[237] European Commission, Green Paper on the Modernisation of EU Public Procurement Policy: Towards a More Efficient European Procurement Market (Brussels, 27 January 2011, COM(2011) 15 final), p. 39, available at https://eur-lex.europa.eu/legal-content/EN/TXT/?uri=CELEX%3A52011DC0015.

[238] Case C-448/01, *EVN AG and Wienstrom GmbH* v. *Republik Österreich* [2003] ECR I-14527, ECLI:EU:C:2003:651.

[239] Ibid., para. 39.

[240] Ibid.

[241] Ibid., para. 41.

[242] Ibid., para. 42.

disproportionately favour non-commercial criteria are not allowed. However, as the author has argued elsewhere,[243] these remarks should merely be understood as raising a suspicion of bad faith where weightings are unusual and not as restricting the general discretion of Member States to balance horizontal and commercial objectives in their choice of award criteria. There is some scope for review of horizontal policy measures under the TFEU and the Directive's proportionality principle, however, as some of these measures may constitute obstacles to trade.[244]

How has the balance actually been struck between national interests in horizontal policies and open market concerns in the design of the EU tendering rules? As mentioned, there has been a recent shift in the balance away from the latter and towards the former.

The shift can be exaggerated. Until quite recently, the Directorate General of the European Commission responsible for public procurement had tended to take a strict approach towards horizontal policies, both in its guidance[245] and in its arguments before the ECJ,[246] but some of its strict interpretations were rejected by some writers, including the present author,[247] by some Member States and contracting authorities,[248] and eventually by the ECJ,[249] and several of the 'new' explicit provisions in the 2004 and 2014 Directives on possibilities for horizontal policies are, in fact, clarifications – for example, on the possibility of using award criteria relating to the whole life cycle of products, including

243 Arrowsmith, *The Law of Public and Utilities Procurement*, vol. 1 (2014), paras. 7-195–7-196.

244 E.g. Case C-346/06, *Dirk Ruffert* v. *Land Niedersachsen* [2008] ECR I-01989, ECLI:EU:C:2008:189. See Arrowsmith, *The Law of Public and Utilities Procurement*, vol. 2 (2018), paras. 20-63–20-68 for an overview of the case law on social and environmental justifications in the procurement context. It is submitted that some measures of a social or environmental nature that relate to the characteristics of the products or services (such as requirements for low-energy light bulbs) may, however, fall within the excluded buying decisions doctrine: see note 50 above.

245 E.g. in European Commission, Interpretative Communication on the Community law applicable to public procurement and the possibilities for integrating environmental considerations into public procurement (COM(2001) 274 final), OJ 2001, No. C333/12.

246 E.g. in Case C-513/99, *Concordia Bus Finland Oy Ab, formerly Stagecoach Finland Oy Ab* v. *Helsingin kaupunki and HKL-Bussiliikenne* [2002] ECR I-7213, EU:C:2002:495.

247 E.g. in S. Arrowsmith, *The Law of Public and Utilities Procurement*, 2nd ed. (London: Sweet & Maxwell, 2006), paras. 19-58–19-60; Arrowsmith, 'Application of the EC Treaty and Directives to Horizontal Policies', pp. 219–220; and also, e.g., Kunzlik, 'The Procurement of "Green" Energy'; McCrudden, *Buying Social Justice*.

248 E.g. in the practices addressed in Case C-368/10, *European Commission* v. *Kingdom of the Netherlands* ECLI:EU:C:2012:284.

249 E.g. in ibid.

production.[250] This aside, however, there has still been a shift that has led to an actual relaxation of restrictions and which also could affect the balance struck in future case law, as discussed below.

This shift has been prompted by a number of related factors, such as pressure for change from some Member States, pressure from those sections of the Commission responsible for EU social and environmental policy, the value of procurement in addressing new problems such as climate change, and the UN's emphasis on 'sustainable' public procurement.[251] The European Commission's 'Europe 2020 strategy for smart, sustainable and inclusive growth'[252] specifically envisaged a role for public procurement in achieving some of the EU's own objectives including a 'resource efficient and low-carbon economy' and innovation, generating support for more flexibility for Member States in these areas of EU concern, as well as leading the EU to adopt other actions to promote these policies through Member State procurement[253] (and in some cases even to *require* Member States to do this).[254] In other words Member States' use of procurement as a policy tool has recently raised not just the

[250] Public Procurement Directive, Art. 67(3), confirmed as already possible in principle under Directive 2004/18 in Case C-368/10, *European Commission* v. *Kingdom of the Netherlands* ECLI:EU:C:2012:284.

[251] For a summary, see United Nations, 'Public Procurement as a Tool for Promoting More Sustainable Consumption and Production patterns' (Sustainable Development Innovation Briefs, Issue 5, August 2008), available at https://sustainabledevelopment.un.org/content/documents/no5.pdf.

[252] European Commission, Communication from the Commission: EUROPE 2020 – A strategy for smart, sustainable and inclusive growth (Brussels, 3 March 2010, COM (2010) 2020 final), available at https://eur-lex.europa.eu/legal-content/EN/ALL/?uri=CELEX%3A52010DC2020.

[253] E.g. establishing specific environmental criteria for including in public procurement on an EU-wide basis, which the Commission has encouraged Member States to endorse and to adopt as part of their own national action plans: see Commission of the European Communities, Communication from the Commission to the European Parliament, the Council, the European Economic and Social Committee and the Committee of the Regions: Public Procurement for a Better Environment (Brussels, 16 July 2008, COM (2008) 400 final), available at http://eur-lex.europa.eu/LexUriServ/LexUriServ.do?uri=COM:2008:0400:FIN:EN:PDF. The aim is both to encourage use of environmental criteria and at the same time avoid distortion of markets through use of common criteria. The Commission has also developed a life-cycle costing tool and guidance to facilitate use of common life-cycle costing methods in the EU. See further the 'Green Public Procurement', available at http://ec.europa.eu/environment/gpp/index_en.htm.

[254] For a review of these requirements, see Arrowsmith, *The Law of Public and Utilities Procurement*, vol. 2 (2018), paras. 20-39–20-54. Illustrations of those introduced in 2014 in the Public Procurement Directive include an obligation to give reasons for every decision not to divide a contract into lots (Art. 46(1)), an obligation generally to take

issue of the balance between Member State interests and the EU's open market interest but also whether EU law allows for sufficient scope for realising the EU's own social and environmental objectives through Member State action. Against this background, the desire to promote and facilitate the effective use of procurement to promote industrial, social and environmental policies was one of the main drivers for the 2014 Directives[255] and is given significant emphasis in the recitals;[256] and those Directives include a number of concrete new possibilities, such as a broader scope for reserving contracts for suppliers providing employment for disadvantaged persons,[257] the possibility for splitting lots among tenderers to assist small companies,[258] and more flexibility in using eco-labels.[259] Subsequently, boosting use of innovative, green and social procurement was designated as one of the top six priorities in the Commission's 2017 public procurement strategy.[260]

As with the balance between open market interests and Member States' commercial interests, interpretation plays an important role. Even prior to the 2014 Directives, Arrowsmith and Kunzlik, as well as arguing for a principle of the equal status of horizontal and commercial policies (and hence the rejection of the 'secondary' policies terminology), as outlined above, highlighted other principles that support a broad interpretation of the scope for horizontal policies, including subsidiarity and the status at the EU level of some of these policy areas[261] (such as environmental policy under Art. 11 TFEU[262] and equality policy under

accessibility criteria into account in specifications (Art. 42(2)) and an obligation to reject abnormally low tenders that violate social or environmental obligations (Art. 69(3)).

255 See Arrowsmith, *The Law of Public and Utilities Procurement*, vol. 1 (2014), para. 3-47.

256 See, for example, Public Procurement Directive, recital 2, referring to facilitating participation of SMEs and enabling 'procurers to make better use of public procurement in support of common societal goals'.

257 E.g. Public Procurement Directive, Art. 20.

258 E.g. Ibid., Art. 46(2).

259 E.g. Ibid., Art. 43.

260 European Commission, Communication from the Commission to the European Parliament, the Council, the European Economic and Social Committee and the Committee of the Regions: Making Public Procurement work in and for Europe (Strasbourg, 3 October 2017, COM(2017) 572 final), pp. 8–9, available at https://eur-lex.europa.eu/legal-content/EN/TXT/?uri=COM%3A2017%3A572%3AFIN.

261 Arrowsmith and Kunzlik, 'Public Procurement and Horizontal Policies in EC Law'.

262 Art. 11 TFEU provides that: 'Environmental protection requirements must be integrated into the definition and implementation of the Union's policies and activities, in particular with a view to promoting sustainable development.'

Art. 8 TFEU).[263] The likelihood of a broad interpretation is now reinforced by the emphasis of the 2014 Directives and the prominence of horizontal policies in the recitals.[264] In this respect, we have seen that in the *EVN/Wienstrom* case the ECJ referred to the existence of an EU policy (on renewable energy) to justify accepting a significant weighting for that policy in the tendering process. As Arrowsmith and Kunzlik have argued, however, the fact that a policy is not an EU policy should not per se affect the outcome; there is no reason why matters of EU concern should enjoy a higher position in the hierarchy of interests than matters of Member State concern (which might be exclusively within the competence of Member States).[265] The fact that Member State procurement is a tool for implementing some policies that are important to the EU merely reinforces, it is submitted, the more general case for a broad scope for horizontal policies within the EU's tendering regime.

It is not clear how far exemptions from the regular tendering procedures are permitted under the Directive for horizontal policy reasons, but the better view is that this is possible only under the Directive's few explicit derogations that are relevant to this – mainly relating to security policies – and not under the Treaty derogations from free movement.[266]

Horizontal Policies and State Aid Member States' interests in horizontal policies also need to be balanced against the EU's interest in ensuring a level playing field in EU markets through the state aid rules which, as we have seen, support the interest in open markets by preventing public contracts from being used to subsidise national industry. Horizontal policy measures in a contract awarded to a national firm may constitute state aid, as indicated in *BAI*, clarifying that awarding a contract on favourable terms for the 'social and cultural' reason of

[263] Art. 8 TFEU provides that: 'In all its activities, the Union shall aim to eliminate inequalities, and to promote equality, between men and women.'

[264] E.g. Public Procurement Directive, recital 2, as noted above. These kinds of references have been cited to support interpretations under the previous directives, e.g. in Case C-324/14, *Partner Apelski Dariusz* v. *Zarząd Oczyszczania Miastai*, ECLI:EU:C:2016:214, ECJ judgment of 7 April 2016, para. 34, although arguably none of these have been decisive to the interpretation adopted.

[265] Arrowsmith and Kunzlik, 'Public Procurement and Horizontal Policies in EC Law'.

[266] See the discussion in Arrowsmith, 'Recommendations for Urgent Procurement in the EU Directives and GPA: COVID-19 and Beyond', in Arrowsmith et al. (eds.), *Public Procurement Regulation in (a) Crisis?*, pp. 88–89.

establishing a ferry service between England and Spain did not automatically preclude the possibility of state aid.[267]

It cannot, however, be assumed that every horizontal policy measure constitutes state aid, as is indicated by the clear recognition of horizontal policies in ECJ case law and in the Directives.[268] Thus, the 'market purchaser' test cannot be solely concerned with the commercial interests of a procurement but must also embrace public authorities' interests in using procurement for horizontal policy reasons (and, indeed, any other approach would require an arbitrary classification of measures as horizontal or commercial). On this basis, it is submitted that a horizontal policy measure does not involve a financial advantage when the additional payment for the horizontal policy benefit merely represents a commercial price for that benefit, and that benefit does not itself take the form of support for particular undertakings.[269] This approach is supported by the analogy of the *Altmark Trans* case law on subsidies for the performance of public service obligations.[270] In general, following the Directives' tendering procedures will demonstrate that there is generally no financial advantage in respect of horizontal policies implemented through contract conditions or award criteria, as the payment for the horizontal policy benefit is priced through the market[271] (although criteria and reservations that favour particular groups of suppliers may be more problematic).[272]

[267] Case T-14/96, *Bretagne Angleterre Irlande (BAI)* v. *Commission of the European Communities* [1999] ECR II-139, ECLI:EU:T:1999:12.

[268] E.g. the possibility of social conditions in contracts recognised in Case 31/87, *Gebroeders Beentjes BV* v. *State of the Netherlands* [1988] ECR 4635, ECLI:EU:C:1988:422, and in, e.g., Public Procurement Directive, Art. 70, and the possibility of set-asides relating to disadvantaged persons as provided for in, e.g., Public Procurement Directive, Art. 20.

[269] Arrowsmith, *The Law of Public and Utilities Procurement*, vol. 2 (2018), para. 20-69; H.-Priess and Von Merveldt, 'The Impact of the EC State Aid Rules on Horizontal Policies in Public Procurement'; Arrowsmith and Kunzlik, *Social and Environmental Policies in EC Procurement Law*, pp. 249–270.

[270] Case C-280/00, *Altmark Trans GmbH and Regierungsprasidium Magdeburg* v. *Nahver kehrsgesellschaft Altmark GmbH, and Oberbundesanwalt beim Bundesverwaltungsgericht* [2003] ECR I-7747, ECLI:EU:C:2003:415.

[271] See, e.g., European Commission, Commission Notice on the notion of State aid as referred to in Art. 107(1) of the Treaty on the Functioning of the European Union, OJ 2016, No. C262/1, available at https://ec.europa.eu/competition/state_aid/modernisa tion/notice_aid_en.html; Ølykke, 'Commission Notice on the Notion of State Aid as Referred to in Article 107(1) TFEU', 197–212.

[272] See Arrowsmith, *The Law of Public and Utilities Procurement*, vol. 2 (2014), para. 20-69.

The European Commission's 2011 Green Paper on modernising public procurement seems to suggest a qualification to this, namely that criteria and conditions that go beyond the subject matter of the contract may involve unlawful state aid. Thus, it states:[273]

> The link with the subject-matter of the contract ensures that the purchase itself remains central to the process in which taxpayers' money is used. This is an important guarantee to ensure that contracting authorities obtain the best possible offer with efficient use of public monies. … At the same time, this guarantee of purchases at the best price ensures a measure of consistency between EU public procurement policy and the rules in the field of State aid, as it makes sure that no undue economic advantage is conferred on economic operators through the award of public contracts.

However, it is submitted that this is incorrect and based on a misunderstanding of the respective roles of the Member States and the EU in balancing commercial and horizontal interests and of the 'link to the subject-matter' rule in the procurement Directives, as discussed above.

The ECJ and subsequent EU measures have taken a different approach to the above when applying state aid in rules to government sales, taking the view that it violates state aid law to attach horizontal policy conditions to these sales, even when these relate to the subject matter of the sale.[274] The ECJ has not articulated the reason for taking this approach in its case law, but the Court's approach may reflect the kind of transparency and market access concerns that we discussed earlier in the present chapter, such as fear of abuse of discretion to set conditions favouring national undertakings. In this respect, the Court's decision is inconsistent with the approach to these matters in the procurement Directives, which – balancing national interests against the EU's interest in open markets – allow horizontal policy conditions. It also seems inappropriate to bring this consideration into play through state aid law; if there is indeed a reason to treat public procurement and sale differently in this respect, then it seems appropriate to give effect to this concern through a general restriction that forms part of the TFEU transparency obligation in relation to the allocation of rights in the sale context, not merely through the state aid rules, and also to allow the seller to rebut the presumption of state aid that might arise if those rules are not applied.

[273] European Commission, Green Paper on the Modernisation of EU Public Procurement Policy, p. 39.

[274] See Chapter 5, Section 5.4.3.1.

2.4.2.4 Efficiency of the Procurement Procedure

We have already mentioned that to some extent an efficient procedure is complementary to other goals in that it will promote participation. Further, a key part of efficient tendering design involves eliminating costs that can be removed *without trade-offs* with other interests.[275] An example is the effective design of flexible procedures, to ensure negotiations are focused on the appropriate issues and therefore to avoid spending resources on negotiations that are not useful. (Early experience with the EU's competitive dialogue procedure in the UK revealed this as a problem with the use of that procedure, with the need to define many aspects of the project and focus negotiations carefully being a key lesson of the UK's experience.)[276]

However, saving costs often also involves balancing procedural costs against other interests. We can also note that sometimes – such as where specifications need changing because discussions with suppliers suggest that most suppliers cannot meet the standards set – the issues present themselves in the form of a need to make changes during an award procedure, where the consequence of not allowing the change is that the procuring entity must either incur significant procedural costs in the form of a retender *or* must choose to sacrifice other national interests, such as value for money (that might, for example, be enhanced by attracting more tenders).

This balance needs to be considered, first, in conducting tendering procedures. An example of a rule that seeks a balance from this perspective is that introduced in 2011 into the UNCITRAL Model Law permitting legalisation of documents to be required only from the winning tenderer (rather than demanding this from all tenderers);[277] this aims mainly to reduce the cost burden on suppliers, but it might, however, delay the contract for the procuring entity.

[275] Another issue that sometimes arises is the allocation of procedural costs between the supplier and the procuring entity (where it must be borne in mind the allocation of costs to the supplier may have an impact on participation and hence on commercial value) – for example, as regards payment for the cost of documents or operating registration systems.

[276] See S. Arrowsmith and R. Craven, 'Competitive Dialogue in the United Kingdom', chapter 3 in S. Arrowsmith and S. Treumer (eds.), *Competitive Dialogue in EU Procurement* (Cambridge: Cambridge University Press, 2012), pp. 181–271, at pp. 265–266.

[277] UNCITRAL Model Law on Public Procurement 2011, Art. 9(7).

The need for a balance is reflected perhaps even more significantly, however, in exemptions from open tendering. Using a procurement method not open to all suppliers can adversely affect both commercial and horizontal policy interests by both reducing the level of competition – potentially excluding the best suppliers – and reducing transparency, which poses a risk to a number of interests. However, the costs of open procedures may be high for both sides; the risks of excluding suppliers who can provide a better deal are low in some markets; and/or any detriment to other interests may be outweighed by the additional costs of open tendering, depending on the size and/or nature of the contract. For this reason, the UNCITRAL Model Law allows procurement methods other than open tendering for reasons of an efficient process (as well as for other reasons, as discussed earlier). For example, 'restricted tendering' (a method that involves merely approaching a limited number of suppliers without a public solicitation but still includes a formal tender) is provided for when 'The time and cost required to examine and evaluate a large number of tenders would be disproportionate to the value of the subject matter',[278] along with an informal request for quotations method for standardised low-value procurement.[279] However, it is also envisaged that wherever possible entities should set up ongoing mechanisms[280] (referred to as 'framework agreements', with a wider use of that term than is found under EU law)[281] for all regular low-value purchasing, for which suppliers are solicited by open solicitation. These mechanisms can often ensure a better overall outcome by providing a system that is both more competitive and transparent than ad hoc restricted tendering and request for quotations yet involves lower procedural costs than repeat open solicitations. Some grounds for single-source procurement are also based on the consideration that cost savings

278 UNCITRAL Model Law on Public Procurement 2011, Art. 29(1)(b).

279 UNCITRAL Model Law on Public Procurement 2011, Art. 29(2).

280 Guide to Enactment of the UNCITRAL Model Law on Public Procurement (2012), e.g. p. 171.

281 The term covers certain arrangements that do not (as EU framework agreements do) involve competition on price and other key terms at the time when suppliers are placed on the system (in order to limit the number of suppliers on the system). (See the definition of EU framework agreements in, e.g., Public Procurement Directive, Art. 33 (1)). That is, it also covers arrangements where competition occurs only when the order is placed – covering, for example, the mechanisms that the EU refers to as dynamic purchasing systems (regulated by, e.g., Public Procurement Directive, Art. 34), which are not within the concept of framework agreements in the EU sense. (On this see UNCITRAL Model Law on Public Procurement 2011, Art. 2(e) and Arts. 58–63.)

in the procedure will outweigh the likely benefits competition, as discussed below.

From an EU perspective, limiting supplier costs supports the objective of removing obstacles to participation in general and for SMEs. Limiting delay and resource costs for national procuring entities, on the other hand, is not in itself an interest of the EU regime. However, Member States' own national interests in this, as well as national interests in limiting suppliers, are – like commercial value and national horizontal policies – important interests that the EU must accommodate in designing its open market rules.

From the EU perspective, recent legislation has given some emphasis to reducing supplier costs. This is seen, most notably, in the 2014 Directives' obligation to accept self-declarations of supplier qualifications (in the form of a Single European Procurement Document),[282] with procuring entities being permitted to require factual verification only after the supplier has provisionally been awarded a contract (which has the same aim as the 2011 UNCITRAL provision limiting legalisation of documents but with a wider scope). It is also seen in measures to increase the use of central information databases to reduce burdens on suppliers in providing information.[283] These can involve some balancing of interests, mainly because of slight delays to the contract for procuring entities as the result of self-declarations or the transfer of some process costs from suppliers to procuring entities where the latter are obliged to consult central databases.

These rules sometimes align with national interests given, in particular, the benefits to national interests from greater supplier participation. However, there is a potential for trade-off where a national assessment of the cost–benefit balance of a particular measure would lead to a different outcome from the EU rule, as where a Member State prefers to verify all qualifications from the outset in a manner that is prohibited under the EU rule on self-declarations to avoid delay. In reality, however, the trade-off is arguably marginal and the evolution of EU procurement law in this area of proof by suppliers is something that can perhaps provide a useful model, based on experience, for the allocation of some other limited rights.

More broadly, the Directives' explicit rules recognise national interests in limiting costs. For example, the rules on framework agreements

[282] Public Procurement Directive, Art. 59.

[283] See ibid., Art. 60.

(which are a variation of regular competitive procedures), most notably, involve a trade-off between the benefits of open competition and procedural costs (in the same way as the comparable UNCITRAL instruments), in allowing 'closed' arrangements for awarding high-value contracts without a new competition[284] (although, like the UNCITRAL rules, they can also reduce the overall costs that need to be traded-off by pushing smaller contracts into a transparent and competitive mechanism). These national interests in limiting costs are also recognised by exemptions from competitive tendering, including where there is only one possible contractor[285] and to give further work to an incumbent without a new procedure: for example, where it could be costly to bring a new contractor on site to do work to deal with unforeseen conditions not provided for in the original contract making it unlikely that anyone else will win any competition,[286] meaning that any costs of a new procedure could be wasted.

However, while these national interests are recognised in principle, the ECJ has shown little sympathy towards arguments based on procuring entity costs when interpreting the rules, particularly when a trade-off with equal treatment considerations is involved. This is reflected in the line of jurisprudence, based on proportionality and since confirmed in the Directives, that precludes general rules for excluding tenders in objective situations that could give rise to conflicts of interest, such as where a tenderer has participated in preparing a specification or where tenderers are owned by the same parent company; instead, the procuring entity must assess the conflict on a case-by-case basis.[287] A similar requirement for a case-by-case analysis of situations, as opposed to the possibility of relying on a general rule, was imposed in *Forposta* in relation to exclusion for grave professional misconduct.[288] These cases reflect a general tendency in ECJ case law to reject a priori considerations of national administrative cost to justify measures affecting the internal market rather than make a balanced assessment of interests. It is also notable that they prioritise equal treatment above limits on discretion,

284 See ibid., Art. 33, and for analysis Arrowsmith, *The Law of Public and Utilities Procurement*, vol. 1 (2014), chapter 11.

285 Public Procurement Directive, Art. 32 (2)(b).

286 As envisaged in Public Procurement Directive, Art. 72(1)(b)(i).

287 Joined Cases C-21/03 and C-34/03, *Fabricom SA* v. *État Belge* [2005] ECR I-1559, ECLI: EU:C:2005:127.

288 Case C-465/11, *Forposta SA and ABC Direct Contact sp. z o.o.* v. *Poczta Polska SA* ECLI: EU:C:2012:801, ECJ judgment of 13 December 2012.

since general rules of the type adopted in these situations by national authorities in preference to a case-by-case approach serve to curtail discretion that could be abused to favour national suppliers.

Further, the ECJ decisions tend to prioritise a formal notion of equal treatment above procedural cost issues even when substantial costs are involved for suppliers as well as procuring entities. Thus, in *VAR* the Court concluded that suppliers submitting products that do not meet a detailed specification but are simply 'equivalent' must provide proof of equivalence in the tender itself, and cannot be permitted to do this merely at appropriate points during the contract[289] – even though in *VAR* this entailed proof of equivalence for more than 2000 vehicle spare parts, some of which might never be needed. The Court invoked the equal treatment principle, the concern being that without proof of equivalence some suppliers, unlike others, would not be subject to a meaningful assessment of compliance at the time of tendering.[290] The ruling curtails the scope for national authorities to balance the procedural costs in specific cases against other national interests by verifying tenders only to the extent that it is warranted in the light of national circumstances (such as likelihood of abuse of discretion) and the features of the specific procurement, such as the nature and degree of commercial or other risks resulting from non-compliance with the specification (such as the disruption that would be caused if the product is later found to be non-compliant).

It should be mentioned, however, that many of the grey areas that require a balance to be made between procedural costs and open market interests – for example, the scope that exists for completing or amending the contract after choosing the winner in flexible procedures[291] – have not been considered by the ECJ. Here, in practice, the balance is determined by national courts or simply by national practice, which may vary between Member States. How the ECJ strikes this balance in future case law could have significant implications for the overall balance of interests under the EU regime.

[289] Case C-14/17, *VAR Srl and Azienda Trasporti Milanesi SpA (ATM)* v. *Iveco Orecchia SpA* ECLI:EU:C:2018:568, judgment of 12 July 2018.

[290] Ibid. The Court differed here from Advocate General Campos Sánchez-Bordona, who prioritised a different aspect of competition, pointing out that the burden on suppliers offering equivalent tenders could give rise to inequality and deter participation by persons offering tenders based on equivalence, and considered that a meaningful assessment could be provided by a declaration of equivalence.

[291] On this point, see competitive dialogue, for example, Arrowsmith, *The Law of Public and Utilities Procurement*, vol. 1 (2014), paras. 8-79–8-82 and 8-103–8-111.

2.4.2.5 Balancing Interests in the Supplier Remedies System

We have so far considered how different interests are balanced in the rules governing use and conduct of competitive tendering, but also important for the overall system is the balance struck in the enforcement system. In most modern regimes, supplier review is the core element of this system and this is thus the focus of this section, especially since a study of procurement has much to offer here and individual enforcement is a core element of the TFEU rules allocating limited rights.

Public procurement is particularly significant in considering individual legal remedies in view of the long experience (since 1989) of designing and revising a bespoke system. The original Remedies Directive of 1989[292] provided a system that, in retrospect, seems on its face largely merely to have anticipated later developments in the general remedies jurisprudence, stating general principles of effectiveness and equivalence and the need for specific powers of interim relief, set aside and damages as elements of effective remedies. Supplier challenges to contracts under the Directives were, of course, already possible under the principle-based enforcement framework of the Treaty prior to 1989, but this was still evolving at that time towards the kind of rules that were made explicit in the Remedies Directive. Arguably, it was in fact the publicity and greater degree of certainty provided by a specific Remedies Directive and consequent Member State measures that had the main impact when the Remedies Directive was first introduced.[293] This led to greater enforcement activity in public procurement, which in turn led to further development of the remedies rules first, through judicial interpretation, especially though the effectiveness principle to add,[294] notably, the 'standstill' requirement[295] (see below) and, secondly, by legislative

292 Council Directive 89/665/EEC of 21 December 1989 on the coordination of the laws, regulations and administrative provisions relating to the application of review procedures to the award of public supply and public works contracts, OJ 1989, No. L395/33 (Remedies Directive).

293 For a historical perspective on this point, see S. Arrowsmith, 'Public Procurement: Example of a Developed Field of National Remedies Established by Community Law', in H.-W. Micklitz and N. Reich (eds.), *Public Interest Litigation before European Courts* (Baden-Baden: Nomos Verlagsgesellschaft, 1996).

294 Stated in Remedies Directive, Art. 1.

295 In Case C-81/98, *Alcatel Austria AG and Others, Siemens AG Österreich and Sag-Schrack Anlagentechnik AG* v. *Bundesministerium für Wissenschaft und Verkehr* [1999] ECR I-7671, ECLI:EU:C:1999:534.

amendments in 2007[296] to incorporate the Court's interpretations and add further innovations. This produced a much more nuanced and effective system geared to the specific context of procurement, as described below, and which the ECJ has indicated is more concrete and robust than that of the Treaty.[297] This can perhaps be seen as a movement from a largely principle-based system found still in the TFEU to a much more rule-based system, which through its precision and certainty achieves much greater effectiveness.

The enforcement system supports, of course, the whole range of interests promoted through the tendering rules – commercial value, integrity and so on – both directly (by correcting violations) and indirectly through its deterrent and interpretative functions and by giving suppliers confidence to participate. The direct interest depends on the precise rule violated and the extent and nature of the consequences of that violation, which can vary widely. Thus in a procedure based on the lowest price, failing to award a contract to the bidder that is the lowest by millions of pounds can have a clear and measurable impact on value. However, proceedings aimed at excluding a rival competitor that has submitted the best offer but omitted an unimportant document for which the tender documents require exclusion support the equal treatment principle with less immediate concrete benefits (and indeed concrete commercial detriment).

The main interest to balance against the above interests is that of an efficient process. In particular, enforcement action involves resource costs both for challenging suppliers and the authority as well as costs in terms of delay to the contract, affecting, in particular, the authority and its stakeholders, the challenging supplier, and other suppliers (in particular, any winning tenderer). The latter costs vary significantly: for example, delay to a procurement of urgently needed medicines is much more problematic than delay to a contract to top up already ample stocks of stationery. As noted, the costs of delay in procurement tend perhaps to be more significant than with other limited rights.

[296] Directive 2007/66/EC of the European Parliament and the Council of 11 December 2007 amending Council Directives 89/665/EEC and 92/13/EEC with regard to improving the effectiveness of review procedures concerning the award of public contracts, OJ 2007, No. L335/31.

[297] As we have mentioned above, in Case C-91/08, *Wall AG* v. *Stadt Frankfurt am Main and Frankfurter Entsorgungs- und Service (FES)* [2010] ECR I-02815, ECLI:EU:C:2009:659, para. 141 of the Opinion of Advocate General Bot and supported in the ruling; Case C-203/14, *Consorci Sanitari del Maresme* v. *Corporació de Salut del Maresme i la Selva* ECLI:EU:C:2015:445, para. 16 of the Opinion of Advocate General Jääskinen.

The approach embodied in the Remedies Directive[298] after decades of experience seeks to balance these interests through a system that is highly effective in correcting specific violations, while promoting resolution of disputes before the contract is concluded.[299] This latter focus is explained largely by the interest in avoiding disruption with its attendant costs but also by national sensitivities over interfering with concluded contracts and the fact that task is still sometimes reserved for the courts rather than bespoke procurement review bodies,[300] making it more difficult and sensitive to correct violations after the contract is concluded.

In the context of violations in a competitive tendering procedure, the system's key elements are: a right of challenge before a review body,[301] with ultimate recourse to a judicial-type body where the initial review body is not judicial in nature;[302] obligations to give suppliers timely information on decisions and the reasons for them;[303] a 'notification and standstill' requirement, which entails notifying participants and providing a period of (usually) ten days before concluding the contract,

[298] The Remedies Directive applies to review procedures relating to contracts of contracting authorities within the scope of the Public Procurement Directive. A separate, very similar, system applies to contracts covered by the Utilities Directive, under Council Directive 92/13/EEC of 25 February 1992 coordinating the laws, regulations and administrative provisions relating to the application of Community rules on the procurement procedures of entities operating in the water, energy, transport and telecommunications sectors, OJ 1992, No. L76/14. Review procedures relating to concessions are also governed by one of these two directives (according to whether or not the concession is in the utilities field): Concessions Directive, Art. 46. A similar remedies system for contracts covered by the Defence and Security Directive is set out in Arts. 55–64 of that Directive.

[299] See, in detail, Arrowsmith, *The Law of Public and Utilities Procurement*, vol. 2 (2018), paras. 22-35–22-304; S. Treumer and F. Lichère (eds.), *Enforcement of the EU Public Procurement Rules*, European Procurement Law Series (Copenhagen: DJØF Publishing, 2011); H. Schebesta, *Damages in EU Procurement Law*, Studies in European Economic Law and Regulation Series (Cham: Springer, 2016); Europe Economics and Milieu, *Economic Efficiency and Legal Effectiveness of Review and Remedies Procedures for Public Contracts: Final Study Report*, Document prepared for the European Commission (Luxembourg: Publications Office of the European Union, 2015; MARKT/2013/072/C, April 2015), available at http://ec.europa.eu/growth/single-market/public-procurement/studies-networks/index_en.htm.

[300] On the approach of different Member States to this, see Europe Economics and Milieu, *Economic Efficiency and Legal Effectiveness of Review and Remedies Procedures for Public Contracts: Final Study Report*.

[301] Remedies Directive, Art. 1(1).

[302] Ibid., Art. 2(9).

[303] E.g. Public Procurement Directive, Art. 55.

to allow a challenge;[304] an automatic prohibition on concluding the contract after challenge to the award or later decisions;[305] the possibility of rapid interim measures even prior to the award (for example, to challenge the specification);[306] the possibility of correcting unlawful decisions;[307] a damages remedy,[308] including for lost profits;[309] and a requirement for the system to be 'rapid',[310] reducing the potential for delay. The system still permits Member States generally to preserve concluded contracts.[311] However, should the system fail to achieve the objectives of resolving disputes before the contract is concluded, to prevent that situation arising from evasion of the system there is also a requirement for the contract to be declared ineffective (at least prospectively) in certain cases in which the procuring entity does not comply with its standstill and automatic suspension obligations.[312]

The balance between the many interests served by effective remedies and the interest in avoiding procedural costs is also implemented further by various limitations on the above, notably by confining the drastic ineffectiveness remedy to where violation of the notification and standstill or suspension deprived the challenger of the possibility of pre-contractual review and there is also a substantive breach of the law affecting the chances of winning the contract;[313] and by allowing review bodies to lift or deny a suspension or deny an ineffectiveness remedy where the negative impact, including on the public interest in proceeding with the procurement, outweighs the benefit of the remedy.[314] This

[304] Remedies Directive, Art. 2a and Art. 2b.
[305] Ibid., Art. 2(3).
[306] Ibid., Art. 2(1)(a).
[307] Ibid., Art. 2(1)(b).
[308] Ibid., Art. 2(1)(b).
[309] Case E-16/16, *Fosen-Linjen AS* v. *AtB AS*, EFTA Court judgment of 31 October 2017; Case E-7/18, *Fosen-Linjen AS, supported by the Confederation of Norwegian Enterprise (Næringslivets Hovedorganisasjon)* v. *AtB AS (Fosen-Linjen 2)*, EFTA Court judgment of 1 August 2019. This confirms the view stated by Advocate General Cruz Villalón in Case C-568/08, *Combinatie Spijker Infrabouw/De Jonge Konstruktie* v. *Provincie Drenthe* [2010] ECR I-12655, ECLI:EU:C:2010:515, judgment of 9 December 2010, para. 110 of the Opinion.
[310] Remedies Directive, Art. 1(1).
[311] Ibid., Art. 2(7).
[312] Ibid., Art. 2d(1)(b).
[313] Ibid., Art. 2d(1)(b).
[314] Ibid., Art. 2d(3) – although this covers economic interests only in certain exceptional cases.

allows review bodies to adjust the balance of interests to the widely varying circumstances of each case.

The general principle of effectiveness has been, and remains, an important tool for the ECJ to fill gaps in the system, dealing, for example, with excessive court fees,[315] and other conditions that provide obstacles to the aims of the system (precluding, for example, a national requirement to use a conciliation procedure before litigation).[316]

However, there are arguably some gaps that it seems desirable to address explicitly, in relation both to procurement and to limited rights in general. The most notable is the fact that, unlike the UNCITRAL Model Law,[317] the Remedies Directives do not provide for a specific time limit for completing review proceedings, leaving this to the general requirement for rapid remedies. This does not provide sufficient certainty to compel all Member States to address this issue, although a European Commission study found sixteen had done so (of these only four set periods longer than thirty days, with eight choosing thirty days and the other four twenty or fifteen days).[318] Setting such time limits is crucial to avoiding a conflict between significant interests in the first place, since if review takes more than a few months to complete – as in England and Wales, for example, even at a time when the UK was an EU Member State – it often requires a choice in individual cases between significant delay to the process or denying an effective remedy to uphold the interests prejudiced by the breach, by denying or lifting a suspension (resolved in the UK mainly in favour of the interest in proceeding with the contract).[319] The conflict is probably more acute in public procurement than in some areas because the public interests involved in proceeding are generally greater but it is still relevant in some other contexts.

Where an authority fails to use the Directives' required competitive tendering procedures, the EU has also developed a nuanced system that

[315] Case C-61/14, *Orizzonte Salute – Studio Infermieristico Associato* v. *Azienda Pubblica di Servizi alla persona San Valentino – Città di Levico Terme* ECLI:EU:C:2015:655.

[316] Case C-410/01, *Fritsch, Chiari & Partner, Ziviltechniker GmbH and Others* v. *Autobahnen- und Schnellstraßen-Finanzierungs-AG (Asfinag)* [2003] ECR I-6413, ECLI:EU:C:2003:362.

[317] UNCITRAL Model Law on Public Procurement 2011, Art. 67(10), making provision for a time limit for completion of independent review.

[318] Europe Economics and Milieu, *Economic Efficiency and Legal Effectiveness of Review and Remedies Procedures for Public Contracts: Final Study Report*, pp. 65–66.

[319] On the UK system, see generally Arrowsmith, *The Law of Public and Utilities Procurement*, vol. 2 (2018), paras. 22-35–22-29 *passim*, and on the operation of suspension specifically, paras. 22-129–22-145.

carefully balances the interests involved. This takes account of the fact that failure to advertise and hold a competition constitutes the most serious type of violation in terms of risks to the open market, as well as to national objectives (so that EU and national interests are to an extent aligned again). This system essentially provides for the remedy of ineffectiveness in all such cases.[320] This is again, however, subject to qualifications to provide a more nuanced balance, which sacrifices the possibility of correction where justified by the possible adverse impact from delay, and in that substitutes sanctions to at least secure a deterrent effect. Thus, there is the same possibility to preserve the contract for public interest reasons as with regular competitive tendering;[321] a possibility for authorities acting in good faith and reasonably to avoid ineffectiveness by notifying the market of their intention to make a direct award and applying a standstill;[322] and a possibility for Member States to cut off the possibility of ineffectiveness six months after the award even when the market could not have known of the violation.[323]

For contracts outside the Directives but covered by the TFEU, including the *Telaustria* transparency obligation, the jurisprudence has clarified, as we noted above, that the Treaty framework for enforcement is not as robust as that provided by the Remedies Directive: while it must not be impossible or unduly difficult to exercise the right to challenge[324] (and the principle of equivalence applies)[325] the Treaty's effectiveness principle does not require application of the Remedies Directive by analogy[326] and, specifically, does not require interim measures and an obligation to terminate unlawful contracts.[327] As with the substantive rules on transparency in procurement, so also with enforcement this principle-based approach leaves somewhat uncertain what exactly the

[320] Remedies Directive, Art. 2d(1)(a).

[321] Ibid., Art. 2d(3).

[322] Ibid., Art. 2d(4).

[323] Ibid., Art. 2f(1)(b). Otherwise, the Member State must effectively allow a month after public notification of the decision for a challenge: ibid., Art. 2f(1)(a).

[324] Case C-91/08, *Wall AG* v. *Stadt Frankfurt am Main and Frankfurter Entsorgungs- und Service (FES) GmbH* [2010] ECR I-02815, ECLI:EU:C:2010:182, para. 64.

[325] Ibid.

[326] Ibid., ECLI:EU:C:2009:659, para. 141 of the Opinion of Advocate General Bot (a position also supported in the ruling in that case); Case C-203/14, *Consorci Sanitari del Maresme* v. *Corporació de Salut del Maresme i la Selva* ECLI:EU:C:2015:445, para. 16 of the Opinion of Advocate General Jääskinen.

[327] Case C-91/08, *Wall AG* v. *Stadt Frankfurt am Main and Frankfurter Entsorgungs- und Service (FES) GmbH* [2010] ECR I-02815, ECLI:EU:C:2010:182, para. 65.

rules are – how a remedy can indeed be made effective in both competitive and non-competitive situations, without necessarily following the Remedies Directive. The differences from the Remedies Directive could be marginal – for example, merely allowing a choice between setting aside concluded contracts and applying a standstill – or could be quite significant. This uncertainty arising out of a principle-based approach under the Treaty also exists with respect to allocation of other limited rights.

The detailed system developed in public procurement for balancing the different interests involved can provide useful insights for other areas of limited rights, but must always be considered in its exact context. Thus, public procurement rules involve the allocation of limited rights in a commercial context and a different approach may be appropriate outside that context. It is also relevant that procurement disputes concern a right allocated at a particular point in time to just one tenderer, so that the dispute has a potential impact on a public authority's ability to proceed with the transaction and on others interested in obtaining the right. This is true of most limited rights but some, such as sales or the grant of exclusive authorisations, have a closer parallel with procurement than others (such as grants, where there might be some flexibility in available funds to correct mistakes without any other impact). Even with this former group, however, there are differences, especially in the likelihood of adverse impact on the public interest from delay, which is a particular problem with procurement although still relevant for some other rights. Remedies for individuals also need to be considered in the context of the overall enforcement system, which for public procurement includes in the EU, for example, a new requirement in the 2014 Public Procurement Directive for national enforcement authorities carrying out various verification and enforcement functions.[328]

2.5 Concluding Remarks

We have suggested that experience in public procurement is particularly useful for several reasons when studying the balancing of interests through competitive tendering. Thus, procurement provides a close analogy for certain other limited rights and involves similar interests; competitive tendering has been extensively used *and* extensively

[328] Public Procurement Directive, Art. 83.

regulated in the procurement context, at both EU and national levels; there is much relevant material to draw on outside the EU context to assist with the critique; and, last but not least, it is from the material on procurement that the ECJ has largely drawn its inspiration in dealing with other limited rights. This all justifies a careful and detailed look at the procurement experience when studying the broad topic of allocation of limited rights.

Against this background, we have reviewed the way in which different interests have been balanced in the procurement context, focusing on some of the key interests involved but considering all interests to some degree. Even this brief review shows that this balancing of interests is a very complex task influenced by, among other things, the complexity of procurement activity and – when balancing interests at the EU level – differences in Member States. There are many areas of controversy, such as the width of discretion to be allowed to Member States for their procuring entities in the light of the potential for abuse of discretion to favour national suppliers and, at the national level, the extent to which discretion should be permitted in balancing commercial and integrity objectives. It is clear that the solutions reached in public procurement should not be copied uncritically, both because of their flaws and controversial nature in some cases and because of the important differences in context between public procurement and certain other types of limited rights. Nevertheless, the wealth of detail and experience embodied in the public procurement rules provides useful lessons and options, and the study of this material is invaluable for considering the balance of interests issues in the context of limited rights more broadly.

3

Licensing

FERDINAND WOLLENSCHLÄGER

3.1 Introduction

As a consequence of regulatory choices made by the State, the exercise of a variety of activities is subject to a licence requirement. This applies to numerous economic activities such as in the area of gambling or public transport, including taxis, but also to activities of a non-economic nature such as constructing a building or possessing weapons, as well as to using natural goods such as in case of mining, carbon emission or fishing, or to access to public infrastructure such as stands at trade fairs and markets or places at university. Such licences are frequently only available in a limited number owing to the limited availability of natural resources, because of State-imposed quantitative restrictions on the exercise of certain activities or due to limited demand for or supply of goods or services by the State. In this case, the issue of allocation arises, which is often of considerable economic, personal or societal relevance and which will be discussed in this chapter. After exploring the concept of licensing (Section 3.2), public interests at stake when allocating limited licences will be systemised with regard to inherent needs as well as to output- and process-related interests (Section 3.3). It will then be analysed whether, and if so how, public interests are optimised by competitive tendering when allocating scarce licences (Section 3.4).[1] In these regards, the variety of sectors and activities concerned not only promises a certain (albeit diverging) amount of material in terms of academic debate, case-law and legislation, but this variety also necessitates a horizontal approach, which makes it possible to generate, at least at a medium level

[1] This chapter is based on previous research by the author; see notably and with further references F. Wollenschläger, *Verteilungsverfahren* (Tübingen: Mohr Siebeck, 2010); F. Wollenschläger, 'EU Law Principles for Allocating Scarce Goods and the Emergence of an Allocation Procedure: Identifying Substantive and Procedural Standards and Developing a New Type of Administrative Procedure' (2015) 8 *REALaw* 205–256.

of abstraction,[2] general insights for allocating limited rights. Which choices has the legislature made, or not made, in terms of competitive tendering, and of defining its modalities? Which balance of interests do these choices reflect? Have competing interests been optimised? This chapter will explore against this background which legal and notably constitutional standards determine these choices and the process of optimising public interests, the issues of creating scarcity, and inviting applications versus direct awards, as well as defining allocation criteria and procedures. The horizontal approach to be taken, however, rules out any in-depth substantive analysis of the specific subject matter.

3.2 The Concept of Licensing

Taking the Oxford English Dictionary as a starting point, a licence may be defined as a 'formal, usually a printed or written permission from a constituted authority to do something, e.g. to marry, to print or publish a book, to preach, to carry on some trade, etc.; a permit'.[3] Not restricted to service activities, this definition is broader than the legal notion of 'authorisation schemes' within the meaning of Article 4(6) of the Services Directive (2006/123/EC). Such a broad understanding would also comprise gun licences or planning permission for a building.

A licensing system allows public authorities to make a prior assessment of a potentially harmful activity in order to check whether, and to ensure that, its exercise complies with the specific regulatory requirements. For instance, a gun owner or an operator of gambling activities must be reliable, or a planned building stable against collapsing. Moreover, under certain licensing systems, the number of available licences is limited, either because a harmful activity is deemed acceptable, or at least tolerable if exercised under quantitative restrictions, such as in the case of limiting gambling licences in order to channel and/or reduce gambling opportunities, or because a harmless activity becomes harmful if exercised without quantitative restrictions, such as in the case of limiting taxi licences in order to prevent a threat to livelihoods in the local taxi trade being caused by excess capacities, in the interest of maintaining its functionality, or in the case of subjecting the use of radio and/or telecommunication frequencies to a licence requirement with only a limited number of licences available in order to guarantee efficient,

[2] On this approach, see Wollenschläger, 'EU Law Principles', 252 ff.

[3] www.oed.com/view/Entry/107943?redirectedFrom=licence#eid (5 December 2024).

non-conflicting frequency utilisation. The examples also reflect a further possible distinction based on the reason of scarcity, namely State-created scarcity and natural scarcity.[4] First, the State may create scarcity in order to achieve specific policy goals (gambling and taxi licences). Second, the State may create (legal) scarcity in cases of natural scarcity by removing the resolution of an allocation conflict from the societal domain and by subjecting it to an allocation scheme (radio and/or telecommunication frequencies).

Following a broad understanding of licensing, a further category may be added, namely scarcity resulting from the State not supplying or demanding an infinite number of goods/services.[5] This is because, broadly defined, licences may also involve an entitlement to use or participate in public infrastructure such as places at university, stands at trade fairs, and markets and land, or admission of medical doctors or hospitals to the public insurance scheme. Such a broad understanding became manifest in the European Court of Justice (ECJ)'s *Promoimpresa* case that was handed down on 14 July 2016, qualifying

> concessions granted by public authorities of State-owned maritime and lakeside property relating to the exploitation of State land for tourist and leisure-orientated business activities [. . .] as 'authorisations' within the meaning of the provisions of Directive 2006/123 in so far as they constitute formal decisions, irrespective of their characterisation in national law, which must be obtained by the service providers from the competent national authorities in order to be able to exercise their economic activities.[6]

The policy choice behind scarcity in these cases especially reflects limited resources and/or a limited need; further policy considerations may, however, also apply, such as guaranteeing an efficient healthcare infrastructure in the aforementioned admission issues.

Finally, it should be noted that public procurement, financial grants (subsidies) and government sales ('privatisation'), which are dealt with in the other sector-specific chapters of this book, do not qualify as licensing systems since they do not permit an action in the sense of the aforementioned definition – at least if it is not to lose its contours.[7] There may, nonetheless, be a certain amount of overlapping, for instance if a

[4] For this categorisation with further references and qualifications, see Wollenschläger, 'EU Law Principles', 205; F. Wollenschläger, *Verteilungsverfahren*, p. 1.

[5] Ibid.

[6] Cf. ECJ, Joined Cases C-458/14 and C-67/15, *Promoimpresa* ECLI:EU:C:2016:558, para. 40 f.

[7] This would also apply to allocating posts in the public service.

concession is awarded that falls under the public procurement regime, or where being included in the public hospital plan is not only key to treating patients under a public insurance scheme but also to gaining access to subsidies (even if the latter may be considered part of the remuneration).

3.3 An Overview of Public Interests

Various public interests play a role in the award of limited licences, which will be analysed on the basis of the set of eleven public interests identified in the introductory chapter and grouped into inherent needs (Section 3.3.1), output-related interests (Section 3.3.2) and process-related interests (Section 3.3.3). It should be noted at the outset that legal concepts and standards, such as respect for fundamental rights, equal and fair treatment or transparency, will be developed in more detail including references in Sections 3.4.1–3.4.3.

3.3.1 Inherent Needs

With regard to inherent needs, a distinction has to be first drawn between the public interests in establishing the limitation in a licensing scheme and in allocating the licence. The inherent need in the former case depends on the reason for scarcity. In case of natural scarcity, the State establishes a licensing scheme in order to prevent unregulated use of the scarce good that is considered detrimental in view of its characteristics. For instance, uncoordinated use of scarce radio and telecommunication frequencies would result in interference, and unlimited exploitation of fish stocks would result in overfishing. In case of scarcity due to limited public demand or supply, sector-specific reasons constitute the limiting factor for public demand or supply. In case of admission of hospitals to the hospital plan granting the right to treat patients who are insured under the public insurance system, and to public subsidies for investment costs, to take one example, limiting plan capacities to the current and expected demand for hospital treatment aims to ensure efficient healthcare provision. The limited availability of stands at trade fairs and markets results from the limited capacity of the specific infrastructure itself, reflecting the State's choice of a specific design (size, categories of goods to be offered). Finally, the inherent need to establish a licensing scheme in case of State-created scarcity results from the characteristics of the regulated activity. Limiting gambling opportunities thus aims to reduce the negative effects of gambling such as addiction, while limiting the number of taxi licences aims to maintain the functionality of the taxi trade endangered by excess capacities.

When it comes to allocating a licence, that is, to determining the criteria for its award, the inherent needs follow from the characteristics of the activity or right to be licenced and thus depend on the subject matter. Two aspects may be distinguished in this regard, that is, qualification criteria as minimum conditions for eligibility (such as economic and financial standing; technical and professional ability; reliability) and comparative allocation criteria to choose the best among the eligible applicants.

When limiting gambling activities in view of the dangers associated with gambling, for instance, certain minimum criteria such as reliability and sound economic standing have to be defined in order to protect consumers and prevent fraud and addiction. When it comes to the comparative allocation criteria, the provider with the best concept has to be chosen with a view to realising these goals. If significant differences in this regard among providers fulfilling the minimum criteria cannot be established, a recourse to formal criteria may be required. When limiting fishing opportunities in order to protect fish stocks, next to minimum eligibility criteria securing a sound operation, a choice could be based on the best concept in terms of achieving the aforementioned goal.

Avoiding overfishing may, however, also be considered a general consideration of environmental protection and may thus not qualify as an inherent need, but as an additional policy objective and hence as an output-related interest. This underlines the fact that it may be difficult to make a distinction between these categories.[8] Such a distinction may undoubtedly serve as a tool to classify allocation schemes and identify changes such as an increasing focus on other than economic goals when it comes to distributing economic goods. This development may also be observed in public procurement law, where the pursuit of non-economic goals such as environmental or social considerations has become increasingly accepted. This is also reflected in terminology, marking a change from their qualification as 'aspects alien to procurement law' to 'secondary considerations' to 'strategic procurement'.[9] Such a distinction must

[8] See also F. Wollenschläger, in P. M. Huber and A. Voßkuhle (eds.), *Grundgesetz-Kommentar*, 7th ed. (Munich: C. H. Beck, 2018), Article 3 GG, para. 54 f.

[9] F. Wollenschläger, 'Europäisches Vergabeverwaltungsrecht', in J. Terhechte (ed.), *Verwaltungsrecht der Europäischen Union*, 2nd ed. (Baden-Baden: Nomos, 2022) § 17, para. 62.

not be overestimated, however. In terms of constitutional standards, an appropriate definition of allocation criteria in line with the standards following from these guarantees is decisive, but not a classification among the aforementioned categories. At any rate, the classification as such must not be used as an argument for more or less stringent standards in terms of justification.[10] Finally, it should be noted that horizontal clauses such as Articles 8 et seqq. Treaty on the Functioning of the European Union (TFEU) obliging the Union to consider certain policy goals, such as environmental protection (Article 11 TFEU), in all its activities further relativise the distinction between inherent needs and achieving additional policies. The same applies to general objectives for State action that are enshrined in national constitutional law, such as with regard to the protection of the natural foundations of life and animals (Article 20a of the German Basic Law [*Grundgesetz* – GG]).

3.3.2 Output-Related Interests

3.3.2.1 Achieving Additional Policies

Additional policy objectives may be identified irrespective of and taking account of the difficulties encountered in distinguishing between inherent needs and additional policy objectives. These often relate to social, environmental, regional or economic aspects. Preference may thus be given to applicants fulfilling certain social or environmental standards, such as paying minimum wages, using environmentally friendly products or techniques, or contributing to climate neutrality. With regard to economic and regional aspects, preference may be given to operators promoting the local or regional economy. Finally, operators offering adequate services in all regions of a country may be prioritised when allocating licences for the use of telecommunication frequencies.

3.3.2.2 Value for Money

In the context of licensing, value for money may have two points of reference, that is, value for money for the public authority and/or for consumers of the licenced activity. If the award of a licence is linked to financial or similar contributions on the part of the public authority, such as subsidies or the opportunity to use public infrastructure, or with fees

[10] Cf. on this, against the background of the German debate on internal and external reasons for distinctions in the context of the general right to equality, Wollenschläger, 'Article 3 GG', para. 54 f.

to be paid by licensees (concession fees or auction proceeds), the public authority may have an interest in selecting the operator promising the lowest costs or the highest revenue for the public. Moreover, the public authority may also have an interest in the conditions offered for the licenced activity constituting value for money for its consumers. The contractual conditions, including the price for users of the telecommunication services, may, for instance, be considered when allocating telecommunication frequencies.

3.3.2.3 Opening of Markets (including Promoting SMEs)

Since licences are often related to economic activities, the State may have an interest in opening up markets and fostering competition, including with a view to licensing the best applicant. This is particularly relevant in markets where there are shortcomings in that regard, for instance in the case of (former) monopolistic or oligopolistic structures such as in the telecommunications sector. What is more, preventing protectionist practices may also play a role against the background of establishing the European Union (EU) internal market.

3.3.2.4 Safeguarding Fundamental Rights

Since public authorities are comprehensively bound by fundamental rights (cf. only Article 51(1) Charter of Fundamental Rights of the European Union (CFR) or Article 1(3) of the Basic Law), these rights must be safeguarded when allocating scarce licences. The State is therefore not free to choose whether to safeguard fundamental rights. These rights are safeguarded if the allocation system is in line with substantive and procedural fundamental rights standards. That having been said, in view of the need to accommodate competing interests in allocation procedures and of the framework-providing character of constitutional law,[11] fundamental rights usually leave room to balance competing public and private interests. The most prominent rights in this regard at the EU level are the freedoms to choose an occupation (Article 15(1) CFR) and to conduct a business (Article 16 CFR), as well as the right to equal treatment (Article 20 CFR).

[11] See on this F. Wollenschläger, 'Verfassung im Allgemeinen Verwaltungsrecht: Bedeutungsverlust durch Europäisierung und Emanzipation?' (2016) 75 *VVDStRL* 187–264 at 207 ff.; F. Wollenschläger, 'Constitutionalisation and Deconstitutionalisation of Administrative Law in View of Europeanisation and Emancipation' (2017) 10 *REALaw* 7–79 at 31 ff.

3.3.2.5 Integrity

The scarcity of a licence in combination with a certain (economic) value of the licence may be an incentive for applicants to seek preferential treatment by employing illegal means such as corruption or collusive tendering. Moreover, inappropriate preferences on the part of the administration may be an issue, an example being favouritism motivated by personal or political considerations. The integrity of the allocation process must therefore be secured by, for instance, transparent criteria and procedures.

3.3.3 Process-Related Interests

3.3.3.1 Equal Treatment

Allocating scarce licences implies unequal treatment insofar as only one or some, but not all, applicants have prospects of receiving a licence. This unequal treatment may, however, be justified if the allocation criteria are adequate in view of the good to be distributed, which depends on the subject matter, notably the inherent needs and output-related interests involved and outlined above. This usually leaves room for more than one form of concretisation. Apart from this substantive dimension, equal treatment also has a procedural dimension and thus constitutes a process-related interest. This is because the allocation procedure has to be designed in such a way as to safeguard equal treatment. This may imply inter alia advertising the award of licences and not granting unjustified advantages to individual applicants such as providing selective information or the opportunity to adjust the bid.

3.3.3.2 Fair Treatment (in addition to Equal Treatment)

As in every administrative procedure, it is vital that applicants be treated fairly. Since an allocation conflict has to be resolved, and thus procedural and substantive standards apply, which follow from the right to equality, it is questionable whether fair treatment calls for standards going beyond those that are requisite for equal treatment.

3.3.3.3 Transparency

Transparency is an important interest in allocation procedures since selecting the best offer is contingent on such transparency. Without an advertisement, for instance, it is not possible to have competition and thus an adequate basis for selecting the best offer. Moreover, transparent criteria reduce the scope for administrative discretion and thus for arbitrariness. Finally, transparency in the shape of a motivated allocation decision is vital as a basis for effective legal protection.

3.3.3.4 Accountability

Accountability, defined in the procurement chapter as 'enabling citizens and other interested parties to establish whether procurement objectives are being met',[12] is also of relevance in the context of licences, albeit not relating to specific aspects.

3.3.3.5 Efficiency of the Process

Finally, efficiency of the process is an important aspect in designing allocation procedures since they (should) aim to bring about efficient allocation. It is highly relevant as a counterbalance to transparency and to further procedural requirements. When interpreted in the light of efficiency, the duty to conduct a transparent procedure does not therefore require maximum transparency. Adequate transparency will suffice when it comes, for instance, to advertising the allocation such as with regard to the appropriate medium or the regional scope of distribution. Moreover, adjusting the bid may be justified for reasons of efficiency.

3.4 Optimising Public Interests: Legal Choices and Assumptions

Having outlined the multi-layered, fragmented legal framework for allocating limited licences (Section 3.4.1), the issue of whether or not tendering should be competitive will be fanned out into two dimensions: first, the creation of scarcity as a basis for competition; second, the choice between inviting applications for limited licences and awarding them directly, thus setting the course for or against competitive tendering (Section 3.4.2). Moreover, how public interests are balanced by competitive (Section 3.4.3) and non-competitive (Section 3.4.4) tendering will be explored.

3.4.1 The Multi-layered, Fragmented Legal Framework

The legal framework for allocating licences is multi-layered and fragmented. In view of the broad variety of subjects qualifying as licences, it is

[12] See Chapter 2, Section 2.3.

not surprising that there is no specific uniform legal framework, unlike, for instance, in public procurement. The applicable set of rules and principles depends on the subject matter of the licence. It may be found at the EU and/or national level, as well as at the constitutional and/or legislative level. Focusing on EU legislation, an initial distinction may be drawn between sector-specific acts, such as for allocating telecommunication frequencies, and acts of a (more) general, cross-sectoral scope, such as the Services Directive, which covers various licences to provide services (Section 3.4.1.1).[13] If no act of secondary EU law applies, substantive and procedural allocation standards still follow – within their scope of application – from primary EU law, and particularly from the fundamental freedoms, but also from EU fundamental rights (Section 3.4.1.2). Moreover, it should be noted that most acts of secondary EU law – despite the ever-increasing significance of EU law for allocation regimes[14] – do not constitute the legal basis for allocation decisions and procedures, but require (legislative) transposition at the national level, with the slot regulation being a notable exception.[15] Thus, even in areas that have become 'Europeanised', national law is still relevant when it comes to allocating limited licences, and this will be explored with reference to the German legal order. Since illustrative aims are pursued, but not comparative ones, this limitation seems justified. Moreover, and this remark also relates to sections further on, the focus on Germany is also due to the advanced state of the debate on allocation procedures, albeit the high degree of constitutionalisation of the German (administrative) legal order needs to be highlighted (Section 3.4.1.3).[16] Finally, the legal framework will be analysed from the perspective of whether a principle-based or rule-based regulation may be observed, and of which approach seems preferable (Section 3.4.1.4).

[13] See, moreover, the ReNEUAL Model Rules on EU Administrative Procedure comprising rules for competitive award procedures [Article III-6(4) and IV-9 ff.].

[14] See on this Wollenschläger, 'EU Law Principles', 209 ff. – the starting point was different, though, see P. M. Huber, 'Gemeinschaftsrechtlicher Schutz vor einer Verteilungslenkung durch deutsche Behörden' (1991) 26 *EuR* 31–62 at 61. See further on supplementing standards of national constitutional law by standards of EU law resulting in a loss of the standard-setting function of the former if EU law reveals itself as stricter (example: allocation regime based on the EU market freedoms for concessions) Wollenschläger, 'Constitutionalisation', 37 ff.

[15] See, e.g., § 27a(1) of the German Aviation Act (LuftVG): 'Airport coordination shall be effected in accordance with the law of the European Union.'

[16] On the high degree of constitutionalisation of the German (administrative) legal order, see Wollenschläger, 'Constitutionalisation', 10 ff.

3.4.1.1 The Legislative Framework at EU Level

Various sector-specific acts of secondary EU law contain rules and principles for allocating scarce licences, namely the European Electronic Communications Code,[17] the Regulation on public passenger transport services by rail and by road,[18] the Directive on the conditions for granting and using authorisations for the prospection, exploration and production of hydrocarbons,[19] the Regulation on the common fisheries policy with regard to fishing opportunities,[20] as well as the air transport rules on ground handling at EU airports[21] and on slot allocation.[22] In view of their purpose, namely to open up markets, these acts of secondary law are primarily intended to realise the market freedoms. That having been said, other aspects of the primary law allocation regime, such as State aid-related aspects in the context of the Passenger Transport Regulation, are also integrated here.

Cross-sectoral significance for allocation procedures attaches, first, to the Services Directive.[23] The Directive extends to the allocation of

[17] Directive (EU) 2018/1972 of the European Parliament and of the Council of 11 December 2018 establishing the European Electronic Communications Code, OJ 2018, No. L321, 17 December 2018, most recently amended by Corrigendum to Directive (EU) 2018/1972, OJ 2020, No. L419, 11 December 2020.

[18] Regulation (EC) 1370/2007 of the European Parliament and of the Council of 23 October 2007 on public passenger transport services by rail and by road, OJ 2007, No. L315, 3 December 2007, most recently amended by Regulation (EU) 2016/2338 of the European Parliament and of the Council of 14 December 2016, OJ 2016, No. L354, 23 December 2016.

[19] Directive 94/22/EC of the European Parliament and of the Council of 30 May 1994 on the conditions for granting and using authorisations for the prospection, exploration and production of hydrocarbons, OJ 1994, No. L164, 30 June 1994, most recently amended by Regulation (EU) 2018/1999 of the European Parliament and of the Council of 11 December 2018, OJ 2018, No. L328, 21 December 2018.

[20] Articles 16 f. Regulation (EU) No. 1380/2013 of the European Parliament and of the Council of 11 December 2013 on the Common Fisheries Policy, OJ 2013, No. L354, 28 December 2013, most recently amended by Council Regulation (EU) 1385/2013 of 17 December 2013, OJ 2013, No. L354, 28 December 2013.

[21] Council Directive 96/67/EC of 15 October 1996 on access to the ground handling market at Community airports, OJ 1996, No. L272, 25 October 1996, amended by Regulation (EC) 1882/2003 of the European Parliament and of the Council of 29 September 2003, OJ 2003, No. L284, 31 October 2003. This directive does go beyond administrative action since it applies to airports irrespective of their (public or private) ownership, cf. Article 1.

[22] Council Regulation (EEC) 95/93 of 18 January 1993 on common rules for the allocation of slots at Community airports, OJ 1993, No. L14, 22 January 1993, most recently amended by Regulation (EC) 894/2002 of the European Parliament and of the Council of 27 May 2002, OJ 2002, No. L142, 31 May 2002.

[23] Directive 2006/123/EC of the European Parliament and of the Council of 12 December 2006 on services in the internal market, OJ 2006, No. L376, 27 December 2006. Cf. for more details and further references Wollenschläger, 'EU Law Principles', 247 ff

licences for 'services supplied by providers established in a Member State',[24] while numerous exceptions *ratione materiae* apply, thus significantly limiting its scope.[25] The Directive contains specific rules on authorisation schemes,[26] also in view of scarcity.[27] Unlike in the context of the EU's fundamental freedoms, the Court has not confined its rules on the freedom of establishment for providers (chapter III) to cross-border situations, but has held that these rules are also applicable 'to a situation where all the relevant elements are confined to a single Member State'.[28]

Cross-sectoral significance for allocating licences also attaches to the EU Procurement Directives if the award of a certain licence falls within their scope of application because it qualifies as a public contract or concession.[29] Since a chapter of this book has been specifically dedicated to public procurement, these rules will not be discussed any further here. It should, however, be highlighted that in particular the inclusion of concessions in the procurement regime under secondary EU law, with the 2014 reform,[30] has expanded its scope with regard to licensing, although it remains controversial when an economic operator has been entrusted with the execution of works or the provision and the management of services, these being prerequisites for a concession.[31] As recital 14 of Directive 2014/23/EU stresses, the mere authorisation to exercise such an activity is not sufficient. Against this background, it is, for instance, controversially debated whether and under what conditions the allocation of casino licences or places for stands at trade fairs and markets qualifies as a concession.[32] As explained elsewhere, an overall

[24] Article 2(1) Directive 2006/123/EC.

[25] Cf. Articles 2(2) and 17 Directive 2006/123/EC – notable exceptions comprise transport services, including urban transport and taxis, healthcare services, gambling activities, certain social services and the exercise of official authority; see further Article 3(1) in case of conflicts with certain acts of secondary EU law.

[26] Articles 4(6) and 9 ff. Directive 2006/123/EC.

[27] See Article 12 Directive 2006/123/EC.

[28] ECJ, Joined Cases C-360/15 and C-31/16, *X* ECLI:EU:C:2018:44, para. 98 ff.; Case C-377/17, *Commission* v. *Germany* ECLI:EU:C:2019:562, para. 57 f.; Joined Cases C-724/18 and C-727/18, *Cali Apartments* ECLI:EU:C:2020:743, para. 56; Case C-62/19, *Star Taxi App* ECLI:EU:C:2020:980, para. 75.

[29] As defined in Article 2(5) Directive 2014/24/EU, OJ 2014, No. L94, p. 65 and Article 5(1) Directive 2014/23/EU, OJ 2014, No. L94, p. 1.

[30] See F. Wollenschläger, in M. Burgi et al. (eds.), *Beck'scher Vergaberechtskommentar*, 4th ed. (Munich: C. H. Beck, 2022), § 105 GWB, para. 2 ff.

[31] See Wollenschläger, '§ 105 GWB', para. 36 ff.

[32] Affirmative for casino licences OLG Hamburg (Higher Regional Court), NZBau 2018, 122, 123; disagreeing for licences for slot machines OVG Münster (Higher Administrative Court),

assessment based on four criteria seems decisive, that is, on (1) the origin of the initiative (economic operator or public authority), (2) the creation of an obligation to perform the service/works, (3) the stipulation of sufficiently precise requirements for the performance of the service/works and (4) the degree of connection of the service/works to the performance of a task in the general interest.[33] The Court has qualified 'a concession for the operation of a lakeside area in order to set up a kiosk, veranda, bathing facilities, jetty and pontoon on the State-owned land around Lake Garda' not as a concession within the meaning of EU procurement law, since it did

> not concern the provision of a particular service by the contracting entity, but an authorisation to exercise an economic activity on State-owned land. [. . .] Such an interpretation is, furthermore, supported by recital 15 of Directive 2014/23. That recital states that certain agreements having as their object the right of an economic operator to exploit certain public domains or resources under private or public law, such as land, whereby the State establishes only general conditions for their use without procuring specific works or services, should not qualify as 'service concessions' within the meaning of that directive.[34]

The Services Directive applies notwithstanding.[35]

3.4.1.2 The Constitutional Framework at EU Level

EU Fundamental Freedoms As has already been explained elsewhere,[36] all allocation procedures that open up the possibility of economic activity are subject to the requirements of the market-freedom-based allocation regime.[37] The fundamental freedom that is relevant in

BeckRS 2017, 112407, para. 49 f.; VGH Mannheim (Higher Administrative Court), GewArch 2022, 28, 29 f.

33 See with further references F. Wollenschläger, 'Vergaberecht und andere Verteilungsregimes: Abgrenzungsfragen an der Schnittstelle von Konzessionsvergaberecht und Öffentlichem Wirtschaftsrecht', in forum vergabee.V. (ed.), *Neunzehnte forum vergabe Gespräche 2018* (Bonn: Bundesanzeiger Verlag, Schriftenreihe des forum vergabe e.V., 2018), vol. 54, p. 113; Wollenschläger, '§ 105 GWB', para. 42 ff.; further J. Wolswinkel, 'Concession Meets Authorisation: New Demarcation Lines under the Concessions Directive?' (2017) 12 *EPPPL* 396–407 at 401.

34 ECJ, Joined Cases C-458/14 and C-67/15, *Promoimpresa* ECLI:EU:C:2016:558, para. 46 ff.

35 Ibid., para. 37 ff. Cf. on the precedence of the concessions regime over the Services Directive recital 57 of the latter and the aforementioned judgment, para. 44 f.

36 See with further references Wollenschläger, 'EU Law Principles', 210 f., on which this section is based.

37 Cf. also ECJ, Case C-463/13, para. 46; Joined Cases C-458/14 and C-67/15, *Promoimpresa* ECLI:EU:C:2016:558, para. 63; M. Szydło, 'The Process of Granting Exclusive Rights in

an individual case is determined by the subject matter of the procedure, while the question of delimitation must not be overestimated in view of the tendencies towards the convergence of market freedoms. The freedoms of establishment (Article 49 et seqq. TFEU) and to provide services (Article 56 et seqq. TFEU) are likely to have the greatest practical significance since most economically relevant licences relate to the permanent or temporary exercise of self-employed activities[38] such as gambling activities, the allocation of stand places at trade fairs and markets, or of concessions in taxi transportation.[39] Beyond the market freedoms, relevance attaches to the general right to free movement (Article 21 TFEU), thus marking a paradigm shift in the fundamental freedoms' integration programme,[40] notably with regard to (limited) access to higher education.[41]

With regard to existing legislation governing (some) allocation procedures, it should be stressed that these pieces of secondary EU law must not be understood as a final codification of the respective area. First, the market freedoms are also relevant within the normed sphere because of their higher ranking, namely as a yardstick of lawfulness and a directive for interpretation and to fill gaps.[42] Second, the existence of legislation does not preclude invoking market freedoms for allocation procedures, which it does not cover, at least as long as an exclusion is not explicitly ordered (and in a manner that is in conformity with primary law); the emergence of an allocation regime for procurement not covered by the EU directives illustrates this.[43]

the Light of Treaty Rules on Free Movement' (2011) 12 *German Law Journal* 1408–1445 at 1419 ff.

38 Cf. on the delimitation only ECJ, Joined Cases C-316/07, C-358/07 to C-360/07, C-409/07 and C-410/07, *Markus Stoß et al.* [2010] ECR I-8069, para. 55 ff.; Joined Cases C-357/10 to C-359/10, *Duomo Gpa Srl et al.* ECLI:EU:C:2012:283, para. 30 ff.

39 On the inapplicability of the freedom to provide services in the transport sector Article 58(1) TFEU: ECJ, Case C-338/09, *Yellow Cab Verkehrsbetrieb* [2010] ECR I-13927, para. 30 ff.; Case C-434/15, *Asociación Profesional Elite Taxi* ECLI: EU:C:2017:981, para. 33 ff., 44 ff.

40 See on this development only F. Wollenschläger, *Grundfreiheit ohne Markt* (Tübingen: Mohr Siebeck, 2007/2017); F. Wollenschläger, 'A New Fundamental Freedom beyond Market Integration: Union Citizenship and Its Dynamics for Shifting the Economic Paradigm of European Integration' (2011) 17 *ELJ* 1–34.

41 See in more detail Wollenschläger, 'EU Law Principles', 230 f.

42 ECJ, Case C-92/00, *Hospital Ingenieure* [2002] ECR I-5553, para. 42 ff.; P. Braun, 'A Matter of Principle(s): The Treatment of Contracts Falling Outside the Scope of the European Public Procurement Directives' (2000) 9 *PPLR* 39–48, at 41 f. and 48.

43 For EU public procurement law, cf. only ECJ, Case C-324/98, *Telaustria* [2000] ECR I-10745, para. 60.

Finally, it should be noted that the fundamental freedoms do not apply to activities that are connected with the exercise of official authority (Article 45(4), Article 51 and 62 TFEU)[44] and require a cross-border element of the award procedure.[45] The Belgacom ruling has, however, relativised the latter by requiring 'the obligation of transparency to be complied with by the concession-granting authority benefits any potential tenderer [. . .], *even where it is established in the same Member State as those authorities*'.[46] It, nonetheless, remains open to debate whether, and if so to what extent, this – potentially far-reaching – interpretation will gain ground.[47]

A final word: Many cases deriving procedural and substantive allocation standards from the market freedoms focus on procurement and concessions beyond the scope of application of the EU procurement directives; the rules and principles derived from the market freedoms are, however, of broader relevance, in particular for licensing, as illustrated by cases (not only) on gambling.[48]

EU Fundamental Rights The award of limited licences is also governed by EU fundamental rights. In contrast with national fundamental rights, they do not (yet) play a comparable role.[49] This may be explained to a certain extent by their limited personal scope of application. While EU institutions, bodies, offices and agencies are always bound by EU fundamental rights, this only applies to Member States – in whose competence the allocation of nearly all limited licences falls – 'when they are implementing Union law' (Article 51(1) CFR). Even if the precise scope of this

[44] On the scope of the derogation, ECJ, Case 149/79, *Commission* v. *Belgium I* [1980] ECR 3881; Case 149/79, *Commission* v. *Belgium II* [1982] ECR 1845; Case C-342/15, *Piringer* ECLI:EU:C:2017:196, para. 54 f.; F. Wollenschläger, 'Unionsrechtliche Grundlagen des Öffentlichen Wirtschaftsrechts', in R. Schmidt and F. Wollenschläger (eds.), *Kompendium Öffentliches Wirtschaftsrecht*, 6th ed. (Heidelberg: Springer, 2024), § 1, para. 59 f.

[45] See, for more details, Wollenschläger, 'EU Law Principles', 211 ff.

[46] ECJ, Case C-221/12, *Belgacom* ECLI:EU:C:2013:736, para. 32 (emphasis added).

[47] For more details and a critical view, see F. Wollenschläger, 'Binnenmarktrelevanz statt grenzüberschreitender Aktivität – eine Neujustierung in der Dogmatik der Grundfreiheiten?', in C. Baldus, F. Kainer and C. Stumpf (eds.), *Privatrecht, Wirtschaftsrecht, Verfassungsrecht: Privatinitiative und Gemeinwohlhorizonte in der europäischen Integration, Festschrift für Peter-Christian Müller-Graff* (Baden-Baden: Nomos, 2015), pp. 443–450; further Wollenschläger, 'EU Law Principles', 212 ff.

[48] See, e.g., ECJ, Case C-64/08, *Engelmann* [2010] ECR I-8219, para. 52 f.

[49] See in detail Wollenschläger, 'EU Law Principles', 232 ff.

condition still remains controversial,[50] there would be substantial scope for application in view of the aforementioned Europeanisation of many allocation procedures. A further and more important reason for the current limited role of EU fundamental rights is the dominance of the EU fundamental freedoms when it comes to setting standards for allocation procedures (next to specific requirements enshrined in EU legislation). Nonetheless, there are also topically relevant requirements under EU fundamental rights that are sure to gain further importance. A confirmation of this is the Court's judgment in the Spika case, handed down on 12 July 2018, where the Court applied EU fundamental rights (Articles 16 and 20 CFR) to scrutinise allocation rules since they limit the possibility of exercising an economic activity and imply differentiated treatment so that they have to be justified.[51]

With regard to specific EU fundamental rights, the right to equality before the law (Article 20 CFR) demands the establishment of proper, equitable allocation criteria, and the allocation procedure to be structured in such a way as to safeguard their implementation in the outcome of the procedure.[52] Moreover, establishing licensing requirements and creating scarcity interfere with the freedom rights applicable to the specific situation. In the case of economic activities such as gambling, these are the freedoms to choose an occupation (Article 15(1) CFR) and to conduct a business (Article 16 CFR), as well as the right to property (Article 17(1) CFR).[53] The restrictions as such (licence requirement and quantitative limitation), as well as the allocation criteria, therefore have to be justified, and they particularly have to be proportionate (Article 52(1) CFR).[54] Furthermore, these freedoms also comprise a procedural dimension (see Sections 3.4.2.2 and 3.4.3.1 for more details), while general rule-of-law requirements of the administrative procedures follow from the right to good administration (Article 41 CFR) – albeit limited to EU

[50] This cannot be discussed in more detail here, see only F. Wollenschläger, 'Grundrechtsschutz und Unionsbürgerschaft', in A. Hatje and P.-C. Müller-Graff (eds.), *Enzyklopädie Europarecht*, 2nd ed. (Baden-Baden: Nomos, 2021), vol. 1, § 13, para. 16 ff.; further Wollenschläger, 'EU Law Principles', 232 ff.

[51] ECJ, Case C-540/16, *Spika et al.* ECLI:EU:C:2018:565, para. 25 ff.

[52] Cf. ECJ, Case C-540/16, *Spika et al.* ECLI:EU:C:2018:565, para. 35.

[53] ECJ, Case C-390/12, *Pfleger et al.* ECLI:EU:C:2014:281, para. 57; Case C-540/16, *Spika et al.* ECLI:EU:C:2018:565, para. 34.

[54] ECJ, Case C-390/12, *Pfleger et al.* ECLI:EU:C:2014:281, para. 58; Case C-540/16, *Spika et al.* ECLI:EU:C:2018:565, para. 36.

institutions.[55] In case of access to public infrastructure, the respective freedom may require equal access – a (positive) dimension that is still underdeveloped at the EU level.[56] Finally, the guarantee of an effective remedy enshrined in Article 47 CFR must be complied with.

3.4.1.3 National Law

Not only are national authorities primarily competent for allocating limited licences, even in Europeanised areas, in view of the predominance of the indirect implementation of EU (administrative) law, but it is also national – and not EU – legislation that constitutes the direct basis on which national authorities allocate limited licences, with the case of allocating slots being a notable exception.[57] National law is therefore of particular relevance: the rules for allocating gambling licences may, for instance, be found in a variety of statutes of the German *Länder*, while the rules for allocating telecommunication licences can be found in the (Federal) Telecommunications Act (*Telekommunikationsgesetz*) or the rules on allocating stand places at markets and fairs in the Federal Trade Code (*Gewerbeordnung*) and in the local government law enacted by the *Länder*. Moreover, national fundamental rights are binding on national authorities and on the legislature when allocating limited licences (including stipulating rules for allocation).

This does not mean that EU law is irrelevant at the national level. First, many allocation procedures transpose EU Directives, such as in case of the allocation of telecommunication licences, so that national law must be in line with the requirements formulated by the EU legislature (and also with EU fundamental rights, the applicability of which is triggered by the implementation of secondary EU law, see Article 51(1) CFR). (Primary and secondary) EU law moreover also formulates standards for allocation beyond cases of transposition of EU law, such as with gambling or stand places at markets and fairs.

[55] Cf. W. Kahl, 'Die Europäisierung des Verwaltungsrechts als Herausforderung an Systembildung und Kodifikationsidee' (2010) supplement 10 *Die Verwaltung* 39–93 at 60 f. with further references. Left open by P. Craig, in S. Peers, T. Hervey, J. Kenner and A. Ward (eds.), *The EU Charter of Fundamental Rights: A Commentary*, 2nd ed. (Oxford: Hart, 2021), Article 41 CFR, para. 41.02 f.

[56] But see at the national (German) level Wollenschläger, *Verteilungsverfahren*, pp. 67 ff.

[57] See, e.g., § 27a(1) of the German Aviation Act (LuftVG): 'Airport coordination shall be effected in accordance with the law of the European Union.'

3.4.1.4 Principle-Based versus Rules-Based Regulation

Reflecting on the legal framework, finally, from the angle of whether a principle-based or rule-based regulation may be observed, and of which approach is preferable, the opposition of a principle- or rule-based regulation in the context of allocating scarce licences has to be questioned first of all. Not only does a comprehensive principle-based regulation exist for all allocation regimes; moreover, a rule-based regulation is a constitutional (and thus principle-based) requirement.

First, EU and national constitutional law formulate substantive and procedural standards for allocating scarce goods which enjoy a comprehensive scope of application and which may be conceived as '*Verteilungsverfassungsrecht*' (allocation constitutional law). All allocation schemes are hence subject to principle-based regulation. It should be noted from a more general perspective that the degree of constitutionalisation of the respective (national) legal order determines the relevance of fundamental rights for allocating limited rights. Fundamental rights play an important role in Germany in view of the high degree of constitutionalisation of administrative law, culminating in an understanding of the latter as 'concretised constitutional law'.[58] Generally speaking, fundamental rights as part of 'administrative constitutional law' fulfil a double function.[59] First, they constitute a yardstick for legislation (mediatising these standards at the application level) against which specific rules have to be tested.[60] Hence, it may be asked whether an auction as an allocation criterion for telecommunication frequencies, limiting licences for taxi operators, or the criteria applied for university admissions, is in line with constitutional standards. Second, fundamental rights may be directly applied if legislation does not provide sufficient allocation criteria or an adequate procedural standard. It is moreover interesting to note that not only (and naturally) in EU primary law, but also in many acts of secondary EU law, only a principle-based approach may be found.[61] Second, a rule-based regulation constitutes a standard required by the constitutional principles applying to allocation schemes

[58] F. Werner, 'Verwaltungsrecht als konkretisiertes Verfassungsrecht' (1959) 74 *DVBl.* 527–533 at 528 f. See on all this and with a nuanced understanding and further references Wollenschläger, 'Constitutionalisation', 7; Wollenschläger, 'Verfassung', 187.

[59] Wollenschläger, 'Constitutionalisation', 22 ff.

[60] See for the primacy of applying EU secondary law ECJ, Joined Cases C-458/14 and C-67/15, *Promoimpresa* ECLI:EU:C:2016:558, para. 58 ff.

[61] See Article 10(1) and (2) and Article 12(1) Directive 2006/123/EC.

since they encompass the duty to develop an allocation concept (see Sections 3.4.2.2 and 3.4.3.1).

True, the duty to develop an allocation concept rules out an allocation without predetermined rules. One, nevertheless, has to bear in mind that rules may be set at different levels. The allocation scheme may be set in (parliamentary) legislation, in executive rules (regulations or guidelines) or individually for and before a specific allocation procedure. The appropriate level of rule-making does not constitute a mere policy choice, but is determined by constitutional law, more specifically the principle of statutory reservation. According to this doctrine, restrictions of a fundamental right and further essential decisions must be based on an Act of Parliament. This does not exclude delegated rule-making, as long as the legislature has taken all the essential decisions.[62] Moreover, it should be emphasised that an allocation scheme may be based on rules set at different levels.

Considering the design of specific allocation schemes, one may observe a more or less tight legislative framework which is to be concretised by the administration. This open legal framework highlights once again the importance of an allocation concept to curtail broad administrative discretion.

That constitutional requirements already demand a rule-based allocation must not be equated with overregulation since the latter does not depend on the existence of the rules, but on their content. Moreover, in view of the foregoing, it should be recalled that rules may be set at different levels so as to allow flexibility. A mere principle-based regulation is problematic in view of legal certainty, the shift of power to the courts applying and concretising allocation principles enshrined in constitutional law, its emergence from a case-by-case regulation (triggered, moreover, by pathological cases) instead of a principled approach and in view of effective enforcement. Express standards undoubtedly result in a higher likelihood of their application and enforcement. The shortcomings of a merely principle-based regulation have become evident in allocation schemes in which the administration acts in the shape of private law. Examples in the context of scarce licences would include the conclusion of lease agreements concerning stands at trade fairs or markets. Public procurement below the EU thresholds and the sale of public goods (real estate and public undertakings in particular) are

62 See for a strict standard BVerfG (Federal Constitutional Court), BVerfGE 147, 253 (309 ff., para. 115 ff.; 321 ff., para. 141 ff.).

further examples over and above this. Often in these cases, despite the conclusion of a private law contract in violation of allocation principles (e.g. without any transparency or by applying illegal allocation criteria), no effective legal protection was offered. This is because the validity of the contract is widely considered not to be affected by disregard for these allocation principles, so that no effective means of primary legal protection are available. Secondary legal protection, that is, damages, does not constitute an adequate remedy since it is hardly possible to prove causation, especially where administrative discretion is exercised.[63]

Gradual improvements may, however, be observed, such as the gradual acknowledgement of allocation standards following from the EU market freedoms, notably in the case of public procurement below the EU thresholds, but also beyond these. Moreover, the applicability of the fundamental right to equality to private law action (procurement) has been acknowledged by the German Constitutional Court, but not until 2006.[64] Finally, in 2016, the same Court advocated the consequence of the nullity of a private law contract in case of violations of fundamental rights and freedoms.[65] Its consequences for multipolar allocation conflicts, however, remain open.[66]

3.4.2 Competitive Tendering, or Not?

Competitive tendering, following the broad definition put forward in the introductory chapter, refers to administrative procedures allocating limited licences and comprising a call for competition. A situation of scarcity must therefore have been created by the State (Section 3.4.2.1). The choice between inviting applications for limited licences, and awarding them, moreover directly sets the course for or against competitive tendering (Section 3.4.2.2).

[63] See on this Wollenschläger, *Verteilungsverfahren*, pp. 658 ff.; Wollenschläger, 'The Allocation of Limited Rights by the Administration: Challenges of Legal Protection', in P. Adriaanse et al. (eds.), *Scarcity and the State* (Cambridge: Cambridge University Press, 2016), p. 93.

[64] See BVerfG, BVerfGE 116, 135.

[65] BVerfG, NVwZ 2016, 1553 – overruling lower instances.

[66] See on this F. Wollenschläger, 'Vertragsnichtigkeit als Fehlerfolge bei grundrechts- und grundfreiheitenwidrigem privatrechtsförmigem Verwaltungshandeln. Ein Paradigmenwechsel für den Unterschwellenvergaberechtsschutz aus Karlsruhe?' (2016) 35 *NVwZ* 1535–1538.

3.4.2.1 Creating Scarcity

Creating (legal) scarcity by restricting the exercise of personal as well as professional freedom and by establishing an allocation regime constitutes a restriction on EU fundamental freedoms and an encroachment on both EU and national fundamental rights in their negative dimension (*Abwehrrecht*).[67] This relates to the requirement of possessing a (scarce) licence to exercise a specific activity, such as to use frequencies as a broadcasting or telecommunication operator,[68] for gambling,[69] or to run a taxi business[70].[71] Such a quantitative restriction needs justification and particularly requires that policy goals be pursued in a proportionate manner. In a market economy, the ECJ has not held the State to be entitled to define a level of supply deemed sufficient; rather, specific reasons of public interest have to be put forward.[72] In that regard, in the case of gambling, the Court has 'recognised that limited authorisation of games on an exclusive basis has the advantage of confining the operation of gambling within controlled channels and of preventing the risk of fraud or crime in the context of such operation'.[73]

In contrast, in the case of limited public demand/supply, such as in the case of allocating stand places at trade fairs or markets, fundamental rights (and freedoms) are affected in their positive dimension, given that participation in public infrastructure is sought; the standard of justification in case of such limitations depends on the specific subject matter, but tends to be lower than in the former case of restricting (negative) freedom, since the State generally enjoys broad discretion with regard to

67 See with further references Wollenschläger, *Verteilungsverfahren*, pp. 54 ff., 107, 124; Wollenschläger, 'EU Law Principles', 217 f.

68 ECJ, Case C-380/05, *Centro Europa 7 Srl* [2008] ECR I-349, para. 95 ff., in particular 100; further, albeit with regard to secondary EU law, ECJ, Case C-560/15, *Europa Way and Persidera* ECLI:EU:C:2017:593, para. 72 ff.

69 See only ECJ, Joined Cases C-338/04, C-359/04 and C-360/04, *Placanica* [2007] ECR I-1891, para. 50 ff.; Case C-203/08, *Sporting Exchange* [2010] ECR I-4695, para. 24; Case C-390/12, *Pfleger et al.* ECLI:EU:C:2014:281, para. 39 ff. (fundamental freedoms) and 57 ff. (fundamental rights); Case C-49/16, *Unibet International* ECLI:EU:C:2017:491, para. 31 ff.

70 See on this and in more detail Wollenschläger, *Verteilungsverfahren*, pp. 380 ff., 385.

71 See further ECJ, Case C-323/03, *Commission* v. *Spain* [2006] ECR I-2151, para. 43 ff.; Case C-169/07, *Hartlauer* [2009] ECR I-1721, para. 33 ff.

72 ECJ, Joined Cases C-338/04, C-359/04 and C-360/04, *Placanica* [2007] ECR I-1891, para. 51; further BVerfG, BVerfGE 11, 168 (188 f.).

73 ECJ, Case C-42/07, *Liga Portuguesa de Futebol Profissional and Bwin International* [2009], ECR I-7633, para. 64.

determining the extent of providing infrastructure (unless a social right exists by way of exception). Finally, putting existent resources to optimum use may be required as a consequence of the State's duty to mitigate scarcity; such a duty has been acknowledged under German constitutional law for allocating places at university.[74]

The need to justify creating scarcity is also addressed in EU legislation. The Services Directive requires a justification for arbitrary State-created scarcity of the possibility of exercising service activities, unlike in the case of shortages resulting from the scarcity of natural resources or technical capacities (cf. Article 11(1)(b); recital 62).[75] The decision on the application of contingents must be based on non-discriminatory considerations that are justified by overriding reasons relating to the public interest and that are proportionate (Article 9(1)).[76] It would not be permissible in accordance with Article 14 No. 5 in this regard to apply contingents to authorisations because of the existence of an only restricted economic need,[77] as has just also been highlighted for EU primary law. This prohibition is, however, placed into perspective to a considerable degree by the fact that the prohibition is not to concern 'planning requirements which do not pursue economic aims but serve overriding reasons relating to the public interest'. Recital 66 cites 'the protection of the urban environment, social policy or public health' as an example of such requirements. This would mean that the number of authorisations to be awarded could not be limited because of a lack of demand, but that this could be done because of a danger to the survival of the (economic)

[74] BVerfG, BVerfGE 33, 303 (331 f.); E 147, 253 (305 ff., para. 103 ff.); Wollenschläger, 'Article 3 GG', para. 180.

[75] This section follows Wollenschläger, 'EU Law Principles', 248 f. Cf. also J. Wolswinkel, 'The Allocation of a Limited Number of Authorisations' (2009) 2 *REALaw* 61–104 at 78 ff.; M. Cornils, in M. Schlachter and C. Ohler (eds.), *Europäische Dienstleistungsrichtlinie Handkommentar* (Baden-Baden: Nomos, 2008), Article 12, pp. 215–223, para. 5, attributes the provision of a limited supply of state services to the first group of cases and therefore to Article 12.

[76] For examples, see recitals 40 and 56.

[77] Article 14 No. 5 prohibits 'the case-by-case application of an economic test making the granting of authorisation subject to proof of the existence of an economic need or market demand, an assessment of the potential or current economic effects of the activity or an assessment of the appropriateness of the activity in relation to the economic planning objectives set by the competent authority; this prohibition shall not concern planning requirements which do not pursue economic aims but serve overriding reasons relating to the public interest'.

sector in question as a result of oversupply.[78] It is, for instance, recognised in healthcare that demand-related access restrictions are permissible in order to ensure that the objectives of 'maintaining a balanced high-quality medical service open to all' or of 'preventing the risk of serious harm to the financial balance of the social security system' are attained. Such planning 'may prove indispensable for filling in possible gaps in access to outpatient care and for avoiding the duplication of structures, so as to ensure medical care which is adapted to the needs of the population, covers the entire territory and takes account of geographically isolated or otherwise disadvantaged regions'.[79] Moreover, to take an example in sector-specific legislation, Article 55(1)(a) of the European Electronic Communications Code obliges the Member States to 'clearly state the reasons for limiting the rights of use, in particular by giving due weight to the need to maximise benefits for users and to facilitate the development of competition, and review, as appropriate, the limitation at regular intervals or at the reasonable request of affected undertakings' (see also Article 46).

Creating (legal) scarcity as a basis for competitive tendering serves inherent needs as well as output-related interests, since the quantitatively unregulated exercise of certain activities is considered detrimental to these goods. To take the example of allocating taxi licences, their limitation is widely considered to be justified in view of the inherent needs to prevent a threat to livelihoods in the local taxi trade being caused by excess capacities, in the interest of maintaining its functionality.[80] Additional policy goals are also put forward: excess capacities may be detrimental in terms of environmental protection, social standards in the taxi trade or quality (value for money). The situation in terms of opening of markets is ambivalent: on the one hand, restricting scope for economic activities restricts market access; on the other hand, limiting access may

[78] See also M. Cornils, in M. Schlachter and C. Ohler (eds.), *Europäische Dienstleistungsrichtlinie. Handkommentar* (Baden-Baden: Nomos, 2008), Article 14, para. 18.

[79] ECJ, Case C-169/07, *Hartlauer* [2009] ECR I-1721, para. 50, 52. Cf. in more detail F. Wollenschläger, 'Patientenmobilität in der Europäischen Union – von der Rechtsprechung des EuGH zur neuen Richtlinie 2011/24/EU über die Ausübung der Patientenrechte in der grenzüberschreitenden Gesundheitsversorgung' (2012) 47 *EuR* 149–183.

[80] See BVerfG, BVerfGE 11, 168 (191); BVerfG, BVerfGE 81, 70 (87 f.); BVerwG (Federal Administrative Court), BVerwGE 79, 208 (210 ff.); Wollenschläger, *Verteilungsverfahren*, pp. 380 ff. with further references. Disagreeing D. Kupfer, *Die Verteilung knapper Ressourcen im Wirtschaftsverwaltungsrecht* (Baden-Baden: Nomos, 2005), pp. 334 ff.

contribute to the functionality of a market. In terms of procedure, removing the solution of allocation conflicts from the societal domain, and subjecting it to an administrative procedure, may contribute to an equal, fair and transparent allocation.

3.4.2.2 Setting the Course for Competitive Tendering: Inviting Applications versus Direct Awards

Competitive tendering, that is, a prior invitation to compete, proves to be the rule stipulated by EU and national law when limited licences are to be allocated by the administration. Exceptions do, however, exist. Opting for competitive tendering reflects specific choices with regard to public interests.

EU Law Sector-specific award regimes often demand an invitation for application, and thus set the course for competitive tendering. The European Electronic Communications Code requires a Member State, if 'limit[ing] the number of rights of use to be granted for radio spectrum', to 'invite applications for rights of use' (Article 55(4)),[81] subject to an exception in cases 'where the granting of individual rights of use for radio spectrum to the providers of radio or television broadcast content services is necessary to achieve a general interest objective as laid down by Member States in accordance with Union law' (Article 48(3)). Similarly, in the case of selecting providers of ground handling services at an airport, Article 11(1)(b) of Directive 96/67/EC formulates a preference for competitive tendering: 'An invitation to tender must be launched and published in the Official Journal of the European Communities, to which any interested supplier of groundhandling services may reply'. An exception to this rule applies in case of in-house-providers.[82] Moreover, authorisations for the prospection, exploration and production of hydrocarbons will, if no exception applies, be 'granted following a procedure in which all interested entities may submit applications' (Article 3 of Directive 94/22/EC). Finally, information on slots to be allocated at coordinated airports has to be made available according to Article 4(7) of Regulation No. 95/93, albeit only 'on request'.

It is not surprising that the cross-sectoral regimes of secondary and primary EU law are more flexible in view of their broader scope of application. The Services Directive contains rules for scarce authorisations

[81] See further Article 7(2) and Article 15 Directive 2002/20/EC.
[82] See Article 11(2) Directive 96/67/EC.

in its chapter (iii) on the freedom of establishment, while specific rules for service providers are not contained in the respective chapter (iv) on the free movement of services. Competitive tendering is the rule when contingents are permissible (see Section 3.4.2.1). This is because, if 'the number of authorisations available for a given activity is limited because of the scarcity of available natural resources or technical capacity, Member States shall', according to Article 12(1) of the Services Directive, 'apply a selection procedure to potential candidates which provides full guarantees of impartiality and transparency, including, in particular, adequate publicity about the launch, conduct and completion of the procedure'.[83] As recital 62 stresses, this pursues 'the aim of developing through open competition the quality and conditions for supply of services available to users'. Article 12(3) of the Services Directive, however, permits the Member States '[s]ubject to paragraph 1 and to Articles 9 and 10' to 'take into account, in establishing the rules for the selection procedure, considerations of public health, social policy objectives, the health and safety of employees or self-employed persons, the protection of the environment, the preservation of cultural heritage and other overriding reasons relating to the public interest, in conformity with Community law'.

A preference for competitive tendering in the sense that it is the rule, and that deviations constitute the exception, may also be derived from primary EU law. Such a transparency requirement may be based on the procedural dimension of the market freedoms and fundamental rights at stake in the respective allocation procedure.[84] An adequate selection in line with the substantive standards following from these guarantees implies that potential applicants are to be informed about the award. Transparency has an instrumental function in such cases since it aims to guarantee an adequate selection (adequate basis for selection and chances of potential participants). Transparency, however, also constitutes a value in its own right in administrative proceedings and is thus a standard in its own right. In this regard, the principle of transparency may be rooted in the right to good administration (Article 41 CFR).

Focusing on the market freedoms which play a dominant role in that regard, a major aspect of their procedural protection is constituted by the 'obligation of transparency', which 'consists in ensuring, for the benefit of

[83] See also Article 10(2)(f) and Article 13 Directive 2006/123/EC.

[84] See in more detail and with further references Wollenschläger, 'EU Law Principles', 222 ff.

any potential tenderer, a degree of advertising sufficient to enable the services market to be opened up to competition and the impartiality of procurement procedures to be reviewed'.[85] According to this formula, the form and scope of publicity depend on the specific subject matter, whereby a (formal) call for tenders is not mandatory.[86] The lack of any advertisement is in breach of Union law unless it can be exceptionally justified, for instance in cases of particular urgency.[87] That creating scarcity may be justified does not mean that an advertisement is not necessary.[88] In an infringement procedure against the Italian Republic, the Court has not accepted renewing old licences for betting on horse races 'without putting them out to tender [. . .]', given that it was not deemed 'necessary in order to preclude operators in the horse-race betting sector from engaging in criminal or fraudulent activities'.[89] In contrast, the Court has accepted a direct award of licences for internet gambling activities 'if the Member State concerned decides to grant a licence to, or renew the licence of, a public operator whose management is subject to direct State supervision or a private operator whose activities are subject to strict control by the public authorities'.[90] Likewise, it has been held permissible

> that the provision of urgent and emergency ambulance services [is] entrusted on a preferential basis and awarded directly, without any advertising, to the voluntary associations covered by the agreements, in so far as the legal and contractual framework in which the activity of those associations is carried out actually contributes to the social purpose and the pursuit of the objectives of the good of the community and budgetary efficiency on which that legislation is based.[91]

[85] ECJ, Case C-324/98, *Telaustria* [2000] ECR I-10745, para. 62; equally Case C-458/03, *Parking Brixen* [2005] ECR I-8612, para. 49; Case C-49/16, *Unibet International* ECLI:EU:C:2017:491, para. 42; Case C-375/17, *Stanley International Betting and Stanleybet Malta* ECLI:EU:C:2018:1026, para. 56 f.

[86] Cf. only joined Cases C-72/10 and C-77/10, *Costa and Cifone* ECLI:EU:C:2012:80, para. 55.

[87] Cf. only ECJ, Case C-458/03, *Parking Brixen* [2005] ECR I-8612, para. 50; Joined Cases C-458/14 and C-67/15, *Promoimpresa* ECLI:EU:C:2016:558, para. 65; Commission Interpretative Communication of 24 July 2006 on the Community law applicable to contract awards not or not fully subject to the provisions of the Public Procurement Directives, OJ 2006, No. C179, 1 August 2006, sub 2.1.4.

[88] See ECJ, Case C-203/08, *Sporting Exchange* [2010] ECR I-4695, para. 47 ff.

[89] ECJ, Case C-260/04, *Commission* v. *Italy* [2007] ECR I-7083, para. 34.

[90] ECJ, Case C-203/08, *Sporting Exchange* [2010] ECR I-4695, para. 59.

[91] ECJ, Case C-113/13, *Spezzino* ECLI:EU:C:2014:2440, para. 56 ff. (quoted from para. 65).

Finally, the advertisement must provide sufficient information on the subject of the award, as well as on criteria that are material to the allocation and to the procedures (duty to develop an allocation concept).[92]

National Law The situation under national legislation varies. The law requires that the imminent procedure, including rules and criteria, be published for the allocation of telecommunication frequencies.[93] The same applies to casino licences according to the rules of the Hess Casino Act (*Hessisches Spielbankgesetz*),[94] whereas there are no rules in the legislation on the allocation of stands at trade fairs/markets.[95] In the latter case, such obligations may be derived from (primary) EU law (see above), and from national constitutional law.[96]

Balancing Public Interests and Competitive Tendering Opting for competitive tendering by inviting applications for limited licences helps satisfy inherent needs and realise output-related interests. It generates a broad basis for selection and thus enhances the chances of finding the best offer according to the predefined allocation criteria, which themselves reflect the aforementioned inherent needs and additional goals. Process- and output-related interests/inherent needs may thus be interdependent. In this sense, recital 62 of the Services Directive, for instance, stresses 'the aim of developing through open competition the quality and conditions for supply of services available to users'. Moreover, competitive tendering opens up markets. Enabling all operators interested in the licence to participate in the competition furthermore contributes to their equal and fair treatment and to the transparency of the procedure. Nonetheless, inviting applications may conflict with efficiency of the process and thus prove ambivalent; this is mitigated by requiring only an adequate degree of transparency (see in more detail below, Section 3.4.3.1) and by allowing for exceptions, such as in case of urgency (see also Section 3.4.4).

92 Cf. ECJ, Case C-336/14, *Ince* ECLI:EU:C:2016:72, para. 87; Case C-49/16, *Unibet International* ECLI:EU:C:2017:491, para. 46; Case C-375/17, *Stanley International Betting and Stanleybet Malta* ECLI:EU:C:2018:1026, para. 56 ff.

93 § 100(3) of the Telecommunications Act 2021.

94 § 5(1) of the Hess Casino Act.

95 Cf. § 70 of the Trades Code and Article 21 of the Bavarian Municipal Code (BayGO).

96 On a duty to advertise limited licences based on the procedural dimension of the right to equality (Article 3(1) of the Basic Law) and on the specific guarantee applicable to the case, see Wollenschläger, *Verteilungsverfahren*, pp. 39 and 84.

3.4.3 *Balancing Public Interests through Competitive Tendering*

The choices to be made and thus the interests to be balanced in the context of competitive tendering are not limited to whether or not to invite applications, but rather procedure (Section 3.4.3.1) and allocation criteria (Section 3.4.3.2) also prove decisive.

3.4.3.1 Competitive Tendering: The Procedural Dimension

Being invited to submit an application, as required by the principle of and the rules on transparency, constitutes a necessary, but not a sufficient condition for enabling competition for limited licences. In fact, further procedural safeguards are essential, which have been acknowledged in constitutional law as well as in non-constitutional legislation. Competing public interests have to be balanced against this background.

The Legal Framework Realising the market freedoms requires designing the administrative award procedure in such a way that opportunities for market access are effectively guaranteed.[97] The ECJ has consequently emphasised the importance of 'open, transparent and non-discriminatory procedures' for market access in a judgment on the allocation of broadcasting frequencies,[98] just as the Commission understands 'a fair and impartial procedure [as] the necessary corollary of the obligation to ensure transparent advertising'.[99] Moreover, the principle of equal treatment has to be respected, meaning 'that all potential tenderers [should] be afforded equality of opportunity'.[100] These general procedural standards imply, for instance, that the material and procedural criteria advertised at the beginning of the award procedure will be applied,[101] that appropriate periods for application are provided for,[102] or that neutrality vis-à-vis

[97] See in more detail and with further references Wollenschläger, 'EU Law Principles', 224 ff.

[98] ECJ, Case C-380/05, *Centro Europa 7 Srl* [2008] ECR I-349, para. 99 ff., in particular para. 105.

[99] Communication, sub 2.2.1.

[100] ECJ, Joined Cases C-72/10 and C-77/10, *Costa and Cifone* ECLI:EU:C:2012:80, para. 57.

[101] ECJ, Case C-6/05, *Medipac-Kazantzidis* [2007] ECR I-4557, para. 53 f.; Joined Cases C-72/10 and C-77/10, *Costa and Cifone* ECLI:EU:C:2012:80, para. 56 f.; Case C-42/13, *Cartiera dell'Adda* ECLI:EU:C:2014:2345, para. 48; Communication, sub 2.2.1 and 2.2.3.

[102] Communication, sub 2.2.1.

tenderers is maintained, for example with regard to negotiations and to access to information.[103]

In addition to the procedural standards following from the fundamental freedoms, EU and national fundamental rights in their procedural dimension (*Verfahrensdimension*) require the administrative award procedure to be designed in such a way as to secure an adequate selection.[104] In order to satisfy this standard, a sufficiently specific, binding allocation concept has to be developed (awareness of a situation of scarcity, definition of allocation object, criteria and procedure). Furthermore, the award has to be sufficiently advertised, whereby the modalities depend on the specific circumstances (see Section 3.4.2.2), and on a procedural design orientated towards neutrality as well as guaranteeing equal opportunities for all applicants (implying the exclusion of persons who have a conflict of interests, or the prohibition of selective information). Moreover, the allocation decision has to be reasoned.[105]

Finally, as emphasised elsewhere,[106] the guarantee of legal protection – being an aspect of the market freedoms as well as a distinct fundamental rights guarantee (Article 47 CFR) – produces advance effects for the administrative procedure, notably in terms of transparency. Effective legal protection requires the procedure to be sufficiently documented and the allocation decision to be motivated.[107]

The aforementioned requirements also appear in various acts of secondary legislation. According to the Services Directive, the allocation criteria must be 'made public in advance' (Article 10(2) of the Services Directive). In terms of authorisation procedures, Article 13(1) of the Services Directive requires them to 'be clear, made public in advance

[103] Communication, sub 2.2.3. See also ECJ, Case C-324/98, *Telaustria* [2000] ECR I-10745, para. 62.

[104] See in more detail and with further references Wollenschläger, 'EU Law Principles', 236 ff.; Wollenschläger, *Verteilungsverfahren*, pp. 38 ff., 82 ff., 107 ff. From the jurisprudence: CFI, Joined Cases T-191/96 and T-106/97, *CAS Succhi di Frutta* [1999] ECR II-3181, para. 72; ECJ, Case C-496/99, *P CAS Succhi di Frutta* [2004] ECR I-3801, para. 108 f.; BVerfG, BVerfGE 116, 135 (153); 116, 1 (16 f.).

[105] CFI, Case T-203/96, *Embassy Limousines* [1998] ECR II-4239, para. 85; CFI, Case T-89/07, *VIP Car Solutions* [2009] ECR II-1403, para. 56 ff., in particular para. 61.

[106] Wollenschläger, 'EU Law Principles', 229–230.

[107] ECJ, Case 222/86, *Heylens* [1987] ECR 4097, para. 15; Case C-340/89, *Vlassopoulou* [1991] ECR I-2357, para. 22; Case C-75/08, *Mellor* [2009] ECR I-3799, para. 59; EGC, Case T-461/08, *Evropaïki Dynamiki* v. *EIB* [2011] ECR II-6367, para. 118 ff.; Communication, sub 2.3.3.

and be such as to provide the applicants with a guarantee that their application will be dealt with objectively and impartially'.

The European Electronic Communications Code stipulates procedural requirements for allocating limited radio frequencies. First, an allocation concept has to be established (Article 55(2) of the European Electronic Communications Code). In terms of procedure, Article 55(7) of the European Electronic Communications Code requires 'a selection procedure which [is] objective, transparent, non-discriminatory and proportionate'. A specific rule to prevent conflicts of interests is contained in Article 11(1)(c) of Directive 96/67/EC.

Balancing Public Interests and Procedural Design An adequate procedural design is vital for realising public interests pursued with the specific allocation regime. If competition was distorted by an undue proceeding, such as by granting selective information to single applicants or by not ruling out conflicts of interests, awarding the licence to the applicant best fulfilling the predefined allocation criteria would be endangered, and thus the realisation of the inherent needs and additional goals associated with it. Moreover, such procedural safeguards contribute to an equal, fair and transparent procedure. This is also true for the duty to motivate the allocation decision, since it requires the authority to comprehensively reflect on its decision and enables judicial control.[108]

That having been said, procedural safeguards may compete with the interest in an efficient procedure. In this sense, a sound balance has to be struck in order to optimise public interests. This is not, however, precluded by the legal framework. Rather, when determining what is adequate in terms of procedural standards, due account has to be taken of the multipolarity of the allocation situation, which means that the interest of applicants and of the administration in an efficient allocation procedure also has to be considered. Hypertrophic procedural standards will therefore not be advocated.[109] This is also implied in the requirement of a proportionate selection procedure following from primary and secondary EU law.[110] Beyond the aspect of efficiency, Article 12(3) of the Services Directive reflects that further interests are also relevant when

[108] See on the requirement of a motivation Wollenschläger, *Verteilungsverfahren*, pp. 584 f.

[109] Wollenschläger, *Verteilungsverfahren*, p. 40. Cf. also Joined Cases C-147/06 and C-148/06, *SECAP et al.* [2008] ECR I-3565, para. 32.

[110] See, e.g., Article 55(7) European Electronic Communications Code.

designing the procedure: 'Member States may take into account [...] considerations of public health, social policy objectives, the health and safety of employees or self-employed persons, the protection of the environment, the preservation of cultural heritage and other overriding reasons relating to the public interest, in conformity with Community law.'

Certain procedural safeguards prove ambivalent in view of optimising public interests, particularly following a strict line with regard to deviations from predefined criteria or to permitting negotiations. On the one hand, such safeguards reduce the possibility of undue influences on the selection procedure and thus ensure that the licence is awarded to the best applicant in a fair, equal and transparent process. On the other hand, negotiations may optimise the outcome, and deviations may be necessary if new assessments are carried out or if circumstances change. Optimising public interests in that regard therefore requires that a careful balance be struck when designing the specific procedure.

3.4.3.2 Competitive Tendering: The Substantive Dimension

Competitive tendering does not only depend on the procedural choices outlined in the preceding sections, such as for inviting applications. In fact, the determination of allocation criteria proves no less decisive for the competitive character of an allocation procedure. The degree of competition may differ, depending on whether formal allocation criteria are applied, such as allocation by lot or on a pro rata basis, or by applying the first-come-first-served principle, or via material allocation criteria such as in a beauty contest. After outlining general legal requirements for determining allocation criteria, two aspects merit particular attention, namely the issues of formal versus substantive allocation criteria, and of (market) access for newcomers. The issue of balancing competing public interests will be discussed against this background.

Legal Framework for Determining Allocation Criteria EU fundamental freedoms as well as EU and national fundamental rights formulate standards for determining allocation criteria. Only an abstract framework can be drawn up here in view of the multiplicity of the subject matters concerned.[111] It should be noted at the outset that the requirements outlined below refer not only to criteria used for a comparative

[111] See in more detail and with further references Wollenschläger, 'EU Law Principles', 218 ff., on which this section is based.

assessment of the applications (i.e. the allocation criteria *sensu stricto*), but to all criteria that are relevant to the award, including minimum conditions for participation in the procedure, or general requirements that all applicants have to fulfil.[112] With regard to the substantive requirements of the EU market freedoms, allocation criteria must neither openly nor indirectly discriminate against foreign applicants (unless the difference in treatment is justified), or unjustifiably restrict market access. Or, to quote the ECJ's judgment on allocating scarce broadcasting frequencies, the allocation has to be carried out 'on the basis of objective, transparent, non-discriminatory and proportionate criteria'.[113] The principles of objectiveness and non-discrimination prohibit criteria that aim to exclude specific tenderers; the requirement of transparency demands the formulation of clear, meaningful award criteria in order, first, to counter barriers to access for interested parties, second, to rule out latitude in decision-making that would enable the allocating authority to engage in arbitrary treatment, and thirdly to make the award decision verifiable.[114] The criterion of proportionality, finally, requires an appropriate material connection to be made between the asset to be distributed and the criteria that are relevant thereto.[115] To give an example, it has been held to be principally justified in the context of gambling to exclude operators who have been convicted of criminal offences.[116] In contrast, requiring gambling operators to have carried out their activities in the Member State in which the licence is to be granted for ten years in order to qualify as a trustworthy operator has been held to be discriminatory,

[112] Cf. for a distinction between (comparative) allocation and (further) granting criteria J. Wolswinkel, 'An Allocation Perspective to Public Law: Limited Public Rights and Beyond' (2014) 8 *ReM* 2014-05.

[113] ECJ, Case C-380/05, *Centro Europa 7 Srl* [2008] ECR I-349, para. 103 f. On the principle of proportionality also Case C-538/07, *Assitur Srl* [2009] ECR I-4219, para. 24 ff.

[114] See only ECJ, Case C-199/07, *Commission* v. *Greece* [2009] ECR I-10669, para. 35 ff.; Joined Cases C-72/10 and C-77/10, *Costa and Cifone* ECLI:EU:C:2012:80, para. 56, 72 ff.; Case C-49/16, *Unibet International* ECLI:EU:C:2017:491, para. 46. See also Case C-375/17, *Stanley International Betting and Stanleybet Malta* ECLI:EU:C:2018:1026, para. 56 f.

[115] Extensively F. Huerkamp, *Gleichbehandlung und Transparenz als gemeinschaftsrechtliche Prinzipien der staatlichen Auftragsvergabe* (Tübingen: Mohr Siebeck, 2010), pp. 226 ff. Cf. also ECJ, Case C-376/08, *Serrantoni* [2009] ECR I-12169, para. 31 ff.; Joined Cases C-72/10 and C-77/10, *Costa and Cifone* ECLI:EU:C:2012:80, para. 69 ff.; Case C-358/12, *Consorzio Stabile Libor Lavori Pubblici* ECLI:EU:C:2014:2063, para. 28 ff.; Szydło, 'Process', 1429 ff., 1439 ff.

[116] ECJ, Joined Cases C-72/10 and C-77/10, *Costa and Cifone* ECLI:EU:C:2012:80, para. 76 ff.; Case C-463/13, *Stanley International Betting Ltd* ECLI:EU:C:2015:25, para. 45 ff.

given that it places foreign operators at a disadvantage without a justification being discernible.[117]

Similar requirements may also be derived from EU and national fundamental rights (see Section 3.4.1.2). First, the right to equality – either as an aspect of a specific freedom right in its participatory dimension (*derivatives Teilhaberecht*) or as a general right to equality (*allgemeiner Gleichheitssatz*; Article 20 CFR; Article 3(1) of the Basic Law) – demands allocation criteria that are adequate in view of the good to be distributed. Moreover, the freedom rights applicable in the specific allocation procedure such as the freedom to conduct a business (Article 16 CFR; Article 12(1) of the Basic Law) require allocation criteria that are adequate and proportionate in view of the licence to be allocated. Again, details depend on the specific subject matter.[118]

The aforementioned requirements also appear in various acts of secondary legislation. With regard to granting limited licences for the use of radio spectrum, Article 55(7) of the European Electronic Communications Code requires 'selection criteria [. . .] which are objective, transparent, non-discriminatory and proportionate'. In case of the provision of ground handling services at an airport, '[t]he selection criteria laid down in the standard conditions or technical specifications must be relevant, objective, transparent and non-discriminatory' (Article 11(1)(a)(2) of Directive 96/97/EC). The Services Directive too requires allocation criteria that 'preclude the competent authorities from exercising their power of assessment in an arbitrary manner' (Article 10(1) of the Services Directive), and are 'non-discriminatory, justified by an overriding reason relating to the public interest, proportionate to that public interest objective, clear and unambiguous, objective, made public in advance, transparent and accessible' (Article 10(2) of the Services Directive).

[117] ECJ, C-49/16 *Unibet International* ECLI:EU:C:2017:491, para. 44 f.

[118] See in more detail and with further references Wollenschläger, 'EU Law Principles', 236 ff.; Wollenschläger, *Verteilungsverfahren*, pp. 36 ff., 107; Wollenschläger, 'Article 3 GG', para. 305 ff.; further S. Boysen, A.-B. Kaiser and F. Meinel, *Verfassung und Verteilung* (Tübingen: Mohr Siebeck, 2015); Huerkamp, *Gleichbehandlung*, pp. 226 ff.; Kupfer, *Verteilung*; N. Malaviya, *Verteilungsentscheidungen und Verteilungsverfahren* (Tübingen: Mohr Siebeck, 2009); M. Martini, *Der Markt als Instrument hoheitlicher Verteilungslenkung* (Tübingen: Mohr Siebeck, 2008); M. Schmidt-Preuß, *Kollidierende Privatinteressen im Verwaltungsrecht* (Berlin: Duncker & Humblot, 2005); A. Voßkuhle, '"Wer zuerst kommt malt zuerst!" Das Prioritätsprinzip als antiquierter Verwaltungsmodus einer modernen Rechtsordnung' (1999) 32 *Die Verwaltung* 21–41.

Formal versus Substantive Criteria A substantive notion of competitive tendering implies that limited licences be allocated according to the merits of the application and thus on the basis of a comparative evaluation (e.g. the most economically advantageous tender in public procurement, qualification of the licensee, auctions, preference for well-established applicants), and not on the basis of formal criteria such as allocation by lot, on a pro rata or pro capita basis, or in rotation.[119]

As a rule, the obligation to apply adequate and proportionate allocating criteria following from the fundamental rights and fundamental freedoms requires substantive criteria to be applied, based on the merits of the application, despite the discretion involved.[120] It should be noted in this regard that, in its ruling in the Bressol case, applying the general prohibition of non-discrimination based on nationality (Article 18 TFEU), the ECJ not only discussed the possible justification of restricting access by nationals of other EU States to higher medical education as such, but also addressed the appropriateness of the allocation criteria applied to select among foreign students, and questioned distribution by drawing lots since this method

> as such, does not take into account [the students'] knowledge or experience. In those circumstances, it is for the referring court to ascertain whether the selection process for non-resident students is limited to the drawing of lots and, if that is the case, whether that means of selection based not on the aptitude of the candidates concerned but on chance is necessary to attain the objectives pursued.[121]

Moreover, according to Article 55(2) of the European Electronic Communications Code, limited licences for using radio spectrum are to be awarded 'by means of a competitive or comparative selection procedure'.

Formal criteria, such as first-come-first-served, seniority, and distribution per capita, pro rata, by lot or in rotation, are easy to administer and guarantee legal certainty and non-discriminatory allocation. They do not, however, account for substantive merits and differences between the

[119] These reflections are based on Wollenschläger, 'Article 3 GG', para. 307 f., and, in more detail, Wollenschläger, *Verteilungsverfahren*, pp. 554 ff., where more references may be found.

[120] Wollenschläger, *Verteilungsverfahren*, pp. 555 f. with further references; further for a priority of criteria based on the merits of the application, Kupfer, *Verteilung*, pp. 355 ff.

[121] ECJ, Case C-73/08, *Bressol et al.* [2010] ECR I-2735, para. 80 f. See already Wollenschläger, 'EU Law Principles', 231.

applications and applicants, which may conflict with the need to select the best offer. Moreover, they may result in too low thresholds for awarding the good, which in turn may lead to misguided incentives (hoarding licences with no intention of using them adequately, or merely for the purpose of excluding third parties; acquisition for resale with windfall profits; no incentive to engage in innovative and competitive behaviour).[122] Such criteria may hence only be applied as subsidiary criteria where there are equally qualified applicants;[123] they may only be applied as the sole criteria if an award based on the substantive merits of the applications is either impossible (absence of rational criteria),[124] not permissible (obligation to maintain neutrality vis-à-vis applicants such as in cases of the use of city halls by political parties or mutually exclusive demonstrations),[125] disproportionate (notably in view of necessary efforts, such as large number of applicants, need for excessive investigations or urgency through no fault of one's own)[126] or unnecessary (sufficient chances of selection for all; short allocation period; availability of alternatives).[127] Specifically with regard to award on a 'first-come-first-served' basis, it may be applied in cases where there are no allocation conflicts, where a fast allocation is needed (e.g. to secure adequate capacity utilisation), or to identify chances.[128] Even allocation by lot may be applied as a last resort, for instance if two bids are ranked equally.[129]

[122] Wollenschläger, *Verteilungsverfahren*, pp. 558 f. with further references; further Martini, *Markt*, pp. 95 ff.

[123] Wollenschläger, *Verteilungsverfahren*, p. 559 with further references; further BVerwG, BVerwGE 45, 331 (340); NVwZ-RR 2006, 786 (786) – at least in that case; BayVGH (Higher Administrative Court of Bavaria), NJW 1984, 680 (682); Kupfer, *Verteilung*, p. 423; Malaviya, *Verteilungsentscheidungen*, p. 137; Martini, *Markt*, pp. 108 f.; Voßkuhle, 'Prioritätsprinzip', 21, 37 f. Less strict OVG Lüneburg (Higher Administrative Court of Lower Saxony), NVwZ 1983, 49 (50); NVwZ-RR 2006, 177 (178 f.).

[124] Wollenschläger, *Verteilungsverfahren*, p. 559 with further references; further Martini, *Markt*, p. 109.

[125] Wollenschläger, *Verteilungsverfahren*, p. 559 with further references; further Martini, *Markt*, pp. 109 f.; Schmidt-Preuß, *Privatinteressen*, p. 422.

[126] Wollenschläger, *Verteilungsverfahren*, p. 559 with further references; further Martini, *Markt*, p. 110; Schmidt-Preuß, *Privatinteressen*, pp. 409, 420 f. Strict Voßkuhle, 'Prioritätsprinzip', 21, 38.

[127] See with further references Wollenschläger, *Verteilungsverfahren*, p. 559.

[128] See for more details and with further references Wollenschläger, *Verteilungsverfahren*, pp. 560 f.

[129] O. Depenheuer, 'Zufall als Rechtsprinzip? – Der Losentscheid im Rechtsstaat' (1993) 48 *JZ*, 171–180, at 177; H. D. Jarass, 'Losverfahren und Grundrechte. Am Beispiel der Spielhallenerlaubnis' (2017) 36 *NVwZ*, 273–280 at 279 f.; Wollenschläger,

Finally, it should be noted that determining a specific substantive allocation criterion also needs justification. The choice between an auction and a selection based on a comparative evaluation of the applications may serve as an example. Auctions may take place if the economic efficiency of using the scarce good (as demonstrated by willingness to pay for the object in question) proves to be an adequate criterion, such as in the case of allocating telecommunication frequencies, but other than in the case of allocating places at universities or posts in the public service;[130] the same applies if auctions are used to determine the market price of a good, and it is primarily financial interests that are at stake, such as in the case of selling real estate.[131] In this regard, Article 55(2) of the European Electronic Communications Code juxtaposes competitive and comparative selection procedures.[132] Moreover, the issue arises of whether pursuing secondary aspects such as environmental considerations is also allowed; this is permissible in principle, but requires a sufficient justification.[133]

In case of gambling, a 'certain number of overriding reasons in the public interest have been recognised by the case-law, such as the objectives of consumer protection and the prevention of both fraud and incitement to squander money on gaming, as well as the general need to preserve public order', provided that they are pursued in a proportionate, consistent and systematic manner.[134] This notwithstanding, Member States enjoy a certain discretion in determining their policy vis-à-vis gambling in view of the diverging approaches in this matter.[135] A set of public interests are set out by Article 17 of Regulation 1380/2013 which are to be considered by the Member States when determining allocation criteria for fishing rights: 'Member States shall use transparent and

Verteilungsverfahren, p. 563 with further references. Cf. for a critical view G. Dürig, in T. Maunz and G. Dürig (eds.), *Grundgesetz*, 1st ed. (Munich: C. H. Beck, 1958), Article 3 GG, para. 231; J. Englisch, in K. Stern and F. Becker (eds.), *Grundgesetz-Kommentar*, 3rd ed. (Köln: Carl Heymanns Verlag, 2019), Article 3 GG, para. 111.

130 Cf. for a comprehensive view Martini, *Markt*, pp. 283 ff. With regard to licences to exercise an occupation, Kupfer, *Verteilung*, pp. 417 ff.; Martini, *Markt*, pp. 675 ff.

131 K. Kruhl, *Die Versteigerung knapper Frequenzen* (Baden-Baden: Nomos, 2003), p. 311; Wollenschläger, *Verteilungsverfahren*, p. 558.

132 See also ECJ, Case C-560/15, *Europa Way and Persidera* ECLI:EU:C:2017:593, para. 65.

133 Cf. only ECJ, Case C-549/13, *Bundesdruckerei* ECLI:EU:C:2014:2235, para. 30 ff.; BVerwG, BVerfGE 116, 202, 227; further Wollenschläger, *Verteilungsverfahren*, p. 203.

134 See only ECJ, Case C-49/16, *Unibet International* ECLI:EU:C:2017:491, para. 36 ff.

135 ECJ, Case C-225/15, *Politanò* ECLI:EU:C:2016:645, para. 39 f. See further Case C-3/17, *Sporting Odds* [2018] EU:C:2018:130, para. 20 ff.

objective criteria including those of an environmental, social and economic nature. The criteria to be used may include, inter alia, the impact of fishing on the environment, the history of compliance, the contribution to the local economy and historic catch levels. Within the fishing opportunities allocated to them, Member States shall endeavour to provide incentives to fishing vessels deploying selective fishing gear or using fishing techniques with reduced environmental impact, such as reduced energy consumption or habitat damage.'

Likewise, a wide range of public interests have to be considered when allocating limited rights for the use of radio spectrum (see Article 55(2) of the European Electronic Communications Code).

To secure effective use of limited resources, some allocation regimes stipulate an obligation, or even a duty, to use the limited right and thus affect the execution stage (see Article 47 of the European Electronic Communications Code, including recitals 122 and 133).

The Issue of (Market) Access for Newcomers The degree of competition when allocating limited licences also depends on the chances of newcomers to gain (market) access. Competing public and private interests, such as in the continuity of a well-established service versus the amortisation of investments, may, however, call for restrictions to be placed on (market) access for newcomers. Two situations merit attention: the issue of determining the duration of a licence, and privileges for established operators. In that regard, fundamental rights and market freedoms prohibit an undue restriction of the chances of newcomers to gain market access, a requirement that does, however, leave room for balancing the aforementioned competing interests.[136]

Concretised for the first situation of determining the duration of the licence, the award may prove disproportionate if its term exceeds the time needed to amortise the investment since the aspect of a fair allocation over time is not taken into account. An excessive duration of the licence would restrict the chances of new applicants to gain access to the market.[137] Such a limitation on determining the duration of a licence may also be found in

[136] Cf. Joined Cases C-660/11 and C-8/12, *Biasci et al.* ECLI:EU:C:2013:550, para. 21 ff.; Case C-156/13, *Digibet Ltd* ECLI:EU:C:2014:1756, para. 32; Case C-540/16, *Spika et al.* ECLI:EU:C:2018:565, para. 32 ff.

[137] ECJ, Case C-323/03, *Commission* v. *Spain* [2006] ECR I-2161, para. 47 f.; further Case C-64/08, *Engelmann* [2010] ECR I-8219, para. 46 ff.; Case C-451/08, *Helmut Müller GmbH* [2010] ECR I-2673, para. 79; Wolswinkel, 'Allocation of a Limited Number', 98 ff.

secondary EU law. According to Article 12(2) of the Services Directive, authorisations 'limited because of the scarcity of available natural resources or technical capacity' are not to place newcomers at an undue disadvantage, that is, they should 'be granted for an appropriate limited period and may not be open to automatic renewal nor confer any other advantage on the provider whose authorisation has just expired or on any person having any particular links with that provider'. The following paragraph, however, allows for an exception if justified by an overriding competing interest such as 'considerations of public health, social policy objectives, the health and safety of employees or self-employed persons, the protection of the environment, the preservation of cultural heritage'. Applying these principles and rules, the Court has rejected an 'automatic extension of existing authorisations of State-owned maritime and lakeside property for tourist and leisure-orientated business activities, without any selection procedure for potential candidates'.[138] Moreover, '[w]here Member States authorise the use of radio spectrum through individual rights of use for a limited period', Article 49(1) of the European Electronic Communications Code requires them to

> ensure that the right of use is granted for a period that is appropriate in light of the objectives pursued in accordance with Article 55(2), taking due account of the need to ensure competition, as well as, in particular, effective and efficient use of radio spectrum, and to promote innovation and efficient investments, including by allowing for an appropriate period for investment amortisation.

Apart from the issue of determining the duration of a licence, allocation systems may also privilege established operators. For instance, slots at coordinated airports are allocated with a preference for air carriers having previously used a specific slot ('grandfathering'),[139] while the remaining slots are distributed to all applicants from the slot pool.[140] A similar preference for established operators may be applied with regard to the allocation of fishing rights.[141] When allocating stands at fairs and markets, national authorities may give preference to applicants who are well known, tried and tested (*bekannt und bewährt*). Privileging former recipients serves an interest in continuity on the part of those recipients,

[138] ECJ, Joined Cases C-458/14 and C-67/15, *Promoimpresa* ECLI:EU:C:2016:558, para. 49 ff. (quotation in para. 57).

[139] See Article 8(2) Regulation No. 95/93.

[140] See Article 10 Regulation No. 95/93.

[141] See Article 17 Regulation No. 1380/2013.

and the interest of the administration and third parties in choosing a tried-and-tested offer. Market access by newcomers is, however, restricted, also to the detriment of innovation. The constitutionality of such criteria hence depends on balancing the aforementioned aspects in the individual case.[142] On this basis, preferring established applicants when allocating stands at fairs and markets is permissible if sufficient chances for newcomers are left.[143] In the Spika case, the Court had to assess the legality of allocating fishing rights according to 'catch levels' in previous years, thus favouring 'historical' operators over new ones.[144] The Court has confirmed, first, that the allocation rules meet an objective of general interest recognised by the Union, namely 'the objective of the common fisheries policy [. . .] to ensure that fishing and aquaculture activities are environmentally sustainable in the long term'. Moreover, an allocation 'based principally on historical share, seeks to ensure that operators who have a fleet of vessels whose fishing capacity is in principle capable of handling the volume of catches corresponding to those opportunities are given priority. That being so, that method is justified by the objective of the common fisheries policy set out in Article 2(5)(d) of Regulation No. 1380/2013 and also makes it possible to maintain economically viable fleets, as referred to in that provision. Furthermore, the adoption of such a method of allocation is also justified by the socio-economic objective set out in Article 2(5)(f) of Regulation No. 1380/2013, in that the preservation of the economic viability of the fleets allows historical operators to continue to operate on the market in question and thus to ensure that a fair standard of living for those who depend on fishing activities is maintained'. Finally, the Court also confirmed the proportionality of the allocation rule, notably in view of the remaining chances for newcomers. Furthermore, Article 3(4) of Directive 94/22/EC allows for privileging holders of a licence for a contiguous area when allocating a licence to prospect or explore for, or to produce,

[142] Wollenschläger, *Verteilungsverfahren*, pp. 556 f. with further references; further Martini, *Markt*, pp. 123 ff.

[143] BVerwG, NVwZ 1984, 585, 585 – more generous GewArch 1965, 30, 31; GewArch 1976, 379, 381; VGH Mannheim (Higher Administrative Court of Baden-Württemberg), NVwZ-RR 2001, 159, 160 f.; BayVGH (Higher Administrative Court of Bavaria), NVwZ 1982, 120, 121 f.; Kupfer, *Verteilung*, pp. 229, 421 f.; Schmidt-Preuß, *Privatinteressen*, pp. 408 f., 777 f.; Wollenschläger, *Verteilungsverfahren*, pp. 332 f. with further references.

[144] See ECJ, Case C-540/16, *Spika et al.* [2018] ECLI:EU:C:2018:565, particularly para. 29, 32, 41 ff., 45 ff.

hydrocarbons in a specific geographical area if justified by geological or production considerations.

In contrast, the ECJ held

> a Member State which, in breach of EU law, has excluded a category of operators from the award of licences to engage in a particular economic activity and which seeks to remedy that breach by putting out to tender a significant number of new licences, [precluded] from protecting the market positions acquired by the existing operators, by providing inter alia that a minimum distance must be observed between the establishments of new licence holders and those of existing operators.[145]

Balancing Public Interests and Substantive Criteria Competing interests have to be balanced when it comes to determining the allocation criteria. In this regard, the inherent needs as well as the further policy goals and interests considered decisive by the State for awarding the licence have to be translated into allocation criteria. The concretisation depends on the specific licence and reflects the respective preferences of the legislature and/or the administration (which have to respect the legal framework outlined above). No generalisation is possible in view of the diverse nature of the subject matter. To dwell on the example of stand places at markets: if they are allocated according to the substantive criterion of their 'attractiveness', inherent needs are served; if extra points are awarded for the particular environmental friendliness of the stand and its services, additional policy goals are considered. (Consumer) Value for money plays a role if this aspect is relevant to the allocation decision. If stand places are allocated by lot, the procedure may be more transparent and efficient than if the decision is taken on the attractiveness of the application. However, disregarding the merits of an application may lead to inherent needs and further policy goals being neglected since the best offer (in substantive terms, i.e. the most attractive or environmentally friendly stand) does not (necessarily) win the competition. The assessment is of course different if all applications in the lottery are equally qualified in substantive terms. This is also decisive for the question of whether equality and fundamental rights are respected. Moreover, if established operators are privileged, the procedure may be more efficient, and also merit-based aspects are considered, if this is

[145] ECJ, Joined Cases C-72/10 and C-77/10, *Costa and Cifone* ECLI:EU:C:2012:80, para. 66. Cf. further Case C-463/13, *Stanley International Betting Ltd* ECLI:EU:C:2015:25, para. 36 ff.

reflected in the fact of being well established. Market access for newcomers is, however, restricted, as is the chance to find the best offer in view of inherent needs and additional policy goals such as promoting innovation.

3.4.4 *Balancing Public Interests through Non-competitive Tendering*

Despite the important reasons in favour of competitive tendering, public interests may be served better in some cases if the licence is awarded directly. First, the interest in an efficient procedure has to be considered since competitive tendering implies a greater administrative effort than does a direct award. Thus, if only one operator is qualified, provided that this can be established without an open procedure, a direct award is permissible. Moreover, procedural efficiency may favour a direct award, as stipulated by Article 3(3)(b) of Directive 94/22/EC, if the licence 'has been the subject of a previous [open] procedure [. . .] which has not resulted in the grant of an authorization'. The interest in procedural efficiency may, however, also be served within a competitive procedure (and thus does not necessarily speak in favour of a direct award) by, for instance, requiring only an adequate degree of transparency in terms of the scope of publicity. Also in case of urgency, a direct award is likely to serve the public interest better than awarding the licence in an inevitably time-consuming open procedure. More generally, it is acknowledged in primary and secondary EU law, as well as in national constitutional law, that overriding reasons related to the public interest may justify a direct award (see Article 12(3) of the Services Directive or Article 48(3) of the European Electronic Communications Code). Against this background, in an infringement procedure against the Italian Republic, the Court did not accept renewing old licences for betting on horse races 'without putting them out to tender [. . .]', as it was not deemed 'necessary in order to preclude operators in the horse-race betting sector from engaging in criminal or fraudulent activities'.[146] In contrast, it was held permissible

> that the provision of urgent and emergency ambulance services [are] entrusted on a preferential basis and awarded directly, without any advertising, to the voluntary associations covered by the agreements, in

[146] Case C-260/04, *Commission* v. *Italy* [2007] ECR I-7083, para. 34.

> so far as the legal and contractual framework in which the activity of those associations is carried out actually contributes to the social purpose and the pursuit of the objectives of the good of the community and budgetary efficiency on which that legislation is based.[147]

Even if licences are awarded directly, transparency may be established by an ex post notice and a motivation, albeit to a limited degree only. Moreover, time limits may be introduced in order to reduce negative effects in terms of opening of markets. Both are the case when public service contracts related to transport by rail are awarded directly.[148]

3.5 Concluding Remarks

Despite the variety of sectors and activities in which licencing systems may be found, general insights for allocating limited rights and optimising public interests in this regard may be identified at least at a medium level of abstraction. We have seen that all allocation regimes are subject to comprehensive principle-based regulation since EU and national constitutional law formulate substantive and procedural standards for allocating scarce licences applying either directly in the absence of legislation, or as a yardstick for legislative choices; the practical relevance of this constitutional layer, which may be conceived as '*Verteilungsverfassungsrecht*' (allocation constitutional law), depends on the degree of constitutionalisation of the respective (national) legal order. Standards and concretisations may also be found in legislation at the national and EU levels. The creation of scarcity by the State, which forms the basis for most allocation regimes, already needs justification against this background. Moreover, competitive tendering, that is, a prior invitation for competition, has proven to be the rule, albeit exceptions may apply. It has also become clear that competitive tendering calls for further procedural safeguards and requires that allocation criteria be determined in an appropriate manner. In these regards, conflicting public (and private) interests have to be balanced in order to optimise them. It is not excluded that public interests may be served better in certain cases by awarding the licence directly, something which the aforementioned constitutional standards do not preclude if sufficiently justified.

[147] ECJ, Case C-113/13, *Spezzino* ECLI:EU:C:2014:2440, para. 56 ff. (quote 65).
[148] See Articles 5(6) and 7(3) and (4) Regulation 1370/2007.

4

Subsidising

JACOBINE VAN DEN BRINK

4.1 Introduction

For many decades, public authorities have tried to achieve public goals by subsidising individuals and organisations for all kinds of activities. Not only at the national level, but also at the European Union (EU) level, there are grant schemes for almost any government policy area thinkable, aimed at entrepreneurship, culture, education, social welfare, agriculture and rural development. For many public authorities, subsidising is a necessary and inevitable way to achieve certain policy goals within those policy areas. Public authorities simply do not have enough capacity to achieve these policy goals by themselves. This shows the general interest which is served by allocating financial grants. However, the societal impact of subsidising does not only lie in serving the general interest. The other side of the medal is that the subsidising of policy goals costs a lot of public money, which has to be borne by the taxpayer. For example, in the period 2021–2027, €95.5 billion has been spent on the EU subsidy programme for research and development, 'Horizon 2020', which is just one of the many European subsidy programmes. Therefore, it is important to guarantee that public money is spent in an efficient and lawful manner.

The overarching public interest which is involved in subsidising is twofold: both the achievement of policy goals and spending of public money in an efficient and lawful manner. However, this overarching public interest consists of several sub-interests, for example the interest of providing equal opportunities to potential recipients. In this contribution, the central question that will be answered is how the legal framework which applies to the allocation of financial grants by public authorities balances these several public sub-interests that derive from this overarching public interest. In order to answer this question, this contribution examines both European subsidy law and subsidy law at the Member State level. Since there is little scientific work available on the legal concept of subsidies across Member States, I will resort to Dutch subsidy law, in particular when illustrating domestic approaches to subsidy law.

This chapter has been structured as follows. First, the concept of subsidising by public authorities will be clarified in Section 4.2. In Section 4.3, an overview is given of the several public sub-interests, which can be deduced from the aforementioned two general public interests. Section 4.4 will discuss which choices have been made in the legal framework and how they affect the achievement of public sub-interests, either through competitive tendering or not. Section 4.5 provides concluding remarks.

4.2 The Concept of Subsidising

The concept of a subsidy or a financial grant[1] can be examined from different perspectives. For an economist, a subsidy is primarily a correction to, or distortion of, the price mechanism.[2] With subsidies, the government aims to raise the consumption or production of a good or service deemed beneficial above the market equilibrium level by stimulating demand, supply or both. For a public administration expert, the subsidy is a policy instrument that, because it lacks direct coercion – the carrot, rather than the stick – sometimes works better than regulation. It may be more effective to subsidise the production or purchase of heat pumps than to prohibit the use of central heating boilers. But what is the subsidy from a legal perspective? This can be illustrated by comparing definitions of subsidies in different jurisdictions. At the EU level, for example, a financial grant is defined as 'a financial contribution by way of donation'.[3] This definition is only applicable to financial grants which are allocated by the European Commission or EU agencies. A general definition of a financial grant allocated by the Member States and financed by the Member States or the EU is lacking at the EU level.[4] Definitions of subsidies used in EU Member States do not necessarily coincide with the

[1] In this chapter, the terms grant and financial grant are used as synonyms.

[2] W. den Ouden, M. J. Jacobs and J. E. van den Brink, *Subsidierecht* (Deventer: Wolters Kluwer, 2021), p. 17.

[3] Article 2, under 33, of the Financial Regulation, European Parliament and Council Regulation 2018/1046, OJ 2018, No. L193/1.

[4] There are a lot of European subsidies that are allocated by the Member States, but financed by the European Union. Examples are the European subsidies financed by the European Regional Development and the European Social Fund. These subsidy schemes are implemented in shared management. See Section 4.2.2.

specific EU definition mentioned above. For example, in the Dutch General Administrative Law Act (GALA) a financial grant has been defined as 'the entitlement to financial resources provided by an administrative authority for the purpose of certain activities of the applicant, other than as payment for goods or services supplied to the administrative authority'. Nonetheless, despite the different definitions of subsidies across jurisdictions, it is possible to discern some key elements that are characteristic of financial grants, which will be discussed in this section.

Entitlement to financial resources: First of all, the award of a subsidy, or a financial grant, implies that it involves the transfer of money. The most common form of a financial grant is the financial contribution by way of donation, or the non-repayable grant.[5] However, the concept of subsidy can also have a broader scope. For example, the guarantee and loan provided by the public authorities can also be considered as a subsidy.[6] After all, in case of the guarantee, the public authority provides an economic advantage (without the guarantee, the bank would not have provided the credit or would have provided it at a higher interest rate) in the form of an entitlement on money (denominated in euros). Although loans have to be repaid and the entitlement to public funds is therefore temporary, a loan is almost always granted for the purpose of the recipient's activities and on terms which are more favourable than those which the recipient would be able to obtain on the free market. Hence, a loan confers an economic advantage as well. Finally, a subsidy in kind could be included in the concept of subsidy. Think, for example, of a municipality that makes a municipal sports facility available to sports clubs free of charge.[7]

Granted to encourage activities with the purpose of achieving public policy goals: Secondly, financial grants are allocated with a particular purpose; public authorities are subsidising to encourage activities to achieve particular public policy goals. This is clearly reflected in the aforementioned Dutch subsidy definition. This means that social benefits and income provisions are not financial grants.[8] They are aimed at guaranteeing a

5 Article 2, under 33, Financial Regulation.

6 This is the case in the Netherlands. See Den Ouden et al., *Subsidierecht*, p. 19. At the EU level, loans and guarantees are considered to be financial instruments. See Article 2, under 29, Financial Regulation.

7 At the EU level as well as in the Netherlands, the subsidy in kind is not included in the legal definition of subsidy. See Den Ouden et al., *Subsidierecht*, p. 20.

8 Den Ouden et al., *Subsidierecht*, p. 30.

certain degree of security of livelihood or purchasing power for private individuals and not, like a financial grant, encouraging or directing certain private activities that are deemed desirable. At the EU level, this element is lacking in the general definition of a grant. However, the element can be found in Article 180 of the Financial Regulation, which concerns grants provided under direct management (i.e. by the European Commission). This article states that grants may be awarded in order to finance an action intended to help achieve a Union policy objective of the functioning of a body which has an objective forming part of, and supporting, a Union policy. Therefore, also at the EU level a financial grant has the aim of achieving public policy goals.

No commercial transaction: Thirdly, a clear distinction needs to be drawn between a financial grant and a commercial transaction. In the latter case, a public authority buys goods or services on the market for a market prize. A financial grant is characterised by the fact that in principle the subsidised activities in itself are not enforceable. In other words, if the beneficiary does not perform the activities, the only sanction will be the repayment of the financial grant. In principle, public authorities do not have the power to enforce the performance of the activities and there is no contract for pecuniary interest. The fact that a subsidy is not considered to be a commercial transaction also means that the amount of the financial grant is in principle not sufficient to finance the activities which will be performed by the beneficiary. This third element makes clear that the financial grant has to be distinguished from public procurement.[9] Public procurement involves contracts for pecuniary interest, that is to say, the exchange of legally enforceable performance.[10] Concerning financial grants, it is in principle not possible to enforce the activities which have been subsidised.

Financial grants as limited rights: There is no necessary relationship between subsidising and limited rights, as public authorities in theory have an unlimited amount of money available. In the end, it is always possible to make more public funds available. Indeed, there are grant schemes on the basis of which public authorities are obliged to award a financial grant whenever the beneficiary meets the granting

[9] However, a financial grant could also qualify as a public procurement in case the beneficiary is obliged to perform the subsidised activities on the basis of an enforceable agreement. See Case C-606/17, *IBA Molecular Italy* v. *Azienda* ECLI:EU:C:2018:843.

[10] Article 2, under 49, Regulation 2018/1046.

criteria.[11] However, for most financial grants there is a limited budget available which has been determined in the grant scheme. This means that not every application for a financial grant can be accepted; the available amount should be allocated among the various grant applications. In that case, a financial grant qualifies as a limited right.

Grant award procedure: The (limited) grant as the outcome of the decision-making process should be distinguished from the grant award procedure. This procedure is usually characterised by the fact that two decisions are necessary before the grant becomes definitive. First, a decision is taken to award the grant, possibly followed by a grant agreement setting out arrangements between the authorities and the grant recipient.[12] At the end of the period in which the eligible activities are carried out, the authorities check whether the activities have been carried out and whether the (administrative) obligations have been fulfilled. Only when this is the case will the grant be determined.[13]

4.3 An Overview of Public Interests Concerning (Limited) Financial Grants

Now we turn to the question of what public interests can be pursued in the (process of the) award of financial grants. In the context of financial grants, a public interest is understood as any goal or constraint that a public authority can take into account when awarding (limited) financial grants.[14]

Achieving public policy goals: It follows directly from the definition of a subsidy that it is always granted for the purposes of pursuing certain policy goals. These policy goals form the 'inherent' public interests at stake in the subsidising process. They can take different substance, aimed at entrepreneurship, culture, education, social welfare, agriculture and rural development. The subsidised activities have to contribute to these underlying policy goals. The activities to be subsidised and their underlying policy goals are usually set by representative bodies. This is an immediate consequence from the prevalent approach: both

[11] See Section 4.4.3.2.

[12] See Article 194 and further, Financial Regulation. For EU subsidies, a grant agreement is mandatory. See for the Netherlands Article 4:29 GALA. In the Netherlands, the conclusion of a grant agreement is voluntary (Article 4:36 GALA).

[13] Article 230, Financial Regulation and Article 4:46, GALA.

[14] See chapter of Wolswinkel, Jansen and Van Ommeren, Section 1.3.

in the EU and in domestic jurisdictions (e.g. the Netherlands), that the award of financial grants to particular policy goals should have a legal basis.[15] This means that spending of public money in the form of financial grants has to be democratically legitimised.

Achieving additional public policy goals: In most cases, a subsidy scheme serves one or more public policy goals which are inherent to the financial grant. It is rather evident that financial grants awarded to stimulate low-energy measures in houses aim to reduce energy consumption. However, most subsidy schemes also aim to achieve additional policy goals or, at least, aim not to jeopardise other public policy goals. For example, it is possible to make explicit in subsidy regulation that public authorities shall take into account equality between men and women when setting up grant schemes[16] or that the objective of the subsidy has to be pursued in line with the objective to protect the quality of the environment.[17] These additional policy goals cannot only play a role in the selection procedure but can also result in additional conditions which have to be obeyed by the grant beneficiary.

Sound financial management: Since ultimately the taxpayer has to bear the cost of subsidising certain activities, it is important to guarantee that these subsidies are spent in an efficient way. The concept of sound financial management, the counterpart of value for money in public procurement law, can contribute to achieving efficient spending of public money. This concept, which has been developed at the EU level, means that financial grants should be awarded in conformity with the principles of economy, efficiency and effectiveness.[18] The principle of economy requires that the resources shall be made available in due time, in appropriate quantity and quality, and at the best price.[19] The principle of efficiency concerns the best relationship between the

[15] Article 58, Financial Regulation and Article 4:23 (1), Dutch General Administrative Law Act (GALA).

[16] See Article 7, European Parliament and Council Regulation 1303/2013, OJ 2013, No. L347/320, laying down common provisions on the European Regional Development Fund, the European Social Fund, the Cohesion Fund, the European Agricultural Fund for Rural Development and the European Maritime and Fisheries Fund and laying down general provisions on the European Regional Development Fund, the European Social Fund, the Cohesion Fund and the European Maritime and Fisheries Fund in conjunction with Article 125 (3)(a) of this Regulation.

[17] Article 8, Regulation 1303/2013.

[18] Article 2(59) in conjunction with Article 33, Financial Regulation.

[19] Article 33(1)(a), Financial Regulation.

resources employed, the activities undertaken and the achievement of objectives.[20] The principle of effectiveness concerns the extent to which the objectives pursued are achieved through the activities undertaken.[21]

The concept of sound financial management can be useful in various stages of the subsidy relationship between the public authority and the beneficiary. First of all, the principle can play a role in the setting up of grant schemes, including the allocation procedure. For example, the relevance of the costs of a project as well as the likelihood to achieve the underlying goals with the proposed activities could be made explicit in the award criteria. Another possibility is that a subsidy scheme determines which costs are eligible. Furthermore, a grant scheme could set flat rates concerning particular costs to avoid, for example, exorbitant hourly rates. Second, the obligations that beneficiaries of financial grants have to fulfil could be governed by the principle of sound financial management. For example, it is possible to demand as a public authority a detailed project administration, which proves that the financial grant has been spent by the beneficiary according to the principle of sound financial management. Furthermore, the beneficiary could be obliged to adapt its remuneration in order not to spend public money on the financing of top incomes. Fourth, the principle of sound financial management can also be an important guiding light in controlling the subsidised project and project administration by public authorities. Finally, the principle of sound financial management could be expressed by the fact that subsidy schemes are evaluated, for example by a court of auditors. In that way, it is possible to assess whether a subsidy scheme has contributed to its intended purpose.

Safeguarding fundamental rights: Awarding financial grants by public authorities should be in conformity with fundamental rights such as the right to non-discrimination. Fundamental rights laid down in the Charter of Fundamental Rights of the European Union (hereafter: the Charter) apply to the EU institutions and EU Member States who award EU financial grants.[22] National authorities who award domestic financial grants are bound by national fundamental rights as well as the European Convention for the Protection of Human Rights and

[20] Article 33(1)(b), Financial Regulation.
[21] Article 33(1)(c), Financial Regulation.
[22] Article 51(1) Charter of Fundamental Rights.

Fundamental Freedoms. The application of fundamental rights to national authorities who implement EU grants follows from Article 51(1) of the Charter. The Commission has stressed the applicability of the Charter on the implementation of the European Structural and Investment Funds – an important category of EU subsidies is financed by these funds – in a Commission notice.[23]

The requirement to safeguard fundamental rights when awarding financial grants means that the public authority should take into account fundamental rights in the process of the allocation procedure. The notion that the awarding of financial grants should be in conformity with fundamental rights has also consequences for the legal protection of beneficiaries. For example, Article 47 of the Charter encompasses the right to an effective remedy to everyone whose rights and freedoms guaranteed by the law of the Union are violated.[24] The right to an effective remedy, for example, means that a rejected applicant of a financial grant should have the opportunity to challenge this rejection before a tribunal.[25]

Integrity: For a long time, financial grants have been considered as the pre-eminent instrument for politicians to 'maintain relationships'. The rationale used to be that authorities had great discretion for what and to whom financial grants would be made available. As a consequence, financial grants were granted to beneficiaries and projects which would not have been awarded financial grants in case the award decision had been based on purely rational arguments. Also, in these days awarding financial grants on other than rational grounds has not been banned. Particularly in a competitive tender where limited grants are awarded, favouritism could still survive, especially in case assessment committees that are involved in the assessment of the quality of the grant application.

Equal opportunities, equal treatment of potential beneficiaries and transparency: The concept of equal opportunities for potential tenderers and transparency, which originated in EU public procurement law, has been broadened in the case law of the Court of Justice not only to

[23] Commission Notice. Guidance on ensuring the respect for the Charter of Fundamental Rights of the European Union when implementing the European Structural and Investment Funds ('ESI Funds'), 2016/C 269/01.

[24] This article is in any case applicable to European subsidies granted by the European Commission and national public authorities.

[25] See Case C-562/12, *Liivimaa Lihaveis MTÜ* v. *Eesti-Läti* ECLI:EU:C:2014:2229.

limited licenses,[26] but also to limited subsidies financed by the EU budget.[27] Concerning EU subsidies, the European regulations state explicitly that grants shall be subject to the principles of equal treatment and transparency. This means that creating equal opportunities and transparency for potential beneficiaries of EU grants is of utmost importance. Public authorities who grant EU subsidies are therefore obliged to take the principles of equal treatment and transparency into account. However, the European regulations concerning EU financial grants provided under shared management are not very clear about the precise meaning of these principles.[28] It is likely that national authorities in drawing up and applying selection procedures and criteria should be inspired by the requirements following from the principles of equal treatment and transparency concerning the allocation of European subsidies in direct management and public procurement, including the case law of the Court of Justice in that respect.[29]

At the national level, the need to offer equal opportunities is also recognised. For example, in the Netherlands, the achievement of equal opportunities for those intending to apply for a subsidy was previously not a key objective of domestic subsidy law. Nowhere in Dutch subsidy law has it explicitly been reflected on what the principle of equal treatment means in the context of allocating limited financial grants. On the contrary, the GALA, which contains general rules on subsidy law, provides several opportunities to award grants without an award procedure. In the absence of a specific legal basis for the grant of those financial grants, there is an inherent risk of the principles of equal opportunities and transparency not being taken into account. At the same time, where legislation is pretty silent, case law indicates that the concept of equal opportunities for potential grant applicants and

[26] Case C-203/08, *Betfair*, [2010] ECR I-04695, ECLI:EU:C:2010:307. See about this development J. E. van den Brink, W. den Ouden, S. Prechal, R. J. G. M. Widdershoven and J. H. Jans, 'General Principles of EU Law', in J. H. Jans, S. Prechal and R. J. G. M. Widdershoven (eds.), *Europeanisation of Public Law* (Groningen: Europa Law Publishing, 2015), pp. 135–260, 252 and further.

[27] Case T-297/05, *IPK International* v. *Commission*, [2011] ECR II-01859, ECLI:EU:T:2011:185.

[28] See Section 4.4.2.1.

[29] J. E. van den Brink, 'Requirements under European Law on the Allocation of Scarce European Subsidies', in W. den Ouden, P. C. Adriaanse and F. J. van Ommeren (eds.), *Scarcity and the State I: The Allocation of Limited Rights by the Administration* (Cambridge: Intersentia, 2016), pp. 127–161, 158.

transparency are also applicable to the financial grant allocation procedure when the financial grant qualifies as a limited right.[30]

Accountability: It is very important that citizens and other interested parties are able to check whether the objectives of financial grants are being met. Comparable to public procurement law, the concept of transparency encompasses an accountability aspect: the transparency concept ensures that the rules of the allocation procedure can be monitored and enforced. The principle of sound financial management is also connected to accountability. To assess whether the principle of sound financial management has been met, it is necessary to be able to determine the extent to which the objectives of the particular grant scheme have been achieved. However, apart from transparency and the principle of sound financial management there are a few additional mechanisms aimed at strengthening the accountability in the context of financial grants. First of all, auditors are entitled to both evaluate the objectives of financial grants and whether the public money has been spent regularly. Second, legislation may provide that beneficiaries of grants have to be published in order to enable citizens and other interested parties to know which beneficiaries the public money has been spent on. Third, legislation can oblige public authorities implementing financial grant schemes to evaluate the scheme every five years. This obligation has been incorporated in the law preventing public authorities from maintaining grant schemes which are not effective.[31] However, one must admit that the evaluation of grant schemes in practice appears to be very difficult.[32]

Efficiency of the process: Subsidising can be a costly process, for example when comparing applications. Also, in the allocation procedure concerning financial grants, there is a public interest in ensuring that the process is carried out efficiently. Arrowsmith has elaborated that efficiency has to be understood as 'without unnecessary or disproportionate delay or waste of resources for public authorities or unreasonable costs for – in the context of financial grants – potential

[30] See Council of State, 2 November 2016, ECLI:NL:RVS:2016:2927 on limited licenses. See about this judgment C. J. Wolswinkel, F. J. van Ommeren and W. den Ouden, 'Limited Authorisations between EU and Domestic Law: Comparative Remarks from Dutch Law', *EPL* 25(4) (2019), 559–586. See Council of State, 11 July 2018, ECLI:NL:RVS:2018:2310 on limited subsidies.

[31] Article 4:24 GALA.

[32] See the report of the Dutch Court of Auditors, *Leren van subsidie-evaluaties (Learning of grant evaluations)*, 13 October 2011.

beneficiaries'.[33] Additionally, in the context of the allocation of financial grants it is important that the benefits of a tender procedure – in the sense that the best project is selected to receive a financial grant – outweighs the costs involved in a tender procedure.

4.4 Optimising Public Interests: Legal Choices and Assumptions

4.4.1 Introduction

The legal framework applicable to the granting of subsidies can both promote and impede the attainment of certain public interests This section will discuss which choices have been made in the legal framework and how they affect the attainment of public interests, either through competitive tendering or not. Competitive tendering in this book is understood as an administrative decision-making process where potential candidates are invited to express their interest in obtaining a subsidy.[34] In Section 4.4.2, I will discuss whether or not a competitive tender procedure is prescribed when allocating subsidies and also whether there is a legal preference for a particular procedure. Section 4.4.3.1 examines how the EU and Dutch legal framework facilitates or restrains an allocating authority in realising or balancing public interests in case financial grants are allocated by a beauty contest. Section 4.4.3.2 will discuss whether the balancing of public interests is different in case financial grants are awarded by other competitive procedures: a first come, first served procedure or the drawing of lots. Finally, Section 4.4.4 deals with subsidies which are directly awarded, without any allocation procedure and without any statutory grant regulation. In that case, potential candidates are not invited to express their interest in obtaining a subsidy and there is no competitive tendering procedure.

In this section, no attention will be paid to state aid law. This is caused by the fact that EU subsidies granted by the European Commission are not regarded as state aid. This is different for EU subsidies which are awarded by the national authorities and subsidies which are financed and awarded by national authorities. However, the fact that these subsidies usually qualify as state aid does not affect the competitive tender

[33] See the chapter of Arrowsmith, Section 2.3.

[34] See the chapter of Wolswinkel, Jansen and Van Ommeren, Section 1.3.

procedure chosen. On the contrary, the subsidy is the ultimate form of state aid. The fact that the grant is distributed by means of a competitive procedure does not alter this. Therefore, the fact that a competitive procedure has been used does not alter the conclusion that a subsidy in principle constitutes state aid. There is one example in state aid law where the competitive tendering procedure chosen has an impact on whether the state aid is compatible with the internal market. Under the General Block Exemption Regulation (GBER),[35] for example, it is in the case of state aid for broadband easier to make use of the exemption from the notification requirement if the subsidy is distributed by means of a competitive tender procedure.[36]

4.4.2 Competitive Tendering or Not?

In this section, a distinction will be made between (1) subsidies awarded directly by the European Commission (direct management),[37] (2) subsidies which are financed by EU money but are awarded by national authorities (shared management)[38] and (3) subsidies which are financed and awarded by national authorities. For all three categories, I will discuss whether or not, and if so, which competitive tender procedure is prescribed when allocating subsidies. A competitive tender procedure is a procedure in which potential recipients have to compete in order to obtain a subsidy. There are several allocation procedures which can be applied by the public authority.[39] It can be a competition on speed ('first come, first served'), a competition on quality ('beauty contest'), a competition on the place on the list resulting from the drawing of lots, or a proportional division. For all these procedures, potential candidates are invited to express their interest in obtaining a subsidy.

35 General Block Exemption Regulation, Commission Regulation 651/2014, OJ 2014, No. L187/1.

36 See, for example, Article 52(6), GBER concerning aid for broadband infrastructures.

37 Article 62(1)(a) and (c), Financial Regulation.

38 Article 62(1)(b), Financial Regulation.

39 Compare P. C. Adriaanse, F. J. van Ommeren, W. den Ouden and C. J. Wolswinkel, 'The Allocation of Limited Rights by the Administration: A Quest for a General Legal Theory', in W. den Ouden, P. C. Adriaanse and F. J. van Ommeren, *Scarcity and the State I. The Allocation of Limited Rights by the Administration* (Cambridge: Intersentia, 2016), pp. 3–25, 11.

4.4.2.1 European Subsidies Awarded Directly by the European Commission (Direct Management)

The European legislative instrument for the implementation of the EU budget – the Financial Regulation – explicitly requires that European subsidies provided by the European Commission are in principle awarded by means of a competitive tender procedure in the form of a beauty contest.[40] This means that only the applications that score best after certain award criteria have been compared will receive a subsidy. However, the Financial Regulation makes a few exceptions to this principle. For example, grants may be awarded without a call for proposals for the purposes of humanitarian aid, emergency support operations, civil protection operations or crisis management aid (Article 195, under a), in other exceptional and duly substantiated emergencies (Article 195, under b) or for activities with specific characteristics that require a particular type of body on account of its technical competence, its high degree of specialisation or its administrative powers (Article 195, under f).

4.4.2.2 European Subsidies Awarded by National Authorities (Shared Management)

In EU legislation applicable to European subsidies which are awarded by national authorities (shared management),[41] there is currently no explicit obligation to use a particular competitive tender procedure. Article 125 (1) of Regulation 1303/2013, which is applicable to the European Regional Development Fund (ERDF), the European Social Fund (ESF) (together referred to as the Structural Funds), the Cohesion Fund and the European Maritime and Fisheries Fund (EMFF), only states that the managing authority shall be responsible for managing the operational programme[42] in accordance with the principle of sound financial management. This principle has been laid down in Article 2(59) in conjunction with Article 33 of the Financial Regulation and means that appropriations shall be implemented in accordance with the principles of economy, efficiency and effectiveness. Furthermore, for the European subsidies financed by the aforementioned EU funds, national authorities

[40] Article 194 in conjunction with Articles 199 and 200, Financial Regulation.

[41] This concerns European subsidies granted by national authorities but financed by the European Union.

[42] An operational programme describes the strategy of a Member State concerning the implementation of a specific European fund. See Article 96, Regulation 1303/2013.

are required to draw up appropriate selection procedures and criteria.[43] This implies that there should be a competitive tendering procedure, but there is no reason that this should be a beauty contest in which applicants are compared on the basis of the quality of their application.

Concerning the European Agricultural Fund for Rural Development (EAFRD), Article 49 of Regulation 1305/2013 states that the managing authority of the rural development programme shall define selection criteria for operations as well. In this provision, it has been explicitly added that selection criteria shall aim for better use of financial resources and targeting of measures in accordance with the Union priorities for rural development. In exceptional and duly justified cases where it is not possible to establish selection criteria due to the nature of the type of operations concerned, the managing authority may define another selection method to be described in the rural development programme.[44] The European Commission held in the 'Guidelines on eligibility conditions and selection criteria for the programming period 2014–2020' with regard to the EAFRD the opinion that the principle of sound financial management implies the use of a competitive tender procedure in the form of a beauty contest.[45] To reduce the costs involved in such procedures, there is flexibility in the selection criteria which are used to determine which projects are the best.[46] Indeed, it is allowed to simplify those criteria in relation to grants of small amounts. However, it is a question of whether reference to the principle of sound financial management in soft law is sufficient to create a duty to apply a beauty contest when allocating financial grants.[47] In view of the principles of legality and legal certainty, EU legislation should oblige Member States explicitly to use such a procedure.

However, this view has been jeopardised by the judgment of the General Court of 3 April 2017.[48] This judgment concerned a dispute between the European Commission and Germany about the application

[43] Article 125(3)(a), Regulation 1303/2013.

[44] Article 49(1), second paragraph, Regulation 1305/2013.

[45] See the Guidelines on eligibility conditions and selection criteria for the programming period 2014–2020 concerning EAFRD, p. 10.

[46] See, for example, the Draft guidelines on eligibility conditions and selection criteria for the programming period 2014–2020, version March 2014, pp. 11–12.

[47] The same applies to an informal view of the European Commission. See Van den Brink, 'Requirements under European Law on the Allocation of Scarce European Subsidies', pp. 141–142.

[48] Case T-28/16, *Germany* v. *Commission* ECLI:EU:T:2017:242.

of a flat rate correction of 10 per cent to the expenditure incurred in Bavaria by the German authorities for 2009–2014 under the EAFRD. The Commission's most important criticism was that the projects financed by the EAFRD were not ranked and that their selection was opaque and therefore not transparent. Germany pleaded before the General Court that the Commission had imposed excessive requirements which did not correspond with the law in force and were not included in the applicable European regulations.[49] However, the General Court referred in its judgment to the principle of sound financial management and held that the selection criteria chosen should make it possible to finance, as a matter of priority, the projects which best meet the objectives of rural development as they result from the European regulation.[50] In other words: authorities have to show that they made a qualitative comparison between projects. This means in any case that allocating EU subsidies financed by the EAFRD on the basis of a first come, first served system or a proportional division is not allowed to grant EU subsidies.

Since Regulation 1303/2013 obliges national authorities to draw up appropriate selection criteria as well, it is plausible that the obligation for national authorities to use a beauty contest when allocating financial grants also applies to European subsidies financed by the ERDF, the ESF, the Cohesion Fund and the EMFF. However, it cannot be denied that the wording of Article 125 of Regulation 1303/2013 differs from the wording of Article 49 of Regulation 1305/2013. Unlike Article 49, Article 125 does not stipulate that selection criteria shall aim for better use of financial resources and targeting of measures in accordance with the Union priorities. Furthermore, the aforementioned guidelines are only applicable to the EAFRD. This means that it remains to be seen whether the General Court or the Court of Justice will hold the opinion that the obligation to use a beauty contest when allocating subsidies applies to other European funds as well.

4.4.2.3 Subsidies Awarded by Domestic Authorities

Whether national authorities are required to apply a competitive procedure will depend on the legislation at issue. In Dutch law, for example, the Dutch GALA contains no general obligation to invite potential candidates to express their interest in obtaining a subsidy. The Dutch GALA only

[49] It concerned the previous regulation which was applicable to the EAFRD: Council Regulation 1698/2005, OJ 2005, No. L277/1.

[50] Case T-28/16, *Germany* v. *Commission* ECLI:EU:T:2017:242, para. 64.

states that in case a subsidy ceiling (the maximum amount available during a given period for the provision of subsidies under a given statutory regulation) is used, the allocation of the available money shall be determined by, or pursuant to, a statutory regulation.[51] Furthermore, the subsidy ceiling shall be notified before the start of the period for which it is fixed.[52] However, the Dutch GALA does not prescribe which procedure should be used to allocate the available public money. It is therefore also possible that the given statutory regulation determines which candidates will be awarded the subsidy.[53]

However, a landmark judgment of the Dutch Council of State of 2 November 2016 has made clear that in Dutch law a legal standard applies that authorities should offer in some way (potential) competitors to tender for an available licence.[54] This legal standard is based on the equality principle, which in this context aims to offer equal opportunities. The Council of State has extended this case law into the domain of public funding of education[55] and limited subsidies.[56] First of all, it follows from this case law that limited financial grants in principle cannot be granted permanently. Furthermore, the authorities have to ensure a degree of advertising sufficient with regard to the availability of the subsidy, the allocation procedure, the application period and the applicable selection criteria. If not, this is contrary to the transparency obligation. This means that the concepts of equal opportunities for potential grant applicants and of transparency are applicable to the financial grant allocation procedure when the financial grant qualifies as a limited right. On the basis of this case law, the obligation to invite potential applicants to express their interest therefore applies to limited subsidies as well.

Furthermore, if the public authorities wish to use an allocation procedure, the GALA has no preference as to which allocation procedure should be chosen. The aforementioned case law of the Dutch Council of State on the principle of equal opportunities does not show any

[51] Article 4:26(1) GALA.

[52] Article 4:27(1) GALA.

[53] In the Netherlands, there are subsidy schemes for one recipient. See, for instance, the Decree on subsidies for the foundation for advice on administrative law jurisprudence on the environment and spatial planning.

[54] Council of State, 2 November 2016, ECLI:NL:RVS:2016:2927. See about this judgment Wolswinkel et al., 'Limited Authorisations between EU and Domestic Law', 559–586.

[55] Council of State, 18 January 2017, ECLI:NL:RVS:2017:86 and Council of State, 20 September 2017, ECLI:NL:RVS:2017:2552.

[56] Council of State, 11 July 2018, ECLI:NL:RVS:2018:2310.

preference either. It is sufficient that the chosen allocation procedure is announced in advance. In practice, Dutch authorities use four allocation procedures: a beauty contest, a 'first come, first served' system, a proportional division and a drawing of lots.[57] Which allocation procedure will be used is usually determined in a specific subsidy regulation set up by the subsidising authorities. In the Netherlands, the first come, first served system is considered to be particularly useful if two conditions are met: (i) the activities for which the subsidy is intended are so well defined in the subsidy regulation that the assessment of the applications is relatively simple for the administrative body and (ii) the characteristics of the applicant are not relevant to the public authority.[58] Indeed, this procedure is a very easy and cheap way to allocate grants. Similar to the allocation of EU subsidies, Dutch subsidising authorities tend to use a beauty contest when they hold the view that it is important that only the best projects receive a financial grant.

Direct Award Is it still possible under domestic law to award subsidies directly, without the use of any competitive tender procedure? In the Netherlands, due to the case law of the Dutch Council of State, the conclusion is that in principle this is not possible when it concerns a limited subsidy, that is, when a subsidy ceiling has been set. However, the Dutch GALA does not oblige to set a subsidy ceiling. It is not yet clear to what extent the principle of equal opportunities can also apply to subsidies for which no subsidy ceiling has been set. For the time being, such grants are often awarded without a competitive tender procedure. In many cases, the absence of a subsidy ceiling and the non-use of a competitive tender procedure coincides with the absence of a legal subsidy scheme. However, this is not necessarily the case because it is also possible to draw up a subsidy scheme for a single subsidy recipient which has a *de jure* or *de facto* monopoly to fulfil the desired activities.[59] Most subsidies which have been awarded directly lack a legal basis. The award of subsidies without a legal basis is permitted under the Dutch GALA.[60] These grants are usually awarded without any competitive tender procedure. First of all, a statutory subsidy scheme may be waived

[57] Den Ouden et al., *Subsidierecht*, p. 307.

[58] Den Ouden et al., *Subsidierecht*, p. 312.

[59] See, for instance, the Decree on subsidies for the foundation for advice on administrative law jurisprudence on the environment and spatial planning.

[60] Article 4:23(3) GALA.

in urgent cases.[61] Second, the Dutch GALA provides for the possibility of granting incidental and budget subsidies without any legal basis.[62] An occasional subsidy is a grant with a limited number of recipients for more or less one-off activities. Think, for example, of the celebration of an association's silver jubilee. The reason for this exception from the requirement of a legal basis for subsidising is that the burden involved in preparing a legislative measure may then become disproportionate in relation to the interests served by strictly enforcing the requirement of a legal basis.[63] Occasional subsidies may be granted for a maximum of four years.[64] Occasional subsidies should therefore be of limited significance: both in terms of the number of recipients and the period for which the subsidy is provided, according to the explanatory memorandum.[65]

A budget subsidy is a grant for which both the recipient and the amount of the grant are expressly mentioned in the government's budget. This is particularly the case for grants awarded to one or a few recipients only. Pursuant to Article 4:23 (3)(c) of the GALA, no legal basis is required for granting a budget subsidy. This means that, in most cases, a budget subsidy is not awarded through a competitive tender procedure. According to the legislator, creating a legal basis would be a relatively heavy burden for the competent legislator, whereas the need for this is less evident if the budget mentions the recipient.[66] This means there is a certain transparency before the subsidy will be awarded. However, budget grants to certain organisations are in practice often awarded for years at a time.[67] This amounts to a subsidy for an indefinite period of time, which seems to be in breach of the aforementioned judgment of the Dutch Council of State on the allocation of limited public rights.[68]

Contrary to the intention of the legislator, the provision of budgetary and incidental subsidies no longer constitutes an exceptional situation in

[61] Article 4:23(3)(a) GALA.

[62] Article 4:23(3)(d) GALA.

[63] Parliamentary Papers II 1993/1994, 23700, 3, p. 43.

[64] The explanatory memorandum states that the duration of occasional subsidies 'as a rule' does not exceed four years.

[65] Parliamentary Papers II 1993/94, 23700, 3, p. 43.

[66] Parliamentary Papers II 1993/94, 23700, 3, p. 42.

[67] An example is the budget subsidy for the NL Confidential Foundation. This organisation has been subsidised every year from the Ministry of Justice and Security's budget at least since 2011.

[68] See Section 4.3.

the Netherlands.[69] Technically, both budget and incidental grants are not limited grants, because there is no subsidy ceiling. Theoretically, public authorities indeed have an unlimited amount of money available. However, the political reality is that agreements have been made on the maximum amount of public money that may be spent in a given period. Furthermore, as far as the budget subsidy is concerned, in many cases public authorities are willing to subsidise just one organisation to carry out the desired activities.[70] For that reason, in Section 4.4.4 the question of which public interests will be served by the direct award of subsidies will be answered.

4.4.3 Balancing Public Interests through Competitive Tendering

4.4.3.1 Balancing Public Interests through a Beauty Contest

The previous section has shown that European subsidies which are awarded directly by the European Commission should be awarded by means of a beauty contest. According to the European Commission and the General Court – at least with regard to EAFRD subsidies – a beauty contest should be used when allocating European subsidies in shared management as well.

The achievement of three kinds of public interests comes to the fore when considering the legal framework for allocating limited subsidies: sound financial management, equal treatment, and transparency and integrity.

Sound Financial Management As has been elaborated in Section 4.3, the principle of sound financial management consists of the principles of economy, efficiency and effectiveness. These principles imply that only the projects which best meet the objectives of the subsidy scheme should be subsidised. A beauty contest makes it possible to make a qualitative comparison between projects that wish to qualify for a grant. In that regard, a beauty contest contributes to sound financial management. The European Commission and the General Court presume that when allocating European subsidies in shared management the use of a beauty contest is obliged to respect the principle of sound financial management.[71]

69 See, for example, Court of Auditors The Hague, Fair Sharing, administrative report and facts report, Follow-up investigation into the granting of subsidies by the municipality of *The Hague*, 24 August 2017.

70 Den Ouden et al., *Subsidierecht*, p. 311.

71 See Section 4.3.

Principles of Equal Treatment and Transparency The use of a beauty contest also means that the principles of equal treatment and transparency are applicable when allocating limited subsidies. After all, the General Court and the Dutch Council of State have ruled that these principles are applicable to the allocation of limited (European) subsidies.[72] However, the applicability of the principles of equal treatment and transparency has only been made explicit in the legal framework applicable to the allocation of EU subsidies.[73] The precise meaning of the applicability of the aforementioned principles has been elaborated in Title VIII of the Financial Regulation which is applicable to grants awarded under direct management. The transparency principle requires that grants shall be awarded following a publication of calls for proposals.[74] Article 194 of the Financial Regulation specifies the contents of the call for proposals. A call should, for example, specify the objectives pursued, the eligibility,[75] exclusion, selection[76] and award criteria[77] and the final date for the submission of proposals. Concerning the beauty contest, the award criteria are most relevant. These criteria shall be such as to make it possible to: (a) assess the quality of the proposals submitted in the light of the objectives and priorities set and of the expected results; (b) award grants to the actions or to the work programmes which maximise the overall effectiveness of the Union funding; (c) evaluate the grant application. In other words: the award criteria make it possible to make a comparison between the quality of the proposals.

As has been elaborated in Section 4.3, the European regulations concerning EU financial grants provided under shared management are less clear about the precise meaning of the principles of equal treatment and transparency. Nonetheless, it is likely that national authorities in drawing up and applying selection procedures and criteria will be

[72] Case T-297/05, *IPK International* v. *Commission*, [2011] ECR II-01859, ECLI:EU:T:2011:185, AB 2011/285, with annotation by A. Drahmann, SEW 2012, 49, with annotation by J. C. A. van Dam and J. E. van den Brink and Council of State, 11 July 2018, ECLI:NL:RVS:2018:2310.

[73] For European subsidies allocated in direct management, see Article 188(a) and (b), Article 189, Financial Regulation.

[74] Article 189(1), Financial Regulation.

[75] See Article 197(1), Financial Regulation: the eligibility criteria shall determine the conditions for participating in a call for proposals.

[76] See Article 198(1), Financial Regulation: the selection criteria shall be such as to make it possible to assess the applicant's ability to complete the proposed action or work programme.

[77] See Article 199, Financial Regulation.

inspired by the requirements following from the principles of equal treatment and transparency concerning the allocation of European subsidies in direct management and public procurement, including the case law of the Court of Justice in that respect. However, specific case law of the Court of Justice has not been available yet.

Even when no EU money is involved, the concept of equal opportunities and transparency is applicable to the allocation of limited subsidies, including the beauty contest.[78] Although these subsidies are not governed by EU principles of equal treatment and transparency,[79] the specific rules derived from this concept resemble the meaning and application of the EU principles of equal treatment and transparency. According to the Council of State, subsidising authorities have to ensure a degree of advertising sufficient with regard to the availability of the subsidy, the allocation procedure, the application period and the applicable selection criteria.[80] For subsidies, this information is usually found in the specific subsidy regulations. However, the concept of equal opportunities for potential beneficiaries and transparency has not yet been explicitly codified into Dutch legislation. Nevertheless, some rules in Dutch legislation can be traced back to these principles. For example, Article 4:26(2) of the GALA states that the allocation method of subsidies should be published at the same time as the subsidy ceiling has been published. However, the GALA makes no further demands on the special subsidy scheme in terms of equality and transparency. Consequently, in that regard the unwritten principles of equal treatment and transparency are applicable. The disadvantage of this principle-based regulation is that the Dutch administrative judge is asked to determine case by case which subsidy schemes comply with the aforementioned principles. This does not only take a lot of effort from the Dutch judges, but it also leads to legal uncertainty and lengthy legal procedures. Perhaps it would be efficient to have this clarity before subsidies have been granted; this could avoid a lot of lengthy judicial procedures and relieve the Dutch judges. However, also when specific rules have been laid down in legislation, judges may still conclude that the

[78] Council of State, 11 July 2018, ECLI:NL:RVS:2018:2310.

[79] Subsidies awarded by the Member States are, of course, governed by the EU state aid rules. Furthermore, it has been discussed in the literature that the EU principles of equal treatment and transparency should also be applicable to subsidies that are paid from national funding. See Van den Brink, 'Requirements under European Law on the Allocation of Scarce European Subsidies', p. 155 and further.

[80] See about this judgment Wolswinkel et al., 'Limited Authorisations between EU and Domestic Law', 559–586.

principles of equal treatment and transparency demand more. The legal certainty offered by rules should therefore not be overestimated.

In conclusion: the allocation of EU subsidies by the European Commission in the form of a beauty contest is governed by very detailed rules based on the principles of equal treatment and transparency (rule-based regulation). The allocation of EU subsidies provided by the Member States has to fulfil the principles of equal treatment and transparency (principle-based regulation). However, it has not been clarified yet by the Court of Justice what this means in practice for national authorities granting EU subsidies. Regarding the allocation of national subsidies, the Dutch Council of State has explicitly judged that national authorities should adhere to the principles of equal treatment and transparency. According to the Council of State, this means that subsidising authorities have to ensure a degree of advertising sufficient with regard to the availability of the subsidy, the allocation procedure, the application period and the applicable selection criteria. This transparency concept is evidently not as comprehensive as the transparency principle in public procurement law.

Integrity As has been elaborated in Section 4.3, it is presumed that in case a financial grant is allocated in a beauty contest, favouritism would be banished. This is especially the case if a beauty contest has been used to select the projects to be subsidised. After all, the idea behind a beauty contest is that only the projects of the best quality are awarded. However, a beauty contest in itself does not guarantee that the rules on integrity are obeyed by the assessors of the grant proposals. In particular in cases where assessment committees are involved in the assessment of the quality of the grant proposals, rules on integrity are of the utmost importance. It is crucial that the assessors of the grant proposals are impartial and independent. Concerning EU subsidies granted in direct and shared management, Article 61 of the Financial Regulation is important. This article holds that financial actors, including national authorities at any level, involved in the EU budget implementation under direct, indirect and shared management, shall take appropriate measures to prevent a conflict of interests from arising in the functions under their responsibility and to address which may objectively be perceived as a conflict of interest. According to Article 61(3) of the Financial Regulation, a conflict of interests exists where the impartial and objective exercise of the functions of a financial actor or other person is compromised for reasons involving family, emotional life, political or national affinity, economic interest or any other direct or indirect personal interest. Article 61(2) of the Financial Regulation holds that where there is a risk of a conflict of interests involving a member of staff of a national authority, the person in question shall refer the matter to their hierarchical superior. Where a conflict of interest is found to exist, the appointing authority or the relevant national authority shall ensure that the person in question ceases all activity in the matter.

For EU subsidies granted in direct management, Article 150 of the Financial Regulation contains more specific rules concerning the selection of grant applications. First of all, application documents shall be evaluated by an evaluation committee, which is appointed by the authorising officer responsible. This committee shall be made up of at least three persons. The members of the evaluation committee evaluating grant applications shall represent at least two organisational entities of Union institutions or Union bodies with no hierarchical link between them, at least one of which does not come under the authorising officer responsible. The evaluation committee may be assisted by external experts; external experts may also be members of the evaluation committee itself, where that possibility is provided for in the basic act. According to Article 150(5) of the Financial Regulation, the members of the evaluation committee and the external experts shall comply with Article 61.

For the different categories of EU subsidies granted in direct management, Article 150 of the Financial Regulation has been elaborated in the specific regulations. Regarding, for example, Horizon 2020, the EU framework programme for Research and Innovation, Article 15(7) of Regulation No. 1290/2013 laying down the rules for participation and dissemination in Horizon 2020, holds that the evaluation of the grant proposals shall be carried out by independent experts.[81] Commission Decision C(2017)4750 makes clear that these independent experts may act as a chairperson or member of the European Research Council (ERC)[82] peer review evaluation panels or as individual experts. The integrity of these independent experts is very important. For that reason, the responsible authorising officer will conclude a contract with the selected experts, which includes a code of conduct.[83] This code of conduct holds, for example, that the expert must work independently,

[81] European Parliament and Council Regulation 1290/2013, OJ 2013, No. L347/81.
[82] ERC stands for 'European Research Council'.
[83] Section 3.2, ERC Rules for Submission & Evaluation, Commission Decision C(2017)4750.

in a personal capacity and not on behalf of any organisation. Furthermore, it is stated that the expert must evaluate each proposal in a confidential and fair way in accordance with the applicable rules. The expert may also not be (or become) involved in any of the actions resulting from the proposal(s) that they evaluated (at any stage of the procedure, including for two-stage calls). Section 2 of the code of conduct deals with the impartiality of the experts. In this section, a few situations are mentioned which will automatically be considered as a conflict of interest. In that regard, a difference has been made between proposals the expert is requested to evaluate (situations under a), proposals the expert is requested to evaluate and all proposals competing for the same call (situations under b) and all proposals under the call in question (situations under c). Furthermore, the ERC Rules for Submission & Evaluation describe that any direct or indirect contact about the peer review evaluation of an ERC call between an applicant legal entity or a principal investigator submitting a proposal on behalf of an applicant legal entity, and any independent expert involved in the peer review evaluation under the same call in view of attempting to influence the evaluation process, is strictly forbidden.[84]

From the foregoing, it appears that when it comes to EU subsidies granted in direct management the integrity rules are very detailed. With regard to EU subsidies granted in shared management, such detailed rules are lacking in the specific EU regulations. This means that only the aforementioned very general rule laid down in Article 61 of the Financial Regulation is applicable. As a consequence, the national law of the various Member States becomes relevant. In the Netherlands, for example, there are no specific integrity rules for the allocation of EU grants. However, the GALA contains several rules about the use of bodies that advise authorities when making all kinds of decisions.

From the Dutch case law on allocating grants in a beauty contest, it appears that rejected applicants often claim that the advisory body, or the expert who has assessed the rejected applications, was not independent and impartial.[85] This shows that in case applications are assessed on quality and a comparison is made between the several applications, the compliance with integrity rules is extremely important. However, it has not been proven yet that the use of competitive tender procedures has achieved a more independent and impartial assessment of grant applications.

[84] Section 3.2, ERC Rules for Submission & Evaluation, Commission Decision C(2017)4750.

[85] See, for a recent example, Trade and Industry Appeals Tribunal, 12 March 2019, ECLI: NL:CBB:2019:100.

While the public interests of sound financial management, equal treatment and transparency and integrity are presumed to be achieved by a beauty contest, the use of the beauty contest could affect other relevant public interests, such as the interest of satisfying (additional) policy goals and the efficiency of the process.

Satisfying (Additional) Policy Goals One of the most important public interests that can be perceived in the (process of the) award of financial grants is the achievement of (additional) policy goals. This should be kept in mind when allocating (EU) subsidies in a beauty contest. The use of a beauty contest bears in the first place the risk that the focus of subsidising authorities is shifted from the achievement of (additional) policy goals to equal opportunities for every applicant and a transparent and impartial tender procedure. Furthermore, it is in general not allowed to adjust a project which receives funding on the basis of a beauty contest. The change of such a project would not comply with the principles of equality and transparency. However, in practice the adjustment of projects is in many cases needed, due to changing circumstances. Refusing the adjustment of subsidised projects could in that case jeopardise the aimed (additional) policy goals. For that reason, Dutch subsidy regulations often contain the rule that a project may be changed, but only after informing the subsidising authority.[86] However, such a rule could be at odds with the principles of equality and transparency.[87]

Efficiency of the Process Second, the use of the beauty contest also affects the efficiency of the process. A beauty contest often needs experts who have to assess the quality of the grant applications. This results in a very time-consuming and therefore expensive procedure.

4.4.3.2 Balancing Public Interests through a First Come, First Served Procedure, a Drawing of Lots or a Proportional Division

A First Come, First Served Procedure Allocating subsidies by the first come, first served principle is a very easy and cheap way to allocate grants. The allocation method can be used in case the subsidised activities

[86] See, for example, Article 37 of the Framework Decision on National Economic Affairs grants (Kaderbesluit Nationale EZ-subsidies).

[87] See Section 4 of the case note of E. M. J. Hardy published in *AB* 2020/11, connected to Trade and Industry Appeals Tribunal, 12 March 2019, ECLI:NL:CBB:2019:101 and A. Drahmann, *Transparante en eerlijke verdeling van schaarse besluiten (Transparent and fair distribution of scarce decisions)* (Deventer: Wolters Kluwer, 2015), p. 185 and further.

have been described very clearly and precisely in the particular grant scheme and the public authority has no preference as to which applicant carries out the activities.[88] In that case, such is the idea, the quality of the projects submitted will not vary much. A good example in this regard is a grant scheme subsidising solar panels or house insulation. In that case, it is not problematic that the first come, first served procedure does not guarantee that public money will end up with the best projects. The use of a beauty contest would be too expensive and indeed run up against the principle of sound financial management and the efficiency of the process.

While the use of the first come, first served allocation procedure could indeed serve the principle of sound financial management and the efficiency of the process, it will not harm the other public interests which have been discussed. The principles of equal treatment and transparency are silent about which allocation system should be used.[89] These principles only demand that the rules which arise out of these principles have to be obeyed when implementing the chosen system.[90] Moreover, in case ranking of the submitted applications is transparent and easy to check for applicants, a first come, first served system will not lead to integrity problems. Indeed, the use of a first come, first served system could avoid many complex judicial procedures.

The Drawing of Lots and a Proportional Division Similarly the drawing of lots and a proportional division could serve the principle of sound financial management, although it is not possible to guarantee that the public money goes to the projects of the best quality only. The fact is, however, that it is often very difficult to determine which project is of the best quality. In addition, threshold criteria can be used in these competitive tendering procedures; projects must meet these criteria before they can take part in a lottery or qualify for a proportional part of the total amount of funding available. In this respect, the drawing of lots and a proportional division can usefully complement the competitive tender procedures discussed earlier.

[88] Den Ouden et al., *Subsidierecht*, p. 307.

[89] Van den Brink, 'Requirements under European Law on the Allocation of Scarce European Subsidies', p. 141.

[90] Ibid., p. 141.

4.4.4 Balancing Public Interests: Direct Award

It follows from Section 4.4.2 that it is sometimes possible to award a grant directly without any competitive tender both at the EU and national level. The most important examples at a national level are the budget and occasional subsidies. The direct award of grants may have consequences for the public interests which have been discussed in Section 4.3. For this section, it is assumed that in case subsidies are awarded directly, there is neither an allocation procedure nor a statutory grant regulation under which the subsidies are granted.

First of all, the direct award of grants is suitable for reaching (additional) policy goals. However, in case a statutory grant regulation is lacking as well, public authorities are not obliged to establish the objectives of these subsidies. Consequently, the objectives of these grants are undefined and unclear. This means that it is not a matter of course to evaluate whether the budget subsidies and incidental grants contribute to the intended policy goal.[91] Therefore, it is difficult for citizens and other interested parties to establish whether the objectives of these grants have been met. Furthermore, it should be kept in mind that the lack of a statutory grant regulation has the consequence that it will be impossible to impose improper obligations[92] in order to reach certain additional policy goals. However, it is possible to impose default obligations (Article 4:37 GALA) and target-related obligations (4:38 GALA).

Second, in case financial grants are not allocated by a competitive tender, it is not guaranteed that the subsidy will be awarded to projects with a certain quality, let alone the best quality. After all, there are no eligibility criteria that the grant proposals should have to fulfil. Furthermore, in cases where a statutory regulation and therefore a legal basis are lacking, the risk is that subsidies are directly awarded without considering properly whether the subsidies are really necessary. This is at odds with the principle of sound financial management. However, in this contribution it has been explored that a competitive tender procedure, especially a beauty contest, could be very expensive. In some cases, not using a competitive tender procedure is very appropriate, especially in case it is clear that there will not be another interested party to conduct

[91] For the Dutch situation, it is important to note that only in case a financial grant is based on a statutory regulation, a report shall be published at least once every five years on the effectiveness and the effects of the subsidy in practice.

[92] Article 4:39 GALA demands a legislative basis for such obligations.

the subsidised activities. This is recognised at both the national and EU level.

A third big disadvantage of the direct award of grants is the fact that it is in general not possible to verify whether a subsidy is awarded on the basis of favouritism. Indeed, in most cases no grant scheme exists, so it is not clear on the basis of which criteria the subsidy is awarded. In the Netherlands, only courts of auditors occasionally investigate on which scale subsidies are directly awarded.[93]

Furthermore, the direct award of subsidies is at odds with the principle of equal opportunities. After all, it lacks an appropriate degree of publicity as regards the availability of the subsidy, the allocation procedure, the application period and the criteria to be applied. In addition, the budget subsidy, which is more or less automatically awarded for many consecutive years to the same beneficiaries, is in fact very similar to a grant awarded for an indefinite period of time. This implies that other potential beneficiaries do not have an equal opportunity to receive a grant.

A final disadvantage is that it is not easy to discover which subsidies are awarded directly. Although the reference in the budget allows theoretically public scrutiny of the grant, the budget documents of, for example, Dutch authorities are in practice very complex and therefore not transparent.

In the end, there is only one big advantage to awarding subsidies directly: the provision of these subsidies is easy and efficient. After all, it is not necessary to make a complex comparison between the several applications, nor the time of submission needs to be determined. However, the lack of a competitive tender procedure could have as a consequence that also projects of low or even bad quality are subsidised, especially in cases where it is not clear to which policy goal the directly awarded subsidy contributes. In that case, public money is easily wasted.

The foregoing means that almost every public interest involved in granting subsidies is not served by the direct award of subsidies. Public

[93] For example, in 2017 the court of auditors of The Hague concluded that approximately half of the subsidies are not granted through a subsidy scheme or specific subsidy regulation. For these subsidies, the awarding rules are insufficiently clear and uniform, according to the court of auditors. See court of auditors, The Hague, *Eerlijk delen, bestuurlijk rapport en feiten rapport. Opvolgingsonderzoek naar de verstrekking van subsidies door de gemeente Den Haag (Fair sharing, administrative report and facts report. Follow-up study on the granting of subsidies by the municipality of The Hague)*, 24 August 2017, RIS 297663, p. 21.

authorities granting such subsidies seem to attach disproportionate value to the lenient and sufficient process. The other public interests disappear into the background. This means that the possibility of awarding subsidies directly should be used very cautiously and only when there are very good reasons to do so, for example when there are only a few possible recipients or when it concerns exceptional and duly substantiated emergencies.[94] Furthermore, these subsidies should only be awarded directly under strict conditions which make it at least possible (1) to establish the public policy to which the subsidy contributes and (2) for potential beneficiaries to call into question the grants already awarded. This means that public authorities should at least be transparent about the subsidies they directly provide, for example by publishing a summary of these subsidies each year.

4.5 Concluding Remarks

In this contribution, the question of which public interests are involved in granting subsidies has been answered. It has been explored how these public interests are secured in cases where grants are allocated by competitive tendering, more specifically the beauty contest and the first come, first served system, the drawing of lots and a proportional division. Subsequently, it has been discussed how these public interests are guaranteed in cases where subsidies are awarded directly. It has turned out that the allocation of subsidies by a beauty contest does most justice to all public interests relevant to subsidisation. In some cases, the balancing of public interests could have as a consequence that the use of first come, first served allocation procedures is preferable. Indeed, this procedure is a very easy and cheap way to allocate grants. The first come, first served method is suitable in case the subsidised activities have been described very clearly and precisely in the particular grant scheme and the public authority has no preference as to which applicant carries out the activities. The drawing of lots and a proportional division could serve the principle of sound financial management as well. The negative impact on the overall quality of the subsidised projects can be mitigated by using threshold criteria.

However, public authorities should be very reluctant to award subsidies directly without any allocation procedure, especially in cases where

[94] Article 195(b) and (c), Financial Regulation. Article 4:23(3)(c) GALA.

also a statutory grant regulation is lacking. Subsidies should be awarded only directly when there are very good reasons to do so. This contribution showed that almost every public interest involved in granting subsidies is not served by the direct award of subsidies. For that reason, the possibility of awarding subsidies directly should be used very cautiously and only when there are very good reasons to do so.

5

Government Sales and Privatisations

ROBERTO CARANTA AND BENEDETTA BIANCARDI

5.1 Introduction

5.1.1 Societal Relevance

States, and more generally public administrations and entities in the public sector (all collectively known as the government), routinely sell goods and assets they do not need any more to perform their public law duties. The government manages to raise some money while often freeing office and other spaces. For instance, Arnold Schwarzenegger, faced with a huge deficit when becoming Governor of California, ordered a complete review of the operations of the State government. Among other things, the report found that the State's warehouses were full of excess property, some from agencies closed down years before.[1] Based on the report, Governor Schwarzenegger issued Executive Order S-10-04.[2] Section 4 thereof charged the California Performance Review, the same task force having drafted the report, 'to identify potentially high value urban properties owned by the State of California, which may be underutilised or which may not reflect a highest and best use, and which may warrant realignment or disposal'. Apparently, the push to sell did not meet the expected results.[3]

Government sale has different economic relevance according to the size of the government concerned. The fact that in the United States (US) reference is made to 'government garage (or yard) sales' attests that government sales

The views expressed by the author are personal and do not represent the views or opinions of the Italian National Anticorruption Authority.

[1] An executive summary of the lengthy report can be read at www.ucop.edu/acadinit/mastplan/cpr/Commission_Perspective.pdf.

[2] Executive Department State of California, 'Executive Order S-10-04', 2004, available at www.library.ca.gov/Content/pdf/GovernmentPublications/executive-order-proclamation/2306-2308.pdf.

[3] S. Geissinger and M. Geissinger, 'State Fails to Carry Out Schwarzenegger's Big Land Selloff', 2008, available at www.eastbaytimes.com/2008/04/13/State-fails-to-carry-out-schwarzeneggers-big-land-selloff/.

tend to be normally low-profile economic activities.[4] As far as we were able to ascertain, these kinds of sales have not attracted much economics research and we could not find relevant economic data. This is hardly surprising. Governments are service providers to the society at large and to needy and at times deserving individuals. The bill for those services is normally not paid by the individual beneficiaries of each service, even when individual beneficiaries may be identified, which is not the case with many services, like defence or law and order. The bill is taken on by taxpayers. Inevitably governments' buying activities greatly surpass their sales in both quantity and complexity. What is interesting from this book's perspective is that, at least in the US, government(s) are moving away from the traditional auction system and embracing new technologies. Indeed, online auctions have become a mainstream option for proactively managing surplus.[5] This ranges from dedicated websites such as GSA auctions, where one can find items from aircraft to tractors and everything in between including fire trucks,[6] to the general e-commerce websites such as eBay.[7]

Privatisation schemes involving undertakings instead require complex transactions going beyond the sale of specific assets and including, for instance, some form of restructuring.[8] Sales as part of more or less large privatisation schemes often reach very relevant economic value when taken in isolation. However, they are often part of wider, nationwide, debt restructuring schemes of significant economic importance.

Unlike public procurement,[9] the overall value of which may fluctuate but is still relatively stable, the value of privatisation very much varies in time and space. At the global level, in 2010 governments across the five inhabited continents raised a record of EUR 159.9 billion through privatisation sales of common stock in State-owned enterprises (SOEs) (share issue privatisations (SIPs) accounted for over three-fourths of this total and included history's largest ever stock offering and the largest corporate security offering of any kind, the EUR 52.4 billion Petrobras seasoned equity offering). In that year, the US raised more proceeds

[4] Executive Department State of California, 'Executive Order S-10-04', 2004, available at www.library.ca.gov/Content/pdf/GovernmentPublications/executive-order-proclamation/2306-2308.pdf.

[5] D. C. Wyld, 'Government Garage Sales: Online Auctions as Tools for Asset Management' (IBM Center for the Business of Government, E-Government Series, 2004), p. 14.

[6] https://gsaauctions.gov/gsaauctions/gsaauctions/.

[7] Wyld, 'Government Garage Sales', p. 77 ff.

[8] See generally K. Bacon, *European Union Law of State Aid*, 3rd ed. (Oxford: Oxford University Press, 2017), p. 352 ff.

[9] See Chapter 2, Section 2.1.

through privatisation sales than any other country. The EUR 33.1 billion raised by European Union (EU) governments represented only 20.6 per cent of the worldwide total, far lower than the long-run average EU share of 43.6 per cent.[10]

These data already show how the business of privatisation may vary widely. Following the 2008 financial crisis, the US government moved fast to acquire large companies too big to fail, but was correspondingly fast in selling them as soon as the economic situation improved. Western European governments, by contrast, had acquired failing or fledgling companies over many decades, first after the 1928 global crises, then after World War II and finally after the oil shocks of the 1970s, consolidating control over many companies (SOEs).[11] Margaret Thatcher turned the tide. Indeed, 'privatization was one of the building blocks of the Thatcherite reforms, which shrank the size of the SOE sector in the UK from 10 percent of GDP to virtually nil'.[12]

During the 1990s, Western European countries pushed ahead 'one of the most extensive and ambitious privatisation programs around the world'.[13] The Maastricht Treaty exercised a strong – albeit indirect – pull towards privatisation. Primary EU law leaves the Member States free to decide what they should own or could sell.[14] However, 'The restructuring and privatization of the SOE sector became necessary not only to modernise the economy, but also to meet convergence criteria' set by the Maastricht Treaty and conditioning entry into the Eurozone 'without politically costly tax increases'.[15] For instance, in the early 1990s Italy began a programme to privatise some of the largest public companies in the Eurozone, a programme that continued into the first half of the next

[10] See, also for specific references, http://firstonline.info/news/files/72.pdf, 1; for further data, see also A. Belke et al., 'The Different Extent of Privatization Proceeds in OECD Countries: A Preliminary Explanation Using a Public-Choice Approach', *FinanzArchiv / Public Finance Analysis* 63(2) (2007), 211–243.

[11] B. Bortolotti and V. Milella, 'Privatization in Western Europe: Stylized Facts, Outcomes, and Open Issues', *Nota di Lavoro* 124 (2006), available at https://papers.ssrn.com/sol3/papers.cfm?abstract_id=936911 and at www.econstor.eu/bitstream/10419/74088/1/NDL2006-124.pdf, 8 ff; concerning Italy, see A. Rinald and M. Vasta, 'Financial Elites and the Italian Corporate Network, 1913–2001', in Y. Cassis and G. Telesca (eds.), *Financial Elites in European Banking* (Oxford: Oxford University Press, 2018), p. 102.

[12] Bortolotti and Milella, 'Privatization in Western Europe', 2 ff.

[13] Ibid., 1.

[14] See generally B. Akkermans and E. Ramaekers, 'Article 345 TFEU (ex Article 295 EC), Its Meanings and Interpretations', *European Law Journal* (2010), 292–314.

[15] Bortolotti and Milella, 'Privatization in Western Europe', 10.

decade. About thirty public companies were involved, and a total of around EUR 100 billion was raised overall.[16]

Another big and sudden wave of privatisation involved Eastern European countries after 1989. 'The collapse of the Soviet Union helped legitimate the kinds of neoliberal economic policies that gained credence in the West under the aegis of the Reagan and Thatcher administrations.'[17] Nobel Prize economist Joseph Stiglitz argued that 'One deeper origin of what became known as the "shock therapy" approach to the transition [from planned to market economy] was moral fervour and triumphalism left over from the Cold War.'[18] However, according to critics of the process, the 'market shock' did not play well with those countries.[19] Their same social fabric was deeply shaken in a process that was hasty if not even faulty.[20]

The EU resorted to privatisation again in the aftermath of the 2008 financial crisis. On a number of occasions, the EU Commission and the International Monetary Fund (IMF) demanded privatisations from rescued countries. For instance, in the case of Portugal, the main agreed policy issues included a three-year joint EU/IMF programme based on three pillars: fiscal adjustment including better control over public–private partnerships and SOEs; reforms of the health system and of public administration; and an ambitious privatisation programme. More generally, the Council routinely recommends restructuring, when not outright privatisation, to Member States facing budget troubles.[21]

16 Data from the Ministry of Finance available at www.dt.tesoro.it/en/attivita_istituzionali/privatizzazioni/.

17 D. M. Trubek, 'The "Rule of Law" in Development Assistance', in D. M. Trubek and A. Santos (eds.), *The New Law and Economic Development* (Cambridge: Cambridge University Press, 2006), p. 92 ff.

18 J. E. Stiglitz, 'Whither Reform? Ten Years of the Transition', 2000, available at http://documents.worldbank.org/curated/en/448681468741326292/pdf/multi-page.pdf, 33; the views Stiglitz takes aim at were consolidated by the World Bank in *From Plan to Market. World Development Report* published for the Bank by Oxford University Press 1996, where the approach followed is defended (see spec. 9 ff).

19 See Stiglitz, 'Whither Reform?', 27; see also D. Kennedy, 'Political Choices and Development Common Sense', in D. M. Trubek and A. Santos (eds.), *The New Law and Economic Development*, p. 150 ff; the author also notes that countries like China and Vietnam which did not go through the 'cure' actually did much better (in economic terms).

20 E.g. for a criticism of the dismantling of the social(ist) safety net during privatisation: L. Damsa, 'The Incomprehensible Post-Communist Privatisation', *Global Journal of Comparative Law* 137 (2014), 178 ff.

21 See, referring to the MoU between Portugal and the EC, R. Olivares-Caminal, 'The EU Architecture to Avert a Sovereign Debt Crisis', *OECD Journal: Financial Market Trends* 2011(2) (2012), 190.

Privatisations in this case can be seen as an iteration of the Washington Consensus, the set of free-market economic policies supported by the IMF, the World Bank and the US Treasury after the fall of the Berlin Wall that has since not escaped harsh criticism.[22]

5.1.2 *Academic Relevance*

Compared to procurement and concessions, sales contracts could be taken as children of a lesser god and indeed they generally attract less attention from the law-makers, the case law and, consequently, from academics.

Still, they deserve a closer look. On the one hand, in their simplicity 'routine' sales are the ideal candidate for testing new approaches, including through technological innovation, to manage contracts enhancing the satisfaction of public interest. In the US, government on-site auctions only brought pitiful financial returns in the past. The Department of Defense has historically recovered only a penny or two of the acquisition costs of military surplus through such sales. Auctions on the web are seen as a game changer.[23] Matching websites are taunted as a tool to dispose of surplus government-owned land.[24] Using technology, however, comes with new and complex legal issues.

On the other hand, the sheer complexity of most privatisation schemes entails a multitude of legal questions to be addressed for the process to benefit the people rather than to create oligarchs.

5.2 The Concept of Government Sale

When defining 'government sales', the notion of 'government' must be taken in a wide sense (see Section 1.1). A 'government sale' occurs not

[22] E.g. concerning specifically social policy, P. Tsoukala, 'Euro Zone Crisis Management and the New Social Europe', *Columbia Journal of European Law* 20 (2013), 31 ff. and spec. 34, arguing that 'the Commission's crisis management measures bears remarkable similarities to reform proposals originated in international development institutions during the 1990s' (see also 42 ff.); for a State-focused study, P. Kozarzewski and M. Bałtowski, 'Change in Economic Policy Paradigm: Privatization and State Capture in Poland', *CASE Working Papers*, 3(127) (2016), (Center for Social and Economic Research, Warsaw).

[23] Wyld, 'Government Garage Sales', 8.

[24] C. Pettit, L. Crommelin, A. Sharam and K. Hulse, 'The Potential of New Technologies to Disrupt Housing Policy', *AHURI Final Report* 308 (2018), 25 (Australian Housing and Urban Research Institute Limited, Melbourne), available at www.ahuri.edu.au/research/final-reports/308.

only when the government, at all levels, is directly involved in the contract, but also when the transaction is carried out by a public undertaking, which owns or controls public assets. The same rules and principles will apply in both instances.[25]

The sale contract is possibly the best known and often simplest contract, corresponding to the very basic *do ut des* scheme, and it may be defined as a contract transferring property rights on a given good or asset from the seller to the buyer against a payment.[26] Therefore, in 'government sales' and unlike in procurement, the government is the seller.[27]

Sale contracts may also be – and this is often the case – part of a larger privatisation scheme,[28] which normally includes a number of transactions going beyond sales contracts and including, for instance, share flotation, partnership agreements, financial guarantees and other similar instruments, and at times administrative decisions, such as (transfer of) concessions, licences or grants. A broad definition of privatisation would include 'any action that moves an enterprise or an economy in the direction of private ownership'.[29] The broad definition leads to distinguishing three kinds of privatisations: through sale of State property, through restitution and through mass or voucher privatisation.[30]

[25] See generally Commission Notice on the notion of State aid as referred to in Article 107 (1) of the Treaty on the Functioning of the European Union (2016/C 262/01), para. 38 ff on the notion of 'State origin'.

[26] A generally accepted definition is brought by Section IV.A. – 1:202: Contract for sale of the *Principles, Definitions and Model Rules of European Private Law. Draft Common Frame of Reference (DCFR)*:

> A contract for the 'sale' of goods is a contract under which one party, the seller, undertakes to another party, the buyer, to transfer the ownership of the goods to the buyer, or to a third person, either immediately on conclusion of the contract or at some future time, and the buyer undertakes to pay the price. Only, unlike what is foreseen under Sub-sec. (3) of Sec. IV. A. – 1:101: Contracts covered, to our ends 'government sales' does include 'contracts for the sale or barter of immovable property or rights in immovable property.

[27] See Chapter 2, Section 2.1.

[28] For a narrow definition of 'privatisation' as 'transfer of ownership of assets to the private sector', see M. M. Shirley, 'The What, Why, and How of Privatization: A World Bank Perspective', *Fordham Law Review* 60 (1992), 24.

[29] World Bank, *From Plan to Market* cit., viii.

[30] W. L. Megginson and J. M. Netter, 'From State to Market: A Survey of Empirical Studies on Privatization', *Journal of Economic Literature* 39 (2001), 339 f.

The focus in this chapter is on the first type of privatisation (privatisation through the sale of State property), even if the other two will be occasionally mentioned.

When assessing the compatibility of the privatisation scheme with the relevant legal framework (see Section 5.4), it is important to look at the entire process. This includes the preparatory measures adopted by the State in order to restructure ('clean') the assets or the company to be sold, measures that could consist, in particular, in write-offs of State debt, debt-to-equity/asset conversion and capital increases (see Section 5.4.2 on prior exposure).

5.3 An Overview of Public Interests

5.3.1 Output-Related Interests

In both business commercial sales and in people garage sales, the essential and straightforward interest is to raise some cash. On the contrary, identifying the inherent public interests lying beyond government sales is more complex. These interests may indeed vary very much. Simple sales often serve different public interests when compared to privatisation schemes. The historical, economic and political conjuncture also affects the interests pursued.

One might argue that Governor Schwarzenegger was trying to sell simply in order to raise money. This interest is the reciprocal of value for money, in that, unlike with public procurement, money is not offered but sought, as much money as the market is ready to offer for the assets sold.

However, unlike private individuals or companies, governments have other effective ways to raise money, and these are called taxes, duties and so on. Nowhere in Executive Order S-10-04 is the need to raise money referred to. Instead, Governor Schwarzenegger recalls why the government owns assets in the first place. According to the recitals in the Order, 'these real property assets are the infrastructure necessary to carry out the services, activities, and programs that California provides to its citizens and visitors'; these assets 'includes priceless parcels of California's breath-taking natural resources, which must be protected for this and all future generations'.[31]

This is, however, only part of the story. There is another potentially powerful inherent interest lurking beneath Executive Order S-10-04 as is

[31] E.g. Available at www.naccho.org/uploads/downloadable-resources/State-of-California-2010.pdf.

made plain by the California Taxpayers Association's reaction to the Order. Founded in 1926, the CalTax is California's largest and oldest organisation representing taxpayers. Established as a nonpartisan, non-profit research and advocacy association, CalTax has a 'dual mission to guard against unnecessary taxation and to promote government efficiency'.[32] In a letter written to Mr Fred Aguiar, Secretary State and Consumer Services Agency (but Governor Schwarzenegger was cc-ed) when the ink of the signature on Executive Order S-10-04 had not yet dried, CalTax expressed its 'enthusiastical support' for the Governor's plan to inventory State property and sell off property that is surplus and unnecessary for the core mission of State government.[33] CalTax stressed the long-term benefits of 'returning' assets to the market; the sale of excess property does not only produce immediate revenue to help stabilise State finances; when 'excess property is restored to the tax rolls, one percent of the sales price will be collected each year in property tax, with a sizeable portion benefiting the State, as less State aid will be needed for schools as a result'.

Clearly avoiding unnecessary taxation may be a public interest behind government sales as relevant as the one calling for government efficiency.[34]

Privatisations offer an even more complex picture of the interests moving governments to sell. Raising cash is often an interest there, and this is normally to reduce deficits. Italy provided a good example of this in the early 1990s. As already recalled, EUR 100 billion were raised and the debt relative to GDP went from 121 per cent in 1994 to 106.4 per cent in 2005; this led to a cumulative decrease of around EUR 30 billion in interest expenditure. As the Italian government avows, multiple reasons lead 'to plan and implement such a broad process of divestment of public companies: the most important was precisely the need to significantly reduce national debt. This objective was pursued in the light of in-depth cost-benefit analyses'.[35]

Here again, value for money, or rather best value for what is sold or value maximisation, is a means to the end of – or the interest in –

[32] www.caltax.org/mission-statement/.

[33] Letter dated 18 May 2004, available at www.caltax.org/AguiarLetter5-18-04.pdf on 23 December 2019.

[34] Google maps, 'California Prison Industry Aut', available at www.google.com/maps/place/California+Prison+Industry+Aut/@38.6921061,-121.1496543,3610m/data=!3m1!1e3!4m5!3m4!1s0x0:0x5e7996b684172aa3!8m2!3d38.6921061!4d-121.1496543.

[35] www.dt.mef.gov.it/export/sites/sitodt/modules/documenti_it/finanza_privatizzazioni/finanza_privatizzazioni/Libro_bianco_privatizzazioni_4603028-1-136.pdf.

reducing the debt. At times privatisations are even used to reduce future costs, so that under certain conditions EU State aid law allows for sales at a negative price, for instance when the costs for winding up the company would be higher than the subsidy given to the seller.[36]

However, raising money was not the reason, or the only or even the main reason why Margaret Thatcher embarked on her huge privatisation programme. Political reasons, and interests, played an outsize role. Privatisations, not unlike nationalisations or collectivisations, are most often the outcome of a polarised political option, and this includes Continental Europe. When the Right came back to power in 1986, 'its program was based on the liberalization of the French economy' which implied 'an ambitious programme of privatizations'.[37]

Looking again at the US, we are provided with an extraordinarily unabashed picture of why privatisation was so strongly pushed. The reference is to Stanley Fisher's working paper on 'Privatization in East European Transformation', which was part of the National Bureau of Economic Research (NBER) research programme in international studies.[38] The opening salvo of the paper set the record right straight away: 'The *creation of a viable private sector*, owning and managing the bulk of the economy's assets, is the essence of the transformation problem in formerly socialist economies. And since virtually all production is currently carried out in the State sector, privatization of State assets is an essential step in the creation of the private sector.'[39] Just to make it clearer, 'revenue is not the main goal; rather it is to move firms rapidly into the private sector, with the intention of increasing their efficiency and that of the economy'.[40] Therefore, a widespread assumption is that 'the purpose of privatization is to achieve a redeployment of assets from

[36] Only future costs borne by a comparable market participant would, however, be relevant; see Case C-334/99, *Germany* v. *Commission* [2003] ECR I-01139, paras. 133 ff; see also Case C-127/16 P, *SNCF Mobilités* v. *Commission* EU:C:2018:165, paras. 110 and 159 ff.

[37] L. Quennouëlle-Corre, 'French Bankers and the Transformation of the Financial System in the Second Half of the Twentieth Century', in Y. Cassis and G. Telesca (eds.), *Financial Elites and European Banking: Historical Perspectives* (Oxford: Oxford University Press, 2018), p. 131.

[38] S. Fisher, 'Privatization in Eastern Europe: Incentives and the Economics of Transition', 1991, available at www.nber.org/papers/w3703; it was also published as part of C. Clague and G. C. Rausser (eds.), *The Emergence of Market Economies in Eastern Europe* (Cambridge, MA: Blackwell, 1992).

[39] Fisher, 'Privatization in Eastern Europe', 1.

[40] Ibid., 13 ff.; the 'efficiency' motive is widespread: e.g. Shirley, 'The What, Why, and How of Privatization', S24; critically Stiglitz, 'Whither Reform?', 30.

the public to the private sector. Under the assumption that assets are used inefficiently by the public sector, privatization should spur productivity and the growth of aggregate output'.[41]

The interest in increasing the role of private actors in the market is often twinned with the desire to develop the equity market. This has been a 'main objective' throughout Europe.[42] For instance, 'the general philosophy of the French privatization's programme was quite original: *the operation primarily aimed at developing economic democracy*, which could be achieved by the access of small savers to the capital of French big firms; *the second aim was to allow employees to partake in a firm's management and benefits*'.[43]

Finally, concerning specifically the sale of wide swathes of land, which, given their economic relevance, is more akin to privatisations than to 'normal' sales, it has been shown that a 'social planner may have other goals beyond efficient land allocation, such as *equity goals, environmental conservation, rural tourism*, etc. For instance, *promoting smallholder farming* has been on the policy agenda of many countries'.[44]

In the examples last referred to, one might well refer to the admittedly rather vague notion of achieving additional policies, keeping in mind, however, that the adjective might be misleading when not plainly wrong. A State might want to sell land precisely to promote smallholder families, this being the main, if not the only, policy interest, so much so that a State might accept to command much less money than it could have attracted by allowing bids from industrial-scale farming conglomerates. Raising money or value maximisation is here a secondary interest, almost an afterthought.

The above discussion should make it clear that, while in procurement the 'inherent' interest may normally be to acquire something to be able to provide a service to the public at large,[45] most often than not in sales and privatisations the immediate and determinant 'reason for which government is willing to award a limited right' is not to dispose of something.

[41] Bortolotti and Milella, *Privatization*, p. 13; Kennedy, 'Political Choices and Development Common Sense', p. 130; this is true of outsourcing generally: F. Wollenschläger, *Verteilungsverfahren* (Tübingen: Mohr Siebeck, 2010), p. 466.

[42] Bortolotti and Milella, *Privatization*, p. 15.

[43] Quennouëlle-Corre, 'French Bankers', 131.

[44] V. Kvartuk and Th. Herzfeld, 'Welfare Effects of Land Market Liberalization Scenarios in Ukraine: Evidence-Based Economic Perspective', *IAMO Discussion Paper* (2019), 14, available at www.econstor.eu/bitstream/10419/195097/1/1662861648.pdf.

[45] See Chapter 2, Section 2.3.

Consequently, neither raising money nor reducing deficits nor creating or strengthening private markets may be considered '*additional policies*'. They may be, according to the circumstances, the main reason for the sale.

In privatisations, the main public interest is widely changing, so much that even value for money (or more correctly, as much money as possible for the given asset, shortly economic gain) may take a backseat, and, indeed, it took a backseat in some historical junctions.[46] This was the case in many post-1989 privatisations when either firms were transferred to managers and workers or 'vouchers' were distributed to the population at large, in both cases entailing little or no financial return for the government concerned.[47]

One interest that is absent from the picture presented so far is the safeguard of fundamental rights, including social rights, which yet might be relevant considering the sheer scale of some of the transactions involved, for instance, in privatisation processes. Lip service only is paid to 'reducing poverty and protecting the environment'.[48] This is hardly surprising since often the privatisation was part of an endogenous or inducted neoliberal agenda not really caring about anything other than market participants' rights.[49]

As Nobel Prize winner Stiglitz pointed out, too often means are confused with ends (or interests). Privatisation should be taken as 'means to the more fundamental ends. It is not just the creation of a market economy that matters but the improvement of living standards and the establishment of the foundations of sustainable, equitable, and democratic development'.[50]

5.3.2 Process-Related Interests

If the reasons – or output-related interests – behind sales and privatisations vary very much from country to country, from time to time and from one transaction to another, the public process-related interests are

46 Bortolotti and Milella, *Privatization*, p. 17.

47 World Bank, *From Plan to Market*, 55 f.

48 Shirley, 'The What, Why, and How of Privatization', S24.

49 D. M. Trubek and A. Santos, 'Introduction: The Third Moment in Law and Development Theory and the Emergence of a New Critical Practice', in D. M. Trubek and A. Santos (eds.), *The New Law and Economic Development*, p. 2, also at 7 ff., discussing the need for a paradigm change.

50 Stiglitz, 'Whither Reform?', 30.

more aligned. This section will be further divided into two subsections: the first illustrating the principles and how they are generally pursued in case of sales of land, buildings or other individual assets; the second analysing how they are enforced in case of privatisation processes.

5.3.2.1 Sale of Land or Individual Assets

In a narrow sense, 'efficiency' may be predicated on the sale/privatisation process itself, the question being whether the process is well designed in terms of the costs/benefits ratio. In a wider sense, 'efficiency' and its different twin 'efficacy/effectiveness' refer to the ability of the process to reach the ends foreseen. Moreover, concerning specifically privatisation, efficiency may, however, be predicated with reference to both the individual transaction and its overall impact on the economy.

'Efficiency', like 'integrity', is a self-evident goal of any – public or private – organisation. Efficiency is a public law general principle in some jurisdictions. A relevant question is whether the goal of efficiency has or has not been achieved. This is a history, not a theory question, and one to be answered with the tools of the economists rather than the lawyers. Critics are judging rather severely a number of privatisation efforts[51] and the achievements of the neoliberal agenda more generally,[52] but some success cases also do exist.[53]

Accountability, a precondition to both efficiency and integrity, is obviously relevant with sales and privatisations. This is about government and the principal/agent conflict is at play here as with any government action.[54]

Transparency links to accountability. This is because the 'account is not rendered discreetly, behind closed doors. Rather, it is in principle open to the general public. The information provided about the actor's conduct is generally accessible, hearings and debates are open to the public, and the forum promulgates its judgment to the public at large'.[55]

[51] E.g. Damsa, 'The Incomprehensible Post-Communist Privatisation'; Kvartuk and Herzfeld, 'Welfare Effects', 13 f. (and further references therein).

[52] E.g. Trubek and Santos, 'Introduction', 16, and more at length Kennedy, 'Political Choices and Development Common Sense', p. 150 f.

[53] E.g. E. Carletti, H. Hakenes and I. Schnabel, 'The Privatization of Italian Savings Banks – A Role Model for Germany?', *Vierteljahrshefte zur Wirtschaftsforschung* 4 (2005), 32.

[54] S. Gailmard, 'Accountability and Principal–Agent Theory', in M. Bovens, R. E. Goodin and Th. Schillemans (eds.), *The Oxford Handbook of Public Accountability* (Oxford: Oxford University Press, 2014), p. 90.

[55] M. Bovens, R. E. Goodin and Th. Schillemans, 'Public Accountability', in M. Bovens, Th. Schillemans and R. E. Goodin (eds.), *The Oxford Handbook of Public Accountability*, 7;

In government contracts, transparency is paramount and its mandate goes beyond accountability and into being instrumental in achieving the ultimate goals of the transaction such as best value for money or highest price for public assets (see Section 5.4) or fostering popular capitalism and so on.[56]

Transparency is normally part of articulated procedural mechanisms known as auction or tendering.

Auctions, and the same is true of tendering, go beyond (*ex ante*) transparency, as they require procedural safeguards both for the integrity of the overall process and for equal and fair treatment.[57] Still, when using auctions, those requirements often boil down to transparency again. Auctions are therefore open and they play out in the presence of the bidders and of curious or nosy members of the general public. The auctioneer is there to ensure that every bidder has the same opportunity for raising their bid. For instance, after 1989 in the Czech Republic small firms were auctioned; the government 'implemented a centrally conceived but locally administered system of open, competitive auctions'.[58]

In many jurisdictions, however, auctions are the preserve of those in the know. Concerning the US again, it has been remarked that 'government auctions have been the province of the "usual suspects"'.[59]

Choosing web-based auctions should in principle remedy these shortcomings and guarantee both the integrity of the process – if the technical tools are adequate – and equal and fair treatment.[60]

In a way fully closing the circle, accountability, transparency, and fair and equal treatment partake in efficiency and integrity.

5.3.2.2 Privatisation Processes

Accountability, transparency and procedural safeguards also apply to privatisations, but how they work depends on whether what is sold is an individual asset – such as a parcel of land or a building or even a small

see also Shirley, 'The What, Why, and How of Privatization', S29 arguing that transparency is central in avoiding abuses and corruption.

56 R. Caranta, 'Transparence et concurrence', in R. Noguellou and U. Stelkens (eds.), *Droit comparé des contrats publics. Comparative Law on Public Contracts* (Brussels: Bruylant, 2010), p. 145, and the contributions collected by K.-M. Halonen, R. Caranta and A. Sanchez-Graells (eds.), *Transparency in EU Procurements* (London: Edward Elgar, 2019).

57 See Chapter 2, Section 2.3.

58 World Bank, *From Plan to Market*, 58.

59 Wyld, 'Government Garage Sales', 8 f.

60 Ibid.

firm – or is instead a large company. If the former, the analogy with standard sales is very close and auctions are usually recommended.[61]

5.4 Optimising Public Interests: Legal Choices and Assumptions

The discussion so far has been nourished from instances from different corners of the world. When analysing the legal regime for sales and privatisations, we need instead to ground the discussion on specific legal orders, the EU and its Member States.

5.4.1 Introduction

The EU legal framework for government sales and privatisation regulates both the processes that shall be followed by public authorities and the limits within which those authorities can pursue the relevant public interests outlined in the previous section. Needless to say, this set of rules is only applicable to the Member States; third countries might instead subject government sales to less or more stringent regulation, as well as to different policies.

In normal circumstances, EU law leaves the Member States free to decide what they should own or could sell. In *Staat der Nederlanden* the Court of Justice recalled that 'the Treaties do not preclude, as a general rule, either the nationalisation of undertakings [. . .] or their privatisation [. . .]'.[62] Article 345 of the Treaty on the Functioning of the European Union (TFEU) establishes the so-called neutrality principle, for which: '*The Treaties shall in no way prejudice the rules in Member States governing the system of property ownership.*' Otherwise said, the State is free to privatise or maintain within the public property a given asset, company, infrastructure and so on.[63]

The financial crisis, however, has led to shelving the neutrality principle on a number of occasions with the EU and the IMF demanding privatisations from countries facing financial difficulties.[64] More generally, the

[61] See, with reference to the successful Mexican privatisation of small firms, Shirley, 'The What, Why, and How of Privatization', S29.

[62] Joined Cases C-105/12 to C-107/12, *Staat der Nederlanden* ECLI:EU:C:2013:677, para. 30.

[63] See Akkermans and Ramaekers, 'Article 345 TFEU (ex Article 295 EC), Its Meanings and Interpretations', 292.

[64] See Olivares-Caminal, 'The EU Architecture', 190; concerning Greece, see now the ESM Stability Support Programme Economic and Financial Affairs, 'Greece, First & Second

Council routinely recommended restructuring, when not outright privatisation, to Member States facing budget troubles.[65]

Article 345 TFEU, in any case, does not have the effect of exempting the Member States' systems of property ownership from the fundamental rules of the Treaty;[66] on the contrary, when public authorities carry out economic transactions in any form, they are subject to EU competition and State aid rules.[67] Therefore, a Member State or one of its articulations that intends to sell some asset is entitled to do so as far as the sale complies with internal market freedoms and does not result in an incompatible State aid to the purchaser.

European Union rules aim at opening up the market for what is on sale to participants from all the Member States. The EU is indeed competent to lay down rules about government sales and privatisations insofar as these transactions can distort the competition on the internal market affecting the trade between Member States, including by giving unfair advantage to one undertaking.[68]

In this EU law framework, the Member States enjoy much discretion on what to sell, but much less room on what they might want to achieve by selling and on how they sell. An interesting case drawing the line between what Member States may or may not do under the TFEU provisions on freedom of establishment concerned the reprivatisation of Transportes Aéreos Portugueses (TAP), the Portuguese airline.[69] Three requirements in the privatisation process were challenged in front of the domestic court. Those clauses required the buyer to (i) ensure

Reviews July 2017 Background Report', Institutional Paper (November 2017) 64, available at www.esm.europa.eu/sites/default/files/2017_11_13_ec_background_report_on_esm_programme_for_greece.pdf.

[65] A table of such recommendations may be found at https://corporateeurope.org/sites/default/files/european_semester_final_recommendations_on_State-owned_enterprises_final.pdf.

[66] Case C-563/17, *Associação Peço a Palavra and Others* EU:C:2019:144, paras. 43 f.; Case C-503/04, *Commission/Germany* ECR I-6153, para. 37; Joined Cases C-105/12 to C-107/12, *Staat der Nederlanden* v. *Essent and others*, paras. 36 ff. See P. Van Cleynenbreugel's analysis of the *Staat der Nederlanden* case: 'No Privatisation in the Service of Fair Competition? Article 345 TFEU and the EU Market-State Balance after Essent', *European Law Review* 39 (2014), 264.

[67] Case C-40/85, *Belgium* v. *Commission* ECLI:EU:C:1986:305, para. 12.

[68] Commission Notice on the notion of State aid as referred to in Article 107(1) of the Treaty on the Functioning of the European Union 2016/C 262/01, OJ 2016, No. C262/1, paras. 7 ff.

[69] Case C-563/17, *Associação Peço a Palavra and Others*; see S. Rodrigues, 'Chronique Actions publiques', *Concurrences* 2 (2019), 5 f.

proper compliance, in good time, with the public service obligations of TAP, including the flight connections between the main national airports and the airports of the autonomous regions, where applicable, and the continuation and further development of the routes serving the autonomous regions, the diaspora and Portuguese-speaking countries and communities; (ii) preserve and promote the growth of TAP enhancing its competitive position as a global air carrier operator; (iii) maintain the integrity, corporate identity and independence of the TAP Group, in particular preserving the TAP trademark and its association with Portugal and ensuring that the headquarters and effective management of the TAP Group remain in Portugal; and (iv) contribute to the growth of the national economy, including maintaining and developing the current national hub as a platform of vital strategic importance in relations between Europe, Africa and Latin America. The Court of Justice held that all the above measures restricted the freedom of establishment.[70] It also held that requiring compliance with public service obligations laid down respecting the requirements of EU law was permissible under EU law,[71] as was, given the peculiarity of bilateral agreements concerning air routes, requiring that the headquarters and effective management of the TAP Group remain in Portugal.[72] The Court instead considered not proven that requiring the keeping and development of the existing national hub was necessary to keep the ties with the Portuguese-speaking third countries.[73] Finally, the Court reaffirmed that purely economic grounds, such as, in particular, promotion of the national economy or its proper functioning, cannot serve as justification for an obstacle to one of the fundamental freedoms enshrined in the Treaties.[74]

No issue of potential State aids rule breach was raised in the *TAP* case,[75] but cases concerning sales and privatisations are often litigated as State illegal aids.

Article 107(1) TFEU provides the general definition of State aid, identifying the four cumulative conditions that must occur: (1) the measure must be granted by a Member State or through State resources;

[70] Ibid., paras. 47 ff.
[71] Ibid., para. 52.
[72] Ibid., spec. paras. 75 ff.
[73] Ibid., paras. 80 ff.
[74] Ibid., para. 70; Case C-201/15, *AGET Iraklis* EU:C:2016:972, para. 72, is referred to.
[75] See A. Doern, 'The Interaction between EC Rules on Public Procurement and State Aid', *Public Procurement Law Review* 3 (2004), 97.

(2) there must be a selective advantage; (3) there must be a (potential for) distortion of competition; (4) there must be an effect on trade between Member States.[76]

The third and fourth conditions, which are 'inextricably linked' and thus generally treated jointly,[77] reveal the connection between free movement principles and State aid rules.[78] So, by ensuring respect for State aid rules, a fair playground for trade (and free movement) is also created.[79]

With specific regard to the second condition, economic transactions carried out by public bodies, including public undertakings, do not confer an advantage on their counterpart and therefore do not constitute aid, if they are carried out in line with normal market conditions.[80] Consequently, for a sale or a privatisation not to entail State aid, public authorities must ensure that the economic transactions involved are done 'on market terms', so that no advantage is given either to the buyer or to the sold company, for instance in terms of foregone revenues (taxes, social contributions or other).[81]

To assess that, the European Court has developed the general market economy operator (MEO) test. With sales of assets, the MEO turns into the market economy vendor principle/test (MEVP),[82] which aims to verify whether a private vendor, under normal market conditions, could have obtained the same or a better price.[83]

[76] *Ex multis*, Case C-280/00, *Altmark* ECR I-7747, para. 75. The relevant notions and the related case law are now comprehensively illustrated in the Commission Notice on the notion of State aid.

[77] Joined Cases T-298/97, T-312/97, etc. *Alzetta* ECLI:EU:T:2000:151, para. 81.

[78] Notice on the notion of State aid, para. 192. If the amount of the aid is too small, it will normally be caught in the *de minimis* regulation exemption.

[79] A breach of State aid rules might indirectly represent a breach of free movement principles. See analysis in Doern, 'The Interaction between EC Rules on Public Procurement and State Aid'.

[80] Case C-39/94, *SFEI and Others* ECLI:EU:C:1996:285, paras. 60 and 61; Case T-274/01, *Valmont* v. *Commission* ECR II-3145, para. 44; Notice on the notion of State aid, para. 74; see for analysis Bacon, *European Union Law of State Aid*, paras. 2.25 ss.

[81] See the leading case C-39/94, *SFEI and Others*, paras. 60–61.

[82] The MEVP is a development of the general '*market economy investor principle*' (MEIP test), which had been originally created by the Court case law to assess the presence of State aid in cases of public investments: see F. Wollenschläger, 'Art. 107 AEUV (Fallgruppen Grundstücksveräußerungen und Privatisierung öffentlicher Unternehmen)', in A. Birnstiel, M. Bungenberg and H. Heinrich (eds.), *Europäisches Beihilfenrecht* (Baden-Baden: Nomos, 2013), para. 471 f.

[83] Notice on the Notion of State aid, para. 74; for a thorough and complete analysis in the topic, see M. Cyndecka, *The Market Economy Investor Test in EU State Aid Law* (Alphen aan den Rijn: Wolters Kluwer, 2016).

An important distinction must, however, be drawn depending on the role of the State in the allocating procedure: the MEO test will only apply when the State is acting as an economic operator, while being excluded in regard to activities carried out as a public authority.[84] To distinguish between the two roles becomes essential, especially when, as in complex restructuring and privatisation processes, the State might play, at different stages, both roles.[85]

Certain types of aid, as foreseen by Article 107(2) of the TFEU, are considered *automatically* compatible with the internal market (automatic compatibility).[86] Other types of aid as foreseen by Article 107(3) *may* be declared compatible with the internal market following a discretionary assessment by the Commission (discretionary compatibility).[87] Article 107(3) outlines a (non-exhaustive) list of categories of aid that might be approved and it represents the legal basis under which most aid measures can be declared compatible. In general terms, governments can be allowed to grant State aid, which 'may increase economic welfare in two main ways; by improving *efficiency* when the market fails to deliver an optimal economic outcome and – depending on social and political preferences – by improving *equity*, when the market outcome is characterized by significant socio-economic inequality'.[88]

[84] See Case C-579/16 P, *Commission* v. *FIH Holding and FIH Erhvervsbank* EU:C:2018:159, paras. 55 ff.

[85] On the distinction and on the rules applicable in case of the State performing mixed functions, see generally Bacon, *European Union Law of State Aid*, paras. 2.26 ff; Notice on the notion of State aid, para. 77. On the aid in favour of restructured, recapitalised or privatised undertakings and, in particular, on the costs of aid that was granted in the past and the subsequent application to the MEO test, see Cyndecka, *The Market Economy Investor Test in EU State Aid Law*, paras. 5.4.2. ff.

[86] This includes (i) aid of a social character for individual consumers; (ii) aid for natural disasters or exceptional occurrences; (iii) aid granted to the economy of certain areas of the Federal Republic of Germany affected by the division of Germany, insofar as such aid is required in order to compensate for the economic disadvantages caused by that division. See for general analysis Bacon, *European Union Law of State Aid*, paras. 3.08 ff.

[87] Bacon, *European Union Law of State Aid*, paras. 3.26 ff.

[88] Bacon, *European Union Law of State Aid*, para. 1.11. Regarding the latter equity objectives, the Commission acknowledges that: 'although specific equity objectives may vary from Member State to Member State, it will often be possible to identify a broad common interest in the pursuit of such objectives. Equity justifications may be demonstrated by statistical indicators illustrating social or regional disparities. These may include GDP per capita, unemployment levels, participation rates in the labour market, poverty indicators, etc.' (Staff discussion paper: guideline outlining the Common principles for an economic assessment of the compatibility of State aid under Article 87.3 (15 May 2009) at 10).

In essence, in order to be declared compatible with the internal market pursuant to Article 107(3)(c) TFEU, aid must be aimed at the development of an activity that constitutes a public interest objective and must be appropriate, necessary and not disproportionate.[89] To assess that, the Commission carries out a fundamental – and highly discretional – balancing test of the measure/scheme. To that purpose – and also arguably to increase the transparency and certainty of the whole process – the Commission has issued a general guideline outlining the Common principles for an economic assessment of the compatibility of State aid under Article 87(3), now Article 107(3) TFEU.[90]

Here the Commission presents the three stages under which such a balancing test is carried out, addressing the following questions: (1) Is the aid measure aimed at a well-defined objective of common interest? (2) Is the aid well designed to deliver the objective of common interest, that is, does the proposed aid address the market failure or other objectives? (i) Is the aid an appropriate policy instrument to address the policy objective concerned? (ii) Is there an incentive effect, that is, does the aid change the behaviour of the aid recipient? (iii) Is the aid measure proportionate to the problem tackled, that is, could the same change in behaviour not be obtained with less aid? (3) Are the distortions of competition and effect on trade limited, so that the overall balance is positive?

In order to assess the impact of the aid, the Commission must identify a counterfactual scenario with which the situation in which the aid is given can be compared. The question to be asked in this context is indeed what the situation will be if no aid is given. Of particular relevance for the present analysis, the Commission acknowledges that

> the aid may be used to cover exit costs and result in disposing of assets and activities (e.g. restructuring). In this case, competitors will benefit and possibly expand their own capacity. Aid may enhance efficiency if the assets of the existing firm are managed better by their new owners and output is produced by more efficient firms. Reciprocally, aid may prevent market exit.[91]

In such general guidelines, the Commission identifies – although it confirms that the assessment must be carried out on a case-by-case

[89] Case T-356/15, *Republic of Austria* v. *European Co* ECLI:EU:T:2018:439; see, for analysis, among others, P. Nicolaides, 'The Compatibility of State Aid with the Internal Market', *European State Aid Law Review* 4 (2018), 534.

[90] Guideline outlining the Common principles.

[91] Ibid., 5.

analysis – a series of operational indicators that can be – and usually are – taken into account by the Commission in order to balance the positive and negative effects of a given aid measure.

These common principles are also developed, with adaptations in the light of the specific policy context, in a number of guidelines, frameworks, communications and so on for specific categories of regional, horizontal and sectoral aid and have been applied in a number of Commission decisions.

The Commission's centralised control over State aids is made possible by Article 108(3) of the TFEU, which establishes the general duty for Member States to notify the measure to the Commission and the corresponding standstill clause, for which the aid measure cannot be implemented until the Commission, in its exclusive competence, has assessed it. If public authorities fail to comply with Article 108(3) TFEU requirements, then the granting measure is to be considered unlawful[92] and, consequently, the aid must be recovered.[93] Therefore, if it turns out that the allocating procedure has not been conducted on market terms and the other elements set out by Article 107 TFEU are respected, then the procedure shall be considered, as a whole, an aid, which is unlawful because it has not been notified. *Vice versa*, compliance with the MEVP test rules out the presence of an advantage, thus the presence of aid altogether.

EU law instruments have generally identified a list of State aids, which are exempted from prior notification under Article 108(3) TFEU. For what is relevant here, the general *de minimis* Regulation adopted by the Commission establishes a set of thresholds below which the measure does not need to be notified.[94] This goes somewhere into explaining why the only sale of assets expressly regulated at the EU level are land sales and privatisation schemes: minor 'garage sales' of movable goods are caught under *de minimis* thresholds.

[92] The current Council Regulation (EU) 2015/1589 of 13 July 2015 laying down detailed rules for the application of Article 108 of the Treaty on the Functioning of the European Union, (so-called Procedural Regulation, OJ 2015, No. L248/9) rules that the duty of notification covers any aid (Article 2(1)), which means any measure fulfilling all the criteria laid down in Article 107(1) TFEU (Article 1).

[93] A subsequent evaluation of the Commission will indeed only have *ex nunc* effects; thus, it will not be able to restore the original invalidity of the granting measure.

[94] Regulation (EU) 1407/2013 on the application of Articles 107 and 108 of the Treaty on the Functioning of the European Union to *de minimis* aid [2013], OJ 2013, No. L352/1; this General '*de minimis*' Regulation came into force on 1 January 2014 and applies until 31 December 2020.

Basically, allocating authorities must comply with both the internal market freedoms and, even more often, with the more specific EU State aid law. The probable reason why EU State aid law is so relevant in this area is linked to the notification duty under Article 108 TFEU and the wider surveillance apparatus for policing possible breaches. Most relevant privatisation cases are brought to the attention of the Commission that way. *TAP* was probably an exception, as issues of State aid were not even raised.

The Commission State aid decision in *Automobile Craiova* mirrors the same issues economic measures are bound to face that were highlighted in *TAP*. In 2007 the Romanian privatisation agency announced the sale of its participation of 72 per cent in Automobile Craiova. The sale was conditioned in particular to minimum production, employment and investment levels. The scoring grid showed that the price offered represented only 35 per cent of the total scoring, with aggregate investments accounting for 25 per cent, the achievement of a production integration level of 60 per cent in the fourth year accounting for 20 per cent and the commitment to a production level of 200,000 cars in the fourth year accounting for 20 per cent. According to the Commission,

> by imposing such conditions and thus accepting that it will not receive the best price for the shares or assets owned by it, the State does not act like a market economy operator, who would try to obtain the highest possible price. Instead, the State chooses to sell the undertaking at a price below the market value. A market economy operator would not have an economic interest in attaching comparable conditions (in particular, such as *maintenance of the level of employment, conditions beneficial for the geographical region concerned or ensuring a certain investment level*) but would sell the company to the highest bidder, who would then be free to determine the future of the acquired company or assets.[95]

It is worth noting that the problem here was not the lack of a competitive tendering procedure, but the conditions attached to it.[96]

While the acquisition of works, goods or services by the State is regulated through detailed secondary rules, such as the procurement

[95] 2008/717/EC: Commission Decision of 27 February 2008 on State aid C 46/07 (ex NN 59/07) implemented by Romania for Automobile Craiova (formerly Daewoo Romania) (notified under document number C(2008) 700) OJ 2008, No. L 239/12, para. 53.

[96] See paras. 55 ff.; also, but this would require further research, it seems that overcapacity in the sector strengthens the rigid approach to conditionality: see para. 59; a similar approach was upheld by Case T-242/12, *SNCF Mobilités* v. *Commission* ECLI:EU:T:2015:1003; then confirmed in Case C-127/16 P, *SNCF Mobilités* v. *Commission*.

directives,[97] government sales and privatisation schemes are not covered by specific EU secondary legislation. However, the general TFEU provisions have been developed in a series of detailed guidance documents issued over the years by the Commission, building on the relevant case law of the Court of Justice.

These soft law instruments are generally binding neither for the Member States and undertakings nor for the Court of Justice.[98] Commission staff working papers are even softer. They are issued for information purposes, but do not represent an official position of the Commission on the issues covered, nor do they anticipate such a position.[99]

The majority of these guidance documents cover State aids generally, while a few apply specifically to sales. The most relevant soft law instruments providing guidance on the matter are:

- Commission Notice on the notion of State aid as referred to in Article 107(1) of the TFEU (2016/C 262/01);
- Guidelines on State aid for rescuing and restructuring non-financial undertakings in difficulty (R&R Guidelines) (2014/C 249/01);
- Commission Staff Working Document, Guidance Paper on State aid-compliant financing, restructuring and privatization of State-owned enterprises (SWD(2012)14);
- Commission Communication on State aid elements in sales of land and buildings by public authorities (97/C 209/03), hereinafter 1997 Communication, now repealed;

[97] See Chapter 2, Section 2.4.1.2.

[98] See Case C-127/16, *SNCF* v. *Commission*, para. 67; also referring to Case C-277/00, *Germany* v. *Commission* EU:C:2004:238, para. 95. In the current Notice on the notion of State aid, the Commission stated that

> this Notice clarifies the Commission's understanding of Article 107(1) of the Treaty, as interpreted by the Court of Justice and the General Court ('the Union Courts'). On issues that have not yet been considered by the Union Courts, the Commission will set out how it considers that the notion of State aid should be construed. The views set out in this Notice are without prejudice to the interpretation of the notion of State aid by the Union Courts; the primary reference for interpreting the Treaty is always the case–law of the Union Courts.
>
> (2016/C 262/01, para. 3)

[99] E.g. Commission Staff Working Document SWD (2012)14 final, point 1.

- Commission's XXIII Report on Competition Policy (Published on 26 March 1995), and
- specific post-crisis temporary rules and guidance for the banking sector following the financial crises.[100]

The present analysis will not go into the last set of measures, which were temporary in nature and concerned privatisations only as the eventual stage of a process starting with the nationalisation of failing or fledgling credit institutions.

The 2014 *R&R Guidelines* as well do not really deal with rules and procedures concerning privatisation or sale of assets. They simply point out that Member States intending to grant restructuring aid must provide a comparison with a credible alternative scenario not involving State aid. Among these possible scenarios, asset disposal and sale to a competitor are expressly mentioned.[101]

This chapter will, instead, focus on the principles and rules outlined in the other pieces of soft law, as well as on the relevant case law and Commission decisions. The specific focus of EU law means that it may have a narrower coverage than national rules on government sales. Still European rules impact the pursuing of other public interests at the national level, which are admissible only if they are not seen as detrimental to achieving the market integration objectives. Therefore, national rules might have a wider coverage and pursue other interests only if they are compliant with EU internal market and State aid rules. This will be specifically addressed in Sections 5.4.3 and 5.4.4.

5.4.2 *Competitive Tendering or Not?*

Having set the relevant legal framework for government sales, it is now possible to address the central questions of the present analysis: (a) Should the sale be done through competitive tendering or there is space for alternative – and still legitimate – mechanisms? (b) How does this framework allow the pursuing of the outlined public interests?

It must be recalled that State aid rules identify the MEO principle, specifically declined as the MEVP test, as the cornerstone around which

[100] Full references at http://ec.europa.eu/competition/State_aid/legislation/temporary.html; a specific application of this set of rules was challenged (and upheld) in Case T-319/11, *ABN Amro Group NV* ECLI:EU:T:2014:186.

[101] Communication from the Commission – Guidelines on State aid for rescuing and restructuring non-financial undertakings in difficulty 2014/C 249/01, point 53.

the allocating procedure shall revolve: to sell at market value is the paramount 'interest' – the only explicitly outlined – by the EU legal framework regarding government sales.[102]

5.4.2.1 Sales of Land, Buildings or Other Assets

In 1997 the Commission issued the first Communication on State aid elements in sales of land and buildings by public authorities, in order to (a) describe a simple procedure allowing the Member State to sell land and buildings in a way that automatically precludes the existence of State aid, (b) to specify which sales should be notified to the Commission to allow for assessment on whether a certain measure amounts as potential State aid, and if so whether it is compatible or not, and (c) to help the same Commission to deal expeditiously with complaints.[103]

The 1997 Communication provided a definition of 'market value': 'the price at which land and buildings could be sold under private contract between a willing seller and an arm's length buyer on the date of valuation, it being assumed that the property is publicly exposed to the market, that market conditions permit orderly disposal and that a normal period, having regard to the nature of the property, is available for the negotiation of the sale'.[104]

The allocating authority had two options to establish the market price and, consequently, to avoid prior notification: (1) a sufficiently well-publicised, open and unconditional bidding procedure, or (2) an independent evaluation based on generally accepted market indicators and valuation standards carried out prior to the sale negotiations.[105]

In relation to the first method, the Communication stated that 'A sale of land and buildings following a sufficiently, well-publicised, open and unconditional bidding procedure, comparable to an auction, accepting the best or only bid is *by definition* at market value and consequently does not contain State aid.'[106]

The requirement that the procedure be 'unconditional' has played an outsize role in this area. Basically, '[r]estrictions may be imposed for the prevention of public nuisance, for reasons of environmental protection or

[102] Wollenschläger, 'Art. 107 AEUV', paras. 475 ff.

[103] Commission Communication on State aid elements in sales of land and buildings by public authorities 97/C 209/03, introduction; see also C. Quigley, *European State Aid Law and Policy*, 3rd ed. (London: Hart, 2015), p. 181 ff.

[104] Ibid., para. II(2)(a).

[105] Ibid., para. II(3).

[106] Ibid., para. I(1).

to avoid purely speculative bids. Urban and regional planning restrictions imposed on the owner pursuant to domestic law on the use of the land and buildings do not affect the unconditional nature of an offer'.[107] Additional restrictions or conditions may be imposed on the buyer 'for the benefit of the public authorities or in the general public interest' only insofar as 'all potential buyers would have to, and be able to, meet that obligation, irrespective of whether or not they run a business or of the nature of their business'.[108]

Two elements stood out in the treatment of conditionality as potential exceptions to a too rigid interpretation of the MEVP: (1) the possibility to exclude 'purely speculative bids' and (2) the possibility to impose additional conditions going beyond what is provided under the applicable legislation or planning rules. However, these exceptions have been proven rather problematic when put into practice.[109]

In relation to the second outlined method, the Communication was at the same time lengthier and less precise when trying to qualify the 'asset valuer' charged with establishing 'the market value on the basis of generally accepted market indicators and valuation standards'.[110]

The 1997 Communication designed the two methods to set the market price as an *alternative*, without a preference being given to one over the other, and they both created a presumption of absence of advantage, thus dispensing from the duty of prior notification.[111]

This whole approach was then tested in both the Commission practice and European Court case law.

[107] Ibid., para. II(1)(b).

[108] Ibid., para. II(1)I.

[109] See Case C-39/14, *BVVG* ECLI:EU:C:2015:470, discussed below.

[110] Commission Communication, 97/C 209/03, para. II(2).

[111] It is interesting to note that in the following landmark *Altmark* judgment (Case C-280/00, para. 93), although related to the conditions that must be fulfilled for compensation for provision of public service obligations not to constitute State aid, the Court of Justice followed somehow a similar approach identifying two ways to establish the market conditions of the compensation to discharge the public service obligation and thus to exclude the presence of aid (the so-called fourth Altmark criterion). In other words, either procurement procedures or benchmarking. See also the Commission Communication on the application of the European Union State aid rules to compensation granted for the provision of services of general economic interest ([2012] OJ C8/4). For general discussion on the matter, see G. S. Ølykke, 'Commission Notice on the Notion of State Aid as Referred to in Article 107(1) TF-U – Is the Conduct of a Public Procurement Procedure Sufficient to Eliminate the Risk of Granting State Aid?', *Public Procurement Law Review* 5 (2016), 197.

Some of the facts of the first relevant case actually predate the Communication.[112] A French partly public-owned company sold for FRF 31 million a large piece of land to a local subsidiary of the Scott Paper Company. That sale was not notified to the Commission under the rules on State aid. About ten years later, Scott sold the plant and the Commission initiated the procedure for illegal State aid, which led to the adoption of a decision declaring the sale incompatible with the common market because of (1) the preferential purchase price (the land's worth was assessed at FRF 39.588 million) and (2) the application of the water treatment levy at a preferential rate. The Commission decision required repayment of the amounts already unlawfully made available to the company.

The Commission decision, which was taken after the 1997 Communication had been enacted, remarked that the land at issue had neither been sold by means of an unconditional bidding procedure nor had been independently valued. Pointing out that it had unsuccessfully attempted to obtain complete information from the French authorities, the Commission determined the amount of unlawful aid to be recovered by comparing the market price of a similar parcel of land with the price actually paid by Scott.[113] This approach was confirmed by the Court of Justice on appeal,[114] which held that, '[a]lthough, as is apparent from the 1997 Commission Communication, use of an independent expert is a method by which an assessment of the market value of land can be obtained', the Commission itself can ground its finding as to the actual value of the land sold on different elements.[115]

The *Scott* judgment is relevant to our ends[116] in that it reaffirmed that 'in order to determine whether the sale of land by the public authorities

[112] Case C-290/07 P, *Commission* v. *Scott* ECR 2010 I-07763.

[113] Ibid., para. 23: the Commission

> relied on the average price paid by the City of Orléans at the time of the three land transactions, between 1975 and 1987, by which it had acquired the land of which the 48 hectares at issue formed part. That amount – FRF 10.9 million – was corroborated by the minutes of the meeting of the City Council of Orléans of 27 May 1994 and roughly tallied with the assessment proposed by the French authorities in their letters of 17 March and 29 May 1997.

[114] It had instead been reversed by the General Court in Case T-366/00, *Scott* v. *Commission* ECR II-797.

[115] Case C-290/07 P, *Commission* v. *Scott*, para. 72.

[116] Even though the 1997 Communication did not feature prominently in the judgment: when assessing the relevance of the acquisition price to set the 'market value' of the land,

to a private individual constitutes State aid, the Commission must apply the private investor test to determine whether the price paid corresponds to the one which a private investor, operating in normal competitive conditions, would be likely to have fixed'.[117]

The determination of the 'market price' of land was at the core also of the following *Seydaland* judgment.[118] The case arose from the agricultural land privatisation in the former Deutsche Demokratische Republik (DDR) and opposed Seydaland to the Bodenverwertungs- und -verwaltungs GmbH (BVVG), that is, a legal person governed by private law, whose shares are held by the *Bundesanstalt für vereinigungsbedingte Sonderaufgaben* (a federal body responsible for special tasks connected with the reunification of Germany). It has the statutory task of privatising land and buildings belonging to the State and used for agricultural and forestry purposes. In order to adapt the system of ownership over agricultural and forestry land at the national level, a law was set introducing different methods for calculating the value of the agricultural land. Seydaland, basing itself on regional reference valuations, asked for a significant price rebate. The BVVG refused to accede to the request arguing that the regional reference valuations did not reflect the prevailing market situation but rather the situation as it was one or two years earlier, since these regional references were only updated every two or more years. Therefore, taking them into account would amount to granting illegal State aids.

A preliminary reference was sent to the Court of Justice asking (i) whether provisions of national law establishing rules to calculate the market price of land are in compliance with State aid rules and (ii) whether the methods foreseen by the German law at stake allowed them to identify the market value of the land. The Court of Justice held that if the national law sets rules for calculating the market value of land for their sale by public authorities, these rules must, in order to comply with Article 87 EC [now Article 107 TFEU], lead in all cases to a price as close as possible to the market value.[119] Indeed, 'while it is clear that the best bid or an expert report are likely to provide prices corresponding to

the Court, while neither disavowing them nor deciding in an inconsistent way, did simply not – yet – consider indications found in the Communication itself.

117 Case C-290/07 P, *Commission* v. *Scott*, para. 68.

118 Case C-239/09, *Seydaland Vereinigte Agrarbetriebe* EU:C:2010:778.

119 Ibid., para. 35.

actual market values [...], it cannot be ruled out that other methods may also achieve the same result'.[120]

Remarkably, the Court added that the market value is theoretical, except in the case of sales to the highest bidder, therefore 'a margin for variation on the price obtained as compared with the theoretical price must be tolerated'.[121] This statement is interesting because it seemingly starts to conceive a sort of hierarchy between the two methods: only the highest bid ensures a sale to market value; any other methods, including export valuations, just approximate it. This line of reasoning will arguably be the basis of both the following case law and of the new Commission notice (see Section 5.4.2.2.).

In the case at hand, the Court sided with the BVVG in considering inadequate a reliance on the regional reference evaluations since 'they do not include a mechanism for updating those valuations which would allow the selling price of the land to reflect in so far possible, the market value of that land, especially when prices are rising sharply'.[122] On the contrary, it considered that reference to a valuation committee is acceptable insofar as 'the workings of that valuation committee result in a determination of the price which is equivalent to the market value, will it be likely to meet the criteria for compatibility with the rules of the Treaty in the area of State aid'.[123]

The judgment in *Seydaland* arguably opened the door to other mechanisms to assess the market value of the land to be sold than those foreseen by the Commission with the 1997 Communication. This by itself did not contradict the Communication, which did not exclude the possibility for a public authority to avail methods other than the twofold alternative methods outlined, but it required to notify the sale to the Commission.[124]

The Commission itself tackled, in a series of decisions concerning land sales, the issue of establishing what might constitute '*generally accepted market indicators and valuation standards*', as well as what could be considered other reliable methods.

[120] Ibid., para. 39.
[121] Ibid., para. 35.
[122] Ibid., para. 43.
[123] Case C-239/09, *Seydaland Vereinigte Agrarbetriebe*, para. 48; the same would apply to a potential third calculation system foreseen by the German legislation, which however is not described in sufficient detail in the judgments: see paras. 49 ff.
[124] Point 3 of the 1997 Communication.

Following the opening of the Court in *Seydaland* and given that the duty of prior notification to every allocating procedure pursuant to other calculation methods was extremely burdensome, the German authorities sought a general Commission's validation of an alternative reference price system implemented by the BVVG: the so-called visual protection surface (VPS) method, which is based on the BVVG database of its previous land sale transactions and whose main explicit objective is to exclude the presence of State aid.[125] The German authorities contended that the VPS method was an accurate alternative to establish the market value of land sold by BVVG, so as to preclude, prima facie, the presence of State aid in such sales transactions, and asked the Commission to take a formal position on that. The Commission considered that the application of the VPS method 'ensures that the price actually paid by the purchaser reflects, in so far as possible, the market value of that land so that no advantage is conferred upon that purchaser as a result of the transaction, thereby precluding the presence of State aid within the meaning of Article 107(1) TFEU'.[126] However, it ambiguously added that since it cannot be definitively ruled out that, in certain cases, the VPS method may lead to a result below market value, the German authorities must ensure that the BVVG shall refrain from applying this method in any such cases.[127] Consequently, it reached the – somewhat tautological – conclusion that the VPS method rules out the presence of State aid *insofar as it the reflects the market value of the land* and in any case, given the limited scope of the VPS database, it added that such conclusion stands solely for the BVVG transactions in its responsibility for the land privatisation programme.[128]

Another fundamental case regarding the establishment of market price, as well as the treatment of the conditionality requirement as defined above, is the *Land Burgenland* judgment.[129] The case deals with a privatisation scheme, that will be specifically outlined and analysed in Section 5.4.2.2; however, the main ruling of the case is a cornerstone in relation to all government sales and, therefore, it shall be anticipated in this section.

[125] Commission response C(2012) 9457 final of 19 December 2012 in relation to measure SA.33167.

[126] Ibid., para. 35.

[127] Ibid., para. 36.

[128] Ibid., para. IV. Conclusion; see also the Notice on the notion of State aid, fn. 164.

[129] Joined Cases T-268/01 and T-281/08, *Land Burgenland* v. *Austria* ECLI:EU:T:2012:90.

The controversy arose from a Commission decision in the field of State aid in connection with the privatisation of Bank Burgenland by the Province of Burgenland through a tender procedure. In the final phase of the tender, two bids were submitted, one by the Austrian company GRAWE (EUR 100.3 million) and a much higher bid by a Ukrainian Consortium (EUR 155 million). The contract was awarded to GRAWE. The Commission found that the sale constituted State aid because, by not accepting the highest bid, the Province of Burgenland did not behave like a private seller operating in a market economy.

In its judgment, the General Court dismissed the actions brought by the Province of Burgenland, the Republic of Austria and the purchaser of the bank. It stated that, 'when the public authority makes use of an open, transparent and unconditional tender procedure, it can therefore be presumed that the market price corresponds to the highest offer, provided that it is established, firstly, that that offer is binding and credible and, secondly, that the taking into account of economic factors other than the price is not justified, such as the off balance-sheet risks existing between the offers'.[130]

In addition to that, the General Court clarified that, in the presence of binding and credible offers, independent studies, irrespective of the author or the date of submission or the analysis method adopted, were irrelevant for determining whether the price paid by the purchaser corresponded with the market price.[131]

The Court of Justice confirmed the reasoning of the General Court in its entirety[132] and it clarified that, even if in principle an expert's report prepared at the time of the transfer may be referred to as an alternative to the result of a public tendering,[133]

> where a public authority proceeds to sell an undertaking belonging to it by way of an open, transparent and unconditional tender procedure, it can be presumed that the market price corresponds to the highest offer, provided that it is established, first, that that offer is binding and credible and, secondly, that the consideration of economic factors other than the price is not justified.[134]

[130] Joined Cases T-268/01 and T-281/08, *Land Burgenland* v. *Austria*, para. 70.

[131] Ibid., para. 73.

[132] Joined Cases C-214/12 P, C-215/12 P and C-223/12 P, *Land Burgenland and Others* v. *Commission* ECLI:EU:C:2013:682.

[133] Ibid., para. 93; the Court refers to Case C-214/07, *Commission* v. *France* ECR I-8357, paras. 59 and 60.

[134] Ibid., para. 94.

If so – and this is the crucial point – there is no need 'to resort to other methods in order to check the market price, such as independent studies'.[135] With this judgment, the hierarchy between the two methods becomes more evident: a sale at market price is best assessed by means of an open and unconditional tendering procedure awarded to the highest bid. An independent evaluation method may be used, but not to overturn the outcome of a bidding procedure.

In *BVVG* the Court of Justice was later confronted with a different and somewhat peculiar case, where it seemingly took a view opposite *Land Burgenland*, introducing an exception to the rule of the finality of the result of a tender procedure in establishing the 'market value'.[136]

The case is already striking in that the BVVG was not the defendant, as it was in *Seydaland*, but the claimant in the proceedings before the national courts. The BVVG had concluded a 'sale and transfer' contract of agricultural land with Mr and Mrs Erbs following a public call for tenders in which they had made the highest bid. The local authority competent to authorise such a sale and the instrument recording that sale refused to approve the transaction on the ground that the price agreed was grossly disproportionate to the agricultural market value of the land at issue, that is, exceeding 'the agricultural market value of the land' at issue by more than 50 per cent. Under the applicable national legislation, adopted with the aim of safeguarding the interests of farmers that prices of the land still available do not become excessive, consent to sale could be refused when the consideration for the sale is grossly disproportionate to the value of piece of land and 'the agricultural market value of the land' corresponds to the price paid for land of the same type and the same situation in a transaction between two farmers. The denial of the authorisation was challenged by both Mr and Mrs Erbs and the BVVG but upheld by the lower courts. The Bundesgerichtshof (Federal Court of Justice) referred the case to the Court of Justice wondering whether the sale of publicly owned property by BVVG at a price below the one established by a public call for tenders amounts to preferential treatment of the purchaser caught under Article 107(1) TFEU.[137]

135 Ibid., para. 95; see also Quigley, *European State Aid Law and Policy*, 184.

136 Case C-39/14, *BVVG*. See also the comment by A. Giraud and S. Petit, 'Public Sales of Land in State Aid Law', *European State Aid Law Review* 1 (2016), 142.

137 As Giraud and Petit, 'Public Sales of Land in State Aid Law', 144, remark, the value of the transaction (about EUR 15,000) was such that most probably the trade among the Member States could not be affected, so State aids rules will anyway not apply.

The Court of Justice started its reasoning by reaffirming *Land Burgenland.*[138] Consequently, it acknowledged that the sale of land to someone not having offered the highest price based on the rule disqualifying tenders grossly exceeding the agricultural value of the land itself may amount to State aid in terms of foregone revenue.[139]

Nonetheless, the Court of Justice accepted that in some specific circumstances the sale to the highest bidder 'does not result in a price which corresponds to the market value of the property'.[140] It is important to stress that the Court did not allow to derogate from the market price criterion, but, echoing the Communication (see Section 5.4.2.1), although not referring to it explicitly, it held that the highest bid that is 'distinctly higher' than both the other bids submitted and the estimated value of the land may have a 'manifestly speculative nature'.[141] Lacking sufficient information on the method followed to estimate the value of the land in the case at hand, the Court referred the case back to the national court to assess whether this was indeed the case. In assessing the value of the land, the German court was directed to make sure that 'the method for valuing the agricultural land includes an update mechanism which takes into account the development of market prices in such a way that the estimate provided corresponds as closely as possible to the current market value of the land'.[142]

BVVG attests to the fact that attempts by the Member States to pursue additional policies when selling land will be treated as State aid. While this leaves open the question of whether the aid might be compatible, compatibility will have in most cases to be assessed by the Commission, following the notification procedure.

BVVG also highlighted the problematic nature of the exception concerning 'purely speculative bids' outlined by the 1997 Communication and its ruling was certainly not the outcome foreseen and desired by the Commission. So much so that its exception and any reference to the case in general have been entirely kept out from the subsequent and now

138 Case C-39/14, *BVVG*, para. 32; the Court refers to Joined Cases C-214/12 P, C-215/12 P and C-223/12 P, *Land Burgenland and Others* v. *Commission*, para. 94.

139 Case C-39/14, *BVVG*, para. 37.

140 Ibid., para. 39.

141 Ibid., para. 40. See also AG Villalon's opinion on case C-39/14, *BVVG*, delivered on 17 March 2015, paras. 69 ff. and Giraud and Petit, 'Public Sales of Land in State Aid Law', 143; see also Quigley, *European State Aid Law and Policy*, p. 184.

142 Case C-39/14, *BVVG*, para. 47; the Court refers here to Case C-239/09, *Seydaland*, para. 43.

applicable Commission Notice. The *BVVG* approach to the possible relevance of a 'purely speculative bid' has not been further followed in the case law, which instead reaffirmed the reasoning and the ruling of the *Land Burgenland* judgment.

The 1997 Communication has been finally repealed by the 2016 Commission Notice on the notion of State aid as referred to in Article 107(1) of the TFEU.[143] This Notice has taken a different approach from the previous Communication, building on the case law meanwhile developed by the Court and the relevant Commission decisions on the matter.

First of all, the Commission chose not to issue another sectoral guidance, but to insert the provisions regarding the sales of *assets, goods and services, or other comparable transactions* (such as the lease of certain goods or the grant of concessions for the commercial exploitation of natural resources) within the general notice on the notion of State aid.

Secondly, the notice locates all these indications in the section regarding the MEO test and in the subsection on the rules *establishing compliance with market conditions*. This reinforces the focal point, already discussed at length, under which the Commission generally wants to tackle the issue of government sales.

Thirdly, it sets a preliminary distinction between (a) situations in which the transaction's compliance with market conditions can be directly established through transaction-specific market data and (b) situations in which, due to the absence of such data, the transaction's compliance with market conditions has to be assessed on the basis of other available methods.

In the first case, it considers that, when a sale is conducted through a competitive, transparent, non-discriminatory and unconditional tender procedure, then its compliance with market conditions can be directly assessed, thus ruling out the presence of selective aid altogether.[144]

143 2016/C 262/01, para. 229.

144 The same applies in case of so-called *pari-passu transactions*, since:

> when a transaction is carried out under the same terms and conditions (and therefore with the same level of risk and rewards) by public bodies and private operators who are in a comparable situation (a 'pari passu' transaction), as may occur in public private partnerships, it can normally be inferred that such a transaction is in line with market conditions. In contrast, if a public body and private operators who are in a comparable situation take part in the same transaction at the same time but under different terms or conditions, this normally indicates that the intervention

The Notice takes a clearer and stricter approach towards conditionality than the previous 1997 Communication, stating that: 'If there is a condition that the buyer is to assume special obligations for the benefit of the public authorities or in the general public interest, which a private seller would not have demanded – other than those arising from general domestic law or a decision of the planning authorities –, the tender cannot be considered unconditional'.[145]

In contrast to the 1997 Communication, the Notice seems not to allow any space for the 'pure speculative bids exception', nor for the pursuing through the sale of any other regulatory policies, such as the prevention of public nuisance or the protection of the environment insofar as they are not already mandated by generally applicable rules. The only relevant criterion for selecting the buyer should be the highest offer, and solely conditions that would be set or considered by private vendors are admissible (such as vendor's sale guarantee or other post-sale commitments).[146]

Transactions have also to be '*in line with the principles of the TFEU on public procurement*'[147] for them to be considered to have been passed according to market terms. This appears to be consistent with the case law of the Court of Justice holding that, even if government sales do not fall within the scope of procurement Directives,[148] they are still bound to respect the general principles of the Treaties, that is, transparency, non-discrimination, fair competition and so on.[149] The enforcement of these principles is here instrumental in ensuring transactions on market terms and better enhancing the enforcement of State aid rules.

The rules for the bidding procedures foreseen in the Notice are quite minimal not just when compared with the very detailed provisions on advertisement and notices (including contract award notices) laid down in Directive 2014/24/EU on public procurement, but also with the 'light

of the public body is not in line with market conditions; see Notice on the notion of State aid, paras. 86 ff.

145 Notice on the notion of State aid, para. 94.

146 Ibid., para. 95.

147 Ibid., para. 89. See Chapter 2, Section 2.3.

148 Cases C-145/08 and 149/08, *Club Hotel Loutraki* ECR 2010 I-04165, para. 59; Case C-451/08, *Helmut Müller* ECR 2010 I-02673.

149 Reference is made both to the landmark *Teleaustria* judgment (Case C-324/98, *Teleaustria* ECR: 2000 I-10745, para. 62) and to the 2006 Commission Interpretative Communication on the Community law applicable to contract awards not or not fully subject to the provisions of the Public Procurement Directives (OJ 2006, No. C179/2).

regime' approach followed for the award of works and services concessions under Directive 2014/23/EU.

However, the Notice sets out a presumption, according to which: 'using and complying with the procedures provided for in the 2014 Public Procurement Directives, can be considered sufficient to meet the requirements above [namely to ensure a competitive, transparent, non-discriminatory and unconditional tender procedure] provided that all the conditions for the use of the respective procedure are fulfilled'.[150] As a consequence, the transaction is presumed not to involve State aid and, therefore, need not be notified.[151]

The Notices, though, set two exceptions where the presumption does not apply: first, in cases where 'it is impossible to establish a market price, such as the use of the negotiated procedure without publication of a contract notice'; secondly, if only one bid is submitted. In the latter case, the Notice considers that

> the procedure would not normally be sufficient to ensure a market price, unless either (i) there are particularly strong safeguards in the design of the procedure ensuring genuine and effective competition and it is not apparent that only one operator is realistically able to submit a credible bid or (ii) the public authorities verify through additional means that the outcome corresponds to the market price.[152]

Apparently, the type of procedures used seems irrelevant and that differs substantially from the Commission's approach in the SGEI Communication.[153] However, the wording of the Notice reveals that the reference to a negotiated procedure without prior notification is not exhaustive, thus leaving space for further exceptions. As observed, 'in reality this exemption constitutes a safety valve for the Commission to

150 Notice on the notion of State aid, para. 93.

151 See analysis in S. Arrowsmith, *The Law of Public and Utilities Procurement*, vol. I, 3rd ed. (London: Sweet & Maxwell, 2014), paras. 4-84 ff.

152 Again the Notice on the notion of State aid, para. 93.

153 2006 Commission Interpretative Communication on the Community law applicable to contract awards not or not fully subject to the provisions of the Public Procurement Directives, above fn; see also Arrowsmith, according to which for contracts excluded there should be as well a presumption that no aid is involved if procedures comparable to those of the procurement directives are followed. However, the author acknowledges that the presumption of compliance 'may not apply for some types of procedures that depart from the fundamental characteristics of the negotiated procedure with a call for competition – even if such procedures adequate to comply with Treaty obligations' (*The Law of Public and Utilities Procurement*, para. 4-84.).

scrutinise suspect contract awards under the State aid rules, even if the public procurement directives have been followed'.[154]

Indeed, the assumption that using procurement procedures rules out – always and automatically – the existence of State aid has been questioned.[155] Furthermore, in case of privatisation processes the Court of Justice has already ruled that using a competitive tender does not always rule out the presence of State aid (see Section 5.4.2.2).

That notwithstanding, the effect of such presumption is to de facto extend the use of procurement procedures also in relation to contracts that had been excluded from the scope of application of 2014 Directives. When Member States sell an asset, land and so on, they do not have to follow procurement procedures *per se*, but if they do so they are *tendentially* considered to be compliant with State aid rules, thus benefiting from the exemption of the burdensome prior notification to the Commission.[156] This inevitably expands the recourse to procurement-like procedures.

The recent parallel cases concerning the botched privatisation of the famous *Nürburgring* in Germany have shed some light on the connection between public procurement rules and the EU regime for sales.[157] The Nürburgring complex consists of a motor-car race track, a leisure park, hotels and restaurants. In 2012 the local court found that the regionally owned entity managing the track was insolvent and decided to proceed with the sale of their assets to Capricorn. A tender process was initiated and concluded with the sale of the assets. A public interest organisation

[154] Ølykke, 'Commission Notice on the Notion of State Aid', 204.

[155] See, among others, Ølykke, 'Commission Notice on the Notion of State Aid'; A. Sanchez-Graells, 'State Aid and EU Public Procurement, More Interactions, Fuzzier Boundaries', in L. Hancher and J. J. Piernas López (eds.), *Research Handbook on European State Aid Law*, 2nd ed. (London: Edward Elgar, 2020); Sanchez-Graells, 'Public Procurement and State Aid: Reopening the Debate?', *Public Procurement Law Review* 21(6) (2012), 205–212; P. E. Hasselgard, 'The Use of Tender Procedures to Exclude State Aid: The Situation under the EU 2014 Public Procurement Directives', *European Public Private Partnership Law Review* 1 (2017), 16; P. Nicolaides and I. E. Rusu, 'Competitive Selection of Undertakings and State Aid: Why and When Does It Not Eliminate Advantage?', *European Public Private Partnership Law Review* 7(1) (2012), 5–29.

[156] Arrowsmith, *The Law of Public and Utilities Procurement*, acknowledges that 'Any presumption that arises based on the nature of the award procedure is, however, *only* a presumption and an economic advantage can be found to exist in light of the specific content of a particular contract' (para. 4-83). In privatisation processes, the advantage might also depend on the State's treatment of the prior exposure of the sold company.

[157] Case C-647/19 P, *Ja zum Nürburgring eV* ECLI:EU:C:2021:666 and C-665/19 P, *Nexovation Inc.* ECLI:EU:C:2021:667.

and a competitor filed a complaint with the Commission, on the ground that the tender process was not open, transparent, non-discriminatory and unconditional. The Commission – and the General Court – saw no harm, but the Court of Justice acknowledged that the investors interested in purchasing the Nürburgring assets had been informed that they would be selected, inter alia, on the basis of the probability of closing the transaction and that one of the factors taken into consideration in that regard was the secured financing of their offer, supported by confirmation of financing partners. So much so that one suitor had been excluded for failing to provide such confirmation. The Court further found that the retained tenderer had only provided a non-binding letter of intent from a financing partner, so much so that it then soon defaulted, without anyone being answerable for its obligations. Therefore, it had received preferential treatment[158] and, on the facts of the case, the Commission could not be satisfied 'that acquisition was made at a price corresponding to the market price, which would be the case if it could be confirmed that the tender process was open, transparent, non-discriminatory and unconditional'.[159]

There is only so much that the *Nürburgring* can tell as to the extent of the parallelism between the requirements of State aids and the procurement procedures. What the Court of Justice considered when assessing whether the procedures met the general principles of competitive tendering was a rather blatant breach of the equal treatment principle.

In the other *Nürburgring* case, juicier issues had been raised. The appellant enterprise claimed that he had been misled about the applicable deadlines and given inaccurate information about existing contracts the buyer would have to live up to. It further lamented that an environmental selection criterion had been introduced subsequently in the tender process, without being communicated to all the tenderers. Finally, it raised a number of further issues about the transparency of the tender procedure. Those included the fact that no announcement of the tender process was made outside the EU; that copies of all the documents for the tender process had not been provided in English and that the same partner in a prominent American law firm had advised both the sellers and Capricorn.

Some of those issues might have brought to light limits to the parallelism between the requirements of State aids and the procurement

[158] Case C-647/19 P, *Ja zum Nürburgring eV*, para. 127.

[159] Ibid., paras. 123 ff.

procedures. A market participant looking for maximum competition and value maximisation would have looked for a worldwide advertisement and possibly translated into English all relevant documents. But neither is required under the public procurement and concession rules as they stand now. On the other hand, the requirement that a measure bears (potential for) distortion of competition is arguably to be understood as a distortion *in* the internal market. Be it as it may be, the Court was content to find a macroscopic breach of the transparency principle and did not go further.

As the Notice on the notion of State aids acknowledges, if the transaction has not been carried out through competitive, transparent, non-discriminatory and unconditional procedures, this does not automatically mean that it does not comply with market conditions[160] or that it involves State aid.[161] Consequently, it allows to prove such compliance through benchmarking or other assessment methods, also including generally accepted standard assessment methodologies.

The Notice reaffirms that these methodologies must be based on the available objective, verifiable and reliable data,[162] which should be sufficiently detailed and should reflect the economic situation at the time at which the transaction was decided, taking into account the level of risk and future expectations.[163] However, it also considers that the appropriate assessment methodology may depend on the market situation, data availability or the type of transaction.

It holds that, in case of sales of land, an independent expert evaluation prior to the sale negotiations to establish the market value on the basis of generally accepted market indicators and valuation standards is in principle satisfactory.[164] This seems to confirm – although it is not stated expressly, as it was in the previous 1997 Communication – that in the case of sale of land the independent expert valuation rules out the duty to prior notification,[165] whereas this methodology is considered not to guarantee such presumption in case of privatisation schemes (see Section 5.4.2.2).

160 Notice on the notion of State aid, para. 97; Case T-488/11, *Sarc* v. *Commission* ECLI:EU:T:2014:497, § 98.

161 See Arrowsmith, *The Law of Public and Utilities Procurement*, para. 4-85.

162 T-274/01, *Valmont Nederland BV* v. *Commission* ECLI:EU:T:2004:266, para. 71.

163 Case T-366/00, *Scott* v. *Commission*, para. 158.

164 Notice on the notion of State aid, para. 103.

165 Ibid., para. 103.

Unlike the 1997 Communication and in accordance with the evolution of the case law, the Notice does not put competitive tendering and the other methodologies on an equal footing. Instead, it sets a hierarchy of assessment methods stating that 'A transaction's compliance with market conditions can be directly established through transaction-specific market information in the following situations: (i) where the transaction is carried out 'pari passu' by public entities and private operators';[166] or (ii) where it concerns the sale and purchase of assets, goods and services (or other comparable transactions) carried out through a competitive, transparent non-discriminatory and unconditional tender procedure.

The Notice stresses that if the specific market information concerning the transaction shows that it does not comply with market conditions, 'it would not normally be appropriate to use other assessment methodologies to reach a different conclusion'.[167] It infers that when the market price is set through an open and unconditional tender, the result (i.e. the selling in favour to the highest bidder) cannot be questioned by using different methodologies, such as the independent evaluation; therefore, neither the Commission nor the selling authority are obliged to resort to other methods in order to check the market price. Rather, they are prevented from doing so. In stating this, the Notice intends to overcome, without even referring to it, the ruling reached by the Court in *BVVG* and to reaffirm *Land Burgenland*.

5.4.2.2 Privatisation Processes

The framework outlined above and the relevant case law of the Court of Justice are in principle applicable to any form of government sale; however, when the sale consists or is part of a larger privatisation scheme, complexity increases and the procedure will follow further specific rules. Privatisations of big assets, including large companies, are way more difficult from the point of view of the procedures to be followed.[168] More often than not privatisation schemes are 'part of an ongoing highly politicised process' and politics determines the choices in the ways they are effectuated.[169]

166 Ibid., para. 86.

167 Notice on the notion of State aid, para. 85, referring to *Land Burgenland* case (GC), paras. 94–95.

168 World Bank, *From Plan to Market*, 50.

169 Megginson and Netter, 'From State to Market', 388. See also M. Andrews, 'State-Owned Banks, Stability, Privatization, and Growth', International Monetary Fund Working Paper, 2005, 20, characterising privatisation as 'a political process'.

A decent approximation to 'normal' is the choice between the placement of shares, possibly floating them on the stock market, and/or through direct sales.[170] It is worth noting that the form of 'direct sale' might involve either negotiations or tendering of the public assets or of the whole company. Privatisation through sale of State property may thus take two main forms: 'The first is direct sales (or asset sales) of State-owned enterprises (or some parts thereof) to an individual, an existing corporation, or a group of investors. The second form is share issue privatisations (SIPs), in which some or all of a government's stake in a SOE is sold to investors through a public share offering'.[171]

But the picture may be much more complicated. For instance, the Polish Act on Commercialization and Privatization 1996 foresees a panoply of privatisation mechanisms, including public offer; public tender; negotiation following public invitation; by accepting an offer in response to an invitation announced by virtue of the provisions of the Act on Public Offerings; a publicly announced auction, if the selling price is not lower than the book value of the shares; sale of shares on a regulated market within the meaning of the Act on Trading in Financial Instruments and so on.[172]

The current Notice on the notion of State aid does not distinguish between sales of land and sales of shares or other assets, but, after setting the general principles applicable to all types of allocating procedures, it deals with some specific issues, which normally emerge in privatisation processes.

This is so, in particular, with the possible prior economic exposure that the sold undertaking might have, since 'the fact that the public body concerned has prior economic exposure to an undertaking should be taken into consideration when examining whether a transaction is in line with market conditions, provided that a comparable private operator could have such prior exposure (for example in its capacity of shareholder of an undertaking)'.[173]

The Court of Justice indeed confirmed that 'a private shareholder may reasonably subscribe the capital necessary to secure the survival of an

[170] See, with reference to the privatisation of banks, Andrews, 'State-Owned Banks, Stability, Privatization, and Growth', 22 ff.

[171] Megginson and Netter, 'From State to Market', 339.

[172] B. McKenzie, 'Doing Business in Poland', 2016, 29, available at www.bakermckenzie.com/-/media/files/expertise/ma-resources/Doing_Business_in_Poland_2016.pdf.

[173] Notice on the notion of State aid, para. 106.

undertaking which is experiencing temporary difficulties but is capable of becoming profitable again, possibly after a reorganization'. Following the same approach, it held that a sale may be completed at a negative price, inter alia through prior recapitalisation by the vendor, and still be, in principle, at market price.[174] The same goes for governments acting as shareholders. As pointed out in Section 5.3, the interest behind privatisation may be to avoid or mitigate future losses.

The Court has, however, early on excluded any balancing of the MEO test with other 'public considerations' since 'in the case of an undertaking whose capital is held by the public authorities, the test is, in particular, whether in similar circumstances a private shareholder, having regard to the foreseeability of obtaining a return and leaving aside all social, regional-policy and sectoral considerations, would have subscribed the capital in question'[175] (but see below for further consideration in relation to *SNCM*).

This means that, under EU law, a privatisation measure by a Member State pursuing economic policy considerations, such as, for instance, benefiting smallholding farmers or fostering popular capitalism, will most probably be found in breach of market freedom and be treated as State aid with very little chances of being found compatible with the Treaty in the ensuing notification procedure as was the case in *BVVG*.[176]

The underlying issue here is how to consider – and somewhat neutralise – the circumstance that an undertaking prior to its restructuring or privatisation might have benefitted from State aid (needless to say the issue becomes more intricate if the State aid is later declared unlawful and needs to be recovered).[177]

This, in turn, recalls the complex distinction between the State acting as a public authority or as a private operator/shareholder, which runs throughout the entire regulation regarding government sales, and State aid in general.[178]

In general terms, the State might indeed concede aid to undertakings, provided that (i) they respect the policies set out at the EU level and (ii) are scrutinised and declared compatible by the Commission (see Sections

[174] Case C-127/16 P, *SNCF Mobilités* v. *Commission*, para. 79.

[175] Case C-234/84, *Belgium* v. *Commission*, para. 14.

[176] Case C-39/14, *BVVG*, ECLI:EU:C:2015:470.

[177] See, for example, Case C-127/16 P, *SNCF Mobilités* v. *Commission*.

[178] On the 'Dual capacity of the State' and the application of the MEO test, see Cyndecka, *The Market Economy Investor Test in EU State Aid Law*, paras. 5.1 ff.

5.4.1 and 5.4.3); in relation to such measures the State acts as a public authority and the MEO test (and its declinations) does not apply. If instead it acts in its quality of shareholder of a given company, it cannot take into account conditions and costs other than those a private operator would consider and bear. The problem arises when the State is a shareholder – thus, is generally responsible for the undertakings' liabilities only up to the value of the subscribed capital – but instead it tries to extend these liabilities and to take into account costs that are not connected with its shareholder position. In other words, when it decides in the counterfactual scenario whether it is more convenient to wind up or to privatise a given entity it improperly takes into account costs (especially social costs deriving from the liquidation process) that it would have not to face as a shareholder but 'in a different stage and dimension' as a public authority.

This was indeed the case with the *Hytasa* judgment where the Court first outlined this dual capacity of the State.[179] The case concerned three Spanish ailing companies, which had received substantial funding from the Spanish government for years. Eventually, due to the chronic unprofitability of the three undertakings, the government decided to privatise them, considering this as the most viable option; this was also because it considered, in the counterfactual scenario of the liquidation, costs such as salaries and unemployment benefits that would be charged to the State in its public authority capacity. To further support the privatisations, the term of the sale included substantial capital injections in favour of the companies.

The Court of Justice held that – even if a parent company may also, for a limited period, bear the losses of one of its subsidiaries in order to enable the latter to close down its operations under the best possible conditions – 'a private investor pursuing a structural policy – whether general or sectoral – and guided by prospects of viability in the long term could not reasonably allow itself, after years of continuous losses, to make a contribution of capital which, in economic terms, proves to be not only costlier than selling the assets, but is moreover linked to the sale of the undertaking, which removes any hope of profit, even in the longer term'.[180]

[179] Joined Cases C-278/92, C-279/92 and C-280/92, *Kingdom of Spain* v. *Commission* ECR 1994 I-04103. Hytasa was the name of one of the three ailing companies.

[180] Joined Cases C-278/92, C-279/92 and C-280/92, *Kingdom of Spain* v. *Commission*, para. 26.

The 2014 Rescue and Restructuring Guidelines[181] have been issued by the Commission precisely on the ground that Member States may seek to maximise the proceeds resulting from privatisation through prior restructuring of the target company, in order to raise the interest with potential buyers. However, Member States cannot do so when they (decide to) sell the company and in the context of such an economic transaction (see Section 5.4.3).[182]

The Court confirmed its approach in the *Gröditzer* judgment, where it found that, in order to establish whether the privatisation of the GS company (whose shares were taken over by a German body governed by public law responsible for restructuring and privatising undertakings in the Länder) for a negative selling price of DEM 340 million involved elements of State aid: 'it is necessary to assess whether, in similar circumstances, a private investor of a dimension comparable to that of the bodies managing the public sector could have been prevailed upon to make capital contributions of the same size in connection with the sale of that undertaking or whether it would instead have chosen to wind it up'.[183] The Court held that in order to do so the liquidation costs to be considered should not include costs linked to the responsibilities of the public authorities, but only costs that a rational market operator would incur. In the case at hand, the Court then concluded that Germany did not properly assess the 'prior exposure' of the GS; hence, its choice to sell it – even if through an open, transparent and competitive tender – instead of winding it up did not respect the MEO test.

It is interesting to note that the Court considered that the subsequent use of an open, transparent and unconditional procedure 'is not such as to challenge the finding that the option of privatising GS at a negative selling price did not satisfy the private investor test and therefore entailed elements of State aid'.[184] Otherwise said, the fact that the allocating procedure is

181 Guidelines on State aid for rescuing and restructuring non-financial undertakings in difficulty (R&R Guidelines) (2014/C 249/01); see also Commission Staff Working Document, Guidance Paper on state aid-compliant financing, restructuring and privatisation of State-owned enterprises, SWD(2012) 14 final.

182 As pointed out, in relation to measures taken in the context of financial crisis 'the objective of combating the financial crisis is, irrespective of how laudable it is, immaterial under the MEIP. Remedying the consequences of the systemic crisis falls within the public policy remit. Thus, accepting it would contradict the core of the MEIP' (Cyndecka, *The Market Economy Investor Test in EU State Aid Law*, para. 5.4.2.3.4).

183 Case C-334/99, *Germany* v. *Commission*, para. 133.

184 Para. 142.

conducted through competitive tendering might not be sufficient since the choice itself to privatise rather than to go into liquidation might amount to a breach of the MEO principle.[185] Therefore, the presumption set out in the 2016 Notice concerning procurement-like procedures needs to be properly interpreted and coordinated with these elements of prior exposure and activities (usually in the restructuring phase) that precedes the tender and that the tender itself is not sufficient to neutralise.

In some rather exceptional cases, the Commission has tried to soften this approach considering that some social costs could in principle be taken into account by market operators when they were, in particular, aimed at protecting the selling public shareholder's brand image.[186]

This was indeed the case in relation to the *SNCM* privatisation process, where the Commission held that:

> large groups of undertakings currently cannot, when they close sites or wind up subsidiaries, disregard the social consequences which such closures or liquidations involve. Accordingly, more often than not they carry out social plans which may include measures for the redeployment of staff, assistance in finding work, redundancy payments and even action at the local economic level, which go beyond the requirements of statutory provisions and collective agreements.[187]

Therefore, the Commission took the view that 'in the event of SNCM's liquidation, such measures would have been introduced which exceeded any statutory obligations with the aim of avoiding *harming the brand image of the holding company* to which it belongs and its ultimate shareholder'.[188]

However, both the General Court[189] and the Court of Justice[190] concluded that the Commission did not provide sufficient evidence to support its conclusions.[191] The General Court acknowledged that 'in a

[185] The issue had already been raised in the *Hytasa* judgment, where, however, the tendering procedure was not considered unconditional, since the sale conditions included an undertaking on the part of the purchasers not to sell the companies during a period ranging from three to four years (see reasoning at paras. 27–28).

[186] See general analysis in Cyndecka, *The Market Economy Investor Test in EU State Aid Law*, para. 5.4.2.4 and the other Commission decisions and case law herein cited.

[187] 2009/611/EC: Commission Decision of 8 July 2008 concerning the measures C 58/02 (ex N 118/02), which France has implemented in favour of the Société Nationale Maritime Corse-Méditerranée (SNCM), OJ 2009, No. L225/180, paras. 267–270.

[188] Para. 270.

[189] Case T-565/08, *Corsica Ferries France* ECLI:EU:T:2012:415.

[190] Joined Cases C-533/12 P and C-536/12, *SNCM and France* v. *CFF* ECLI:EU:C:2014:2142.

[191] See also analysis in T. Bruyninckx, 'Quality Requirements to the Application of the "Private Investor Test"?', *European State Aid Law Quarterly* 14(2) (2015), 291.

social market economy, a reasonable private investor would not disregard, first, its responsibility towards all the stakeholders in the company and, second, the development of the social, economic and environmental context in which it continues to develop'.[192] However, the Court considered that 'the assumption of the burden of those additional costs, because of legitimate concerns, cannot follow an exclusively social, even political, objective, as it would otherwise go beyond the framework of the private investor test'.[193] Therefore, the protection of the brand image of a Member State as a global investor in the market economy cannot constitute by itself sufficient justification to demonstrate the long-term economic rationale of the assumption of additional costs. Furthermore, the Court stresses the difference between the image of the company itself (which might be taken into consideration provided that there is an economic rationale attached to it) and the brand image of the Member State, as referred to by the Commission (whose protection cannot constitute a valid objective under the MEO test and it might instead distort competition).[194]

Concerning the procedures to be followed to avoid State aid scrutiny, guidance is offered by the 2012 'Commission Staff Working Document Guidance Paper on State aid-compliant financing, restructuring and privatization of State-owned enterprises',[195] which, in turn, builds on the 1993 Commission's XXIII Report on Competition Policy.[196] This report has remained the main guidance regarding privatisation processes, and it is still currently referred to both by the Commission[197] and by the case law of the Court of Justice.[198] Accordingly, the Commission distinguished, in principle, three different methods of privatisation: (1) through the sale of shares on a stock exchange, which, as a rule, excludes aid; (2) through a tender procedure, which must be open, transparent

[192] Ibid., para. 82.

[193] Ibid., para. 84.

[194] Ibid., para. 85.

[195] SWD(2012)14 final.

[196] Publications Office of the European Union, 'EU Publications', available at http://bookshop.europa.eu/is-bin/INTERSHOP.enfinity/WFS/EU-Bookshop-Site/en_GB/-/EUR/ViewPublication-Start?PublicationKey=CM8294650.

[197] See, as a recent example, the Decision regarding the privatisation of the HSH Nord Bank (State aid no. SA.29338, SA.44910 and SA.52288 (2018/N) – Germany Sale of HSH Nordbank AG, C(2018) 7783), available at https://ec.europa.eu/competition/elojade/isef/case_details.cfm?proc_code=3_SA_44910.

[198] *Ex multis*, see Case *Land Burgenland*, paras. 19 ff.

and unconditional, while the undertaking must be sold to the highest bidder; (3) through a sale preceded by an expert evaluation.[199]

To ensure consistency with State aid rules, the preferred privatisation method is the sale of shares on the stock exchange;[200] however, this is not always possible or expedient.

The alternative is the, already familiar, open, transparent and unconditional competitive tender. The Commission Staff Working Paper provides a number of cumulative conditions that 'should be observed in order to exclude, without further examination, the presence of State aid and thus prior notification to the Commission'.[201]

The procedure must first be open to all comers. In no case may there be discrimination based on the nationality of prospective buyers of the shares or assets (thus confirming the interaction and the shared goals with the principles of free movement, see above).

The procedure must also be transparent: 'Bidders must be given enough time and information to carry out a proper valuation of the assets as the basis for their bid'.[202] The tender must be sufficiently well publicised, meaning that, according to the circumstances, it must be advertised 'over a reasonably long period' in the national or international press and/or other appropriate publications. Additionally, for privatisation that may attract investors from abroad, the tender 'should also be made known through agents addressing clients on a Europe-wide or international scale'.[203]

The Commission Staff Working Paper is somehow trying to pre-empt what might be a *BVVG*-type exception, clearly stating that 'company/ assets must be sold to the highest bidder'.[204] The same could be said regarding the treatment of conditionality: it is repeated that, to avoid State aid implications, 'the conditions (express or *de facto*) related to

[199] European Commission, *XXIII Report on Competition Policy of 1993*, pp. 255–261; see Cyndecka, *The Market Economy Investor Test in EU State Aid Law*, para. 5.4.1.

[200] See also Quigley, *European State Aid Law and Policy*, p. 183.

[201] SWD(2012)14 final, point 5; later on, the Working Paper adds that 'If the conditions above are not complied with, privatisations carried out by trade sales must be notified to the Commission'.

[202] Ibid.

[203] Ibid.

[204] SWD(2012)14 final, point 5. Notably, the Working paper was issued prior to the *BVVG* case, which showed how such 'purely speculative bid' exception might lead to the subversion of the result of a tendering procedure, a result that, as contended, was not properly foreseen nor desired by the Commission.

privatisation must be of such kind that all potential buyers would be able to meet them'.[205]

By insisting on the highest price and therefore return maximisation, the Working Paper seems to rule out the legality of conditions going beyond applicable legislation and concerning, for instance, environmental or social interests. More specifically, the Working Paper expressly excludes industrial policy conditions limiting the choices of the potential buyer. Tenders are considered conditional when making 'it practically impossible for a potential investor intending to follow a different industrial strategy to win the bid simply by offering the highest price', and refers to its decision in the *Automobile Craiova* case.[206]

The concerns that Member States might still pursue illegal industrial policy practices even when apparently retreating from the market may be well grounded. Those concerns are more acute when what is sold is not just land or buildings, but undertakings actually offering goods and services on the market and employing hundreds of workers. The same will be the case when the privatisation is pursued in a manner other than through stock-exchange flotation or through open, transparent and unconditional competitive tender.[207]

The Staff-Working document provides a set of relevant examples where it considers that the above conditions are not respected; hence, where the presence of State aid cannot be excluded and the sale needs to be notified to the Commission:

> This is so in particular in case of (i) sales after negotiation with a single prospective purchaser or a number of selected bidders; (ii) sales preceded by the writing-off of debt by the State, other public enterprises or any public body, and sales preceded by the conversion of debt into equity or capital increases (see section above on preparatory measures); and (iii) sales on conditions that are not customary in comparable transactions between private parties.[208]

[205] Ibid.

[206] 2008/717/EC: Commission Decision of 27 February 2008 on State aid C 46/07 (ex NN 59/07) implemented by Romania for Automobile Craiova (formerly Daewoo Romania) OJ 2008, No. L 239/12; 1999/720/EC, ECSC: Commission Decision of 8 July 1999 on State aid granted by Germany to Gröditzer Stahlwerke GmbH and its subsidiary Walzwerk Burg GmbH, OJ 1999, No. L 292/27 is also referred to.

[207] SWD(2012)14 final, point 5.

[208] Ibid.

The Court of Justice confirmed this approach in the complex *SNCF* judgment.[209] In essence, Sernam, one of the controlled companies of the Société Nationale des Chemins de fer Français (SNCF) group (the French national State-owned railway company), had been granted a State aid measure within the context of a restructuring plan. Later, the Commission found out the aid had been misused but outlined two possibilities under which the aid measure could have been declared compatible with the internal market. One of the possibilities given by the Commission to 'neutralise' the misused aid was to sell 'en bloc' all assets of Sernam at market price through a transparent and open procedure to a company that had no legal link with the SNCF.[210] However, Sernam's economic situation failed to elicit any proposals based on a positive valuation in the call for tenders conducted on SNCF's behalf by a bank. All the offers submitted under that open and transparent procedure concluded that the value was very negative and no binding offers were submitted. In particular, there were two offers: one by candidate 4, which valued the assets at minus EUR 65.2 million and another offer by a consortium established by candidate 5, who was associated with Sernam's management team (Financière Sernam), which valued the assets at minus EUR 56.4 million. As no firm offer had been submitted, the decision was taken to continue the discussions solely with the consortium. Later on, however, candidate 5 informed SNCF that it was not able to submit a binding offer, not even a conditional one. Financière Sernam then submitted a different binding autonomous offer at a sensibly lower value of minus EUR 95.5 million. Eventually, SNCF decided to conclude the sale with Financière Sernam accepting its second 'solo offer'.

The Commission issued a decision contesting, among other things, that the sale process had not been the result of an open, transparent procedure under market terms. SNCF challenged the decision before the General Court, which considered that the discussions should have logically continued with the 'last interested party' and therefore SNCF should have turned to candidate 4, which had participated in the procedure from the start and submitted a preliminary second-round offer of minus EUR

[209] Case T-242/12, *SNCF Mobilités* v. *Commission*; then confirmed in Case C-127/16 P, *SNCF Mobilités* v. *Commission* EU:C:2018:165. See analysis in J. A. Vaglio, 'MEOP, Economic Continuity and Distortions of Competition in the Sernam Case', *European State Aid Law Review*, 3 (2019), 418.

[210] Case C-127/16 P, *SNCF Mobilités* v. *Commission*, para. 7; Article 3, para. 2 of *Sernam* 2 Decision.

65.2 million; the fact that the candidate did not submit a firm offer was considered to be irrelevant. The Court of Justice upheld the first instance judgment. After reaffirming that the question of whether a specific tender procedure has been open, transparent and unconditional has to be answered on the basis of 'a body of indicia specific to the circumstances of each case',[211] the Court considered that since in the present case the successful bid did not originate from a candidate who had participated autonomously in the tendering procedure from the beginning of that procedure, then the requirement of an open and transparent procedure had not been observed.[212]

It is worth mentioning that SNCF contended that 'EU law authorises the award of contracts to an economic operator without prior publicity or competition following the failure of a procedure, even where the operator did not participate in that first procedure and without this constituting a breach of the principles of openness and transparency'.[213] Hence, those principles should a fortiori be deemed to have been observed where the assets have been transferred, as in the case at hand, to a party that has participated in the process initially as part of a consortium from which the other party withdrew in the course of the procedure and later as an autonomous bidder. The Court, however, chose not to rule on such a potential analogy, since it regarded the circumstance that the appellant did not participate autonomously to the tender from the beginning as a sufficient ground to reject the applicant's argument.[214]

Concerning other assessment methodologies, it is worth remarking that the Working Paper does not consider recourse to an expert valuer as an alternative and sufficient mechanism to avoid State aid scrutiny (and the prior notification) in privatisation processes.[215] This method is

211 Case C-127/16 P, *SNCF Mobilités* v. *Commission*, para. 68 (see also C-277/00, *Germany* v. *Commission*, para. 95).

212 Ibid., para. 69. See also AG Mengozzi's opinion in Case C-127/16 P, *SNCF Mobilité*, delivered on 20 July 2017, para. 66.

213 Case C-127/16 P, *SNCF Mobilités* v. *Commission*, para. 64.

214 This outcome seems in line with the current Article 26(4)(b) of Directive 2014/24/EU of the European Parliament and of the Council of 26 February 2014 on public procurement and repealing Directive 2004/18/EC Text with EEA relevance, OJ 2014, No. L94/65; see, however, the discussion of A. Sanchez Graells, 'Do EU Procurement & State Aid Rules Conflict on Possibility of Consortium Members "Go It Alone"?', 2018, available at www.howtocrackanut.com/blog/2018/3/20/do-eu-public-procurement-and-state-aid-rules-conflict-on-the-possibility-for-consortium-members-to-go-solo-c-12716-p.

215 See also XXIII Commission Report on competition, para. 403.

normally limited to simpler transactions, like the sale of land and buildings, as confirmed also in the later Commission Notice on the Notion of State aid.[216]

Another leading case is the already mentioned *Land Burgenland* judgment, whose facts now deserve to be presented in more detail. The HYPO Bank Burgenland AG was a regional bank wholly owned by Land Burgenland and, according to Austrian legislation, it was liable as a deficiency guarantor for all the bank's liabilities. After two unsuccessful attempts, in 2005 Land Burgenland launched a third privatisation procedure with the publication in the press of a call for tenders and with the assistance of a leading bank advisory group. Bids were received from Grazer Wechselseitige Versicherung (GRAWE), an Austrian undertaking, and from a Consortium consisting of two Austrian undertakings and two Ukrainian joint-stock companies. Those offers were subject to an individual examination and following contractual negotiations, which ended on 4 March 2006. On the recommendation of the advisor, the contract was awarded to GRAWE despite the purchase price offered being significantly lower than the one offered by the Consortium. The advisor suggested preferring GRAWE on its reliability concerning both the payment of the purchase price and the continuation of the operation of the bank. That was relevant for the Land that had provided a guarantee in case of default of the bank.

Informed by the Consortium, the Commission initiated the formal examination procedure to determine whether GRAWE had received a selective advantage. According to the Commission, a private vendor might accept the lower bid instead of the higher bid in two situations: (a) when it is obvious that the sale to the highest bidder is not reliable, and (b) in other situations where a private vendor would take into account factors other than the price.

Concerning (a), the Commission dismissed the worries expressed by the advisor, and concerning (b), the private vendor test would not allow Land Burgenland to take into account the risks stemming from potential liability to make payment under a guarantee which had been classified as State aid in a previous decision.[217] According to the Commission, the role of the State as the seller of an undertaking and its obligations in its capacity as a public authority should not be mixed up.

216 Notice on the notion of State aid, para. 103.

217 Commission Decision C(2003) 1329 final of 30 April 2003, relating to aid E 8/02, was adopted, OJ 2003, No. C 175/8.

Confirming the first instance judgment,[218] the Court of Justice reaffirmed that 'when applying the private investor test, it must be determined whether the measures in question are those which such an investor, who counts on making a profit in the short or long term, could have granted'.[219] However, 'by granting aid, a Member State pursues, by definition, objectives other than that of making a profit from the resources granted to an undertaking belonging to it, it must be held that those resources are, in principle, granted by the State exercising its prerogatives as a public authority'.[220]

Of specific interest in relation to privatisation is the issue of the determination of the market price, which the Commission had identified on the sole basis of the Consortium's bid. The Court of Justice recalled its settled case law on the market economy investor principle (MEIP) test.[221] Then, it reaffirmed that even if an expert's report prepared at the time of the transfer may be referred to as an alternative to the result of a public tendering,[222]

> where a public authority proceeds to sell an undertaking belonging to it by way of an open, transparent and unconditional tender procedure, it may be presumed that the market price corresponds to the highest offer, provided that it is established, first, that that offer is binding and credible and, secondly, that the consideration of economic factors other than the price is not justified.[223]

If so, there is no need 'to resort to other methods in order to check the market price, such as independent studies'.[224]

5.4.3 Balancing Public Interests

In the previous section, it was clarified that, for what concerns process, the EU law-preferred avenue is a competitive and transparent bidding procedure, to which placement of shares on the stock market is equated. The analysis will focus on State aid.

218 Joined Cases T-268/08 and T-281/08, *Land Burgenland and Austria* v. *Commission*.
219 Ibid., para. 48; see also para. 52, where the precedents are discussed.
220 Ibid., para. 56.
221 Ibid., para. 92; the Court refers to Case C-390/98, *Banks* ECR I-6117, para. 77, and Case C-277/00, *Germany* v. *Commission*, para. 80.
222 Ibid., para. 93; the Court refers to Case C-214/07, *Commission* v. *France* ECR I-8357, paras. 59–60.
223 Ibid., para. 94.
224 Ibid., para. 95; see also Quigley, *European State Aid Law and Policy*, p. 184.

The present section outlines a set of both process- and output-related public interests that the Member States can pursue through government sales while complying with EU law. The paramount goal of EU State aid law is the compliance with the MEO test. In terms of public interests, this means that EU law pursues raising money or value maximisation/minimisation of future costs as output interests. Process is the way to assess the achievement or otherwise of these interests. Under EU law, process-related interests are allowed and favoured insofar as they are instrumental in ensuring transactions under market terms. Other output-related public interests such as additional policies may be pursued by the Member States insofar as they are not inconsistent with the MEO principle or, if they are, may be allowed by the Commission under Article 107(3) TFEU.

A first, more complex subsection will analyse the full interplay among the relevant interests allowed by the use of competitive tendering or analogous mechanisms such as floating on a stock market. The following subsection will outline which process-related interests are still relevant when different mechanisms are used by Member States for selling or privatising.

5.4.3.1 Through Competitive Tendering

The previous sections presented what is to be considered a competitive tendering in case of government sales and which characteristics it shall have in order to comply with the relevant EU legal framework. This section will now examine whether an open, transparent, well-publicised and unconditional tendering procedure allows the allocating authorities to pursue other public interests.

Competitive tendering procedures in general are structurally designed based on rules derived from process-related interests such as transparency and fair and equal treatment in order to achieve both process-related interests, such as accountability, integrity and efficiency, and output-related interests such as value for money.[225] The enforcement of these principles is in turn instrumental in ensuring transactions on market terms and better enhancing the enforcement of State aid rules. This explains why the relevant EU framework revealed a strong favour towards competitive tendering procedures.

[225] See in general Arrowsmith, *The Law of Public and Utilities Procurement*, paras. 3–12 ff.; A. Sanchez-Graells, *Public Procurement and the EU Competition Rules* (London: Hart, 2015), pp. 101 ff.

As a matter of fact, an MEO is by definition searching for the best value for money. In turn, the pursuit of the best value for money partially corresponds to the principle of raising money or value maximisation/minimisation of future costs, which, as shown, might drive government sales and privatisations (see Section 5.3). Also, the concept of best value for money relates to that of government efficiency, insofar as it allows governments to get the most out of what they sell. If so, then also other interests, such as, for instance, the reduction of national debts, avoiding unnecessary taxation and possibly also developing capital markets (but not popular capitalism), are better pursued by means of a competitive tendering.

The same results are achieved when the government sale involves floating shares on the stock market. Indeed, the Commission working paper on privatisations considered the sale in the stock exchange as the most suitable sale methodology (although arguably the focus there was strictly on State aid law compliance).[226]

The underlying idea at the EU level is that competitive tendering procedures allow better to achieve the best value for money when compared to direct sales or other non-competitive tendering procedures, irrespective of the 'object' tendered and the conditions attached to it. Noteworthy, procurement procedures are also based upon this fundamental assumption.

Competitive tendering procedures are also designed to comply with the process-related interests of transparency and accountability and their corollaries, as well as to that of equal treatment. In relation to the achievement of such interests, competitive tendering procedures clearly represent a more suitable option and the Notice itself makes express reference to the general principles of the Treaties on public procurement, that is, transparency, non-discrimination, fair competition and so on.[227]

More generally, the Notice aims at re-establishing a high degree of convergence with public procurement law and especially with procurement procedures. Arguably, nothing less than those standards might be now considered sufficient to meet State aid requirements, and, in turn, these standards might allow ensuring transparency, accountability and so on. The presumption laid down by paragraph 93 of the Notice arguably determines the effect of extending the application of procurement procedures also to some excluded contracts such as government sales.

[226] Commission Staff Working Paper, 11.

[227] Notice on the notion of State aid, para. 89.

EU State aid law is built around a strong synergy between developed procedure-related interests and output-related interests consistent with the MEO. As it stands now, it is suspicious, when not outright hostile, towards those various interests related to additional policies. This translates into the prohibition of conditionality set by the 2016 Notice but built upon the predominant case law.

This approach drives a wedge between EU State aid and public procurement law.[228] Paragraph 174 of the Notice clarifies that tenders are unconditional only if they do not contain any conditions that the buyer is to assume special obligations for the benefit of the public authorities or in the general public interest, which a private seller would not have demanded, other than those arising from general domestic law or a decision of the planning authorities. A number of provisions in the 2014 procurement and concessions directives instead allow public buyers to pursue environmental and social policies – part of what are labelled as additional considerations in the present research – while requiring that the specific conditions set out in the tender are linked to the subject matter of the public contract and comply with the transparency principle.[229] The same interest of best value for money does not need to be understood merely in strictly economic terms and the use of procurement-like procedures remains neutral in regard to the interests pursued.[230]

Concerning government sales through competitive tenders, the Notice instead focuses exclusively on the highest price criterion and strictly related economic criteria (e.g. the binding and credible nature of the offer).

The approach set out by the Notice seems to rule out the possibility of pursuing or balancing any substantial interest other than value

[228] As noted,

> In the light of the definition of 'relation to the subject matter of the contract' in art. 67(3) in the Public Contracts Directive, which adopts a broad definition, a possible clash between the Commission's interpretation of the rules on State aid and the public procurement directives could be identified. The reason for the strict approach from the Commission could be explained by the fact that the market economy operator ('MEO') principle is the template used.
>
> (Ølykke, 'Commission Notice on the notion of state aid', 204)

[229] See Chapter 2, Section 2.3.

[230] See comments to Articles 18, 42, 43, 67, 68 and 70 in R. Caranta and A. Sanchez-Graells (eds.), *European Public Procurement: Commentary on Directive 2014/24/EU* (London: Edward Elgar, 2021).

maximisation/minimisation of future costs, since 'to accept that the State acted as a mirror image of a private investor, the transaction as a whole must be free of any terms reflecting public policy objectives because no private investor or vendor would ensure anything more than a profit increase for itself'.[231]

This approach runs counter sustainability concerns. It is argued that a State, when selling as much as when buying, may not simply be motivated by strictly economic considerations. On the contrary, it might well want to take into account other general interests, including what in public procurement are now called 'strategic considerations'. Therefore, the State might want to pursue different public goals through the sale of assets, including a better or more efficient use of some land or building through the involvement of private parties. As a seller, the State may, for instance, require that the land sold stays accessible to the general public or that the building is affected by community services. This will for sure depress the price since some potential buyers, while 'able to meet that obligation', might well be unwilling to do so and others will only be ready to pay less. However, when a competitive tendering procedure is used, the winning bidder cannot be said to have received any favour, so the situation should fall outside the notion of State aid under Article 107 TFEU.

True, a 'conditional sale' does not automatically amount to unlawful State aid and it is not necessarily forbidden, but it rules out the presumption of the absence of any aid.[232] And the consequent duty to notify to the Commission impacts the time frame for the transaction, increasing it significantly and possibly affecting its effectiveness.

This links to the further question: Can the Commission conclude that the sale *itself* was a form of compatible aid? In other words, can Member States pursue objective(s) of common interest *by means of* the sale/privatisation transaction?

The issue is connected, once again, with the dual capacity of the State (see Section 5.4.2.2). The answer provided both by the Commission and

[231] I. Platis, 'What Is the Optimum Market Price Standard for State Aid Purposes', *State aid hub* (10 December 2015); see also P. Nicolaides, 'The Challenge of Calculating a Market Price', *State aid hub* (25 August 2015).

[232] S. Arrowsmith points out (although in relation to procurement activities) that 'if the procuring entity does not use a procedure that is appropriate to create a presumption that the transaction does not involve state aid, this does not, of course, mean that the state aid *is* involved. Nor, it is submitted, there is even a presumption that there is state aid' (*The Law of Public and Utilities Procurement*, para. 4-85).

by the case law seems essentially negative, as *Hytasa* and the following decisions and judgments have shown. Nor does the line of reasoning followed in the *SNCM* judgment contradict this approach. Compatible aid measures can, therefore, in principle be allowed to rescue and restructure firms in difficulty with the aim of raising the interest of potential buyers. Therefore, for instance, compatible aids can be granted in the prior phase of rescue and restructuring of a given company.[233] But the sale transaction must take place on market terms.

The Commission has not always been consistent with the aforementioned approach. It seemingly departed from that in Decision n. 507/2015 in the context of a land development project.[234] The contested measure concerned the land lease and sale of buildings in Germany. The transaction was concluded between Neuwoges (a limited liability company whose shares are fully owned by the local municipality and whose statutory obligation is to secure sufficient housing supply) and two property companies. The Commission concluded that there was no State aid because the transaction was carried out on market terms. It, however, went further on in its assessment, examining whether an aid in similar conditions could have been considered compatible. It concluded considering that Neuwoges had pursued an object of common interest, connected with its statutory obligation to secure sufficient housing supply and that the measure pursued was appropriate, necessary and proportionate.[235]

233 See in general Guidelines on State aid for rescuing and restructuring non-financial undertakings in difficulty (R&R Guidelines). For a (partial) positive assessment, see, for instance, 94/653/EC: Commission Decision of 27 July 1994 concerning the notified capital increase of Air France, OJ 1994, No. L 254/73; 97/81/EC: Commission Decision of 30 July 1996 concerning aid granted by the Austrian Government to Head Tyrolia Mares in the form of capital injections, OJ 1997, No. L 25/26 2005/418/EC: Commission Decision of 7 July 2004 on the aid measures implemented by France for Alstom, OJ 2004, No. L150/24; Commission Decision 2005/941/EC of 1 October 2004, '*Bull*', OJ 2005, No. L342/81; 2005/407/EC: Commission decision of 22 September 2004 on the State aid which the United Kingdom is planning to implement for British Energy plc, OJ 2005, No. L142/26; 2005/345/EC: Commission Decision of 18 February 2004 on restructuring aid implemented by Germany for Bankgesellschaft Berlin AG, OJ 2005, No. L116/1. Most recently see also Commission Decisions of 26 and 29 November 2015, adopted in State aid control procedures SA.43363 and SA.43364.

234 Commission Decision 2015/507/EU of 16 September 2014 on the measure SA.23129 – (12/C) (ex 12/NN) (ex CP 141/2007) implemented by Germany, OJ 2015, No. L 89/37.

235 Critically, P. Nicolaides, 'Land Development', 20 April 2015, available at http://stateaidhub.eu/blogs/stateaiduncovered/post/2051; more generally on the topic: P. Nicolaides, 'State Aid Implications of Public Investment in Land Development & Social Housing', *Journal of European Competition Law & Practice*, 10(10) (2019), 609.

The approach here followed by the Commission has, however, been strongly criticised essentially because it affirmed at the same time that the transaction had been made under market terms (thus, the public seller acted as a private operator) and that the sale pursued a public policy (thus, the public seller entered the transaction as a public authority). As pointed out, the respect of market firms seemingly rules out the existence of a market failure, hence the need for public intervention with aid measures. These observations highlight once again the incompatibility between the two roles played by Member States.

Summing up the findings so far, process-related interests are embedded in the design of a competitive bidding procedure. Mimicking the working of the competitive market, competitive tendering procedures act as a mechanism for the maximisation of desired outcomes. Desiderata need to be included in the specifications before launching the procedure. Those specifications, rather than the procedure itself, provide the balance among potentially conflicting interests. However, EU law limits what the Member States may desire. As *Automobile Craiova* shows, it is not enough for a tendering procedure to be open and competitive for EU State aid law to be complied with.[236] Conditionality may be an issue. If the privatisation procedure is conditional, some outcome-related interests will be scrutinised by the Commission according to the following table, which focuses on the output-related interests in the context of sales and privatisations (Table 5.1).

5.4.3.2 Through Non-competitive Tendering

The previous section has shown that public interests, notably process-related interests but also output-related interests, are more efficiently pursued by means of competitive tendering, which – in theory and often in practice as well – acts as a mechanism for the maximisation of desired outcomes. Arguably, such interests are less effectively achievable through non-competitive tendering procedures.

That is certainly the case for transparency and, possibly, for fair and equal treatment and for accountability. Indeed, the existing independent evaluation mechanism appears to be rather opaque when compared with the open, transparent and well-publicised tendering procedure. Even if it still allows recourse to such methodology, the Commission Notice does not provide any clarification. Some guidance might still be found in the

236 2008/717/EC, para. 71.

Table 5.1 *State aid and conditionality*

Value maximisation/minimisation of future costs	NOT State aid
Reduction of national debts	NOT State aid insofar as value maximisation is achieved (as a collateral benefit thereof)
Avoiding unnecessary taxation	NOT State aid insofar as value maximisation is achieved (as a collateral benefit thereof)
Developing capital markets	NOT State aid insofar as value maximisation is achieved (as a collateral benefit thereof)
Sustainability, especially environmental	State aid to be screened for compatibility
Fundamental rights	State aid to be screened for compatibility
Securing sufficient housing supply	State aid to be screened for compatibility
Developing popular capitalism	Incompatible State aid
Encouraging/protecting smallholder farmers or more generally small and medium-sized enterprises (SMEs)	Incompatible State aid
Protecting local workers	Incompatible State aid
Requiring additional non-mandatory benefits for workers	Incompatible State aid
Encouraging/protecting local economic development	Incompatible State aid, unless it regards the development of disadvantaged regions covered by regional aid,[a] in which case it must be screened for compatibility

[a] See Communication from the Commission Guidelines on regional State aid 2021/C 153/01 (C/2021/2594), OJ 2021, No. C 153/1.

previous 1997 Communication, which on the matter stated that: 'An "asset valuer" is a person of good repute who: (i) has obtained an appropriate degree at a recognised centre of learning or an equivalent academic qualification, (ii) has suitable experience and is competent in valuing land and buildings in the location and of the category of the asset'.[237] The 1997 Communication further required the asset valuer to be independent of the public authority selling the land and/or building.[238]

[237] Commission Communication on State aid elements in sales of land and buildings by public authorities 97/C 209/03, § II(2)(a), OJ 1997, No. C 209/3.

[238] See Wollenschläger, 'Art. 107 AEUV', para. 481 f.

Concerning instead output-related interests, the picture is the same as the one drawn in the previous subsection and the table therein insofar as potentially incompatible State aids are concerned.

A few additional aspects need to be briefly dealt with. One might easily assume that, since an open, well-publicised and transparent tender creates more competition, the price obtained through competitive tendering would *generally* be higher. However, as the case law concerning privatisation processes has shown, tendering procedures might not always result in a binding offer, especially when the asset sold is not so appetible. Thus, the government might have to then turn to other allocating strategies. Also, there might well be public interests that are better achieved with direct and targeted sales even if such a transaction might be deemed to be against the relevant EU law framework. This is especially the case of large privatisations, which are politically motivated and politics determines the choices in the ways they are effectuated.[239]

The choice most suited for a given privatisation is therefore guided based on different trade-offs between, on the one hand, equal treatment and transparency (and accountability) and, on the other hand, 'efficiency'. The latter is here understood as the ability of the process to reach the ends foreseen and, as already shown, ends pursued through privatisation are many and motivated by politics. For instance, according to the World Bank, in the early United Kingdom (UK) privatisation drive, direct sales to '"strategic" or "core" investors were also favoured because they would bring in revenue and *turn the firm over to "real" owners possessing the knowledge and incentives to govern the company efficiently and the capital to restructure it*'.[240] These sales often involve the presence of 'advisors', and their level of transparency is variable depending on the jurisdiction where they take place, but for sure it is lower than auctioning assets or floating shares.

[239] See Andrews, 'State-Owned Banks, Stability, Privatization, and Growth', 20, characterising privatisation as 'a political process'. Even though economic constraints may also play a role, for instance floating was rarely used in Eastern European countries due to the underdeveloped character of local stock markets: World Bank, *From Plan to Market*, 54; for a detailed, if now somewhat outdated, analysis of the different tools used to privatise industries, L. Anderloni, 'Methods of Privatisation Optimisation of the Objectives of Sellers and Investors and the Role of Financial Institutions', in R. Ruozi and L. Anderloni (eds.), 'Banking Privatisation in Europe: *The Process and the Consequences on Strategies and Organisational Structures*' (Berlin: Springer, 1999), p. 45.

[240] World Bank, *From Plan to Market*, 53 (emphasis added).

Even the Commission may exceptionally be ready to accept the use of evaluators. In the case of the privatisation of Alitalia, the Italian flagship airline, the Commission was ready to accept an arrangement under which the sale was monitored by a trustee charged with checking that the sale itself took place at market price.[241]

Still, allocating procedures other than competitive tendering are not *per se* able to overcome the strict EU law approach, including towards conditionality, so that, concerning output-related interests the table in Section 5.4.3 is fully applicable to sale based on experts' evaluation or benchmarking. Only, concerning specifically privatisations, the transactions will be automatically classed as potentially incompatible State aid.

5.5 Concluding Remarks

While this chapter did not attempt a rigorous comparative study nor was based on one, the research showed that sales and even more privatisations may answer to a very wide array of general interests. Some of the output-related interests identified are peculiar to our area, such as, for instance, the desire to redesign the borders between the State and the market to the benefit of the latter or to lessen tax pressure. Process-related interests, instead, tend to be common to other areas such as public procurement and might be considered to constitute elements of a *jus commune* of public contracts.

Some of the process-related interests, such as equal treatment and transparency, correspond to general principles in many jurisdictions and certainly in the EU. The same is true of the relevant internal market rules, including the non-discrimination principle, which is the basis for equal treatment.[242] The principle of proportionality is also relevant to assess whether measures restricting market freedoms taken to protect worthy general interests are legitimate. As recalled, internal market case law is limited concerning sales and privatisations, and in *TAP*, the Court of Justice stopped short of applying the proportionality test, rather referring to detailed secondary law (Section 5.4.1). State aid law, while grounded on general principles or at least broad theories, such as the MEO principle, is instead characterised by very detailed case law and Commission guidance instruments.[243]

241 This solution withstood challenge in Case T-123/09, *Ryanair* v. *Commission* ECLI:EU:T:2012:164; appeal dismissed in Case C – 287/12, *Ryanair* v. *Commission* ECLI:EU:C:2013:395, see Bacon, *European Union Law of State Aid*, para. 2.68.

242 On the relevance of discrimination in our area: Wollenschläger, 'Art. 107 AEUV', para. 475.

243 Wollenschläger, 'Art. 107 AEUV', para. 475.

The case law and guidance instruments severely curtail the options open to the Member States, especially insofar as output-related interests are concerned. There emerges a strong preference for a competitive tendering procedure, although, at the same time, the current Notice on the notion of State aid allows a somewhat wider spectrum of alternative methodologies to assess the compliance with market terms.

It is argued that the strict approach to conditionality adopted by the Commission extends the parallel with the private vendor too far, well beyond what is needed to avoid distortions in the competition between the Member States. It is submitted that the Commission fails to appreciate that the notion of market economic operator is to be used to assess whether an advantage – to be understood as an 'economic benefit' – has been conferred.[244] It is counterintuitive to treat obligations in the public interest as 'advantages' and this even more so since the latter is defined as 'an improvement in the economic and/or financial position of the undertaking'.[245]

These aspects could and should of course be considered in the procedure following the notification of the State aid, which is due once the exception does not apply. The length and uncertainties of the scrutiny will, however, have a chill effect on the Member States often pressed to privatise their assets and industries.

It is questionable whether such an approach is consistent with the overall Horizon 2020 strategy and the newer European Green Deal and it is submitted that EU State aid law does not only fail to contribute to the achievement of sustainable development but actually hinders it. The latter document indeed highlighted the need to review the relevant State aid guidelines, including the environment and energy State aid guidelines.[246] The very recent 2022 Communication from the Commission on Guidelines on State aid for climate, environmental protection and energy seems to be most conservative and stop much short of making State aid rules an instrument to achieve societal interests.[247]

[244] Notice on the notion of State aid, para. 66; however, para. 74 of the same Notice conflates the notion of (lack of) advantage with that of transaction 'in line with normal market conditions'; see also paras. 76 ff.

[245] Bacon, *European Union Law of State Aid*, 29, where references to the case law may be found.

[246] Communication from the Commission to the European Parliament, the European Council, the Council, the European Economic and Social Committee and the Committee of the Regions the European Green Deal, COM/2019/640 final, para. 2.2.2.

[247] Communication from the Commission – *Guidelines* on State aid for climate, environmental protection and energy 2022, 2022/C 80/01.

PART II

Connecting Limited Rights

6

Limited Rights

Scope of Application

STEVEN VAN GARSSE AND ILENIA VANDORPE

6.1 Introduction

The government, as an organisation that officially manages and controls a country or a region,[1] enjoys a particularly privileged position. This position allows it to collect taxes, expropriate real estate and other assets, exercise coercion subject to legally predefined conditions and so on. But a government can also regulate economic or spatial life through a licence: prohibiting activities, subjecting them to special conditions, creating exclusive rights and so on.

In connection with the above, the government enjoys a lot of financial power to ensure its functioning and to carry out its policies. A government will usually finance its actions and policies mainly with funds that it collects through various mechanisms such as taxes. In order to realise its public purpose(s), the government can choose to use the collected funds to purchase certain services, works or deliveries, or to grant these funds to citizens, companies and other private actors in order to realise a specific project (via subsidies). In addition, the government also owns a lot of real estate. The government can include its property in its policy choices by possibly granting rights of use to this property to third parties. In addition, the government can decide to valorise part of its real estate through sales and other related transactions.

The actual granting (whether or not in exchange for a quid pro quo) of funds, rights of use, goods and licences by the government

[1] Cambridge Dictionary, 'Government', last accessed 23 May 2022, available at https://dictionary.cambridge.org/dictionary/english/government.

implies the granting of an (often) economic advantage to certain market players and, consequently, potentially the denial of this advantage to others. Given that the number of interested actors will often be greater than the number of beneficiaries, this concerns an allocation of rights in a situation of scarcity. Consequently, a discussion on an appropriate distribution mechanism arises.

Despite the limited nature that characterises all of the above-mentioned governmental acts, the other contributions in this book have already shown that the limited rights identified here (namely public contracts, concessions, sale of assets, subsidies and licences) are not entirely identical in content.

This observation forms the starting point of this contribution, which, however, distinguishes itself from the other contributions in this book by its objective. This contribution attempts to provide some insight into the existence or non-existence of the possibility of a common distribution mechanism[2] that starts from the different nature of the limited rights mentioned above.[3] This question is very important for practice and academia. Depending on the results of our analysis, other questions can become relevant, for example whether or not it would be feasible or even desirable for certain regulatory frameworks (and consequently, possibly certain limited rights) to converge in such a way that they (could) even merge into one. This could enhance legal certainty reducing conflicts between regulations and could lead to administrative simplification.

To achieve our goal, this contribution addresses the following two questions. First, the question of how limited rights relate to each other in the light of their supranational definition(s), of their various characteristics distilled from the said definition(s) and of the purpose and extent of their regulation (Section 6.2). Next, the question is asked whether the definition(s), characteristics and regulation of limited rights actually facilitate the creation of a common distribution framework, or whether they prevent it. In this connection, a look will also be taken, for the sake of comparison, at relevant developments under Dutch law (Section 6.3). After dealing with both questions, this contribution ends with a brief conclusion.

[2] General principles or specific rules by which limited rights would be distributed.

[3] And not from the various foundations, as is the case in other contributions in this book.

6.2 Substantive Relationship between the Listed Limited Rights

6.2.1 Introduction

6.2.1.1 General Remarks

In Part I of this book, extensive attention has already been paid to (some) common categories of limited rights, namely by Arrowsmith,[4] Caranta and Biancardi,[5] van den Brink[6] and Wollenschläger.[7] Building further on the insights already obtained in the aforementioned part, we now turn our attention to the way in which these various limited rights relate to each other in terms of content.

The delimitation of limited rights is subject to two opposing tendencies. On the one hand, governmental actions and the various transactions associated with them are becoming increasingly complex and hybrid.[8] This, of course, makes it more difficult to qualify a certain governmental action as one limited right or another. On the other hand, the importance of an accurate identification and qualification of limited rights, with a view to identifying the correct framework and ensuring legal certainty, is growing. In fact, the applicable legal framework is always constructed on the basis of the specific nature of the limited right in question, so that inaccurate identification and qualification and the consequent application of an erroneous legal framework may attribute characteristics and legal effects to the limited right concerned that are incompatible with its nature. As a result of their different nature, some limited rights are more extensively regulated than others.[9]

Indeed, this regulatory tendency means that it is increasingly important to know whether, and if so which, specific regulation applies to a particular limited right or whether compliance with certain principles[10] is

[4] See Chapter 2.
[5] See Chapter 5.
[6] See Chapter 4.
[7] See Chapter 6.
[8] E.g. in the context of public–private partnerships (PPP) projects where the government uses both private and public law instruments. See, inter alia F. Lichère (ed.), *Public-Private Partnership: Report of the XVIII Congress of the International Academy of Comparative Law* (Brussels: Bruylant, 2011), p. 532.
[9] On licenses, see Articles 9–14 of Directive 2006/123/EG of the European Parliament and of the Council of 12 December 2006 on services in the internal market, OJ 2006, No. L 376/36.
[10] Regulation, by its very nature, is often much more extensive than principles, so that, in contrast to principles, it will, normally, limit governmental action more strictly.

sufficient. When existing, the applicable regulation will often play an important role in determining the nature of the relationship that arises between the government and the beneficiary of the limited right through the grant of that right, and in the possible enforceability of the limited right concerned.

For the above reasons, it comes as no surprise that the number of delimitation disputes and the corresponding number of court decisions are on the rise.[11]

The characteristics (including any definitions) of the various limited rights (i.e. public contracts and concessions as forms of public procurement, sale of assets, subsidies and licences), as well as the applicable regulatory framework governing each of them, are discussed below. The order in which the aforementioned limited rights are discussed in this contribution is the same as the order in which the various individual rights were discussed in Part I of this book.

In the below analysis, we mainly start from (the difference with) public contracts, since this subject matter is the most extensively regulated and often gives rise to demarcation questions with regard to the other limited rights. In discussions about the applicable framework, in a search for legal certainty, there is in practice, on the one hand, sometimes a tendency to resort to the regulations applicable to public contracts as these are regulated clearly and extensively (Arrowsmith).[12] On the other hand, there is sometimes a tendency to just not qualify the transaction as a public contract, hoping to escape strict regulations.[13]

[11] By way of example, reference can be made to the general trend towards an increase in the total number of cases pending before the Belgian Council of State, see 'Activity report 2019–2020 Council of State', 15. This Council is to a large extent competent in Belgium for disputes concerning public contracts and concessions. A similar movement is also occurring in the Netherlands, see: F. J. van Ommeren, 'Concessies 2.0: de concessie op de grens van de vergunning, de overheidsopdracht en de subsidie', (2020) *Nederlands Tijdschrift voor Bestuursrecht*, 10, 639–648. There is also a general increase in the number of cases in the European Court of Justice, see Court of Justice of the European Union, 'The year in review – annual report 2021', last accessed 23 May 2022, available at https://curia.europa.eu/jcms/upload/docs/application/pdf/2022-05/qd-aq-22-001-en-n.pdf.

[12] See the chapter of Arrowsmith, Section 2.1.

[13] S. van Garsse, *De concessie in het raam van de publiek-private samenwerking* (Brugge: die Keure, 2007), p. 320. However, making such re-qualification legally conclusive is becoming increasingly difficult due to, on the one hand, the many rulings of the European Court of Justice on the qualification issue and, on the other hand, the increasing codification via the European Directives.

6.2.1.2 A Specific Note on Public Procurement

Public procurement is defined by Arrowsmith[14] as the activity of a public authority in purchasing goods or services from an external source. It therefore includes the acquisition of works, services and products via public contracts. Based on this broad definition, Arrowsmith also includes acquisitions through concession arrangements. Conceptually, however, this approach is not free from criticism. After all, in concessions the emphasis is on the granting of exploitation rights (for a work or a service) rather than the acquisition of works, supplies or services to support the operation of the government.

In practice, when a concession is granted, the government relinquishes the exploitation of a work or service – a task that it would normally have undertaken itself – to a private company that, through payment of third-party beneficiaries for the use of the work or service concerned, can build its own revenue model around it.

In view of this operational nature, the legal concept of the concession is therefore considered in various legal systems as a way of having public services managed by private parties and therefore, in essence, a way of organising the government, rather than a way of providing the government with resources to operate through a commercial transaction.[15] Given its different object and purpose, the concession cannot simply be equated with classic public contracts, as regulated for decades at national and supranational levels.

In the following, the two legal concepts are therefore dealt with separately as part of the demarcation, all the more so since the current legal frameworks are anything but identical.[16]

[14] See Chapter 2 of Arrowsmith.

[15] See, for example for France, X. Bezancon, *2000 ans d'histoire du partenariat public-privé* (Paris: Presse de l'école nationale des Ponts et chaussées, 2004), p. 284. See also R. Caranta and P. Patrito, 'An Intellectual History of Concessions and PPP Law' in P. Bogdonawicz, R. Caranta and P. Telles (eds.), *Public-Private Partnerships and Concessions in the EU* (London: Elgar, 2020), p. 18.

[16] Inter alia on concessions; S. de La Rosa (ed.), *L'endradrement des concessions par le droit europeéen de la commande publique* (Paris: Société de la legislation compare, 2014), p. 220; S. van Garsse, 'Concessions and Public Procurement' in C. Bovis (ed.), *Research Handbook on EU Public Procurement Law* (Cheltenham: Edward Elgar, 2016), p. 593; L. Vitora (ed.), *Service Concessions in the EU: A Comparative Study of the Transposition of Directive 2014/23 on the Award of Concession Contracts into National Law* (Navarra: Thomson Reuters/Aranzadi, 2018); P. Bogdonawicz, R. Caranta and P. Telles (eds.), *Public–Private Partnerships and Concessions in the EU* (Cheltenham: Edward Elgar, 2020), p. 221.

6.2.2 *Public Contract*

6.2.2.1 Definition and Characteristics

The current public contract Directives[17] define public contracts as 'contracts for pecuniary interest concluded in writing between one or more economic operators and one or more contracting authorities and having as their object the execution of works, the supply of products or the provision of services'. From this definition, it is possible to deduce the various characteristics that may lead to the qualification of a legal act as a public contract within the meaning of the applicable Directives.

A first characteristic is that there must be a written contract for pecuniary interest. This means that the public contract Directives apply where, first, there is a concordance of wills between two different persons, the contracting authority and the supplier, and, second, the commercial relationship that is created consists in the supply of products, services or works for pecuniary remuneration. In other words, there are mutual acts of performance, the creation of rights and obligations for the parties to the contract and interdependence of their respective acts of performance.[18] According to the European Court of Justice, there is only a public contract if the contractor(s) concerned is/are chosen at the expense of other persons on the basis of objective criteria.[19]

A second characteristic, which already follows in part from the first, is that the purpose of a public contract is to *purchase* goods, services or works. In a public contract, the right granted by the government generally can take the form of a payment of a certain sum of money to the person whose offer is accepted and with whom the contract is concluded.[20] In the case of a concession, however, the right granted by the public authority does not consist of a right to a payment, but of the right

[17] Article 2(5) of Directive 2014/24/EU of the European Parliament and of the Council of 26 February 2014 on public procurement and repealing Directive 2004/18/EC, OJ 2014, No. L 94/65 and Directive 2014/25/EU of the European Parliament and of the Council of 26 February 2014 on procurement by entities operating in the water, energy, transport and postal services sectors and repealing Directive 2004/17/EC, OJ 2014, No. L 94/243.

[18] Opinion of Advocate General Cosmas of 18 November 1999 in Case C-107/98, *Teckal* ECLI:EU:C:1999:344.

[19] Case C-9/17, *Tirkkonen* ECLI:EU:C:2018:142; Case C-410/14, *Falk Pharma* ECLI:EU:C:2016:399.

[20] C. E. C. Jansen, 'Allocation of Limited Rights form a European Public Procurement Law Perspective' in P. C. Adriaanse, F. J. van Ommeren, W. den Ouden and C. J. Wolswinkel (eds.), *Scarcity and the State I: The Allocation of Limited Rights by the Administration* (Cambridge: Intersentia, 2016), pp. 239–275.

to (continue to) exploit a service or a work which is the subject of the concession (see below).

A third feature that seems to be derived from the above definition is that there can only be a public contract if the contract in question is concluded between one or more economic operators and one or more contracting authorities. It is clearly stated in the public contract Directives[21] that the sole fact that both parties to an agreement are themselves public authorities does not exclude the application of procurement rules. However, the application of these rules should not interfere with the freedom of public authorities to perform the public service tasks conferred on them by using their own resources, which includes the possibility of cooperation with other public authorities. For this reason, exceptions[22] have been included in the public contract Directives that exclude certain agreements between public authorities from the scope of the public procurement rules. One of these exceptions concerns the so-called horizontal cooperation between contracting authorities. In order to be able to speak of a cooperation and consequently invoke this exception, all public bodies party to the (cooperation) agreement have to jointly participate in the cooperation. In the so-called *Remondis* judgment,[23] the European Court of Justice points out that this condition cannot be considered fulfilled when the only contribution made by some public bodies party to the agreement is limited to reimbursing costs. In this case, the exemption of horizontal cooperation cannot be applied, and this act would rather seem to be the acquisition of a service by the contracting authority concerned, which pays a remuneration for it. Consequently, it is a public contract and the relevant Directives apply.[24]

A fourth characteristic of a public contract is that, as a result of its conclusion, the contractor is obliged to perform certain actions, which

[21] Recital 31 of the Directive 2014/24/EU of the European Parliament and of the Council of 26 February 2014 on public procurement and repealing Directive 2004/18/EC, OJ 2014, No. L 94/65.

[22] Article 12 of Directive 2014/24/EU of the European Parliament and of the Council of 26 February 2014 on public procurement and repealing Directive 2004/18/EC, OJ 2014, No. L 94/65. Also W. A. Janssen, *EU Public Procurement Law & Self Organisation* (The Hague: Eleven International Publishing, 2018).

[23] Case C-429/19, *Remondis GmbH* v. *Abfallzweckverband Rhein-Mosel-Eifel* ECLI:EU:C:2020:436.

[24] Case C-429/19, *Remondis GmbH* v. *Abfallzweckverband Rhein-Mosel-Eifel*, paras 29, 30 and 38.

the contracting authority may enforce, if necessary. If the contractor defaults, a contracting authority usually has, under national law, various tools available to sanction the said contractor (penalties, fines, etc.) and even to force him to perform the contract.[25] Moreover, depending on the national framework, the contracting authority may even carry out the contract itself at the contractor's expense and risk or have it carried out under the same conditions by one or more other companies.[26] Despite the fact that the initial contractor will not be involved in these methods of performance, he will have to bear the costs and risks involved. Such a performance obligation and toolkit of sanctions are also typically found in concession contracts (see below).

In order to determine whether the above characteristics are present and therefore whether or not there is a public contract within the meaning of the relevant legal framework, a functional approach is used. This means that the purpose of the contract must be taken into account when assessing whether the above-mentioned characteristics, and thus a public contract, are present or not.

If, for example, a contracting authority concludes an agreement for the provision of services by another contracting authority that is still under its control at the time of purchase, but shortly afterwards is largely owned by a private company, this is still a public contract.[27] In fact, this contract does not concern the joint fulfilment by the public authorities concerned of tasks of general interest, but the purchase of services from a legal entity that is largely controlled by a private enterprise. From that perspective, this contract has the same function as a public contract, namely the purchase of services in support of the operation of the government. The assessment of the existence of a public contract is functional in the sense that it must take into account all the phases characterising the conclusion of the contract and its purpose.

In determining whether or not there is a public contract, the legal qualification of the contract under national law is irrelevant. The definition of a public contract and the consequent application of the public contract Directives fall within the domain of European law. For example, according to the European Court of Justice, there is a public

[25] See, for example in Belgium, Article 44 of the Royal Decree Performance.
[26] Ibid., Article 47(2).
[27] Case C-719/20, *Commission of the European Communities* v. *Republic of Austria* ECLI:EU:C:2022:372; Case C-29/04, *Commission of the European Communities* v. *Republic of Austria* ECLI:EU:C:2005:670.

works contract if the contract in question shows that the works are carried out with the intention of integrating commercial and service activities, so that the contract is deemed to fulfil an economic function, regardless of the national law qualification given to that contract.[28]

6.2.2.2 Regulation

Given the multitude of public authorities, and consequently the large number of public contracts published, public procurement is of great economic and social importance. As a result, public procurement lends itself to corruption, for example by awarding contracts at excessively high prices to companies linked to the government in order to channel money to civil servants involved.

Public contracts have long been regulated in many countries in order to fight corruption as well as to ensure an efficient spending of governmental resources.[29]

Since the early 1990s, the importance of European regulation has increased enormously, although, as Arrowsmith rightly points out earlier in this book, this is (mainly) due to another objective, namely to create a European internal market in which free movement and the opening of markets without distorted competition are guaranteed.[30] It follows that the limited nature of public contracts was/is not the primary incentive to regulate public contracts.[31]

In order to achieve this European single market, the European legislator endeavours to regulate as many aspects of public contracts as possible (from awarding to, recently, even performance[32]).[33]

[28] Case C-220/05, *Jean Auroux and Others* v. *Commune de Roanne* ECLI:EU:C:2007:31, paras. 40–41.

[29] See for Belgium: D. D'hooghe, *De gunning van overheidscontracten en overheidsopdrachten* (Brugge: die Keure, 1997), p. 106; Van Garsse, *De concessie in het raam van de publiek-private samenwerking*, p. 320. See for France: H. Lemesle, 'Réglementer l'achat public en France (xviiie-xixe siècle)', (2010) *Genèses* 3, 8–26.

[30] Also S. Arrowsmith, *The Law of Public Procurement and Utilities Procurement*, Vol. I (London: Sweet & Maxwell, 2014), p. 150; S. Evers Hjelmborg, P. Stig Jacobson and S. Troels Poulsen, *Public Procurement Law: The EU Directive on Public Contracts* (Copenhagen: DJØF Publishing, 2006), pp. 22–23.

[31] Directive 2014/24/EU of the European Parliament and of the Council of 26 February 2014 on public procurement and repealing Directive 2004/18/EC, OJ 2014, No. L 94/65, recital 2, which addresses the issue of scarcity indirectly.

[32] More specifically a modification of contracts.

[33] Directive 2014/24/EU of the European Parliament and of the Council of 26 February 2014 on public procurement and repealing Directive 2004/18/EC, OJ 2014, No L 94/55 and Directive 2014/25/EU of the European Parliament and of the Council of 26 February

6.2.3 Concession

6.2.3.1 Definition and Characteristics

According to the applicable European legislation, a concession is defined as a contract for pecuniary interest concluded in writing by means of which one or more contracting authorities or contracting entities entrust the performance of works or the provision and the management of services to one or more economic operators the consideration for which consists either solely in the right to exploit the work or services that are the subject of the contract or in that right together with payment.[34] Several characteristics can be deduced from this definition which, once present, lead a given contract to be considered as a concession within the meaning of the applicable regulations.

The first characteristic, namely that there must be a written contract for pecuniary interest, is largely the same as for public contracts. In the case of a concession, too, there must be an agreement of will between the contracting authority and the beneficiary of the concession, the relationship between the two being characterised by the mutual performance of interdependent services.

An important difference with a public contract (second characteristic) is the object of the reciprocal services. Contrary to a public contract, the beneficiary of a concession cannot be obliged to exploit certain *supplies*,[35] but only to offer certain services or carry out certain works and exploit those. In fact in order to be able to speak of a concession, the contracting authority must in return grant the right to exploit the works or services in question (whether or not free of charge).[36] Concessions, therefore, presuppose an exploitable activity, and not just any service or work (e.g. in the case of the operation of a car park through user fees).[37] Whether the fee that the concessionaire can collect from third parties in connection with its operation is of a private or public law nature is irrelevant to the

2014 on procurement by entities operating in the water, energy, transport and postal services sectors and repealing Directive 2004/17/EC, OJ 2014, No. L 94/243.

[34] Article 5(1)(a) and (b) of Directive 2014/23/EU of the European Parliament and of the Council of 26 February 2014 on the award of concession contracts, OJ 2014, No. 94/1.

[35] One could also argue that supplies are not exploitable (from an economic point of view).

[36] Case C-225/15, *Criminal proceedings against Domenico Politanò* ECLI:EU:C:2016:645, para. 30.

[37] Case C-458/03, *Parking Brixen GmbH* v. *Gemeinde Brixen and Stadtwerke Brixen AG* ECLI:EU:C:2005:605; Case C-274/09, *Privater Rettungsdienst und Krankentransport Stadler* v. *Zweckverband für Rettungsdienst und Feuerwehralarmierung Passau* ECLI:EU:C:2011:130, para. 25.

qualification as a concession.[38] However, the mere granting of such a right of exploitation as a quid pro quo within the contract concluded is not sufficient for it to be classified as a concession. In fact, this right of exploitation must be accompanied by a complete or substantial transfer of the operating risk from the contracting authority to the concessionaire. If the contracting authority does not do this, the transaction in question may be reclassified as a public contract.[39] The operational risk may be very limited (e.g. in sectors with regulated tariffs[40]), but it must be present in any event.[41] Such a risk exists if, when the concession is awarded, there is a possibility that the concessionaire will not, under normal operating conditions, recoup its investments and the costs incurred in operating the works or services it provides, even if part of the risk remains with the contracting authority.[42] In other words, the contracting authority may not relieve the concessionaire of all potential loss, for example by guaranteeing a minimum revenue equal to or higher than the investments and costs incurred by the concessionaire in performing the concession or by providing a guarantee to the concessionaire as to the profitability of the investments and costs incurred.[43] Thus, the recouping by the concessionaire of these investments and costs must be subject to the vagaries of the market and may therefore consist of a demand risk, a supply risk or a combination of both. In the case of a demand risk, this concerns the risk of actual demand for the works or services that are the object of the contract. Supply risk, on the other hand, refers to the possible situation in which, for example, the provision of the services does not meet the demand of the target audience.[44] Whether or not an operating risk exists can be assessed taking into account the net present value of all investments, costs and revenues of the concessionaire.

[38] Case C-206/08, *Wasser- und Abwasserzweckverband Gotha und Landkreisgemeinden (WAZV Gotha)* v. *Eurawasser Aufbereitungs- und Entsorgungsgesellschaft mbH* ECLI: EU:C:2009:540, para. 55.

[39] C-274/09, *Privater Rettungsdienst und Krankentransport Stadler* v. *Zweckverband für Rettungsdienst und Feuerwehralarmierung Passau* ECLI:EU:C:2011:130, para. 26.

[40] Directive 2014/23/EU of the European Parliament and of the Council of 26 February 2014 on the award of concession contracts, OJ 2014, No. 94/1, recital 19.

[41] Case C-206/08, *Wasser- und Abwasserzweckverband Gotha und Landkreisgemeinden (WAZV Gotha)* v. *Eurawasser Aufbereitungs- und Entsorgungsgesellschaft mbH* ECLI: EU:C:2009:540, para. 77.

[42] Directive 2014/23/EU of the European Parliament and of the Council of 26 February 2014 on the award of concession contracts, OJ 2014, No. 94/1, recital 18.

[43] Ibid., recital 19.

[44] Ibid., recital 20.

However, what is not decisive in terms of the required exploitation risk are risks related to poor management,[45] non-compliance with the agreement by the concessionaire or cases of force majeure. These risks are inherent to any type of contract, be it a public contract or a concession.[46] In practice, there may be an operating risk, for example, if the level of user fees is not set unilaterally by the service provider but is determined in consultation with, for example, social security bodies.[47]

A third feature that may be deduced from the above definition is that a concession can only exist if the contract is concluded between one or more economic operators and one or more contracting authorities. As with public contracts, the rules applicable to concessions stipulate that the sole fact that both parties to the contract have the status of public authorities does not exclude the application of the concession Directive. Here too, the application of the concessions Directive should not interfere with the freedom of public authorities to perform their public service tasks by using their own resources, which includes the possibility of cooperation with other public authorities.[48] For this reason, the concession Directive also contains exceptions that exclude certain agreements between public authorities from this framework. The terms of these exceptions are almost identical[49] to those contained in the public contract Directives.[50]

A fourth characteristic of a concession is that the concessionaire, as a result of the conclusion of the contract, is obliged to perform certain services or carry out certain works. If the concessionaire fails to do so, the contracting authority may, under national law, penalise the concessionaire on the basis of the contract documents (penalties, fines, etc.). In addition, national provisions even allow the contracting authority to force the concessionaire to fulfil his obligations. If desired or necessary,

[45] Case C-274/09, *Privater Rettungsdienst und Krankentransport Stadler* v. *Zweckverband für Rettungsdienst und Feuerwehralarmierung Passau* ECLI:EU:C:2011:130, para. 38.

[46] Directive 2014/23/EU of the European Parliament and of the Council of 26 February 2014 on the award of concession contracts, OJ 2014, No. 94/1, recital 20.

[47] Case C-274/09, *Privater Rettungsdienst und Krankentransport Stadler* v. *Zweckverband für Rettungsdienst und Feuerwehralarmierung Passau* ECLI:EU:C:2011:130.

[48] Directive 2014/23/EU of the European Parliament and of the Council of 26 February 2014 on the award of concession contracts, OJ 2014, No. 94/1, recital 45.

[49] Article 17 of Directive 2014/23/EU of the European Parliament and of the Council of 26 February 2014 on the award of concession contracts, OJ 2014, No. 94/1.

[50] Article 12 of Directive 2014/24/EU of the European Parliament and of the Council of 26 February 2014 on public procurement and repealing Directive 2004/18/EC, OJ 2014, No. L 94/65.

the contracting authority can, depending on the applicable national legal framework, even perform the service itself or have it performed by third parties, at the expense and risk of the defaulting concessionaire.[51] In this respect too, concessions are similar to public contracts.

6.2.3.2 Regulation

The assessment of whether or not the contract is a concession, as defined by the applicable regulations, is also based on a functional approach. Therefore, it is necessary to check whether the finality of the contract falls within the current European law definition of a concession. As in the case of public contracts, this approach abstracts from a possible national law qualification of the contract concerned. For example, the European Court of Justice has explicitly ruled that the question of whether there is a service concession must be assessed solely on the basis of European law.[52]

As mentioned earlier in this contribution, concessions have historically often been seen as a special technique for public authorities to entrust the management of public services to external entities under conditions they set. Despite the great economic importance that the granting of exploitation rights by contracting authorities possesses or can possess, it is striking that concessions, in contrast to public contracts, are little regulated.[53] This can be explained by the idea that prevailed for a long time in some countries that concessions, especially service concessions, were associated with the right of the contracting authority to organise itself in a certain way and that, in the exercise of their powers, contracting authorities should have great freedom to choose a partner *intuitu personae*. This made regulation very delicate. Spurred on by the European legislator, a (limited) general framework has nevertheless been established. One reflex was to start from the existing regulation of public contracts. The idea was that concessions were a variant of public contracts. However, given the fundamentally different subject matter of

[51] Cf. Belgium Article 71, §1, 2° and 3° Royal Decree of 25 June 2017 '*betreffende de plaatsing en de algemene uitvoeringsregels van de concessieovereenkomsten*' [on the award of public contracts in the classic sectors], *Official Gazette* 29 June 2017.

[52] Case C-274/09, *Privater Rettungsdienst und Krankentransport Stadler* v. *Zweckverband für Rettungsdienst und Feuerwehralarmierung Passau* ECLI:EU:C:2011:130, para. 23.

[53] At the national and European level. For example, Directive 2014/23/EU of the European Parliament and of the Council of 26 February 2014 on the award of concession contracts, OJ 2014, No. 94/1 is half the size of Directive 2014/24/EU of the European Parliament and of the Council of 26 February 2014 on public procurement and repealing Directive 2004/18/EC, OJ 2014, No. L 94/65.

concessions and public contracts, this approach has been controversial from both a historical and a legal perspective and continues to arouse national opposition.[54]

Moreover, the regulatory impulse given in 2014 to concessions seems, in fact, to have been driven mainly by the consideration that a persistent legal uncertainty should be resolved as far as possible in order to avoid distortions in the internal market.[55] This legal uncertainty arose not only at the level of the concession itself, namely due to the application of a different legal framework to service concessions on the one hand and to works concessions on the other,[56] but also due to the interpretative difficulties concerning the distinction between a public contract and a concession.[57] Consequently, the awarding of a concession does not seem to have been regulated at the European level, or at least not primarily, because of the sole fact that concessions are limited rights, but rather out of a desire to ensure greater legal certainty and, consequently, to achieve a certain degree of harmonisation.

The fact that the European legislator tried to find a balance between the need for legal certainty on the one hand and giving the Member States sufficient freedom on the other is clearly expressed in the applicable Directive 2014/23/EU. This Directive provides only for limited regulation of concessions. This is evident at several levels. First of all, in contrast to the public contract Directives, this Directive does not impose any fixed award procedures. A contracting authority is reasonably free to award a concession that falls within the scope of this Directive, as it contains few detailed rules, and its regulation is mainly based on general principles. Of course, this applies not only to the award procedure, but to everything that this Directive regulates. Secondly, the European legislator has severely limited the scope of this Directive both *ratione materiae* and *ratione pecuniae*. Indeed, important sectors such as water are excluded from the application of this Directive.[58] But even if a certain contract is

[54] Inter alia H. Courivaud, 'La concession de service public "à la française" confrontée au droit européen', (2004) *Revue internationale de droit économique* 4, 395, 434. See also the Belgian Council of State No. 248.196, 2 September 2020 and No. 216.544, 29 November 2011. See also S. Van Garsse, *De concessiewet* (Brussels: Politeia, 2021), pp. 32–37.

[55] Directive 2014/23/EU of the European Parliament and of the Council of 26 February 2014 on the award of concession contracts, OJ 2014, No. 94/1, recitals 1 and 4.

[56] Ibid., recital 4.

[57] Ibid., recital 18.

[58] Article 11 of Directive 2014/23/EU. Concessions are not regulated in this sector.

not excluded substantively from this Directive, for instance not covered by the exclusion relating to the water sector, it may still be that the provisions of this Directive do not apply to the contract in question, purely because of the fact that this contract does not exceed a certain value. For example, a service concession must exceed the threshold of EUR 5,382,000 (excluding value-added tax (VAT)),[59] whereas for a public service contract this threshold is much more limited (EUR 215,000 (excluding VAT)).[60]

6.2.4 *Sale of Assets*

6.2.4.1 Definition and Characteristics

The sale of assets is defined by Caranta and Biancardi[61] as the contractual transfer of ownership of a given asset from the vendor to the buyer in return for payment of a price. This definition is based on Article IV.A. – I.202 of the Principles, Definitions and Model Rules of European Private Law – Draft Common Frame of Reference (DCRF) prepared by the Study Group on a European Civil Code and the Research Group on Existing EC Private Law.[62] However, there is no definition enshrined in European legislation, as is the case for public contracts and concessions.

From the above description, various characteristics can be derived that (may) cause the qualification as a sale of assets.

A first characteristic is that a sale of assets gives rise to reciprocal obligations between the various parties involved, as a result of which the agreement concluded can be regarded as a contract for pecuniary interest.

A second aspect that characterises a sale of assets is the opposite role that the government will fulfil, compared to public procurement. When applied to the government in its capacity as provider of limited rights, it will here be qualified as a seller and the (private) actor acquiring the property right to the asset as a buyer. Read in conjunction with the

59 Commission Delegated Regulation (EU) 2021/1951 of 10 November 2021 amending Directive 2014/23/EU of the European Parliament and of the Council in respect of the thresholds for concessions, OJ 2021, No. L 398/21.

60 Ibid. The difference can also be explained from an economic point of view. They have a different risk profile.

61 See the chapter of Caranta and Biancardi, Section 5.2.

62 The definition is: 'A contract for the "sale" of goods is a contract under which one party, the seller, undertakes to another party, the buyer, to transfer the ownership of the goods to the buyer, or to a third person, either immediately on conclusion of the contract or at some future time, and the buyer undertakes to pay the price.'

previously discussed definition of a public contract, the government here fulfils a role that is fundamentally different from the role it assumes in the procurement of public contracts. In the case of public contracts, the government is in fact *purchasing* certain items, whereas in the case of sale of assets it puts (parts of) its assets on the market. This different direction (and consequently the different purpose of these agreements), that is, accruing to the government in the case of public contracts, or repelling in the case of sale of assets, is related to the different aims the government seeks to achieve with these agreements. While, as already mentioned, the government uses public contracts (mainly) to support its services, the motive for a sale of assets is different (e.g. to generate a maximum amount of revenue; e.g. if the government concerned has a lot of debts, the sale of assets is an easy way to remedy this to some extent).

As regards the third aspect, namely the status of the parties, the description of sale of assets does not expressly state this. It could possibly be deduced from this that the parties to the sales contract, in principle, include both private parties and other public authorities.[63]

A fourth characteristic of the sale of assets is that, once the sales agreement has effectively been concluded, the government can force the buyer of the asset to perform its obligations. However, this enforceability is generally limited to the buyer's obligation to pay the agreed price.

On the basis of this analysis, particularly as regards the subject of the sales contract, as well as the different role of the government and the purpose of the transaction, the distinction between public procurement on the one hand and sale of assets on the other seems, at first sight, to be quite clear. This distinction also seems fairly clear to the European Court of Justice. For example, in the *Müller* judgment the Court explicitly ruled that the sale of an unbuilt or built-up plot of land by a public authority to an undertaking does not constitute a public contract. In doing so, the Court emphasised the different status of the authority required for qualification as a public contract, namely that the authority in question must in that case act as a buyer and not as a seller.[64]

But appearances can be deceptive. In practice, situations occur in which a sale of assets could be reclassified as a public contract or as a

[63] This can be explained because of the generic nature of this directive. There is no focus on a specific legal relationship.

[64] Case C-451/08, *Helmut Müller GmbH* v. *Bundesanstalt für Immobilienaufgaben* ECLI:EU:C:2010:168, para. 41.

concession, with the result that the (strict provisions of the) Directives must be followed.

This is the case if the public authority concludes more than just a sale agreement. This means, for example, that a contracting authority, which does not have to be the same as the party to the sale agreement, markets a public contract directly related to the good or property subject to the sale. Such a situation gave rise to the previously mentioned *Müller* judgment of the European Court of Justice. This case concerned the sale and renovation of old barracks. The Court recalled here the functional approach to public contracts and stated that the application of the public contract Directives is not immediately excluded in a situation such as the one at issue in this judgment, namely where there would be two governmental actions regarding the same property, consisting of, on the one hand, the sale of the relevant land and, on the other hand, the award of a public works contract concerning that same land.[65] It is important to note here that the mere fact that both contracts can be considered as a whole, given their subject matter, and that their concrete qualification can therefore also be assessed globally, does not mean that there is effectively a single large public contract. The necessary characteristics of a public contract must still be present. The Court recalls this also in this judgment, stating that the classification as a public contract requires the existence of a contract for pecuniary interest, which implies, for example in the case of a public works contract, that the contracting authority pays a sum of money which constitutes a consideration for the execution of works as an act to which the chosen contractor is bound.[66] The execution of works, as the subject of the contract, must then provide the contracting authority with a direct economic benefit. Thus, the works do not necessarily have to be materially or physically carried out for the contracting authority concerned. The said economic interest may manifest itself in various ways. It can manifest itself when the contracting authority (1) becomes the owner of the works carried out, (2) is able to dispose of the works in view of its public purpose, (3) is able to profit from the future use or transfer of the works in question, (4) has participated financially in the realisation of the works, or (5) is exposed to risks of economic failure of the works in question.[67] Next, a qualification as a public contract requires that the selected contractor directly or

[65] Ibid., para. 82.
[66] Ibid., para. 48.
[67] Ibid., paras. 50–52.

indirectly[68] undertakes to perform the agreed works and that such performance can be legally enforced.[69]

With regard to the distinction between the sale of assets and the concession, the *Müller* judgment mentioned above also provides the necessary insights. Here, the European Court of Justice points out that, in principle, a contracting authority cannot grant a concession for the exploitation of a property if that property does not belong to it, but to a private operator. An owner of land who, in such a case, does not have the capacity of a public authority, already has the right to exploit the property of which he is the owner. The government, in the event that it is not the owner of the property in question, cannot in principle dispose of the exploitation of, for example, the work carried out. The existence of a concession implies a necessary transfer of the right of exploitation, which cannot take place if the authority in question does not even possess this right initially.[70]

6.2.4.2 Regulation

Unlike, for example, public contracts, the sale of assets is not extensively regulated at the European level. The little existing regulation is mainly motivated by the consideration of avoiding the provision of State aid through the sale of public assets. State aid is present under Article 107(1) TFEU if (1) the Member State grants aid in any form whatsoever to an undertaking performing an economic activity; (2) this aid is granted through State resources; (3) these State resources provide an economic advantage to the undertaking(s) concerned which it/they would not have obtained through normal commercial activity; (4) the aid is selective (i.e. it applies only to one or more undertakings, a particular sector, etc.); (5) the aid threatens to distort or distorts competition by affecting trade between Member States. On the basis of this definition, the sale of assets may in certain cases involve State aid. As this led to the examination of several sales contracts by the European Commission, the latter has drawn up a general guideline[71] for Member States to clarify how a sale of assets

[68] For example if the contractor hires a subcontractor instead of using its own means.

[69] Case C-451/08, *Helmut Müller GmbH* v. *Bundesanstalt für Immobilienaufgaben* ECLI: EU:C:2010:168, paras. 60–63.

[70] Ibid., paras. 72–74.

[71] Commission Communication on State aid elements in sales of land and buildings by public authorities, OJ 1997, No. C 209/3. This Communication is now replaced by the Communication referred to in the following footnote.

can be carried out without unlawful State aid on the part of the selling government.[72]

In order to achieve the stated objective of the regulation on the sale of assets, the applicable legal provisions are aimed at creating sufficient competition between all potentially interested buyers in order to obtain the highest price.[73] This objective on the part of the European regulator makes it clear that here, too, the limited nature of this limited right is not, in fact, primarily at the root of the creation of the applicable regulations.

6.2.5 *Subsidies*

6.2.5.1 Definition and Characteristics

Unlike in public procurement, from a European law perspective, grants are not defined unambiguously, but in one way or another, depending on the applicable regulatory framework.[74] For example, the European Regulation on the financial rules applicable to the general budget of the Union describes a grant as 'a financial contribution by way of a donation'.[75] The European Commission's summary note to the aforementioned regulation states, somewhat more comprehensively, that '[g]rants are direct financial contributions from the European Union budget awarded by way of a donation to third-party beneficiaries (usually non-profit-making organisations) engaged in activities that serve EU

[72] Commission Notice on the notion of State aid as referred to in Article 107(1) of the Treaty on the Functioning of the European Union, OJ 2016, No. C 262/1.

[73] Ibid.

[74] The European Commission has now adopted a Proposal for a Regulation with the aim of regulating foreign subsidies that distort the internal market (COM/2021/223). Despite the fact that the applicable definition of a (foreign) subsidy is also based on the concept of 'financial contribution', this definition, given the objective of this Regulation, contains additional elements compared to other definitions. This definition reads as follows: 'For the purpose of this Regulation, a foreign subsidy shall be deemed to exist where a third country provides a financial contribution which confers a benefit to an undertaking engaging in an economic activity in the internal market and which is limited, in law or in fact, to an individual undertaking or industry or to several undertakings or industries' (Article 2 of the Proposal).

[75] Regulation of the European Parliament and of the Council 2018/1046 on the financial rules applicable to the general budget of the Union, amending Regulations (EU) No. 1296/2013, (EU) No. 1301/2013, (EU) No. 1303/2013, (EU) No. 1304/2013, (EU) No. 1309/2013, (EU) No. 1316/2013, (EU) No. 223/2014, (EU) No. 283/2014, and Decision No. 541/2014/EU and repealing Regulation (EU, Euratom) No. 966/2012, OJ 2018, No. L 193/1.

policies'.[76] The definition of grants, as already mentioned in this book by Van den Brink,[77] is somewhat consistent with this last definition of the European Commission.[78]

Also from the above definitions, several characteristics can be distilled which can lead to the qualification of a certain limited right as a subsidy.

A first characteristic is that a government provides financial resources through a subsidy. These resources can take different forms. Van den Brink[79] rightly points out that a subsidy may not only exist if a direct flow of funds is created between the government and the recipient of the subsidy, but also if, for example, the government acts as a guarantor on behalf of the recipient vis-à-vis the bank, enabling the recipient to obtain a loan which they would not have been able to take out without government assistance.

A second element that characterises a subsidy is that the granting of financial resources is not done randomly, but with the aim of supporting certain activities that fall within public policy goals. In this respect, the subsidy differs from public procurement because the beneficiary of the financed activities is not directly the government itself, but in the majority of cases[80] a third party alien to the relationship between the government and the subsidy recipient. For example, a sports club applies for a grant. The public authority grants a subsidy for the purpose of constructing sports infrastructure. The beneficiaries of this subsidised activity will

[76] European Commission, 'Before you apply: EU funding for beginners,' last accessed 28 December, available at https://ec.europa.eu/info/funding-tenders/how-apply/you-apply-eu-funding-beginners_en. Some definitions use the same point of view, although in slightly different terms, e.g. the definition of the UK Department of Economics and Finance: 'A grant is a financial transfer used to fund an activity because *that activity is in broad alignment with the funder's objectives*' [italics added] (HM Treasury, *Improving Financial Relationships with the Third Sector: Guidance to Funders and Purchasers* (London: HM Treasury, 2006), p. 5).

[77] See the chapter of Van den Brink, Section 4.2.

[78] Subsidies, according to this definition, are 'the allocation of financial resources by the government for the purpose of undertaking certain activities in furtherance of public policy goals, without these resources constituting a compensation for goods, works or services which the beneficiary of the subsidy has (potentially) provided to the government'.

[79] See the chapter of Van den Brink, Section 4.2.

[80] Given the specific objectives that a government tries to achieve through granting a subsidy, the beneficiary of the financed activity can, in certain cases, also be the subsidy recipient itself. Think, for example, of a subsidy for the installation of solar panels. It is the grant recipient itself that mainly benefits (alongside possible third parties) from the subsidised solar energy.

be (mainly) third parties, namely the members of the sports club. This system is substantially different in public procurement where the government purchases goods, works or services to support its own operations or where it manages its own services.

The latter aspect is linked to the third characteristic of a grant, which is that, unlike in public procurement, its award does not in principle create a contract for pecuniary interest between the government and the subsidy recipient. A decision by a government to award a subsidy merely creates an obligation for the government to actually pay that grant for a certain period of time or at a given moment. However, such a decision does not impose any obligation on the recipient of the subsidy to actually carry out the activities for which the subsidy was granted. Consequently, the award of a subsidy does not give rise to any reciprocal obligations between parties.

However, the absence of reciprocal obligations does not prevent the granting authority from having means available if the recipient of the subsidy does not behave as the government has originally intended (fourth characteristic). If the subsidised activities are not carried out, the authority can always demand repayment of the subsidies initially granted. In addition, if necessary, the government can always withdraw the subsidy.[81] The obligation of the government to actually disburse the promised grants only applies to the extent that the beneficiary of the grant continues to comply with the conditions set by the government.

In the light of the above, the distinction between public procurement and subsidies seems fairly easy to make. In practice, however, this is not always possible. For example, in order to obtain some control over the spending of the subsidies received, the government can conclude an implementation agreement with the subsidy recipient.[82] Such an agreement imposes a performance obligation on the beneficiary of the grant, which also exists for the contractor in case of a public contract or a

[81] A. Drahmann, *Transparante en eerlijke verdeling van schaarse besluiten* (Deventer: Wolters Kluwer, 2015), p. 154.

[82] The conclusion of an implementation agreement can therefore increase the practical relevance of a grant. See, for instance, an agreement between the City of Ghent and a non-profit organisation concerning the organisation of summer camps: https://ebesluitvorming.gent.be/document/5ee78629937e551d0726f0a2;jsessionid=BB7BA9FAD58AB5844616757583801DDBE9 (consulted on 12 January 2022). See further J. E. van den Brink and L. W. Verboeket, 'Subsidie of aanbesteding? Subsidie met uitvoeringsovereenkomst kan een aanbestedingsplichtige overheidsopdracht zijn', (2019) *Administratiefrechtelijke Beslissingen*, 319, para. 2.

concession.[83] Another aspect that may bring a subsidy within the scope of public procurement is the extent to which the amount paid by the government covers the cost of performing the subsidised activity. If a government fully finances the activity at a market price (cost with profit margin), this could possibly be qualified as a public contract.[84]

An illustration of the thin line between subsidies and public contracts can be found in a judgment of the European Court of Justice of 18 October 2018 (*IBA Molecular* judgment).[85] The facts of this case are as follows: in 2015, the Italian region of Veneto transferred a sum of EUR 700,000 to the religiously inspired institution 'Sacro Cuore'. The contract implementing this funding provided that 'Sacro Cuore' had undertaken to manufacture and supply a particular medicinal product to several public hospitals. Sacro Cuore was not entitled to demand payment from the hospitals other than a flat-rate delivery charge of 180 EUR. The question the Court of Justice had to answer was whether this contract was a contract for pecuniary interest as defined in the public procurement Directives. The Court ruled that this was such a contract without any doubt. As explained earlier, a public contract exists if there is an exchange of performances. The fact that the remuneration is limited to a partial reimbursement of the costs incurred in performing the contract does not affect this. This ruling must be endorsed. Contrary to what is usually the case with a subsidy, the government here actually reimbursed, under the guise of financing, services of which it was the ultimate beneficiary (i.e. the public hospitals within the region that were supplied with the medicinal products). It can also be pointed out that in return for funding, the beneficiary of these funds was obliged to spend them in a well-defined manner. Moreover, these funds covered almost all the costs associated with the provision of the services.

6.2.5.2 Regulation

In contrast to public procurement, subsidies are not extensively regulated at the European level. Here too, the European regulator has paid

[83] See footnotes earlier in this contribution.

[84] Drahmann, *Transparante en eerlijke verdeling van schaarse besluiten* p. 156. The market-based remuneration here is a payment by the government, as the beneficiary of the financed activities. Consequently, the second characteristic of a grant is absent here.

[85] Case C-606/17, *IBA Molecular Italy Srl* v. *Azienda ULSS n. 3 and Others* ECLI:EU:C:2018:843.

attention to how interference with State aid can be avoided.[86] Besides that, the national and European legal frameworks mainly regulate how and which amount of subsidies can be granted. As van den Brink rightly points out, the granting of subsidies can serve various purposes. Logically, these purposes will prompt the government to regulate the allocation of subsidies. Regulation will often make it possible for the government to check whether the activity for which the subsidy was requested is in line with the intended public policy goals, whether the subsidy is actually spent on the activities concerned and is not used for other purposes, to create clarity and transparency about when a certain subsidy can be granted to whom, and so on. Thus, as with the other legal forms discussed, the limited nature of a subsidy was/is not the primary consideration for creating its legal framework.[87]

6.2.6 *Licences*

6.2.6.1 Definition and Characteristics

A definition of licences can be found in the conjunctive reading of the recitals of the European Concession Directive and the European Services Directive. For example, the Concession Directive defines licences, to which licences under the Services Directive also belong,[88] as an act by which the government, on request of an economic operator and not on its own initiative, establishes the conditions for the exercise of an economic activity, leaving the economic operator free to exercise the licensed activities or not.[89] In conjunction with the relevant recitals of the European Services Directive, a public authority gives a licence in practice, for example, if the natural resources available or the technical possibilities are limited.[90] Consequently, the following items, among others, can be

[86] Commission Notice on the notion of State aid as referred to in Article 107(1) of the Treaty on the Functioning of the European Union, OJ 2016, No. C 262/1.

[87] In comparison with public procurement, this statement is even more valid. Subsidies can also be of a non-limited nature (e.g. if there is no maximum amount, the number of possible subsidy recipients is not limited, etc.).

[88] Recital 39 of the Directive of the European Parliament and of the Council 2006/123/EG, 12 December 2006 on services in the internal market, OJ 2006, No. 376/36 (further: Services Directive).

[89] Directive 2014/23/EU of the European Parliament and of the Council of 26 February 2014 on the award of concession contracts, OJ 2014, No. 94/1, recital 14. Express reference here is made to the Services Directive.

[90] Recital 62 of the Services Directive.

regarded as a licence: telecommunication and radio frequencies, time slots at airports, CO_2 emission rights and so on.

From the above definition, several characteristics can be derived that will determine whether a certain limited right can be qualified as a licence or not.

A first characteristic is that, in contrast to public procurement, the granting of a licence by the government does not create a contract for pecuniary interest. In this case, the public authority merely grants permission to an economic operator to carry out a certain economic activity. This qualification as an authorisation influences the degree of enforceability of the relevant activity by the government (for further explanation, see the fourth characteristic of licences).

A second element characterising a licence is the purpose with which the government actually grants it. Unlike in the case of public procurement, a licence will (mainly) serve the economic operator and not the licencing authority. Indeed, with a licence, the licencing authority does not seek to support or organise its own services, but rather to organise a limited market in an objective manner by setting general admission conditions. This aim is already achieved by the mere creation of the licence, whereas in public procurement the mere creation of the concession or public contract cannot achieve the aim of supporting or organising the public service without going through a whole award procedure.

The third characteristic of a licence is the capacity of the party to whom the authority grants the licence. Indeed, the party applying for a licence is explicitly referred to in the above definition as an 'economic operator'. At first sight, a difference could be discerned when compared to the other limited rights,[91] but if the concept of 'economic operator' were to be interpreted in accordance with the European competition law concept of 'undertaking', a public authority could also be described as such, if it were to offer goods or services on the market[92] and to apply for a licence on that basis. From this point of view, the applicant for a licence would not necessarily have to be a private operator.

A fourth characteristic of a licence, which partly follows from the first element, is the different, less active, role that the government fulfils compared to public procurement. Despite the fact that when granting a

[91] Indeed, from the above definitions of public contracts, concessions, sale of assets and subsidies, it can be deduced that these limited rights can be present both in the relationship between governments and private persons as just between governments.

[92] See, for example, T-319/99, *Fenin* v. *Commission* ECLI:EU:T:2003:50.

licence, as is the case with the award of a concession, the government gives a right to perform certain acts, the government will not be able to legally enforce the economic activity authorised by the licence. Indeed, the licensee, unlike the beneficiary of a concession, is free to carry out the economic activity or not.[93] Consequently, if the economic operator does not comply with the conditions imposed in the licence, this can only result in the loss of the licence. There will be no question of carrying out the activity or activities concerned at the expense and risk of the operator, as is the case with public procurement. Of course, the government is free, after taking away the licence from the initial holder, to grant the licence to another economic operator if the latter meets the conditions set by the government. This will often be the case when it comes to licences for economically very advantageous or necessary activities, such as, for example, the allocation of time slots at airports or the licence for the execution of emergency services.

On the basis of the above characteristics, the distinction between licences and public procurement seems fairly easy to make. This is also confirmed in practice, where the demarcation between licences and public procurement rarely gives rise to problems.

The delineation between licences and concessions has also been addressed in several cases that the European Court of Justice had to assess.

In this respect, the *Belgacom* judgment is particularly interesting. In this case, several public authorities had concluded an agreement with a private operator which gave this operator the exclusive right to exploit cable networks for remote distribution and gave it television activities and subscribers as well. This transfer was accompanied by an obligation on the part of the operator to carry out the transfer. In this judgment, the European Court of Justice subtly points out the element that determines whether or not a certain public act is classified as a concession or as a licence. Indeed, the Court states that if the economic operator was not required by the public authorities to perform the transferred activities, it would be a licence and not a concession.[94] Also in other cases, the

[93] In this respect, the granting of a licence shows some resemblance to the sale of assets, with the difference that a licence will often be granted for a certain period of time, whereas with a sale of assets the buyer acquires a basically perpetual right of ownership.

[94] Case C-221/12, *Belgacom NV* v. *Interkommunale voor Teledistributie van het Gewest Antwerpen (INTEGAN) and Others* ECLI:EU:C:2013:736, recital 33. However, according to the Court, this does not affect the applicability of the obligation of transparency.

obligation to perform – and thus the legally enforceable nature of the relevant economic activity – emerges as an important element in assessing the demarcation between a licence and a concession.

The question of the dividing line between licences and concessions was also addressed in the so-called *Promoimpresa* judgment of 14 July 2016.[95] This case concerned authorisations granted by the government for the operation of a domain area for tourist–recreational purposes. According to the Court, these public acts can be classified as authorisations[96] within the meaning of the Services Directive, as they are formal decisions by the public authorities which operators must obtain in order to be able to carry out an economic activity for tourism and recreation purposes. These are not agreements aimed at imposing the performance of a specific activity (for the benefit of public authorities), for which a party obtains a right of exploitation with an associated risk of exploitation. The authority in question merely grants permission to carry out an economic activity in a given area.[97]

As regards the distinction between licences and public contracts, reference can be made to the *Politano* judgment of 8 September 2016.[98] This case concerned the granting of licences for the provision of betting and gambling services. As the Court of Justice and the Advocate-General rightly pointed out, the services which are the subject of those licences, namely the provision of betting and gambling services, are not provided for the benefit of the licensing authority. In this respect alone, a licence differs from a public contract, where it is at the request of the public authority that the selected contractor carries out certain well-defined works, services or supplies. In this regard, reference can once again be made to what the Concession Directive says on this subject, namely that a licence is not granted at the initiative of the authority concerned, but at the request of one or more economic operators.[99] However, what the Court seems to have omitted, and what could have strengthened its argument, is the reference to the freedom of the licensee to exercise or

[95] Joined Cases C-458/14 and C-67/15, *Promoimpresa srl and Others* v. *Consorzio dei comuni della Sponda Bresciana del Lago di Garda e del Lago di Idro and Others* ECLI: EU:C:2016:558.

[96] Including a license, which is one of the possible authorisations within the meaning of the Services Directive (recital 39 of the Services Directive).

[97] See also recital 57 of the Services Directive.

[98] Case C-225/15, *Domenico Politano*, ECLI:EU:C:2016:645. See also recital 51 of the opinion of Advocate General Wahl of 16 June 2016 in this case, ECLI:EU:C:2016:456.

[99] Recital 14 of the Directive 2014/23/EU.

not the economic activity concerned and the concomitant lack of legal enforceability vis-à-vis the public authorities. This is also an important difference with public procurement.

6.2.6.2 Regulation

Licences differ from public procurement not only in terms of content, but also in the degree of regulation. Contrary to what is the case for public procurement, the European legislator has not created one all-encompassing framework for (almost) all licences. Because of the very diverse number of sectors in which the government may be required to grant licences, ranging from the telecommunications and radio sector to the gambling sector, licences are regulated in a fragmented way. With the aforementioned Services Directive, however, the European legislator took a step in the right direction and tried to create a fairly general framework for the granting of licences that give access to the performance of certain service activities. The primary incentives on the part of the European regulator for creating this framework appear to be the removal of barriers to the European internal market and the guarantee of the freedom of establishment and freedom to provide services between the Member States.[100] Here again, scarcity does not seem to have been a primary consideration in regulating the granting of licences through the Services Directive. Contrary to the other legal concepts discussed, it seems clearer that scarcity does constitute an important *subsidiary* consideration here. For example, recital 62 of the Services Directive states that, when the number of available authorisations for an activity is limited due to scarcity, a selection procedure must be organised to choose between different candidates and thus improve the quality and conditions of the services offered to users through the functioning of the free market.

6.3 The Development of a Common Regime from the Nature and Characteristics of the Limited Rights under Discussion?

As demonstrated earlier, it is not always easy to distinguish between different limited rights. Despite this increasing complexity, there is, at the same time, an increasing need for accurate identification and qualification of the different legal concepts. Given this need for legal certainty, some limited rights have been subject to increasingly extensive regulation.

[100] Recitals 7 and 12 of the Services Directive.

However, this regulatory tendency is, as follows from what was explained earlier, mainly fragmented, in the sense that the extent to which the legislator intervenes depends very much on the nature and the characteristics of the limited right in question, as well as on the objective that the regulator wishes to achieve. For example, reference was made to the regulation of public procurement, which is very precise and extensive, as opposed to the limited regulation of the sale of assets.

The question now is whether the overarching notion of 'limited right', despite the different nature and characteristics of the legal concepts discussed here, causes, or is already causing, an evolution towards a common regime that can provide guidance in the distribution of all limited rights.[101]

In recent years, a consensus seems to have developed in the literature that it is increasingly possible to speak of an overarching framework that regulates the distribution of the various limited rights. Some authors do not hesitate to take a clear position on this. Wollenschläger, for example, states unequivocally that a cross-sectoral distribution regime has already been established.[102] Other authors put it somewhat more conditionally and speak of a slow but sure trend towards harmonisation.[103]

In our opinion, arguing that driven by European law, a regime would exist or would further develop to regulate the distribution of all limited rights is taking too big of a leap. On the one hand, it is stated that there is one overarching European framework, but on the other hand, this common regime is applied to limited rights, each of which, as demonstrated earlier, has its own special, distinguishable nature and characteristics. In our opinion, making the limited rights discussed subject to the

[101] See also F. J. van Ommeren, 'Bestuursrecht is verdelingsrecht. Iets over het onderscheid tussen publiek- en privaatrecht' in A. A. J. de Gier a.o. (ed.), *Goed verdedigbaar. Vernieuwing van bestuursrecht en omgevingsrecht* (Deventer: Kluwer 2011), pp. 98–99, who even takes the position that administrative law is essentially distributional law and the considerations of C. J. Wolswinkel, 'Verdelingsrecht en algemeen bestuursrecht: Naar een algemeen deel verdelingsrecht?' in T. Barkhuysen, B. Marseille, W. Den Ouden, H. Peters and R. Schlossels (eds.), *25 jaar Awb in eenheid en verscheidenheid* (Deventer: Wolters Kluwer, 2019), pp. 805–814.

[102] F. Wollenschläger, 'EU Law Principles for Allocating Scarce Goods and the Emergence of an Allocation Procedure', (2015) *REALaw*, 8(1) 205.

[103] P. C. Adriaanse, F. J. van Ommeren, W. van Ouden and C. J. Wolswinkel, 'The Allocation of Limited Rights by the Administration: A Quest for a General Legal Theory' in P. C. Adriaanse, F. J. van Ommeren, W. van Ouden and C. J. Wolswinkel (eds.), *Scarcity and the State I: The Allocation of Limited Rights by the Administration* (Cambridge: Intersentia, 2016), pp. 3–25.

application of a single common distribution framework wrongfully abstracts from the heterogeneity that arises with regard to the different nature that each of these limited rights possesses and the purpose that the government aims to achieve with each of these rights. For example, the purpose of public contracts is to provide (additional) support to the government, whereas by means of a sale of assets the government wishes to divest itself of certain assets, often to increase efficiency. As explained in detail above, the other limited rights also have a different purpose. Various examples are conceivable in which the nature and characteristics (including the intended purpose) of the limited rights cannot be reconciled and may therefore clash. Consequently, we feel there is a risk of artificially combining fundamentally different rights into one.

Parallel to tendencies at the European level, important legal developments are taking place within the national legal frameworks of Member States. These developments may possibly be (partly) inspired by evolutions at the European level, but will have their own focus (e.g. by the use of a different legal basis), because of the way in which the legal system concerned is structured.

In this context, one can point to the recent developments in Dutch law on the distribution of limited rights. Here, we clearly see that in (purely) internal situations there is a tendency to abstract from the different nature and characteristics of certain limited rights and an evolution towards a common distribution regime. Moreover, contrary to what is the case from a European law perspective, this regime is not based on different foundations that are brought together into one, but has a pre-existing principle, namely the principle of equality, as its legal basis.

An important pivotal point in the development of a Dutch common distribution framework is the so-called *Speelautomatenhal Vlaardingen* judgment by the Dutch Council of State. This case concerned the granting of two licences for the operation of a gaming hall in the municipality of Vlaardingen. The mayor had not 'put these licences on the market' but had awarded them directly to a certain private party. A third party, to whom the licence had not been granted, was of the opinion that the mayor's actions were not legally valid and therefore requested the annulment of the mayor's decision to grant these licenses. The Administrative Jurisdiction Division ruled that 'Dutch law contains a legal standard to the effect that, *when distributing limited licence(s), the administration must in some way offer (potential) interested parties the opportunity to compete for the permit(s) available. [...] This legal norm is based on the principle of equality*, which in this context aims to offer equal opportunities.' (own emphasis). This principle then gives rise to an obligation of transparency that imposes various specific requirements on the way in which an 'appropriate degree of publicity' can be achieved (including the timeliness of publication, clarity on distribution criteria, etc.).[104]

However, the development of a distribution framework in Dutch law is not limited to the distribution of licences. We also see that important jurisprudential steps are being taken with regard to the sale of assets. In this respect, reference can be made to the judgment of the Dutch Supreme Court of 26 November 2021. In this case, the municipality of Montferland sold a property that had a very good location as part of a redevelopment plan. This sale took place without the municipality having organised a public procedure for this purpose. The Dutch Supreme Court ruled here that '*when entering into and performing private-law contracts, a public body must observe the general principles of proper administration and thus the principle of equality*'. This therefore also applies to the decision with whom and under what conditions it concludes an agreement for the sale of real estate belonging to it. 'It follows from the principle of equality – which in this context means offering equal opportunities – that a public body that intends to sell a property belonging to it must offer space to (potential) candidates to compete for this property if there are several candidates for the purchase of this property or if it is reasonable to expect that there will be several candidates'.[105] Here, too, it is stated that in order to offer a truly equal opportunity, the government must ensure an adequate degree of publicity.

In our opinion, the above-mentioned judgments show that a development is taking place within the Dutch legal system towards a common distribution framework. Both in the distribution of licences and in the case of a sale of assets, the government is obliged, on the basis of the principle of equality, to offer (potential) bidders the necessary space for competition. This framework therefore seems to abstract from the different nature and characteristics of both limited rights.

Given that the principle of equality, which seems to form the basis of a common framework for the distribution of licences and sales of assets, should normally, as a general principle of administrative law, guide all government action, the question arises whether the aforementioned

[104] Council of State, 2 November 2016, ECLI:NL:RVS:2016:2927.
[105] Supreme Court, 26 November 2021, ECLI:NL:HR:2021:1778.

distribution regime should simply be transferred to the granting of other limited rights (e.g. public contracts, concessions and subsidies).

Despite the fact that the principle that the government should provide space for competition to (potential) bidders could easily be transferred to the other rights discussed, we believe that the very different nature and characteristics of these limited rights prevent a truly common distribution framework in practice. The obligation of the government to provide space for competition will have to be given a different concrete meaning in the light of the specific nature and characteristics of the relevant limited right.

That a harmonised distribution framework is not so obvious is already apparent from the existing rules with which a government must comply if it wishes to place limited rights in a position of limited competition (hereafter: the exceptions).

In our opinion, one cannot speak of one common regime if the guiding principle (i.e. offering sufficient room for competition) is the same, but the exceptions, which deviate from this principle to a certain extent, differ greatly depending on the relevant limited right. In this way, the distribution of one limited right can be very different from the distribution of another limited right. This can be explained by the fact that the exceptions originate from different regulations, which, given the nature of the limited right concerned, take a different approach.

For example, in public procurement law, a whole range of exceptions have been developed that (seem to) allow the government to award a public contract with less or without any form of competition.

The best-known exception is undoubtedly the in-house exception that originated in the well-known *Teckal* judgment[106] of the European Court of Justice. A second example is the exception of horizontal public–public cooperation. Other exceptions within European and national public procurement law are based on not reaching certain threshold values (small contracts) or allowing modifications (e.g. extensions, etc.). For small contracts, for example, reference can be made to the exception of the 'accepted invoice' as it exists in Belgian law.[107] This exception implies that contracts with an estimated value of less than EUR 30,000 (excluding VAT) can be awarded in a much more flexible manner, with limited competition.

[106] Case C-107/98, *Teckal Srl* v. *Comune di Viano and Azienda Gas-Acqua Consorziale (AGAC) di Reggio Emilia* ECLI:EU:C:1999:562.

[107] Article 92 of the Law on Public Procurement.

As public procurement law is often used as a source of inspiration for (the solution of) distribution issues, it is no coincidence that some authors have tried to transpose certain exceptions from public procurement law (or at least to investigate whether certain exceptions can be transposed) to other limited rights.[108] After all, distribution regimes of other limited rights have few, if any, exceptions. Take, for example, the Services Directive, which, at first glance, always seems to be based on the highest possible level of competition when it comes to the way in which licences are granted, and seems to leave almost no room for any exception(s). Given the different nature and characteristics of the relevant limited rights, such an exercise, aimed at transferring all the exceptions that apply to public contracts to other limited rights, is therefore not obvious.

If one were to opt, following Dutch law, to base an overarching distribution framework for all limited rights on the principle of equality, the question arises as to what impact this would have on the existing exceptions. As already mentioned, the equality principle means that, when distributing limited rights, a government, in principle, has to offer everyone an equal chance to acquire the relevant limited right. Within the Dutch law doctrine of limited rights, offering equal opportunities seems to be a rather general obligation with little room for exceptions. In the previously mentioned *Didam* judgment,[109] the Dutch Supreme Court ruled that it follows from the principle of equality that a public authority that intends to sell an asset belonging to it *must* offer space to (potential) interested parties to compete for the asset in question (own emphasis). According to the Court, this obligation in principle already applies when there is only a reasonable expectation that there will be several interested parties. Since this is not a certainty, the government is advised to offer equal opportunities in (almost) every case. The only case in which the Supreme Court does not require the government to start a full procedure with all its formalities is when it can be established on the basis of objective, verifiable and reasonable criteria that there is only one serious party who can purchase the asset in question. However, because the government really has to provide the necessary evidence, this exception seems to be rather empty in practice. The question is now how this

[108] R. Wildemors and C. J. Wolswinkel, 'Inbesteding bij schaarse vergunningen? Institutionele excepties op de transparantieverplichting', (2019) *Nederlands Tijdschrift voor Europees Recht*, 3/4, 119–127.

[109] Supreme Court, 26 November 2021, ECLI:NL:HR:2021:1778.

evolution will manifest itself in other situations of scarcity, which, for example, do not involve a sale of assets.

One may wonder what the impact is of the application of the principle of equality, as a basis for a common distribution regime, on the exceptions that allow a lesser degree of competition. Also from the perspective of European law, new questions will arise if a general principle of administrative law such as the principle of equality forms the basis for an overarching distribution framework of different limited rights. For example, the question arises as to how the exceptions for the award of low-value public contracts should be approached from this new angle.[110] Given that the regulation of public procurement (at the national level) was motivated by the objective to prevent favouritism in the award of contracts, a reduction in organised competition can easily be justified as the risk of corruption is logically lower for low-value contracts. However, a strict approach based on the principle of equality, as outlined above, risks putting such exceptions under pressure, since the obligation to provide equal opportunities is linked to the notion of scarcity that characterises a public contract as such and therefore also applies to small contracts.

6.4 Concluding Remarks

The above discussion shows the importance of properly distinguishing the different limited rights discussed in this book. The nature and characteristics of each limited right, as well as their mutual relationship, were extensively discussed, mostly starting from public procurement law.

Subsequently, the development of an overarching distribution framework, as identified increasingly in legal doctrine, was covered. The authors of this contribution formulated several critical reflections, which can be reduced to the view that the different nature and characteristics of the limited rights as well as the current diversity in legal regimes make a common distribution mechanism not self-evident.[111]

110 See also Arrowsmith, *The Law of Public Procurement and Utilities Procurement* (Vol. I), pp. 272–278; L. Bolzonello and E. Canali, *The Opacity of Transparency: Issues of Application of the Principle of Transparency to Public Contract Awards Falling Outside the Scope of Directive 2004/18* (Maastricht: Maastricht Centre for European Law, 2012), pp. 14–18.

111 Namely, how detailed the overarching distribution framework will be in nature.

The (as yet) imperfect harmonisation and the lack of an adequate common distribution framework with overarching exceptions led to many new, often complex, legal questions and associated legal uncertainty. Moreover, as Arrowsmith rightly points out in her contribution to this book, grafting a common distribution framework onto the principle of equality (which abstracts from the different nature and characteristics of the limited rights involved) risks creating tension between the various interests that a government must pursue.[112] On the one hand, the principle of equality will require the government to offer equal opportunities to interested parties, possibly even for low-value contracts, as discussed above. Organising such equality requires special efforts on the part of the public authorities, as well as the necessary time and resources. On the other hand, the next principle applies that a public authority must act in a financially efficient manner, since its operation is (mainly) financed by taxpayers' money. If the idea of equal opportunities is applied in an absolute way, as is increasingly the case, this second principle may be neglected and the authority may be forced to organise a (costly) procedure knowing that the costs incurred can never be compensated by the possible benefits obtained as a result of organising competition.

Perhaps modern technologies and automation[113] can solve this in due time, or the wider acceptance of alternative distribution mechanisms, such as first come, first served, can offer partial solutions.[114] But today's conclusion is that these digital platforms do not yet exist and the organisation of competitive bidding procedures is increasingly emphasised. Time will tell how this issue will evolve.

[112] See the chapter of Arrowsmith, Section 2.5.

[113] See already G. Racca, 'The Role of IT-Solutions in the Award and Execution of Public Procurement Rules below Thresholds and List B Services: Overcoming E-barriers' in D. Dragos and R. Caranta (eds.), *Outside the EU-Procurement Directives–Inside the Treaty* (Copenhagen: DJØF Publishing, 2012), p. 373.

[114] Because the government has to invest less time and resources and automatic systems take over the role of the government to some extent.

7

Balancing Public Interests through Limitation, Allocation and Execution of Limited Rights

JOHAN WOLSWINKEL

7.1 Introduction

Competitive tendering is considered an adequate, even preferred, mechanism for governments to make a sound and solid choice between potential recipients of governmental rights that are available in limited quantity only (such as public contracts and certain licences and subsidies). Competitive tendering, it is presumed, allows governments to realize several public interests that are all at stake when awarding these 'limited rights', such as value for money and other (additional) policies, equal treatment and transparency. However, given the multitude of public interests involved, it should not come as a surprise that it is often impossible to realize all these public interests to their full extent. In fact, realizing one public interest can come at the expense of other public interests. Because of these interconnections between public interests, it is important to identify which relative weight is put on the different public interests involved in the award of limited rights.

This question cannot be answered straightforwardly, however, as the relative weight and the exact configuration of public interests depend on the limited right at stake. For example, the public interest of 'value for money' plays a key role in public procurement dealing with the award of public contracts, whereas this public interest is much less developed when so-called limited licensing schemes are concerned. This might not only be due to the inherent characteristics of the limited right at stake, but also to the applicable legal frameworks governing the award of these limited rights.

There is an additional reason why this question cannot be answered straightforwardly. In order to understand and explain the differences between limited rights when the realization of public interests is involved, comparison of these different limited rights should not be restricted to the actual 'allocation' stage, to which competitive tendering applies as a mechanism to make a choice between applicants. To explain the relative weight attached to public interests when awarding limited rights, this allocation stage, through competitive tendering or not, should be considered as part of a bigger 'life cycle' of limited rights. Within this life cycle, allocation decisions are preceded by some limitation decisions, as limited availability of rights is a necessary precondition for allocation. The issue of which public interests could or should be pursued when awarding limited rights, through competitive tendering or not, might therefore also be determined by the choices made in the preceding limitation stage. For example, where the number of licences is restricted for the sake of public safety, this public interest has already been realized partially, irrespective of the outcome of the allocation procedure. What is more, government rights such as concessions or licences often establish a long-term (legal) relationship between governments and recipients, such that choices made in the allocation stage will cast a shadow on the execution stage, that is, the stage where the limited rights that have been awarded are actually 'in use' for the exercise of certain activities. For example, whether or not it is possible to modify a limited right after its award (e.g. by prolongation) will also depend on the choices made by the allocating authority in the initial allocation stage.

The decomposition of the award process into these three stages of limitation, allocation and execution provides a useful analytical framework for the question of how public interests are pursued when limited rights are awarded. This framework helps to understand the dynamics and interdependencies between these stages for different types of limited rights, which contributes to explaining differences in the award of these limited rights when pursuing public interests. What is more, this analytical framework also helps to critically interrogate differences between the applicable legal regimes governing the award of limited rights: Are these differences justified by the differences inherent to the various types of limited rights or should the various legal regimes converge to one another?

To answer these questions, this contribution has been structured as follows. First, it compares four different types of limited rights (subsidies, licenses, public contracts and government sales) as far as the pursuit of public interests is concerned (Section 7.2). This comparative section mainly brings together results from the different chapters in Part I of this edited volume. While this comparison has been structured to expose some (but not all) of the interdependencies between the public interests involved, it does not involve a separate legal analysis of the applicable legal regimes.[1] Next, Section 7.3 will discuss to what extent and in what way the applicable legal regime covers the realization of public interests in the three different stages involved in the life cycle of limited rights (i.e. limitation, allocation and execution). Finally, Section 7.4 will discuss the interdependencies between these different stages, which vary across the different types of limited rights. These findings will shed light on the variations between limited rights when pursuing and realizing public interests. In the concluding Section 7.5, new pathways for legal development are sketched.

7.2 Interdependencies between Public Interests

7.2.1 Many Interdependencies

Several public interests can be pursued when awarding limited rights, such as value for money, equal treatment and opening of markets. Some of these public interests (such as value for money or opening of markets)[2] have a more outcome- or output-oriented character, whereas other public interests are more process-oriented (such as equal treatment or transparency). The different chapters in Part I of this edited volume show there are many interdependencies between these public interests. In some cases, these interdependencies consist of a considerable amount of overlap or parallelism between public interests. In other cases, the attainment of certain public interests is squarely at odds with the attainment of other public interests.

Considering first the subset of so-called process-related public interests (equal treatment, fair treatment, transparency, accountability and efficiency of the process), it turns out that these interests are certainly not unique for the award of limited rights, but have a particular meaning and weight in that distributive context. This contextualization of process-related interests also has an impact on their mutual interplay. For example, Arrowsmith questions the added value of distinguishing transparency as a separate public interest in the context of awarding limited rights, as it is merely a means to achieve other public interests, such as

[1] See Chapter 2 of Arrowsmith, Chapter 3 of Wollenschläger, Chapter 4 of Van den Brink and Chapter 5 of Caranta and Biancardi for the analysis of public contracts, licences, subsidies and government sales, respectively.

[2] With references to Section 2.3 of the chapter of Arrowsmith, Wolswinkel, Jansen and Van Ommeren identify eleven different public interests involved in the award of limited rights in Chapter 1.

equal treatment of tenderers and accountability.[3] Moreover, given the enormous weight attributed to equal treatment when awarding limited rights, the added value of distinguishing fair treatment as a separate public interest is not always clear, although this value is sometimes found in guarantees of due process during and after the allocation process. But even after re-ordering and re-interpreting these process-related interests, a potential tension between these interests remains. This holds in particular for transparency, equal treatment and accountability on the one hand and efficiency on the other hand: where transparency can contribute to equal treatment and accountability, it can at the same time harm the efficiency of the process since a call for competition can be the start of an expensive and time-consuming process of comparing applications.[4]

Switching our attention to the subset of so-called output-related interests, there is a similar challenge in relating public interests to each other. Arrowsmith, for example, argues that the output-related interests of safeguarding fundamental rights is not an interest that can be balanced against other considerations in regulating public procurement, but is a value that must be fully respected in all cases.[5] In the same vein, Wollenschläger poses that the State is not free to choose whether or not to safeguard fundamental rights, even though fundamental rights usually leave some room for balancing competing public and private interests.[6] Other output-related interests than safeguarding fundamental rights (such as value for money, integrity, opening of markets and (other) additional policies) could be balanced, not only against other output-related interests, but also against process-related interests. This can be illustrated by the example of integrity. Caranta and Biancardi conclude that the process-related interests of accountability, transparency, fair treatment and equal treatment partake in integrity,[7] while Wollenschläger argues that the integrity of the allocation process must be secured by transparent criteria and procedures.[8] Van den Brink considers the public interest of integrity on its own by problematizing subsidies as the pre-eminent instrument for public authorities to 'maintain relationships',[9] but Arrowsmith highlights the close relationship

[3] See Section 2.3 of the chapter of Arrowsmith.
[4] See, for more detail, Chapter 9 of Buijze.
[5] See Section 2.3 of the chapter of Arrowsmith.
[6] See Section 3.3.2.4 of the chapter of Wollenschläger.
[7] See Section 5.3.2.1 of the chapter of Caranta and Biancardi.
[8] See Section 3.3.2.5 of the chapter of Wollenschläger.
[9] See Section 4.3 of the chapter of Van der Brink.

between integrity and other 'output-related' interests, as integrity problems often have an adverse impact on the attainment of other public interests, including value for money in implementing commercial or horizontal objectives.[10]

Thus, even at first sight, several interdependencies between public interests become visible: between process-related interests, between process- and output-related interests and between output-related interests. These interdependencies are not one-directional: transparency, for example, can harm the efficiency of the process, but can also contribute to it. In the following of this section, the analysis will focus on the dynamics between several output-related interests. The reason therefore is that unlike process-related interests, which are focusing on the allocation process only, these output-related interests give reason to consider the allocation of limited rights as part of a bigger life cycle aimed at the realization of certain public interests. In particular, this analysis of output-related interests will focus on the interplay between four public interests: (i) ensuring inherent needs, (ii) value for money, (iii) so-called additional policies and (iv) opening of markets.

7.2.2 *Value for Money as an Inherent Need?*

First of all, the relationship between value for money and so-called inherent needs of limited rights deserves attention. To acquire something (a good or service) as a government is considered as the need inherent to the award of a public contract. Government sales reflect an opposite need, as governments want to get rid of something when selling public assets. However, to get rid of something is usually not the main reason for government sales. As Caranta and Biancardi point out, other public interests such as raising money, reducing deficits, creating or strengthening private markets or promoting smallholder families in land sales may be the main reason for sale, according to the circumstances. The public interest of value for money, which translates into raising money or value maximization (best value for what is sold) in the context of government sales, may overlap with the inherent need of governmental sales.[11] With regard to public contracts, Arrowsmith argues that value for money (in relation to commercial aspects of the contract) covers several dimensions: apart from the actual acquisition of certain goods and services (hence the 'inherent

[10] See Section 2.3 of the chapter of Arrowsmith.

[11] See Section 5.3.1 of the chapter of Caranta and Biancardi.

need'), it implies ensuring (i) that goods or services procured are both suitable for purpose and not over-specified, (ii) that they are acquired on the best possible terms, which may involve considering not just price but also other commercial elements such as quality and delivery time, and (iii) that the supplier actually provides the goods or services on the agreed terms. Thus, value for money is intrinsically linked to the actual acquisition of goods and services under public contracts.[12]

This overlap between the inherent need of limited rights and value for money is less evident for the two other limited rights considered in this volume: licences and subsidies. The main reason to authorize something is to keep control over certain activities to safeguard certain public interests, while subsidies are primarily meant as a financial incentive to stimulate certain activities, again for the sake of certain public interests. Although the monetary element is inherent to subsidies, the interest of value for money is usually separated from the inherent need of promoting certain activities. Van den Brink translates this interest of value for money into a distinct public interest of 'sound financial management', which aims at ensuring an efficient spending of public money.[13] As far as licensing is concerned, value for money seems only loosely related to the public interests underlying the licensing scheme at stake. Wollenschläger points out that value for money may have two points of reference, that is, value for money for the public authority or for consumers of the licensed activity. If the award of a license is linked to financial or similar contributions on the part of the public authority, the public authority may have an interest in selecting the operator promising the lowest costs or the highest revenue for the public. Moreover, the public authority may also have an interest in the conditions offered for the licensed activity constituting value for money for its consumers.[14] In any case, the interest of value for money does not seem to be omnipresent in limited licensing: although some licensing schemes hint at the importance of the optimal or efficient use of resources (e.g. 'effective and efficient use of radio spectrum' in the area of telecommunications), which can be considered an operationalization of value for money in the context of licensing, this 'efficient use' is certainly not a key consideration in all limited licensing schemes.[15]

[12] See Section 2.3 of the chapter of Arrowsmith.

[13] See Section 4.3 of the chapter of Van den Brink.

[14] See Section 3.3.2.2 of the chapter of Wollenschläger.

[15] The output-related interest of efficient use of the resource should be distinguished from the process-related interest of efficiency of the award procedure.

7.2.3 Positioning Additional Policies

Where value for money can be easily linked with the inherent need of certain limited rights, it is more difficult to relate 'additional policies' thereto. In general, additional (or horizontal) policies refer to public interests that are not *necessarily* connected with the objective for which the limited right involved is granted. In the context of public contracts, Arrowsmith describes how additional policies have been increasingly recognized, both under national and EU legislation. In particular, she points out that the EU objective of opening markets for competition needs to be balanced not only against Member State interests in commercial value for money (and integrity), but also to a certain extent against Member States' interests in pursuing their own horizontal policies (including the support of their national industry). EU law has traditionally been keen on putting constraints on the pursuit of additional policies by Member States, but increasingly requires Member States to promote horizontal policies of EU interest, such as preventing climate change, supporting small and medium-sized enterprises (SMEs) and promoting accessibility. Thus, public procurement is used as a tool to support or promote a variety of industrial, social or environmental objectives that are not *necessarily* connected with the objective for which the goods or services themselves are acquired.[16]

A general distinction between inherent needs and additional policies is less easy to draw when licensing is concerned, due to the enormous variety in licensing schemes: a public interest that might count as the inherent need of one licensing system (e.g. requiring permission for the sake of environmental protection) is not necessarily the inherent need of another licensing scheme. Therefore, it should be settled on a case-by-case basis whether certain public interests are intrinsically connected with the motives underlying the licensing scheme and should therefore not be classified as additional. The same holds for subsidies: the specific objective for which a subsidy is granted will determine whether a certain public interest is inherent to a certain subsidy scheme or not.[17]

In the context of governmental sales, the interest of achieving additional policies has received separate attention in European Union (EU)

[16] See Section 2.3 of the chapter of Arrowsmith, who distinguishes between value for money in relation to the commercial aspects and achieving and implementing 'additional' policies in an effective and efficient way.

[17] See Section 4.3 of the chapter of Van den Brink, who distinguishes between the achievement of public policy goals and the achievement of additional policy goals.

State aid law. According to the Commission Notice on the notion of State aid, a tender for the sale of assets, goods or services is unconditional when a potential buyer is generally free to acquire the assets, goods or services to be sold and to use them for its own purposes, irrespective of whether or not it runs certain businesses. If, however, there is a condition that the buyer is to assume special obligations for the benefit of the public authorities or in the general public interest, which a private seller would not have demanded (other than those arising from general domestic law or a decision of the planning authorities), the tender cannot be considered unconditional. When public bodies sell assets, the only relevant criterion for selecting the buyer should therefore be the highest price, also taking into account the requested contractual arrangements (e.g. the vendor's sales guarantee or other post-sale commitments).[18] Thus, the EU State aid regime does not seem to offer much room for taking into account additional policies in government sales.[19]

7.2.4 *Opening of Markets as an Additional (EU) Policy?*

As Arrowsmith points out, the objective of opening markets for competition is a public interest promoted by EU law, which needs to be balanced against Member State interests in realizing commercial value for money, domestic horizontal policies and integrity. With regard to limited licensing schemes, both the caselaw of the European Court of Justice (ECJ) on the compatibility of licensing schemes with the four market freedoms (goods, services, capital and workers) and secondary EU legislation, notably the Services Directive,[20] confirm that opening of markets is a key concern of EU law. With regard to government sales, opening of markets is promoted through the EU State aid regime rather than through the market freedoms. As Caranta and Biancardi argue, the EU is competent to lay down rules about government sales and privatizations insofar as these transactions can distort the competition on the internal market affecting the trade between Member States, including by giving unfair advantage to one undertaking.[21] Thus, the central aim of

[18] Commission Notice on the notion of State aid as referred to in Article 107(1) of the Treaty on the Functioning of the European Union, OJ 2016, No. C262/1, paras. 94–95.

[19] See also Section 5.4.2.1 of the chapter of Caranta and Biancardi.

[20] Directive 2006/123/EC of the European Parliament and of the Council of 12 December 2006 on services in the internal market, OJ 2006, No. L376/36.

[21] See Section 5.4.1 of the chapter of Caranta and Biancardi.

the State aid rules is here to prevent the sale of assets being incompatible with the internal market.

Given this emphasis in EU law on opening of markets in the context of public contracts, limited authorizations and governments sales, it is striking that Van den Brink does not discuss the public interest of opening up markets for competition separately when providing an overview of the public interests involved in the award of subsidies.[22] Admittedly, the impact of the free movement provisions is not straightforward for the award of subsidies. As the Court ruled in *ARGE*:

> [. . .] as a rule aid is granted to undertakings established on the territory of the Member State granting it. Such a practice, and the consequent unequal treatment of undertakings of other Member States is thus inherent in the concept of State aid. It does not, however, amount in itself to covert discrimination or a restriction on freedom to provide services within the meaning of Article 59 of the Treaty.[23]

But even where subsidy schemes as such do not constitute a restriction to free movement, these schemes can be at odds with the free movement provisions of the Treaty on the Functioning of the European Union (TFEU), which are the building blocks for the internal market. For example, the ECJ has considered a subsidy scheme where dwellings in another Member State were excluded from eligibility for subsidy for owner-occupied dwellings incompatible with Articles 21, 43 and 49 TFEU.[24]

Furthermore, subsidy schemes fall within the scope of EU State aid law more than once. According to Van den Brink, a subsidy is even the ultimate form of State aid. For State measures (including subsidy schemes) to be classified as State aid within the meaning of Article 107 TFEU, several conditions need to be fulfilled: (i) the existence of an undertaking, (ii) the imputability of the measure to the State, (iii) its financing through State resources, (iv) the granting of an advantage, (v) the selectivity of the measure and (vi) its effect on competition and trade between Member States.[25] Consequently, subsidy schemes targeted at

[22] See Section 4.3 of the chapter of Van den Brink.

[23] Case C-94/99, *ARGE Gewässerschutz* v. *Bundesministerium für Land- und Forstwirtschaft*, ECLI:EU:C:2000:677, para. 36

[24] Case C-152/05, *Commission of the European Communities* v. *Federal Republic of Germany*, ECLI:EU:C:2008:17, para. 31.

[25] See for more detail on these requirements the Commission Notice on the notion of State aid as referred to in Article 107(1) of the Treaty on the Functioning of the European Union, OJ 2016, No. C262/1.

natural persons not involved in an economic activity will not constitute State aid. Furthermore, State funding that does not have an effect on competition and trade between Member States is not incompatible with the internal market. However, a State measure is already considered to distort or threaten to distort competition when it is liable to improve the competitive position of the recipient compared to other undertakings with which it competes.[26] Likewise, it is sufficient that aid is liable to affect trade between Member States. The relatively small amount of aid or the relatively small size of the receiving undertaking does therefore not as such exclude the possibility that trade between Member States might be affected.[27] However, subsidy schemes are considered not to constitute incompatible State aid if the aid granted to a single undertaking over a given period of time does not exceed a certain fixed amount (so-called *de minimis* aid), as this kind of aid is deemed not to have any effect on trade between Member States and not to distort or threaten to distort competition.[28]

Despite these relatively low thresholds for subsidy schemes to enter the scope of EU State aid law, not every scheme is therefore incompatible with the internal market. In particular, EU State aid law allows for State measures to be compatible with the internal market when this aid is granted for certain purposes.[29] Thus, where the EU State aid regime promotes the public interest of opening markets and aims to prevent distortion of fair competition, it does not fully neglect other public interests (whether additional or not). Thus, in the context of government sales, even where attempts by Member States to pursue additional policies will be treated as State aid, this aid might be compatible with the

[26] Ibid., para. 187.

[27] Case C-518/13, *Eventech Ltd* v. *The Parking Adjudicator* ECLI:EU:C:2015:9. For more detail, refer to P. C. Adriaanse, 'The Influence of EU State Aid Law on the Allocation of Limited Rights by National Authorities', in P. C. Adriaanse, F. J. van Ommeren, W. den Ouden and C. J. Wolswinkel (eds.), *Scarcity and the State I. The Allocation of Limited Rights by the Administration* (Cambridge: Intersentia, 2016), pp. 229–231.

[28] Recitals 1 and 3 Commission Regulation (EU) No. 1407/2013 of 18 December 2013 on the application of Articles 107 and 108 of the Treaty on the Functioning of the European Union to *de minimis* aid, OJ 2013, No. L352/1.

[29] Council Regulation (EU) 2015/1588 of 13 July 2015 on the application of Articles 107 and 108 of the Treaty on the Functioning of the European Union to certain categories of horizontal State aid (codification), OJ 2015, No. L248/1, followed by Commission Regulation (EU) No. 651/2014 of 17 June 2014 declaring certain categories of aid compatible with the internal market in application of Articles 107 and 108 of the Treaty, OJ 2014, No. L187/1.

internal market under certain conditions.[30] In other words, EU State aid law contains some (limited) room for pursuing other additional policies than opening of markets. Examples thereof could be the need to promote the execution of an important project of common European interest or the need to facilitate the development of certain economic activities or of certain economic areas, provided this aid does not adversely affect trading conditions to an extent contrary to the common interest.[31] This balancing approach in EU State aid law is essentially similar to the evaluation of restrictions under EU free movement provisions: where restrictions to market freedoms (goods, services, workers, capital) are in principle forbidden, such restrictions can still be justified by overriding reasons relating to the public interest.[32]

7.2.5 Explaining the Differences: Beyond Allocation

The previous subsections show that the relative weight and the exact configuration of public interests depend on the limited right at stake. For example, the need for realizing value for money is omnipresent in the context of public contracts and government sales, whereas the applicability of this public interest is less evident in the context of subsidizing and – even more – licensing. By contrast, public interests that are sometimes considered as additional in public procurement are more than once the most important reasons for which a licence or subsidy is granted (and sometimes a government asset is put up for sale).

To some extent, these non-identical configurations of public interests can be explained by the legal regime applicable to the award of the limited right at stake. Where EU law has entered the scene, which is the case most prominently with public procurement law, the relative weight of opening markets for competition seems to increase. For limited rights which are less often subject to (detailed) obligations under EU law, the different public interests might be balanced in another way. Nonetheless, assuming that the applicable legal regime is shaped, at least to some extent, by the inherent characteristics of the limited right at stake, it is necessary to move beyond the differences in legal regimes and

30 See Section 5.4.1 of the chapter of Caranta and Biancardi.

31 Article 107(3)(b) and (c) TFEU.

32 See already Case C-55/94, *Reinhard Gebhard* v. *Consiglio dell'Ordine degli Avvocati e Procuratori di Milano* ECLI:EU:C:1995:411, para. 37.

to focus on the question of how the inherent characteristics of the limited right shape the balancing of public interests.

In order to further understand how differences in the characteristics of limited rights have an impact on the pursuit of public interests, it is useful to distinguish between different stages in the life cycle of limited rights. Where competitive tendering deals with the stage of 'allocation', that is, the choice of who will receive a scarce good and who will not, allocation decisions are preceded by some kind of limitation decision. The distinction between 'first-order' and 'second-order' decisions is useful here: where first-order decisions determine the total amount of the good to be allocated, second-order decisions specify how to allocate this good.[33] First-order decisions therefore deal with limitation, and second-order decisions with allocation. Considering that the award of limited rights will establish a legal relationship between governments and private parties, an additional category of 'third-order' decisions can be distinguished, referring to decisions taken by the government after the limited right has been allocated to a private party.[34] In line with these first-order, second-order and third-order decisions, we can distinguish between first-order, second-order and third-order objectives in the pursuit of public interests. In the remainder of this chapter, we will consider how these different levels of objectives are intertwined and impact the pursuit of public interests.

7.3 A Three-Stage Process

7.3.1 Limitation

Any scheme of limited rights presupposes a limitation to the number of rights available for grant. Merely by setting a maximum, public authorities can already pursue public interests, irrespective of the successive allocation. For example, when the number of taxi driving licences is limited to a maximum, the impact of this kind of transport on public traffic and road safety will be limited (assuming that every licensee can use only a limited number of cars). This process of setting a maximum has therefore distinct value in the pursuit of public interests, although the

[33] J. Elster, *Local Justice: How Institutions Allocate Scarce Goods and Necessary Burdens* (New York: Russell Sage Foundation, 1992), p. 139.

[34] Elster, *Local Justice*, p. 141, adds another category of third-order decisions: decisions by potential recipients of a scarce good that affect either the need for it or their likelihood of receiving it.

relative importance of this first-order decision depends on the limited right at stake.

At one edge of the spectrum, public contracts and government sales can be situated. The issue of limitation or establishing the 'size' of the contract is not primarily a legal one.[35] Where acquisition is central to the definition of procurement of public contracts,[36] there is no legal requirement that public authorities should acquire more or less than they actually do. Instead, the decision about the amount needed and the decision whether or not to purchase these goods or services from an external source are up to the public authority itself.[37] The absence of limitation decisions in public procurement law is not surprising, as – instead of being at its very heart – limitation is a precondition that procurement law takes for granted without questioning it. In *Falk Pharma*, the ECJ stressed the notion of exclusivity as being essential to the public procurement regime:

> Essentially, the risk of favouring national economic operators which that directive seeks to preclude is closely connected to the selection which the contracting authority intends to make from the admissible tenders and to the exclusivity which will result from the award of the contract concerned to the operator whose tender has been accepted or to the economic operators whose tenders have been accepted, in the case of a framework

[35] This does not mean that the issue of limitation (or delineation) is legally irrelevant in the context of public contracts. For example: since the EU Public Procurement Directive applies only if the estimated value of the contract exceeds the applicable monetary threshold (Article 4 of Directive 2014/24/EU of the European Parliament and of the Council of 26 February 2014 on public procurement and repealing Directive 2004/18/EC, OJ 2014, No. L94/65), the 'size' or volume of the contract matters for the applicable legal regime. In the same vein, Article 46 Public Procurement Directive allows for the possibility of dividing a contract into lots (on the basis of either size or subject matter), thereby not increasing the overall pie, but creating more (and smaller) pieces available for grant. For more detail, refer to Ignacio Herrera Anchustegui, 'Division into Lots and Demand Aggregation – Extremes Looking for the Correct Balance?', in Grith Skovgaard Ølykke and Albert Sanchez-Graells (eds.), *Reformation or Deformation of the EU Public Procurement Rules* (Cheltenham: Edward Elgar, 2016), 125–145 and C. E. C. Jansen, 'Stretching the Proportionality Principle: How Dutch Law Facilitates the Participation of SMEs in Public Procurement' (2022) 31 *Public Procurement Law Review* 214–238.

[36] R. Caranta, 'The Changes to the Public Contract Directives and the Story They Tell about How EU Law Works' (2015) 52 *Common Market Law Review* 391–460 at 446–448. See also Section 2.2 of the chapter of Arrowsmith, who characterizes public procurement as the activity of a public authority in purchasing goods or services from an external source.

[37] As Arrowsmith notes in Section 2.2 of her chapter, a broad understanding of public procurement also considers the identification of an authority's need for certain goods or services, which can be understood as determining the size of the public contract.

> agreement, that constituting the objective of a public procurement procedure.[38]

Thus, the ECJ considered as apparent that the *choice* of a tender and, thus, of a successful tenderer is intrinsically linked to the regulation of public contracts by that directive and, consequently, to the concept of 'public contract'.[39] This means that the legal regime on the award of public contracts is tailor-made for a decision context where the need for 'choice' and 'selection' is given. If this context is absent, principles of equal treatment and transparency do still apply, but in a different way as the need for organizing competition for a scarce good does not exist any more.[40]

For government sales, a similar reasoning applies. As Caranta and Biancardi argue with reference to Article 345 TFEU and the case-law of the ECJ,[41] the State is free to privatise or keep for itself a given public asset. Thus, there is no general legal requirement obliging public authorities to sell certain assets (goods, lands, buildings). Where the primary interest is to raise money, the amount of assets available for sale will be determined by the amount of money the government aims to raise with the selling process or by other policy considerations in favour of the sale of government assets.

It seems therefore fair to conclude that – due to the 'limitation' that is inherent to these two kinds of rights in the sense that these rights cannot 'exist' without limitation – public interests are not very present in the limitation stage as far as public contracts and government sales are concerned. To put it somewhat differently, the 'default' position for public contracts and government sales is *not* that private parties should in principle have access to a right that is limited for some reason. Instead, the 'default' position here is that a public authority is free in its decision to provide services itself instead of procuring them and in its decision to make its assets available for sale. Only as far as governments decide to enter the market and engage with external parties, they are bound

[38] Case C-410/14, *Dr. Falk Pharma GmbH* v. *DAK-Gesundheit* ECLI:EU:C:2016:399, para. 36 and Case C-9/17, *Maria Tirkkonen* ECLI:EU:C:2018:142, para. 29.

[39] Case C-410/14, *Falk Pharma GmbH* v. *DAK-Gesundheit*, para. 38 and Case C-9/17, *Maria Tirkkonen*, para. 30. See also Case C-436/20, *ASADE* ECLI:EU:C:2022:559, para. 68.

[40] Case C-410/14, *Falk Pharma GmbH* v. *DAK-Gesundheit*, paras. 43–47.

[41] Case C-105/12, *Staat der Nederlanden* v. *Essent NV (C-105/12), Essent Nederland BV (C-105/12), Eneco Holding NV (C-106/12) en Delta NV (C-107/12)* ECLI:EU:C:2013:677.

by certain obligations in order to ensure fair competition and equal treatment.

The 'default' position for licenses seems to be completely different. Creating scarcity is a necessary first step in the awarding process, as Wollenschläger describes extensively.[42] From a legal point of view, creating a licensing scheme is already considered an impediment to free movement, as service providers have to ask for permission before they can start their economic activity. Such a licensing scheme is therefore a restriction to free movement that needs to be justified.[43] A limitation of the number of licences (in other words: creating scarcity) is considered an *additional* restriction to free movement, since it *tends to limit* the number of service providers.[44] Consequently, this additional but usually non-discriminatory restriction needs to be justified by an overriding reason relating to the public interest and should be proportionate, that is, both suitable and necessary to attain this public interest.[45]

However, separate attention for this 'limitation decision' seems to be somewhat marginal in the Services Directive. Although this directive introduces a distinction between limited licenses because of overriding reasons relating to the public interest (Article 11) and limited licences because of scarcity of available natural resources and technical capacity (Article 12), it does not make very clear to what extent these 'quantitative restrictions' should be justified.[46] According to Wollenschläger, the need for justification of artificial scarcity ('because of overriding reasons relating to the public interest') will be higher than the need for justification of 'natural or technical scarcity',[47] even though the exact size of the limitation also deserves some justification in the latter case. The Electronic

[42] See Section 3.4.2.1 of the chapter of Wollenschläger.

[43] Article 9(1) Services Directive.

[44] Case C-169/07, *Hartlauer Handelsgesellschaft mbH* v. *Wiener Landesregierung and Oberösterreichische Landesregierung* ECLI:EU:C:2009:141, para. 36; Case C-570/07 and Case C-571/07, *José Manuel Blanco Pérez and María del Pilar Chao Gómez* v. *Consejería de Salud y Servicios Sanitarios and Principado de Asturias* ECLI:EU:C:2010:300, paras. 55–58, Case C-539/11, *Ottica New Line di Accardi Vincenzo* v. *Comune di Campobello di Mazara* ECLI:EU:C:2013:591, para. 27 and Case C-50/21, *Prestige and Limousine SL* v. *Área Metropolitana de Barcelona et al.* ECLI:EU:C:2022:997, para. 63.

[45] Case C-570/07 and Case C-571/07, *José Manuel Blanco Pérez and María del Pilar Chao Gómez* v. *Consejería de Salud y Servicios Sanitarios and Principado de Asturias* ECLI:EU:C:2010:300, para. 61.

[46] For more detail, see C. J. Wolswinkel, 'The Allocation of a Limited Number of Authorisations: Some General Requirements from European Law' (2009) 2 *REALaw* 61–104 at 78–87.

[47] See Section 3.4.2.1 of the chapter of Wollenschläger.

Commerce Code, for example, stipulates that Member States shall 'clearly state the reasons for limiting the rights of use, in particular by giving due weight to the need to maximise benefits for users and to facilitate the development of competition, and review, as appropriate, the limitation at regular intervals or at the reasonable request of affected undertakings'.[48] Wollenschläger suggests that this public interest of ensuring the optimal use of resources is an immediate result of the creation of scarcity: putting existent resources to optimum use may be required as an immediate consequence of the State's duty to mitigate scarcity.[49]

Finally, subsidies take an intermediate position in this respect. Like licensing schemes, subsidy schemes can have either an open-ended or a closed character. Therefore, it is an explicit choice of governments whether or not to use a maximum, although domestic law might require a limitation to the total amount of subsidies available for certain activities. In general, the choice for a maximum will be understandable and justified, given the need to restrict government expenditure. The exact size of that maximum is also hardly regulated, although some kind of principle of 'economy' (as part of the principle of sound financial management) may act as a legal constraint here, requiring that the resources used in the pursuit of certain activities are made available in due time, *in appropriate quantity and quality*, and at the best price.[50] But even where the limitation decision as such is hardly regulated for limited subsidies, this decision itself might invoke the EU State aid regime. Since making a choice between potential recipients is inherent to limited subsidies, this will imply that a 'selective advantage' within the meaning of State aid law is conferred to certain parties. In this respect, it is important to highlight the definition of 'competitive bidding process' in the General Block Exemption Regulation, which explicitly includes limitation in the sense that 'the budget or volume related to the bidding process is a binding

[48] Article 55(1)(a) of the Directive (EU) 2018/1972 of the European Parliament and of the Council of 11 December 2018 establishing the European Electronic Communications Code, OJ 2018, No. L321/36.

[49] See Section 3.4.2.1 of the chapter of Wollenschläger.

[50] Article 33 of the Financial Regulation in Regulation (Eu, Euratom) 2018/1046 of the European Parliament and of the Council of 18 July 2018 on the Financial Rules Applicable to the General Budget of the Union, Amending Regulations (EU) No. 1296/2013, (EU) No. 1301/2013, (EU) No. 1303/2013, (EU) No. 1304/2013, (EU) No. 1309/2013, (EU) No. 1316/2013, (EU) No. 223/2014, (EU) No. 283/2014, and Decision No. 541/2014/EU and Repealing Regulation (Eu, Euratom) No. 966/2012, OJ 2018, No. 193/1.

constraint leading to a situation where not all bidders can receive aid'.[51] Thus, limited budget or volume is an important driver for the EU State aid regime and its exemptions to be applicable.

7.3.2 *Allocation*

As far as the allocation stage is concerned, it is clear that publishing a call for competition implies the need to develop allocation criteria[52] in order to make a choice between competing parties.[53] The immediate question then is which allocation criteria can be used to award a limited right.[54] As far as the award of public contracts is concerned, EU legislation is clear about the kind of allocation criteria that can be taken into account. According to Article 67(1) of the Public Procurement Directive, the award of public contracts should be based on the *most economically advantageous tender.* This most economically advantageous tender – from the point of view of the contracting authority – is identified on the basis of the price or cost, using a cost-effectiveness approach, and may include the best price–quality ratio, which shall be assessed on the basis of criteria, including qualitative, environmental and/or social aspects, linked to the subject matter of the public contract in question. Thus, where the most economically advantageous tender can have price only as the award criterion, at least the award criteria should be linked to 'the subject-matter of the public contract in question', thereby excluding procedures such as a lottery or a first come, first served award. Arrowsmith explains that the underlying rationale for the requirement that award criteria should be linked to the subject matter of the contract, which was originally introduced

[51] See Article 2(38) of Commission Regulation (EU) No. 651/2014 of 17 June 2014 declaring certain categories of aid compatible with the internal market in application of Articles 107 and 108 of the Treaty, OJ 2014, No. L187/1, describing such a process as 'a non-discriminatory bidding process that provides for the participation of a sufficient number of undertakings and where the aid is granted on the basis of either the initial bid submitted by the bidder or a clearing price'. See, for more detail, Section 7.4.1.

[52] In fact, a further distinction can be made in the allocation stage between the choice of the allocation criteria and the application thereof.

[53] In the context of direct award to a single operator, there is no need to determine allocation criteria for a choice between several operators.

[54] See Section 3.4.3.2 of the chapter of Wollenschläger, who calls this the 'substantive' dimension of the allocation stage. To be sure, allocating authorities can also use threshold criteria in the allocation procedure to secure certain public interests.

through the ECJ's case-law,[55] has never been clearly articulated. However, the risk of abuse when formulating allocation criteria is one plausible explanation, as curtailing abuse of discretion was in fact the reason for the public procurement directives' original restrictions on award criteria. Thus, Arrowsmith argues that the origins of the rule that award criteria should be linked to the subject matter of the contract, should not be found in the public interest of creating value for money.[56]

In the case of government sales, the preference for a certain award criterion is even more strict. The sale of governmental assets should in principle be based on the *highest price* in order not to classify as State aid.[57] Apart from some opportunity to disregard purely speculative bids, there is hardly room to take into account other considerations than the highest price in order to avoid the classification of State aid. However, as mentioned before in Section 7.2.3, the classification as State aid does not necessarily imply that this aid is incompatible with the internal market, as allocation criteria could be chosen that contribute to the additional policies the EU State aid regime explicitly allows for.

As far as limited licenses are concerned, general EU legislation is hardly guiding as to the contents of the allocation criteria. The Services Directive, for example, merely states that Member States *may* take into account, in establishing the rules for the selection procedure, considerations of public health, social policy objectives, the health and safety of employees or self-employed persons, the protection of the environment, the preservation of cultural heritage and other overriding reasons relating to the public interest, in conformity with EU law.[58] An obligation to use such 'substantive' allocation criteria seems absent, thereby also providing room for allocation procedures such as a lottery or a first come, first served procedure. Sector-specific legislation is hardly more concrete. The Electronic Communications Code, for example, requires Member States to apply 'selection criteria [. . .] which are objective, transparent, non-discriminatory and proportionate'.[59] While the elements of 'objective'

[55] See, for example, Case 31/87, *Gebroeders Beentjes BV* v. *State of the Netherlands* ECLI:EU:C:1988:422.

[56] See Section 2.4.2.3 of the chapter of Arrowsmith.

[57] Case C-39/14, *BVVG Bodenverwertungs- und -verwaltungs GmbH* ECLI:EU:C:2015:470, para. 32. See also Joined Cases C-214/12 P, C-215/12 P and C-223/12 P, *Land Burgenland and Others* v. *Commission* ECLI:EU:C:2013:682, para. 94.

[58] Article 12(3) Services Directive.

[59] Article 55(7) Electronic Communications Code.

and 'transparent' do not relate directly to the contents of the criteria but have a more procedural character, the requirement that selection criteria should be non-discriminatory clearly relates to the substance of the allocation criteria used, as it excludes criteria that make direct or indirect distinction on the grounds of nationality. The most interesting element here is the requirement of 'proportionality'. While this requirement is often mentioned in EU legislation, also with regard to licensing schemes,[60] it establishes a substantive connection with the underlying public interest when applied to allocation criteria, as the criterion should be both suitable and necessary to pursue the public interest at stake.[61]

Interestingly, however, there is hardly any case-law on the impact of the requirement of proportionality on the choice of the allocation criteria. The exception in this respect is the judgment of the ECJ in *Bressol*, which is also discussed by Wollenschläger. As this case dealt with the admission of students to medicinal studies (instead of licensing schemes for economic activities), the ECJ applied the general prohibition of non-discrimination based on nationality (Article 18 TFEU) and the right of every Union citizen to move and reside freely within the territory of the EU Member States (Article 21 TFEU) instead of the corollary provisions on free movement. Interestingly, the ECJ did not only consider a limitation to the number of positions available for non-resident students, but also considered the allocation criteria used in the selection procedure, hence both the first-order limitation and the second-order allocation decision. In particular, it addressed the appropriateness of the allocation criteria to select among foreign students and questioned distribution by drawing lots since this method as such does not take into account the knowledge or experience of prospective students. According to the ECJ, the referring court had to ascertain whether the selection process for non-resident students is limited to the drawing of lots and, if that is the case, 'whether that means of selection based not on the aptitude of the candidates concerned but on chance is necessary to attain the objectives pursued'.[62]

60 Article 9 Services Directive.

61 Cf. Article 15(3) Services Directive. See also Case C-391/20, *Cilevičs and Others*, EU:C:2022:638, para. 65.

62 Case C-73/08, *Nicolas Bressol and Others and Céline Chaverot and Others* v. *Gouvernement de la Communauté française* ECLI:EU:C:2010:181, para. 80. See already, F. Wollenschläger, 'EU Law Principles for Allocating Scarce Goods and the Emergence of an Allocation Procedure: Identifying Substantive and Procedural Standards and Developing a New Type of Administrative Procedure' (2015) 8 *REALaw* 205–256 at 231.

Consequently, Wollenschläger argues that as a rule, the obligation to apply adequate and proportionate allocation criteria requires *substantive criteria* to be applied, based on the merits of the application, despite the discretion involved.[63] The criterion of proportionality would require an appropriate 'material connection' to be made between the asset to be distributed and the criteria that are relevant thereto. Formal criteria, such as first come, first served, seniority, distribution per capita, pro rata, by lot or in rotation, although easy to administer and guaranteeing legal certainty and non-discriminatory allocation, do not account for substantive merits and differences between the applications and applicants, which may conflict with the need to select the best offer. According to Wollenschläger, this priority of substantive allocation criteria implies that formal, non-substantive criteria can only be applied if the application of substantive criteria is impossible, not permissible, disproportionate or unnecessary. While this argumentation makes sense, it should be noted that this view has not been supported in case-law or EU legislation so far. Instead, case-law of the ECJ seems less pronounced when it comes to the contents of the allocation criteria. In *Bressol*, for example, the Court merely seemed to express some preference for a selection procedure based on the aptitude of the candidates instead of a lottery, *given* the quality objective underlying the limited number of rights.[64] Thus, it made the choice of the allocation criteria (hence the second-order allocation decision) dependent on the public interest underlying the limitation of the number of rights (hence the first-order limitation decision).

As far as subsidies are concerned, Van den Brink takes a similar outspoken approach to Wollenschläger. In the case-law on subsidies awarded by EU authorities, she traces a preference for a beauty contest. In *Germany* v. *European Commission*,[65] the General Court considered that the principle of 'sound financial management' implies that

[63] See Section 3.4.3.2 of the chapter of Wollenschläger.

[64] See with reference to Article 21 of the Consolidated version of the Treaty on the Functioning of the European Union, OJ 2008, No. C115/57 instead of to the fundamental freedoms: Case C-73/08, *Nicolas Bressol and Others and Céline Chaverot and Others* v. *Gouvernement de la Communauté française* ECLI:EU:C:2010:181, para. 81, in which case the Court instructed the referring court to ascertain whether the selection process for non-resident students is limited to the drawing of lots and, if that is the case, whether that means of selection based not on the aptitude of the candidates concerned but on chance is necessary to attain the objectives pursued, being the maintenance of a balanced high-quality medical service open to all citizens (para. 62).

[65] Case T-28/16, *Germany* v. *European Commission* ECLI:EU:T:2017:242.

budgetary appropriations should be used in accordance with the principles of economy, efficiency and effectiveness, since the latter principle is intended to ensure the best ratio between the means employed and the results obtained. Compliance with those principles requires that the selection criteria chosen should make it possible to finance, as a matter of priority, the operations 'which best meet' the objectives of rural development. Van den Brink criticizes this reasoning of the General Court from the perspective of legality, arguing that the principle of 'sound financial management' is not mentioned explicitly in the applicable regulation on rural development.[66] However, the General Court stresses that secondary EU legislation should be interpreted consistently with the TFEU, which refers explicitly to the principle of 'sound financial management' in Article 317. As far as subsidies awarded by national authorities are concerned, Van den Brink argues that the principle of sound financial management also allows for first come, first served allocation, the drawing of lots or a proportional division. According to her, first come, first served allocation is suitable in cases where the subsidized activities have been described very clearly and precisely in the particular grant scheme and where the allocating authority has no preference as to which applicant carries out the activities. The drawing of lots and a proportional division could equally serve the principle of sound financial management, since the negative impact on the overall quality of the subsidized projects of such non-substantive procedures could be mitigated by threshold criteria, excluding applicants from funding if they do not meet these minimum requirements. Overall, this would mean that subsidizing (as well as licensing) is currently still (slightly) more open to non-substantive allocation criteria than public contracts and government sales.

[66] Council Regulation (EC) No. 1698/2005 of 20 September 2005 on support for rural development by the European Agricultural Fund for Rural Development (EAFRD), OJ 2005, No. L277/1. According to Article 33 of the Financial Regulation, appropriations shall be used in accordance with the principle of 'sound financial management' and thus be implemented respecting the following principles: (a) the principle of economy, which requires that the resources used by the Union institution concerned in the pursuit of its activities shall be made available in due time, *in appropriate quantity and quality*, and at the best price; (b) the principle of efficiency, which concerns the best relationship between the resources employed, the activities undertaken and the achievement of objectives; and (c) the principle of effectiveness, which concerns the extent to which the objectives pursued are achieved through the activities undertaken.

7.3.3 Execution

The allocation stage will result in the award of a limited right, which can be 'exercised' subsequently by the recipient of that right. It is clear that public interests also extend to this 'execution' stage. In fact, output-related interests are aimed at achieving results in this final stage, for example through realizing value for money or additional policies (public health, protection of the environment, etc.). However, this will not always run smoothly, such that public authorities will be faced more than once during the execution stage with the question of whether or not to take additional 'third-order' decisions to secure the attainment of public interests.

As Arrowsmith points out with regard to public contracts, ensuring commercial value also involves some control over contract execution since a failure at the execution stage – whether because of non-delivery or change of terms (e.g. price increase) – can undermine the value achieved through the initial allocation of the right. She observes that compared with the allocation stage control over this execution stage has relied traditionally less on transparency and legally enforceable general rules.[67] However, the Public Procurement Directive of 2014 has introduced detailed rules[68] which codify and elaborate rules on contract amendments, developed by the ECJ as corollary rules of the general principles of equal treatment and transparency.[69] These provisions impede contract amendments without organizing new competition, except in specified cases in which there is either considered no risk to the open market objectives (e.g. where change has been provided for in advance in transparent review clauses[70]) or in which this interest of fair competition is considered to be outweighed by other public interests, such as continuity of supply. Contract amendments due to unforeseeable circumstances can be considered an example of this latter category.[71]

Interestingly, the case-law of the ECJ with regard to the execution of public contracts has not been applied so far to other limited rights, at

[67] See Section 2.4.2.2 of the chapter of Arrowsmith, pointing out that UNCITRAL Model Law on Public Procurement 2011 does not deal with this phase.

[68] Article 72 of the Public Procurement Directive.

[69] Case C-454/06, *pressetext Nachrichtenagentur GmbH* v. *Republik Österreich (Bund), APA-OTS Originaltext – Service GmbH, APA Austria Presse Agentur registrierte Genossenschaft mit beschränkter* ECLI:EU:C:2008:351.

[70] Article 72(1)(a) of the Public Procurement Directive.

[71] Article 72(1)(c)(i) of the Public Procurement Directive.

least not explicitly. For example, the Services Directive does not contain any provision on the modification of authorizations (except for the provision that a limited license cannot be prolonged automatically).[72] However, the *Wall* judgment on concessions agreements (which were not regulated by EU secondary legislation at that time)[73] indicates that the prohibition to amend a contract substantially is considered a direct result of the principle of equal treatment. This would imply that this prohibition, just like the obligation to invite applications through a call for competition,[74] also applies to limited licenses: they cannot be amended substantially after their award without organizing a new call for competition.

Nonetheless, this perspective that the principle of equal treatment opposes substantive modification of limited rights after their award, has not been codified in concrete rules for other limited rights than public contracts. Van den Brink, for example, argues with respect to subsidizing that the adjustment of projects is in many cases needed due to changing circumstances, since refusing the adjustment of subsidized projects could hinder the realization of certain (additional) policy goals. However, from the perspective of the principles of equality and transparency, it is in general not allowed to adjust a project which receives funding on the basis of a beauty contest. She therefore argues that the mere existence of an obligation to inform the subsidizing authority in case of a change to the subsidized project, could be at odds with the principles of equality and transparency.[75] However, this would not be problematic if the subsidizing authority uses this notification as a starting point to evaluate whether or not the proposed amendment has been substantial and in compliance with the principle of equal treatment.

Finally, the case of government sales is somewhat different here. Unlike lease or rental of government assets, the sale of government assets is a one-off activity: after the sale has been completed, there is no legal relationship any more between the selling government and the acquiring party. In this respect, it is worth repeating that according to the

[72] Article 12(2) of the Services Directive.

[73] Case C-91/08, *Wall AG* v. *La ville de Francfort-sur-le-Main and Frankfurter Entsorgungs- und Service (FES) GmbH* ECLI:EU:C:2010:182. For concession contracts, this obligation has been codified now in Article 43 of the Concessions Directive (Directive 2014/23/EU of the European Parliament and of the Council of 26 February 2014 on the award of concession contracts, OJ 2014, No. L94/1).

[74] Case C-203/08, *Sporting Exchange Ltd* v. *Minister van Justitie*, ECLI:EU:C:2010:307.

[75] See Section 4.4.3.1 of the chapter of Van den Brink.

Commission the only relevant criterion in the allocation stage for selecting the buyer is the highest price. The Commission explicates that this criterion can also take into account the requested contractual arrangements, for example the vendor's sales guarantee or other post-sale commitments. However, a condition that the buyer is to assume special obligations for the benefit of the public authorities or in the general public interest, which a private seller would not have demanded (other than those arising from general domestic law or a decision of the planning authorities), does not classify as such a post-sale commitment.[76] But the issue of third-order decisions taken in the execution stage to secure the attainment of public interests seems to be less present here.

7.4 Connecting the Stages

7.4.1 Limitation and Allocation

The preceding section shows that the different public interests at stake when awarding limited rights have different weights not only in the allocation stage, but also in the preceding limitation stage and in the subsequent execution stage. Even though the Court considered in *Engelmann* that different characteristics of 'limited award' are *distinct* restrictions to the fundamental freedoms that must be examined *in turn*,[77] it is worth unravelling the interdependencies between these

[76] Commission Notice on the notion of State aid as referred to in Article 107(1) of the Treaty on the Functioning of the European Union, OJ 2016, No. C262/1, para. 95.

[77] Case C-64/08, *Criminal proceedings against Ernst Engelmann* ECLI:EU:C:2010:506, para. 43, with respect to limitation, duration and call for competition. See also Case C-323/03, *Commission of the European Communities* v. *Kingdom of Spain* ECLI:EU: C:2006:159, para. 44, with respect to selection criteria in addition to limitation and duration; Case C-203/08, *Sporting Exchange Ltd* v. *Minister van Justitie*, para. 58, with regard to limitation versus call for competition. See also for the distinction between the lawfulness of the limitation and the lawfulness of the grant of these limited rights: B. J. Drijber and H. Stergiou, 'Public Procurement Law and Internal Market Law' (2009) 46 *Common Market Law Review* 805–846, at 826, and G. Skovgaard Ølykke, 'Is the Granting of Special and Exclusive Rights Subject to the Principles Applicable to the Award of Concessions? Recent Development in Case Law and Their Implications for One of the Last Sanctuaries for Protectionism' (2014) 23 *Public Procurement Law Review*1, 1–20, at 6, who correctly distinguishes between the organization of the market and the choice of the provider. See also C. J. Wolswinkel, 'From Public Contracts to Limited Authorisations and Vice Versa: Exploring General Award Requirements from the EU Court's Corollary Approach' (2015) 24 *Public Procurement Law Review*5, 137–163, at 140.

different stages to explain the relative weight attached to public interests when awarding limited rights.

Let us start with the interdependencies between limitation and allocation. Regulation of the limitation decision ('creating scarcity') seems most developed as far as licenses are concerned. This is not surprising, since public contracts and government sales presuppose the existence of limited demand or supply, while subsidization also faces monetary boundaries. The public interests underlying the creation of a licensing scheme as such, either to ensure some quality or to ensure capacity regulation, will usually be guiding in the decision to limit the number of authorizations available for grant. For example, in the context of the regulation of gambling activities, overriding reasons like the prevention of gambling addiction and the combat of fraud, are considered legitimate reasons both to adopt a licensing scheme and to limit the number of licenses.[78] Thus, some public interests will already be secured to a certain extent by the first-order limitation decision, thereby putting less pressure on the second-order allocation decision to choose the relevant allocation criteria.

However, it should be realized that limitation and allocation cannot always be distinguished easily. Licensing (or eligibility) criteria[79] in 'open' licensing schemes can act as de facto allocation criteria. In general, each licensing criterion establishes a threshold that an applicant should meet: once the applicant meets this (absolute) threshold, he is eligible for the award of that right.[80] This can be referred to as the distinction between *selection* and *admission*. According to Elster, a selection procedure compares individuals against each other, usually by producing a ranking list, and accepts them by starting at the top and going down the list until the good is exhausted. By contrast, an admission procedure compares individuals against an absolute threshold and offers the good to all those and only those who exceed the threshold.[81] However, under certain

[78] See, for example, Case C-49/16, *Unibet International Ltd* v. *Nemzeti Adó- és Vámhivatal Központi Hivatala* ECLI:EU:C:2017:491, para. 39.

[79] See also Section 3.4.3.1 of the chapter of Wollenschläger, who discusses Article 10 of the Services Directive in this respect.

[80] Terminology is not univocal here: public procurement law distinguishes selection and award criteria, subsidy law eligibility and selection criteria.

[81] Elster, *Local Justice*, p. 24, also discusses 'placement', which regulates the allocation of non-scarce, heterogeneous goods, ensuring that each individual ends up with some unit of the good.

conditions, admission can amount to selection. Therefore, Elster distinguishes between *pure* and *impure* admission procedures. In *pure* admission procedures, the threshold is chosen because it is substantially appropriate. In *impure* admission procedures, by contrast, admission is used as a proxy for selection, with the threshold being chosen with a view to matching the number of applicants with the number of places.[82] Although there can be valid reasons to use a proxy selection criterion instead of a pure selection criterion,[83] this use of 'open' authorization schemes shows that the distinction between limited and open schemes should be somewhat relativized.

A fundamental question is whether the public interest underlying the limitation of the number of rights should also return in the allocation stage and, if so, why. As far as licensing schemes are concerned, it seems safe to conclude that the ECJ has paid more attention to the limitation of rights than to the allocation of rights so far. Much case-law on gambling licences, for example, deals with the question of whether a monopoly is justified.[84] In the aforementioned case of *Bressol*, the Court evaluated capacity restrictions for foreign students to higher education in Belgium and considered that Articles 18 and 21 TFEU preclude national legislation, which limits the number of non-resident students in Belgium who may enrol for the first time in medical and paramedical courses, unless that legislation is justified in the light of the objective of protection of public health. In particular, according to the Court, a selection process for non-resident students by the drawing of lots, which is based not on the aptitude of the candidates concerned but on chance, is not self-evident, but should be necessary to attain the objectives pursued by the system of guaranteeing high-level quality of healthcare services.[85] Thus, the Court reviewed the allocation criteria in the light of the public interests underlying the limitation decision.

In *Blanco Pérez and Chao Gómez*, the Court examined allocation criteria *as part of* the justification of the maximum number of authorizations. In particular, these allocation criteria were evaluated in the light of

[82] Elster, *Local Justice*, p. 25.

[83] Ibid.

[84] See, e.g., Case C-3/17, *Sporting Odds Ltd* v. *Nemzeti Adó- és Vámhivatal Központi Irányítása* ECLI:EU:C:2018:130.

[85] Case C-73/08, *Nicolas Bressol and Others and Céline Chaverot and Others* v. *Gouvernement de la Communauté française* ECLI:EU:C:2010:181, paras. 81–82.

the *suitability* of this quantitative restriction.[86] The Court considered this first-order decision as suitable since the attainment of the objective sought by the two quantitative restrictions was furthered through the application of certain criteria at the stage of selecting licensees for new pharmacies (second-order decision). Thus, the ECJ relied on the contents of the allocation criteria in assessing the lawfulness of a limitation to the number of rights.

Thus, this (scarce) case-law of the ECJ provides for an argument to use the requirement of *suitability*, which is part of the proportionality test, to establish a connection between the first-order decision of limitation and the second-order decision of allocation. Already in *Gambelli*, the Court held that the suitability test is passed only if the restriction reflects a concern to limit activities 'in a consistent and systematic manner'.[87] These elements of consistency and coherence can be used as an argument to connect the allocation criteria with the limitation decision. In particular, if the allocation criteria are not aimed at (further) pursuing the public interests underlying the limitation decision, then this limitation decision could be considered not consistent and therefore not suitable and proportionate to attain these public interests.

The connection between the limitation and the subsequent allocation stage is also relevant in the context of subsidizing. First of all, Section 7.3.1 showed that the EU State aid regime comes into play once a subsidy scheme limits the amount of money available for subsidizing a certain activity (which will usually be the case). Under those conditions, there is a *selective* advantage as some parties will receive funding while others will not. Interestingly, Van den Brink points out that the European Commission has identified in its General Block Exemption Regulation[88] several examples of competitive bidding for subsidy schemes (e.g. in the context of renewable energy and broadband infrastructures), which are identified as compatible with the internal market.[89] Although Van den

[86] Case C-570/07 and Case C-571/07, *José Manuel Blanco Pérez and María del Pilar Chao Gómez* v. *Consejería de Salud y Servicios Sanitarios and Principado de Asturias* ECLI:EU:C:2010:300, paras. 63–64, 86–87 and 92–93. See Section 7.3.1.

[87] Case C-243/01, *Criminal proceedings against Piergiorgio Gambelli and Others* ECLI:EU:C:2003:597, para. 67.

[88] Commission Regulation (EU) No. 651/2014 of 17 June 2014 declaring certain categories of aid compatible with the internal market in application of Articles 107 and 108 of the Treaty, OJ 2014, No. L187/1.

[89] According to Article 3 of the General Block Exemption Regulation (Commission Regulation (EU) No. 651/2014 of 17 June 2014 declaring certain categories of aid

Brink does not discuss the reasons for this exemption, it is interesting to dive into these reasons. Based on the recitals, it seems that distortions to competition (and trade) are considered limited if aid is granted on the basis of a competitive selection procedure.[90] Thus, while the mere fact that a competitive procedure has been used does not alter the conclusion that a subsidy in principle constitutes State aid, the use of competitive bidding is still very relevant here as it may determine whether or not this State aid is compatible with the internal market. In the same vein, the Commission considers explicitly in the context of the necessity and proportionality of the aid that the selection of beneficiaries through a competitive, transparent and non-discriminatory procedure will be considered as 'a positive indicator'.[91] Thus, also as far as subsidizing is concerned, limitation and allocation should not be considered in isolation.

7.4.2 Allocation and Execution

While limitation and allocation are intertwined, especially in the case of limited licensing schemes and also to some extent in the case of subsidy schemes, interdependencies between the stages of allocation and execution are less evident. However, legal attention for so-called third-order decisions, taken *after* the decision to award a public contract, has increased in public procurement law over time. The Public Procurement Directive of 2014 contains provisions on 'contract performance' next to 'conduct of the procedure'.[92] In particular, Article 72 addresses the issue of modification of contracts. According to this provision, public contracts may be modified without a new procurement procedure where the modifications, irrespective of their monetary value, have been provided for in the initial procurement documents in clear, precise and

compatible with the internal market in application of Articles 107 and 108 of the Treaty, OJ 2014, L 187/1), aid schemes are compatible with the internal market within the meaning of Article 107(2) or (3) of the Treaty and exempted from the notification requirement of Article 108(3) of the Treaty provided that such aid fulfils all the general and specific conditions laid down in this regulation.

90 See recitals 61 and 71 of the General Block Exemption Regulation.

91 Communication on 'Criteria for the analysis of the compatibility with the internal market of State aid to promote the execution of important projects of common European interest', OJ 2021, C 528/10, para. 41.

92 Chapter III and chapter IV of the Public Procurement Directive.

unequivocal review clauses.[93] Modification of a public contract is also possible where the modifications, irrespective of their value, are not substantial. According to Article 72(4), a public contract is considered substantial where it renders the contract materially different in character from the one initially concluded. This is the case, *inter alia*, where the modification introduces conditions that, had they been part of the initial procurement procedure, would have allowed for the admission of other candidates than those initially selected or for the acceptance of a tender other than that originally accepted or would have attracted additional participants in the procurement procedure.[94] Thus, in procurement law, whether or not a third-order decision amending a limited right is justified during the execution stage depends on the way the allocation procedure has been organized initially.

For other limited rights, this connection between second-order allocation decisions and third-order execution decisions is less developed. Nonetheless, EU law provides some clear indicators that the prohibition of substantial amendments also applies to other limited rights.[95] Even though this prohibition originated in the ECJ's case-law on public contracts,[96] it has also been applied as a corollary of the principle of equal treatment of tenderers and the obligation of transparency to concession agreements, which were not covered by secondary EU law at that time.[97] Thus, this prohibition could also be applied to amendments of limited licenses, as a corollary of the Articles 49 and 56 TFEU. In the same vein, as Van den Brink stresses, it could be argued that a substantial amendment of a subsidy disrupts the equal treatment of tenderers that has been realized in the allocation stage through competitive tendering.[98]

The execution stage therefore raises the question of which weight should be given to the different public interests over time. Interestingly,

[93] Article 72(1)(a) of the Public Procurement Directive.

[94] For more detail, see Piotr Bogdanowicz, *Contract Modifications in EU Procurement Law* (Cheltenham: Edward Elgar, 2021).

[95] See also Wolswinkel, 'From Public Contracts to Limited Authorisations and Vice Versa', 160–161.

[96] Case C-454/06, *Pressetext Nachrichtenagentur GmbH* v. *Republik Österreich (Bund), APA-OTS Originaltext-Service GmbH and APA Austria Presse Agentur registrierte Genossenschaft mit beschränkter Haftung* ECLI:EU:C:2008:351, paras. 34 and 35.

[97] Case C-91/08, *Wall AG* v. *La ville de Francfort-sur-le-Main and Frankfurter Entsorgungs- und Service (FES) GmbH* ECLI:EU:C:2010:182, paras. 37 and 38. See currently Article 43 of the Concessions Directive.

[98] See Section 4.4.3.1 of the chapter of Van den Brink.

process-related interests such as equal treatment and transparency have been put forward by the ECJ to justify the prohibition of substantial amendments. In *Succhi di Frutta*, the ECJ even considered that a contracting authority has to comply strictly with the criteria that it has itself laid down on that basis not only in the tendering procedure per se, but also, more generally, up to the end of the stage during which the relevant contract is performed.[99] However, even though that is not the approach taken by the ECJ, one could also argue that the relative weight of these process-related interests decreases over time, especially if other, output-related interests, such as value for money and additional policies, call for modification of limited rights. To some extent, this rebalancing approach is visible in the Public Procurement Directive, which allows for modification of public contracts where the need for modification has been brought about by circumstances which a diligent contracting authority could not foresee, provided that the modification does not alter the overall nature of the contract and that any increase in price is not higher than half of the value of the original contract.[100]

In general, a new public interest seems to enter the scene in this execution stage, which is the interest of *legal certainty*. While this public interest has not been put forward often in the context of limited rights, which has often been dominated by the principle of equal treatment, it is not entirely absent there.[101] In fact, the execution stage requires again and again to rebalance the need for legal certainty (or equal treatment), on the one hand, and the need for flexibility to adapt to changing needs (including additional policies), on the other hand. Once the allocation of limited rights is considered a balancing exercise, it should not be excluded in advance that the outcome of that balancing exercise can change over time, such that other public interests prevail over the public interest of equal treatment as established in the allocation stage.

7.5 Concluding Remarks: In Isolation or Conjunction

Balancing public interests when awarding limited rights is not merely a matter of organizing a competitive tendering procedure adequately, as

[99] Case C-496/99 P, *Commission of the European Communities* v. *CAS Succhi di Frutta SpA* ECLI:EU:C:2004:236, para. 115.

[100] Article 72(1)(c) Public Procurement Directive.

[101] See, for example, Joined Cases C-72/10 and C-77/10 *Criminal proceedings against Marcello Costa and Ugo Cifone* ECLI:EU:C:2012:80, para. 78.

the role of these public interests is not limited to the actual allocation of limited rights. Instead, several public interests also play a role in the preceding limitation stage or have a 'trickle-down' effect in the consequent execution stage. This trickle-down effect can also be reversed: if certain public interests are also relevant in the execution stage, which is by definition the case with so-called output-related interests, the question is how this relevance can be anticipated in the allocation stage.

This contribution has therefore started from the assumption that in order to understand and explain the differences between limited rights when the realization of public interests is involved, comparison of these different limited rights should not be restricted to the actual 'allocation' stage, but should extend to the preceding limitation stage and the consecutive execution stage. Considering the different output-related public interests involved, the interests of value for money and opening markets for competition have been developed most strongly for public contracts and government sales. For licenses and subsidies, other public interests (sometimes referred to as additional policies, but sometimes also considered as the key interests underlying licensing or subsidy schemes) are more dominant. Particularly as far as licensing is concerned, the decision to limit the number of available rights in order to pursue certain public interests seems to attract more legal attention than the decision on how to allocate these limited rights. By contrast, especially with regard to public contracts, the decisions taken in the allocation stage have a large impact on the possibility for allocating authorities to amend limited rights during their 'execution' stage, thereby running the risk of absolutizing equal treatment at the expense of other public interests.

Balancing public interests is not merely an issue of balancing public interests in the stage of allocating limited rights through competitive tendering. For some limited rights, in particular limited licenses, the limitation stage seems equally important for pursuing public interests. For other limited rights, such as public contracts and government sales, limitation is inherent to these limited rights. These inherent differences between types of limited rights should be taken into account when considering differences in the applicable legal regimes and the relative weight attached to public interests in the allocation stage. At the same time, general legal principles can be applied in a flexible way, taking into account these inherent differences. One particular way forward to connect the stages of limitation and allocation is to further develop the requirement of *suitability* (as part of the proportionality principle), which requires that activities are limited 'in a consistent and systematic manner'. This requirement forces allocating authorities to consider the allocation stage in conjunction with the limitation stage. Another way forward, especially to connect the execution stage with the allocation stage, is to put central the public interest of *legal certainty* when considering whether an amendment to a limited right is allowed or not. Admittedly, this public interest should pay attention to the interests of both the holder of the limited right and those who did not obtain that right, but absolutizing the public interest of equal treatment should be avoided in this execution stage as public interests need to be balanced against each other continuously, also after limited rights have been awarded. Thus, the challenge for allocating authorities is to balance public interests not merely in the stage of (competitive) allocation, but throughout the entire life cycle of limited rights.

8

European Union Law and Granting Limited Rights to Provide Services of General Interest

What Role for National Law?

JOHAN VAN DE GRONDEN

8.1 Introduction

In the first chapter of this volume, it is outlined that limited rights may occur in four forms: public contracts, (limited) authorisations, financial grants and asset sales. Furthermore, it is made clear in the chapters written by Arrowsmith,[1] Wollenschläger,[2] Van den Brink[3] as well as Caranta and Biancardi[4] that the impact of EU law on these rights has increased over the years. When shaping their policies on these matters, the Member States must observe European Union (EU) law and their room for manoeuvre could be limited.

This raises the question of how EU law relates to the national rules on limited rights. Does EU law restrict the room for manoeuvre for Member States considerably or does it give significant leeway for national action? It goes without saying that this question is very broad and can be addressed from different angles. In the present volume, much attention is paid to the role of public interests, such as social policy and environmental protection. In her contribution, Arrowsmith refers to these policies as horizontal policies in order to ensure that their values are equal with the objectives to be achieved by EU economic law.[5] Therefore, public interest objectives are defined as non-market goals in this contribution. These goals concern issues that, for example, fall within the scope of the Rule of Reason

[1] See Chapter 2 of Arrowsmith.
[2] See Chapter 3 of Wollenschläger.
[3] See Chapter 4 of Van den Brink.
[4] See Chapter 5 of Caranta and Biancardi.
[5] Chapter of Arrowsmith, Section 2.3.

approach (overriding requirements in the public interest) developed by the European Court of Justice (ECJ) in free movement law,[6] which means that no aims of purely economic nature are pursued.[7]

In order to do justice to the complicated relationship between economic and public/horizontal interests, this contribution focuses on services of general interest (SGIs). Many Member States have in place special policies and laws for such services. On many occasions, SGIs are provided by a limited number of operators. In other words, limited rights play an important role in national policies dealing with the provision of SGIs. Access for all must be guaranteed, when it comes to these services, and granting limited rights to specific operators serves this purpose. Admittedly, also conferring financial benefits (state aid) may enable operators to provide SGIs. In many cases, however, limited rights are regarded as an important means to ensure the continuous provision of SGIs, often even combined with financial benefits. In this contribution, limited rights are defined as exclusive or special rights within the meaning of Article 106(1) of the Treaty on the Functioning of the European Union (TFEU): an exclusive right means that only one operator is entitled to supply particular services or goods, whereas a special right confers this supply to a limited group of operators.[8] As a result, a special or exclusive right may substantially affect the ability of other enterprises to exercise the economic activity concerned in the same geographical area under equivalent conditions.[9] One of the core provisions dealing with SGIs is Article 106(2) TFEU, and, accordingly, the TFEU conforms that a close connection exists between this concept on the one hand and exclusive and special rights on the other hand. Although limited rights and SGIs do not overlap completely, these concepts coincide to a large extent. In the first part of this volume, public procurement contracts, limited authorisations, financial grants and asset sales (government sales and privatisations) have been explored. In the light of the definition used for the concept of limited

[6] See Section 8.4.1 of this chapter.

[7] See C. Barnard, *The Substantive Law of the EU: The Four Freedoms*, 7th ed. (Oxford: Oxford University Press, 2022), p. 169 and pp. 505–507.

[8] These definitions can be derived from Article 1(f) and (g) of Directive 2006/11 on the transparency of financial relations between Member States and Public Undertakings, OJ 2006, No. L318/17. See also Case C-327/12, *SOA Nazionale Costruttori* [2013] ECLI:EU:C:2013:827, para. 41 and Case C-545/17, *Mariusz Pawlak* [2019] ECLI:EU:2019:260, para. 43. See also Chapter 1 of Wolswinkel, Jansen and Van Ommeren.

[9] See para. 41 of the *SOA Nazionale Costruttori* judgment and para. 43 of *the Mariusz Pawlak* judgment.

rights, this contribution mainly focuses on limited authorisations and financial grants insofar as these grants are given in order to finance the exercising of limited rights to provide SGIs. Public procurement contracts are included in the analysis as far as concessions/exclusive rights are concerned. The role played by asset sales is limited to the extent that these assets are used to finance the supply of SGIs.

In Europe, the States bear special responsibility for ensuring that these services are provided. In the Quality framework on SGIs the Commission has put forward that SGIs are services and goods that '. . . public authorities of the Member States classify as being of general interest and, therefore, subject to specific public service obligations . . .'.[10] This comes down to services and goods that are regarded to be of special interest and the provision of which are, accordingly, entrusted by the State to a specific operator or specific group of operators in the benefit of its citizens. For example, in many Member States the provision of ambulance or certain other health services is entrusted to a limited group of operators. The same is true for the disposal of waste. Also in industries, such as the postal sector and transport, exclusive or special rights to provide SGIs are granted. In other words, in a wide range of branches the public authorities of the EU Member States make use of limited rights in order to guarantee the access to specific SGIs.

As is apparent from the foregoing chapters, the EU rules that are of importance in this respect are part of EU internal market and competition law. The public procurement directives are adopted in order to establish an internal market for public contracts. On top of that, in the previous chapters reference is made to the Services Directive[11] as well as to EU competition law, more specifically EU state aid law. For that reason, EU internal market and EU competition law are at the heart of the analysis to be carried out.

In the light of the foregoing, the central question of this contribution is which discretion the Member States have when granting limited rights to provide SGIs under EU internal market and competition law. This contribution starts with discussing which SGIs fall within the scope of the EU internal market and competition rules. Then, it will be examined which

[10] European Commission, Communication from the Commission to the European Parliament, the Council, the European Economic and Social Committee and the Committee of the Regions: A Quality Framework for Services of General Interest for Europe (Brussels, 20 December 2011, COM(2011) 900 final), p. 3.

[11] Directive 2006/123 on services in the internal market, OJ 2006, No. L376/36.

obligations are imposed by these rules on the Member States. Subsequently, it will be explored to what extent the Member States may derogate from these obligations. The contribution will end with some conclusions.

8.2 The Scope of EU Internal Market and Competition Law

The question of scope is of great importance, as it concerns the fundamental question of whether SGIs should be made subject to market forces according to EU law. In order to find out whether the EU internal market rules apply to SGIs, the concept of service in EU law must be analysed. According to Article 57 TFEU, a service for the purpose of the Treaty is a service that is normally provided for remuneration, which constitutes consideration for the service in question, normally agreed upon between the provider and recipient.[12] As a result, the EU internal market rules apply to services having an economic dimension.[13] In other words, the question of whether SGIs should be made subject to market forces is addressed by examining whether the service at issue is of an economic nature in EU internal market law.

To my mind, the concept of services within the meaning of the Treaty is interpreted by the ECJ in an expansive way. The case law of the ECJ entails that every service that potentially can be provided on the market is an economic service. A very important case, which is also relatively unknown, is *Freskot.*[14] At issue was a public compulsory insurance scheme covering natural risks in the agriculture sector. It concerned risks resulting from calamities and disasters in agriculture. The bodies managing the scheme did not provide services for economic consideration given the intense State regulation: the rates were fixed in national law and the levies were imposed by tax law. Nevertheless, the Treaty provisions on free movement could be applicable. In the view of the ECJ, this was the case insofar as the compulsory scheme covers insurable natural risks.

In other words, insurable risks prompt the applicability of the Treaty provisions on free movement. It sufficed that the service could potentially be supplied on the market for the Treaty provisions on free movement to apply. A similar decision was taken by the ECJ in *Kattner*

[12] See Case 263/86, *Belgian State* v. *Humbel* [1988] ECR 05365, ECLI:EU:C:1988:451, para. 17.

[13] Barnard has pointed out that an economic link must be demonstrated. See Barnard, *The Substantive Law of the EU*, pp. 294–295.

[14] Case C-355/00, *Freskot* [2003] ECR I-05263, ECLI:EU:C:2003:298.

Stahlbau.[15] Of great interest is also the judgment in the *Watts* case,[16] which was about the reimbursement of the costs of a British patient who had undergone treatment in a French hospital. Here, the ECJ held that the question of whether the National Health Service (NHS), which is the managing body in British healthcare, provides services for economic consideration could be left open. What matters is that the patient concerned moved from the UK to France in order to receive hospital treatment there. Medical services can be provided on the market and, as a result, EU free movement law kicks in. Of interest is also the case law of the ECJ on education and free movement. Educational services being part of an official State system are predominately financed by the government. Consequently, they are not provided for economic consideration.[17] In contrast, educational services that are largely financed by private means are of an economic nature and do fall within the ambit of EU internal market law.[18] For example, private universities supply economic services.

In sum, SGIs that can be provided on the market are subject to EU internal market law. In this respect, it must be noted that EU internal market law includes harmonisation measures, such as the Services Directive, which refers to the concept of service within the meaning of the Treaty for delineating its scope. Thus, in *Kirschstein* the ECJ held that the Services Directive applied to a private institution of higher education, as its educational services were financed by private funds.[19] A similar decision concerning the applicability of the Services Directive to educational services was taken by the ECJ in *The Hungarian Law on higher education*.[20]

The Services Directive has a lot in common with the Treaty provisions on the free movement of services and the freedom of establishment. Nevertheless, it should be pointed out that a significant difference

[15] Case C-350/07, *Kattner Stahlbau GmbH* v. *Maschinenbau- und Metall- Berufsgenossenschaft* [2009] ECR I-01513, ECLI:EU:C:2009:127.

[16] Case C-372/04, *Watts*, 16 May 2006, ECLI:EU:C:2006:325. Case C-372/04, *Watts* v. *Bedford Primary Care Trust and Secretary of State for Health* [2006] ECR I-04325, ECLI:EU:C:2006:325.

[17] See, e.g., Case 263/86, *Belgian State* v. *Humbel* [1988] ECR 05365, ECLI:EU:C:1988:451 and Case C-109/92, *Wirth* v. *Landeshauptstadt Hannover* [1993] ECR I-06447, ECLI:EU:C:1993:916.

[18] See, for instance, Case C-153/02, *Neri* v. *European School of Economics (ESE Insight World Education System Ltd)* [2003] ECR I-13555, ECLI:EU:C:2003:614.

[19] See Case C-393/17, *Kirschstein* [2019] ECLI:EU:C:2019:593, paras. 53–63.

[20] See Case C-66/18, *The Hungarian Law on higher education* [2020] ECLI:EU:C:2020:792, paras. 194 and 195.

between these sets of rules lies in the fact that a directive must be transposed into national law;[21] such an obligation does not apply to the Treaty provisions on free movement. It is settled case law that in the event of an implementation failure a directive provision cannot of itself impose obligations on an individual, even if it has direct effect.[22] In other words, a directive provision has no horizontal effect.[23] As a result, EU law does not require that a domestic court sets aside a provision of national law in a dispute between private parties. Thus, in *Thelen Technopark Berlin*[24] the ECJ held that the competent national court was not obliged to disapply a provision of German law, although this provision was in violation of Article 15 of the Services Directive. Consequently, in the event of incompatibility of a provision of national law with the Services Directive, a litigant can only rely upon this directive *vis-à-vis* the competent authorities of an EU Member State and is empty-handed in disputes only involving private parties, such as private service providers and private customers. It goes without saying that this considerably limits the scope of the Services Directive.

For the purposes of the subject of limited rights, the EU public procurement rules are also of relevance. It would be beyond the scope of this contribution to discuss the scope of these rules, which are explored by Arrowsmith in her contribution, in great detail.[25] However, it is clear from the drafting of Directive 2014/24 on public procurement ('Public Procurement Directive')[26] that the economic dimension plays an important role in this regard. Contracting authorities (being public bodies in a very broad sense)[27] must subject the procurement of various public contracts to the procedures set out in this directive.[28] According to Article 2 under 5, public contracts are defined as contracts that are concluded for pecuniary interest (in writing) between economic operators and contracting authorities (with respect to the execution of works, the supply of products or the provision of services). In the same vein,

[21] See Article 288 TFEU.

[22] Case C-91/92, *Faccini Dori* [1994] ECR I-03325, ECLI:EU:C:1994:292.

[23] See P. Craig and G. De Búrca, *EU Law: Text, Cases and Materials*, 7th ed. (Oxford: Oxford University Press, 2020), pp. 238–240.

[24] Case C-261/20, *Thelen Technopark Berlin* [2022] ECLI:EU:C:2022:33.

[25] See Chapter 2 of Arrowsmith.

[26] Directive 2014/24 on public procurement, OJ 2014, No. L94/65.

[27] This is apparent from Article 2(1) of the Public Procurement Directive.

[28] See, for example, Public Procurement Directive, Article 4.

Directive 2014/23 on the award of concession contracts ('Concessions Directive')[29] sets out that an integral part of the concept of concession is constituted by the pecuniary interest involved in the conclusion of the contracts between the contracting authorities and the economic operators.[30] Also here the economic dimension is an important matter for determining the applicability of the relevant rules. Only services that are normally provided for economic consideration could fall within the scope of the Concessions Directive.[31]

In EU competition law, an approach to economic activities similar to the one in EU internal market law is in place. According to settled case law, the competition rules apply to undertakings, which are entities engaged in economic activities.[32] An economic activity is defined as the offering of goods and services on a market.[33] Accordingly, the interpretation of the concept of undertaking is decisive for the scope of EU competition law. In my view the case law of the ECJ on the concept of undertaking boils down to examining whether a good or service may be offered potentially on the market.[34] For example, in *Ambulanz Glöckner*[35] the ECJ pointed out that the ambulance services under review were provided by commercial enterprises in the past and concluded for that reason that organisations providing these services must be regarded as undertakings. In contrast, according to settled case law the exercise of official authority does not amount to an economic activity, as such exercise belongs to the exclusive competences of the State.[36] Undertakings cannot offer services on the market mirroring the exercise of State prerogatives. Another limitation of the concept of undertaking is related to social security.[37] If a social security scheme predominately is based on the principle of solidarity and subject to substantial State control, the bodies managing these schemes are not engaged in economic

[29] Directive 2014/23 on the award of concession contracts, OJ 2014, No. L94/1.

[30] See Article 5(1) of Concessions Directive.

[31] See Case C-436/20, *ASADE* [2022] ECLI:EU:C:2022:559, paras. 59–67.

[32] See, e.g., Case C-41/90, *Höfner* [1991] ECR I-01979, ECLI:EU:C:1991:161.

[33] See, for example, Case 118/85, *Commission* v. *Italy* [1987] ECR 02599, ECLI:EU:C:1987:283.

[34] See J. W. van de Gronden, 'Services of General Interest and the Concept of Undertaking: Does EU Competition Law Apply?', (2018) 41 *World Competition* 199.

[35] Case C-475/99, *Ambulanz Glöckner* [2001] ECR I-08089, ECLI:EU:C:2001:577.

[36] See, e.g., Case C-343/95, *Diego Calì* [1997] ECR I-01547, ECLI:EU:C:1997:160.

[37] On this matter, see Van de Gronden, 'Services of General Interest and the Concept of Undertaking', pp. 203 and 204.

activities.[38] In contrast, if such a scheme is based on a mix of solidarity and competition, the managing bodies do qualify as undertakings for the purposes of EU competition law.[39] Until very recently, the Union courts applied the social security approach developed in competition law only to bodies managing social security schemes and not to providers of services. However, in *Casa Regina Apostolorum*[40] the General Court held that the providers of the medical services under review (hospitals) did not qualify as undertakings, as they operated within a legal framework that was predominately based on the principle of solidarity. The aim to ensure universal coverage was at the heart of the healthcare system concerned, and the provision of the services at issue was financed by public means. In my view, the line of reasoning of the General Court comes down to extending the social security approach (originally developed for managing bodies) to providers of services (and goods). In its judgment in *Casa Regina Apostolorum*,[41] the ECJ contended that the ruling of the General Court was not vitiated by an error of law and, accordingly, its ruling was not annulled. This judgment may be the first step of the ECJ to extend the social security approach to healthcare providers.

In sum, the national laws governing the limited rights regarding SGIs must be compatible with EU free movement and competition law, insofar as these services are of an economic dimension. SGIs that are not of an economic nature, such as public insurance schemes covering uninsurable risks and educational services predominately financed out of the public purse, are immune from the EU rules dealing with the freedom of service provision and competition. This means that these EU rules do not impose obligations on the Member States when taking measures with regard to SGIs not being of an economic nature.

In this regard, it must be pointed out that economic SGIs are referred to as services of general economic interest (SGEIs) in the Treaties.[42]

[38] See, for example, Joined Cases C-159/91 and C-160/91, *Poucet and Pistre* [1993] ECR I-00637, ECLI:EU:C:1993:63 and Joined Cases C-262/18 and C-271/18, *SZP/VZP* [2020] ECLI:EU:C:2020:450.

[39] See, for instance, Case C-67/06, *Albany* [1999] ECR I-05751, ECLI:EU:C:1999:430; Joined Cases C-115/97 – C-117/97, *Brentjens* [1999] ECR I-06025, ECLI:EU:C:1999:434 and Case C-219/97, *Drijvende Bokken* [1999] ECR I-06121, ECLI:EU:C:1999:437.

[40] Case T-223/19, *Casa Regina Apostolorum* [2021] ECLI:EU:T:2021:315.

[41] Case C-492/21, *Casa Regina Apostolorum* [2023] ECLI:EU:C:2023:354.

[42] See, for example, Article 106(2) TFEU, Article 14 TFEU, and Article 36 of the Charter of the Fundamental Rights of the EU. See also the Communication from the Commission to the European Parliament, the Council, the European Economic and Social Committee

In other words, SGIs are composed of SGEIs and non-economic SGIs. In what follows, attention will be paid to only SGEIs. This implies that at this stage of the analysis the following conclusion may be drawn. The Member States enjoy a wide margin of discretion when it comes to regulating limited rights in order to guarantee the universal provision of non-economic SGIs, such as the benefits of statutory pension schemes and of statutory social security schemes. The EU rules dealing with the freedom of service provision and competition do not apply to the way these rights are designed. It should be pointed out, however, that it cannot be excluded that other rules or principles of EU law may be relevant. The EU Charter of fundamental rights or the principle of equal treatment laid down in Article 18 TFEU, for example, could come into play in the event that a national statutory scheme of social security has a negative impact on non-discrimination matters or on the protection of fundamental rights. Also issues may arise under the EU rules for the free movement of persons (e.g. the Treaty provisions on the free movement of workers). It should be stressed that these issues may result from the way the rights of Union citizens of other Member States are regulated by the national legislation concerned. If the access to labour markets for these citizens or their migration rights are restricted, the EU rules for the free movement of persons could be infringed.[43] In such cases, the problem lies, however, not in the creation of an exclusive or special right to provide SGIs but rather in the entitlements given by national schemes to persons from other Member States.

8.3 The Obligations Resting with the Member States with Regard to SGEIs

Which requirements must the Member States observe when granting limited rights? How should, for example, the right to provide ambulance services or educational services predominately financed by private means be designed? In my view, two sets of national rules and measures governing these systems must be distinguished. The first set concerns regulatory requirements for the operation of SGEIs. Regulatory requirements are often laid down in licences given to enterprises but could also be found in national legislation. Obligations are imposed upon SGEI

and the Committee of the Regions: A Quality Framework for Services of General Interest for Europe (Brussels, 20 December 2011, COM(2011) 900 final), p. 3.

[43] See in this respect, for example, Case C-67/14, *Alimanovic* [2015] ECLI:EU:C:2015:597.

operators in order to guarantee the high quality of the services rendered, the protection of the users, the access to the services, etc. In other words, these regulatory requirements govern the way the SGEIs are supplied by the operator. Although the requirements concerned are drafted by the legislature having particular SGEIs in mind, similar requirements are also found in national laws dealing with services not being SGEIs. The second set of rules is about the access to the right to provide SGEIs. These rules focus on the creation and award of limited rights. This award may be combined with giving financial grants to the operator selected.

Both the EU internal market and competition/state aid rules are of importance for assessing the compatibility of national limited rights with European law. When it comes to EU internal market law, it must be pointed out that once a particular matter is subject to full harmonisation, the national laws governing this matter must not be assessed under the Treaty provisions on free movement but under the relevant EU directives and regulations.[44] In, for example, *CASTA*[45] the ECJ examined whether the grant of a particular right to provide ambulance services was harmonised by the EU public procurement rules or not. In the latter case, the legal framework for review was constituted by the Treaty provisions on free movement (and by some general obligations of the Directive which was then in place; these obligations amounted to a very limited level of harmonisation). In the event this grant was harmonised, the EU public procurement rules would apply. In the same vein, in *Promoimpresa*[46] the ECJ held that the concessions given in order to exploit State-owned property for tourist and leisure purposes had only to be assessed in the light of the Treaty provisions on free movement, insofar as this matter was not governed by the Services Directive.[47] In other words, when identifying which EU legal framework is in place, great attention must be paid to the question of whether and to what extent a certain matter is harmonised.

However, when it comes to SGEIs, only a few harmonisation measures are relevant, as many of these measures are related to matters that are regarded to be part of the competences of the Member States. With an exception to sectors such as the financial branch, telecommunications,

[44] See e.g. Case 5/77, *Tedeschi* [1977] ECR 01555, ECLI:EU:C:1977:144, paras. 34 and 35 and Case C-475/12, *UPC* [2014] ECLI:EU:C:2014:285, para. 63.

[45] Case C-50/14, *CASTA* [2016] ECLI:EU:C:2016:56.

[46] Joined Cases C-458/14 and C-67/15, *Promoimpresa*, 14 July [2016], ECLI:EU:C:2016:558.

[47] See para. 62 of the *Promoimpresa* judgment.

energy and public transport, the Treaty provisions on free movement continue to play an important role for SGEIs. Harmonisation measures that may have a great impact on SGEIs in general, at least potentially, are the Services Directive and the Concessions Directive. Therefore, also (some) attention to these pieces of EU legislation will be paid.

8.3.1 Regulatory Requirements in Relation to EU Internal Market and Competition Law

As is known, the ECJ's interpretation of the prohibition not to restrict free movement is based on a market access test.[48] Every measure that renders the access to the market or the exercise of the right to provide services on the market more difficult is deemed to restrict free movement.[49] This means, for example, that quality requirements an operator has to observe are restrictive.[50] It is very common, for example, that national laws oblige providers of economic educational services to comply with specific standards in order to protect the high level of education. For providers from other Member States, these requirements are an obstacle: they are also obliged to comply with standards laid down in their home state laws. It goes without saying that also (arbitrary) discriminatory requirements are not in line with the free movement rules. For instance, imposing conditions on providers that are harder to meet for foreign than for domestic operators is considered to be restrictive.[51]

Two observations must be made in this regard. The first one is that although sound reasons of public policy may underpin the need to impose particular standards upon providers of SGEIs, this does not call into question their restrictive nature for foreign operators. Nevertheless, the restrictions may be justifiable on the basis of exceptions. The second observation is that the Treaty provisions on free movement only apply

[48] See, e.g., Barnard, *The Substantive Law of the EU*, pp. 429–442.

[49] See, for example, Case C-76/90, *Säger* [1991] ECR I-04221, ECLI:EU:C:1991:331 and Case C-384/93, *Alpine Investments* [1995] ECR I-01141, ECLI:EU:C1995:126.

[50] See, for example, Case C-55/94, *Gebhard* [1995] ECR I-04165, ECLI:EU:C:1995:411; Joined Cases C-171 and C-172/07, *Apothekerkammer des Saarlandes* [2009] ECR I-04171, ECLI:EU:C:2009:316; and Case C-439/99, *Commission* v. *Italy* [2002] ECR I-00305, ECLI:EU:C:2002:14.

[51] See, for example, Case 205/84, *Commission* v. *Germany* [1986] ECR 03755, ECLI:EU:C:1986:463. On this matter, see also Barnard, *The Substantive Law of the EU*, p. 428.

insofar as the trade between the Member States is influenced. The purely internal situation is not covered by these Treaty provisions.

This observation must be nuanced in the light of the Services Directive, as also is put forward by Wollenschläger in his contribution to the present volume.[52] In *Visser Vastgoed*,[53] the ECJ has decided that the provisions of the Services Directive dealing with establishment do apply to internal situations. Domestic providers are, as a result, entitled to rely on these provisions of the Services Directive. For particular SGEIs this finding is of great importance. Admittedly, services, such as healthcare, are excluded from the scope of the Services Directive. Other SGEIs, such as the provision of economic educational services, are not. Consequently, domestic providers of those services can challenge their national laws and policy measures under the Services Directive.

To a large extent, the provisions of the Services Directive dealing with the freedom of establishment mirror the case law of the ECJ on free movement. It should be noted, however, that there are some striking differences.[54] In contrast with Article 49 TFEU (containing the ban on restricting the freedom of establishment), the Services Directive lays down three sets of obligations with regard to the permanent provision of services: rules for authorisation schemes (Articles 9–13), a ban on certain requirements (Article 14) and a duty to evaluate 'suspect requirements', which means that these requirements are only permitted if justified on public interest grounds (Article 15).[55] Under the Services Directive, authorisation schemes and the conditions attached to authorisations are only permitted if they are necessary with a view to a public interest objective.[56] Article 14 of the Directive prohibits national requirements, such as direct and indirect discriminatory requirements, the direct or indirect involvement of competing operators in the granting of authorisations[57] and an economic needs test. It is apparent from *Rina*

[52] Chapter of Wollenschläger, Section 3.4.1.1.

[53] Joined Cases C-360/15 and C-31/16, *Visser Vastgoed* [2018] ECLI:EU:C:2018:44.

[54] The Directive provisions governing the freedom of establishment are discussed in, for example, Barnard, *The Substantive Law of the EU*, pp. 452–461.

[55] The term 'suspect requirements' is taken from Barnard, *The Substantive Law of the EU*, p. 459.

[56] See in this respect Articles 9 and 10 of the Services Directive.

[57] It is apparent from the wording of Article 14(6) of the Services Directive that this ban does not apply to professional bodies and associations acting as the competent authorities and to the consultation of entities, such as chambers of commerce and social partners, on matters others than individual applications for authorisations.

Services[58] that these requirements are not justifiable and, accordingly, a Member State including them in national legislation violates EU law.[59] In contrast, the requirements listed in Article 15(2) of the Services Directive may be justifiable. This means that these requirements are not permitted, unless, as is stated by Article 15(3), they are necessary with regard to an overriding reason of public interest, proportionate and non-discriminatory. Interestingly, Article 15(4) sets out that the need to provide SGEIs is also capable of justifying the requirements listed in section 2 of that provision.

In this respect, it must be noted that pursuant to Article 17 under 1 of the Services Directive, this piece of EU legislation does not apply to SGEIs provided on a temporary basis. Article 16 Services Directives, which deals with free movement of services under this directive, is therefore not relevant for SGEIs. As a result, the temporary provision of SGEIs is not harmonised by the Services Directive and, accordingly, the national laws dealing with this have to be reviewed under the Treaty provisions on the free movement of services.[60] Of interest in this regard is that in *Commission* v. *Hungary (mobile payment services)*,[61] the ECJ accepted that a Member State enjoys great discretion in designating services as SGEIs, since it did not examine whether the services under review in this case could be supplied by the market satisfactorily.[62]

Another important complicated matter that has to be brought up is related to the absence of horizontal effect of directive provisions. In Section 8.2 of this contribution, it was put forward that according to the ECJ in *Thelen Technopark Berlin* a provision of the Services Directive cannot be invoked in a dispute between private parties. Accordingly, national regulatory requirements cannot be challenged on the basis of the Services Directive, if the litigant has taken (a) private service provider(s) to court. Such legal actions may only be successful, if a competent authority of an EU Member State is targeted.

It is clear from the foregoing that at the EU level a complicated legal framework is in place, as the provision of SGEIs on a permanent basis

58 Case C-593/13, *Rina Services* [2015] ECLI:EU:C:2015:399.

59 See in this regard also Case C-325/20, *BEMH* [2021] ECLI:EU:C:2021:611, paras. 26 and 27.

60 See Case C-171/17, *Commission* v. *Hungary (mobile payment services)* [2018] ECLI:EU:C:2018:881, para. 63.

61 Ibid.

62 See K. Vriesendorp, 'Article 16 of the Services Directive: The Potential and Future of a Dormant Provision', (2023) 48 *European Law Review* 69.

falls within the scope of the Services Directive, whereas the provision of SGEIs on a temporary basis is covered by the Treaty provisions on free movement. This is the result of the choices made at the drafting stage of the Services Directive. In my view, no compelling reasons exist for this divide between the freedom of establishment and free movement of services. At the heart of SGEIs are values, such as universal access and high quality. National legislation dealing with the supply of these services does not, as a rule, make a distinction between operators supplying these services on a permanent or temporary basis on the territory of the country concerned. The unfortunate consequence of the complicated set-up of the Service Directives provisions on SGEIs is, therefore, that national legislatures are obliged to observe two sets of EU rules, that is, the Services Directive and the Treaty provisions on free movement, when drafting national SGEI laws. For that reason, in my view the artificial divide between SGEIs supplied on a permanent and temporary basis introduced by the Services Directive should be reconsidered by the EU. This divide complicates the task of Member States to ensure access to SGEIs needlessly.

Another complication to be addressed in my view is related to the absence of the horizontal effect of the provisions of the Services Directive. It should be borne in mind that every national provision violating a prohibition laid down in the Services Directive amounts to the incorrect implementation of this directive. The unfortunate point is that such failures can only be questioned *vis-à-vis* the competent authorities of a Member State. The Union legislature can easily solve this problem by laying down the prohibitions that are now contained in the Services Directive in a regulation; the latter instrument of EU law is capable of itself imposing obligations on private entities.[63]

8.3.2 Access to Limited Rights in EU Internal Market and Competition Law

The creation and award of limited rights to provide SGEIs must be assessed under EU internal market law and a special provision of competition law dealing with exclusive and special rights, which is Article 106 (1) TFEU. Insofar as the award of the limited right to provide SGEIs

[63] This follows from Article 288 TFEU, which provides that regulations have general application.

involves financial grants (in order to finance these SGEIs), EU state aid law comes into play.

8.3.2.1 The Creation and Award of Limited Rights to Provide SGEIs

Does a system of exclusive or special rights give rise to restrictive effects under EU internal market law? The answer to this question is affirmative. It must even be pointed out that two types of restrictive effects must be identified: the limitation of the number of providers and transparency issues in the award process.[64]

Limitations of the Number of Providers The fact that only one operator or a small group of operators is entitled to provide certain SGEIs makes the access to the market of other suppliers, including those from other Member States, impossible. In EU internal market law, the ECJ has drawn from this the conclusion that free movement is restricted.[65] In *Freskot* (already mentioned), for example, the compulsory nature of the scheme gave rise to a restriction, as insurance companies from other Member States cannot offer similar insurance cover in the Member State concerned. Providing this service was the exclusive right of a private organisation wholly owned by the State concerned. Exclusive rights are only valid insofar as they can be justified by an exception.

Similar conclusions must be drawn, if the Services Directive applies. This is the case if the limited right concerns a service not excluded from the scope of this directive. As is set out by Wollenschläger in his contribution to the present volume, the Services Directive lays down specific rules for limited rights.[66] Article 15(2)(d) of this EU measure provides that Member States may not reserve the access to a service activity to a particular provider or providers, unless this is justified by public interest reasons. For that reason, the ECJ held in *Commission v. Hungary (mobile payment services)* (already mentioned) that the exclusive right to provide particular SGEIs granted by the Member State

[64] See J. W. van de Gronden, 'Free Movement of Services and the Right of Establishment: Does EU Internal Market Law Transform the Provision of SSGI?', in U. Neergaard, E. Szyszczak, J. W. van de Gronden and M. Krajewski (eds.), *Social Services of General Interest in the EU* (The Hague: Springer, 2013), pp. 123–160, at p. 153.

[65] See, for example, Case C-203/08, *Betfair* [2010] ECR I-04695, ECLI:EU:C:2010:307, paras. 22–24 and Joined Cases C-721/19 and C-722/19, *Sisal* [2021] ECLI:EU:C:2021:672, para. 35.

[66] See the chapter of Wollenschläger, Section 3.4.2.2.

concerned was covered by this Directive provision. As already stated several times, according to *Thelen Technopark Berlin* the provisions of the Services Directive do not have horizontal effect. In my view, this does not mean, however, that a competing operator is not entitled to challenge a decision by which a competent authority of an EU Member State has granted an exclusive right to a private service provider. It should be pointed out that such legal action is taken against the state body having granted the exclusive right at stake, rather than against a private operator. The possible adverse consequences resulting from the proceeding against this state body for the enterprise being granted the exclusive right concerned are of an indirect nature, which is acceptable in the view of the ECJ.[67]

If the limited right is contained in a concession, the Concessions Directive may be applicable. It should be noted that the applicability of this directive excludes that the Services Directive applies.[68] A concession implies that a right to provide particular services is transferred by a public authority to an enterprise and that this enterprise enjoys a certain economic freedom in exercising the right granted while being exposed to the risk of operating of the services concerned.[69] In the event a concession is at issue, a public body has acquired for itself or for the benefit of the general public services or goods[70] and the economic operator awarded the concession is obliged to carry out the activities concerned. In contrast, authorisations being covered by the Services Directive presuppose that only permission is given to exercise an economic activity.[71] The Concessions Directive[72] contains specific requirements that must be observed by a public authority while granting such rights.

As for competition law, the Treaty lays down specific rules governing national measures limiting the number of market operators. Article 106 (1) TFEU contains a provision of competition law specifically dealing with exclusive and special rights. It stipulates that Member States are not

[67] This can be derived from Case C-201/02, *Wells* [2004] ECR I-00723, ECLI:EU:C:2004:12. On this matter, see Craig and De Búrca, *EU Law*, pp. 243 and 244.

[68] See Joined Cases C-458/14 and C-67/15, *Promoimpresa* [2016] ECLI:EU:C:2016:558, paras. 44–48 and recital 57 of the Services Directive. On this matter see also the chapter of Wollenschläger, Section 3.4.1.1.

[69] See para. 46 of the *Promoimpresa* judgment.

[70] See R. Caranta, 'The Changes to the Public Contract Directives and the Story They Tell about How EU Law Works', (2015) 52 *Common Market Law Review* 391–459 at 446.

[71] See paras. 47 and 48 of the *Promoimpresa* judgment.

[72] Directive 2014/23 on the award of concessions contracts, OJ 2014, No. L94/1.

allowed to grant an exclusive or special right in such a way that other Treaty provisions, especially those on competition, are infringed. Accordingly, Article 106(1) TFEU has no independent effect and must be applied in conjunction with other rules laid down in the TFEU.[73] The ECJ has mainly applied Article 106(1) in combination with Article 102 TFEU, which bans the abuse of a dominant position. The case law on these two provisions is highly complicated, as it should be established that the State, when shaping the limited rights, has obliged or made the undertaking concerned to abuse its dominant position.[74] Given the complexity of this test, it is difficult to find a violation of Article 106(1) TFEU. For that reason, the majority of the national measures involving limited rights have been reviewed under the Treaty provisions on free movement in recent years.[75] The striking conclusion is, therefore, that Article 106(1) TFEU, which is specifically designed to deal with limited rights, does not have such a considerable impact on these rights as EU internal market law has.

Transparency Principle The ECJ has derived from the free movement rules and the principle of non-discrimination the obligation for the Member states to give providers from other Member States the opportunity to compete for the granting of limited rights.[76] If such rights are awarded by the State without a competitive procedure, the transparency principle is violated, provided that a certain cross-border effect occurs.[77] In *Romaqua Group*,[78] the ECJ seems to have accepted that even Article 106(1) in conjunction with Article 102 TFEU also requires a competitive tendering procedure for the granting of exclusive rights. Transparency

[73] See, e.g., Case C-250/06, *United Pan-Europe Communications* [2007] ECR I-11135, ECLI:EU:C:2007:783, paras. 14–17.

[74] See, e.g., Case C-475/99, *Ambulanz Glöckner* [2001] ECR I-08089, ECLI:EU:C:2001:577, para. 39.

[75] On this matter, see H. Schweitzer, 'Services of General Economic Interest', in M. Cremona (ed.), *Market Integration and Public Services in the European Union* (Oxford: Oxford University Press, 2011), pp. 16–18 and J. W. van de Gronden and C. S. Rusu, *Competition Law in the EU: Principles, Substance, Enforcement* (Cheltenham: Edward Elgar, 2024), pp. 477–479.

[76] See, for example, para. 47 of the *Betfair* judgment (mentioned above). Cf. B. J. Drijber and H. Stergiou, 'Public Procurement Law and Internal Market Law', (2009) 46 *Common Market Law Review* 805–846 at 825 and 826.

[77] See, e.g., Case C-347/06, *ASM Brescia* [2008] ECR I-05641, ECLI:EU:C:2008:416, paras. 59 and 62.

[78] See Case C-510/22, *Romaqua Group* [2023] ECLI:EU:C:2023:694.

must be guaranteed in the process of the award of limited rights. This principle is mainly developed in cases concerning games of chance and not in the context of SGEIs. It is apparent, however, from the general wording used in the case law that the transparency principle also applies to other exclusive and special rights, such as the right to carry out SGEIs. Accordingly, the approach developed by the ECJ for exclusive and special rights dealing with games of chance also applies to limited rights involving SGEIs. Against this backdrop, it has to be concluded that the award of an exclusive right or a special right to provide a particular SGEI must, as a rule, be made subject to a competitive procedure. It should be noted that this could give providers from other Member States a great opportunity to get access to various SGEI sectors. It must be stressed that the transparency principle entails that economic operators from other Member States have equal opportunity to be granted limited rights in a particular Member State.

Apart from the transparency principle developed in EU free movement law, it should be pointed out that the Services Directive also contains an obligation having a lot in common with this principle. Pursuant to Article 12 of the Services Directive, Member States must apply a selection procedure to potential candidates, if the number of authorisations available for a service activity is limited because of the scarcity of the available natural resources or technical capacity. Although this provision governs all kinds of limited authorisations, it is also relevant for limited rights to provide SGEIs that are covered by the Services Directive. The selection procedure of Article 12 must be conducted in an impartial fashion and has to be transparent, which in particular means that adequate publicity is given about the launch, conduct and completion of the procedure. To my mind, this means that operators are given equal opportunity to compete for the authorisation concerned. Recital 62 of the Services Directive specifically mentions the requirement of open competition.[79] The first section of Article 12 of the Services Directive, moreover, underlines that the selection procedure is applied to potential candidates; this implies that competitiveness must play a role in this procedure. Accordingly, it is not surprising that the ECJ held that the automatic renewal of authorisations falling within the scope

[79] See also European Commission, *Handbook on Implementation of the Services Directive of the Commission* (Luxembourg: Publications Office of the European Union, 2022), p. 45, available at https://op.europa.eu/en/publication-detail/-/publication/60e2d020-6c6f-11ed-9887-01aa75ed71a1.

of this provision is not permitted.[80] In my view, Article 12 of the Services Directive entails that the granting of limited rights to provide SGEIs caught by this Directive must be subjected to a competitive procedure.

Furthermore, Article 11 of this directive states that the duration of an authorisation must be unlimited in time, unless the number of authorisations is limited by an overriding reason relating to the public interest. In *Trijber and Harmsen*,[81] the ECJ has derived from this obligation that the duration of the authorisation period must be limited, if a national authority has limited the number of authorisations for reasons of public interest. The reason for this is that the access to the market must not be made impossible for other service providers. The access to the market must be secured for service providers. To my mind, this means that the transparency principle is at the heart of this case law: newcomers must get a fair chance to access the market.

As already pointed out, the Concessions Directive applies in the event that a public authority has concluded a contract in order to ensure that an operator carries out activities for the benefit of the general public or for itself. In such circumstances, the granting of the limited right concerned amounts to mutually binding obligations.[82] The public authorities must make known their wish to award a concession by means of a concessions notice pursuant to Article 31(1) of the Directive. Consequently, the principle of transparency also applies to concessions.[83] Interestingly, Articles 74 and further of the Concessions Directive deal with public contracts for social services, health services, educational services and other sensitive services. In *ASADE*[84] the ECJ was called upon to interpret these provisions, and it held, by referring to the special status of SGEIs, that Member States were allowed to reserve the participation in the procedure for the award of a public contract to provide certain social services (or other services falling within the scope of Article 74 of the Directive) to private non-profit organisations (provided that certain conditions were met).[85] However, the ECJ also stressed that it followed from Article 76 of the Concessions Directive that the award of

[80] See paras. 49–57 of the *Promoimpresa* judgment. See also Article 12(2) Services Directive.

[81] Joined Cases C-340/14 and C-341/14, *Trijber and Harmsen* [2015] ECLI:EU:C:2015:641.

[82] Cf. Recital 14 of the Concessions Directive.

[83] See also J. Wolswinkel, 'From Public Contracts to Limited Authorisations and Vice Versa: Exploring General Award Requirements from the EU Court's Corollary Approach', (2015) 24 *Public Procurement Law Review* 137–163 at 151.

[84] Case C-436/20, *ASADE* [2022] ECLI:EU:C:2022:559.

[85] Case C-436/20, *ASADE*, para. 95.

the public contract must take place through a competitive tender.[86] It is clear from this discussion that competitive procedures are required on the basis of the Concessions Directive.

8.3.2.2 Financial Grants and EU State Aid Law

The award of limited rights to provide SGEIs may be combined with giving financial grants to the undertakings entrusted with an SGEI mission in order to guarantee the adequate financing of the supply of these rights. Under EU law these grants qualify as state aid. Consequently, Articles 107–109 TFEU, provisions of which are discussed in the contribution of Caranta and Biancardi to the present volume, apply.[87] This entails that, in principle, pursuant to Article 108(3) TFEU, the national measure concerned must be notified to the Commission.[88] In *Altmark*,[89] however, the ECJ has developed a special approach to SGEIs assuming that financial support given with a view to SGEIs aims at compensating the costs incurred with the supply of these services. The economic benefits given do not constitute state aid if the following conditions are satisfied: (1) the undertaking concerned is charged with the provision of an SGEI, (2) the parameters of the amount of the compensation are calculated in an objective and transparent way, (3) the compensation does not go beyond what is necessary and (4) if the task to provide the SGEI concerned has not been granted in accordance with a public procurement procedure, the amount of compensation is determined on the basis of the expenses of a well-run undertaking. As is apparent from the contribution of Caranta and Biancardi,[90] in EU law the market price may be established through a tendering procedure or an evaluation based on generally accepted market indicators. It is not a surprise, therefore, that the fourth *Altmark* condition underlines the importance of public procurement and the costs of a well-run company.

It is apparent from these conditions that following a public procurement procedure or other type of competitive procedure is not required in order to benefit from the *Altmark* approach. Admittedly, applying the public procurement rules entails that the fourth condition of this

[86] Case C-436/20, *ASADE* [2022] ECLI:EU:C:2022:559, paras. 96 and 97.

[87] See the chapter of Caranta and Biancardi, Section 5.4.1.

[88] See, for example, Case C-179/20, *Fondul Proprietatea* [2022] ECLI:EU:C:2022:58, paras. 107–111.

[89] Case C-280/00, *Altmark* [2003] ECR I-07747, ECLI:EU:C:2003:415.

[90] See the chapter of Caranta and Biancardi, Section 5.4.2.1.

approach is met. Also, in the second condition of *Altmark*, transparency plays a role, as this condition requires that the parameters of the compensation concerned must be objective and transparent. However, the references made in *Altmark* to transparency do not entail that a competitive procedure must be organised, as is prescribed in EU free movement law. The fourth condition of the *Altmark* ruling specifically allows for either organising a public procurement procedure or calculating the costs of the compensation to be given on the basis of the costs of an efficient company. Giving the choice between these two methods would not have made sense, if tendering was compulsory according to the second *Altmark* condition. In my view, the transparency requirement of this condition comes largely down to clearly outlining which criteria must be fulfilled to be eligible for a particular compensation. The references made to transparency in *Altmark* are not related to a call for competition.

In sum, organising a public procurement procedure could prevent issues of EU state aid law from arising, as is also apparent from the analysis carried out by Arrowsmith in her contribution[91] and by Caranta and Biancardi in their contribution to the present volume.[92] However, the absence of such a procedure does not automatically trigger the applicability of Article 107(1) TFEU. It should be noted that Van den Brink has argued in her contribution to the present volume that according to the General Court of the EU the principle of transparency applies to the allocation of limited European subsidies.[93] It should be stressed that this case law concerns the legal framework governing the grant of EU subsidies. In other words, these matters relate to the economic benefits given through funds or other resources managed by the EU and are, accordingly, not connected with the economic benefits given by Member States to undertakings in cases arising under Articles 107–109 TFEU.

In this regard, it must be recalled that this contribution deals with limited rights to provide SGEIs. It is not sensible anymore to organise a competitive procedure for granting compensation for covering the costs incurred with the operation of an SGEI mission, once the limited right

[91] See the chapter of Arrowsmith, Section 2.4.1.2. Arrowsmith points out in this section that, nevertheless, it cannot be excluded that public procurement activity could constitute state aid. The receipt of a public contract may amount to an advantage that an operator would not have obtained under normal market circumstances.

[92] Chapter of Caranta and Biancardi, Section 5.4.3.1.

[93] See the chapter of Van den Brink, Section 4.4.3.1. She refers to Case T-297/05, *IPK International* [2011] ECR II-01859, ECLI:EU:T:2011:185.

connected with this compensation has already been granted on the basis of a competitive procedure. My point is that no independent obligation to organise a competitive procedure can be derived from Articles 107–109 TFEU. This conclusion is of interest in the event that the award of the limited right concerned has not been subject to a call for competition (because an exception could be relied upon).[94] Also, this conclusion is relevant for the financing of SGEIs not being subject to limited rights (a subject that falls outside the scope of the present contribution).

8.4 Derogations from the Obligations of EU Internal Market and Competition Law

As limited rights to provide SGEIs could give rise to effects that are qualified as restrictive under EU internal market and competition law, it is of great importance to examine the exceptions. At first, it will be examined to what extent regulatory requirements could be justifiable, and then attention will be paid to the measures governing the access to limited rights.

8.4.1 *Justifying Regulatory Requirements*

It may be assumed that as a rule the regulatory requirements imposed on SGEI providers are aimed at realising public interest goals, such as access for all and a high standard of service provision. If a Treaty provision on free movement is infringed, exceptions laid down in, for example, Articles 51 and 52 TFEU, and the Rule of Reason (overriding requirements of general interest) can be invoked. Relying on these exceptions is only successful if the proportionality principle is met. The national laws under review must be suitable for attaining the public interest goal concerned and do not go beyond what is necessary.[95] The Member States must prove whether it may reasonably be concluded from the evidence submitted that the means chosen are appropriate and that the objectives set cannot be achieved by less restrictive measures.[96] It must be examined '... objectively, through statistical or ad hoc data or by other

[94] On these exceptions, see Section 8.4.2.2 of this chapter.

[95] See, for example, *Gebhard* (mentioned above) and Case C-231/20, *MT* [2021] ECLI:EU:C:2021, para. 43.

[96] See, e.g., Case C-333/14, *Scotch Whiskey Association* [2015] ECLI:EU:C:2015:845, para. 56.

means . . .' whether this is the case.[97] The interventions made by the Member States must be based on sound and convincing arguments.

In examining the suitability, the ECJ assigns great value to the consistent and systematic drafting of the laws at hand.[98] It may be argued that by doing so the ECJ makes the national SGI measures subject to principles of good administration. On the one hand, national discretion is acknowledged for the Member States when organising an SGEI sector. On the other hand, the Member States must come up with a coherent system, which, in my view, limits the room for clinching deals and achieving compromises in the politcal process. The approach based on consistent and systematic drafting is also used by the ECJ when interpreting the provisions of the Services Directive dealing with the exceptions regarding the restrictions of the freedom of establishment.[99]

In sum, it may be assumed that in many cases the Member States will be able to justify the regulatory requirements imposed on SGEI providers. Nevertheless, it is of great interest that Member States pay special attention to the design of their systems and the arguments on which restrictive measures are based. Peculiar loopholes must be taken out and weak points have to be addressed. The need for this is even more pressing in the event that the Services Directive applies, since domestic suppliers are also able to challenge national SGEI systems, as internal situations are covered by this piece of EU legislation.

Basing market interventions that have been adopted with a view to the continuous provision of SGEIs on convincing evidence is also key to success under the Services Directive, as is apparent from, for example, *CNAE*. In this case, it had to be examined whether there was sufficient proof for the claim that the quantitative and territorial restrictions under review were necessary in order to ensure that the SGEIs concerned would be provided in less attractive areas.[100] In this regard, an important case in point is *Cali Apartments*.[101] According to French law, letting apartments for a short stay to tourists was subject to prior authorisation. This requirement was reviewed in the light of Article 9 of the Services

[97] See Case C-148/15, *Deutsche Parkinson Vereinigung* [2016] ECLI:EU:C:2016:776, para. 36.

[98] See, for example, Case C-169/07, *Hartlauer* [2009] ECR I-01721, ECLI:EU:C:2009:141 and Case C-570/07, *Blanco Pérez and Chao Gómez* [2010] ECR I-04629, ECLI:EU:C:2010:300.

[99] See Case C-293/14, *Hiebler*, 23 December 2015, ECLI:EU:C:2015:843.

[100] See Case C-292/21, *CNAE* [2023] ECLI:EU:C:2023:32, paras. 72 and 73.

[101] Case C-727/18, *Cali Apartments* [2020] ECLI:EU:C:2020:743.

Directive. The intervention was considered to be justifiable, as it contributed to the achievement of public interest objectives connected with social housing. It was of relevance that the authorisation scheme was confined to big cities (having more than 200,000 inhabitants), where housing problems capable of putting under pressure the access to social dwelling places occurred. The interpretation given by the ECJ of the requirement of Article 10(2)(g) that the national conditions of an authorisation scheme are transparent and accessible is very illuminating.[102] It suffices in the ECJ's view that the national applicable measure '[. . .] effectively enables any interested person to be informed immediately of the existence of legislation likely to affect access to, or the exercise, of the activity concerned [. . .]'.[103] Consequently, Article 10(2)(g) of the Services Directive is complied with, if an economic operator is able to know in advance which conditions must be met. It should be pointed out that in the context of Article 10(2) Services Directive transparency refers to access to information on the applicable laws and not to competitive procedures for granting limited rights.

8.4.2 *Justifying Restrictions of the Access to Limited Rights in EU Internal Market and Competition Law*

Justifications are also available for the restrictions resulting from the creation and award of limited rights. Although the issues at play largely overlap with those discussed in the previous section, it will be shown that new questions also arise.

8.4.2.1 Justifying Creation and Award of Limited Rights to Provide SGEIs

To start with, attention should be paid to the justifications in relation to the creation of limited rights. Then, the role of justifications in the award process has to be discussed.

Justifying the Limitations of the Number of Providers In the same vein as with the regulatory requirements, the Member States can invoke exceptions to justify the restrictions resulting from limiting the number of providers. This means that it must be demonstrated that a general interest goal is at issue. Moreover, the principle of proportionality must

102 See paras. 104–107 of the *Cali Apartments* judgment.
103 See para. 107 of the *Cali Apartments* judgment.

be met, including the approach based on consistent and systematic drafting. It must be made clear, for instance, that an exclusive right to provide a pension scheme or to provide ambulance services is proportionate.

The classical argument for such a right is that universal provision must be guaranteed. Such arguments can perfectly be assessed under Article 106(2) TFEU, which is specifically concerned with the operation of SGEI missions and stipulates that the need to provide these services may justify derogations from several prohibitions contained in the Treaty, such as the competition and internal market rules. In its competition law judgments, the ECJ has accepted that competition may be restricted if this is necessary with a view to the supply of the SGEIs at hand under economically acceptable circumstances.[104] This means that the Member States were allowed to resolve problems of cherry-picking. In *Ambulanz Glöckner*, for instance, the ECJ held that the exclusive right under review prevented that commercially oriented providers of ambulance services would concentrate on the most profitable services and leave the permanent provision of emergency transport of patients to the provider entrusted with an SGEI mission.[105]

It is striking that in free movement cases concerning exclusive and special rights Article 106(2) TFEU is not applied. However, the ECJ has approached the issues at play in free movement cases from the angle of the 'classic' exceptions in free movement law, which are the rule of reason (also known as overriding requirements of general interest) and Treaty provisions, such as Article 52 TFEU (which deals with public policy, public security and public health). Nevertheless, in its interpretation of these exceptions the ECJ accommodated arguments that are typical of Article 106(2) TFEU. In *Freskot*,[106] for example, which concerned a compulsory insurance scheme for natural risks, the ECJ held that the design of this scheme was aimed at guaranteeing a minimum level of cover of risks for all farmers at an adequate level. Therefore, the insurance scheme under review was justifiable. Of great interest was the question of to what extent the cover provided by this scheme concerned risks that could be dissociated from other risks without compromising the social object pursued.[107] In my view, this test comes down to

[104] See, for example, Case C-475/99, *Ambulanz Glöckner* [2001] ECR I-08089, ECLI:EU:C:2001:577, para. 57.

[105] See paras. 58–65 of the *Ambulzanz Glöckner* judgment.

[106] Case C-355/00, *Freskot* [2003] ECR I-05263, ECLI:EU:C:2003:298.

[107] See para. 71 of the *Freskot* judgment.

examining whether the provision of the compulsory insurance cover could be carried under economically acceptable circumstances. Such reviews are very common under Article 106(2) TFEU, as already stated. Furthermore, in cases concerning social security the ECJ has even accepted that the aim of preserving the financial equilibrium (balance) of a social security scheme constitutes a Rule of Reason exception.[108] One of the core elements of preserving the financial balance is to prevent that commercial enterprises would offer insurance cover to wealthy or healthy persons leaving persons who are less fortunate to the operator being entrusted with a special task. This is exactly the problem of cherry-picking, which also plays an important role in assessments under Article 106(2) TFEU. Accordingly, the arguments that were significant for shaping Article 106(2) TFEU can also be used for justifying exclusive and special rights on the basis of the Rule of Reason.

Justifying Not Observing the Transparency Principle To what extent is not subjecting the award of exclusive or special rights to a competitive procedure justifiable? It is accepted in the case law of the ECJ in free movement cases that no competitive procedure is organised, if the limited right concerned is awarded to a State body or an organisation controlled by the State.[109] This is known as in-house and quasi-in-house provision.[110]

Are the Rule of Reason and Treaty exceptions, such as Article 52 TFEU, also capable of justifying non-compliance with the transparency principle? In cases such as *Betfair*, the ECJ held that this was not the case, as awarding a limited right to an operator on the basis of a competitive procedure does not prevent the State from imposing on this operator standards that are necessary for attaining specific public interest goals. As long as it is guaranteed that these standards are observed, it does not matter which operator is selected.[111] Consequently, departing from a strict reading of the reasoning in *Betfair* one may conclude that the absence of a competitive procedure cannot be justified by the Rule of Reason or a Treaty exception. The conditions attached to an exclusive

[108] See, e.g., paras. 85–91 of the *Kattner Stahlbau* judgment (mentioned above).

[109] See para. 59 of the *Betfair* judgment (mentioned above).

[110] See Drijber and Stergiou, 'Public Procurement Law', pp. 811 and 812. See also S. Hötte, 'Ode to Liberty? – The Determination of Services of General (Economic) Interest and the "Make-or-Buy" Decision', (2020) 45 *European Law Review* 487–506 at 491 and 492.

[111] See paras. 57 and 58 of the *Betfair* judgment. Cf. Case C-64/08, *Engelmann* [2010] ECR I-08219, ECLI:EU:C:2010:506, para. 47.

right or special right are in themselves sufficient for achieving the goals set by the State. The aim of these conditions is to achieve particular public interest goals and, accordingly, granting a limited right to the incumbent without organising a call for competition is not necessary for attaining the goals set.

It should be stressed, however, that this line of reasoning was developed in cases concerning games of chance and that, for obvious reasons, such services do not constitute SGEIs. In subsequent case law, the ECJ has moderated its view as to whether Rule of Reason or Treaty exceptions may be relied upon in disputes involving the transparency principle. In *Belgacom*, it held that the absence of a competitive procedure '. . . might, exceptionally, be allowed . . .' on the basis of these exceptions.[112] In the case at issue, the ECJ, however, rejected the claim that public interest goals were at stake.

On the findings made in *Belgacom*, the ECJ further built in the judgments *Azienda Sanitaria*[113] and *CASTA*.[114] These judgments concerned the provision of SGEIs, that is, ambulance services. Here, the ECJ did not rule out that the absence of a competitive procedure could be justifiable on the basis of the Rule of Reason. In these cases, it was of great interest that in the national system under scrutiny the ambulance services were provided for by non-profit operators (charity organisations).[115] In the view of the ECJ, it had to be established that the absence of profit-seeking is necessary for attaining the social purpose at play, that is, access for all to emergency ambulance services; to what extent this mattered had to be examined by the national referring judge.[116]

In *UNIS* a great opportunity for elaborating on the approach developed in *Sanitaria* and *CASTA* was missed. In this case, the ECJ held that the selection by social partners of one operator for providing cover of particular risks for workers risks and health insurance (also SGEIs in my view) amounted to an exclusive right. The management of

[112] See Case C-221/12, *Belgacom* [2013] ECLI:EU:C:2013:736, para. 38. See also J. Wolswinkel, 'Concession Meets Authorisation: New Demarcation Lines under the Concessions Directive?', (2017) 12 *European Procurement & Public Private Partnership Law Review* 396–407 at 398.

[113] Case C-113/13, *Azienda Sanitaria* [2014] ECLI:EU:C:2014:2440.

[114] Case C-50/14, *CASTA* [2016] ECLI:EU:C:2016:56.

[115] See paras. 57–62 of the *Azienda Sanitaria* judgment and paras. 63–65 of the *CASTA* judgment.

[116] See paras. 52–63 of the *Azienda Sanitaria* judgment and paras. 57–66 of the *CASTA* judgment.

this cover was based on a collective agreement. This collective agreement was declared generally binding by the French Minister of Social Affairs. As this decision amounted to granting exclusive rights to the provider selected by the social partners and the award of these rights had not been subject to a competitive procedure, free movement was restricted, since the transparency principle was not complied with. It is striking that the French government did not mention any justification ground and, therefore, the ECJ did not examine whether the French system was justifiable. The *UNIS* case shows that Member States wishing to uphold the system of selection of providers of social insurance by employers and trade unions have to come up with sound reasons for the necessity of this system.

At the current stage of the case law it remains uncertain under which conditions the award of exclusive or special rights does not need to be subjected to a competitive procedure on the basis of the Rule of Reason or a Treaty exception. Further case law must be awaited. In my view, the provision of social rights, such as pension and social security benefits, requires that the operators concerned make large and long-term investments, entertain stable engagements with the beneficiaries (in order to guarantee access to particular entitlements) and have specific expertise. It is of utmost importance that persons affiliated with a pension or social security system and paying contributions to such systems may trust that they receive the benefits due. It cannot be excluded from the outset this may be put under pressure, if frequently a new provider is selected. As a result, when deciding on the matter of justification grounds in cases concerning the transparency principle and limited rights to provide SGEIs, the ECJ should examine with great care whether these investments, engagements and expertise are respected in competitive procedures. It should be avoided at all costs that the continuous and stable provision of SGEIs closely related to the social welfare state is put under pressure. What works in cases dealing with exclusive rights to provide games of chance (not being SGEIs), may fall short in, for example, social security and healthcare cases (where, in many Member States, services that qualify as SGEIs are at issue). On the other hand, the transparency principle should not be set aside if following a competitive procedure will not (significantly) harm the functioning of SGEIs. In my view, it is of great interest that in cases similar to *UNIS* a thorough and in-depth debate is conducted before the ECJ, in order to address all issues at play in an all-encompassing fashion. To my mind, the outcome of this debate could be that not complying with the transparency principle in cases concerning limited rights to provide particular SGEIs is justifiable on the ground that the stable and continuous provision of these services must be guaranteed. The specific nature of certain SGEIs may justify that a call for competition is not the right course of action. It is of utmost importance that a Member State confronted with litigation against one of its SGEI schemes prepares its case in an excellent way and presents the ECJ with all relevant arguments and reasons for derogating from the transparency principle in a comprehensive way. It is of great importance that the ECJ judgment that will balance the competition concerns and the proper supply of SGEIs will be based on a proceeding where a legal debate of high quality has been conducted.

In Section 8.3.2.1 of this contribution, it was outlined that the Services Directive lays down provisions for selection procedures that mirror the transparency obligation developed in free movement law. Article 12 of this Directive requires a competitive selection procedure for certain limited rights, while it flows from Article 11 that the duration of the authorisation must be limited in the event that the number of authorisations has been limited for reasons of public interest. The question arises whether exceptions are available in order to derogate from these provisions of the Services Directive. According to settled case law, as already stated, once a matter is harmonised the free movement rules, including the exceptions, do not apply any more. As a result, derogating from obligations laid down in an EU directive or regulation is only permitted, insofar as this directive or regulation allows for this. As the Services Directive does not contain any exception to the obligations laid down in Article 12 as well as in Article 11, it is not permitted not to follow the procedures prescribed in these provisions in my view. However, it should be noted that Article 12(3) of the Services Directive provides that a Member State may take into account, in establishing the rules for the selection procedure, considerations related to, for example, public health, social policy and environmental protection. The wording of this provision does not make any mention of the possibility of not following a selection procedure though. This implies that Member States are permitted to base the selection criteria (partly) on these public interest considerations but are not allowed to decide not to subject the granting of limited authorisations to a competitive procedure. This view is supported by the ruling of the ECJ in *Promoimpresa*, where it held that Article 12(3) was not capable of justifying the automatic renewal of an authorisation leading to allocating scarce rights when no selection procedure was organised at the time of the initial grant of this authorisation.[117]

As was also pointed out in Section 8.3.2.1 of this contribution, the Concessions Directive obliges the public authorities of the Member States to grant concessions in a competitive way. In contrast with the Services Directive, the Concessions Directive does provide that derogations are permitted in specific circumstances.[118] These derogations are set out in, for example, Article 31(4) of the latter Directive and concern matters, such as the absence of competition for technical reasons. Accordingly, public authorities wishing not to follow a competitive procedure must verify which exceptions are laid down in the Directive on the award of concessions contracts.

8.4.2.2 Justifying Giving Financial Grants

In *Altmark* the ECJ has, as was already stated, adopted a special approach to the interpretation of Article 107(1) TFEU and, by doing so, has given some leeway to the Member States to finance the provision of SGEIs. If a particular financial grant does not benefit from this approach, a couple of exceptions can be relied upon.[119] Of special interest is the Commission Decision on Public Services Obligations,[120] which sets out the conditions regarding specific SGEIs, such as hospital and social services. If those conditions are satisfied, the obligation to notify financial grants to the Commission is lifted. In fact, this Decision contains an exemption for the ban on granting state aid to undertakings. In this Decision, emphasis is put on, *inter alia*, introducing efficiency mechanisms, as the calculation of the compensation due must be based on commonly accepted accounting principles and overcompensation must be avoided.[121] It should be stressed that Article 4 of the Decision, which deals with the entrustment of the task to provide SGEIs, does not require that the compensation is given through a competitive procedure. It does stipulate that the act of

[117] See paras. 53–55 of the *Promoimpresa* judgment (mentioned above).

[118] See also Wolswinkel, 'Concession Meets Authorisation', p. 406.

[119] On this matter, see, e.g., E. Szyszczak, 'Introduction', in E. Szyszczak and J. W. van de Gronden (eds.), *Financing Services of General Economic Interest. Reform and Modernization* (The Hague: Asser Press, 2013), pp. 1–34, at pp. 15–31.

[120] See the Commission Decision of 20 December 2011 on the application of Article 106(2) of the Treaty on the Functioning of the European Union to State aid in the form of public service compensation granted to certain undertakings entrusted with the operation of services of general economic interest, OJ 2012 L7.

[121] See Articles 6 and 7 of the Commission Decision on Public Services Obligations.

entrustment sets out what the nature and the contours of the SGEI mission are and how compensation is calculated.[122] Transparency must be given with regard to the set-up of this mission and the financial benefits. This goes, however, not so far as that various operators should have had the opportunity to compete for the compensation.

The EU framework for SGEIs,[123] which specifies how the Commission will exercise its competences under Article 106(2) TFEU to approve national measures financing SGEIs, does also not require that SGEIs are granted through competitive procedures. It does set out some transparency obligations, which come down to providing information on the nature of the SGEI missions and the compensations concerned. These obligations highly mirror what is set out in the Commission Decision on Public Services Obligations (governing specific SGEIs).[124] Moreover, the EU framework for SGEIs specifies that the Commission will only approve national measures, if the applicable Union rules on public procurement are complied with.[125] Also in line with the Commission Decision on Public Services Obligations, in the EU framework for SGEIs the importance of efficiency is stressed.[126] The Commission is prepared to approve the national measures financing SGEIs, if efficiency is a key element in the way the compensation is calculated.

It should be pointed out that a national state aid measure is only justifiable on the basis of Article 106(2) TFEU if it is notified to the Commission in advance.[127] Strikingly, in cases concerning the Treaty provisions on free movement as well as Article 106 TFEU, a national court has the authority to assess whether the restrictive measures under review are justifiable on the basis of Article 106(2) TFEU, while this competence does not exist in state aid law cases. The reason for this difference lies in the fact that in EU state aid law the Commission has the sole power to examine whether a national measure is compatible with the internal market.

[122] Other transparency obligations entailing the duty to provide specific information are contained in Article 7 of the Commission Decision on Public Services Obligations.

[123] See the Communication from the Commission on a European Union framework for State aid in the form of public service compensation, OJ 2012 C8/15.

[124] See for these obligations, for example, paras. 16, 17, 21–60 of the EU framework for SGEIs.

[125] See para. 19 of the EU framework for SGEIs.

[126] See points 21–43 of the EU framework for SGEIs.

[127] See Joined Cases C-434/19 and C-435/19, *Poste Italiane* [2021] ECLI:EU:C:2021:162, paras. 33 and 73.

In sum, under the current EU state aid rules considerable leeway exists for financing SGEIs and, accordingly, giving financial grants. Nevertheless, the interventions of the Member States must be well-defined and efficiency-driven, whereas the nature of the SGEI missions and the compensations given are clear from the outset. It should be noted that at the time of the writing of this contribution the Commission was in the midst of reviewing the EU rules for national subsidies given for the supply of health and social services of general economic interest.[128] Accordingly, it cannot be excluded that in due time the Commission Decision on Public Services Obligations and the EU framework for SGEIs will be amended.

8.5 Conclusions

As is apparent from the foregoing, non-economic SGIs are not impacted by the EU rules for the freedom of service provision and competition. However, SGEIs ('economic SGIs') are not immune from these rules. The analysis carried out shows that the EU legal framework governing the national limited rights to provide SGEIs is very complicated. The reason for this is that this matter is partly harmonised by various EU measures, such as the Services Directive, and partly remains subject to the Treaty provisions on free movement. In general, the case law on free movement sets out a comprehensive set of rules, which clarify under which circumstances limited rights to provide SGEIs are lawful. A great dearth of case law is developed and explains, for example, that the applicable national laws must be drafted in a consistent and systematic fashion. However, in my view the case law on the transparency principle based on the EU free movement rules is still surrounded by some difficulties. The most significant issue is whether the award of limited rights to provide SGEIs without organising a competitive procedure is justifiable under certain circumstances. It is fully understandable that no exception may be relied upon in the event that an exclusive right to organise games of chance has not been made subject to such a procedure. However, SGEIs concern essential services, such as pension schemes and healthcare services. The provision of these services requires huge investments and specific expertise. In *Azienda Sanitaria* and *CASTA*, the ECJ seems to have realised that

[128] See the Press Release of 1 December 2022 'Commission publishes results of evaluation of State aid rules on services of general economic interest applicable to health and social services and to small aid amounts', IP/22/7233.

the logic as applied in cases on games of chance cuts no ice in cases concerning SGEIs. In my view, it is of great interest that case law is further developed on this matter and due consideration is paid to the special position of SGEIs. It should be recalled that Article 14 TFEU provides that the supply of SGEIs must be guaranteed both in EU and national law. An important asset of SGEIs is that providing these services contributes to social and territorial cohesion according to this Treaty provision.

The adoption of harmonisation measures, such as the Services Directive and the Concessions Directive, complicates the EU rules on limited rights. Member States have to comply with a fragmented set of obligations when designating SGEIs. The provisions laid down in these Directives do not seem to accommodate SGEI concerns in a comprehensive and coherent way. Although the case law of the ECJ requires that national legislation is based on consistent and systematic drafting, it could be argued that such drafting is – for a part – absent when it comes to, for instance, SGEIs and the Services Directive. It is to be wished for that the Union legislature will improve this drafting. Special attention should be paid to the question of whether and, if so, under which circumstances the award of limited rights to provide SGEIs does not have to be made subject to a competitive procedure. Moreover, it should also be considered whether the prohibitions contained in the Services Directive should be moved to an EU regulation. This would solve the problems occurring in cases where implementation failures regarding the Services directive are raised in disputes between solely private parties. The unfortunate point is that the provisions of the Services Directive do not have horizontal effect.

Furthermore, it is apparent from the analysis carried out that the granting of compensation for providing SGEIs does not need to be made subject to a competitive procedure. Neither the famous *Altmark* ruling nor the measures adopted by the Union legislature, such as the Commission Decision on Public Services Obligations and the EU framework for SGEIs, require this. It should be pointed out that some transparency, meaning that information and some clarity are provided, must be given according to the EU state aid rules. The conclusion is that, whereas the obligation to award limited rights through a competitive procedure plays a central role in EU internal market law, this is not true for EU state aid law.

In sum, the Member States enjoy a wide margin of appreciation in shaping limited rights. Insofar as those rights do not concern economic activities, the freedom of the Member States is hardly impacted. But also when it comes to economic activities, their freedom is considerable. If the national laws governing the limited rights to provide SGEI are drafted in a consistent and systematic way, a fair chance exists that they are compatible with EU law. Moreover, the financial grants meeting the *Altmark* conditions or the criteria laid down in other EU measures dealing with SGEIs are permitted. In my view, the most significant limitation of the room for manoeuvre results from the transparency principle. This principle requires that in many procedures leading to the award of limited rights for supplying SGEIs, competitive procedures must be organised (with an exception to in-house and quasi-in-house provision). In fact, this is a revolutionary conclusion but the full potential of this finding is not clear, as the case law on this issue is not crystallised yet. As was already stated, new developments not only related to case law but also to EU legislation, such as the Services Directive, are needed in order to provide more transparency on how limited rights to provide SGEIs must be awarded.

9

The Transparent Allocation of Limited Rights

What Types of Transparency Promote Public Interests?

ANOESKA BUIJZE

9.1 Introduction

Transparency is an overarching norm in the allocation of limited rights. This may be because transparency is important in its own right, but perhaps more importantly, the transparent allocation of limited rights has many benefits. In this volume, Arrowsmith points this out repeatedly in her contribution, and it is also reflected in the introductory chapter of this volume, where it is stated that 'In short, the dominating idea is that a competitive procedure between interested parties will enable government to put "their" rights in the hand of those who value them most, while at the same time enabling them to realise other public interests than value for money.'[1] Indeed, transparency can contribute to the realization of all of the public interests defined by Arrowsmith. However, transparency is usually not the *only* way to promote these interests. Moreover, transparency is a multifaceted concept: there is a multitude of transparency obligations, ranging from the obligation to provide access to documents to the general public to the prohibition to change the terms of a public contract after the award procedure has ended and the contract has been awarded. In fact, there are different types of transparency, and not all types promote all the public interests discussed in this volume. Finally, transparency can also have adverse consequences, public interests can be harmed by too much or the wrong kinds of transparency. Therefore, one would expect to see those transparency obligations that contribute to the interests that the law aims to promote, and those interests can differ depending on the specific right that is being allocated as well as the specific legal instruments that regulate its allocation.

[1] See the chapter of Wolswinkel, Jansen and Van Ommeren, Section 1.3.

Indeed, the chapters by Arrowsmith, Wollenschläger, van den Brink, and Caranta and Biancardi show that transparency obligations differ, depending on the type of right that is being allocated and the specific legal framework that is applicable. These differences are sometimes subtle and sometimes require further clarification. At other times, however, they are stark. A central tenet in this book is that transparency is a precondition for competitive allocation. Thus, the obligation to be transparent about there being an opportunity to acquire a limited right might be considered quite fundamental. Yet, even to this obligation we see exceptions for almost all of the rights discussed. Van den Brink points at financial grants that are awarded without any competitive procedure, Caranta and Biancardi discuss the figure of direct sales, and Arrowsmith shows that in exceptional circumstances, public authorities can invite parties they themselves select to submit a tender. For limited authorizations, however, the room for exceptions seems to be more limited.[2] The Services Directive in particular seems to leave no room for it.[3] Although the same basic transparency obligation applies, there are differences in the extent to which exceptions to this obligation are acceptable.

Such differences are to be expected. To the extent that transparency is a means to an end, transparency obligations should contribute to the interests that a particular legal framework seeks to promote. As is shown in the contributions in Part I of this book, transparency is a rather broad concept and encompasses a host of different obligations. These obligations contribute to the realization of different interests, in different ways. Sometimes, a particular transparency obligation is essential to achieve an interest. In many cases, however, there are alternative means available. In addition, some transparency obligations may have harmful effects. If the latter is the case, that may be a good reason to opt for an alternative mechanism. To put it in another way: one needs different transparency obligations, depending on what public interests one feels are most important to achieve.

The differences in transparency obligations observed in the abovementioned chapters can shed light on the way public interests have been, or can be, optimized in the applicable legal framework. As an example, the rules regarding transparency in the allocation of authorizations, particularly within the scope of the Services Directive, emphasize the rights of economic operators directly involved in the allocating

[2] Although not unheard of, see Case C-203/08, *Betfair* ECLI:EU:C:2010:307.

[3] See the chapter of Van de Gronden, Section 8.4.2.

procedure, whereas the other fields either balance these rights against other interests involved or allow public authorities room to engage in this balancing exercise themselves.

This contribution is structured as follows: Section 9.2 will discuss the different transparency obligations that are discussed in this volume, and Section 9.3 presents a way to classify these obligations. Section 9.4 will discuss how transparency contributes to realizing the public interests distinguished by Arrowsmith. It will also discuss whether the transparency obligations that must be observed when allocating grants, authorizations, sales and public contracts contribute to these interests. Finally, Section 9.5 will analyse these findings: Do the differences in transparency obligations when allocating different types of rights reflect differences in how public interests are or should be optimized, or are there, rather, inexplicable differences that cannot be explained by the characteristics of the right that is being allocated?

9.2 Transparency Obligations

The authors in this book identify a wide variety of transparency obligations:

- transparency about the decision to create a right;
- transparency about the decision to create scarcity;
- transparency about the availability of the opportunity to acquire a limited right;
- the need for rules governing the allocation procedure (notions of rule-based governance);[4]
- transparency about the rules governing the allocation procedure;
- transparency about selection and allocation decisions.

9.2.1 Transparency about the Decision to Create a Right

Before a right can be awarded, it must be created. The decision to acquire goods or services or to sell an asset must be taken, or a grant or authorization scheme must be created. In public procurement, the

[4] This obligation seems to be the odd one out, because it does not concern the communication of information. If one understands transparency as a tool to make government behaviour observable and predictable for citizens, the coherence between this obligation and the others becomes clear.

decision on what goods and services to purchase falls outside of the scope of this project.[5] European Union (EU) law has nothing to say on what goods and services public authorities choose to procure, and it leaves the decision on whether to procure goods and services through the market or to produce them in-house to the authorities of the member states. Such decisions are of course subject to general transparency obligations enshrined in constitutional and administrative law, such as the duty to give reasons and the obligation to publish information based on freedom of information acts. When creating an authorization scheme, deciding to sell assets, or when creating a grant scheme, more specific transparency obligations are in place. The reasons for these obligations differ though. Wollenschläger reminds us that authorization schemes limit the freedom to provide services, and as such, they require justification. Transparency about the decision to create an authorization scheme facilitates accountability. Actors can control whether the authorization scheme actually contributes to the realization of a public interest and is not merely a barrier to market access for non-nationals. For grants, van den Brink describes that a legal basis is required for most subsidies, to ensure democratic representation in the decision about what public interests are promoted. Caranta and Biancardi show that in asset sales, the reasons to privatize an undertaking must be transparent, to ensure that a market economy operator (MEO) would also sell and that the sale does not constitute state aid.

9.2.2 Transparency about the Decision to Create Scarcity

Although scarcity can be a given, sometimes it is created. This is especially true for authorization schemes. However, limited authorization schemes limit the freedom to provide services to an even greater extent and must again be justified. Member states must be transparent about their reasons to limit the number of available authorizations, to ensure that the limitation actually contributes to the public interest. For grants, the situation is slightly more complicated. If they are awarded on the basis of a grant scheme, the available budget needs to be included in the legal measure creating that scheme. Again, this allows for democratic control over the height of the available budget and ensures that public interest is taken into account when deciding on the budget. For budget

[5] See the chapter of Arrowsmith, Section 2.2.

subsidies, which van den Brink in her contribution defines as a grant for which both the recipient and the amount of the grant are expressly mentioned in the government's budget,[6] there is no explicit ceiling, which means that there is no transparency about the decision to limit the available budget. Indeed, it is not transparent what the budget actually is. The same is true for incidental subsides, which van den Brink defines as a grant with a limited number of recipients for more or less one-off activities, such as the celebration of a silver jubilee.[7] For procurement and asset sales, scarcity is considered as a given. Governments do not have unlimited assets for sale, nor do they have unlimited demand for goods and services. As such, transparency about the decision to create scarcity is not required.

9.2.3 *Transparency about the Availability of the Opportunity to Acquire a Limited Right*

This is a necessary condition for competitive allocation procedures, so whenever a competitive procedure is required, so is transparency about the availability of the opportunity to acquire a limited right. In public procurement law, occasional exceptions are allowed, but the possibilities for awarding a contract without competition are severely limited and the choice must be justified.[8] For authorizations, exceptions to the obligation to award them using a competitive procedure seem extremely hard, and under the Services Directive maybe impossible, to justify.[9] For grants and asset sales, there is no general obligation in EU law for member states to allocate these using competitive procedures, and therefore, there is no

[6] See the chapter of Arrowsmith, Section 2.4.2.2.

[7] Ibid.

[8] Ibid. Reasons that warrant exception to the need to have a 'standard' procurement procedure: the authority's needs require adapting readily available solutions; the nature, the complexity or the legal and financial make-up of the contract or risks attached; technical specifications cannot be established with sufficient precision using established standards; urgency; research and development contracts for supply; purchases from a commodity market or on particular advantageous terms because of winding up or similar; purchases needed to avoid incompatibility or technical difficulties; procurement from a winner of a design contest; allowing further works, supplies or services to be added to an existing contract where a change of supplier would cause significant inconvenience.

[9] See the chapter of Van de Gronden, Section 8.4.2. Outside of the scope of the Services Directive, *Betfair* shows that the award of a gambling monopoly to a private operator without the use of a competitive procedure can be allowed, provided that its activities are subject to strict control by the public authorities (Case C-203/08, *Betfair*, para. 59).

obligation to publish the opportunity, at least not based on EU law.[10] On the other hand, if allocating authorities want to use a competitive procedure, they will have to be transparent about the opportunity to acquire the right. For asset sales, a competitive allocation procedure violating the transparency requirement could be designated as state aid.[11] The same is true for grants, and in this case, a lack of transparency could also violate national law.[12]

9.2.4 Existence of Rules Governing the Allocation Procedure (Notions of Rule-Based Governance)

The existence of rules governing the allocation procedure will help ensure that procedures are conducted according to pre-established rules. This will prevent arbitrariness and promote integrity. The mere existence of these rules will not create transparency; for that, they have to be published. It is, however, a necessary condition for transparency. In addition, rule-based allocation can prevent arbitrariness and discrimination independent of whether they are made public or not, as long as they are observed.[13] The obligation to conduct allocation procedures according to pre-established rules exists for all four rights, but some differences can be observed. In public procurement, for example, the procedural rules are largely determined at the EU level. However, particularly detailed award criteria are not always required. Sometimes, authorities will not know yet exactly what they need, and they can negotiate a preferred solution with market parties. All rules that are in place though, whether they are included in the procurement directives or were drafted by the contracting authority, must be observed. There is little room for exceptions, and the rules cannot be changed during the procurement procedure. For authorizations, the principle of transparency requires that rules about the procedure and award criteria are created, but EU law gives little guidance

[10] See the chapter of Arrowsmith, Section 2.4.2.2 and the chapter of Caranta and Biancardi, Section 5.4.2.1.

[11] See the chapter of Caranta and Biancardi, Section 5.4.2.1.

[12] See the chapter of Van den Brink, Section 4.4.3.1. Dutch national law may impose even stricter obligations on public authorities to award limited rights using a transparent competitive procedure than EU law. Indeed, the Dutch Supreme Court has recently ruled that public authorities have to create a transparent, competitive procedure when selling land as well. See HR 26 November 2021, *Didam* ECLI:NL:HR:2021:1778.

[13] A. Buijze, *The Principle of Transparency in EU Law* (Utrecht: Utrecht University, 2013), p. 131.

on their content. However, these rules must meet strict transparency criteria: all the conditions and detailed rules of the award procedure must be drawn up in a clear, precise and unequivocal manner, so that, first, all reasonably informed tenderers exercising ordinary care can understand their exact significance and interpret them in the same way.[14] There does not seem to be room for the equivalent of a negotiated procedure, which by its nature is less transparent at the start of the procedure about the award criteria that are eventually going to be applied. When allocating limited authorizations, all applicable rules must be observed, the same as when procuring goods or services. The difference between the fields is that for authorizations, public authorities must draft detailed selection and award criteria in advance, even if they have only a vague idea of what criteria would allow them to best serve the interests they want to serve.

For grants, if there is a legal basis for the grant, there should be rules about how it will be allocated. To some extent, this is also true for budget subsidies and incidental subsidies, in the sense that the general rules on administrative decision-making or budgeting are applicable. The latter sets of rules may not be as suitable to ensure equal opportunity to acquire a grant, but they do allow for accountability, and can contribute to the integrity of the decision-making process. For asset sales, if there is a competitive procedure, there must be rules on how the procedure will be conducted and what award criteria will be used. Or rather, perhaps, there are rules for what award criteria must be used: the highest price.

As Caranta and Biancardi show, EU law leaves precious little room to take any other interests into account.[15] For direct sales, there are rules on how the price should be determined, which contribute to the realization of mostly the same interests. These rules also ensure that economic operators face the same conditions on the market (level playing field), but not that they have an equal opportunity to buy the asset that is up for sale. For grants and asset sales, it is uncertain how detailed these rules need to be, although for grants, van den Brink shows that the rules provide some leeway for those situations where it is hard to establish objective award criteria. In those cases, the focus is instead on the integrity of the assessment committee. This option offers less transparency to interested parties about how the grant will be awarded, but it does

[14] Case C-49/16, *Unibet International Ltd.* v. *Nemzeti Adó- és Vámhivatal Központi Hivatala* ECLI:EU:C:2017:491, para. 46.

[15] See the chapter of Caranta and Biancardi, Section 5.5.

allow the creation of grant schemes to promote public interests that are hard to capture in detailed and unambiguous award criteria.

9.2.5 Transparency about the Rules Governing the Allocation Procedure

If there is an obligation to draft rules governing the allocation procedure, these must also be made public. This is true for all four rights discussed in this book, with no room for exceptions.

9.2.6 Transparency about Selection and Allocation Decisions

There is usually some level of transparency about all government decisions, in the sense that they must at least be made known to their addressees. For allocation decisions at the end of a competitive procedure, there are additional obligations in place though. The decision to award a contract, authorization or grant after a competitive procedure should be notified to all parties who were involved in the procedure. Contracting authorities are obliged to draft an individual report for every contract they award, detailing the reasons for all decisions taken during the award procedure, including the decision to use a non-standard procedure, which they must send to the Commission upon its request.[16] In the case of asset sales, in many cases, the decision to sell an asset must also be notified to the Commission. If it was not awarded by means of a competitive procedure, the obligation to notify the Commission is even more common.[17] For grants, we see that incidental subsidies are only made public to their recipient. Budget subsidies are in the budget, which allows democratic control.[18]

9.3 What Is Transparency?

The inventory of transparency obligations in the previous section shows that transparency is a broad concept. Transparency requirements vary widely, from the obligation to publish the opportunity to acquire a limited right, to the prohibition to change contract terms after the award

[16] Article 84 of Directive 2014/24/EU on public procurement and repealing Directive 2004/18/EC, OJ 2014, No. L 94/65.

[17] See the chapter of Caranta and Biancardi, Section 5.4.2.1.

[18] See the chapter of Van den Brink, Section 4.4.2.3.

of a contract.[19] Nevertheless, there is a common core that unites these obligations: transparency is always concerned with the availability of, access to and quality of information.[20] Transparency, in the context of the allocation of limited rights, requires public authorities to ensure information related to the allocation of limited rights is available, accessible and of sufficient quality. However, this leaves some questions unanswered, and the definition is insufficient to determine what concrete obligations public authorities should observe. To whom should they be transparent, what information should be made available, at what moment in time, and are exceptions to the obligation to be transparent allowed? Should the information they make public be of a certain quality? The answer to these questions is determined by the underlying interests, both public and private, the realization of which transparency promotes.[21]

We see that the target of the transparency obligations discussed in the previous section varies. Often, transparency is aimed at economic operators who may participate in the allocation procedure, but there are also transparency obligations targeting the Commission, when there is a suspicion of state aid, or the general public, in the case of budget subsidies. The obligations also differ with regard to what information should be made public, for example, the opportunity to acquire a limited right, the award criteria, the rules governing the procedure, the way in which public interests have been balanced against the interests of service providers. The same is true for the quality of the information that has to be provided, in particular where the level of detail provided on the award criteria is concerned. The moment at which transparency should be provided also varies. Ex-ante transparency is needed for competitive procedures, but ex-post transparency will usually be sufficient for non-competitive allocation. The reasons for the transparency obligations also vary, although one obligation can and often does serve multiple purposes. We have also seen that exceptions to transparency obligations are sometimes allowed. The acceptability of such exceptions varies.

9.3.1 *Types of Transparency*

To understand the plethora of transparency obligations, it is useful to distinguish different types of transparency depending on the way in

[19] Case C-495/99 *Commission* v. *CAS Succhi di Frutta SpA* ECLI:EU:C:2004:236.
[20] Buijze, *The Principle of Transparency in EU Law*, p. 30.
[21] Ibid., p. 35.

which they contribute to the realization of the various policy interests discussed in this book. I devised such a typology elsewhere.[22] The typology is based on two observations: first, transparency contributes to the realization of public interests in two distinct ways, or, in other words, it has two different functions for the recipients of information.[23] It allows its beneficiaries to make well-informed decisions regarding their own actions, and it allows them to observe the behaviour of public authorities, which is a necessary condition for holding them accountable. Second, within EU law, transparency contributes to three major overarching interests: the proper functioning of democracy, the proper functioning of the internal European market and the realization of fundamental rights.[24] This results in six types of transparency obligations. For each of these types, it is possible to answer the questions identified above: Why should public authorities be transparent? To whom, about what and when should they observe quality standards? What sort of exceptions can be justified? And are there alternative means that can help realize the same interests in those cases where transparency is not desirable?

In the context of the allocation of limited rights, this typology is useful in several ways. First, it shows that transparency can assist its beneficiaries in two distinct ways. Transparency either can assist them in decision-making or allows them to monitor the actions of public authorities. The first function of transparency is intimately connected to competitive allocation procedures: the publication of opportunities, rules about procedures and award criteria allows economic operators to decide whether to pursue such opportunities. For this to work, transparency must be provided ex-ante: interested parties must have access to the information before they make their decisions in order to profit from that access.[25] The second function of transparency, to allow for monitoring and control, is straightforward: by being transparent about the criteria upon which the award of a limited right is based, interested parties can control whether the authority awarding the right has, in fact, applied these criteria.[26] This contributes to accountability and integrity and helps to ensure that outcome-related interests such as value for

[22] Ibid., p. 35.
[23] Ibid., p. 54.
[24] Ibid., p. 76.
[25] Ibid., p 54.
[26] Ibid., p. 56.

money are realized, provided that the selection and award criteria were properly designed to contribute to those interests. For this second function of transparency, ex-post transparency is sufficient. In addition, transparency is not necessarily targeted at the economic operators involved in the allocation procedure. Other parties may be equally well-positioned to exercise control.

Second, the typology can help to understand the concrete transparency obligations that public authorities should observe vis-à-vis economic operators when allocating limited rights, namely, the obligations that are required to ensure the proper functioning of the internal European market, as shown in the following paragraph.

9.3.2 *Helping Economic Operators to Optimize Their Decisions*[27]

Transparency allows economic actors to make informed decisions about the utilization of their resources. Transparency is required to the extent it contributes to efficiency or, alternatively, to economic operators realizing their rights. Transparency targets all economic actors equally. The scope of the obligation extends to information that is relevant to economic operators to assess the consequences of their actions. Information should be made public in time to allow them to incorporate the information in their decision-making process. Information should be made public on the initiative of the authority, since economic actors will not know to look for the information unless it is made public and because this is the only way to ensure equality between economic operators. The information provided should be of sufficient quality to allow them to know what their legal rights and obligations are. Exceptions to transparency are allowed to protect other interests, for example the right to privacy of others and efficiency (transparency may hamper efficiency: costs of additional transparency outweigh its benefits). In addition, other public interests may justify exceptions, such as national security in the case of procurement of military equipment. How easy it is to justify these exceptions will depend on both the value attached to the functioning of the internal market and the value attached to the rights of the economic operators who are potentially involved in the procedures.

27 This section and the following are based on Buijze, *The Principle of Transparency in EU Law*, in particular appendix I.

9.3.3 Helping Economic Operators Monitor the Behaviour of Public Authorities

In addition, transparency allows economic operators to see whether public authorities are complying with the rules. The scope of this obligation would be to be transparent about information that relates to actions of public authorities that affect the economic operator, that is, all allocation-related information. The information should be made public either in time to allow economic actors to try to affect the outcome of the procedure (but this is not always required), or ex-post, to make judicial review possible. Information should be made public at the initiative of the public authority, since they know what information economic operators need to review whether the rules are being complied with. The quality of the information should be such that economic operators can understand the reasons for a decision and challenge them. Exceptions can be justified to protect the interests of others (privacy), efficiency (the cost of additional transparency outweighs the benefits) or the public interest.

Alternatives to transparency towards economic operators are available. Courts, administrative supervisors and special advocates can act as fiduciaries who safeguard the rights of economic operators in case there are reasons to not make information available to them. Opting for passive transparency, where economic operators request information if they are interested in it, can be an alternative to active transparency but only if there are reasons to limit active transparency.

Again, making exceptions to transparency obligations when transparency aims to contribute to the smooth functioning of the internal market, but is actually inefficient, should be easy. However, as Arrowsmith points out, if one attaches intrinsic value to transparency, fair treatment and the rights of economic operators to have access to allocating procedures, there are reasons to adopt a level of transparency that is less than efficient.[28]

9.4 Transparency's Contribution to Achieving Public Interests

So how do these different types of transparency obligations contribute to achieving public interests? Wolswinkel et al. follow Arrowsmith in distinguishing three types of public interests in their introduction to this

[28] See the chapter of Arrowsmith, Section 2.3.

volume: inherent need, outcome-related interests such as value for money, additional policy goals, the opening of markets, safeguarding fundamental rights and integrity, and process-related interests such as equal treatment, fair treatment, accountability, efficiency and transparency.

The process-related interests identified in this volume usually contribute to the outcome-related interests, but not always. Equal treatment usually promotes value for money, but not always. Transparency usually contributes to the process-related interests and therefore, indirectly, to the outcome-related interests. Transparency usually contributes to efficiency, but not always. To further complicate the picture, various types of transparency contribute to different public interests.

In the following, I will first explore whether the classification of transparency as a public interest makes sense. The subsequent paragraphs discuss transparency's contribution to the realization of the other process-related interest, to inherent need and to the outcome-related interests.

9.4.1 *Transparency as a Public Interest?*

There is no consensus about whether transparency has intrinsic value. In this volume, Arrowsmith and Caranta and Biancardi take the view that it is merely a means to an end, whereas Wolswinkel et al. and Wollenschläger argue it (also) has intrinsic value. The distinction is important: as Arrowsmith points out, if transparency has intrinsic value, that provides an argument to demand it even if it has no net benefit: 'As a *separate* objective, it may justify costs – for example, financial costs of publishing information – that go beyond what is warranted by their contribution to other specific objectives such as financial savings or an actual reduction in corruption.'[29]

Wolswinkel et al. argue that transparency could be understood as a public interest relating to 'client satisfaction', where the clients involved are the competing economic operators who are directly involved in the allocation process.[30] Wollenschläger points out that transparency is an aspect of good administration, and as such, European law considers it a human right.[31] In a similar vein, the equal treatment of economic operators is considered a fundamental right, and therefore, so is transparency to the extent that it is required to ensure that equal treatment.

[29] Ibid.

[30] See the chapter of Wolswinkel, Jansen and Van Ommeren, Section 1.3.2.

[31] See the chapter of Wollenschläger, Section 3.4.2.2.

I would argue, however, that this does not make transparency an intrinsic public interest, but rather that it is instrumental in promoting the private interests and, indeed, the fundamental European rights of market operators. Upholding these rights may well be a public interest, but it does not make transparency an intrinsic value. Designating it as such creates two problems: first, it will lead to too much transparency where transparency does not, in fact, contribute to the interests of these private parties, or where transparency is harmful to other interests and there are alternatives to protect the interests of these private parties. Second, it blurs the image when transparency is harmful to the rights of other private parties. When transparency is given intrinsic value as a public interest, the rights of these third parties are then balanced against an abstract public interest, rather than against the rights of other private parties.

9.4.2 Process-Related Interests

Transparency facilitates accountability and fair and equal treatment, and contributes to efficiency. Accountability in turn contributes to the realization of the output-related interests discussed below, but also to fair and equal treatment as well as, potentially, efficiency. Efficiency is relevant for the realization of all other public interests: promoting or protecting these interests has a cost. The lower that cost is, the more resources are left to promote and protect other interests.[32]

It is important that public authorities can be held accountable for their allocation decisions. Accountability has no agreed-upon definition. For this contribution, I will use the definition provided by Bovens. He defines accountability as a relationship between an actor and a forum, in which the actor has an obligation to explain and to justify their conduct, the forum can pose questions and pass judgment, and the actor may face consequences.[33] The forum can vary. It can be a court, civil society, a different administrative authority or even the general public.[34] In the context of this contribution, administrative accountability, legal accountability and democratic accountability are the most relevant. When the

[32] A. Buijze, *On the Justification and Necessity of Legal Effectiveness Norms* (Utrecht: Utrecht University, 2008).

[33] M. Bovens, 'Analysing and Assessing Accountability: A Conceptual Framework 1', *European Law Journal* 13(4) (2007), 447–468, 449.

[34] Bovens, 'Analysing and Assessing Accountability: A Conceptual Framework 1', 447–468, 449.

Commission acts as an accountability forum vis-à-vis the member states, that constitutes administrative accountability. Where the legislator needs to draft rules regarding the allocation of limited rights, there is democratic accountability. Where allocation decisions are challenged before the courts, there is legal accountability. To facilitate accountability, the actor has to be transparent towards the forum. However, for legal accountability it is necessary that a third party brings the case before the court. Therefore, transparency must also be observed towards interested parties.

Transparency contributes to accountability, because without it, the accountability forum cannot pass judgment on the actions of the actor. The target of the concrete transparency obligations required for that will differ though, depending on the accountability forum. This means that transparency does not necessarily have to target the economic operators involved in the allocation procedure. In state aid, for instance, member states are required to be transparent vis-à-vis the Commission, which will review their compliance with the state aid rules. Different accountability fora will emphasize the importance of compliance with different norms. While the Commission will impose consequences if member states interfere with the functioning of the internal market, private parties will go to court if their individual rights are harmed by the actor's actions.

In addition, ex-post transparency is sufficient to facilitate accountability. An accountability forum can only pass judgment on the behaviour of an actor after the fact. This means that many of the transparency obligations that are characteristic of the allocation of limited rights are not needed to ensure accountability. There is no need to publish the availability of a limited right to ensure public authorities are held accountable for their allocating decisions, nor is it necessary to be upfront about the award criteria towards the economic operators involved in the procedure, as long as a proper accountability forum can review afterwards that nothing untoward has been going on. General administrative law principles, like the duty to give reasons and the principle of due care, will be sufficient for that.

9.4.2.1 Transparency's Contribution to Efficiency

Efficiency is understood here as obtaining an objective at minimum cost. Although some of the authors in this volume juxtapose efficiency and transparency, they can go hand in hand.[35] Transparent allocation

[35] See the chapter of Wollenschläger, Section 3.3.3.5 and the chapter of Van den Brink, Section 4.4.3.1.

procedures will often lower costs. Economic operators who are potentially interested in acquiring a right can make an informed estimate of whether they have a chance to actually win the procedure, and therefore of whether it is worth their while to submit a proposal. Economic operators who conclude that they have little chance of winning the right can refrain from submitting a proposal, saving them money and time.[36] On the other hand, a competitive procedure requires an investment from all parties who want to participate in the allocating procedure, including the allocating authority. The more complex the procedure, the greater this investment. The gains from transparent allocation procedures must therefore be balanced against the costs they involve.[37]

9.4.2.2 Transparency's Contribution to Equal Treatment's Contribution to Efficiency

In the context of the allocation of limited rights, transparency is intimately connected with equal treatment. Indeed, without transparency, equal treatment in a competitive procedure is impossible. To ensure equal treatment, the opportunity to acquire a limited right must be made public to all potentially interested parties. The rules of the procedure and the award criteria must be made known and must be phrased in such a manner that all interested parties will understand them in the same way.

It is important to understand, however, that although equal treatment without transparency is difficult to imagine, transparency without equal treatment is quite possible.[38] Imagine a procedure where the allocating authority makes it known that only national undertakings can acquire a right. This is a clear violation of the principle of equal treatment. Transparency, however, does still have advantages in such a situation. It will still facilitate the accountability of the allocating authority: having the rule out there in public will allow an accountability forum to judge whether the rule was complied with. Transparency still contributes to efficiency: it is clear that foreign undertakings need not apply, which saves them time and money.

[36] See the chapter of Arrowsmith, Section 2.3.

[37] See also the chapter of Arrowsmith, Section 2.3.10 and the chapter of Van den Brink, Section 4.3.

[38] Buijze, *The Principle of Transparency in EU Law*, pp. 149–150.

9.4.2.3 Transparency's Contribution to Fair Treatment

The right to fair treatment is comprised of several elements, some of which require transparency. The right to be heard before an adverse decision is taken, for instance, requires transparency about the fact that such a decision is about to be taken as well as the grounds for that decision. Indeed, the availability of information about the allocation procedure to economic operators involved in the procedure might be said to be necessary for fair treatment as well. As a process-related interest that helps boost the quality of administrative decisions, fair treatment helps ensure that both the rights of parties involved in the allocating procedure and the interests of the allocating authority are realized, but it might also have intrinsic value.

9.4.3 Inherent Need

A minimum level of transparency is required to satisfy the inherent need of any allocation procedure. At the very minimum, the party that is awarded a limited right through a unilateral decision should be made aware of this. When there is a bilateral decision, public authorities should also be transparent ex-ante to establish whether there are parties that are interested in acquiring the right. A baseline level of transparency is needed to satisfy the inherent need of allocation procedures. In practice, the level of transparency required when allocating limited rights far surpasses this baseline.

On the other hand, transparency requirements can make it more difficult to satisfy the inherent need of an allocation procedure. Caranta and Biancardi discuss an example of this, where a competitive procedure resulted in there being no binding offers.[39] Public procurement offers rules for the same eventuality: where a tender results in no offers, the procuring authority is then justified to use the less transparent negotiated procedure without prior notification.[40]

Transparency's adverse effect on the realization of the inherent need is closely related to the efficiency of the procedure, which may be harmed by too much transparency. An overly detailed procedure for allocating grants, for example, may scare away potential applicants who are

[39] Case T-242/12 *SNCF Mobilités* v. *Commission* ECLI:EU:T:2015:1003, as discussed in Chapter 5.

[40] See the chapter of Arrowsmith, Section 2.4.2.2.

deterred by the sheer amount of paperwork involved. But even a fairly simple competitive procedure may deter applicants, if the chances of them acquiring the right are slim and out of their control, as may be the case for a lottery.

9.4.4 Output-Related Interests

9.4.4.1 Value for Money and Additional Policies

Although value for money and the realization of horizontal policies can be separated, the manner in which transparency contributes to their realization is similar. Therefore, they are discussed together. Based on the contributions by Arrowsmith, Wollenschläger, Van den Brink, and Caranta and Biancardi, we can make four observations.

First, value for money and additional policy goals can be realized through a competitive procedure where the submitted tenders are compared on their merits. Transparency is necessary for such procedures to work. Second, the meaning of value for money is not always clear beforehand, and it can be hard to determine how to translate horizontal policy goals in concrete rules and award criteria. Third, value for money may also be realized through other, less transparent allocation procedures. Finally, EU law does not necessarily promote value for money, but it does allow member states to promote this value. Although value for money can be a consequence of following EU-prescribed allocation procedures, it is not the aim. The first two of these observations must be elaborated upon.

To facilitate a competitive procedure, allocating authorities must be transparent about the opportunity to acquire a right, the rules governing the procedure, the award criteria and the allocation decision. In addition, rule-based allocation is required. Essential for competitive allocation then is the need for ex-ante transparency aimed at economic operators who may want to be involved in the allocation procedure. Ex-ante transparency allows economic operators to identify opportunities and to assess whether it is worth their while to submit a proposal. It allows public authorities to identify the best candidate, although again, all too elaborate procedures might scare potentially suitable candidates away due to their inefficiency.

To maximize value for money and the realization of horizontal policy goals through a competitive procedure, the allocating authority must have a (very) clear idea of what it wants. It must make public beforehand on what criteria it will base its allocation decision and even how these criteria will be weighed. However, it may be difficult to establish this beforehand. For grants, one might say that a granting authority gets value for money if its subsidy makes the greatest contribution possible to whatever public interest it is trying to achieve. Van den Brink more or less equates value for money with the requirement of sound financial management, where the subsidy is only spent on projects that actually contribute to the public interest, which is best achieved through a beauty contest. She also points out that it is in fact difficult to determine which projects do this.[41] Take the example of research grants. Even if an agreement was reached on the purpose of such a grant – for instance, subsidizing research that will further the energy transition – it is impossible to predict in advance which research projects will actually achieve this goal. Perhaps then, it is no surprise that EU law does not contain a blanket obligation to award all grants by means of a competitive procedure.

For authorizations, the issue of value for money seems even more complicated. Wollenschläger proposes that value for money could mean the lowest cost for the customers of the recipient of the available authorizations, or the best value for money for the consumer, in the sense that contractual conditions for service consumers are also taken into account.[42] If we accept his proposal, that raises the question of how the allocating authority would determine value for money for consumers. Would they award a gambling license to the operator who provides the best mix of odds that the customer wins, thrill, and safeguards against gambling addictions? How would they even know the preference of the end consumer? How could they possibly design award criteria that guarantee the winner of the allocation procedure best meets these preferences?

In short, the meaning of value for money is not always clear beforehand. The same is true for what award criteria would best contribute to the realization of horizontal policy goals. If this is the case, transparency has little added value for realizing this interest. Public procurement has procedures available for when procuring authorities face similar problems, such as when they want an innovative solution for a problem that is not yet on the market. Public procurement law provides conditions under which they can cooperate on a solution together with market

[41] See the chapter of Van den Brink, Section 4.3.
[42] See the chapter of Wollenschläger, Section 3.3.2.2.

parties.[43] A similar procedure seems to be lacking for grants and authorizations, although in the case of grants, public authorities could take this approach for budget subsidies and incidental subsidies, even in the absence of rules requiring them to do so.

Note, then, that value for money can be promoted by other means as well. Arrowsmith mentions the relational approach that is common in private procurement, which achieves the same goals as competitive allocation in public procurement.[44] The budget subsidies Van den Brink discusses in her contribution may well rely on the same mechanism to function.

Alternatively, public authorities may use 'neutral' allocation procedures, like lotteries, that do not promote value for money or horizontal policies. However, as discussed in further detail in Section 9.5.1, these procedures are not as neutral as they may seem, and alternative modes of allocation may be more advantageous overall.

9.4.4.2 Opening of Markets

The opening of the European market is an important interest at the EU level. It is, in fact, the primary goal of the public procurement directives.[45] Having such a European-wide market, where economic operators from all member states compete on an equal footing for public contracts, will guarantee the best prices for procuring authorities and will increase overall welfare in the EU.[46] The competitive allocation of rights will contribute to opening the markets: it will ensure that rights are awarded to the most suitable candidate, no matter its nationality, rather than one that the allocating authority is already familiar with. Achieving this interest again requires ex-ante transparency, as economic operators all over the EU must be made aware of the opportunity as well as the rules governing the procedure.

A slightly more broad conception of this interest is the overall functioning of the internal European market. This does not only require that

[43] See the chapter of Arrowsmith, Section 2.4.2.2.

[44] See the chapter of Arrowsmith, Section 2.4.1.1.

[45] C. Jansen, 'Allocation of Limited Rights from a European Public Procurement Law Perspective', in P. Adriaanse, F. J. van Ommeren, W. den Ouden and C. J. Wolswinkel (eds.), *Scarcity and the State: The Allocation of Limited Rights by the Administration* (Cambridge: Intersentia, 2016), pp. 239–275.

[46] D. Robert Cooter and T. Ulen, *Law and Economics*, 6th ed. (Boston: Addision-Wesley, 2012), p. 38. See also Caranta and Biancardi in Section 5.3.1 of their chapter, and their reference to the work of Stiglitz.

member states refrain from discriminating against non-nationals, it also requires them to interfere with the market as little as possible. This is reflected most prominently in the prohibition of state aid, which, by its definition, gives an advantage to one or more economic operators that is not available to others.

Once again, although opening up markets is generally beneficial, there is a cost involved. Publishing opportunities to sell two pencils and a bouquet of flowers in the Official Journal is a bit much. For rights that have limited transboundary importance, EU law therefore does not require as involved a procedure, and allocating authorities can suffice with a lower level of transparency. This is true for public procurement, where contracts under a certain threshold are exempted from the scope of the directives, and to some extent also for sales and grants, which can be granted under the *de minimis* exception without risk of being classified as forbidden state aid. For allocating limited authorizations, the picture looks a bit different. The Services Directive has no equivalent exception and is applicable even in purely internal situations.[47] This discrepancy cannot be explained, I feel, by the characteristics of the services market, but rather by a different valuation of the rights of economic operators.

9.4.4.3 Safeguarding Fundamental Rights

Transparency can contribute to realizing fundamental rights in much the same manner that it contributes to realizing the interests of economic operators. It can either ensure that people have information available that they need to realize their fundamental rights for themselves, or it can help them assess whether a decision affecting their rights was taken on the right grounds and whether they want to challenge it in a court. On the other hand, transparency can result in the violation of fundamental rights, in particular the right to privacy.[48]

When allocating limited rights, fundamental rights can play a role in different ways. First, there is the emerging right to good administration, which includes a right to (some types of) transparency. Second, transparency

[47] Joined Cases C-360/15 and C-31/16, *Visser Vastgoed* ECLI:EU:C:2018:44.

[48] See, for example, E. Julie Cohen, 'Privacy, Visibility, Transparency, and Exposure', *The University of Chicago Law Review* 75(1) (2008), 181–201; A. Rouvroy and Y. Poullet, 'The Right to Informational Self-Determination and the Value of Self-Development: Reassessing the Importance of Privacy for Democracy', in S. Gutwirth, Y. Poullet, P. Hert, C. Terwangne and S. Nouwt (eds.), *Reinventing Data Protection?* (Dordrecht Springer, 2009), pp. 45–76.

is necessary for the realization of the right to equal treatment and the freedom to provide services. Third, fundamental rights can play a role as horizontal policy goals.[49] Finally, transparency and competitive allocation may have adverse consequences for the fundamental rights of third parties.

Transparency is an aspect of the right to good administration.[50] As such, it gains additional weight, and it becomes harder to justify exceptions to transparency obligations based on the argument they do not support the public interest or are not needed for the realization of policy goals.[51] The same is true for the right to equal treatment. Ex-ante transparency is necessary to ensure that all economic operators have an equal opportunity to acquire a right. This requires transparency about the opportunity to acquire a right. In addition, all interested operators who meet the minimum requirements must be allowed to participate in the allocation procedure. This is true even though competitive procedures are not always needed to promote value for money or horizontal policy goals. A transparent, competitive procedure becomes compulsory purely to satisfy the principle of equal treatment. Any type of competitive procedure will do though; a beauty contest is not necessary. Lotteries are equally acceptable, as is first come, first served. These procedures are not well suited to optimize other interests, like value for money or horizontal policy goals,[52] but as Arrowsmith pointed out, those were not goals of EU law to begin with.

We can now see that the rather curious transparency obligations related to the allocation of limited authorizations under the Services Directive can be explained by the emphasis the latter puts on the rights of service providers. They benefit from competitive procedures, in the sense that they get an equal opportunity to acquire a right, even when these procedures are not designed to optimize public interests.

Nevertheless, transparency, or rather, competitive allocation, can have adverse consequences for the rights of others, or even the rights of

[49] See Section 9.4.4.1.

[50] See the remark in the chapter of Wollenschläger, Section 3.4.2.2, on the foundation of the principle of transparency.

[51] See also the chapter of Arrowsmith, Section 2.3.10.

[52] A. Jimenez and Fernandez-Bermejo, 'The Allocation of Limited Public Rights: An Analytical and Constitutional Approach', in P. C. Adriaanse, F. van Ommeren, W. den Ouden and J. Wolswinkel (eds.), *Scarcity and the State: The Allocation of Limited Rights by the Administration. Ius Commune: European and Comparative Law Series* (Cambridge: Intersentia, 2016), pp. 27–54, 45.

economic operators themselves. Wollenschläger provides an example of this when he discusses the allocation of fishing rights.[53] In that case, the Court of Justice allowed an exception to the rule that all economic operators should have equal opportunity to acquire these rights. Note that the Services Directive does not always leave room for such exceptions, even though small-business holders might indeed be equally as dependent on their license to provide services.[54] Indeed, it may not always be in the best interest of the rights holders themselves to have their right to equality of opportunity emphasized over all their other interests.

In addition, third-party rights may be affected. One of the consequences of the competitive allocation of limited rights is that the rights holder will change every so often. Customers are forced to switch service providers. This might mean they can no longer go to their favourite fish stand at the market, that their subsidized music lessons will now be offered by a different organization, or that their pension provider changes. Clearly, the impact of that change varies, depending on the type of service that is provided. Van de Gronden points to the interests of consumers in the continuity of service of general economic interest (SGEI) provision, which should, perhaps, merit an exception to the rule that authorizations are allocated through a competitive procedure.[55] I agree with him wholeheartedly. In addition, it is worth pointing out that at least under the Services Directive, the protection of the right to equal treatment of economic operators comes at a cost: both the other interests of these economic operators and the interests of third parties are disregarded.

9.4.4.4 Integrity

Integrity is an important value in the allocation of limited rights, and it is traditionally closely related to transparency. The idea that transparency promotes integrity can be traced back to Bentham, who argued that public scrutiny promotes virtue in public officials and reduces the chance of dishonest behaviour.[56] Hence, transparency prevents arbitrariness, discrimination and corruption, and contributes to norm-compliance.

[53] Case C-540/16, *Spika and others* ECLI:EU:C:2018:565.

[54] Services Directive, Article 12. For artificial scarcity, there may be a possibility of making exceptions, although this room seems limited as well, Joined Cases C-458/14 and C-67-15, *Promoimpressa* ECLI:EU:C:2016:558.

[55] See the chapter of Van de Gronden, Section 8.5.

[56] See S. Baume and Y. Papadopoulos, 'Bentham Revisited: Transparency as a Magic Concept, Its Justifications and Its Skeptics', *Transatlantic Conference on Transparency Research* (2012) for an extensive treatment of Bentham's work on transparency.

Therefore, integrity also contributes to the realization of other output-related interests.

To achieve integrity, ex-post transparency will usually be sufficient. As with accountability, it is not necessary that the transparency obligations designed to promote integrity target economic operators involved in an allocation procedure, although such obligations will also contribute to integrity. The notion of rule-based governance is also important to promote integrity.

However, transparency is not the only way in which one can realize integrity. Caranta and Biancardi and Van den Brink show alternative mechanisms for preserving the integrity of allocating authorities in cases where it is difficult to be transparent about scoring award criteria (Van den Brink) or where it is difficult to assess whether a market price has been established correctly (Caranta and Biancardi).

In other words, compromising on transparency is not the same as compromising on integrity.

Moreover, rule-based allocation of limited rights may be more transparent and promote integrity, but it has downsides as well. This is illustrated by a case about the allocation of a limited authorization for a casino that recently came before the Dutch Council of State.[57] One of the award criteria used was the effort put into the prevention of nuisance. The actual measures that were to be put into place were not defined, to allow room for innovation and alternative solutions. The winner of the procedure had proposed a cashless system and was scored high on this criterion. The plaintiff argued that he had no way of knowing that to have a fair chance of winning the procedure, he needed to include a cashless system in his proposal. He argued that the award criteria were not sufficiently clear and unambiguous and thus violated EU law. Although I have argued elsewhere the plaintiff was right,[58] the plight of the municipality is real. Requiring it to draft award criteria that take all potential measures to prevent nuisance into account requires an immense investment of time and effort and can stifle innovation. Similarly, Arrowsmith points to the example of rules forbidding or limiting discussions with suppliers. Such discussions, she points out,

[57] Council of State, 20 November 2019, ECLI:NL:RVS:2019:3918.

[58] A. Buijze, 'Transparant waartoe? Over de toegevoegde waarde van transparantie voor het realiseren van publieke waarden', in A. Buijze, A. Drahmann, J. Wolswinkel, N. Bontje and E. Pietermaat (eds.), *Transparantie en openbaarheid* (The Hague: Boom juridisch, 2022), pp. 51–52.

'can be useful to ensure a specification is workable, enable products or services offered to be best adapted to the public authority's needs or prevent bid-rigging, leading to better value for money'.[59] Requiring public authorities to draft detailed rules, in particular detailed award criteria, to promote integrity can therefore lead to lesser value for money, a disproportionate investment of time and effort by public authorities, and a lack of innovative solutions being offered. That may be an acceptable sacrifice to prevent abuse of power and discriminatory practices, but it may well be possible to prevent these from occurring by using other means, such as the safeguards that are in place to prevent abuse of the negotiated procedure and the competitive dialogue in the procurement directive.

The same can be said about the obligation to exclude offers because of a mistake: although this may prevent abuse of power and discrimination, it may also lead to less value for money if otherwise appealing offers are excluded because of a simple mistake.[60] Deviating from the rule could lead to a better outcome.

9.5 Discussion

What can we learn from the analysis provided in the previous paragraphs? First, transparency obligations are common when allocating limited rights. The transparent allocation of limited rights contributes to accountability, efficiency and fair and equal treatment. When used in a competitive procedure where offers are compared against each other, transparency contributes to value for money and the realization of horizontal policies. It is essential to the opening of markets, as well as the realization of the fundamental right to equal treatment of economic operators. Finally, it contributes to integrity. On the other hand, too much or the wrong kind of transparency can be detrimental to achieving value for money, horizontal policies and the rights of third parties as well as those of economic operators involved in the allocation procedure. Where this is the case, alternatives to transparency that also contribute to accountability and integrity may be desirable. The legal framework often recognizes this. There are a number of issues that warrant further discussion: first, the alignment of different interests, in particular the alignment of public and private interests; and, second, the apparent differences in the value attached to the public interests distinguished in

[59] See the chapter of Arrowsmith, Section 2.3.10.
[60] See the chapter of Arrowsmith, Section 2.4.2.2.

this volume, depending on the legal regime that is applicable to the allocation of a specific right.

9.5.1 *On the Alignment of Public and Private Interests*

Transparent, competitive allocation procedures contribute to the realization of many different public and private interests. However, occasionally these interests conflict. Perhaps this is not surprising, but as Wolswinkel et al. point out in their introduction to this volume:

> [. . .] the dominating idea is that a competitive procedure between interested parties will enable governments to put 'their' rights in the hands of those who value them most while at the same time enabling them to realize other public interests than value for money.[61]

Unfortunately, this is not always possible. Arrowsmith has concluded as much in the context of public procurement: transparent, rule-based allocation procedures that promote the opening of the market, equal treatment and integrity can sometimes make it more difficult to achieve value for money and horizontal policies. This is not necessarily a bad thing; one might conclude that when these interests conflict, they must be balanced against one another, and naturally, one or the other must prevail.

However, the phrasing by Wolswinkel et al. reveals a complexity that remains obscured when we frame this as a balancing of public interests: the idea that transparent, competitive allocation procedures result in rights being allocated to those parties who value them the most. This point is perhaps best illustrated with the example of an auction: whoever is willing to pay the most for a limited right gets it. In public procurement, the idea is that the economic operator who is willing to accept a contract at the lowest price is also the economic operator who values that contract the most. The allocating procedure gives this economic operator the opportunity to show the allocating authority just how much he values acquiring the right. Thus, transparent, competitive allocation procedures not only achieve public interests, they are also fair towards the private parties that want to acquire a limited right. Whoever is best able to meet the demand of the allocating authority wins the right, whether that authority is looking for the cheapest chair or for the most socially responsible community centre operator.

[61] See the chapter of Wolswinkel, Jansen and Van Ommeren, Section 1.1.3.

However, the above examples show that perhaps the easiest way to determine which economic operator values a right the most is to assess their willingness to pay. But the fact that an economic operator values a right the most does not mean he needs it or deserves it the most, nor, in fact, does it mean that he will create the greatest societal value when the right is allocated to him. The first point is, of course, a well-known criticism from economic theory on how difficult it is to assess how much someone values something.[62] While I have recently spent a couple of hundred euros on a new cell phone, that does not merit the conclusion that I value that phone more than someone with less disposable income who currently does not own a phone would value it. Thus, auctions and other allocating methods that depend on assessing willingness to pay do not necessarily result in rights being allocated to those parties who value them the most. And indeed, all competitive allocation procedures rely on this to some extent: entering the allocation procedure carries a cost. Time has to be spent to identify opportunities when they are published, to read and understand the rules governing the procedure and the award criteria, and to draft a proposal. This investment may or may not pay off: the risk that the right is awarded to someone else is very real. Parties who are unable to make this investment may value a right, but it will not be awarded to them. This will result, for example, in licences to provide services being allocated to those parties who can make the investment required to participate in the procedure and who are able to carry the risk of not receiving a particular licence. In the Netherlands, this has already resulted in small enterprises opting not to participate in lotteries, because they cannot carry the risk of not receiving the authorization.[63] Indeed, competitive allocation may well structurally benefit larger undertakings, who can spread the risk of not receiving a particular right, and are better able to carry the investment costs.[64] This is especially true for procedures that respect the right to equal treatment, but do not take other public

[62] See, e.g., A. Sen, 'The Discipline of Cost-Benefit Analysis', *Journal of Legal Studies* 29 (2000), 931–951, 945–946; C. Sunstein, 'Cognition and Cost-Benefit Analysis', *Journal of Legal Studies* 29 (2000), 1059–1103, 1088.

[63] Omroep Gelderland, 'Viskraam voor het laatst op markt in Kerkdriel: doodsteek voor ondernemers', 2019, available at www.gld.nl/nieuws/2426542/Viskraam-voor-het-laatst-op-markt-in-Kerkdriel-Doodsteek-voor-ondernemers.

[64] The problem is well-known in public procurement, and there exist some mechanisms to address it. See, e.g., European Commission, Directorate General for Internal Market, Industry, Entrepreneurship and SMEs, *SME Needs Analysis in Public Procurement: Final Report* (Luxembourg: Publications Office, 2021).

interests into account, with lotteries being the clearest example. This is not necessarily a bad thing. There may be advantages to such an allocation system. However, it is important to realize that allocating rights to private parties who value them the most is not the same as allocating rights to parties that deserve or need them the most, nor with allocating them to the parties that we feel 'should' receive them.

The second issue is that the fact that an economic operator values a right the most does not mean he will create the greatest societal value when the right is allocated to him. As an example, let us take a look at the auction of radio frequencies. The highest bid for these frequencies will come from the party that thinks it can make the most money from advertising. This earning potential might be there because the winner broadcasts a programme that many people enjoy listening to, but it might also be because it targets people with high expendable incomes. Ensuring that radio frequencies are allocated to broadcasters who target the well-off probably does not constitute a public interest. Of course, public authorities can ameliorate this problem. They are not limited to awarding rights based on willingness to pay, except perhaps for asset sales, but can use selection and award criteria to assess the quality of tenders and applications for licenses and grants they receive. For example, when auctioning radio frequencies public authorities can place conditions on the actual programming. They can reserve lots for classical music, jazz or folk. They can prioritize grants to organizations that employ vulnerable groups, or award licenses to companies that have strict public health measures in place. However, every interest that is taken into account in the allocation procedure requires work on behalf of the allocating authority that has to translate this interest in selection and award criteria. Moreover, what this does is change the characteristics of the right parties compete for. They are no longer vying for a right to supply coffee to the government, but for the right to supply coffee in a manner that does not harm people or the planet. The weakness of using willingness to pay as a selection criterion does not disappear.

That an economic operator values a right the most does not mean he needs it or deserves it the most, nor, in fact, that he will create the greatest societal value when the right is allocated to him. In addition, it means that the interest in acquiring a limited right of private actors who 'value' a right the most does not necessarily coincide with the public interest, other than the opening of markets. Rather, these interests need to be balanced against one another.

To conclude: ensuring that rights are allocated to the private parties who value them the most does not necessarily contribute to the realization of public interests. This is especially true when allocating limited authorizations. In public procurement and asset sales, finding the candidate who values a right the most, where 'value' is understood as having a high willingness to pay, does in fact contribute to the public interest in at least one very direct manner: lower prices or higher income for the state.

9.5.2 *Striking the Balance: On Optimizing Public Interests*

The transparency obligations that apply to the allocation of different types of limited rights reflect the fact that the legal regimes governing that process attach different values to different public interests. The obligations in asset sales are primarily determined by the need to prevent member states from distorting the market. For public procurement, it is the need to open up the market. For authorizations, it is the right of economic operators to have an equal opportunity to acquire a right. For grants, sound financial management is key, which is essentially a combination of value for money and efficiency. This results in stark differences in transparency obligations.

In addition, the regimes differ in the extent to which they allow public authorities room to balance various interests against one another. The procurement directives prescribe detailed procedures for the allocation of government contracts. These rules determine the margin of discretion that procuring authorities have available to balance public interests. Where transparency threatens the efficiency of the procedure, or the ability of member states to achieve value for money, exceptions to the principle of transparency can be justified.

When selling assets, public authorities are severely limited in what interests they can take into account. Transparency obligations are tailored to ensure the state aid rules are complied with, and exceptions to these rules cannot be justified. The one exception is the possibility of opting for direct sales. But although EU law shows a preference for competitive allocation, it provides little guidance for when direct sales are acceptable and when instead competitive allocation is required. Caranta and Biancardi suggest direct sales may be more appropriate for achieving certain interests, whereas tenders favour different interests, in particular transparency, equal treatment and accountability. That means member states are still, to some extent, free to determine what public interests they give precedence to.

For grants, authorities have a large margin of discretion when balancing the various interests involved in allocating them. That raises questions though, about how to strike that balance when the right to equal treatment of potential recipients conflicts with other interests. Are incidental and budget subsidies allowed at all? Van den Brink is quite critical in her answer to that question, arguing that most public interests, except perhaps efficiency, are harmed by the practice. I do not share her pessimism. In particular for budget subsidies, democratic debate should guarantee such subsidies actually promote the public interest, not unlike the legal basis required for grants that are awarded through competitive allocation schemes. Even the fact that these subsidies are in practice more or less granted for an unlimited period of time may be justifiable, if the interest in continuity of service provision of the people who profit from the activities organized with the grant carries much weight.[65] For incidental subsidies, one might argue these should be reserved for special opportunities, not unlike the exception in public procurement law for execution sales. Moreover, the type of transparency associated with competitive allocation procedures, ex-ante transparency towards economic operators, is not needed to achieve accountability and integrity, or compliance with norms protecting the public interest. The problem seems to be not so much that incidental subsidies and budget subsidies exist – allocating limited rights without a competitive procedure can sometimes serve the public interests – but rather that their use is largely unregulated.

For limited authorizations, although the emphasis on the rights of economic operators is very strong, other public interests are always at play. The decision to make only a limited number of licences available is an infringement of the freedom to provide services and therefore needs to be justified. Transparency ensures that it is possible to establish whether the number of authorizations available does in fact serve the public interest and therefore safeguards the freedom to provide services, which is the main purpose of the Services Directive. Thus, allowing the creation of scarcity under the Services Directive is already an example of balancing interests: if the freedom of economic operators were to prevail, limiting the number of licenses available would not be an option. The very fact that scarcity exists implies a balancing of interests.

[65] Compare the argument to Chapter 8 of Van de Gronden about the importance of service continuity in the provision of SGEIs.

Although the allocation of limited authorizations theoretically allows for the public interest in terms of value for money and horizontal policy goals to be taken into account when designing the allocation procedure and determining award criteria (in fact, the very fact that a limited authorization scheme is allowed to exist is a reflection of the fact these interests are relevant), the manner in which this can be done is unclear. Public procurement law provides public authorities with procedures that balance member states' interests in realizing value for money and horizontal policy interests against the interests of opening up the market, which requires the equal treatment of economic operators. The allocation of limited authorizations on the other hand must comply with strict transparency requirements, but EU law contains no detailed procedures. That means member states themselves have to strike the balance between these interests, but finding that balance is hard. In particular, the effects of seemingly simple allocation procedures, such as lotteries and first come, first served, are hard to assess. They may seem neutral with regard to their contribution to value for money and horizontal policies, but they may have unintended consequences for the public interest, as discussed above. In addition, with the allocation of limited authorizations there seems to be no room for exceptions to the obligation to provide transparency about the opportunity to acquire a right of the kind that public procurement does allow in order to allow member states the room to strive for value for money/horizontal policy goals. Limitations to transparency are allowed, however, when they are inspired by efficiency considerations. As Wollenschläger points out, there is no obligation to provide maximum transparency, but rather adequate transparency when it comes to, for instance, the advertising of the opportunity to acquire a right.

To conclude, the legal regime applicable to the allocation of limited authorizations strikes a different balance between the various public and private interests than the other regimes. The right to equal treatment and the freedom to provide services are front and centre, at the cost of promoting other interests. This might be a conscious choice, but it is also quite possible that it is an unintentional consequence of developments in case law,[66] where the diverging balancing of values was not sufficiently acknowledged by the courts. Intentional or not, we must now be on our guard that the precedence given to the rights of the economic

[66] Joined Cases C-360/15 and C-31/16, *Visser Vastgoed* ECLI:EU:C:2018:44.

operators directly involved in the procedure, at the expense of the interest of other third parties as well as the public interest, does not extend further beyond the scope of the Services Directive, at least not without careful consideration of the consequences.[67] In addition, the Services Directive itself may need to be revised on this point.

The less demanding obligations when allocating grants can be criticized because they do not promote equal opportunity to the extent that the rules for allocating authorizations do, especially within the scope of the Services Directive. However, it must be taken into account that these rules have a strong focus on promoting the right to fair and equal treatment of service providers and are less suitable to promote value for money, horizontal policies, the rights of third parties and even at times the remaining rights of service providers themselves. Before arguing that the transparency obligations related to the allocation of limited authorizations should inspire transparency obligations in other fields, one would do well to consider the downsides of this approach.

[67] See also Chapter 8 of Van de Gronden's heartfelt plea for a more lenient approach to SGEIs than the one resulting from the analogous application of the obligations in the Services Directive.

10

Regulating Competitive Tendering of Limited Rights

Principle-Based, Rule-Based and Integrated Approaches

CHRIS JANSEN, RIANNE JACOBS AND FRANK VAN OMMEREN

10.1 Introduction

When governments decide to allocate limited rights through competitive tendering, the law compels them to observe the principles of non-discrimination, equal treatment, transparency and proportionality. The contributions in Part I of this book show that, as far as licences, subsidies and government sales are concerned, EU law has not developed these principles into detailed rules, unlike the domain of public contracts. We assume that the situation is very similar in national law. Differing regulatory approaches are followed, resulting in different legal frameworks that can be qualified in terms of either principle-based or rule-based systems, with the caveat that variations of both types of systems can be discerned, even within a single legal framework that deals with a particular limited right.

Given these differences, it seems possible – at least in theory – to position legal frameworks on a sliding scale, with principle-based only systems at one end and fully detailed rule-based systems at the other. The relevance of identifying a legal framework's position on this scale is clear. If a framework is only principle-based, this provides the government with a considerable degree of discretion when making decisions during a competitive allocation process, provided that the principles of non-discrimination, equal treatment, transparency and proportionality are taken into account. If a legal framework has all the features of a fully detailed rule-based system, it instructs the government to take a particular course of action for almost every decision that can be made in the process.

In this chapter, we explain these differing regulatory approaches and investigate the extent to which they can be problematized considering the central theme of this book. Governments allocate limited rights through competitive tendering to meet various public interests.[1] In pursuing these interests, governments have to consider the above-mentioned principles and any rules that can be derived from them. This book seeks to answer the question of how this legal framework might affect the realization of public interests.[2] Our contribution analyses the extent to which this differs depending on the nature – either principle-based or rule-based – of the legal framework. We draw lessons from the outcomes to assist legislators in developing potential legal frameworks that governments could then observe in relation to the competitive allocation of limited rights.

This question and the objective of our analysis prompt us to make three clarifying remarks regarding this contribution's focus and method.

First, we focus on a different relationship than most of the other contributions in this book. Their focus is on the relationship between the government – public administration – and its capacity as the purchaser of goods, works or services, the seller of goods and other property rights or the grantor of licences or subsidies, on the one hand, and private citizens, companies or social institutions, interested in acquiring a public contract, government property, a licence or a subsidy on the other. Comparatively, our contribution focuses primarily on the relationship between legislators and governments allocating public contracts, property rights, licences and subsidies. After all, we are primarily interested in the amount of discretion governments are allowed within the relevant legal framework when they decide to allocate limited rights through competitive tendering. This means that the government itself – the public administration – is the addressee of the rules set by the legislator; private citizens, companies and social institutions are not. However, this does not mean that their position is irrelevant from the perspective of the relationship between the legislator and the government allocating limited rights. Private citizens, companies and social institutions interested in acquiring these rights play important roles as third parties, given that their relationship with the allocating government is the object of the legal framework set by the legislator.

[1] See the chapter of Wolswinkel, Jansen and Van Ommeren, Section 1.3.1.

[2] Ibid.

Second, our analysis primarily focuses on the legal framework set by the European Union (EU). We understand that EU law limits the discretion of allocating governments in its member states, but it also provides a framework within which national legislators may further restrict that discretion. We have not investigated whether or to what extent the national legislators of the member states have indeed done so. Our analysis is based on the generic and sector-specific EU legal framework, as can be deduced from the contributions from Arrowsmith, Wollenschläger, Van den Brink, Caranta and Biancardi. Moreover, our analysis is limited to parts of the framework that limit the discretion of the allocating government. This does not alter the fact that the interaction between EU law and national law is highly relevant to our contribution. After all, as we noted, EU law does not follow a rule-based approach for all of the limited rights dealt with in this book. Insofar as EU law does not do so, however, it cannot be ruled out that the discretion of allocating governments is further and perhaps even predominantly restricted by national law.

Third, our analysis takes the competitive allocation of public contracts as a starting point. The reason for this is that this domain has experienced relatively extensive regulatory developments over a long period of time. These developments initially resulted in a principle-based only system at the level of EU law. This allowed governments a considerable degree of discretion when allocating contracts by means of competitive tendering. Moreover, this system allowed national legislators to provide for additional and more restrictive rules within the EU principle-based framework. Subsequently, the latter framework gradually developed into rules, which were used to instruct governments about particular courses of action when allocating contracts. For some contracts, these rules have become increasingly detailed as time has progressed. This is particularly true of public contracts and contracts in utilities. Their development has resulted in a legal framework that has features of a fully detailed rule-based system. This has even triggered the question – potentially preluding a further stage of development – of whether it is wise to have such a system and whether it might be preferable to downsize the legal framework to a more principle-based system.[3]

[3] S. Arrowsmith, *The Law of Public and Utilities Procurement: Regulation in the EU and UK*, 3rd ed. (London: Sweet & Maxwell, vol. 1, 2014), pp. 234–235. F. van Ommeren, 'Challenges for the National Legislator: The Allocation of Limited Rights by the Administration', in P. Adriaanse, F. van Ommeren, W. den Ouden and J. Wolswinkel

The structure of this chapter is as follows. First, we provide assumptions about principle-based and rule-based systems in general, and we elaborate on their features and distinctions (Section 10.2). Next, we analyse the use of both types of systems in the domain of competitive allocation of public contracts (Section 10.3). Following this analysis, we describe (Section 10.4) and reflect on (Section 10.5) the application of principle-based and rule-based orientated legal frameworks in the domain of competitive allocation of government sales and privatizations, licenses and subsidies. Finally, we summarize our main findings (Section 10.6).

10.2 Principle-Based and Rule-Based Systems: General Features and Distinctions

10.2.1 Introduction

In this section, we examine the difference between principle-based and rule-based regulation. Why do we refer to a regulation as principle-based or rule-based, and why do legislators opt for one of the two systems or a combination of them? For the sake of clarity, we would like to point out that this section is not about the use of principle-based and rule-based systems in the specific context of the competitive allocation of limited rights by the government. This is covered in Sections 10.3 and 10.4. Before those two sections, we would like to explain the difference between principled-based and rule-based regulation in a general sense.

10.2.2 What Makes a Regulation Principle-Based or Rule-Based?

Regulations based on a principle-based approach state in an abstract and generally formulated way what purpose or result should be achieved by their addressee. By contrast, regulations based on a rule-based approach prescribe in concrete and detailed terms how the addressee should act. An essential feature of principle-based regulation is therefore that it allows the addressee considerable discretion, while an essential feature of a rule-based regulation is that it allows the addressee only little, if any, discretion. These descriptions should be regarded as archetypes. In practice, many combinations occur, because much legislation consists

(eds.), *Scarcity and the State I: The Allocation of Limited Rights by the Administration* (Cambridge: Intersentia, 2016), p. 91.

of both principles and rules, and because a combination may form part of a statute in one and the same place. Although the labels 'principle-based' and 'rule-based' are often used for legal regimes as a whole, it is in fact better, or at least more accurate, to look at the level of specific legal provisions to determine what character they have.

Some authors also describe rules as 'applicable in an all-or-nothing fashion'.[4] Because rules are detailed and prescribe what action should be taken or what the legal consequences are if certain facts occur, care must be taken to ensure that they do not conflict. Rules that conflict with each other cannot continue to coexist. If any principles are in mutual conflict, they must be weighed up against each other. Even if they are in conflict, they can continue to coexist. Dworkin articulated this as follows:

> Principles have a dimension that rules do not – the dimension of weight or importance. When principles intersect [. . .], one who must resolve the conflict has to take into account the relative weight of each. This cannot be, of course, an exact measurement, and the judgment that a particular principle or policy is more important than another will often be a controversial one. Nevertheless, it is an integral part of the concept of a principle that it has this dimension, that it makes sense to ask how important or how weighty it is.[5]

Although it is easy in theory to differentiate between principles and rules, in practice it is far from simple to determine whether a regulation, or part of a regulation, should be qualified as rule-based or principle-based. This is because many regulations are combinations of both approaches, given that they contain both principles and rules. In any such combination, a goal is often formulated in one or more principles; there are also rules to which the addressee must adhere in order for the goal to be reached. These could be commands (such as annual reporting obligations concerning results that have already been achieved) or prohibitions (such as a prohibition against carrying out certain activities without a licence). Moreover, statutory provisions often take the form of rules, while at the same time their implementation is in the form of a principle. An example that comes to mind is the rules on statutes of limitations. They are generally formulated as hard and fast rules, but it concerns in essence the effect of the principle of legal certainty; there must come a time when

[4] Ronald M. Dworkin, 'The Model of Rules' (1967) 35(14)*University of Chicago Law Review* 2; J. Braithwaite, 'Rules and Principles: A Theory of Legal Certainty' (2002) 27 *Australian Journal of Legal Philosophy* 50.

[5] Dworkin, 'The Model of Rules', 27.

it is no longer possible to invoke a claim from the past. The rules designated as commands and prohibitions (above) can in some cases also have the effect of a principle. To make a distinction between provisions that are principle-based or rule-based, background knowledge is required of the matter covered by regulation and the starting points and objectives on which it is based. Because regulations usually consist of both types of rules, it is often better to refer to an integrated system of principles and rules.[6]

10.2.3 Why Do Legislators Opt for a Principle-Based or Rule-Based System?

Literature on principle-based and rule-based systems contains a range of arguments for both approaches. Arguments for a principle-based approach state that principles can often be formulated in simple and general terms and can then be applied flexibly because of their general formulation. In this connection, it is also frequently stated that a more principle-based system prevents over- and under-inclusiveness. It is important too that principle-based systems provide scope for addressees to achieve the goal in question in a manner of their own choosing. It is stated that this scope can promote innovation, although it is perhaps better to say that it does not inhibit the innovation of products, services or processes by addressees. Another claim made is that this system prevents loophole behaviour and box-ticking, by which it is meant that principle-based regulations compel addressees to behave in a manner intended by the regulation that, if it were rule-based, could allow them to evade the regulation by giving a strict interpretation of it. Finally, it is important whether regulations are set at the level of EU law or that of the member states; in an international context, it is often easier to reach agreement about principles than about rules.[7]

[6] See Van Ommeren, 'Challenges for the National Legislator: The Allocation of Limited Rights by the Administration', p. 90.

[7] Heath P. Tarbert, 'Rules for Principles and Principles for Rules: Tools for Crafting Sound Financial Regulation' (2020) 10 *Harvard Business Law Review* 5–9; John Pearson Allen, 'Rules- or Principles-Based Regulation? Factors for Choosing the Best Language Strategy' (2015) 56 *Canadian Business Law Journal* 375, 376–382; John M. Conley, Lodewijk Smeehuijzen, Cynthia. A. Williams and Deborah E. Rupp, 'Can Soft Regulation Prevent Financial Crises: The Dutch Central Bank's Supervision of Behavior and Culture' (2019) 51 *Cornell International Law Journal* 773, 799–800.

The main argument that is put forward for a rule-based system is the legal certainty that such a system offers to parties subject to the law. In general, rules are clearer than principles, making it easier to comply with them. It is easier to adhere to the hard and fast 'you may drive at 50 kph here' rule than to the 'you may not endanger road safety' principle. It is also easier to determine when enough has been done to comply with a rule. In this connection, it is sometimes argued that hard and fast rules can give protection against being held liable, by customers, for example, because it is easier to demonstrate that these hard and fast rules have been complied with.[8]

The above arguments are highly abstract, but that is never the case for the choice between a more, or less, rule- or principle-based system. After all, such a system is always designed with a view to resolving a particular problem in a particular area of the law. We note that in the different fields of the law, the question arises (or has arisen) as to whether a choice has to be made between rules that allow greater discretion and detailed hard and fast rules, in various guises and at various times. Of particular prominence is the discussion regarding the regulation of the financial markets after the worldwide financial crisis of 2008.[9] Before the financial crisis, it was principle-based regulations that were preferred, but more rule-based regulations came into favour after the crisis. The financial markets are not the only area in which regulations were preferred that allowed greater discretion, only to be followed by more rule-based regulations. Conversely, however, there are also occasions when the large number of detailed rules in a particular area of the law gives rise to an examination as to whether regulations that allow greater discretion could be used. Whenever detailed rules are perceived as complicated and become outdated because of the fast rate of technological development, the question arises of whether this can be tackled with regulations that allow greater discretion. This occurred in the 1990s in various countries in respect of environmental laws,[10] employment

[8] Tarbert, 'Rules for Principles and Principles for Rules', 9–10; Allen, 'Rules- or Principles-Based Regulation?', 376–380.

[9] Conley et al., 'Can Soft Regulation Prevent Financial Crises'; J. Black, 'Forms and Paradoxes of Principles-Based Regulation' (2008) 3 *Capital Market Law Journal*, 425–457; I. Mason, 'Principles Based Regulation – Will It Work?', in C. Skinner (ed.), *The Future of Investing in Europe's Markets after MiFID* (West Sussex: Wiley & Sons, 2007), pp. 85–92.

[10] This can be derived from the Protocol on environmental protection to the Antarctic Treaty, available at www.antarctica.gov.au/about-antarctica/law-and-treaty/the-madrid-

laws[11] and food safety laws[12] and led to the inclusion in various laws of 'duty of care' provisions. These are provisions that oblige their addressees to exercise care for a particular interest formulated by law and that are formulated in such a way that they have multiple options on how to do so. In the field of tax law, too, ever-increasingly detailed rules on the prevention of tax evasion resulted in a discussion in various member states, including the UK, on the question of whether a more principle-based approach would be more effective in countering unwanted loop-hole behaviour.[13]

10.3 Public Procurement

10.3.1 Introduction

In this section, we examine the use of principle-based and rule-based systems in the context of EU regulation of competitive public procurement. We focus in particular on the regulations in the Directives 2014/24/EU and 2014/25/EU that significantly affect the procurement of ordinary public contracts and contracts in utilities above a certain value.[14] This is because these regulations appear to restrict governments'

protocol/; Barbara Beijen, 'Seeking Coherence among Environmental Directives', in M. G. W. M. Peeters and R. Uylenburg (eds.), *EU Environmental Legislation: Legal Perspectives on Regulatory Strategies* (Abingdon: Edward Elgar, 2014), pp. 71–73.

11 This can be derived from Council Directive 96/82/EC of 9 December 1996 on the control of major-accident hazards involving dangerous substances, OJ 1997, No. L10/13.

12 This can be derived from European Commission, Green Paper on the General Principles of Food Law in the European Union (Brussels, 30 April 1997, COM(97) 176 final); Regulation (EC) 178/2002 of the European Parliament and of the Council of 28 January 2002 laying down the general principles and requirements of food law, establishing the European Food Safety Authority and laying down procedures in matters of food safety, OJ 2002, No. L31/1; Nicole Coutrelis, 'EU "New Approach" also for Food Law?', in B. M. J. van der Meulen (ed.), *Governing Food Chains through Contract Law, Self-Regulation, Private Standards, Audits and Certification Schemes* (Wageningen: Wageningen Academic Publishers, 2011), pp. 381–389.

13 Stenographer's report of the scientific part of the meeting of the Dutch Association for Tax Research, held on 13 February 2014 in Amsterdam. The report is available in Dutch at https://belastingwetenschap.nl/media/1541/vbw-13-februari-2014-stenografisch-verslag.pdf. The discussion was themed around principle-based provisions in misappropriation situations as an alternative to concrete regulations. The same discussion was also held in Great Britain: Judith Freedman, 'Improving (Not Perfecting) Tax Legislation: Rules and Principles Revisited' (2010) 6(6) *British Tax Review* 717–719.

14 Directive 2014/24/EU of the European Parliament and of the Council of 26 February 2014 on public procurement and repealing Directive 2004/18/EC, OJ 2014, No. L94/65 ('Public Procurement Directive') and Directive 2014/25/EU of the European Parliament

discretion much more than do those relating to public contracts for social and other specific services, which are also regulated by these two Directives,[15] and to concessions regulated by Directive 2014/23/EU.[16] What we would eventually like to discover is whether and, if so, to what degree the regulatory approaches we find influence the level of discretion and therefore the ability of governments to achieve their procurement objectives, thereby serving public interests. We will first give an outline overview of the decisions that typically accompany a competitive public procurement process (Section 10.3.2). We will then show that EU law does not interfere with the 'what' or the 'why' of public procurements, but only the 'how' (Section 10.3.3). Based on the above, we can then further analyse EU law against the background of the difference between principle-based and rule-based approaches. Our analysis will show that there are different ways of regarding regulation as an integral approach (Section 10.3.4). We will then attempt to explain why the EU legislator has opted for this approach (Section 10.3.5). This brings us finally to the question about the possible impact of the selected approach on the ability of governments to achieve their procurement objectives (Section 10.3.6).

10.3.2 What Decisions Are Typically Made during a Competitive Public Procurement Process?

Any government proposing to procure goods, services or work must base its procurement decisions on the objectives it is seeking to achieve in the context of the specific interests it is seeking to serve. This requires a tailor-made approach, even though in abstract terms the way in which the procurement process is organized is always the same.[17]

Once a government has decided on a competitive procurement process, it will first have to design it and then carry it out. Decisions made by governments in that context generally relate to the same subjects. They

and of the Council of 26 February 2014 on procurement by entities operating in the water, energy, transport and postal services sectors and repealing Directive 2004/17/EC, OJ 2014, No. L94/243 ('Utilities Directive').

15 Public Procurement Directive, Arts. 74–77 and Utilities Directive, Arts. 91–94.

16 Directive 2014/23/EU of the European Parliament and of the Council of 26 February 2014 on the award of concession contracts, OJ 2014, No. L94/1 ('Concessions Directive').

17 For more details on this, see C. Jansen, 'Allocation of Limited Rights from a European Public Procurement Law Perspective', in P. Adriaanse, F. van Ommeren, W. den Ouden and J. Wolswinkel (eds.), *Scarcity and the State I: The Allocation of Limited Rights by the Administration* (Cambridge: Intersentia, 2016), pp. 241–243.

first involve the requirements that economic operators that are interested in the contract must meet in order to be considered for it. These requirements concern the competencies they must possess (qualitative selection criteria), any circumstances that would give rise to their exclusion from the process (exclusion grounds), and the quality of the goods, services and work they are offering with their tender (technical specifications). Another important topic about which governments will have to decide is that of the evaluation methods and award criteria that they use to select the best tender.

Decisions made by governments regarding the aforementioned requirements and criteria can be divided into draft and implementation decisions. Whenever a procuring government makes draft decisions, it sets the requirements and criteria in the light of its procurement objectives and the related public interests. It then informs economic operators that are interested in the contract of these requirements and criteria. Whenever a government makes implementation decisions, it uses the same requirements and criteria to evaluate the tenderers and their tenders. The government will have to evaluate and establish whether one or more of the exclusion grounds apply to any of the tenderers, whether a tenderer meets the qualitative selection criteria, whether their tenders meet the technical specifications, and which of the tenders ranks best after the award criteria have been applied. In the light of the outcomes of these evaluations, implementation decisions are made in the form of the exclusion of tenderers, the declaring invalid or rejection of tenders and the awarding of the contract to one of the tenderers. Just as governments publish their draft decisions (the requirements and criteria), they do the same with regard to their implementation decisions – the outcomes of their evaluation of the tenderers and their tenders, based on the same requirements and criteria.

10.3.3 EU Law Restrictions on Levels of Discretion: What Do They Relate to (and What Not)?

The problems associated with EU regulations on public procurement and how they are reflected in the national laws of the member states have long been studied from the perspective of the restrictions imposed by these regulations on governments when making their procurement decisions. However, if we wish to make a pronouncement on the question of whether and, if so, to what degree the various regulatory approaches used by the EU affect the ability of governments to achieve their procurement objectives and therefore serve public interests, then we should focus not just on the restrictions but consider first and foremost the starting point that procuring governments have discretion.[18]

Whenever a government is proposing to procure a contract of certain cross-border interest, it must use a competitive allocation procedure in accordance with EU law. This obligation does not alter the fact that EU law allows governments, in principle, to determine their own procurement needs and how – with what goods, services or works – these needs should be met.[19] This also applies to the public interests that governments seek to serve through the acquisition of these goods, services and works, as well as the various priorities they wish to pursue in that context. Although EU law highlights these interests and how competitive procurement can be used by governments to serve them,[20] it ultimately does not hinder governments from making their own policy decisions in this context. In short, EU law does not interfere with the 'what' or the 'why' of competitive public procurement.

Where EU law does interfere – and this is the exception to the aforementioned starting point – is the 'how' of competitive public procurement. This is because the draft and implementation decisions made by governments in order to arrive at the correct procurement result may not lead to discrimination on the grounds of nationality or to unequal treatment of economic operators interested in the contract. The corollary of this is that procurement decisions must be transparent and proportional. The objective sought by the EU legislator through these restrictive conditions is to promote the development of healthy and effective competition between economic operators in order to create a European single market for public contracts. It is assumed here that this is a different objective to those that governments themselves seek to attain through their competitive procurement procedures.

10.3.4 Restricting Discretion: Principle-Based, Rule-Based or Integrated Approach?

From the above, it follows what the result is that a government must achieve, whenever it has to apply a competitive procurement procedure in

[18] See S. Kelman, 'Reinventing Government, 25 Years On: Has the Procurement System Improved?' (2018) 27 *Public Procurement Law Review* 101.

[19] Jansen, 'Allocation of Limited Rights from a European Public Procurement Law Perspective', pp. 243–244.

[20] Concessions Directive, Recitals (3); Public Procurement Directive, Recitals (2); and Utilities Directive, Recitals (4).

line with EU law. When making its decisions, it must be guided by its own procurement objectives but at the same time ensure effective competition.

Continuing from our observations in Section 10.2, we can now analyse the EU regulation of public procurement in more detail in the light of the distinction we made in that section. We refer to the distinction between regulations that state in an abstract and general way that governments must achieve the result described above, and that give governments a great deal of discretion (principle-based approach), and regulations that prescribe in a specific and detailed manner how governments must act in order to achieve the aforementioned result, and that allow little, if any, discretion (rule-based approach).[21] At first sight, it looks as though the distinction is the same as that between the regulations based on the Treaty on the Functioning of the European Union (TFEU), for all contracts of certain cross-border interest with a financial value below the relevant thresholds referred to in the directives, and those based on the directives on contracts with a financial value that exceeds these thresholds. After all, a feature of the directives is their 'high level of detail', which suggests a rule-based approach that is distinct from the principle-based approach that we find in the provisions of the TFEU,[22] in particular in relation to the fundamental freedoms. The fact that these Treaty provisions, unlike the directives, do not focus specifically on the context of competitive public procurement does not alter the fact that the directives are based on them.[23] However, a closer examination at the level of specific provisions shows that the directives bear testimony to an integrated approach in different ways.[24] We develop this in more detail below.

First, the directives opt for an integrated approach, in the sense that they contain the principles of non-discrimination, equal treatment, transparency and proportionality,[25] as well as the detailed rules that derive from them, and which allow governments less discretion than do the underlying principles themselves.

Second, it is notable that the directives have a strong rule-based approach as far as the traditionally most important contracts in cross-border procurement practice – public contracts and contracts in

[21] Section 10.2.2.

[22] See the chapter of Arrowsmith, Section 2.4.1.2.

[23] Concessions Directive, Recitals (4); Public Procurement Directive, Recitals (1); and Utilities Directive, Recitals (2).

[24] Section 10.2.2.

[25] Concessions Directive, Art. 3(1); Public Procurement Directive, Art. 18(1); Utilities Directive, Art. 36(1).

utilities – are concerned,[26] while the regulations relating to the more recent contracts for social and other specific services and for concessions are inclined much more towards a principle-based approach.[27]

The third striking aspect – and from here, we refer solely to ordinary public contracts and contracts in utilities that come under the scope of Directives 2014/24/EU and 2014/25/EU – is that not every principle has been expanded to the same degree in the directives into more detailed rules that restrict governments' discretion more than do the principles themselves. This has taken place mostly in respect of the transparency principle – we will return to this below – but to a much lesser extent with regard to the non-discrimination principle,[28] the principle of equal treatment[29] and the proportionality principle.[30] An additional factor is that in many cases the rules, as far as these principles are concerned, go no further than repeating the obligation on governments to observe the underlying principle in the specific context of a procurement decision covered by the rules, without any concrete description of the actions or non-actions that governments are expected to take.

This brings us to a final observation in relation to the integrated approach found in Directives 2014/24/EU and 2014/25/EU. It is undeniably true, as Arrowsmith submits, that '[t]hey contain a huge amount of detail [. . .] across all stages of the allocation process'.[31] At the same time, however – and we deal with this below – we note that the rules in these directives allow governments greater discretion as far as some types of procurement decision are concerned for the purpose of achieving the result mentioned at the start of this section, than they do with regard to other decisions.

By developing the foregoing observations on the basis of the distinction made in Section 10.3.2 between procurement decisions according to

[26] The level of detail of the rules of the Public Procurement Directive barely differs from that of the Utilities Directive; see also the chapter of Arrowsmith, Section 2.4.1.2.

[27] In relation to the latter, see Public Procurement Directive, Arts. 74–77; Utilities Directive, Arts. 91–94; and Concessions Directive, Arts. 19–30.

[28] See, for example, Public Procurement Directive, Arts. 22(1), 29(5), 30(3), 30(6), 30(7), 42, 43(1)(b), 46(2), 56(1)(b), 58(3), 65(2), 68(2)(a) and 80(3). See also Utilities Directive, Arts. 40(1), 48(3), 48(6), 48(7), 49(4), 58, 60, 61(1)(b), 65(2), 83(2)(a) and 97(3).

[29] See, for example, Public Procurement Directive, Arts. 24, 29(5), 30(3), 31(4), 41 and 56(3). See also Utilities Directive, Arts. 42, 48(3), 49(4), 51(2), 59 and 76(4).

[30] For a detailed analysis of the directives, see C. Jansen, 'Stretching the Proportionality Principle: How Dutch Law Facilitates the Participation of SMEs in Public Procurement' (2022) 31 *Public Procurement Law Review* 217–218.

[31] See the chapter of Arrowsmith, Section 2.4.1.2.

their nature and subject, the following nuanced picture emerges, as far as Directives 2014/24/EU and 2014/25/EU are concerned.

The directives contain mostly detailed rules that restrict governments' discretion as far as the draft of the content of their requirements and criteria is concerned. As we noted earlier, governments may tailor this draft according to their own procurement objectives and the specific interests related to them, but the objective of EU law imposes a limit: governments must guarantee effective competition in the context of their procurement activities. This means they may not devise requirements or criteria that discriminate according to nationality, that result in any other kind of unequal treatment of economic operators, or that are insufficiently linked to the subject matter of the contract. To prevent governments from doing this, the directives limit the aspects to which some of the requirements and criteria may be related.[32] This has not happened in the case of other requirements and criteria, but the directives do prescribe in detail the procedural and substantive preconditions that must be observed when setting the content of the requirements and criteria.[33] For this latter method, the directives also determine in many cases how governments should specifically ensure that the requirements and criteria are objectively clear,[34] wherever their discretion as far as other requirements and criteria are concerned is restricted only in an abstract sense by the transparency principle. Along the same lines described above, we find elsewhere in the directives detailed rules that restrict governments' discretion with regard to the requirements they may set in relation to evidence used by economic operators to demonstrate that they meet the aforementioned requirements and criteria.[35]

The directives also have many detailed rules that considerably restrict governments' discretion with regard to the publication of their requirements and criteria and of other relevant information. These publication and information obligations can be regarded as elaborations of the transparency principle. The same applies to the rules that restrict discretion

[32] See, for example, the exhaustive lists in Art. 57 (exclusion grounds) and Art. 58 (selection criteria) Public Procurement Directive. See also Utilities Directive, Arts. 78–80.

[33] See, for example, Art. 42 (technical specifications), Art. 43 (labels) and Art. 67 (contract award criteria) Public Procurement Directive. This is not the case in Art. 70 (special conditions relating to the performance of a contract). See also Utilities Directive, Arts. 60, 61 and 82.

[34] This is particularly the case with regard to the technical specifications and labels, in the sense that governments will have to reconcile them with existing standards.

[35] Or, in the case of the exclusion grounds, that they do *not* actually apply to them.

with regard to the publication of the results of the evaluations of both the tenderers and their tenders, based on the previously drafted and published requirements and criteria. What is noticeable, however, is that the directives contain relatively far fewer detailed rules regarding the content of the decisions that governments can make in carrying out evaluations as such.[36] This means that the level of governments' discretion regarding the taking of these implementation decisions appears to be limited only by the principles. However, this does not mean that governments have much discretion in relative terms with regard to these decisions. This is because, in a number of important cases, the European Court of Justice (ECJ) has distilled rules from the principles that governments must observe whenever they have to decide whether or not to exclude tenderers from further participation in the tendering procedure on the basis of the qualitative selection criteria or exclusion grounds,[37] whether or not to declare tenders invalid in the light of the technical specifications,[38] or whether or not to ascribe a value to a valid tender on the basis of the award criteria that would result in it being ranked as the best.[39] Essentially, all these rules that have emerged from the ECJ amount to a requirement whereby governments must strictly adhere to the design decisions they have made and published during the earlier stages of their procurement process.[40]

10.3.5 Why Has the EU Legislator Opted for an Integrated Approach?

In the light of the arguments mentioned in Section 10.2 for the use of principle- or ruled-based approaches,[41] some guesswork is needed to find the arguments on which the choices made by the EU legislator referred to in Section 10.3.4 are based.[42] What is clear, though, is that the EU

[36] Important exceptions to this are, for example, the detailed rules of Art. 57 (exclusion grounds) and Art. 69 (abnormally low tenders) of Public Procurement Directive. Compare also Utilities Directive, Arts. 78–80 and Art. 84.

[37] Case C-336/12, *Manova* ECLI:EU:C:2013:647, para. 40; Case C-171/15, *Connexxion Taxi Services* v. *Netherlands* ECLI:EU:C:2016:948, para. 38.

[38] Case C-599/10, *SAG ELV Slovensko* ECLI:EU:C:2012:191, paras. 35–41.

[39] Case C-448/01, *EVN AG and Wienstrom GmbH* v. *Republik Österreich* [2003] ECR I-14527, ECLI:EU:C:2003:651, para. 48.

[40] Case C-496/99P, *CAS Succhi di Frutta* [2004] ECR I-3801, ECLI:EU:C:2004:236, paras. 113–115.

[41] See Section 10.2.3.

[42] This is even more the case given that no detailed reference has been made on the matter in recent decades, as far as we have been able to ascertain. An exception is Concessions Directive, Recitals (1), (4) and (8).

legislator has, from the very beginning, drafted the coordination of national procedures for public contracts above the financial thresholds, and later for contracts in utilities, by setting rules that restrict governments' discretion primarily by means of the transparency principle.[43] This development continued in the subsequent generations of directives and led to the integrated approach of the kind we have already described. In that context, we understand too the comments by Arrowsmith, who regards 'rule-based decision-making that limits discretion' as one of the four dimensions of 'the concept of transparency' that she distinguishes.[44]

Following on from that, it could be argued that the EU legislator has found it sufficient, with a view to achieving effective competition, to provide additional rules that oblige procuring governments to make clear in particular the requirements and criteria they set, as well as the results of their evaluations based on these requirements and criteria. The clearer this information is to the economic operators concerned, the better able they will be to verify themselves whether, and to what extent, governments have honoured the principles of non-discrimination, equal treatment and proportionality in their procurement decisions. It would then seemingly not be necessary – at least as far as all types of requirements and criteria devised by governments are concerned[45] – for their level of discretion to be restricted even more, in the sense of additional rules being made that prescribe how they draft their requirements and criteria in concrete terms so that they comply with the aforementioned principles. That is certainly not necessary as far as decisions made by governments regarding the implementation of that draft are concerned. A rule that essentially obliges governments, when evaluating tenderers and their tenders, to strictly observe their own draft, means that their discretion is restricted to exactly the right degree, given the result that the EU legislator is seeking to achieve through that rule.

Following on from the above, it could also be argued that the rationale behind some of the choices made by the EU legislator could be found in the most important arguments referred to in Section 10.2.3. As far as ordinary public contracts and contracts in utilities are concerned, we refer, for example, to the fact that the directives impose considerable

[43] See Recitals (9) and (10) of Council Directive 1971/305/EEC of 26 July 1971 concerning the coordination of procedures for the award of public works contracts, OJ 1971, No. L185/5.

[44] See the chapter of Arrowsmith, Section 2.3.10.

[45] That may be different if it were possible to find a connection with existing standards.

restrictions on governments' discretion, in the sense that they prescribe in detail how governments must provide insight into the results of their draft and implementation decisions. These restrictions on governments' discretion have resulted in a well-functioning control mechanism that promotes legal certainty. At the same time, this mechanism offers the possibility of giving governments a little more room for policy – with the advantages that this entails – in the sense that governments may in principle determine their own requirements and criteria, provided they are compatible with the principles of non-discrimination, equal treatment and proportionality. Particularly notable here is that the balance between legal certainty and discretion may apparently differ, depending on whether a contract above the relevant financial threshold (rule-based) or below that threshold (principle-based) is involved, and whether the contract has the character of an ordinary public contract or contract in utilities (rule-based) or is for social and other specific services or a concession (principle-based). The EU legislator also apparently recognizes this difference, in the recitals for the Concessions Directive, for example,[46] but this does not explain why with one type of contract there is a greater need for discretion for governments – at the expense of legal certainty – than with another.

10.3.6 What Is the Impact of the Integrated Approach on Procurement Objectives?

In Section 10.3.3, we noted that, in principle, EU law allows national governments to determine their own objectives and the public interests they seek to serve through their procurements. At the same time, EU law sets conditions under which governments may do this. This raises the question of whether EU law can have a negative impact on the ability of governments to achieve their procurement objectives and, if so, whether that impact would be greater if regulations were of a more rule-based character.

It is suggested in the literature that this would indeed be the case.[47] In that connection, we refer to two important issues relating to

[46] See Concessions Directive, Recitals (1) and (8).

[47] See S. Arrowsmith, 'The EC Procurement Directives, National Procurement Policies and Better Governance: The Case for a New Approach' (2002) 27 *European Law Review* 3. See also the chapter of Arrowsmith in this book, Section 2.3.10 and Section 2.4.2.2, in which she refers to S. Kelman, *Procurement and Public Management: The Fear of Discretion and*

government procurement regulation: (1) the restriction on bilateral communications with potential or actual tenderers during the procurement process;[48] and (2) the restriction on tenderers from making corrections to their tenders after they have been submitted.[49] In essence, it is assumed that if EU law were to provide greater scope for proper communication and correction opportunities than is currently the case, governments would be better placed to achieve the best price–quality ratio for their procurements. Although similar restrictions on levels of discretion with regard to the competitive allocation of other limited rights hardly seem to be a problem,[50] it is to be expected that the issues referred to are relevant outside the domain of government procurement as well.[51] For that reason, we will briefly examine these issues.

As far as the first issue is concerned, it should be stated at the outset that the directives give governments a great deal of scope for communicating with potential and actual tenderers while drafting their requirements and criteria.[52] This gives them a strong starting position from which they can manage the realization of their procurement objectives. However, as soon as the requirements and criteria have been published, that scope is much more limited.[53] In these circumstances, the directives do allow potential and actual tenderers to submit questions and comments resulting from the design of the procurement process, after which the government must publish its response to every potential tenderer. This multilateral communication can help achieve a sound balance

the Quality of Government Performance (Washington, DC: The AEI Press, 1999), p. 28; S. Kelman, 'Remaking the Federal Procurement System' (2002) 31 *Public Contract Law Journal* 581. She also refers to S. L. Schooner, 'Fear of Oversight: The Fundamental Failure of Businesslike Government' (2001) 50 *American University Law Review* 627. In the Netherlands, this position is held by Telgen and Stolwijk (amongst others). For detailed literature references, see C. Jansen, 'Over het vermeende dilemma tussen de doelmatigheid en de rechtmatigheid van de overheidsinkoop', in E. Manunza and F. Schotanus (eds.), *The Art of Public Procurement. Liber Amicorum in Honour of Prof. Dr. Jan Telgen* (Enschede: University of Twente, 2018), pp. 171–183.

48 See also the chapter of Arrowsmith, Sections 2.3 and 2.4.2.2.

49 Ibid., Section 2.4.2.2.

50 We have not found any references to this in Chapters 3, 4 and 5 of Wollenschläger, Van den Brink, and Caranta and Biancardi.

51 See also the chapter of Arrowsmith, Section 2.4.2.2.

52 See, for example, Public Procurement Directive, Art. 40, and Utilities Directive, Art. 58.

53 At least when a government uses one of the standard procurement procedures. In the event of the directives permitting the use of the competitive procedure with negotiation or the competitive dialogue procedure, the opportunities for bilateral communications are greater.

between the various relevant interests. However, it could also be argued that the directives offer governments too much scope for the purpose of responding insufficiently to questions and comments from tenderers. The sought-after balance between the relevant interests appears to be better served by rules that create clear parameters for effective multilateral communications, rather than an expansion of the opportunities for bilateral communications after the design of the procurement process has been published. To the extent that the purpose of these communications is to deal with the consequences of ineffective choices that governments have included in their designs, an expansion would not resolve the actual problem. What is needed for that, first and foremost, is professionalization of public procurement. Governments that have professionalized their procurement processes generally give greater consideration to the draft of their requirements and criteria in advance. This means they run less of a risk of having to improvise their procurement process on a 'learning from their mistakes' basis and being controlled by circumstances.

As far as the second issue is concerned – the restriction on allowing corrections to mistakes in tenders – it has to be admitted that such a restriction can have an impact on the ability of governments to achieve their procurement objectives. However, it is not clear how easing this restriction would help achieve a better balance between the various interests without at the same time conceding the starting point principle that governments should strictly adhere to the design of their previously published procurement process.[54] Any easing would also affect the integrity of the procurement process, which in due course would undermine the procurement objectives themselves. What we have noticed, however, is that exceptions to the rules, on which grounds corrections to mistakes in tenders are permitted, allow governments to a significant degree to decide whether allowing corrections in a specific case is compatible with the principles underlying the rules.[55] From the point of view of legal certainty, it would actually be better to advocate a more rule-based approach to this issue.

[54] Apart from the fact that the design may not provide for any possibility of correcting mistakes in tenders if this would result in a new tender being submitted, see ECJ Case C-599/10, *SAG ELV Slovensko* ECLI:EU:C:2012:191.

[55] See Public Procurement Directive, Art. 56(3) *in fine*. Compare also Utilities Directive, Art. 76(4).

Taking everything into account, we believe, contrary to what is suggested in the literature cited above, that the impact of EU law on the ability of governments to achieve their procurement objectives is not very problematic. However, we would like to point out the following. The drafting of non-discriminatory, proportional and transparent requirements and criteria obviously comes at a price. The same applies to the evaluations carried out on the basis of these requirements and criteria, so that the results of these evaluations can be shown in a transparent manner. After all, professional knowledge and skills are needed to be able to make procurement decisions that are compatible with the regulations. The latter requires investments that in many cases yield no immediate added value as far as the procurement objectives governments seek are concerned; it is even possible that such investments will come from the budget intended for the objectives themselves. In the long term, these investments may help improve the level of professionalism and therefore the ability of governments to make decisions that are in line with the regulations. It should also be pointed out that any such investments can be limited, the more the regulations are of a rule-based character. After all, the concomitant restriction of discretion simplifies the making of decisions by governments, promotes the lawfulness of such decisions and helps limit the costs involved in eliminating the consequences of unlawfully made decisions.[56] Clearly, a balance has to be found here: having too many rules leads to greater costs.

10.4 Licences, Subsidies and Government Property

10.4.1 Introduction

In the previous section, we examined the use of principle-based and rule-based systems in the context of EU regulation of competitive public procurement. The findings of that examination offer an inspiring angle for an additional investigation into the use of such systems in the context of competitive allocation by governments of other rights:[57] licences, subsidies and property rights. What we would like to discover through this investigation is whether and, if so, to what degree the various

[56] In this connection, compare the decision by the Dutch legislator to expand the codified proportionality principle in the directive to more detailed rules that restrict the government's discretion in the country's public procurement legislation. See Jansen, 'Stretching the Proportionality Principle', p. 216.

[57] See also the chapter of Arrowsmith, Sections 2.1 and 2.3.

regulatory approaches influence governments' level of discretion and their ability to achieve their objectives and therefore to promote the associated public interests they pursue with the competitive allocation of a licence, a subsidy or a property right.

It is by no means a given that governments allocate these rights competitively. This is most obvious in the sale of government property, as with procurement of public contracts. After all, as soon as a government has decided on a sale, it automatically restricts the number of rights it will grant. This is not the case with the awarding of licences and subsidies: the starting point is that the government must first decide to set a ceiling on the number of rights it will award. Often, however, there is no reason to do this, or the government simply neglects to do so, and there is therefore no maximum number of licences or subsidies that can be awarded. In these cases, governments are able to achieve the public interests they intend to promote through the awarding of these rights without the need for the rights to be allocated competitively. And even if a government has set a ceiling, which can result in a scarcity, it does not mean it has to allocate rights competitively or that it is legally bound to do so in order for the relevant interests to be served. It is possible, but is not necessarily so.[58]

With a view to the purpose of this contribution, we focus in this section solely on cases where governments have set a maximum number of rights they will award, before carrying out a competitive allocation. We examine the actual structure of the competitive allocation process (Section 10.4.2), the EU legal framework relevant to that process (Section 10.4.3), the rationale of the restrictions on the discretion of the allocating government contained therein (Section 10.4.4), and how these restrictions can be valued in the light of the difference between principle-based and rule-based approaches (Section 10.4.5).

We repeat the comment we made in Section 10.1 that we realize that the interaction between EU law and national law is greatly important for the topic of our contribution. EU law, after all, not only sets limits to the discretion of governments that allocate licences, subsidies and property rights, but also offers a framework in which national legislators can impose further restrictions. Following on from this, it should be remembered that the differences between the member states in these areas are fairly large. The latter is true not just in relation to the granting of rights,

[58] See the chapter of Wolswinkel, Jansen and Van Ommeren, Section 1.1.3.

but also – and much more importantly – the regulation culture. It depends to a significant degree on the national regulation culture whether legislators in the relevant member state prefer a more principle-based or a more rule-based approach, or an integrated one, and how much discretion is given to the government in question as the party awarding licences, subsidies and property rights. Such a culture depends in part on the degree to which legislators regard the relevant governments as suitable or trustworthy to be given more, or less, discretion.

With regard to the foregoing, we have not investigated whether, or to what degree, national legislators have further restricted the discretion permitted by EU law. Our analysis below assumes the prevailing EU legal framework, as described by Wollenschläger, Van den Brink, and Caranta and Biancardi in their contributions to this book.

10.4.2 Structure of the Competitive Allocation Process

As is the case in the competitive procurement of a public contract, it is obvious that in the case of the competitive allocation of a licence, a subsidy or a property right, a government will base its allocation decisions on the objectives it is seeking to realize through the awarding of these rights, also given the specific public interests attached to these objectives. Both Wollenschläger and Caranta and Biancardi show that the difference between the 'inherent needs' and the 'additional policy objectives' associated with the competitive allocation of a licence and a property right is not always clearly defined.[59] Wollenschläger also notes that the difference is not so relevant from the perspective of the requirements imposed by law on competitive allocations.[60]

Although not all of the aforementioned authors examine in detail the structure of the competitive allocation process in the case of a licence, a subsidy or a property right, we believe it can be assumed that this process too will consist of both a design and implementation phase.[61] Generally speaking, the process will run along the same lines: the government first drafts the requirements and criteria for the potential applicants and their

[59] See the chapter of Wollenschläger, Section 3.3.1, and the chapter of Caranta and Biancardi, Section 5.3.1.

[60] See the chapter of Wollenschläger, Section 3.4.3.1.

[61] Compare the chapter of Wollenschläger, Section 3.3.3.1, and the chapter of Caranta and Biancardi, Section 5.4.3.1.

applications, publishes them, uses them to evaluate the applicants and their applications, makes allocation decisions based on the outcomes of the evaluations and finally publishes these decisions. Furthermore, it is important to note that, to the extent that governments try to exercise control over the objectives they aim to achieve through the awarding of the rights, they will mainly do so through the design of the allocation process. This may involve differences of emphasis, depending on the specific nature and characteristics of the right being awarded, the objectives pursued by the government and the related public interests.[62]

It can also be assumed that the allocation process includes both a qualitative and a competitive phase. As far as the qualitative phase is concerned, its design may relate to the minimum requirements that potential applicants must meet and to the requirements that their actual applications will have to meet. Decisions made by governments in this connection will, as stated, very much depend on their context. When awarding certain rights – such as subsidizing the purchase of solar panels by homeowners or the sale of superfluous goods – both the status of the applicants and the substance of their applications will often be irrelevant to the government, in contrast to when awarding certain licences.

Once the government has informed potential applicants of the aforementioned minimum requirements and the applicants have submitted their applications, the government will use the requirements to evaluate the content of the applications and, possibly, the applicants themselves.[63] The government will then only admit applicants to the competitive phase who meet the minimum requirements.

Supplementary to the design of the qualitative phase, governments may also decide to exercise control over their objectives through the design of the competitive phase. If a government does so, this will be apparent from the fact that it has drafted criteria on which basis it will carry out a comparative evaluation of the applications in order to select the best one or ones.[64] Such draft will generally be based on the price offered by or requested by the applicant, the quality of the application or

[62] Jansen, 'Allocation of Limited Rights from a European Public Procurement Law Perspective', pp. 274–275.

[63] In the event that the status or position of an applicant is of importance to the government, the evaluation may be carried out in phases. If that is the case, the government invites only applicants to submit applications who meet the requirements in relation to their position. For example, see Section 10.3.2 *in fine* in relation to public procurement.

[64] See the chapter of Wollenschläger, Sections 3.3.1 and 3.4.3.2, and the chapter of Van den Brink, Section 4.4.3.1.

a combination of these. Again, the government will be guided, when deciding upon the draft of the criteria, by the objectives it is seeking to realize through the awarding of the right in question.[65] In the case of the sale of government property, the government will as a rule be seeking to realize a maximum financial yield and for that reason opt for the criterion of price.[66] However, it cannot be excluded that the government will seek to apply qualitative criteria as well. In the case of the competitive allocation of a subsidy, it is obvious – given the nature of the right – that the government will select the best application or applications with the help of a quality-based criterion.[67] With the competitive allocation of licences, the government may decide to prioritize financial criteria or quality-based criteria, depending on the nature and the interests affected by the licence in question.[68]

It is also the case that, in the context of the design of the competitive phase, governments will not always opt for an allocation criterion with the intention of exercising control over the objectives they pursue with the awarding of the right. For example, a government will not do so if it is indifferent to the content of the applications being considered for selection. This may be apparent, for example, from the fact that a government is basing its selection decision on the 'first come, first served' principle.[69] Such an allocation method may be used when certain licences and subsidies are being allocated.[70]

10.4.3 EU Legal Framework

As soon as governments decide to competitively allocate licences, subsidies or property rights, they may have to deal with EU law. What EU law does not offer is a specific and uniform legal framework, of the kind that applies to the competitive procurement of public contracts. To the extent that EU law provides for rules, they are often highly fragmented.[71]

[65] See also the chapter of Wollenschläger, Section 3.4.3.2.
[66] See the chapter of Caranta and Biancardi, Section 5.3.1.
[67] See the chapter of Van den Brink, Sections 4.4.2 and 4.4.2.1.
[68] See the chapter of Wollenschläger, Section 3.4.3.2, who states that generalisations are not possible because of the great variety of licensable rights.
[69] This will also be the case if the government bases its decisions on the drawing of lots.
[70] In this connection, see the chapter of Wollenschläger, Section 3.4.3.2, and the chapter of Van den Brink, Sections 4.4.2 and 4.4.4.
[71] Chapter of Wollenschläger, Section 3.4.1.

This is most clearly evident in the competitive allocation of licences. Depending on the object of the licence, the allocation process may come, for example, within the scope of sector-specific secondary EU legislation[72] or the cross-sectoral Services Directive.[73] The rationale of this legislation is found mainly in the aim of the EU to create the internal market.[74] Wollenschläger points out that most of this secondary EU legislation does not provide a legal basis for the competitive allocation of licences or for the allocation decisions made in that context: it is the national laws of the member states, in which the legislation is converted, that provides that basis.[75] To the extent that a licence does not come within the scope of the aforementioned secondary EU legislation or – to the extent that it does – the legislation does not provide for a regulation,[76] primary EU law becomes relevant, in particular the fundamental Treaty freedoms that are also related to the aforementioned rationale.[77] In the next sections, we will be discussing what the aforementioned EU legal framework means for the discretion of governments when they decide to competitively allocate licences.

As far as the issuing of subsidies is concerned, Van den Brink points out the relevance of state aid law for national subsidies and subsidies that are issued in shared management. Subsidies awarded directly by the European Commission are not designated as state aid.[78] From her

[72] See the chapter of Wollenschläger, Section 3.4.1.1, referring to Directive 2018/1972/EEC on the European Electronic Communications Code, amended by Directive 2002/20/EC; Regulation (EC) 1370/2007 on public passenger transport services by rail and by road amended by Regulation 2016/2338; Directive 94/22/EC on the conditions for granting and using authorizations for the prospection, exploration and production of hydrocarbons, amended by Regulation 2018/1999; Regulation (EC) 1380/2013 on the Common Fisheries Policy, amended by Regulation 1385/2013; Directive 96/67/EC on access to the ground handling market at Community airports, amended by Regulation 1882/2003; and Regulation (EC) 95/93 on common rules for the allocation of slots at Community airports, amended by Regulation 894/2002.

[73] Directive 2006/123/EC of the European Parliament and of the Council of 12 December 2006 on services in the internal market, OJ 2006, No. L 376/36.

[74] See the chapter of Wollenschläger, Section 3.4.2.

[75] See the chapter of Wollenschläger, Sections 3.4.1 and 3.4.1.3. To this extent it can be argued that, though some licensing systems are based on EU directives, it should also be remembered that most licensing systems are national in nature.

[76] Chapter of Wollenschläger, Section 3.4.1.2.

[77] Chapter of Wollenschläger, Sections 3.4.1 and 3.4.1.2. According to Wollenschläger, most relevance in practice will accrue to the freedom of establishment and the freedom to carry out services. Wollenschläger also refers to the relevance – albeit slighter – of the EU fundamental rights; see Section 3.4.1.2.

[78] See the chapter of Van den Brink, Sections 4.4.1 and 4.4.3.1.

contribution, we infer that the method by which subsidies are allocated is irrelevant as to whether a subsidy qualifies as state aid. Whenever a government opts to competitively allocate a subsidy,[79] it is therefore state aid. However, if the European Commission has stated that the aid is compatible with the objectives of the internal market, no unlawful state aid is said to have been made.[80] Van den Brink also points out that subsidies issued directly by the European Commission always had to be allocated by means of a beauty contest.[81] European subsidies issued in shared management may be subject to additional rules based on secondary EU legislation for the allocation process.[82] To the extent that this is not the case, relevance accrues to the general principles of equal treatment and transparency in accordance with case law of the Court.[83] In addition, governments can derive inspiration, according to Van den Brink,[84] from rules in the Financial Regulation that, as stated, determine in detail how the European Commission must competitively allocate subsidies.[85] With regard to the framework described above, in the next sections we will be discussing its significance for the level of discretion of governments when competitively allocating subsidies.

This brings us to the sale of government property. Caranta and Biancardi show, in that context, that the fundamental Treaty freedoms and state aid law set the limits of government discretion in the light of the realization of the internal market objective.[86] Contrary to the domains

[79] As stated, that is the premise on which this contribution is based. We will therefore not be examining any further the obligations imposed by EU law on governments, discussed by Van den Brink, to allocate grants competitively. For more on this, see her chapter, Section 4.4.2.2.

[80] See the chapter of Van den Brink, Section 4.4.1.

[81] Art. 194 in conjunction with Arts. 199 and 200 of the Financial Regulation, European Parliament and Council Regulation 2018/1046, OJ 2018 No. L193/1. See the chapter of Van den Brink, Section 4.4.2.1.

[82] Chapter of Van den Brink, Section 4.4.2.2, referring to Regulation (EC) 1303/2013 applicable to the European Regional Development Fund, the European Social Fund (together referred to as the Structural Funds), the Cohesion Fund and the European Maritime and Fisheries Fund; Regulation (EC) 1305/2013 concerning the European Agricultural Fund for Rural Development (EAFRD).

[83] See the chapter of Van den Brink, Section 4.4.3.1, with a reference to Case T-297/05, *IPK International* v. *Commission* [2011] ECR II-01859, ECLI:EU:T:2011:185.

[84] See the chapter of Van den Brink, Section 4.4.2.2.

[85] European grants awarded by the European Commission involve what is known as 'direct management'; see the chapter of Van den Brink, Sections 4.4.1 and 4.4.2.1.

[86] See the chapter of Caranta and Biancardi, Section 5.4.1.

discussed above, primary EU law has not been developed into secondary EU legislation with regard to the sale of government property. What has been provided, however, are soft-law instruments that give governments guidance on selling their property.[87] From this, it appears that the use of a competitive allocation process, in accordance with the Treaty principles that apply to the procurement of public contracts, is one way of ensuring that the sale is in line with primary EU law, and with state aid law in particular.[88] The significance of this legal framework for the discretion of governments involved in a competitive sale is dealt with in the next sections.

10.4.4 *Rationale of EU Law Restrictions on Discretion*

From the previous section, it appears that the rationale behind the principles and regulations of EU law that governments may have to deal with whenever they competitively allocate licences, subsidies or property rights, lies in the aim of the EU in creating the internal market. Given that objective, the principles and regulations are based both on the fundamental Treaty freedoms and on competition law that contains state aid law.[89] In the context of the subject of this contribution, the effect of these various principles and regulations, given their underlying common objective, is always the same: when making their allocation decisions – regardless of the nature of the law governing the competitive allocation process – governments may not discriminate against potential applicants by nationality and are obliged to treat all applicants equally. As part of that process, governments will also have to observe the transparency and proportionality principles when making allocation decisions.[90] As far as

[87] Chapter of Caranta and Biancardi, Section 5.4.2.1, with a reference to the 2016 Commission Notice on the notion of State aid (2016/C 262/01) and the Commission Staff Working Document Guidance Paper on State aid-compliant financing, restructuring and privatization of State-owned enterprises, SWD(2012) 14 final, which builds on the Commission Report XXIII on Competition Policy 1993.

[88] See the chapter of Caranta and Biancardi, Section 5.4.2.1, with a reference to the Commission Notice of 2016, para. 89.

[89] See also P. Adriaanse, F. van Ommeren, W. den Ouden and J. Wolswinkel, 'The Allocation of Limited Rights by the Administration: A Quest for a General Legal Theory', in P. Adriaanse, F. van Ommeren, W. den Ouden and J. Wolswinkel (eds.), *Scarcity and the State I: The Allocation of Limited Rights by the Administration* (Cambridge: Intersentia, 2016), pp. 17–22.

[90] Chapter of Wollenschläger, Sections 3.3.3.1, 3.3.3.3, and 3.4.3.1; Chapter of Van den Brink, Sections 4.3 and 4.4.3.1; Chapter of Caranta and Biancardi, Sections 5.4.3.1 and 5.5 ('a jus commune of public contracts').

the allocation of subsidies is concerned, reference should also be made to the principle of sound financial management.[91]

This means the objective that the EU legislator seeks to achieve through the aforementioned principles and regulations is essentially the same as that of the EU legal principles and regulations that apply to competitive public procurement. In that context, we have shown that this objective is not only different from the procurement objectives pursued by governments themselves, but that EU law does not stop national governments from determining what these objectives are, what public interests they intend to serve through these objectives, and what emphases they wish to place in that context. In other words, EU law does not interfere with the 'what' or the 'why' of competitive public procurement, only the 'how'. In their contributions, Wollenschläger and Van den Brink show that things are barely any different with regard to the competitive allocation of licences or subsidies.[92] This is also the case, in principle, as far as the competitive sale of government property is concerned; at least, if a government designs the allocation process in such a way that the property right is awarded to the applicant making the highest offer. To the extent that a government is aiming for non-economic objectives and interests through its competitive allocations, Caranta and Biancardi state that the apparently limited scope that EU law provides for governments to do so is a problem.[93]

10.4.5 Restricting Levels of Discretion: Principle-Based, Rule-Based or Integrated Approach?

From the contributions by Wollenschläger, Van den Brink, and Caranta and Biancardi, it seems that the EU legal framework that was discussed in the previous sections – unlike the framework we looked at for competitive

[91] Chapter of Van den Brink, Section 4.4.2.2.

[92] Chapter of Wollenschläger, Sections 3.4.2.1 and 3.4.2.2. Wollenschläger believes indeed that lawful use of the instrument of competitive allocation as such is a necessary precondition for achieving the objectives that the granting of the right is intended for. Compare the chapter of Van den Brink, Section 4.4.4, and the chapter of Caranta and Biancardi, Section 5.4.3.1.

[93] Chapter of Caranta and Biancardi, Sections 5.4.1, 5.4.2.1, 5.4.2.2, and especially 5.4.3.1: 'This approach drives a wedge between EU State aids law and public procurement law. [...] It is argued that a State, when selling as much as when buying, may not simply be motivated by strictly economic considerations.'

public procurement[94] – has a mostly principle-based orientation. This is certainly true of the competitive allocation of licences and government property rights and, to a somewhat lesser degree, of the awarding of subsidies. We explain this below.

As far as the domain of licences is concerned, the contribution by Wollenschläger shows the following for those cases in which a licence does not come within the remit of secondary EU legislation or – to the extent that it does – for which legislation makes no provision. For these cases, it follows from case law of the ECJ that the restrictions on governments' discretion do not go beyond the general principles that we mentioned in the previous section.[95] From the contribution by Van den Brink, it seems that things are no different as regards the competitive allocation of European subsidies that do not come under the scope of secondary EU legislation.[96] To the extent that the competitive allocation of a licence or European subsidy does fall under the remit of secondary EU legislation, the analysis of the aforementioned provisions by Wollenschläger[97] and Van den Brink[98] suggests that the restrictions on governments' discretion have an equally principle-based character. By contrast, the provisions of the Financial Regulation, which are only relevant for the competitive allocation of European subsidies by the European Commission, are more rule-based in character.[99] Finally, Caranta and Biancardi point out that the soft-law instruments for the

[94] Section 10.3.3. See Jansen, 'Allocation of Limited Rights from a European Public Procurement Law Perspective', p. 249; See the chapter of Arrowsmith, Section 2.1.

[95] Chapter of Wollenschläger, Section 3.4.3.1. Wollenschläger is referring here, in particular, to the draft of the allocation process.

[96] Chapter of Van den Brink, Section 4.4.3.1.

[97] See the chapter of Wollenschläger, Section 3.4.1.4: Directive 2006/123/EC, Arts. 10(1) and 10(2) (draft decisions) and Art. 12(1) (draft and implementation decisions). See also Section 3.4.2.2: Directive 2018/1972/EEC, Arts. 7(2) and 55(7) (draft and implementation decisions); Directive 96/67/EC, Art. 11(1)(a) (draft and implementation decisions); Directive 94/22/EC, Art. 3(6) (implementation decisions), Arts. 5(1) (draft decisions) and 5(3) (implementation decisions); and Regulation (EC) 95/93, Art. 4(2) (draft and implementation decisions).

[98] See the chapter of Van den Brink, Section 4.4.2.2: Regulation (EC) 1303/2013, Art. 125 (3)(a)(ii) (draft and implementation decisions) and Regulation (EC) 1305/2013, Art. 49 (draft and implementation decisions).

[99] See the chapter of Van den Brink, Section 4.4.3.1: the principles of equal treatment and transparency are formulated in Art. 188(a) and (b) of the Financial Regulation. They then form the framework for the most important draft and implementation decisions (set out in more detail in Arts. 189–200) taken by governments when competitively allocating grants.

sale of government property may be linked to the Treaty principles that apply to public contracts,[100] but are limited to a principle-based approach.[101]

10.5 Integrated Reflections from the Perspective of the Regulation of Public Procurement

Whenever a government wishes to award a licence, a subsidy or a property right through a competitive allocation process, it must design and then implement that process. What these processes have in common is that the government first drafts the requirements and criteria for the potential applicants and their applications, publishes them, uses them to evaluate the applicants and their applications, makes allocation decisions based on the outcomes of the evaluations and finally publishes these decisions. When making all the aforementioned decisions, the government will have to observe the principles of non-discrimination, equal treatment, transparency and proportionality.[102]

Given the principle-based character of the EU legal framework, governments have considerable discretion when allocating licences, subsidies or property rights, at least when compared to the discretion that EU law allows governments in the case of public procurement. Obviously, things will be different if national law includes other additional regulations. What we have also noticed is that any restrictions on governments' discretion – regardless of whether they are based on one or more of the principles or on rules derived from the principles – do not in themselves prevent governments from achieving their objectives and interests through competitive allocations.

[100] See the chapter of Caranta and Biancardi, Section 5.4.2.1: paras. 89–96 of the 2016 Commission Notice on the notion of State aid (2016/C 262/01) (draft and implementation decisions).

[101] Chapter of Caranta and Biancardi, Section 5.4.2.1: 'The rules for the bidding procedures foreseen in the Notice are quite minimal not just when compared with the very detailed provisions on advertisement and notices (including contract award notices) laid down in Directive 2014/24/EU on public procurement, but also with the "light regime" approach followed for the award of works and services concessions under Directive 2014/23/EU.'

[102] This is apart from the question of whether EU law impedes the objectives and public interests that a government is seeking to serve through its competitive allocation. We refer here to the restrictions that could apply to the sale of government property resulting from state aid law; see Section 10.4.4 with a reference to the chapter of Caranta and Biancardi.

This then brings us to the question of the extent to which the earlier analysis of the regulatory approach to the domain of public procurements has yielded any useful insights for possible approaches to other domains that feature in this book. After all, having considerable discretion enables governments not just to take effective and lawful allocation decisions, but also *not* to do so.

It is important to know – and this is in keeping with the contributions by Wollenschläger, Van den Brink, and Caranta and Biancardi[103] – that the transparency principle is the key driver, which can be operated to better manage effective and lawful decisions by the government at every stage of the allocation process: governments must state as clearly as possible in advance what they are planning to do before actually doing what they have said they will do, and showing retrospectively, again as clearly as possible, what they have done. A legal framework with a more rule-based orientation could give governments greater direction, especially as far as the design of the allocation process is concerned. The more direction governments get in this context, the easier it is for them to incorporate transparency in their decisions, and the easier it will be for applicants to have the opportunity of verifying whether such decisions are in accordance with the other principles.[104]

Given the latter possibility, there is apparently less need for a rule-based approach, to the extent that its purpose is to give governments greater direction when making decisions in accordance with the other principles – those of non-discrimination, equal treatment and proportionality. As far as that is concerned, however, it is possible to consider things differently. Ultimately, the most suitable regulatory approach will depend very much on the circumstances of each case. This includes such aspects as the nature of the right being allocated and of the requirements and criteria on which basis allocation decisions must be made, together with the level of professionalism of the responsible individuals in the government insofar as it affects their ability to make these decisions in an effective and lawful manner. An example that comes to mind is the difference in the level of professionalism needed to evaluate and compare applications on the basis of the price being offered or requested

[103] Chapter of Wollenschläger, Section 3.4.2.2; Chapter of Van den Brink, Section 4.3; Chapter of Caranta and Biancardi, Section 5.3.2.1. See also Section 10.3.5, with a reference to the chapter of Arrowsmith.

[104] See the chapter of Wollenschläger, Section 3.4.3.1; Chapter of Van den Brink, Section 4.3.

compared to an evaluation and comparison based on qualitative criteria.[105] The extent of the risk that the aforementioned individuals are not sufficiently qualified to make effective and lawful decisions is also a relevant circumstance. That in itself contains the risk that the government, when making its decisions, is focused entirely on complying with the principles and the detailed rules derived from them, and then losing sight of the objectives it was seeking to realize through the allocation process.[106] We are also mindful of the extent to which applicants for rights will be able to verify whether, and to what degree, draft and implementation decisions that governments make as part of an allocation process are in compliance with the requirements set by law. Also relevant is the extent of the transaction costs that are incurred by all the actors involved in managing the aforementioned risks, in relation to the benefits yielded by the costs.[107] We also refer to the degree to which a principle lends itself to be developed into rules by which governments' discretion can be restricted and standardized. The transparency principle perhaps lends itself better to this than does the principle of equal treatment, for example.

Another important insight is as follows. The discretion that governments have during the implementation phase of an allocation process is restricted to a significant degree – even in the case of a principle-based approach – by the design decisions they have made and published at an earlier stage.[108] This means that governments are not allowed to reverse

[105] Van den Brink asks in this connection for particular attention to be paid to the prevention of conflicts of interest between applications and assessors; see Chapter 4, Section 4.4.3.1.

[106] See the chapter of Van den Brink, Section 4.4.3.2. For more on this, see Jansen, 'Over het vermeende dilemma tussen de doelmatigheid en de rechtmatigheid van de overheidsinkoop', pp. 171–183.

[107] See Section 10.3.6. See also the chapter of Wollenschläger, Sections 3.3.3.5 and 3.4.3.1; Chapter of Van den Brink, Section 4.4.3.2. See the nuanced comment by Van den Brink in Section 4.4.3.1

> The disadvantage of this principle-based regulation is that the Dutch administrative judge is asked to determine case by case which subsidy schemes comply with the aforementioned principles. This takes not only a lot of effort of the Dutch judges, but also leads to legal uncertainty and lengthy legal procedures. Perhaps it is more efficient to have this clarity before granting subsidies at all; this could avoid a lot of lengthy judicial procedures and relieve the Dutch judges. However, also when specific rules have been laid down in legislation, judges still may conclude that the principles of equal treatment and transparency demand more. The legal certainty that rules can offer should therefore not be over-estimated.

[108] Section 10.3.4.

decisions they have made, even when they have acquired new knowledge as a result of changing circumstances.[109] The foregoing does not alter the fact that it would be useful if the legal framework gave governments greater insights into the decisions it can and cannot make in this context.[110]

10.6 Concluding Remarks

Whenever rule makers start regulating the competitive allocation of the rights referred to in this book – with a view to ensuring fair and transparent competition – they restrict the discretion of the allocating governments. This will particularly be the case if they select a rule-based approach in that context. The statement in the literature that legislators and rule makers, in so doing, are restricting the ability of governments from realizing the objectives they are seeking to attain through this competition is, in our view, an oversimplification. However, legislators and rule makers must realize that regulating competitive allocations of limited rights requires a tailor-made approach, based on the starting points and principles discussed above – the tailor-made aspect is not the leader but the closer. Following on from this, we recommend that when regulating a specific domain, other domains should be considered as well – with a view to both the underlying differences and the similarities. This way, a great deal can be learned from each other. Moreover, this approach can help bring about a more overarching and coherent vision on the competitive allocation of rights by governments.

[109] In their chapters, Wollenschläger and Van den Brink refer to problems that touch on a question that we addressed in Section 10.3.6: acquiring further knowledge may tempt governments to not uphold or even to deviate from requirements and criteria that they have already published. See the chapter of Wollenschläger, Section 3.4.3.1 *in fine*: 'Thus, optimising public interests in that regard requires a careful balance when designing the specific procedure.' Van den Brink is more emphatic, referring, like us, to the difficulty in reconciling the various interests, see Chapter 4, Section 4.4.3.2.

[110] Section 10.3.6.

For EU product safety concerns, contact us at Calle de José Abascal, 56–1°,
28003 Madrid, Spain or eugpsr@cambridge.org.

www.ingramcontent.com/pod-product-compliance
Lightning Source LLC
LaVergne TN
LVHW011658200926
848484LV00004B/990

* 9 7 8 1 0 0 9 4 4 3 7 7 7 *